Intellectuals and the Crisis of Politics in the Interwar Period and Beyond

Intellectuals and the Crisis of Politics in the Interwar Period and Beyond

A Transnational History

Balázs Trencsényi

Great Clarendon Street, Oxford, OX2 6DP,
United Kingdom

Oxford University Press is a department of the University of Oxford.
It furthers the University's objective of excellence in research, scholarship,
and education by publishing worldwide. Oxford is a registered trade mark of
Oxford University Press in the UK and in certain other countries

© Balázs Trencsényi 2025

The moral rights of the author have been asserted.

All rights reserved. No part of this publication may be reproduced, stored in a retrieval system,
transmitted, used for text and data mining, or used for training artificial intelligence, in any form or
by any means, without the prior permission in writing of Oxford University Press, or as expressly
permitted by law, by licence or under terms agreed with the appropriate reprographics rights
organization. Enquiries concerning reproduction outside the scope of the above should be sent
to the Rights Department, Oxford University Press, at the address above.

You must not circulate this work in any other form
and you must impose this same condition on any acquirer.

Published in the United States of America by Oxford University Press
198 Madison Avenue, New York, NY 10016, United States of America

British Library Cataloguing in Publication Data
Data available
Library of Congress Control Number: 2024947346
ISBN 9780198929482
DOI: 10.1093/9780198929512.001.0001

Printed and bound by
CPI Group (UK) Ltd, Croydon, CR0 4YY

Links to third party websites are provided by Oxford in good faith and
for information only. Oxford disclaims any responsibility for the materials
contained in any third party website referenced in this work.

The manufacturer's authorised representative in the EU for product safety is
Oxford University Press España S.A. of El Parque Empresarial San Fernando de Henares, Avenida
de Castilla, 2 – 28830 Madrid (www.oup.es/en or
product.safety@oup.com). OUP España S.A. also acts as importer into Spain
of products made by the manufacturer.

Contents

1. Introduction: The Faces of Crisis	1
2. The Morphology of Modern Crisis Discourses	18
3. Crisis of the Mind and Spirit	32
4. Crisis of Capitalism	73
5. Crisis of Social Cohesion	99
6. Crisis of Liberalism	116
7. Crisis of Democracy	167
8. Crisis of Socialism	194
9. Crisis of the Nation-State and the International System	218
10. Long Shadows of the Interwar Crises	241
11. Conclusion: The Politics of Crisis	274
Select Bibliography	*294*
Index	*317*

1
Introduction

The Faces of Crisis

Aside from *Angelus Novus*—blown by the "storm rising from Paradise" as memorably described by Walter Benjamin—Paul Klee drew many other angels, especially toward the end of his troubled life.[1] They are tragic or comic, suffering, contemplating, or impishly smiling, constituting a veritable mirror world to the human one. One of these is called *Angel in Crisis II* (*Krise eines Engels II*, 1939). It is very sketchy, but still powerful; it evokes, but also subverts, some of the classic iconographic features of angelic creatures.[2] Klee's angel seems to hide behind its defensively closed wings, which (in traditional iconography) are usually depicted as being spread outward, symbolizing the transmission of divine grace. Its head is unnaturally turned upward, possibly alluding to the piercing ambiguity of the multi-layered canopy of divine spheres above it—which can confer both redemption and eternal damnation—while also evoking the metaphor of the "world turned upside down." It craves to ascend higher in the divine hierarchy, but a heavy weight hanging—in a somewhat grotesque manner—from its nose prevents it from taking off.

Angel in Crisis is thus immobilized, being wedged between upwardness and downwardness, and equally between past and future. As celestial hierarchies and ontological securities are suspended, this transcendent creature, like its human homologues, is left alone in agonizing fear and insecurity. Being in crisis thus implies a temporal and spatial suspense. The look of Klee's black-and-white *Angel in Crisis* is markedly different from his more colorful *Angelus Novus*, turned toward the past, whose "eyes are staring, his mouth is open, his wings are spread. [. . .] But a storm is blowing from Paradise; it has got caught in his wings with such violence that the angel can no longer close them."[3] *Angel in Crisis* is left rather expressionless by the artist—it is neither smiling nor crying, and its eyes are turned inward. It is important to note that, as does the overwhelming majority of Klee's angels, *Angel in Crisis* dates from the fateful year 1939. It can be thus interpreted as closing the parentheses of the interwar period that had been symbolically opened by *Angelus Novus* in 1920, with its ambiguity of the retrospective gaze toward the horrors of the Great War and the messianic expectation of a universal regeneration to come.

Remarkably, the Bern collection of Klee's works contains two portrayals of an *Angel in Crisis*, implying that crisis might well have different faces.[4] This book is about these different faces and what surrounds this angel—different from the historical

Intellectuals and the Crisis of Politics in the Interwar Period and Beyond. Balázs Trencsényi, Oxford University Press.
© Balázs Trencsényi (2025). DOI: 10.1093/9780198929512.003.0001

2 Intellectuals and the Crisis of Politics

debris that mesmerized the eyes of *Angelus Novus*: human communities struggling with insecurities regarding their past and future, challenged by intellectual as well as physical dislocation, and the plethora of ideas and visions they generate and exchange as part of their effort to make sense of what is happening to them. Trying to grasp the complexity of these past reflections and interactions, I seek to offer an insight into what goes beyond the current diagnoses of crisis, delineating the morphology, tracing the multiple genealogies, and pondering on the present political and cultural implications of these discourses that have become so prevalent in the twentieth century.

The concept of "crisis" has a complex history, bridging classical Antiquity and political modernity in an intriguing way.[5] Reconstructing the modern discourses of crisis gives us a unique insight into the underlying logic of key political and intellectual controversies that have come to shape our world. In this respect, Reinhart Koselleck's hypothesis, originally focusing on the long shadows of the Enlightenment, but also seeking to discern the (patho)genesis of political modernity as such, might also be tested on other periods and different cultural contexts. Did the emergence of the discourse of crisis signal—and at the same time contribute to—the radical transformation of modern political thinking and action by shifting their horizons of expectation?[6] And did this transformation contribute to the tragic developments of the twentieth century? Reflecting on these questions, rather than staying within the framework delineated by the binary of *Kritik* and *Krise*, and being somewhat skeptical of the underlying antimodernist connotations of Koselleck's seminal early work, here I propose not a "pathogenetic" reconstruction, but rather an inquiry both into the destructive and the creative sides of framing key components and institutions of modernity as crisis-ridden.

Importantly, discourses of crisis are not only frameworks for temporalizing,[7] but also for spatializing, modernity, and thus can be turned into vantage points for a transnational analysis of intellectual history. Along these lines, one needs to analyze how references to crisis shed light on key assumptions that characterize a given historical moment while also pointing to "symbolic geographies" (i.e., contrasting Orient and Occident, or "centers" and "peripheries"), which go beyond closely knit local/national milieux and thus unveil transnational entanglements.

There is an obvious need for a geographically and thematically more comprehensive re-narration of European intellectual history, weaving Eastern, Southeastern, Western, Northern, and Southwestern perspectives together and de-centering the dominant narrative that takes Western European positions and developments as normative and adds the others as "exotic" peripheries.[8] Studying the ways crisis was experienced, conceptualized, and negotiated might contribute to an understanding of how competing visions of time and history shaped and continue to shape political thinking and, conversely, how political and social reconfigurations have framed our assumptions about temporality and spatiality. In this sense, this book was also written in dialogue with a number of recent attempts to rethink transnational political and intellectual history, focusing especially on the persistent epistemological frames that structure political and cultural debates.[9]

The classic historiographic narrative of "systemic crisis" that led to the collapse of liberal democracy focused on Weimar Germany, describing it as eminently crisis-ridden and taking at face value the endemic statements of various contemporaneous political subcultures about disorientation, disintegration, and an impending catastrophe.[10] Jacobson and Schlink put it succinctly: "The short history of the Weimar Republic is above all a history of its crises."[11] This picture, however, has been increasingly questioned by scholars who emphasize the illocutionary force of representing crisis (i.e., rather than predictions of what was to come, crisis discourses were meant to unify and mobilize their target audience to make a concerted effort to avoid the catastrophe).[12]

From another methodological angle, there has been a growing emphasis on the open-ended horizons of Weimar politics, arguing that radical ideological criticism could go together with a *de facto* acceptance of the existing institutional frameworks. While democracy was heavily contested, its fall was far from being predetermined.[13] Along these lines, we might try to nuance our image of the interrelationship between discourses and historical processes. Following Koselleck's interventions, and due to the dramatic decline of historiosophical grand narratives (such as Marxism) in the last decades, there has been an increasing scholarly consensus that it was not some crisis existing "out there" that generated crisis discourses in the interwar period. Rather, these discourses had their own intrinsic dynamic and did not merely mirror the historical developments unfolding in front of the eyes of those who employed this conceptual framework. Instead, crisis discourses came to be conceived as catalysts of processes that challenge and eventually even dissolve an existing political order.

A radical version of this "revisionist" position could even go so far as to argue that "crisis" was a discursive weapon frequently used and abused—one that was often completely (and sometimes intentionally) detached from the actual political and social dynamics it claimed to describe. Those who link this type of historical analysis to the present often talk of the "inflation" (or even the complete emptying out) of the meaning of crisis as an explanatory concept.[14] From another perspective, crisis is actually real and quite common, but not to be over-dramatized, as it is concomitant to the democratic process.[15] Recently, it has also been theorized as a metahistorical category derived from individual psychology, denoting for the political community a serious existential challenge, which can be overcome with creativity, self-reflection, and adjustment; whereas inflexibility and the proliferation of compensatory mechanisms (such as self-victimization) can aggravate it, leading to self-destruction.[16] Undoubtedly, for an increasing number of observers, our world is becoming ever more crisis-ridden. What is more, we also seem to face a multiplicity of crises: climate, energy, demography, parliamentary politics, state institutions, identity, etc., each of which may even amplify the other's impact and deal a devastating blow to our civilization.[17]

The divergence of these perspectives points to a growing disconnect between the use of crisis as a reified category and the historicizing and contextualizing drive that came to dominate the more hermeneutically or discursively oriented social sciences and humanities. The former is typically present in policy-oriented research and in

4 Intellectuals and the Crisis of Politics

public discourse, with references to crises "out there" to be "managed" or "contained." For the latter, crisis is merely in the "eye of the beholder." This disconnect exemplifies a more general rift between academic and public discourses and has led to the growth of mutual distrust and in some cases also the breakdown of meaningful communication between them.

The ongoing discussion on the epistemological status and political force of key concepts greatly influenced me in my work (in fact, I even had the good luck to meet Koselleck several times in the late 1990s) and I drew on these insights when casting out my own net of comparative intellectual history, seeking to catch various discourses stemming from Western and Eastern Europe. Nevertheless, I also had an underlying assumption (perhaps linked to my own East Central European experiences) that we should try to nuance even further the way we describe the interrelationship of discourses and historical processes. While agreeing with the suggestion to be more cautious in using crisis both as a political concept or an analytical term, it is still undeniable (shown also by the Covid-19 pandemic situation and the consequences of the 2022 Russian aggression in Ukraine) that there are historical moments characterized by the compression of the horizons of time and space, the anxiety caused by the co-existence of many possible scenarios, a loss of sense of causal relationships, and thus a pervasive feeling of individual and collective disorientation experienced by many contemporaries. It is not by chance that the key question of the literature on the topic is whether the proliferation of crisis discourses might be read as a "crisis" itself. My suggestion is indeed taking agency seriously—to perceive crisis not as some sort of inherent and impersonal dynamic, but as a series of "speech-acts" of sorts.[18] This does not mean, however, that we should reject its analytical force altogether, as it reflects the self-perception and emotionality of actors in a given historical situation, providing an interpretative key to read the different processes unfolding around them. In some ways, one can locate crisis precisely in the field of tension between the objective and subjective, normative and descriptive, explainable and unexplainable, as well as the conceptual and structural dimensions. The interwar period, characterized by the radicalization of political discourse in all possible directions and by traumatic socioeconomic and sociocultural disturbances and breakdowns, provides us with particularly rich material to reflect on these questions.

The rise of transnational and global historical approaches in the last two decades triggered several attempts to link the different economic, social, and political layers of what came to be described as the "interwar crisis" in a broadly transnational narrative. In *The Great Interwar Crisis* Robert Boyce focuses mainly on diplomatic history between 1922 and 1933 to analyze the entanglements and eventual breakdown of the international economic and political system and argues that the fall of the security framework—which guaranteed the functioning of an increasingly globalized economy—was due to the concatenation of a number of factors linked to the misreading of national interests and each other's intentions by key players on the "world stage."[19] With a somewhat divergent focus and methodology, Adam Tooze offers a narrative of the roots of the interwar crisis, stressing the importance of the final years

Introduction: The Faces of Crisis 5

of the First World War.[20] Here, too, global entanglements are studied from the perspective of the sustainability of frameworks of cooperation. But Tooze's focus is more on the clash between the defenders of the new world order and the "insurgents" who successfully exploited the internal contradictions of the new political and economic framework (e.g., calling for the intervention of the nation-state at the moment of the collapse of the international financial system).

What is common in many of these new transnational approaches is that they see crisis not so much as a total breakdown, but rather as a space for innovation. Crisis is thus often analyzed retrospectively not as the end of a period, but more as the beginning of something new. While most of these transnational approaches focus on diplomacy and economic decision making in their search to shed new light on the post-Great War order—which has been traditionally characterized as eminently crisis-ridden—I offer a different perspective by turning to the discursive frames, narrative tools, analytical categories, and self-representations of historical actors who contributed to the framing of this period in terms of a world crisis.

To be sure, it is evidently untrue that an "objective" crisis automatically generates "subjective" crisis narratives. It is also far-fetched to argue for the other extreme position—that representations of crisis are completely disengaged from the socioeconomic, cultural, and political processes and are only used as discursive weapons to subvert the political order. Reflections on the social, economic, cultural, and spiritual tendencies of the period were rooted in diverse scholarly methods (from political economy to sociology, history, and cultural philosophy) and often offered intriguing contextual and/or causal analyses. Furthermore, born under conditions of extreme urgency, these were efforts to make sense of the world. While we should not forget that framing certain social, economic, or cultural processes as threats to the existence of a community could well be a conscious manipulation, it is hard to deny that in any historical moment there are highly divergent ways and epistemic patterns to construct reality as a crisis, and their intellectual and moral qualities are far from homogeneous.

Thus, conceiving of discourses of crisis as representations that challenge and possibly even explode an existing political order does not imply that they are interesting merely as intellectual landmines used for conscious or unconscious subversion. One must make important distinctions, both between the different ideological frameworks and between theories and ideologies of crisis. In this way, one can provide a more pluralistic take on the different ways the imagery of crisis became embedded in modern political discourse.[21] Although it is hard to draw the border between ideological and analytical statements, it is still important to consider that the occurrence of the concept of crisis might indicate very different ideological and mental frames. Likewise, while liberal, conservative, socialist, communist, and fascist diagnoses were in some ways part of the same discussion, and often intersected with each other, they should not be equated as different sides of the same pathology, relativizing their respective moral and intellectual weight. Nor can they be merged with those sociological or historical projects that sought to describe and analyze phenomena in the

6 Intellectuals and the Crisis of Politics

past or the present as crisis-ridden, even if those who put forward these analyses were themselves far from being ideologically neutral.

Reaching beyond the "usual suspects" (such as Oswald Spengler, Karl Jaspers, Paul Valéry, José Ortega y Gasset, Antonio Gramsci, or John Maynard Keynes), this book follows a wider range of—more or less well-known—intellectuals and political thinkers who conceptualized the interwar developments in terms of a crisis (e.g., Raymond and Robert Aron, Otto Bauer, Walter Benjamin, Nikolay Berdyaev, István Bibó, Henri de Man, Guglielmo Ferrero, Ernst Fischer, René Guénon, Béla Hamvas, Friedrich von Hayek, Käthe Leichter, Karl Mannheim, Mihail Manoilescu, Wilhelm Medinger, Ludwig von Mises, Alva and Gunnar Myrdal, Bogdan Radica, William Rappard, Wilhelm Röpke, Louis Rougier, Alexander Rüstow, Pitirim Sorokin, Adriano Tilgher, Jenő Varga, Angela Vode, Alfred Weber, Florian Znaniecki, and Ferdynand Zweig), representing different national and transnational contexts as well as extremely divergent intellectual and political positions. In their work we find competing models of reality, which obviously should not be mistaken for Reality as such. But we should nevertheless do more than just lump them together and claim that they were all manipulators of public opinion. We should likewise go beyond simply registering and cataloguing their divergences taxonomically. Bringing together thinkers from such divergent contexts, and with markedly different histories of their reception in mainstream historical narratives of political and social thought, is also intended as a "de-provincializing" tool. Some are commonly described as central figures of the European intellectual canon, while others—usually those who did not move to Western Europe or the United States—are considered peripheral, if mentioned at all. This approach invites the reader to reconsider the history of European political thought from an unconventionally multifocal perspective. This is even more important because many of the problems and dilemmas of liberal democracy and political modernity, central to interwar crisis discourses, were felt in a particularly acute way precisely in the countries that were considered "peripheral."

By including a rather extensive list of internationally lesser-known thinkers as well, this book seeks to go beyond the predictable references and present a much more complex texture of the transnational intellectual debates in the interwar period. This involves recovering already-forgotten conversations and pointing to indirect links and parallels, some of which were less obvious even for the very actors of the period. By analyzing how these thinkers constructed reality, and thereby engaging with them in a sort of retrospective dialogue, we can thus hope to learn something not only about the speakers, but also about the world they inhabited and sought—often desperately—to make sense of.

Extending the textual corpus way beyond the list of "usual suspects" also entails that it is impossible to reconstruct the arguments of these thinkers in their entirety. My aim is, however, to put their conceptualization of crisis in the broader context of their work as well as into the intertextual web of other conceptualizations. The fact that in most European languages the vernacular notion for crisis is derived from the original Greek word (Bg., Srb., and Ukr. *криза*, Cz. *krize*, Cro. *kriza*, Nl.

and Esp. *crisis*, Fr. and Por. *crise*, Ger. *Krise* or *Krisis*, Ita. *crisi*, Pol. *kryzys*, Rom. *criză*, Slo. *kríza*, Swe. *kris*; the predictable outliers are Hungarian with *válság*, but also *krízis*, Finnish with *pula* or *kriisi*, and Irish with *géarchéim*) makes it relatively easy to compare conceptualizations both diachronically and synchronically. Thus, I employ the tools of conceptual history, but the final aim is neither just signaling the diachronic transformation of a single concept along the lines of *Begriffsgeschichte*, nor reconstructing the pivotal philosophical arguments characteristic of the more traditional streams of intellectual history, but more of a contextual analysis of political languages, taking into account the transnational and transdisciplinary interplay of discourses. The focus is not on mere concepts but understanding the complex intellectual and political moves of people who framed the situation around themselves as a crisis. Such an in-depth textual and contextual analysis is unavoidably selective as the number of possible sources is nearly endless. Tellingly, Hungarian philosopher Béla Hamvas (1897–1968) compiled an annotated bibliography in 1937–38 about the different branches of "crisis literature"—from philosophy, aesthetics, and history to psychology, economics, and demography—and listed almost 1,000 relevant entries in German, English, French, and Hungarian alone.[22] Rather than engaging with all of them individually, which would be humanly impossible, this book seeks to trace different ideological streams and debates in a variety of national and transnational contexts by using an extensive textual corpus in sixteen European languages.

Focusing mainly on discourses and conceptualizations, this interpretative framework cannot aim at a comprehensive interpretation of social mentalities either, as it would be problematic to extrapolate the mindset of a society as a whole from the representations of crisis crafted by individual intellectuals and subcultures.[23] At the same time, there is a correlation between the intensity of intellectual discourses around crisis, the proliferation of the term in the public sphere, and its politicization.[24] While I do not intend to argue that the feeling of crisis was shared by each and every member of the societies in question, it seems plausible to assume that in the interwar period the idea of crisis became linked to the political, social, economic, and cultural spheres, and that moments of intensive political tension came to be conceptualized as a crisis by actors of various political and ideological camps. Furthermore, I seek to show that there was an increasing tendency to link these crisis phenomena both conceptually and ideologically, resulting in the discourse of "general" or "total" crisis.

Starting from the reconstruction and contextualization of individual utterances—and exploring their multi-level interrelationships with each other and with their different interpretative communities—is akin to Michael Werner and Bénédicte Zimmermann's methodological precept of "pragmatic induction"[25] put forward as a central element of the program of *histoire croisée*. However, while *histoire croisée* as it was conceived was usually predicated upon an entanglement of two contexts (particularly the French–German "dialogues" from the mid-nineteenth century onward), here I needed to develop an interpretative framework that accommodated the interplay between over a dozen national cultures and the many actors who crisscrossed them.

8   Intellectuals and the Crisis of Politics

Expanding the typical geographical and discursive horizons of crisis-centered studies of the interwar period, this book offers an alternative to the traditional "concentric" ways of writing European intellectual history around the axis of British, French, and German "classics" and their radiating influence. Instead, different conversations and complex threads of interaction are mapped in a polycentric way, establishing personal or structural connections but also remaining sensitive to the "asynchronous synchronicity" of different intellectual positions. In this sense it is also an experiment in devising a new way of thinking about Europe and European history, going beyond the usual binaries of East/West, center/periphery, European/non-European, local/global, and national/transnational. All this also implies the destabilization of the very framework of "European intellectual history" in terms of a Euro-centric and asymmetric grand narrative contrasting the "Old Continent" to the "Rest of the World." Many of the actors and intellectual debates I sought to trace had ramifications and connectivities beyond what is traditionally considered to be Europe. At the same time, Europe remained a central point of reference in these conversations and for most participants it had a pivotal historical and even "historiosophical" role in shaping the global crisis dynamics and epistemologically ordering reflection on this very same dynamic.

The "European dimension" of the intellectual history presented here is, in this sense, not an "incomplete" or "deficient" global history, let alone a "quasi-national" grand narrative supplanting the teleology of nation-formation with the equally problematic master narrative of Europeanization, with certain countries and cultures sooner or later becoming "admitted to the club" and others remaining "excluded" for the time being (or forever). Rather, it marks out a flexible unit of analysis to reconstruct a complex and multi-layered discourse that had a strong inherent tendency to treat European developments as a *pars pro toto* of the entire world. At the same time, this multiplicity of discourses also means that Europe is not a single and disjunct ideational construct shared by all participants. Thus, it should not be assumed but thoroughly historicized. One can find many competing images of Europe (and its many subdivisions), which also indicates, overall, how historically precarious and ideologically loaded our most common symbolic geographical terms are.[26]

Historicizing and spatializing these crisis discourses might also give us some practical hints regarding the way crisis can be used as an interpretative term. While overusing the concept hollows it completely of its meaning, in certain situations the reference to "crisis" might still help our reflection on past occurrences with a modest expectation of identifying some similarities and differences with our present predicament. It is at once too imprecise to follow blindly the concept's analogies when trying to cope with our current challenges; however, it may still offer more than just accidental resemblances.

All this helps us to critically reassess Koselleck's powerful and captivating theoretical contribution.[27] An obvious question in this regard concerns the German historian's reading of the Enlightenment "backwards" from the French Revolution (and in a less explicit way also from the breakthrough of totalitarian regimes). Most scholars of the Enlightenment would be nowadays more cautious to posit such a clear-cut and one-directional line, pluralizing both the notion of Enlightenment itself (identifying conservative, radical, clerical and anti-clerical, etc., forms)[28] and reflecting on the remarkable regional differences which also influenced the outlook of various ideological streams. One might contrast the French context to the Scottish, Rhenian, Prussian, Bohemian, Neapolitan, Polish, and Greek developments to get an overwhelmingly variegated picture of ideological and attitudinal plurality in the Enlightenment. This also opens up a much more polyphonic representation of the roots of political modernity—namely, that in different contexts the Enlightenment had very different historical impacts, as Enlightened ideas and tropes were also reframed by later cultural and ideological streams like Romanticism and Positivism. Once we get such a colorful picture, it will be much harder to draw any straightforward conclusion from the analysis of the work of French *philosophes* regarding the "pathogenesis" of modern political thought over the entire European continent.

Going beyond the image of a comprehensive shift from premodern to modern political languages once and for all around the early nineteenth century, a starting hypothesis of this project is the existence of a "second *Sattelzeit*" roughly between 1890 and 1945 characterized by new ways in which concepts were temporalized and dynamized, undermining the linear modernist narrative and generating cyclical and other "anti-modernist" visions of history.[29] One can identify a number of conceptual features and narrative frames of the "second *Sattelzeit*," bringing along a reconfiguration of the structure of political thought and speech around the turn of the century:

1. Atemporalization (anti-historicism, the ontologization of the national past).
2. Serialization (the use of tropes like the "second renaissance" and generational discourses).
3. Hierarchization (contrasting asymmetrically elites versus masses, minorities versus majorities, centers versus peripheries).
4. Biologization (using organic metaphors, the symbolism of "gardening," eugenics).
5. Sacralization (the reappearance of the topos of "elect nationhood," the charismatic cult of the leader, etc.).

This is important in the sense that we can also identify multiple conceptual ruptures and not only a linear continuity between the eighteenth and the twentieth centuries. A case in point is the shift in the function of nationalist discourse from the more universalist and emancipatory implications characteristic of the early nineteenth century toward the exclusivist and antidemocratic version (envisioning a zero-sum game between competing national projects) at the end of the nineteenth century and beyond. This makes it possible to see the interwar anti-modernist projects neither as accidental nor as the only possible outcomes of the *Dialektik* of modernity. By far, not all the actors analyzed in this book assumed such anti-modernist positions. In fact, the period was characterized by the co-existence of different temporalities (premodern, modern, anti-modern): the "contemporaneity of the non-contemporaneous," to use Bloch's famous formula. But even the most committed partisans of political modernity had to face the challenge that a significant part of their public had lost its confidence in the vision of linear progress. It is also important to mention that, in this framework of interpretation, the end of the First World War is not an absolute breaking point, but more of a moment of the transformation of political and institutional contexts, opening new horizons and radicalizing existent tendencies.[30]

If one further nuances the assumption of one fundamental—and arguably fatal—shift from premodernity to modernity, it also becomes possible to devise a more complex model of the interplay of intentions and unintended consequences. In Koselleck's depiction, there is a certain tension between the hypertrophy of terms that fuse objective and subjective levels of agency (he talks of "Enlightenment criticism" that "experienced, promoted and determined" crisis),[31] and the claim that the long-term implications of critical discourses remained hidden from the very historical actors who employed them. He thus casts them as actors of a tragedy and makes them somewhat comparable to sorcerer's apprentices who launch processes they cannot control.

This ambiguity regarding agency is deepened by the moral language used by Koselleck alluding to dishonesty—"ostensibly," "hypocritic"—implying both deception and self-deception in playing down the political implications of their ideas. Seeking to preserve their own sphere of free-thinking from interference by the authoritarian state, these *philosophes* eventually developed a meta-political discourse of moralism which deconstructed the frameworks of traditional politics aimed at avoiding the type of ideological civil war that characterized the seventeenth century. As is well documented, this picture had many common traits with Carl Schmitt's radical anti-modernist critique, one of the young Koselleck's main intellectual models and inspirations.[32] It is not by chance that Koselleck castigated his "anti-heroes" for their permanent indecision and proliferation of an "eternal debate": Schmitt memorably offered this very depiction in his *Political Romanticism*.

Reflecting on Koselleck's model from the vantage point of the interwar period also makes it possible for us to "re-embed" his interpretation in the interwar debates on the crisis of liberal democracy and modernity. This is all the more important because the very project of the Koselleckian *Begriffsgeschichte* of crisis seems to reveal a "blind spot" with regard to precisely this era (also not unrelated to the biographies of Otto Brunner and Werner Conze, Koselleck's main interlocutors in this project).[33] It is telling that in his entry on "crisis" in the *Geschichtliche Grundbegriffe*, Koselleck argues that, in the interwar period, one cannot find truly innovative uses of the concept.[34] This "blind spot" in the historicization of crisis might also be linked to Koselleck's criticism of the intellectuals launching the crisis discourse for perpetuating an endless debate and avoiding what for him (and for Schmitt) was constitutive of politics, namely decision.[35] However, one might also raise the question of whether the deterioration of political relations during the interwar period was due to the lack of decision of the political elites or the contrary: the proliferation

Introduction: The Faces of Crisis **11**

of decisionism and the readiness to draw inhuman conclusions from these radical individual and collective resolutions.[36]

Koselleck's *oeuvre* remains fundamental in many historiographical domains, such as the field of conceptual history in general and the study of the conceptualization of crisis in particular. However, pointing to the historical and political entanglements of his project also allows us to problematize some of the key assumptions of his analysis, such as the causal relationship of critique and crisis, the problem of agency, or the temporalization of the model of conceptual transformation.[37] All this cannot be separated from his insights about the "state of permanent crisis" characterizing world history, which he memorably diagnosed in the very first sentence of his *Critique and Crisis*.[38]

While keeping a distance from triumphalist or "pathogenetic" grand narratives of political modernity, it is still important to think in terms of a more comprehensive framework, which makes it possible to study different ideological projects relationally. Historicizing and pluralizing ideologies such as liberalism, conservatism, populism, or socialism also implies finding genealogical and analogical links among them. This makes it possible for us to have a more reflective stance toward some of the key problems that triggered remarkable debates in the interwar years (and which continue to shape our present political discussions): the rise of "illiberal democracy," the limits of majoritarianism, the mental/cultural versus institutional preconditions of democracy, and the relationships among different types of liberalism (cultural, social, economic). Reconstructing these interwar discussions is also important because they contributed to the formation of two ideological configurations that came to exert a notable influence on the political culture of the early twenty-first century: populism and neoliberalism. My aim is to facilitate this dialogue over temporal and geographical distance, taking the multiplicity of experiences seriously and not erasing the considerable differences, but also reflecting on what keeps these different conceptualizations and articulations together.

All of this has obvious stakes for our current political and cultural predicament, increasingly permeated by crisis discourses and the overall conviction that the different "faces" or manifestations of crisis have converged into a permanent state of "crisis-riddenness." It is indicative that the word "permacrisis" was declared the word of the year by *Collins Dictionary* in 2022.[39] Simultaneously, Tooze's analytical data visualizations of the various aspects of what he came to label as "polycrisis" became veritable bestsellers way beyond the academic sphere.[40] Therefore, the combination of synchronic and diachronic aspects of reconstruction is meant to contribute to a better understanding of the early twenty-first-century "politics of crisis" in general, and the rise of new authoritarian projects in particular. I seek to problematize those over-deterministic interpretations, still rather common especially in the media, that derive the political conditions of certain countries from some sort of unavoidable authoritarian destiny or fateful path-dependency; but also the presentist ones that are prevalent among many social scientists, whose model of causality—reduced to a very small number of variables—factors out the contextual relevance of any former sociocultural or ideological configuration in the analysis of these

12   Intellectuals and the Crisis of Politics

"hybrid regimes," as if similarity with any previous authoritarian project was merely accidental.

Finally, given the exponential growth of scholarly works on the entanglement of crisis, neoliberalism, and populism, the reader is invited onto a historical journey that may contribute to a more nuanced understanding of their multi-layered relationship. Most importantly, I intend to disprove those unilinear causal models that make reductive assertions that crisis produces populism, populism and/or (neo)liberalism produces crisis, or (neo)liberalism triggers populism. What I argue instead is that, with time, these ideological threads became interconnected with the discourse of crisis in such a way that it has become increasingly hard to imagine them without each other. In this sense, the accumulated historicity of their relationship is not just a timely research topic for historians to untangle but is central to our understanding of the very texture of ideas, symbols, tropes, enemy images, and horizons of expectation that define what can be said politically and how in the present.

* * *

This book was conceived and written in very particular circumstances. Coming from Hungary—and working at the Central European University, which the Hungarian government of Viktor Orbán forced into exile after 2017—I have been surrounded by the rhetoric of crisis (of democracy, of liberalism, of institutions, of education, of identity, etc.) for quite some time. As I went ahead with my research, the unfolding of the Covid-19 pandemic from spring 2020 onward added another—now truly global—level to the discussion on crisis. Finally, the full-scale Russian invasion of Ukraine, starting on February 24, 2022, brought along yet another dramatic shift, posing the troubling question of whether the period between 1989 and 2022 might be considered as another "interwar period."

As social distancing turned into the "new normal," luckily it did not imply intellectual distancing, and I had the opportunity to continue exchanging ideas with several friends and colleagues. I am particularly grateful to the institutions that hosted me in Berlin in 2020: the Wissenschaftskolleg zu Berlin and the Centre Marc Bloch. The emerging collective of the CEU Democracy Institute, which took up the mission of the university in Budapest, made it possible for me to link my work to many ongoing research initiatives in the field of democratization and de-democratization. I have been working in close contact with the members of the project we launched at the CEU Democracy Institute in the spring of 2021: "A Never-Ending Story? Mapping Crisis Discourses in East Central Europe, 1918–2008." I am grateful to the enthusiastic team of doctoral students (Lucija Balikić, Una Blagojević, Isidora Grubački, and Anna Orsolya Sudár) acting as co-organizers and to all the participants of this project who shared their ideas with us through our numerous zoom research meetings.[41] Furthermore, the students in my graduate seminars on "Discourses of Crisis" held at CEU in the fall of 2020 and of 2021 contributed to my work with innumerable bright questions and observations. Likewise, with students and colleagues involved in the Invisible University for Ukraine project we learned together "by doing" how various modalities of academic and existential solidarity can help in an unprecedented crisis.

Among my friends and colleagues, I thank especially Pál Ács, Sorin Antohi, Mónika Baár, László Bruszt, Holly Case, Aurelian Crăiuțu, András Czeglédi, Iván Zoltán Dénes, Michael Freeden, Róbert Gulyás, Maciej Janowski, Victor Karády, Liisi Keedus, Gábor Klaniczay, László Kontler, Michal Kopeček, János Mátyás Kovács, Marc Lazar, Joep Leerssen, Zsófia Lóránd, Tibor Mezei, Diana Mishkova, Virág Molnár, Jan-Werner Müller, Vladimir Petrović, Eva Piirimäe, István Rév, Matthias Riedl, István Sántha, Martin Schulze-Wessel, Ostap Sereda, Olga Shevchenko, Ondřej Slačálek, Renáta Uitz, Jakob Vogel, Diána Vonnák, Lea Ypi, and Tetiana Zemliakova for their input over the years. I had the privilege to present various chapters of this book in seminars and workshops at LSE London (2017), Centre Marc Bloch, Berlin (2019), Oxford European Studies Centre, St Antony's College (2022), Sciences Po, Paris (2023), the University of Tartu (2023), the Helsinki Collegium for Advanced Studies (2023), the Institute of Political Science at Charles University, Prague (2024), the Institute of History of the Polish Academy of Sciences in Warsaw (2024), and the School of Government and International Affairs, Durham University (2024).

Cody Inglis helped a lot with language editing and with many useful comments, while Benedek Pál assisted me in identifying and accessing rare books in various European libraries. Writing this book during a period of pandemic and the Russian full-scale invasion of Ukraine, which will most probably enter the history books as a prolonged period of global crisis, I am particularly grateful to my family, my mother Ildikó, my father Imre, my wife Oksana, and our son Márk, for having kept together and preserved a modicum of normality.

Notes

1. Boris Friedewald, *Die Engel von Paul Klee* (Cologne: DuMont, 2011).
2. Klee suffered from scleroderma in the late 1930s, making it increasingly hard for him to paint in a nuanced way. On his later period, see ibid., 70–92.
3. Walter Benjamin, "Theses on the Philosophy of History," in Hannah Arendt, ed. *Illuminations: Essays and Reflections*, trans. Harry Zohn (New York: Schocken Books, 1999 [1968]), 257. The most engaging interpretation of Benjamin's angelology is by his friend Gerschom Scholem in "Walter Benjamin and His Angel," in *On Jews and Judaism in Crisis: Selected Essays* (New York: Schocken Books, 1976), 198–236.
4. *Angel in Crisis I* (dated December 1, 1939) is less known, held in private collection, but also deposited in Zentrum Paul Klee in Bern. It is rather like *Angel in Crisis II* in its basic features but somewhat less self-enclosed. I warmly thank Olga Shevchenko for calling my attention to it.
5. For a recent overview of the different (mostly Western European) contexts of crisis in the history of political thought, see Cesare Cuttica and László Kontler, eds., *Crisis and Renewal in the History of European Political Thought* (Leiden: Brill, 2021). For an informative literature review of the different interpretative trends dealing with crisis,

14 Intellectuals and the Crisis of Politics

see Jérôme Heurtaux, Rachel Renault and Federico Tarragoni, "États de crise," *Tracés* 44 (2023): 9–27.

6. Reinhart Koselleck, *Critique and Crisis: Enlightenment and the Pathogenesis of Modern Society* (Cambridge, MA: MIT Press, 1988).

7. Michael Freeden pointed out that Koselleck's work focused almost exclusively on the temporalizing aspects of the concept of crisis. See Michael Freeden, "Crisis? How Is That a Crisis!? Reflections on an Overburdened Word," *Contributions to the History of Concepts* 12, no. 2 (2017): 12–28. For a recent assessment of the linkages between Koselleck's work and the "spatial turn," see Niklas Olsen, "Spatial Aspects in the Work of Reinhart Koselleck," *History of European Ideas* 49, no. 1 (2023): 136–51.

8. The research team of the ERC Starting Grant project "'Negotiating Modernity': History of Modern Political Thought in East-Central Europe" (2008–2013) reflected precisely on this problem. See Balázs Trencsényi et al., *A History of Modern Political Thought in East Central Europe*, vols. 1–2 (Oxford: Oxford University Press, 2016–18).

9. An important work in this vein is Holly Case, *The Age of Questions* (Princeton: Princeton University Press, 2018). For broader methodological considerations, see Samuel Moyn and Andrew Sartori, eds., *Global Intellectual History* (New York: Columbia University Press, 2013), and Darrin M. McMahon and Samuel Moyn, eds. *Rethinking Modern European Intellectual History* (Oxford: Oxford University Press, 2014).

10. The paradigmatic work is Detlev J. K. Peukert, *The Weimar Republic: The Crisis of Classical Modernity* (New York: Hill & Wang, 1992). While in methodological and generational terms it represents a very different project, Peter E. Gordon and John McCormick, eds., *Weimar Thought: A Contested Legacy* (Princeton: Princeton University Press, 2013) also starts from the presupposition that the Weimar crisis was experienced more profoundly than elsewhere.

11. Arthur J. Jacobson and Bernhard Schlink, eds., *Weimar: A Jurisprudence of Crisis* (Berkeley: University of California Press, 2000), 7.

12. "Weimar's crises should be understood as the products of the people who diagnosed them and not as factors that can be used in explanations of Weimar's collapse." Rüdiger Graf, "Either-Or: The Narrative of 'Crisis' in Weimar Germany and in Historiography," *Central European History* 43, no. 4 (2010): 614. See also his *Die Zukunft der Weimarer Republik: Krisen und Zukunftsaneignungen in Deutschland 1918–1933* (Munich: Oldenbourg Verlag, 2008), as well as Moritz Föllmer and Rüdiger Graf, eds., *Die "Krise" der Weimarer Republik: Zur Kritik eines Deutungsmusters* (Frankfurt a. M.: Campus Verlag, 2005). See also Peter Fritzsche, "Historical Time and Future Experience in Postwar Germany," in Wolfgang Hardtwig, ed., *Ordnungen in der Krise: Zur politischen Kulturgeschichte Deutschlands 1900–1933*, (Munich: Oldenbourg, 2007), 141–64, who criticizes Peukert's classical narrative and argues that the imaginary of the crisis needs to be taken into account as well.

13. See, e.g., the pioneering works by Tim B. Müller and Adam Tooze, eds., *Normalität und Fragilität: Demokratie nach dem Ersten Weltkrieg* (Hamburg: Hamburger Edition HIS, 2015) and Jens Hacke, *Existenzkrise der Demokratie: Zur politischen Theorie des Liberalismus in der Zwischenkriegszeit* (Berlin: Suhrkamp, 2018).

14. The claim of conceptual inflation was already voiced in the 1970s and 1980s. Morin talked about the "crisis of the concept of crisis," gradually expanding to all spheres and losing its explicatory value: "Le mot 'crise' s'est répandu de proche en proche, envahissant toute chose sociale, toute notion . . . ce terme diagnostic a perdu toute vertu explicative"; See

Edgar Morin, "Pour une crisologie," *Communications* 25 (1976): 135, 153. See also the often-quoted article by Renate Bebermayer, "'Krise'-Komposita—verbale Leitfossilien unserer Tage," in *Muttersprache* 90 (1980): 189–210.

15. See Guillermo O'Donnell, "The Perpetual Crises of Democracy," *Journal of Democracy* 18, no. 1 (2007): 5–11.

16. Jared Diamond, *Upheaval: How Nations Cope with Crisis and Change* (London: Allen Lane, 2019).

17. For the idea of the cumulative nature of crises, see Jeremy Adelman and Anne-Laure Delatte, "The Crisis of Our Crises," *Project Syndicate* (September 7, 2015), available at https://www.project-syndicate.org/commentary/global-crises-international-integration-by-jeremy-adelman-and-anne-laure-delatte-2015-09 and Adam Tooze, "Welcome to the World of the Polycrisis" *Financial Times* (October 28, 2022), available at https://www.ft.com/content/498398e7-11b1-494b-9cd3-6d669dc3de33

18. From a different analytical and political perspective, this is also a key point made in Janet Roitman's *Anti-Crisis* (Durham, NC: Duke University Press, 2013). At the same time, reflecting on the recent proliferation of the concept, she is extremely skeptical of the analytical value of the notion.

19. Robert Boyce, *The Great Interwar Crisis and the Collapse of Globalization* (Basingstoke: Palgrave Macmillan, 2009).

20. Adam Tooze, *The Deluge: The Great War and the Remaking of Global Order, 1916–1931* (London: Penguin Books, 2015).

21. Freeden, "Crisis," 16.

22. Béla Hamvas, ed., *A világválság—Die Weltkrise. Aktuális kérdések irodalma a Fővárosi Könyvtárban. Literatur von Zeitfragen in der Stadtbibliothek Budapest*, 53. (Budapest: Budapest Székesfőváros Házinyomdája, 1938).

23. Eric Hobsbawm criticized Richard Overy's *The Morbid Age* for conflating an intellectual discourse of crisis with an overall societal mood: "Looking for a central 'mood' as the keynote of an era does not get us closer to reconstructing the past than 'national character' or 'Christian/Islamic/Confucian values'. They tell us too little too vaguely." Eric Hobsbawm, "C (for Crisis)," *London Review of Books* 31, no. 15 (August 6, 2009), 12–13, available at https://www.lrb.co.uk/the-paper/v31/n15/eric-hobsbawm/c-for-crisis

24. According to Google Books' Ngram Viewer, in the English corpus the two high points of frequency are 1917 and 1932, in German 1918 and 1932, while in French 1921 and 1932. In the Hungarian Arcanum Database, the high point is also 1932, with a slightly less powerful surge in the late 1910s.

25. Werner and Zimmermann define "pragmatic induction" as "starting from the object of study and the situations in which it is embedded, according to one or more points of view—previously defined, it is true, but subject to continual readjustments in the course of empirical investigation." Michael Werner and Bénédicte Zimmermann, "Beyond Comparison: *Histoire Croisée* and the Challenge of Reflexivity," *History and Theory* 45, no. 1 (2006): 47.

26. On the possible links between symbolic geographical categories and conceptual history, see Diana Mishkova and Balázs Trencsényi, "Conceptualizing Spaces within Europe. The Case of Meso-Regions," in Willibald Steinmetz, Michael Freeden, and Javier Fernández Sebastián, eds., *Conceptual History in the European Space* (New York: Berghahn, 2017), 212–35.

16　Intellectuals and the Crisis of Politics

27. The latest and most comprehensive engagement with Koselleck's theoretical legacy is Stefan-Ludwig Hoffmann, *"Der Riss in der Zeit": Kosellecks ungeschriebene Historik* (Berlin: Suhrkamp, 2023).

28. Franz Leander Fillafer, "The Enlightenment on Trial: Reinhart Koselleck's Interpretation of *Aufklärung*," in Q. Edward Wang and Franz Leander Fillafer, eds., *The Many Faces of Clio: Cross-Cultural Approaches to Historiography: Essays in Honor of Georg G. Iggers* (Oxford: Berghahn Books, 2007), 322–45.

29. This is also the working hypothesis in Diana Mishkova, Balázs Trencsényi, and Marja Jalava, eds., *"Regimes of Historicity" in Southeastern and Northern Europe: Discourses of Identity and Temporality, 1890–1945* (Basingstoke: Palgrave Macmillan, 2014). In his monograph on Weimar liberals, Jens Hacke also identifies a second *Sattelzeit*. See Hacke, *Existenzkrise der Demokratie*, 25.

30. Detlev Peukert also alluded to this in his *Weimar Republic*. Likewise, Hungarian dissident and intellectual historian Miklós Szabó provided such a historical interpretation of the Hungarian political right in his *Az újkonzervativizmus és a jobboldali radikalizmus története—1867–1918* [The History of Neo-Conservatism and Right-Wing Radicalism, 1867–1918] (Budapest: Új Mandátum, 2003). The book was mostly written in the 1970s but was published only posthumously.

31. Koselleck, *Critique and Crisis*, 122.

32. By now there are numerous excellent studies focusing on various aspects of Koselleck's intellectual contexts and trajectory. For a general overview, see Niklas Olsen, *History in the Plural: An Introduction to the Work of Reinhart Koselleck* (New York: Berghahn Books, 2012). On his links to the German radical conservative tradition, especially Schmitt, see Sebastian Huhnholz, *Von Carl Schmitt zu Hannah Arendt?: Heidelberger Entstehungsspuren und bundesrepublikanische Liberalisierungsschichten von Reinhart Kosellecks Kritik und Krise* (Berlin: Duncker & Humblot, 2019). On his understanding of crisis and politics and their entanglement, as well as the similarity of "crisis" as a metahistorical category in Koselleck and the Schmittian *Ausnahmezustand*, rooted in Koselleck's attempt at "historicizing historicism," see Gennaro Imbriano, *Der Begriff der Politik: Die Moderne als Krisenzeit im Werk von Reinhart Koselleck* (Frankfurt a. M.: Campus, 2018).

33. Both were influenced by the methodology of *Volksgeschichte* ("ethno-history" or "folk history"), which in turn had strong political resonance on the extreme right. Austrian medievalist Otto Brunner (1898–1982) devised a powerful methodological challenge to the nineteenth-century liberal nationalist historical grand narrative and was a vocal supporter of Nazi policies in the late 1930s. After the war, he held the prestigious chair of medieval history in Hamburg. Werner Conze (1910–1986) was a prominent social historian with a special focus on the history of Eastern Europe. Having studied in Königsberg, he worked within the paradigm of *Ostforschung*—which was increasingly Nazified—and legitimized the ethnic cleansing of German-occupied Eastern European territories during the Second World War. After the war, he became professor at Göttingen and later rector at Heidelberg, serving also as the President of the German Historical Society in the 1970s. For Brunner, see James Van Horn Melton, "From Folk History to Structural History: Otto Brunner (1898–1982) and the Radical-Conservative Roots of German Social History," in Hartmut Lehmann and James Van Horn Melton, eds., *Paths of Continuity: Central European Historiography from the 1930s to the 1950s* (Washington, DC: German Historical Institute, 1994), 263–92; for Conze, see Irmline Veit-Brause, "Werner

Conze (1910–1986): The Measure of History and the Historian's Measures," in ibid., 299–344.

34. From the nineteenth century onward, Koselleck saw "few corresponding gains in either clarity or precision" regarding the conceptualization of crisis. See Reinhart Koselleck and Michaela W. Richter, "Crisis," *Journal of the History of Ideas* 67, no. 2 (2006): 397. This is the English translation of the original: Reinhart Koselleck, "Krise," in Otto Brunner, Werner Conze, and Reinhart Koselleck, eds., *Geschichtliche Grundbegriffe: Historisches Lexicon zur politisch-sozialen Sprache in Deutschland*, vol. 3: *H–Me* (Stuttgart: Klett-Cotta, 1982), 617–50. On the possible roots of the reticence of Koselleck and his co-editors to engage with the interwar conceptual transformation, see Anson Rabinbach, "Rise and Fall of the Sattelzeit: The *Geschichtliche Grundbegriffe* and the Temporality of Totalitarianism and Genocide," in Dan Edelstein, Stefanos Geroulanos, and Natasha Wheatley, eds., *Power and Time: Temporalities in Conflict and the Making of History* (Chicago: University of Chicago Press, 2020), 103–21.

35. One might also consider the limited engagement with spatial concepts in the design of the *Geschichtliche Grundbegriffe* as yet another "blind spot," not unrelated to the intensive concern with spatiality and spatial concepts by Carl Schmitt during the Second World War, in the context of genocidal territorial expansion.

36. An analogous question is posed by Andrew S. Gilbert, *The Crisis Paradigm: Description and Prescription in Social and Political Theory* (Cham: Palgrave Macmillan, 2019), 61–100.

37. See Hartmut Kaelble, "Europa in der Krise. Zivilisationskrise—Integrationskrise—Krisenmanagement," in Thomas Mergel, ed., *Krisen Verstehen. Historische und kulturwissenschaftliche Annäherungen* (Frankfurt: Campus Verlag, 2012), 131–44.

38. Koselleck, *Critique and Crisis*, 5.

39. David Shariatmadari, "A Year of 'Permacrisis,'" *Collins Language Lovers Blog*, November 1, 2022, available at https://blog.collinsdictionary.com/language-lovers/a-year-of-permacrisis/

40. "A problem becomes a crisis when it challenges our ability to cope and thus threatens our identity. In the polycrisis the shocks are disparate, but they interact so that the whole is even more than the sum of the parts." Adam Tooze, "Welcome to the World of the Polycrisis," *Financial Times*, October 28, 2022, available at https://www.ft.com/content/498398e7-11b1-494b-9cd3-6d669dc3de33. For the global echo of the notion, see "This is Why 'Polycrisis' is a Useful Way of Looking at the World Right Now," available at https://www.weforum.org/agenda/2023/03/polycrisis-adam-tooze-historian-explains/; "Why 'Polycrisis' Was the Buzzword of Day 1 in Davos," available at https://time.com/6247799/polycrisis-in-davos-wef-2023/

41. The outcome of this project is Balázs Trencsényi, Lucija Balikić, Una Blagojević, and Isidora Grubački, eds., *East Central European Crisis Discourses in the Twentieth Century. A Never-Ending Story?* (London: Routledge, 2024). I thank Routledge for allowing me in this book to use some passages from my contribution, "Crisis without Catharsis? Crisis Discourses and the Problem of Modernity in Interwar East Central Europe," (pp. 27–54), dealing with East Central European authors.

2
The Morphology of Modern Crisis Discourses

As has been established by conceptual history research, the notion of "crisis" has a remarkably long career and reaches back to classical Antiquity.[1] However, for a long time the notion had a primarily medical referentiality, implying in the progress of an illness a turning point that could lead to recovery but also to death. In classical Greek, the word is etymologically linked to "critique," which also implied separating, telling things apart from each other, both in the sense of contest and of decision between alternative options. We can still capture this semantic link in expressions like "critical situation." In the Middle Ages, crisis assumed an eschatological referentiality as well, pointing to the Last Judgment as a final "crisis" of mankind.

The Emergence of the Modern Concept

Politicized in the eighteenth century, crisis became an important concept of Enlightenment social thought, linked to the birth of the public sphere and thus intimately tied to the rise of political modernity. However, the oft-quoted appearance of the notion in Jean-Jacques Rousseau's *Émile* ("The crisis is approaching, and we are on the edge of a revolution") shows an ambiguity, being at the liminal zone between premodern and modern semantic connotations.[2] Reinhart Koselleck's central hypothesis about the moralization of politics in the Enlightenment is clearly supported by the way the concept of crisis appears here in *Émile*, in the context of an argument advocating introspection to find one's real self, while contrasting the image of the criminal driven by despair and society sustaining the criminal order that drives him to commit a crime, judging the latter much more morally despicable than the criminal. It is this quest for the "real self" that Rousseau sets as a main target of education, arguing that only in this way one can prepare a child for preserving his/her moral integrity even if the social and political conditions change radically.

Conspicuously, Rousseau links crisis to the concept of "revolution," which would occur in the future. Nevertheless, revolution still had a connotation of the turn of fate, traditionally associated with the wheel of fortune, and there is very little in this usage that indicates an open-ended futural projection that came to characterize political modernity as analyzed by Koselleck in view of the transformative period of the *Sattelzeit*. It is this semantic ambiguity that colors the use of the notion of crisis as

---

Intellectuals and the Crisis of Politics in the Interwar Period and Beyond. Balázs Trencsényi, Oxford University Press.
© Balázs Trencsényi (2025). DOI: 10.1093/9780198929512.003.0002

well: crisis is not only the opening of historical progress but refers to the turning upside down of the social hierarchies—with the great becoming small and the small becoming great.

This ambiguity is visible in Rousseau's other works, such as the *Considerations on the Government of Poland and on its Proposed Reformation* (completed in 1772; published only posthumously). Crisis also appears here as a transformation projected onto the future, one which could be read in terms of the starting point of an open-ended progress—"The nation will date her second birth from the terrible crisis from which she is emerging"[3]—but this is nuanced by other uses referring to the past: "Every free state in which no provision has been made for great crises is in danger of perishing with every storm. Only the Poles have been able to convert their very crises into a new means of safeguarding their constitution."[4] The second meaning fits more into the classical republican model of constitutional regeneration and restoration of "first principles." But even the allusion to "second birth" in the first quote occurs in the context of the contrast between ancient patriotic zeal and modern moral indifference.

Rousseau's conceptualization can thus be perceived as Janus-faced, having both a future-oriented and a classical (temporally cyclical) component. In some ways, this is the case with English-born American radical publicist Thomas Paine's (1737–1809) use as well. To be sure, the very title of his series of pamphlets, and the famous first sentences of the first issue—"[These] are the times that try men's souls. The summer soldier and the sunshine patriot will, in this crisis, shrink from the service of their country; but he that stands by it now, deserves the love and thanks of man and woman"[5]—turned crisis into a central notion of political analysis and mobilization. At the same time, the notion does not appear frequently in the pages of the series and even then mostly in a localized meaning—far from the all-encompassing rhetoric implied by the first issue.

Subsequently, crisis became an increasingly important concept in various political and cultural discourses throughout the nineteenth century, changing its function and connotations to a certain extent over time. Several authors employed the notion of crisis in the context of their broader investigations into the course of world history. Thus, in developing the late Enlightenment construction of stadial history further, Henri de Saint-Simon (1760–1825) contrasted organic and crisis-ridden historical periods. He conceived of crisis as a profound reconfiguration accompanied by ideological and social disorientation, reaching beyond national confines:

> ... for, gentlemen, you cannot conceal from yourselves that the crisis which faces the human mind is common to all the enlightened peoples, and that the symptoms which appeared in France, during the terrible explosion which occurred there, can be detected at the present moment by an intelligent observer in England, and even in Germany.[6]

The mid-nineteenth century saw a veritable boom in economic crisis theories. French statistician Clément Juglar (1819–1905), who was trained as a medical doctor (which might have also played a role in turning his interest toward the concept of

20 Intellectuals and the Crisis of Politics

crisis), drew on datasets from the most industrialized countries to establish economic cycles and the regularity of commercial crises.[7] He became interested in economic disturbances in the revolutionary year of 1848 and subsequently turned to study economic crisis phenomena with statistical means. In his main theoretical work, published in 1863, Juglar sought to ascertain the "general causes, the development, explosion, and the liquidation of crises."[8] With regard to their main causes, Juglar pointed to unbridled speculation and the overexpansion of industry and trade, triggering a dynamic of excessive spending, which however at some point led to a breakdown and a subsequent return to a more balanced situation by liquidating the excesses.

Writing simultaneously with Juglar, but representing a very different theoretical position, Karl Marx (1818–1883) also employed the concept of crisis in his critical analysis of capitalism. Already in "Wage Labour and Capital," published at the end of the revolutionary period of 1848–49, Marx talked of crisis as an occurrence indicating the internal contradictions and limits of the capitalist system:

> . . . in the same measure in which the capitalists are compelled, by the movement described above, to exploit the already existing gigantic means of production on an ever-increasing scale, and for this purpose to set in motion all the mainsprings of credit, in the same measure do they increase the industrial earthquakes, in the midst of which the commercial world can preserve itself only by sacrificing a portion of its wealth, its products, and even its forces of production, to the gods of the lower world—in short, the crises increase.[9]

Marx continued to work on the theory of crisis in his mature works as well, such as the second volume of *Capital*. His most detailed exposition of crisis theory can be found in his *Theories of Surplus Value*, where he engaged with the theoretical legacy of classical political economy (Jean-Baptiste Say, David Ricardo, James Mill) and put forward an explanation focusing on overproduction and arguing that crises were necessary occurrences in a capitalist money economy. Like his earlier argument, he paid special attention to the global dimensions of crisis: "In the crises of the world market, the contradictions and antagonisms of bourgeois production are strikingly revealed."[10]

Marx described crisis as a destructive process, which made the unity of seemingly separate but still interlinked phases (e.g., buying and selling, supply and demand) visible. In this interpretation, the economic system based on monetary transactions experienced moments when one phase was not followed automatically by the other (e.g., a product was manufactured without there being an immediate buyer). Indeed, for the socialist theoretician, the principal cause of crisis was the contradiction between the "impetuous development" of productive powers and the limitations of consumption, inherent also to his idea of the gradual sharpening of the class conflict with an ever-richer and ever-smaller minority of capitalists and the increasingly proletarianized masses, which could only be resolved by a final crisis in the future that would overhaul the capitalist system altogether.

For Swiss historian Jacob Burckhardt (1818–1897), too, crisis denoted a historically significant transformation, and thus he looked for such conjunctures of transformative forces in various historical moments, starting with classical Antiquity.[11] He identified barbarian incursions and population movements (describing the *Völkerwanderung* as the paradigmatic case) as instances of "primitive crises," destroying older forms but also dynamizing history by triggering development. The usual reading of Burckhardt's use of the notion of crisis points out that he endowed crisis with positive and future-oriented transformative connotations—"The crisis itself is an expedient of nature, like a fever"[12]—in contrast to later streams of radical conservative cultural pessimism, which linked crisis to decline, often in spiritual and racial terms. Nevertheless, Burckhardt's vision also had darker shades, particularly in view of his equation of transformative crises with regenerative wars. Overall, he considered war as a motor of progress that restores the real forces of the nation and argued that peace held for too long could lead to disconcertion (*Entnervung*) and the proliferation of unhealthy social elements (*Notexistenzen*) who "thicken the air" and "pollute the blood of the nation." In this context, Burckhardt's qualification that, when possible, it is preferable to wage a just and defensive war does not alter the picture he provides, shaped as it is by social Darwinism combined with a measure of anthropological pessimism. This is even clearer from the next qualification, where he points out that modern wars were generally too short and did not affect bourgeois existence, thus they only postponed the "real crisis."[13] Needless to say, all of this attains special acoustics in view of the Great War half a century later, which indeed was greeted by many participants and observers as a possibility to "clear the air" and refresh the biological and spiritual energies of their respective nations.

Burckhardt was an atypical thinker in many ways, but his thinking about crisis anticipated some of the most important tropes of the *fin-de-siècle* discussion. For instance, the concept of crisis was inserted into a debate on social transformation and the loss of function of traditional elites. This was linked to a sweeping image of the advent of mass society, eroding traditional hierarchies and social norms and leading to the demise of rational politics, replaced by an appeal to irrational mass emotions.[14] An important aspect of this debate concerned the social and political role of intellectuals. On the one hand, this reflected the emergence of a new social group with specific consciousness and peculiar socioeconomic characteristics, emerging as a response to what was framed as the "crisis" of traditional elites (most obviously in the French context, which is also the best documented).[15] On the other hand—especially in societies beyond Western Europe—it pointed to the growing gap between traditional popular culture (based on a dominantly rural sociocultural milieu) and educated urbanites who uncritically embraced modernity. This latter tension was often conceptualized in terms of the emergence of "two cultures." Especially in the wake of collective traumas (e.g., the 1905 Russian Revolution) this discourse of internal rupture came to be framed as a comprehensive political, intellectual, and moral crisis caused by the superficiality of modernization and the dysfunctionality of the new elites. As the Russian liberal political economist Petr Struve (1870–1944) puts it:

> The detestable triumph of reaction has moved many of us to forget or keep silent about the mistakes of our revolution. Nothing could be more dangerous than forgetfulness, nothing more thoughtless than silence. "Political impressionism" is the only name for this attitude; it must be opposed by an analysis that transcends the impressions of the moment in order to study the moral essence of the political crisis into which the intelligentsia has led our country.[16]

Thus, at the European semi-peripheries, this (self-)criticism often boiled down to a castigation of the imitative and inauthentic nature of emerging modern intellectual cultures and social mores in these societies, which had undergone a swift Westernization on the surface while leaving deeper structures untouched (this is the meaning of the famous metaphor launched by the Romanian *Junimist* intellectual movement in the late nineteenth century: "forms without substance").[17]

At the turn of the twentieth century, in many European contexts, East and West alike, the crisis of political modernity came to be described in biopolitical terms: a demographic shift leading to overpopulation and a decline in the health of the nation which needed to be treated by eugenicist measures.[18] Importantly, medical language was also changing toward the end of the nineteenth century, shifting from the binary of health/sickness to normality/abnormality, opening up the space for an even more comprehensively organicist conceptual framework that could also be transferred to the analysis of societies.[19] The biopolitical framing of crisis also brought another important element, namely connecting generational discourses with the trope of spiritual and biological decline and a criticism of democratic institutions. This has been documented to a great extent for France (e.g., the famous "Agathon's Report" from 1912) and Italy (in the political language of pre-First World War integral nationalists like Enrico Corradini), but it appeared in other countries as well, such as in Serbia, where the pre-1914 Yugoslavist discourse put the recovery from the crisis of the body politic at the top of the agenda for the young and nationally conscious generation.

By the 1910s the link between generational and anti-parliamentary crisis discourses became solidified. Different variants of integral nationalism put forward a vision of national crisis and rejuvenation, breaking with nineteenth-century modalities of nation-building. From this perspective too, the Great War is much less of a turning point than is usually presumed. Zeev Sternhell, among others, argues that the vision of a crisis of civilization and the anti-materialism that became common denominators of fascist ideologies was already present at the turn of the century, as faith in the individual and optimistic views of progress were gradually abandoned in the context of the rise of mass society.[20]

However, these ideological components received a further twist in the interwar period. This conceptual transformation is obvious if one compares the use of the concept of crisis during the First World War and its subsequent usages in the interwar years. For instance, in 1917 Swedish conservative and pro-German geopolitical writer Rudolf Kjellén (1864–1922) published his wartime articles under the title

Studien zur Weltkrise, but the notion referred here mainly to the political and military clash between the two alliances.[21] He argued that the war was a "great crisis that has to be decided either on one side or the other."[22] He linked the unfolding world crisis (*Weltkrise*) to the emergence of the national principle (*Nationalitätenprinzip*) as a new legitimizing framework of politics but rejected the narrative of the Entente about the liberation of oppressed small nations. He subscribed instead to the idea of *Mitteleuropa* (drawing on Friedrich Naumann's eponymous book published in 1915), which he considered to be a unificatory framework for the core of Europe.

Going directly against this discourse and seeking to deconstruct *Mitteleuropa* as an instrument of German domination, Tomáš G. Masaryk (1850–1937), a key ideologist of the other side in the World War, also used crisis in his programmatic texts about war aims, for example, his 1915 inaugural lecture launching the School of Slavonic Studies at the University of London.[23] The ideological conflict notwithstanding, Masaryk's reference to the "Crisis of Europe" resembled Kjellén's in the sense that it did not reach beyond the war itself. This is all the more interesting as Masaryk had a remarkable track record of using the concept as a keyword in his political essayism directed at the Czech public before the war, most importantly in his *Naše nynější krize* (Our Current Crisis), written two decades earlier, criticizing the Czech liberal nationalist mainstream.[24] Without too much further unpacking of the concept, the conventional pairing of the notion of crisis with the war is perhaps most obvious in Winston Churchill's encompassing narrative *The World Crisis* (which he started to write in 1914), where—the prominence of the concept in the title notwithstanding—crisis is not an explanatory term in any way.[25]

We can observe the same dynamic in a different geopolitical context, too—of Spain remaining neutral in the conflagration of the First World War. During the war, prominent writer and public intellectual Ramiro de Maeztu (1875–1936) published *Authority, Liberty and Function in the Light of the War*, based on a series of articles originally printed in the journal *New Age*.[26] De Maeztu's book was intended as a diagnosis of the deep political and spiritual disorientation of the liberal world order in the context of the war, evincing the author's search for an ideological "third way" (which he calls the "functional principle") between liberalism and authoritarianism, which he also localized in the two warring camps. When the volume was republished in Spanish in 1919, the title was changed to the much more concise *La crisis del humanismo*. Nevertheless, the very notion of crisis barely features in the text, and usually refers to specific contexts like England and not to the general predicament of European civilization. Moving from Fabianism toward an increasingly right-wing corporatist position, de Maeztu tends to use the binary of "order" and "disorder" instead of "crisis" as a central normative frame.

It is also symptomatic that the diagnosis of radical cultural transformation put forward by the young Karl Mannheim (1893–1947) in his 1917 lecture "Soul and Culture," while having all of the components of interwar discourses of cultural crisis (e.g., the analysis of alienation between objective and subjective reality—taken from Georg Simmel's writings—or the feeling of the loss of meaning of older forms and the search for new ones), could still be formulated without employing the concept of "crisis" itself.[27]

In this sense, the end phase of the war meant an important conceptual turning point, while the interwar period witnessed quantitative as well as qualitative shifts in the circulation of crisis discourses. As one of the most accomplished historians of modern conceptualizations of crisis, Rüdiger Graf argued, activating already-existing discursive patterns, the discourse of crisis gradually became more comprehensive, moving from a predominantly economic reference to cover most spheres of human existence.[28] While in the mid-1910s the concept of crisis was not so much present in economic knowledge-production, as we will see, one of the main tropes of interwar crisis discourses was indeed the claim that different sectoral crises merged into a comprehensive and therefore much more profound systemic disorder, linking economy, culture, society, and foreign politics. Along these lines, Graf suggests that we can talk of the gradual "globalization" and "singularization" of the concept of crisis.[29] At the same time, it is also important to see that even these overarching statements about a multi-sectoral crisis depended on the particular perspective of the speaker: a philosopher could describe the crisis of scientific cognition as the root of all other cultural and social disturbances; an economist could point at the proliferation of state interventionism; while a social theorist might have identified the breakthrough of mass society as the ultimate common denominator of all crisis symptoms.

The Specificities of the Interwar Conceptualization

Drawing on Michael Freeden's argument about the plurality of political functions and ideological emplotments of the concept of crisis,[30] we need to search for an interpretative framework that is sensitive both to continuities and ruptures, ideological and contextual differences, and to transnational interferences. In the following, I sketch out the main lines of such a framework in terms of a working hypothesis that needs to be tested further both in view of the various local contexts as well as in terms of its global relevance. A central tenet of my argument is that discourses of crisis combine analytical and mobilizing functions in a highly compelling manner. This means also that it would be too easy to dismiss them as merely propaganda slogans—we must take them seriously even if we cannot take them at their face value.

By now it has become more or less consensual in the scholarly community that the interwar discourses of crisis were not projecting an unavoidable doomsday, but rather sought to discern a transformative moment that might result in collective regeneration provided that the given political or cultural community successfully mobilizes its human, spiritual, and material resources in the "right direction."[31] This did not exclude the imagery of irretrievable decline, but it usually referred to certain social or cultural subgroups or strata, and even in this case the hope of a miraculous recovery often loomed behind the text. At the same time, crisis discourses were not merely rallying cries of various political and meta-political camps but were often embedded in serious intellectual projects to shed light on the complex social, cultural, political, and economic processes unfolding at a given moment.

Along these lines, I argue that a discourse of crisis is neither the cause nor merely an indicator of social and political conflicts. Rather, it is a representation of reality and a narrative framework of temporalization (compressing time and identifying both ruptures and continuities) and spatialization (for instance, when talking of the "crisis of Europe," as Masaryk did, or of the "decline of the West" in the case of Oswald Spengler and his followers) used by different historical actors, which in turn need to be analyzed in order to better understand the thinking and sociopolitical agency of these actors. Key features of this perception of crisis are a sense of rupture, the experience of time pressure (the conflation of the horizons of past, present, and future), a growing uncertainty in establishing causal relationships (finding that the same phenomena can be linked to different causal chains), and a feeling of fragmentation of the public sphere when representatives of different interpretations of the world or of the given situation are unable to communicate their experiences, falling captive to their own autarchic language-games. For the "insiders," these language-games give perfect explanations for everything, but for the "outsiders" they usually make very little sense. Regarding the spatial dimension, modern discourses of crisis contain implicit or explicit symbolic geographical projections (linking global and local developments, speaking of the rise or decline of geographical and political units, pointing to the threat posed by neighbors, etc.). Tracing these projections, we can also follow the transformation of national self-representations over time as well as the change of the image and relevance of broader frameworks, including Europe.

To analyze the different temporal and spatial frameworks; political, cultural, and social functions; and conceptual connotations of these crisis discourses, I propose a taxonomy based on "discursive localizations" and not so much on ideological streams (liberal vs. socialist vs. fascist visions, etc.), as I sought to avoid representing these ideological streams as monological. Furthermore, the most original voices are often hard to place into an ideological box, and it is also tedious to employ the same taxonomy transnationally—what in one context qualifies as liberalism might well be considered socialism or conservatism in another. Graf also detected these overlaps and discerned four "definitions of crisis" in the Weimar context—nationalist, socialist, European, spiritual/moral—but also pointed to their considerable interferences, as in the case of national socialism.[32] In fact, the dialogues, overlaps, and interferences between different ideological streams that transcend the traditional ideological lines of demarcation often constitute the most interesting and characteristic feature of the period in question.

While in the interwar period most ideological streams opted for some notion of crisis or an adjacent term (e.g., transition, transformation, crossroads) as part of their conceptual apparatus, there are also ideologies that turned it into the very core of their conceptual framework. In the following, I pay special attention to the entanglements of two such ideological streams—populism and neoliberalism—as being built around diagnoses of "general crisis." Given the magnitude and latitude of existing scholarly literature on populism and neoliberalism, and particularly the exponential growth of academic interest in the last decade, it would be futile to try to come up with any sort of consensus definition. Most of the scholars who deal with these notions register a conceptual indeterminacy, polysemy,[33] or as Pierre Rosanvallon puts it with regard to populism, "*flottement semantique*."[34] Partly this is due to the fact that there is an obvious discrepancy between the rather select few ideologists who assumed the label of populism or neoliberalism to describe their own position and the many authors who used these tags with reference to others.

Rather than just registering the presence of these labels in the political debate on crisis, I seek to insert these ideological streams into a differentiated picture of political modernity, paying special attention to underlying shifts in the perception of history (or, using François Hartog's terminology, "regimes of historicity"). In this respect, one might also pose the question of whether the four interpretative possibilities of the modern crisis concept identified by Koselleck ("a chain of events leading to a culminating, decisive point," "a unique and final turning-point of history," "a critical situation," and "a historically immanent transitional phase")[35] and their (inter)relationships remained unaltered in the context of a radical shift of historical sensitivities in the interwar years. Koselleck read the twentieth-century usages as fitting into "the frame of philosophies of history already established in the previous (nineteenth) century."[36] While his assertion that "'crisis' continues to demonstrate the ongoing novelty of our epoch, still perceived as a transitional stage,"[37] seems to be applicable to the interwar years as well, there were also interesting new developments. In the following, these interwar discussions are analyzed both in view of their rootedness in the generic processes of political modernity and the specific features distinguishing them from earlier intellectual and conceptual configurations.

Analyzing crisis discourses with reference to the differentiation and multilayeredness of political modernity makes it possible to identify moments of intensive conceptual transformation other than the early nineteenth-century *Sattelzeit* memorably analyzed by Koselleck and his colleagues. In contrast to the open-ended visions of the post-revolutionary era in the early nineteenth century and the organicist evolutionary metaphors characterizing the positivist understanding toward the end of the nineteenth century, the problematization of the future-oriented model—becoming increasingly prevalent after the turn of the twentieth century—was reflected also in the reconfiguration of crisis discourses.

The transformation of temporal frames and ideological contexts created novel modalities, such as the proliferation of the imagery of unresolved crisis, creating a permanent suspension in time, which could only be broken by a truly cataclysmic event. In that sense, rather than referring to a transition from one political/social/cultural configuration to another, crisis came to denote the recurrence (or even "eternal return") of irresolvable transition situations. Likewise, anti-modernist ideologies that emerged from the 1910s onward offered structurally different resolutions of the crisis than modernist ones. For example, they tended to negate—or suggested opting out of—historicity altogether. These ideological modalities are most obvious in the various constructions of "national metaphysics" proliferating in the 1920s–1930s.

Instead of projections of resolving the crisis and entering the next phase of evolution, the period in question witnessed the rise of "retrospective prophetism," where the overcoming of the crisis was predicated upon the recovery of a previously abandoned or "lost" tradition. The resonance of the crisis discourse with the fundamental criticism of political modernity was central especially to the populist understanding of history, working both with positive and negative *Sonderweg* theories as an alternative to bourgeois liberalism. In a less direct way, however, it can also be seen in the interwar discussion about the validity of the liberal tradition among those who became associated with neoliberalism, suggesting a break with the recent past to restore the "essence" of their ideological orientation. This retrospective modality evidently resonated with the "restorative" features of pre-modern prophetism, but also combined it with elements that were unmistakably linked to modernity, especially the active choice implied when opting for a certain layer of tradition. In this sense, even the most straightforward restorative claim to the immediacy and authenticity of pre-modern life had to be mediated through the experience and institutions of modernity.

Another anti-modernist modality was related to the consciousness that it was exactly by radicalizing the conflicts, and thus in some sense even proactively aggravating the ongoing crisis, that any lasting solution to the overall social and cultural disorder could be expected. This is very clear both in the radical leftist and rightist (conservative revolutionary) visions, seeking to turn the crisis into a transformative moment by destroying the existing system. But it was also present in less predictable contexts, such as the mainstream liberal or liberal conservative expert narratives of the economic slump, where "crisis" was perceived as a necessary process of cathartic self-purging. Destroying the unprofitable branches of investment, crisis came to be perceived as some sort of quasi-apocalyptic "Last Judgment" of the market, which had to be allowed to run its own course without trying to alleviate its consequences and thus only prolonging it.

The interplay of these modernist and anti-modernist modalities embedded in the crisis discourse had repercussions also beyond 1945. Hence, the reconstruction of these discussions might offer clues also to the more recent configurations of the crisis discourse. While the bulk of this book is about the complex discursive developments of the interwar years, its aim is far from being "antiquarian" in the sense of merely seeking to discern various modalities of crisis discourses in the distant or not-so-distant past. Instead, it is meant to contribute to the contextualization of ideologies and political discourses that thematized crisis after the Second World War, and to relate it to our current predicament. Thus, in the concluding chapters I take a long-term perspective well beyond the interwar years and argue that it is not by chance that these two above-mentioned ideological traditions, linked intimately to interwar crisis discourses rose to such prominence after the end of the Cold War. However, we must also pay attention to the differences. While there are obvious conceptual and ideological continuities, it is also important to consider changes in the underlying assumptions of political thinking and action over the last hundred years.

Without doubt, the twenty-first-century variants of neoliberalism and populism are radically different from their precursors a century before. This also makes it

28 Intellectuals and the Crisis of Politics

hard to give a universally applicable definition of these notions. It is characteristic of the debate around these two ideological streams that different analysts looking at different geographical and historical configurations came up with very divergent renderings. As a result, there has been increasing academic peer pressure to abandon them altogether as unscientific. However, their pivotal presence in public discourse has still made them too important to be left completely to non-academic "laymen." Taking all this into account, my book is not intended to offer a comprehensive meta-theory of populism or neoliberalism, but rather relies on "pragmatic induction" in relating these ideological streams to each other through their formative experiences, and various interpretations, of crisis. This reconstruction also provides intellectual resources for a historically reflective use of these labels, even in present-oriented analytical operations within the fields of political science, sociology, or anthropology. A possible gain from this would be to problematize the recurrent assumption that they are ideologically completely "flat" or serve only as "empty signifiers" or "placeholders" to be filled with whatever ideological content one chooses. Instead, I point to several ideological components rooted in the formative experiences of the interwar years that shaped the ways adherents of these streams structure reality.[38]

In addition to identifying common formative experiences, I explore various ideological and personal links between these two streams. Significantly, some of the key authors, whose work focused on crisis before—and after—1945, such as Wilhelm Röpke, were central ideologists of both. Along these lines, I hope to shed some historical light on the phenomena that puzzled most observers in the last two decades: the entanglement of seemingly incompatible, or even openly antagonistic, neoliberal and populist elements in the ideological compositions of new autocratic projects from East Central Europe to Latin America.

Such a historicization offers important clues not only for the epistemic community of historians, but also for those looking to understand our current political dynamic. It gives us tools to compare responses to what seemed to be an all-encompassing process of dissolution of ideological and institutional frameworks with current developments, which are increasingly framed as part and parcel of a "polycrisis." Importantly, employing such a historical perspective should not necessarily amount to the total relativization or deconstruction of the concept. Rather, it might help us develop a more reflective use of the very notion of crisis in political debates, preventing its heedless overuse and conceptual inflation and saving it for interventions when its deployment does have analytical force and mobilizing emotional impact.

Notes

1. On the conceptual history of crisis, apart from Reinhart Koselleck's seminal *Critique and Crisis*, see also Reinhart Koselleck and Michaela W. Richter, "Crisis," *Journal of the History of Ideas* 67, no. 2 (2006): 357–400, and Ernst Wolfgang Orth, "Krise," in Christian Bermes and Ulrich Dierse, eds., *Schlüsselbegriffe der Philosophie des 20.*

Jahrhunderts (Hamburg: Meiner, 2010), 149–73. For its localization in various political and historical contexts, see also Thomas Mergel, ed., *Krisen verstehen: Historische und kulturwissenschaftliche Annäherungen* (Frankfurt: Campus, 2012); Henning Grunwald and Manfred Pfister, eds., *Krisis! Krisenszenarien, Diagnosen und Diskursstrategien* (Munich: Fink, 2007); Poul F. Kjaer and Niklas Olsen, *Critical Theories of Crisis in Europe: From Weimar to the Euro* (London: Rowman & Littlefield, 2016); and Andrew S. Gilbert, *The Crisis Paradigm: Description and Prescription in Social and Political Theory* (Cham: Palgrave Macmillan, 2019).

2. Jean-Jacques Rousseau, *Emile, or Education*, trans. Barbara Foxley (London: J. M. Dent and Sons, 1921, 157.

3. Jean-Jacques Rousseau, "Considérations sur le Gouvernement de Pologne, et sur sa réformation projetée," in *Collection complète des oeuvres* (Geneva, 1782), vol. 1, 440; available at https://www.rousseauonline.ch/pdf/rousseauonline-0006.pdf; for the English translation, see *Considerations on the Government of Poland and on its Proposed Reformation*, 11, available at https://css.ethz.ch/en/services/digital-library/publications/publication.html/125482

4. Ibid., 480; English trans., 29.

5. Thomas Paine, "The American Crisis," (December 23, 1776), available at https://www.ushistory.org/Paine/crisis/c-01.htm

6. Claude-Henri de Saint-Simon, "Letters from an Inhabitant of Geneva to his Contemporaries" [1803], in *The Political Thought of Saint-Simon*, ed. Ghita Ionescu (Oxford: Oxford University Press, 1976), 74.

7. On the broader intellectual context, see Daniele Besomi, "Clément Juglar and his Contemporaries on the Causes of Commercial Crises," *Revue européenne des sciences sociales* 47, no. 143 (2009): 17–47.

8. Clément Juglar, *Des Crises commerciales et leur retour périodique en France, en Angleterre, et aux États-Unis* (Paris: Guillaumin, 1862), 4.

9. Karl Marx, "Lohnarbeit und Kapital," in Karl Marx and Friedrich Engels, *Werke*, Vol. 6 (Berlin: Dietz Verlag, 1959), 423; first published in the "Neue Rheinische Zeitung" in April 1849.

10. Karl Marx, *Theorien über den Mehrwert*, in Karl Marx and Friedrich Engels, *Werke*, vol. 26.2 (Berlin: Dietz Verlag, Berlin, 1967), 500. English translation available at https://www.marxists.org/archive/marx/works/1863/theories-surplus-value/ch17.htm

11. Jacob Burckhardt, "Die geschichtlichen Krisen," in Jakob Oeri, ed., *Weltgeschichtliche Betrachtungen* (Pfullingen: Neske, 1949), 199–251. The text was published posthumously based on the lectures Burckhardt held between 1868 and 1872.

12. Burckhardt, "Die geschichtlichen Krisen," 234. I followed Mary D. Hottinger's translation from *Reflections on History* (London: Allen & Unwin, 1950 [1943]), 158.

13. On Burckhardt's concept of crisis, see John R. Hinde, *Jacob Burckhardt and the Crisis of Modernity* (Montreal: McGill–Queen's University Press, 2000).

14. For an overview on the late nineteenth-century visions of crisis, see John W. Burrow, *The Crisis of Reason: European Thought, 1848–1914* (New Haven: Yale University Press, 2000).

15. Christophe Charle, *Naissance des "intellectuels," 1880–1900* (Paris: Minuit, 1990).

16. Petr Struve, "The Intelligentsia and Revolution," in Nikolai Berdiaev et al., *Vekhi (Landmarks)*, ed. and trans. Marshall S. Shatz and Judith E. Zimmermann (London: M. E. Sharpe, 1994), 125.

30　Intellectuals and the Crisis of Politics

17. See Diana Mishkova and Roumen Daskalov, "'Forms without Substance': Debates on the Transfer of Western Models to the Balkans," in Roumen Daskalov and Diana Mishkova, eds., *Entangled Histories of the Balkans*, vol. 2: *Transfers of Political Ideologies and Institutions*, (Leiden: Brill, 2013), 1–97.

18. See Marius Turda, *Modernism and Eugenics* (London: Palgrave Macmillan, 2010).

19. Robert A. Nye, "Degeneration and the Medical Model of Cultural Crisis in the French Belle Époque," in Seymour Drescher, David Sabean, and Allan Sharlin, eds., *Political Symbolism in Modern Europe: Essays in Honor of George L. Mosse* (Somerset: Taylor & Francis Group, 1982), 19–43. Cammarano also points to the framework of "organicist positivism" as the main catalyst of crisis discourses. See Fulvio Cammarano, "Crisi politica e politica della crisi: Italia e Gran Bretagna 1880–1925," in Paolo Pombeni, ed., *Crisi, legittimazione, consenso* (Bologna: Il Mulino, 2003), 81–131.

20. See Zeev Sternhell, *Neither Right nor Left: Fascist Ideology in France* (Berkeley: University of California Press, 1987).

21. Rudolf Kjellén, *Studien zur Weltkrise* (Munich: Bruckmann, 1917).

22. Kjellén, "Die Welthistorische Buchschluss des Jahres 1915," in *Studien*, 10.

23. T. G. Masaryk, *The Problem of Small Nations in the European Crisis: Inaugural Lecture at the University of London, King's College* (London: The Council for the Study of International Relations, 1916).

24. Tomáš G. Masaryk, *Naše nynější krize. Pád strany staročeské a počátkové směrů nových* [Our Current Crisis: The Fall of the Old Czech Party and the Opening of New Directions] (Prague: Čas, 1895).

25. Winston Churchill, *The World Crisis*, vols. 1–5 (London: Thornton Butterworth, 1923–31).

26. Ramiro de Maeztu, *Authority, Liberty and Function in the Light of the War* (London: G. Allen & Unwin, 1916).

27. Károly Mannheim, *Lélek és kultúra* [Soul and Culture] (Budapest: Benkő, 1918). The lecture was given at the Free School of the Human Sciences (Szellemi Tudományok Szabad Iskolája) in Budapest, an institution that grew out of the circle of friends around György Lukács and Béla Balázs, the Sunday Circle (Vasárnapi Kör).

28. See Graf, *Die Zukunft* and Graf, "Die 'Krise' im intellektuellen Zukunftsdiskurs der Weimarer Republik," in Föllmer and Graf, eds., *Die "Krise" der Weimarer Republik*, 77–106.

29. Graf, "Either-Or," 608.

30. Michael Freeden argues that crisis is "filtered through" by different political ideologies: for liberals, it frustrates free human development; for conservatives, it implies too much change; for socialists, it is rooted in the systemic crises of capitalism; for greens, in the imbalance in nature; for anarchists, in power concentration; for fascists, in racial miscegenation; for the religious, in profanity; and so on. See Freeden, "Crisis?" 22.

31. Rüdiger Graf, "Optimismus und Pessimismus in der Krise—der politisch-kulturelle Diskurs der Weimarer Republik," in Wolfgang Hardtwig, ed., *Ordnungen in der Krise: Zur politischen Kulturgeschichte Deutschlands 1900–1933* (Munich: Oldenbourg, 2007), 115–40; and Fritzsche, "Historical Time," in ibid., 141–64.

32. See Graf, "Die 'Krise' im intellektuellen Zukunftsdiskurs der Weimarer Republik," 91.

33. Rogers Brubaker, "Why Populism?," *Theory and Society* 46, no. 5 (2017): 357–85.

34. Pierre Rosanvallon, *Le siècle du populisme: Histoire, théorie, critique* (Paris: Éditions du Seuil, 2020), 9.

35. Koselleck and Richter, "Crisis," 371–2.
36. Ibid., 398.
37. Ibid.
38. Devising the methodological approach of my book, I drew also on Michael Freeden's thoughtful analysis of the morphology of ideologies, and of the central concepts around which they are organized, as well as his understanding of "decontestation" of the meaning of such key concepts as a constitutive element of political debate. See Michael Freeden, *Ideologies and Political Theory: A Conceptual Approach* (Oxford: Clarendon Press, 1996), 47–91.

3
Crisis of the Mind and Spirit

The interwar period witnessed a proliferation of arguments about the underlying spiritual causes of the socioeconomic crisis experienced after the First World War—accentuating the disorientation of the "European mind" and the concomitant decomposition of Western civilization. Philosophers and cultural essayists produced many different versions of this argument, depending on their ontological and political preferences.[1] At the same time, they all strove to insert crisis into a broader temporal framework, describing it as the end/beginning of an era (for instance, of post-Renaissance individualism), and drawing parallels between the present and various previous periods of transformation. A key feature of these discourses was the stress on the "crisis of values" over the "crisis of structures."[2] Naturally, this diagnosis positioned philosophers of culture as the most qualified specialists of crisis phenomena. The philosophical diagnosis of crisis could be framed rather apolitically, pointing more to epistemological issues, such as the case of Edmund Husserl's (1859–1938) famous book on *The Crisis of European Sciences and Transcendental Phenomenology* (1936),[3] but it was more typical to insert this into a meta-political framework, as was the case also with Martin Heidegger (1889–1976), Husserl's eminent and controversial disciple.

The Crisis of European Identity

In the years following the First World War, a central modality of the crisis discourse, rooted in the devastating experience of the conflagration, focused on the disintegration of European culture and society. During the First World War, it was still possible to bring together radical cultural criticism (combining nihilism and conservative aestheticism) with a pan-European vision of reconciliation under the aegis of a philosophical crisis discourse. This can be seen in the somewhat cryptic essay on the "crisis of European culture," published in 1917 by the German poet and philosophical writer Rudolf Pannwitz (1881–1969), who was inspired especially by Stefan George and Friedrich Nietzsche.[4] Pannwitz was also a precursor of later crisis debates in the sense that his vision of European culture was constructed with a special attention to the non-European civilizational "others." He was particularly impressed by Asian spirituality, and his text was permeated by references both to classical Chinese and Indian religious and philosophical thought (from Buddha to Confucius and Laozi) but also contemporaries, like Gu Hongming (1857–1928), the Chinese traditionalist

---

Intellectuals and the Crisis of Politics in the Interwar Period and Beyond. Balázs Trencsényi, Oxford University Press.
© Balázs Trencsényi (2025). DOI: 10.1093/9780198929512.003.0003

thinker and friend of Leo (Lev) Tolstoy (1828–1910). Importantly, in contrast to the interwar conservative revolutionaries, Pannwitz's critique of modernity was linked to a vision of transcending national particularisms: the way out of the crisis was to create a European unity that would make it possible to overcome petty national conflicts while preserving the organic multiplicity of European culture.

After 1918, however, under the impact of a lost war and thinking in the framework of the contrast between *Kultur* and *Zivilisation*—a central element of wartime German intellectual propaganda—conservative German intellectuals described the postwar world in terms of a period of cultural dissolution on the national as well as the European level. In fact, in the German context, many liberals also subscribed to the discourse of crisis in terms of dissolution while rejecting the rightist and leftist radicalisms mushrooming in the wake of the fall of the imperial order. A case in point is the postwar cultural–political essays of Ernst Troeltsch (1865–1923), the leading German liberal Protestant intellectual.[5] His most influential text from the period was on the "crisis of Historicism," linking his analysis of the internal contradictions of the historicist worldview which had dominated German culture in the nineteenth century to the overall political and cultural malaise of the early twentieth.

Referring to the methodological debate of the turn of the century on the relationship of historical and natural sciences, dominated by neo-Kantianism,[6] Troeltsch pointed to the self-destructive impact of scientism on historical thinking. He identified a growing rupture between over-specialization under the pressure of scientism and the craving for synthesis, satisfied by dilettante history (*Dilettantenhistorie*), which rejected the conventions of academic knowledge-production. All of this resonated with a broader process of the "dissolution of the idea of humanity," the "anarchy of values," "ideological chaos," and a "fight of all against all":

> Realists, Moderns, *Völkisch* and Expressionists are against the Ancients, the admirers of Christianity are fighting each other and modern culture, and the Dionysian and Apollonic regenerators of Antiquity against Christianity and Modernity at the same time.[7]

While most actors loudly proclaimed the universal validity of their belief systems, the manifest incompatibility of these truth claims led to the proliferation of radical value relativism. Troeltsch also identified several radical ideological projects seeking to transcend this relativism, namely French integral nationalism's attempt to universalize the particular, British neo-traditionalist Christianity, Italian Futurism, and the Soviet collectivist experiment.[8] But for Troeltsch, predictably, the deepest crisis—and consequently the most desperate search for a new ideology—characterized the German case. The main directions of this search he identified were "anti-historicism," radical rationalism, *Völkisch* nationalism, and irrational spiritualism.

In contrast to these purported remedies which sought to offer a return to dogmatism and self-isolation, Troeltsch remained committed to universalism and argued for the renewal of the relationship between history and philosophy: "While Historicism calls for ideas, Philosophy does so for life. Through such a connection both can

34   Intellectuals and the Crisis of Politics

be assisted."[9] The struggle against radical relativism could not invalidate a historical perspective, and so the way out of the crisis for Troeltsch could only lead through a more reflexive historical consciousness. His universalist stance also implied a conciliatory tone toward the Western powers defeating Germany. Thus, in his political essays of the early 1920s, he referred to Great Britain and the United States (both marked by Protestant culture) as the models (with all their internal contradictions) of a more organic development.

While in the German context this feeling of dissolution could be linked—although could not be reduced—to the catastrophic end of the First World War, in the victorious countries, too, many intellectuals shared the feeling of a loss of orientation caused by the war, and reflected upon the collapse of the vision of linear progress that had characterized the late nineteenth century. A paradigmatic early text along these lines is "The Crisis of the Spirit" by French poet, writer, and philosopher Paul Valéry (1871–1945).[10] Valéry started his reflections with a reference to the First World War, which in his interpretation had led to the "loss of European consciousness." While the military and economic crisis was eventually overcome with the end of the war (a claim to which most of his German interlocutors would have hardly subscribed), the spiritual crisis remained and even became more tangible in most spheres of life. Nevertheless, Valéry did not link the origins of this crisis to the outbreak of the war. In his interpretation, its roots reached much deeper to the structures of modernity; this, in turn, was characterized by the coexistence of incompatible life and knowledge principles.

While, during its ascendance, Europe—being the synthesis of divergent intellectual traditions, such as Greek aesthetics, Roman law, and Christian morality—was able to harmonize seemingly incompatible elements such as chivalry and equality, fantasy and logical strength, skepsis without pessimism, or mysticism without resignation, the symptoms of crisis started to appear well before the turn of the twentieth century. In contrast to some other narratives of the decline of Europe at the time, Valéry's definition of Europe was normative–cultural and not ethnic–racial. Europe, for him, was most of all a community of values and attitudes. In Valéry's interpretation, a key component of Europeanness was the evolution of science as an autonomous sphere of curiosity and creativity. A main indicator of the loss of dynamism was exactly the change of the function of science. In the last period of European modernity, science lost its autonomy and became an instrument—of the forces of the market or of political power.

Valéry's argument was paradigmatic as it contained most components of the interwar discourse of cultural/spiritual crisis in a nutshell. These are *historicization/serialization* (locating the origins of crisis in some sort of turning point, and tracing the process of its unfolding as a historical sequence while pointing to the need for a "new" classicism, Middle Ages, humanism, Renaissance, etc., as its possible overcoming), *spatialization* (projecting the crisis features on a given geographical entity and contrasting it to other entities), and *hierarchization* (setting the decomposition of the social and cultural system against an allegedly more coherent and unitary configuration led by authentic elites, described as "non-crisis"). Still, Valéry's argument did not include *biologization* or *sacralization*. These elements would return in different configurations throughout the interwar period, and the narratives predicated on them were to define the intellectual and often also the political implications of a given discourse of crisis.

The central trope of historicization pointed to the beginning of a new era, one that would replace the previous configuration of values and mentalities. Of course, where this beginning was located could be highly divergent: one extreme was Heidegger's ontological "*Sonderweg* theory" of the entire Western philosophical tradition, contrasting the pre-Socratic philosophers as the last period of authentic philosophical thinking to what followed ever after. The more typical positions however usually located the starting point of the actual crisis at the origins of modernity (albeit the exact timing of these origins could diverge widely). Comparisons flourished between the contemporary situation and previous instances of political and social upheaval, depicting the collapse of certain sociocultural institutions or configurations as prefiguring the current crisis. For instance, Italian liberal historian and journalist Guglielmo Ferrero (1871–1942) talked of the disintegration of a fundamental form of Western culture and society, contrasting the peace system successfully closing the Napoleonic wars to the failure of the peacemakers in 1919–20.

Such comparisons often had explicitly anti-modernist implications. Thus, in 1920 Austrian Catholic conservative social philosopher Othmar Spann (1878–1950) argued that his period witnessed a moment of universal crisis "not only of this or that country, this or that political party, state form or reform policy," but a crisis of "our general way of thinking."[11] Spann compared the unfolding "crisis of the *Zeitgeist*" to the breakthrough of Renaissance Humanism, emerging as a reaction to the crisis of medieval Christianity. Now, it was precisely Humanism's turn to be overtaken by a new collectivistic principle which had not, however, acquired strong ideological contours just yet, but could be perceived as the radical negation of the rule of individualism characterizing the modern period—a *Gegenrenaissance* in Spann's terms.

The anti-modernist "*Ur-Text*" of the interwar crisis literature was undoubtedly Oswald Spengler's (1880–1936) *The Decline of the West*. Spengler was the most internationally visible German conservative intellectual of the post-World War I period and had a considerable impact from Ireland to Ukraine. Importantly, while the two volumes (published in 1918 and 1922, respectively) had powerful repercussions in various national contexts and were considered the most compelling depiction of crisis-ridden culture and politics in the West, the very notion of crisis was not that central to the text. In fact, it was used by Spengler in most cases with reference to an internal cultural or political conflict that could be resolved by a new configuration. In this sense, while he became famous for his gloomy imagery of irretrievable decline, Spengler's notion of crisis evoked the Burckhardtian use in the sense of a dramatic historical turning point, rather than an apocalyptic "end of history."

Spengler's main contention was that if one wanted to grasp the real nature and dimensions of the crisis of the present, one needed to assume a perspective which was able to look at the morphology of historical forms as they evolved over thousands of years.[12] From this elevated viewpoint, individual events—no matter how dramatic, such as the Great War—were only the "external forms" of the historical crisis, rooted in longitudinal processes of transformation.[13] At the same time, for Spengler, the propensity of historicization inherent to contemporary Western civilization was in itself a marker of crisis. Historicization in modern Western culture also implied individualization; this process of fragmentation—getting lost in particular questions and insights without facing the totality of culture—was precisely a key symptom. Individualization, in his reading, eventually pointed to a comprehensive spiritual crisis, encapsulating the whole Western world, and opened the way for the rise of the East (Russia in particular) and the start of a new civilizational cycle.

Crisis was thus far from being equated only with decadence. It could rather imply a dramatic transformation creating something fundamentally new or starting a new cycle of history. In his *Esquema de las crisis* (Scheme of Crises), Spanish philosopher José Ortega y Gasset (1883–1955) analyzed the century between 1550 and 1650 as a crisis-ridden transition to modernity, drawing a parallel between the two liminal periods marking the beginning and end of modernity, locating the latter in the early twentieth century.[14] Closer to academic knowledge-production and more unambiguously liberal, the influential work *La Crise de la conscience européenne, 1680–1715* (The Crisis of the European Conscience) by French literary historian Paul Hazard (1878–1944) also conceptualized crisis (although, in contrast to the title, the word itself rarely occurs in the body of the text) as a radical shift of intellectual horizons—within a short, compressed time frame predating the usual timeline of the Enlightenment—from a civilization based on duties to one based on rights, from classicism to rationalism and sentimentalism.[15]

Combining a cyclical and an evolutionary perspective, Russian émigré sociologist Pitirim Sorokin (1889–1968) living in the United States described the present as a transitory period comparable to the rise of modernity: in his terminology, this meant the shift from sensate to ideational culture, while in the previous transition from the twelfth to the sixteenth century, it was the other way round: the sensate took over from the ideational.[16] Similarly, German economist and political thinker Wilhelm Röpke (1899–1966) argued that the outcome of the interwar crisis could lead to a cyclical return of more human proportions in European civilization, which had characterized the eighteenth century and which he contrasted to the nineteenth-century obsession with imperial power and expansion.[17]

As for spatialization, the central tension was between localizing crisis in the national context in contrast to broader (European or global) frames. Predictably, those who were engaged in a cultural–philosophical approach were more likely to reject the idea that crisis could be contained by national frontiers and pointed instead to the transnational nature of the roots and symptoms of the crisis. A case in point is Ortega's argument that the crisis posed a challenge to the Europeans "as Europeans," since national differences were diminishing and the only way out from the crisis was by creating a new European cultural and political project. While most crisis discourses still focused on Europe, alternative geographical frames were also suggested that transcended the European geographical horizons. A common reference along these lines was to the United States, often embedded in the trope of "Americanization."

The attention to supranational frames did not mean that these thinkers abandoned national frameworks altogether. They often continued to think of nations as different manifestations of a Hegelian Absolute Spirit, and they also often assigned special roles to certain national communities both as epicenters of the crisis and possible triggers of recovery. This ambiguity could be seen in the work of German intellectuals, such as globe-trotting Baltic German philosopher Hermann Graf von Keyserling (1880–1946), whose sweeping tableau of the search for spiritual recovery in Europe went together with a special focus on German national identity, in need of fundamental rethinking after the collapse of the German Empire in 1918.[18]

Polish sociologist and social philosopher Florian Znaniecki (1882–1958)—most famous for the monumental *The Polish Peasant in Europe and America* co-written with William I. Thomas—also developed an analysis of civilizational crisis after the First World War, combining national and universalist perspectives in a peculiar manner. In his 1921 essay on the fall of Western civilization, he depicted a normative image of Western development in terms of free creation, manifested in political terms in democracy and the growth of social solidarity, while registering a number of threats that seemed to set back this civilizational process.[19] First and foremost, he pointed to the growth of materialism, which undermined both cultural creation and political liberties, resulting in a homogenizing mass rule and the rise of "racial imperialism," an expansive and intolerant form of nationalism. In his revised text in the early 1930s he reframed this in terms of a crisis discourse, but in contrast to many contemporaries he held on to the image of crisis as a future-oriented transformative experience.[20] He rejected both the conservative and revolutionary solutions to the cultural and political disorientation of his times, arguing that these seemingly antagonistic positions were both seeking to establish a "stable equilibrium," which was characteristic of premodern societies but could not be a model for the future. Instead, Znaniecki put forward to concept of "fluidity" (*płynność*), which meant a permanent creative adaptation to the changing conditions and an openness to exchange and learning. The envisioned direction of human development was thus toward a supranational cooperation, dominated by spiritual culture and capable of renewing itself in all its spheres of life, from religion to science, economics, and politics. Eventually this was supposed to result in a fundamental anthropological transformation, creating a "new man" and a "new civilization."

While this argument was markedly universalistic, Znaniecki's thought also had a national angle. In his 1933 "Poland in the World Crisis," he stressed the need for certain nations to take the lead in overcoming the global spiritual and political crisis.[21] He listed the usual suspects, but rejected all of them: France was too self-centered and self-serving; England was too traditionalistic; Italy was excessively vain in its cult of the Roman past; Soviet Russia was destructive of its own traditions; Germany was sinking into hatred; and the United States experienced a huge rift between its

38 Intellectuals and the Crisis of Politics

idealism and the actual social realities. From this perspective, Znaniecki saw the possibility for Poland to emerge as a catalyst of global transformation, not so much by its political or economic strength (as it was a small country which recently regained its liberty) but rather *because* of these features, that is, Poles could only achieve anything by cultivating the spirit of cooperation. It was not imperial greatness, but rather the common effort of "free nations" that could lead toward such a future. Poles could draw on their past, from the Jagiellonian model of multinational statehood to the early modern tradition of religious tolerance and the romantic messianic program of fighting for the liberation of all oppressed peoples, to serve as such a catalyst. In this sense, it was possible to harmonize the national and universalist commitments, but only by transcending the nation-state as the envisioned final stage of historical development.

As opposed to Znaniecki's future-oriented democratic humanism and pro-Western rhetoric, radical conservative discourses also employed civilizational crisis as a key trope but rejected democracy and described the Western development as a dead end. Arguably the most radical anti-modernist version of the philosophical crisis discourse—merging temporal and spatial frames in a peculiar manner—came from René Guénon (1886–1951).[22] Inspired by various spiritualist and religious doctrines ranging from occultism to Taoism, and Hinduism and especially Islam, Guénon emerged as a key figure of the French traditionalist scene, with a remarkable transnational impact. While his cultural horizons were unusually inclusive, the political implications of his writings became increasingly radically conservative.

Guénon pointed to the proliferation of crisis discourses in postwar Europe and saw this as the sign of a growing awareness in Western civilization of its own decomposition. He evidently felt himself vindicated in this development:

> Many no longer doubt the possibility of a world crisis, taking the latter word in its most usual acceptation, and this in itself marks a very noticeable change of outlook: by sheer force of circumstance certain illusions are beginning to vanish, and we cannot but rejoice that this is so, for it is at any rate a favorable symptom and a sign that a readjustment of the contemporary mentality is still possible—a glimmer of light as it were—in the midst of the present chaos.[23]

However, in contrast to most authors, he did not search for the causes of this disorientation in the recent past, let alone the First World War, and argued instead that it indicated a much deeper civilizational decline, encompassing the whole epoch of modernity, starting in the fourteenth century.[24] This means that for Guénon, rather than the starting point of the crisis, the Renaissance and the Reformation were already manifestations of a decadence that started earlier with the dissolution of the hegemonic Christian *Weltanschauung*. This temporal frame was also spatialized, contrasting the decomposing West with the East, which preserved its spiritual integrity:

> In the present state of the world then we have on the one hand all the civilizations that have remained faithful to the traditional standpoint—namely the civilizations of the East—and on the other a veritably anti-traditional civilization, namely that of the modern West.[25]

Predictably, Guénon considered the growing interest in these Eastern traditions to be the indicator of spiritual regeneration. In his view, modernity was approaching the final phase of its existence—the climax of the crisis—that had already provided the possibility of transformation. This transformation meant a return to the authentic tradition of sacrality abandoned by Western civilization. This tradition also had political implications, as it entailed a hierarchical social organization. Democracy in the sense of the rule of the majority was a typical product of the modern spiritual disorientation, as it contradicted the principle of elites, who were the natural leaders of any society. Likewise, Guénon described nationalism as essentially a Western and modern phenomenon and looked for a more transnational framework of regeneration. He pointed to the Catholic Church as the only available institution that could fulfill this mission, provided it reverted to its own authentic roots, perhaps through engaging in dialogue with Eastern spiritual traditions.[26] Eventually, however, this call for synthesis remained unheeded, and in 1930 Guénon moved to Cairo, where he was initiated into Sufi esotericism, married into a pious Muslim family, and withdrew from the European public sphere.

Although representing highly divergent political positions, both Znaniecki and Guénon sought to reframe the relationship of the constitutive elements of civilization. Many other cultural philosophical discourses also engaged in such an effort of hierarchization, rooted in the experience of the loss of civilizational unity. On a different level of abstraction, we can see this also in Edmund Husserl's introductory part to *The Crisis of European Sciences*,[27] where he argued that this crisis did not principally concern science as such, but rather the relationship of science and human existence. While in the Renaissance this relationship had been intact, during the Enlightenment the belief of the universality of the new philosophy was lost. As the specialized sciences established themselves by offering new vistas in interpreting various natural phenomena, post-Enlightenment metaphysics failed to provide a comprehensive picture accommodating these developments. In Husserl's understanding, however, the mission of philosophers was to create a unitary "philosophy," and not "philosophies." He used the famous metaphor of philosophers being the "functionaries of mankind" in terms of realizing a coherent and integrative worldview. While usually on a different level of abstraction, most cultural crisis discourses of the interwar years were also based on the craving for a unitary image of the different spheres of human existence, projecting various models of reintegration.

Such philosophical constructions were (as a rule) less openly context-bound than the political and economic conceptualizations of crisis, which rather responded to distinct historical twists and turns. One can nevertheless trace certain patterns in the transformation of the philosophical crisis discourses by comparing the texts stemming from the early postwar years (exemplified by Valéry's essay) to the ones from the late twenties, mid-thirties, and early forties, all responding to somewhat different intellectual challenges and being rooted in different intellectual and political contexts.

A paradigmatic text exemplifying the attitudes and horizons of the late-1920s, linking philosophical and political considerations, is Ortega's bestselling essay, *The Revolt of the Masses*.[28] Crisis is a pivotal concept in this text, which starts with the statement that the rise of mass rule in Europe is "the greatest crisis that can afflict peoples, nations, and civilizations."[29] Nevertheless, written before the peak of the Great Depression, the feeling of imminent collapse was much less omnipresent here as it would become afterward.

Like Valéry, Ortega also pointed to the multisectoral nature of crisis, present not only in the sphere of politics but also in the intellectual moral, economic, and religious spheres. For him, the main cause was the fundamental sociocultural transformation of Europe, with the "multitude becoming visible in the places previously reserved for minorities," leading to a situation where the influence of previous social and cultural elites became minimized: "there are no longer protagonists; there is only the chorus."[30] It is important to stress, however, that rather than some sort of passéist conservative utopia, Ortega's text did not crave for the lost privileges of the nobility of the *ancien régime*. He firmly distinguished the "spiritual nobility" from the actual one, pointing out that, historically, most privileged groups quickly lost their spiritual and moral exemplarity and became "vulgar." Further, he also did not deplore the actual progress of civilization, as he accepted the democratization of pleasures and commodities as an immense achievement, indicating the general rise of the civilizational level, but still considered the concomitant massification of politics and culture as potentially self-destructive.

The political implication of massification was the break-up of the unity of liberalism and democracy: while democracy in the nineteenth century was tempered by liberalism and the rule of law, the emerging "hyperdemocracy" of the twentieth century did not tolerate any hindrances to mass rule. Ortega repeatedly stressed that this diagnosis should not be conflated with a narrative of decline (commonly linked in the 1920s to Spengler's work). He negated the existence of pre-existing "periods of plenitude" as "optical distortion" and stressed that his criticism was not aimed at restoring any past configuration but instead to break with the past once and for all. Marked by the processes of acceleration and the compression of space and time, the present was not inferior to the past, but rather that it failed to fulfill the high expectations associated with it: the present thus felt "superior to other times, inferior to itself."[31] The sentiment of crisis in Ortega's interpretation was precisely due to this mismatch of expectations and reality: in contrast with the nineteenth century, when progress seemed to be following a linear track, the developmental direction of the post-First World War era seemed much less clear, and the reopening of horizons was often perceived as disorientation and eventually decadence: "No one knows toward what center human things are going to gravitate in the near future, and hence the life of the world has become scandalously provisional."[32]

For Ortega, coming to terms with the fact that progress was not automatic was essential for the future of human civilization. While scientific discoveries were commonly held to be forthcoming almost by default, he believed they were the result of the work of a select group of highly qualified and creative individuals. If society allowed itself to be deceived about the automatism of scientific progress and demolished the last bastions of creative individuality, the result would have been civilizational collapse and "barbarization."[33] This was linked to the gradual specialization of the spheres of scientific inquiry, as scholars were losing the possibility of the integral interpretation of the universe and their work became mechanistic, being restricted to specific subfields.

Education was a key factor in countering this: it was not enough to transmit technological skills but also a creative spirit needed to be cultivated that could counteract the principles of mass society and mechanization. The rise of self-sufficient masses in the late nineteenth century was unavoidable and implied the progress of civilization, but the imposition of the values of these masses ("vulgarity") on all spheres of life, including culture, was something new and could lead to catastrophic consequences. Culture presumed some external standards to which one could appeal, but "vulgarity" negated this; barbarism was exactly the absence of such standards. Ortega derived from this the rise of anti-liberal ideologies (e.g., syndicalism, fascism) that rejected the existence of external value systems and cultivated pure force (and "direct action") as the source of political power. The growth of violence inherent to the dominance of "mass-men" in his interpretation was also linked to the unprecedented expansion of the modern state. Ortega described liberal democracy as being rooted in the effort "to live in common and take each other into account," which entailed the principle of the self-limitation of power, that is, "the determination to share existence with the enemy."[34] In contrast, anti-liberalism (being central to both Bolshevism and fascism) was a regressive ideology, seeking to revert to a pre-liberal world, which Ortega considered impossible. Instead, he argued for the "*Aufhebung*" of liberal democracy: "Europe needs to preserve its essential liberalism. This is the condition for superseding it."[35]

In the last part of his book, Ortega set out his vision of such a post-liberal order as a way out of the impasse caused by mass society. He focused on the creation of a new European political framework, offering a new level of convergence beyond the nation-state. In his understanding, the ambitions of big European nations converged around creating a new supranational order, which was hindered by the existing nation-state framework. This was also a response to those discourses of crisis which deplored the loss of European dominance after the Great War. Ortega transferred his notion of crisis as the loss of self-assuredness to this tension as well: the prevalent feeling of decadence in European intellectual circles was aggravated by the recognition of the particularity of national positions.[36]

For Ortega, although he was acutely aware of the specific Spanish crisis (described in his famous 1921 essay *España invertebrada [Invertebrate Spain]*), the European crisis was not the sum total of the crisis of particular nations, as many French and German authors would have argued, but exactly the disfunction of the national

42 Intellectuals and the Crisis of Politics

framework as the dominant political and cultural structure.[37] Moving beyond the nation toward a more encompassing and dynamic civilizational framework was in line with Europe's *longue durée* development, set in motion in classical antiquity with the tension between city and countryside and only partially resolved by the emergence of the Roman imperial project. In this context, Ortega contrasted Caesar's vision favorably to republican particularism but also distinguished it from the past-oriented Augustan program, which preserved rather than superseded the frame of mind of the city-state. Along these lines, Ortega sketched out a constructivist definition of the nation, criticizing even Ernest Renan's (1823–1892) conception of the daily plebiscite as not future-oriented enough. He rejected the retrospective projection of common markers (such as race and language) as constitutive of the nation, arguing that they were the result of nation-building, not its precondition ("not what we were yesterday, but what we are going to be tomorrow, joins us together in the state"[38]). The obvious implication was that the ethnic heterogeneity of European nations was not a hindrance to a common European political project. To the contrary, a common polity rooted in shared will would lead to the reinforcement of a mutual European mentality, which in Ortega's opinion was already taking shape: "We are more influenced by what is European in us than by what is special to us as Frenchmen, Spaniards, and so on."[39]

From this perspective, the upsurge of nationalism was also a crisis symptom. It was a regressive counter-reaction, "nothing but a mania, a pretext to escape from the necessity of inventing something new,"[40] to overcome the insecurity caused by general disorientation and the inability to realize a common European project. This made the crisis even deeper. Hence, the real danger posed by Bolshevism was precisely its alternative supranational vision to mobilize European forces to create a new unity. For Ortega, this was a false and regressive solution: it fused the European ideology of Marxism with the rule of backward and essentially non-European masses.

The conceptualizations analyzed above had repercussions across Europe, with Spengler, Valéry, or Ortega featuring in many works, creating a common framework of reference and an increasingly synchronized discussion of authors coming from various national cultures. A good illustration of this is provided by the East Central European reception of their texts. Rather than just reiterating their arguments, most of their interlocutors in these countries sought to apply them critically to questions they were interested in, often comparing and even contrasting them to each other. For example, Romanian social theorist Petre Andrei (1891–1940) wrote on cultural and educational crises, (mis)reading Spengler as a "prophet of decline" while asserting that the ongoing crisis was not the end of Western civilization.[41] He pointed to Georg Simmel's theory of the conflict of subjective and objective culture as a more adequate description of the situation, arguing that the core of the crisis was the growing gap between technological and moral development, which was made all the more obvious by the traumatic war experience. To chart the way out of the crisis, and in line with his political orientation on the left of the agrarian populist tradition, Andrei considered the task of universities to facilitate social mobility. This would create a more integrated new elite, which could continue the tradition of Western high culture. Andrei also envisioned the infusion of fresh and organic life forces from the peasantry, thus projecting the structural opposition of Occident and Orient in Spengler onto the intra-state contrast of multi-ethnic urban society and organic countryside.

Philosopher Nicolae Bagdasar (1896–1971), another prominent Romanian intellectual, also revisited European crisis discourses with a special focus on German (Spengler, Simmel, Husserl) and French (Valéry and Henri Massis) authors, pointing to the Great War as the collective experience that made the general European cultural crisis manifest.[42] Similar to Andrei, Bagdasar was also critical of Spengler for his "hermetic" separation of civilizational cycles and also for his simplistic reading of the nineteenth century as mechanistic, arguing that it was rather early modern culture with its rationalism which was mechanistic. Resonating with Husserl's argument, Bagdasar pointed to the disproportionate development of sciences and spiritual activities, designating the lack of a single unitary idea as the main indicator of crisis. But he also rejected the image of an overall crisis of modernity, asserting that development always presupposed the struggle of existing values. In this context, crisis was a normal phenomenon of the clash of old and new forms.[43]

The crisis literature of the postwar decade had multiple political and intellectual agendas and was far from being a conservative anti-modernist project. In fact, some of these texts and authors were seeking to salvage liberalism and democracy, and the discourse of the decline of the West or of Europe did not necessarily imply either an expectation of imminent collapse, or the fascination with a non-European other. At the same time, there were also certain features shared by these authors, such as the problematization of European cultural and political development. Along these lines, there was an urge to critically reconsider the historical traditions and turning points constitutive of the European canon, from the Greek and Roman antiquity to the Middle Ages, the Renaissance, the Enlightenment, and the nineteenth-century intellectual reconfigurations. Second, there was an acute sense of the conflict between the creative individuals and minorities, carrying the authentic traditions and capable of renewing them, and what was perceived as the deluge of mass society. Finally, the cultural crisis discourses of the postwar decade were generally critical of the nation-state as a limited and limiting framework of social and cultural existence, unable to answer the more fundamental questions that were posed on a higher, civilizational level.

A New Age of Crisis and Criticism

The dramatic economic and political developments of the early 1930s deepened the sentiment of crisis all over Europe. While Ortega could still argue that parliamentary democracy had no practical alternative, parliamentarism's loss of legitimacy in Central Europe and elsewhere exposed totalitarian ideologies on both left and right as powerful challengers of the postwar order.

44 Intellectuals and the Crisis of Politics

The growing despair and rampant insecurity influenced German existentialist philosopher Karl Jaspers's (1883–1969) study on the "spiritual situation of the time."[44] In contrast to Ortega, who was more skeptical about the existence of previous epochs of temporal and spiritual unity, Jaspers was more prone to contrast the pre-modern and modern periods in terms of a loss of harmony. He understood the feeling of crisis as rooted in the perception of a permanently changing world in an epoch that had lost the possibility of finding peace in transcendence. With this loss, the material world remained the only place for self-realization, and unceasing change brought on feelings of impotence (*Ohnmacht*).

For Jaspers, crisis was conceptually closely connected to criticism—taking the form of "critique of the present" (*Zeitkritik*), which contrasted the reality of the *present* to alternative trajectories of *potential* realities. He linked the perspective of *Zeitkritik* to Christian universal history, unfolding along the lines of the "plan of Salvation." In the sixteenth century, with the rise of Renaissance humanism, this vision was first challenged, and classical antiquity re-emerged as a normative framework. The plan of Salvation became secularized in the Enlightenment, while Jean-Jacques Rousseau's perspective questioned the linear vision of moral progress. Jaspers explored the transformation of the understanding of historical change through the French Revolution, which promised an unprecedented expansion of human agency but through its heedless violence created disenchantment. He also looked at an array of nineteenth-century philosophers and historians, such as Georg Wilhelm Friedrich Hegel, Johann Gottlieb Fichte, Søren Kierkegaard, Nietzsche, Alexis de Tocqueville, and Jacob Burckhardt, identifying a strong stream of *Kulturkritik* present already in the late nineteenth century. The forms of authority in the nineteenth century "completely melted away in the fire of criticism."[45] After the turn of the century, the sentiment of crisis became all-pervasive. While seemingly successful, and for some time obscuring the symptoms of crisis, the global expansion of European civilization in the nineteenth century had ushered in a persistent feeling of loss of continuity with previous eras. In Jaspers's understanding, the crisis unfolding in the twentieth century was incomparable with previous instances of civilizational decline (e.g., Rome) precisely because of European expansion in the 1800s and the repercussions of its truly global spiritual and political developments. At the same time, he admitted that different peoples assessed their situations differently as their experiences could not be completely synchronic.

Jaspers's analysis of the key features of the crisis identified several motifs encountered in previous depictions of the "crisis of the European mind": mass existence (*Massendasein*), rationalization (*Rationalisierung*), and mechanization (*Mechanisierung*). These processes catalyzed an attitude where the satisfaction of needs is considered automatic, and all goods and experiences are deemed objects to be purchased. Massification dissolves the unity of individuals by their functions and reduces humanness to the general (*Allgemeine*). Jaspers connected the cult of youth to this dissolution of individuality, thus redescribing a typical trope of his time as a key crisis symptom. This fit into the broader picture of the collapse of temporal horizons as a central feature: future and past all collapsed into the present and human existence had lost its temporal embeddedness. The entangled processes of massification, rationalization, and mechanization undermined the traditional patterns of social existence: instead of *Kameradschaft*, more amorphous human partnerships became dominant. Simultaneously, a new type of rulership emerged, based not on open violence but on a more subtle principle—the "diffusion of responsibilities" (*Verteilung der Verantwortungen*). The omnipresent and bureaucratized control mechanism (described as "*Apparat*") pulverizes resistance but cannot establish total control over all social actors. Jaspers acknowledged that a completely planned society and total social control were impossible because of various unpredictable events—here he even raised the possibility of an unprecedented epidemic.

Jaspers's vision of crisis was thus composed of both a long and traumatic process of cultural and civilizational transformation as well as the accidental occurrence of certain events that challenged the newly emerging framework. He pointed to the proliferation of crisis symptoms around himself: state crisis, cultural crisis, the crisis of being human (*Menschsein*), the uprooting of national cultures, the "dominance of the average," and the prevalence of experience over existence. His proposed remedy was via philosophical reflection—focusing neither on divinity nor on the world as such, but on the very existence of the human being. As Jaspers was inspired by Husserl's phenomenology, it is unsurprising that they shared the belief that philosophy was the "royal way" to recreate a unitary perception on life. In contrast to psychology, anthropology, and sociology—which could only provide partial knowledge about particular spheres of human existence—philosophy was the only adequate form of self-knowledge, making it possible to overcome the conflict of "Being" and "Consciousness." Similarly, Jaspers rejected liberalism, socialism, conservatism—the prevalent ideologies and "worldviews" of his time—as partial and having limited relevance for individual life choices. What he proposed instead was an *Existenzphilosophie*, which was meant to transcend ideological fragmentation and the specialized branches of scholarship, focusing on the human being.

While Jaspers did not draw direct political conclusions from his analysis, the dramatic developments of the early 1930s did trigger a number of German conservative philosophical reflections that framed the local and global situation in terms of a spiritual and political crisis, something to be overcome by a fundamental transformation, that is, a "Conservative Revolution," for example, Spengler's *Year of Decision*.[46] The bulk of the text was written in 1929, well before the Nazi takeover yet marked by a diffuse expectation of fundamental change. With the collapse of the Weimar Republic, Spengler found himself in an ambiguous position. He reveled in watching the dissolution of the democratic regime he hated but was also dissatisfied with Hitler's emerging new order. He thus positioned himself as a source of creative criticism (*schöpferische Kritik*), stressing that 1933 was just the beginning of the transformation and one should not confuse mobilization (*Mobilmachung*) with triumph (*Sieg*).

46 Intellectuals and the Crisis of Politics

Spengler's book, published in the fatal year of the collapse of the Weimar Republic, focused on the complex entanglement of crisis and "creative" criticism (which he distinguished from doctrinaire criticism based on ideological convictions). He stressed at the very beginning of the text that from "a planetary perspective," the raging economic crisis was only part of a more fundamental challenge, which was to determine the destiny of the world (*Weltschicksal*). This also prompted him to argue that one needed to put the German situation into a broader context.

The discourse of crisis Spengler employed was therefore based on his general vision of historical transformation, where cycles of civilization end with catastrophes "of unfathomable dimensions."[47] While the world crisis of the late 1920s was usually described with regard to the dysfunctions of certain spheres (e.g., production and consumption, state apparatus, or the international system) for Spengler it fit into the broader historiosophical pattern he had sketched out before, indicating a global transformation (changing the world order, "*imperium mundi*"), comparable to the shift from the Roman republican regime to the *Principatus*. From this perspective, the key phenomena of the post-First World War order in Germany and beyond—such as democracy, parliamentarism, and self-government—were symptoms of a transitional vacuum, to be eventually replaced by a new transcendent order.

Overall, Spengler argued that all high cultures were based on military force. Hence all political actions were about power, though some were veiled: he referred to the pacifists, whose seeming rejection of violence did not prevent them from seeking to extirpate militarists. Power was meant to be exercised by heroic individuals, while the masses were mere instruments of their creative work. Importantly, Spengler also linked *Kritik* and *Krise* conceptually in this work, describing criticism as an antithesis of creation, and pointing to Rousseau and Kant as "ideologists" and starters of a "new age of *Kritik*." While previous generations of conservative thinking would have contrasted cosmopolitan Enlightenment to organic Romanticism, Spengler drew a line of continuity between them, describing Romanticism as lacking the feeling of reality. Thus, for him, the entire period since the eighteenth century precipitated a process of decline, including the pre-1914 *belle époque* (*Friedezeit*).

While his criticism of the Enlightenment and Romanticism were rooted in the radical conservative ideology of the 1910–1920s (ranging from Charles Maurras to Carl Schmitt), his focus on creative violence also brought him rather close to the Nazi cult of violence, albeit with some important differences. He was bitterly ironic about professional politicians and party leaders as being contaminated by modern mass society and described mass party propaganda (both its radical leftist and rightist version) as a sign of crisis. He also tried to differentiate his concept of race from Nazi racism, and instead of the Aryan discourse subscribed to by the Nazis, he contrasted European populations and people of color, while also envisioning the rise of Japan to the status of superpower.

Heidegger's crisis discourse was also framed in view of the search for a philosophical position capable of restoring the lost metaphysical (and, by implication, socio-political) unity. As Hans Sluga points out, Heidegger's approach was deeply rooted in the German discussion going back to Fichte's conception in *Addresses to the*

German Nation (1806) of the interplay of philosophical and political spheres.[48] Sluga argues that Fichte's text brought together four conceptual clusters (crisis, nation/race, leadership, order) and to a large extent preformatted the later debates. Similarly mediating between the philosophical and political spheres, Heidegger's understanding of crisis was linked to the "fatal confusion" of Western culture, and he considered its impact as specifically acute in Germany. Especially in his texts born in the context of the Nazi takeover, he also expressed his hope that a German spiritual renewal would have world-historical importance.

As Sluga documents, after 1933 crisis became a central notion of the various German streams that competed for the status of "official philosophy."[49] Among the paradigmatic figures were Alfred Baeumler (1887–1968), director of the Institute of Political Pedagogy in Berlin, whose work focused on the creation of a German nationalist philosophical canon based on the work of Nietzsche, and Ernst Krieck (1882–1947), focusing on education and implementing the Nazification of the university in Frankfurt am Main, serving also as editor of the ideological journal *Volk im Werden*. There were important differences between these streams, but none of them managed to achieve full hegemony. The regime itself wavered between different ideological options within the broader National Socialist framework; however, they all operated with a temporal frame, which described the rise of the new regime as a solution not only for Germany, but also having global repercussions. This meant that the cultural pessimism of the 1920s, prevalent in the radical nationalist camp, was superseded by a discourse of new beginnings and regeneration, describing the crisis as a transformational process that would open a road toward a new world order.

Likewise, the discourse of crisis was also deployed on the German cultural Left. The collective project of the journal *Krise und Kritik*, launched by Bertolt Brecht (1898–1956) and Walter Benjamin (1892–1940) in 1930, together with the writer Bernard von Brentano (1901–64) and the theater director and critic Herbert Ihering (1888–1977), was intended as a broadly conceived progressive intellectual platform to engage with different social and cultural crisis phenomena in a comprehensive manner.[50] As Benjamin put it retrospectively,

> [t]he journal was planned as an organ in which experts from the bourgeois camp were to undertake to depict the crisis in science and art. This was meant to demonstrate to the bourgeois intelligentsia that the methods of dialectical materialism are dictated to it by its own most necessary characteristics—necessities of intellectual production, research, and existence.[51]

The list of envisioned contributors included many key figures of the Weimar intellectual scene, from Siegfried Kracauer and Ernst Bloch to Erwin Piscator and Kurt Weill.[52]

The programmatic document of the journal explicitly connected the concepts of criticism and crisis: "The journal's field of activity is the present crisis in all areas of ideology, and it is the task of the journal to register this crisis or to bring it about, and this by means of criticism."[53] At the same time, there was considerable dissent regarding the political and cultural agenda to be derived from this analysis. An obvious tension was between Brecht and especially Benjamin, who both remained critical of the dogmatic Stalinist rhetoric which labeled social democrats as "social fascists" and rejected a broader cooperation with non-communist progressives, and those intellectuals who followed the "general line" of the Party.[54] The aesthetic implications were also obvious, in the sense that Brecht and Benjamin were unwilling to subordinate their literary judgment to the emerging socialist realist dogmatism, and hoped to keep the journal open to authors who were far from fitting into the communist mainstream. Remarkably, Brecht contrasted the multi-perspectivity of James Joyce and Alfred Döblin favorably to the realism of Thomas Mann (1875–1955), arguing that the works of the former represented "attempts to emerge from the crisis, but they are, regarded separately, also the crisis in themselves."[55] Eventually these tensions—together with the precarious economic situation in the midst of the Depression—demotivated publishers from embarking on the new endeavor, and scrapped the project of the journal. But the intellectual agenda developed by the circle around it had strong repercussions in the German leftist intellectual culture of the early 1930s and, with the forced exile of many key figures, these effects were felt globally.

While the political convictions of the circle around *Krise und Kritik* were antagonistic to the radical right, morphologically their crisis discourse had many common features with that of the conservative revolutionaries. Thus, crisis in the vision of the prospective editors was indeed a moment of decision, an opportunity to demolish ideology and provide the possibility of a revolutionary transformation. At the same time, the editors were also acutely aware of the threat posed by the radical right and planned to pay extensive attention to the strategies and politics of the Nazis, especially in view of their takeover of the regional administration in Thuringia.[56] In this sense, crisis also gained a more sinister connotation in the sense of the premonition of a civil war, with unpredictable and potentially catastrophic consequences.

An attempt to provide an immediate theoretical reaction to the rise of national socialism, albeit finalized and published only decades later, was by the leading Marxist philosopher Georg (György) Lukács (1885–1971) on the rise of "fascist philosophy" in Germany.[57] Born in Budapest, Lukács spent the early 1930s in Berlin as an emissary of the Comintern, returning to Moscow after Hitler's takeover. His interpretative model was based on the notion of the gradually sharpening crisis of capitalism, which led to a final confrontation between revolutionary and counter-revolutionary forces.

While Lukács did not develop a self-standing theory of crisis, key elements of his thinking on this topic appear in his articles from the 1930s. He drew on the Marxian analysis of economic crisis developed in the *Theories of Surplus Value*, converting it into a more generic rendering of the dialectic relationship of individualization and totality, a key theme in his thinking from the 1910s onward:

> ... in periods when capitalism functions in a so-called normal manner and its various processes appear autonomous, people living within capitalist society think and experience it as unitary, whereas in periods of crisis, when the autonomous elements are drawn together into unity, they experience it as disintegration. With the general crisis of the capitalist system, the experience of disintegration becomes firmly entrenched over long periods of time in broad sectors of the population which normally experience the various manifestations of capitalism in a very immediate way.[58]

In the context of the acute crisis, confronted with the processes of disintegration, the bourgeois camp abandoned its previous support for parliamentary democracy and turned to the most reactionary wing of the (petty) bourgeoisie—the fascists. Fascism in this reading was the expression of the subjective anti-capitalism of these social strata, which, however, objectively reasserted the capitalist system in its most reactionary, monopoly–capitalist form. This binary opposition was also used by Lukács to reject the liberal and social democratic positions as "objectively" supporting the survival of bourgeois capitalism and thus unavoidably slipping toward fascism. These fascist tendencies were detectable not only in political rhetoric and violence, but also in the ideological superstructure (i.e., the philosophical thought of German intellectuals) increasingly dominated by irrationalism. Lukács's intransigent Stalinist position (among others, criticizing his own previous neo-Hegelian writings) was obviously influenced by the catastrophic collapse of the Weimar Republic. Seeking to formulate a comprehensive criticism, Lukács sketched out a broad picture of the different philosophical streams, starting with Nietzsche as the earliest and arguably most original critic of rationalism before moving to different varieties of *Lebensphilosophie*, the irrationalist evolution of neo-Kantianism and neo-Hegelianism, and culminating in Spengler's authoritarianism and eventually in Rosenberg's racial mythology. The crisis of capitalism thus catalyzed the crisis of thinking, undermining the bourgeois democratic position and leaving only two possible directions of development—communism or fascism. While this text focused on German thinkers, Lukács's interpretation of the radicalization of social and ideological contradictions in the period of acute crisis was not limited to Germany. He also argued that if the socialist revolutionary transformation was hindered, France and Great Britain would also soon encounter the strengthening of fascist tendencies.[59]

Another important figure in the Weimar Republic's leftist intellectual scene, Karl Mannheim, originally also from Budapest, employed crisis as a key heuristic concept in *Ideology and Utopia*, the formative text of the "sociology of knowledge." However, Mannheim sought to operationalize this concept without falling into the trap of "catastrophism," which characterized the anti-modernist crisis literature on the right as well as the communist messianism on the left.[60] In fact, his position was subsequently criticized as anti-Marxist by the intellectuals around the emerging Frankfurt School.

50 Intellectuals and the Crisis of Politics

In the introductory chapter, "Preliminary Approach to the Problem," which he appended in 1936 to the English edition of his book, Mannheim contrasts the unitary mental and social structures characterizing premodern societies to the emergence of internally differentiated societies and points to the mutually conditioned nature of material and cultural phenomena. The dissolution of homogeneous societies with their hierarchical value system led to the competition of different images of the world articulated by representatives of different social groups. This was often described as chaos and decomposition, but according to Mannheim it was rather the catalyst of progress: "This general uncertainty was by no means a symptom of a world doomed to general decay, but it was rather the beginning of a wholesome process which marked a crisis leading to recovery."[61]

The process of social differentiation characterizing modernity led to unprecedented conflicts between these competing representations of reality, some seeking to legitimize the existing order while others challenged it. This resulted in an extraordinary situation—a "final intensification of the intellectual crisis," which was "characterized by two slogan-like concepts 'ideology and utopia.'" Mannheim sought to analyze and eventually overcome them by making social actors go beyond their own socially constituted biases.[62] According to Mannheim, it was illusion to believe that crisis could be resolved by merely reinforcing the ideological or utopian attitudes:

> A fearful and uncertain concealment of contradictions and gaps will no more lead us out of the crisis than the methods of the extreme right and left, who exploit it in propaganda for the glorification of the past or future, forgetting for the moment that their own position is subject to the same criticism.[63]

Facing crisis reveals the possibility of self-reflection: "There is a point where the movement of life itself, especially in its greatest crisis, elevates itself above itself and becomes aware of its own limits."[64] From this perspective, Mannheim offered the sociology of knowledge as a tool of this self-reflection, facilitating a more systematic engagement with the social problems of the time:

> Crises are not overcome by a few hasty and nervous attempts at suppressing the newly arising and troublesome problems, nor by flight into the security of a dead past. The way out is to be found only through the gradual extension and deepening of newly won insights and through careful advances in the direction of control.[65]

This argument resonated with the conception developed in his next book, *Man and Society*, which contains a self-standing chapter on the sociological causes of the present cultural crisis.[66] Here Mannheim turns to the question of social transformation, pointing out the contradiction between two key principles shaping the sociopolitical imaginary of the epoch, namely *laissez-faire* and state intervention, which in his opinion led to the revolt of irrational masses against the institutional system and the emergence of dictatorial regimes.[67] The resolution of the crisis resulting from the clash of these principles was, in his opinion, a synthesis of liberal democracy with the technology of modern social planning.

With the rise of right-wing and left-wing totalitarian regimes, the feeling of decline and cultural pessimism that characterized the conservative critics of liberal democracy until the early 1930s could take an anti-totalitarian direction as well. Dutch historian Johan Huizinga (1872–1945), who became internationally famous with *The Waning of the Middle Ages* (1919), a captivating portrayal of late medieval Burgundian court culture, offered a complex interpretation of crisis as a cultural and historical phenomenon. In his analysis of the modern "spiritual distempers" from 1935, he combined the perspective of *Kulturkritik* with a reflection on historical knowledge, which also influenced later historiographic discussions on crisis.[68] Registering the medical—Hippocratic—origins of the term, Huizinga developed a morphology of crisis, distinguishing the process of decomposition from the visible signs (symptoms). In contrast to the cultural mood before 1910, which was generally optimistic, and even in the early postwar years, which brought a sense of relief, in his own present Huizinga registered the vanishing of the concept of progress from the horizon of expectation. While he rejected the contrast of culture and civilization, similar to Spengler or Ortega, he put crisis into a *longue durée* historical framework. He linked it to medieval eschatological conceptions and pointed to the secularization of the concept of history based on the conceptual change of "Revolution."

In contrast to the classical vision of history, the modern understanding was that historical progress was irreversible, hence crisis became perceived as a phase of fundamental transformation in this developmental scheme. These crisis-ridden periods were not identical. For instance, earlier crises (those around 1500 and between 1789–1815) were less marked by the feeling of cultural disintegration than that unfolding in the twentieth century. In some ways, the period marking the end of classical Antiquity and the rise of the Middle Ages was more comparable, but still, these two eras were bridged by the continuity of Christian religion and imperial functions. Huizinga's understanding of the novelty of the contemporary crisis was that the rift between the past and the future was much more dramatic.

In some ways comparable to Ortega's or Husserl's analysis, Huizinga also pointed to the growing gap between life and knowledge as a key feature of the crisis. The progress of science did not lead to the integration of its results into the texture of human culture but rather triggered a clash of knowledge and existence.[69] Applied sciences became dominant, undermining a more integrated scientific vision and its concomitant critical capacity. This led to the proliferation of superficial explanatory frameworks, typically naturalist, which reduced the complexity of the world to a limited number of factors. From his perspective, (neo)romantic cultural and political theories—which often turned to racial determinism—exemplified such a reductionist naturalism.[70] In turn, Huizinga also rejected Freudian psychoanalysis as inimical to the procedure of scientific verification.

The epistemological crisis was aggravated by the subordination of science to technology and politics: for Huizinga, this was exemplified by the development of bacterial warfare and the overall politicization of scientific research, especially in the dictatorial regimes. The loss of science's moral prestige created a general tendency toward anti-intellectualism and the merger of fiction and history, resulting in the

52 Intellectuals and the Crisis of Politics

popularity of the concept of myth and the parting of the ways between the aesthetic and rational spheres. The disappearance of rational standards also generated political voluntarism, which Huizinga already traced in the work of Burckhardt and Nietzsche, and the shift of the Darwinist conception of the struggle for survival from animal species to collective sociopolitical entities, like nations and states. In this context, Huizinga also criticized Schmitt's theory of the political, which focused on the binary opposition of friend versus enemy, arguing that this definition was contingent on the existence of a political entity and left the question of internal cleavages within a state unresolved—for instance, separatist groups who sought to become an independent state. Here, he evidently missed the racist implications of Schmitt's theory. In general, however, his criticism was vocal enough, castigating the demoralization of politics which negated virtue and heroism and undermined the sheer coexistence of humans, which in turn by necessity must be based on mutual trust.

As for the question of regeneration, Huizinga shared the perspective—prevalent in the interwar years—that the rise and decline of civilizations was cyclical in nature. He thus registered the symptoms of crisis as a promise of renewal. The way out of crisis was thus both forward and backward: regeneration required a return to the principles of classical European civilization by a process of internal purification and a "new asceticism," rejecting the exaggeration of power and pleasures. In this sense, like Ortega, Huizinga also argued for a more emphatic internationalist position, fighting against national egoism, while he also made it clear that this did not imply the elimination of nations but rather the harmonization of their interests and interaction in a more encompassing international framework.

Huizinga's vision also had international repercussions. Hungarian essayist Béla Hamvas eagerly read German, French, and Italian authors who wrote on the spiritual crisis of humankind from different philosophical and political perspectives. These ranged from the liberal Ortega, the personalist Jacques Maritain (1882–1973), and the Orthodox existentialist Nikolay Berdyaev (1874–1948), to the radical rightists Baeumler and Julius Evola (1898–1974), as well as Guénon. Hamvas was highly critical of the spiritual fragmentation of modernity, stressing that relativism in physics and the formlessness of modern art were two sides of the same coin, and expressed his craving for an epoch of harmony.[71] He also adhered to a vision of general crisis transcending different life-spheres:

> . . . there is no crisis in family life, in society, in public morals: in the family, society, and public morals there are human beings experiencing a crisis for whom the entire situation of the world is crisis-ridden.[72]

At the same time, he rejected the passéist turn toward a pre-existing societal or cultural model, and thus also went against the potential radical conservative political implications of the anti-modernist criticism he otherwise professed. This is the point where he found Huizinga particularly inspiring, even if he registered his own distance from the Dutch historian's rationalist thinking based on the contrast of reason and myth.[73]

Hamvas concurred with Huizinga in his argument about the irreversibility of the historical process, as against the "myth of eternal return." Hamvas considered those historiosophical works that professed the program of such a return to be "tinkerish" and characteristic of the modern age losing its professional standards. His political argument also converged with Huizinga's conservative liberalism criticizing authoritarian leaders as destructive of their communities and praising instead the contenders of the statist regimes permeated by the "passion of truth."[74] The only way to avoid crisis was through catharsis. The future was inscrutable, and neither retrospective utopias nor totalitarian visions of collective regeneration could offer such an experience—only a profoundly self-critical intellectual and spiritual introspection.

It was also possible to build a conservative/anti-modernist yet also anti-totalitarian crisis discourse with reference to Nietzsche's contrast of the spiritless "last man" and the heroic "superman" (*Übermensch*). Reflecting on the intellectual origins of Nazism and the Second World War, the German-born Eric Voegelin (born Erich Vögelin, 1901–85) made such an attempt in "Nietzsche, the Crisis and the War."[75] Having left his Vienna university position after the Anschluss and settling in the United States, he characteristically fought a two-front war, both against the Nazi ideologists claiming Nietzsche's legacy, and also against those liberal or communist critics who blamed the genocidal expansionism of Germany on philosophical influences, particularly the author of *Also sprach Zarathustra*. To make his point, Voegelin developed an interpretation of a comprehensive crisis of Western modernity, rereading Nietzsche as one of the most perceptive precursors of this diagnosis, and at the same time a staunch critique of German nationalism.

What is more, Voegelin also drew on Nietzsche to sketch out the possible political implications and use of the crisis discourse itself. For him, conceptualizing crisis was not just descriptive but also normative:

> ... the phenomenon which is apt to arouse political sentiments is the transformation of a latently critical into a consciously critical situation through the creation of symbols which purport to describe the crisis. [...] Calling attention to a crisis by inventing the terminological apparatus for its description has the effect of a "challenge" to "overcome" it (*Überwinden* is one of the fundamental ideas of Nietzsche), and accepting the challenge means the adoption of an attitude which inevitably will be "destructive" of the attitudes and beliefs which constitute the crisis.[76]

Agony or Regeneration? Constructing a European Canon of "Crisis Literature"

The conservative anti-totalitarian position had prominent adherents in the second half of the 1930s. But it became gradually clear that the political weight of this position was limited and could hardly stave off the rise of the extreme right, which also

54   Intellectuals and the Crisis of Politics

used conservative tropes, evoking a mythical period of harmony in the past but combined it with a much more radical rejection of the existing institutions of political modernity (most of all, parliamentarism). As a result, the conservative position became increasingly desperate.

Polish intellectual Marian Zdziechowski's (1861–1938) "catastrophism" embodied this desperation. A literary historian who specialized in Slavic cultures in a European context, he had a strong link both to Catholic modernism at the turn of the century and pre-revolutionary Russian intellectual streams (having studied in Dorpat/Tartu and St. Petersburg). In his interwar writings, drawing on Spengler, Ferrero, Gustave Le Bon, Berdyaev, and Gonzague de Reynold (1880–1970), he depicted a comprehensive picture of civilizational decline of the West, starting with the French Revolution and reaching its climatic point in Bolshevism.[77] His understanding of crisis was that of an indicator of an even more comprehensive reconfiguration with apocalyptic overtones, caused by the massification of society and culture. In this sense, the First World War was far from being a catalyst; rather, it was the beginning of the final phase of decomposition. At the same time, he did not derive from this any vision of national–collectivist regeneration. Rather, he described capitalism, nationalism, and Bolshevism as crisis symptoms of the very same irreversible process of dehumanization and de-Christianization.

Zdziechowski's ideas were linked to the broader Polish "catastrophist" stream in the 1930s and 1940s, including such luminaries of Polish and European culture as Witkacy (Stanisław Ignacy Witkiewicz, 1885–1939) and the young Czesław Miłosz (1911–2004).[78] In their work, however, the concept of crisis was overshadowed by apocalyptic symbols and expectations. These expectations were dramatically reinforced by the outbreak of the Second World War (Witkacy committed suicide upon hearing the news of the Soviet invasion of Poland in September 1939). In Miłosz's paradigmatic poems, such as the 1944 *A Song on the End of the World*, time and history come to a final standstill in a metaphysical sense, even if the people do not realize it.[79]

The feeling of despair is also palpable in the very title of the Croat intellectual (and son-in-law of Ferrero) Bogdan Radica's (1904–93) book of conversations *The Agony of Europe*.[80] Publishing his book when the Second World War was already raging, but his own country was still out of the warfare, Radica offered a broad panorama of European intellectual positions preoccupied with the crisis of values and institutions. While he used the metaphor of agony, Radica's understanding of crisis was not necessarily linked to terminal illness (prefiguring the end of civilization). He understood it rather as a moment of despair and disorientation when "one order is being destroyed, while the other is not yet visible."[81] In his opinion, "Old Europe" was moribund, a condition he linked to the defeat of "Spirit" by "the most brutal material forces." What was once a synthesis of Athens, Rome, and Christianity came to be dominated by Sophism, Caesarism, and the decline of religious sentiment. While these tropes were obviously not original, Radica's voice was atypical in the sense that he framed Europe not so much from the inside out, but vice versa, reflecting on the ambiguity of Western self-positioning and the in-betweenness of his own culture (and also being particularly sensitive to other cases of ambiguity, such as that of Spain). Along these lines, he reviewed the multiplicity of European intellectual and political traditions, searching for future-oriented engagements with crisis phenomena and contrasting different generational, national, and ideological perspectives.

The first part of his book contains a series of conversations with his father-in-law, Ferrero, first published in Italian in 1939.[82] In these conversations, the Italian anti-fascist émigré thinker resumed the key themes of his political–historical analyses from the 1920s and 1930s (*La tragedia della pace* (1923); *Discorsi ai sordi* (1925); *Aventure. Bonaparte en Italie, 1796–1797* (1936); and *Reconstruction. Talleyrand à Vienne, 1814–1815* (1936)). Using Roman history as the closest parallel to the developments in contemporary Europe, Ferrero developed a theory based on the contrast of civilizations of quality and quantity. He stressed that real progress was through qualitative steps—whereas quantitative growth was just a "parenthesis." Along these lines, the Italian thinker described the nineteenth century as "Promethean," focusing mainly on material growth, and culminating in the First World War, which dealt a radical blow to European civilization. He contrasted the early modern wars, which were to a certain extent "humanized," and which pursued limited strategic aims, to the conflagration between 1914–18, which (he opined) was the first total war. Conversely, the peace architecture closing early modern wars up to the Napoleonic Wars was able to create a lasting international order by employing a mutually acceptable principle of peace-making. In contrast, the First World War was only seemingly concluded with the collapse of Central and Eastern European dynasties, but instead created a permanent ideological and political insecurity that resulted in a lasting, crisis-ridden period characterized by the growth of voluntarism, cynicism, and the cult of violence.

Drawing on his analysis of the Congress of Vienna as a model of peace-making, Ferrero argued that the main political and intellectual task was to recreate a lasting "European balance."[83] Praising the classicist political culture of the Enlightenment, which entailed self-limitation and rational compromise, he was highly critical of Romanticism, which in his opinion was at the root of totalitarianism. Likewise, in contrast to Ortega, who praised Caesar for breaking with the paradigm of the city-state, Ferrero (evidently responding to the Italian fascist narrative of a continuity between Caesar and Mussolini) saw in the Roman politician the archetype of amoral politics. For him, Caesarism was particularly dangerous in the era of mass politics. Along these lines, he depicted Louis Napoleon as the direct precursor of fascism. Characterizing the transitional period between monarchy and democracy, totalitarian regimes used democratic means, such as the plebiscite, but their aim was not democratic: they sought to legitimize the rule of the tyrant. The transitional nature of totalitarianism also meant that it was not there to stay for long. Thus, Ferrero's abhorrence of the inhuman potential of totalitarian dictatorship notwithstanding, his crisis discourse—as transmitted by Radica—was not about an irredeemable civilizational catastrophe but instead a serious and multi-level challenge to European civilization, which necessitated an equally powerful intellectual response that could become a lasting basis for future political and social action.

56 Intellectuals and the Crisis of Politics

Proceeding from Ferrero to other prominent European intellectuals, Radica offers a veritable catalogue of crisis discourses, taking up different themes which were important for the oeuvre of these authors, while also pointing to common motifs such as the conflict of culture and politics. Along these lines, the conversation with Thomas Mann focused on nationalism and the mass movements of the late nineteenth century, which in Mann's interpretation were particularly destructive of spirit and reason. He also castigated the vitalist philosophical legacy of Nietzsche and Henri Bergson as a gateway to totalitarianism, arguing that the contrast of the vital forces of the primitives to "over-refined" modern culture and the cult of primitivism was not conducive to universal regeneration but self-destruction. Connected to this, he described the German relationship to the core of European civilization—which he deemed classical and Catholic—as highly ambiguous, but also pointed to a stream in German culture that was fully compatible with these values (symbolically linked to the figure of Johann Wolfgang von Goethe), in contrast to the "anti-Europeanism" of Nietzsche and his followers.

Radica was aware that, before he had turned vocally anti-fascist, Mann expressed more ambiguous opinions of European civilization and the place of Germany in Europe, especially in the 1918 *Reflections of a Nonpolitical Man*. Similarly, when talking to Benedetto Croce (1866–1952), the most important Italian intellectual critical of fascism, Radica did not shy away from posing the question regarding the responsibility of the Italian philosopher for the ideological radicalization of his country, pointing out that the neo-idealist school he created had in a way prepared the ground for Gabriele D'Annunzio's radical nationalism, which could be considered a precursor of fascism.

The dialogue with Croce focused mainly on the crises of thinking and of culture from the perspective of historicism. For Croce, history was the most integrated way of knowledge, while historicism, humanism, and liberalism were all part of the same intellectual thread. Liberalism in his reading was of course quite different from the actual liberal political formations that were collapsing in many European countries from the mid-1920s onward. According to Croce, while liberalism in the philosophical sense was not in crisis, liberal *politics* indeed was crumbling, caused mainly by the rise of mass society, mass politics, and the concomitant loss (starting with the Bismarckian combination of authoritarianism and social welfare policies) of the privileged position of enlightened elites who sought to rule according to the dictates of reason and individual freedom. But the collapse of liberal political forces was not the death of liberalism; rather, it was a symptom of chaotic transformation.

In his Paris exile, Berdyaev, in a much less optimistic voice, spoke of the crisis of man, which he derived from the destruction of Christian humanism by democratic capitalism and totalitarianism. He worked with a much more Manichean model than Ferrero, Mann, or Croce, contrasting "paganism" and Christianity as the only two possible—and mutually exclusive—directions for mankind. Along these lines, he painted an apocalyptic picture of the doom of capitalism together with its chief ideological adversaries—totalitarian communism and fascism—all being rooted in the same pagan materialism. According to Berdyaev, the only resolution was Personalism, understood as the philosophical motor of Christian revival. Instead of the core of Europe, dominated by materialism, this revival was expected to come from the peripheries. Irrespective of the communist regime, Berdyaev identified Russia as the carrier of the mission of universal regeneration (contrasting the institutional church, which was disappearing, and "mystical Christianity," which in his opinion was expanding even under totalitarian pressure) and Spain as the other pole of spirituality. While the cult of mysticism and the focus on Russia's messianic mission were atypical among the interlocutors of Radica's book, in political terms Berdyaev's position was not that far from his peers, such as Ortega or Mann, as he envisaged a European federation as a way out of the crisis.

Radica provocatively put the Russian thinker next to the pacifist humanist physician and writer Georges Duhamel (1884–1966), whose vision of Europe was diametrically opposed to Berdyaev's. Duhamel asserted that the core of Europe was overlapping with the French wine regions: Burgundy, Champagne, and Normandy. From his perspective, the East posed a mortal danger of fomenting subversive revolutionary and religious movements. For Duhamel, Russia was the Other of Europe, and even in his first meeting with Radica in 1928 (after Duhamel had published *Le Voyage de Moscou*), he was still convinced that—because of the cultural differences— Bolshevism could not be transferred to Western Europe. Resuming the conversation in 1936, as French society was increasingly permeated by feelings of crisis, Duhamel seemed less optimistic and talked about the "virus of Moscow, Berlin, and Rome," stressing that a divided French society was unprepared for the impending assault of the "barbarians."[84] Finally, in 1938, reflecting on the Munich crisis, he contrasted two possible scenarios: a triumphant militarism destroying European civilization, or some sort of restoration of a European balance of forces with France as its keystone.

Overall, most voices registered by Radica saw the solution of the crisis in some sort of supra-national rearrangement of Europe. Ortega thus reiterated his vision of a new liberalism as a reaction to the totalitarian challenge, promoting his vision of European federalism. Likewise, French political geographer from Alsace, André Siegfried (1875–1959) talked of the crisis of Europe in terms of losing its economic and political dynamism after the Great War. Siegfried linked this to the collapse of the nineteenth-century global economic system and its division of labor, with the concomitant fall of English commercial hegemony and the rise of industrial protectionism. In this new context, European democracies needed to reposition themselves, sustain their global leadership in technological innovation, and reinforce their moral commitment to the freedom of speech and thought, which also catalyzed innovation in the industrial domain. In this respect, he contrasted the "healthy democratic" northern zone of Europe to the "pathological" (southern and eastern) regions, where efficiency was pursued by abandoning the liberal democratic value system.

Salvador de Madariaga (1886–1978) was yet another cosmopolitan thinker who identified himself with liberalism, albeit with a strong conservative inflection. He rejected Francoist "national fascism" but also socialism, pointing to Anglo-Saxon liberalism as the model to follow. Like Ortega, he considered European federalism as

58 Intellectuals and the Crisis of Politics

a way out of the crisis, stressing that linguistic differences were bigger than those of mentality. Maritain was also positioned by Radica in the context of the Spanish Civil War, as the French Catholic thinker memorably raised his voice in favor of the Republican government.[85] Reframing the contrast of rational Catholicism and irrational Protestantism prevalent in the discourse of the radical conservatives around the Action Française, the European crisis in Maritain's rendering was due to a clash of anthropocentric rationalist humanism (manifested in Cartesianism) and "irrationalism" (similar to Maurras, the main ideologist of Action Française, Maritain linked irrationalism to Martin Luther and Rousseau). Nationalism in his understanding was a manifestation of irrationalism and Nazism was the product of Luther's subjectivist inwardness (*interiorité*), transferred to the sphere of biology. Again, Maritain's suggested remedy was the federalization of Europe—a chance missed after the First World War.

Another French Catholic intellectual turning in an anti-fascist direction during the Spanish Civil War, François Mauriac (1885–1970) expressed similar positions. For him, postwar France entered a period of spiritual and political crisis, but he saw the signs of a Christian revival which also entailed the rejection of totalitarianism. Taking a more ambiguous position both politically and philosophically, Miguel de Unamuno (1864–1936) focused on the tragic contradictions of civilization, encapsulated by his famous notion of "Donquijotism." Transcending the Spanish cultural context, it denoted eternal struggle and agony, rooted in the contradiction of Western civilization and Christianity. Agony, the central metaphor of Radica's book, was also taken from this context, albeit without its theological implications.

Radica's other interlocutors, who also defined themselves as liberal, described the clash of totalitarianism and liberalism as a crisis, which could result in the disintegration of civilization but also a rejuvenation of Europe. Thus, for instance, Julien Benda (1867–1956) linked liberalism to classicism, depicting the root of totalitarianism as a "sensual/irrational deviation." He pointed to the liberal democrats' loss of self-confidence, in contrast to the adherents of totalitarianism who firmly believed "in their own valor and their principles."[86] Benda inserted this into a *longue durée* historical framework, linking the liberal democratic side to the tradition of rationalist thought, including Socrates and Plato, medieval theology, the Port-Royalists, the doctrines of the French Revolutionaries, and the Dreyfusards while drawing an equally direct line of irrationalism connecting the Sophists, the Renaissance philosopher Pomponazzi, the anti-Cartesian reaction, French materialism, Fichte, and Herder with—Hitler!

Italian liberal émigré Count Carlo Sforza (1872–1952) also created a historical framework, contrasting Giuseppe Mazzini's (1805–72) universalist patriotism—which he evidently used as a transnational ideological and symbolic framework to sustain a liberal anti-fascist platform—to fascist self-centeredness. For him, crisis was first and foremost the moral degradation of political elites and the collapse of international solidarity. As an example, he cited the reticence of Western European democracies to support the US government in its efforts to sanction the Italian aggression in Ethiopia.[87]

Socialist philosopher and literary scholar Adriano Tilgher (1887–1941) was yet another Italian interlocutor of Radica who derived the global crisis from the collapse of civilizational standards and the rise of the cult of violence, which became evident after 1914.[88] For him, the core of the crisis was the clash of two contradictory dynamics: the simultaneous expansion of violent nationalism and the progress of European unification. Rooted in a Marxist analysis, Tilgher linked the intensification of nationalism to the transformation of the global economy. The interconnection of economic and political competition pushed the state toward protectionism and made both the bourgeoisie and the proletariat dependent on that protection, which then prompted the use of nationalistic arguments and led to imperialistic expansionism. In turn, this could only be countered by political and economic democratization.

Moving to the right, Swiss Catholic conservative de Reynold described the essence of crisis as a conflict between Europe and Asia, describing racism and Bolshevism as instances of the "paganization" of Europe. Radica also included Maurras, the main intellectual of the French right, but he evidently kept his distance, describing his interviewee as a "Mediterranean *condottiere*" who failed to create action out of his ideas. Maurras reiterated his well-known criticism of the French Revolution as the key turning point toward the political and spiritual decline of Europe. In contrast to the liberal voices in the book—full of anxiety in view of the crisis of democracy unfolding globally in the 1930s—Maurras saw his own critical stance vindicated. He criticized democratic states for being incapable of conducing foreign policy successfully, and in general failing to make and execute decisions in a moment of external and internal pressure. He stressed the need for personal authority as an integrative force, especially in big nations with multiple interests and conflicts.[89] Authority was cemented by the emotional and eventually biological adherence of the population to a common national framework, bridging the two main components of his ideology: integral nationalism and monarchism. At the same time, Maurras also subscribed to some version of the federalist discourse, asserting that France had a mission in Europe to create a new harmony of the national and supranational (Catholic) perspectives.

Radica also talked to Giovanni Papini (1881–1956), another Catholic intellectual on the extreme right. Having started his intellectual career in avant-gardist circles in Florence, the Italian Papini combined certain tropes of futurism with radical conservatism. In their first conversation from 1928, Papini talked about individual crises as symptoms of a global crisis and stressed the need for a truly universal catastrophe to make people conscious of their sinfulness and thus catalyze a spiritual and political regeneration.[90] Looking for possible models, he rejected the Bolshevik program of transformation as materialistic and eventually self-destructive, but praised Mahatma Gandhi for launching an oriental spiritual revolution that could serve as a blueprint for the merger of traditionalism and future-oriented visions.

As for Italy, Papini considered the creation of a truly unified nation-state and society as the most important task of the fascist regime. Resuming the conversation with Radica a decade later, he became more ambitious in linking Italian fascist policies to

60   Intellectuals and the Crisis of Politics

the project of global palingenesis. While democracy was fragmenting the nation, Caesarism was unifying it, and, by adopting Caesarism to modern conditions, fascism offered a new synthesis of antiquity and modernity. Consistent with this imperialist turn, the contrast between European and non-European nations became more explicit. Papini noted the rise of non-European forces after the Great War, but still upheld the "European mission" to teach and direct other peoples. What is more, he sought to harmonize Italian nationalism with imperialist Eurocentrism, deriving the task of the spiritual unification of Europe from the legacy of Dante and Machiavelli.

Russian émigré writer and Orthodox thinker Dmitriy Merezhkovskiy (1865–1941) was closer to Western conservative revolutionary streams than Berdyaev and converged with Papini on the hope for an apocalyptic transformation, but predictably described Russia as the epicenter of universal regeneration. While most Western European radical conservatives considered Russia as the source of non-European contamination, Merezhkovskiy contrasted the Russian "spiritual revolution" (creating a fictitious link between Slavophilism, Fyodor Dostoevsky, and the February Revolution) to the anti-Russian (Semitic, materialist) Bolsheviks, whose spiritual father he found in Tolstoy, the "prophet of chaos." Merezhkovskiy characterized Bolshevik rule as ephemeral and contradictory for the Russian soul, and hoped for a "Slavic Napoleon" to rise who would achieve a global spiritual and political revolution.

Perhaps the most interesting feature of Radica's kaleidoscopic overview of European cultural and philosophical crisis discourses in the 1930s is that, even though the political and epistemological positions of his interlocutors were extremely divergent, they shared a common conceptual language—not only because of the questions and editorial interventions of Radica. Most of them linked crisis in one way or another to the fall of European hegemony, moral disorientation, the lack of common values, and the growth of violence. At the same time, they also saw in it a chance for cultural, political, and spiritual regeneration. Who was identified as the main culprit for causing the crisis, and the possible catalyst of regeneration, was of course dependent on the political orientation of the respective thinker, but the structure of the narrative in pointing to a previous moment of equilibrium, a gradual process of corruption reaching almost complete dissolution, and articulating the hope that exactly the gravity of the situation would galvanize new energies of reconstruction was omnipresent—and strongly resonated with romantic metahistorical narratives. What is more, while the historical width and depth might have been different, key reference points, such as classical antiquity, the Renaissance, the Enlightenment, or the First World War, remained central to most narratives.

Crisis of Religiosity

As in Radica's analysis of Maritain, Papini, Merezhkovskiy, or Berdyaev, the philosophical diagnoses were often linked to the discourse of the crisis of religiosity, or of particular denominations. The clash of traditionalist, modernist, and anti-modernist visions was particularly visible in these debates, with many interesting border-crossings between theology and philosophy (as in the case of Personalism). Again, the political implications were often outspoken, for instance, in the debates on the nationalization of religion. While some critiques took up a universalist position and castigated the nationalist turn of the clergy, others argued exactly for an even closer inter-relationship between nationalism and religion, amounting to the sacral-ization of the nation as a way out of the spiritual crisis. While the discussion on the crisis of religion also had considerable repercussions in the interwar period, it was far from being a novel phenomenon. It was more of a new chapter in a prolonged debate, reaching back well into the nineteenth century, on the problems posed by modernity, above all the inadequacy of previous forms of religiosity in the new conditions and, in turn, the disappearance of religious sentiment from society.

The first theme was at the center of the positivist challenges against religious dogma in the second half of the nineteenth century. It entailed various projects of rationalization and historicization, represented by such pivotal figures of the period as Renan, for whom the crisis was of a political nature. Renan identified its cause in the *Kulturkampf* of the 1870s, with Pope Pius IX's exaggerated concentration of power on the one hand—seeking to buttress his hegemonistic claims theologically and reasserting Catholic dogmas as irrational—and, on the other, the sovereignty claims of the German state, represented by the equally hegemonistic chancellor Otto von Bismarck. With the acceptance of papal infallibility, "the papacy wanted to place itself outside of nature," while the emerging German nation-state, rooted in Protes-tantism, achieved its highest self-confidence in the very same historical moment when it defeated France militarily. The result was a frontal clash between Church and State. Such a struggle had repercussions well beyond the German context, creating also an internal split within the Catholic community between those who accepted the infallibility dogma and those who rejected it.[91] For Renan, the way out of this crisis was to follow liberal precepts, separate church and state, and allow full liberty of conscience, which he believed would also undermine the hegemonic claims of the papacy.

Responding also to this positivist criticism, the second half of the nineteenth century saw the emergence of various streams of theological modernism, address-ing what they perceived as the crisis of traditional religiosity. However, at the turn of the century various counter-movements emerged, which considered theo-logical modernism as a part of the problem rather than the solution. Theological modernism's rationalist penchant was described as a slippery slope leading to sec-ularization and the loss of religious sentiment altogether. For the anti-modernists, the crisis of religion was caused exactly by the convergence of social moderniza-tion and the rationalist/historicist deviation of theological thought. The emerging anti-modernist theological currents, such as the Dutch neo-Calvinist movement, stressed the importance of emotions and irrational belief as constitutive. For them, it was only possible to overcome the crisis if one could recreate a more immedi-ate experience of the divine, characteristic of earlier ages. The most paradigmatic school of thought framing this program of religious revival in terms of a discourse of crisis was Swiss Calvinist theologian Karl Barth's (1886–1968) "neo-orthodoxy," which in the 1920s became internationally well-known as the "theology of crisis."[92] For Barth, as he described it in his famous *Epistle to the Romans*,[93] the main agenda was to recreate a more immediate relationship with transcendence, breaking through the conventional institutional structures and mental frameworks of mediation. God's sovereignty was absolute, and humans could not aspire to understand—let alone influence—divinity. Hence the infinite despair of the religious person, which was only assuaged by divine grace. Crisis in this sense was not externalized as cultural or theological disorientation but internalized as constitutive of the experience of transcendence. Barth's "theology of crisis" also meant a challenge to the historicist trends dominating the late nineteenth century both in the theological realm and more broadly in German social and cultural thought. This challenge was most coherently formulated by the Lutheran theologian Friedrich Gogarten (1887–1967).[94]

While Barth had a huge impact also beyond denominational borders, distinct denominations experienced different developments that came to be framed as crisis. In the case of Protestantism, this was commonly linked to the clash of modernist and anti-modernist streams, the former putting emphasis on the compatibility of religion and reason, while the latter asserting that faith was a fundamentally different faculty than rational thinking. Importantly, in political terms these two positions were not unambiguous. Modernist rationalism could be taken up by conservative elites and irrational anti-modernism could have anti-authoritarian implications (as in the case of Barth and his followers, who inspired anti-Nazi streams in Protestantism).

As for Catholicism, the dividing lines were somewhat different, hence the perception of crisis was also based on different experiences. Theological modernism was not able to break through in the late nineteenth century because of the strong dogmatic and political conservative backlash in the 1870s and 1880s. The anti-modernist ideological campaign culminated in the 1910 "Oath Against Modernism" by Pope Pius X, who lashed out against the rationalization and historicization of religious faith.[95] As a result, crisis was often depicted not as a clash of modernism and anti-modernism, but more in terms of a confrontation of traditional Catholicism and various mass ideologies (especially communism and fascism) that both challenged the position of the Church and were perceived to have replaced traditional religious belief as a framework of orientation. A suggested solution was a sort of spiritual third way between modernism and traditionalism that was most powerfully formulated by the philosophical school of Personalism. Seeking to mediate between individualism and collectivism, Personalism also intersected with political "third way" discourses. In the early 1930s it had a markedly anti-liberal orientation, but by the second half of the 1930s some of its leading representatives became vocally anti-totalitarian, linking the metaphysical and political connotations of personal freedom. A key text of this movement published in 1936 by Emmanuel Mounier (1905–50), "The Personalist Manifesto" also contained ample references to crisis.[96] In Mounier's understanding, Personalism was not a closed doctrine but a variety of perspectives cutting across the ideological alternatives of the day, namely fascist and communist totality and decadent bourgeois liberalism. The unfolding crisis was thus a possibility for a complete spiritual and ideological overhaul, that of "remaking the Renaissance":

> Historically, the crisis that presses upon us is more than a simple political crisis or even than a profound economic crisis. We are witnessing the cave-in of a whole area of civilization, one, namely, that was born towards the end of the Middle Ages, was consolidated and at the same time threatened by the industrial age, is capitalistic in structure, liberal in its ideology, bourgeois in its ethics.[97]

The most concise statement linking the discourse of crisis and the program of reviving Catholicism as a catalyst of democratic thought came from Maritain,[98] who blamed the process of de-Christianization for the emergence of left- and right-wing totalitarianisms. These movements disregarded the divine element in the human being, rooted in the incarnation of God, and sought to instrumentalize their fellow humans for political aims. He chose Schmitt's theory of *Politik* based on the contrast of friend and enemy to illustrate this "godless" totalitarian logic. From this perspective, crisis denoted the moment of seeming hegemony of these ideologies, which threatened human civilization with self-destruction. However, Maritain saw in the return to a Christian humanism a solution that focused on human dignity and could be translated into the political sphere as "Christian democracy." He was fully aware of the fact that the ideological combination he proposed did not fit into the usual left–right division and so legitimized this syncretism with a reference to the contemporaneous crisis: "[I]n such epochs of general crisis as ours, it is especially necessary that the effort of the spirit transcends the worm-eaten frames of psychological or party-political dispositions."[99] It is indicative of the multi-layeredness of ideological positions that Maritain referred to American political thinker Walter Lippmann (1889–1974). While Lippmann became a key intellectual source for the French neoliberals in the mid-1930s, he also resonated with Maritain's Christian democratic position on questions such as the importance of human rights. Overall, Maritain saw the fight for Christian liberty as a French ideological mission against Russian Bolshevism, Italian fascism, and German Nazism, as well as a possible way to create a common European framework.

The crisis discourse of French personalism had repercussions in East Central European Catholic intellectual circles as well. An illustration for this is provided by the 1936 "Congress of Lithuanian Catholic Scientists and Science Enthusiasts" in Kaunas, which brought together a wide range of representatives from the Catholic intelligentsia and the Church hierarchy itself, including Archbishop of Kaunas Juozapas Skvireckas.[100] The contribution by leading Lithuanian Catholic philosopher Stasys Šalkauskis (1886–1941) offered a complex landscape of intellectual references. Having studied in Moscow and Fribourg, and thus combining Eastern and Western European sources of inspiration, he drew especially on Maritain,

64   Intellectuals and the Crisis of Politics

as well as on nineteenth-century French Catholic thinker Ernest Hello and on de Reynold, together with Russian Orthodox philosophical and theological voices, mainly Berdyaev and Vladimir Solovyov.[101]

Šalkauskis described crisis as a period of transformation—one when new ideas struggle to break through the existing social and cultural order. As an adept of personalism, he rejected putting the blame on external factors and called for introspection to find the root of crisis in oneself. Giving a historical dimension to this introspection, he pointed to the loss of medieval spirituality after the rise of Renaissance anthropocentrism. He saw the Catholic intellectual tradition as the principal source of regeneration, even though he considered the actual answers given by his fellow Catholics as insufficient and "clumsy." Therefore, he did not call for a simple return to the Middle Ages but argued for a new synthesis to be worked out by "updating" the Catholic position. This synthetic intention also had political implications, as his criticism of "godless" modernity was compatible with a certain sympathy for a "national democracy," partly because of the obvious ideological and geopolitical threat coming from the direction of the Soviet Union and Nazi Germany. At the same time, many of Šalkauskis's students, such as Antanas Maceina (1908–87), gradually moved toward a more radical nationalist position, combined with a Catholic corporatist social agenda.

In Eastern Orthodoxy, the modernist theological streams were less successful even though in the Balkans at the turn of the century liberal nationalism as a political orientation was often shared by prominent clergymen.[102] But due to the absence of a powerful liberal theological stream, modernism and anti-modernism came to overlap in Orthodoxy. New types of Orthodox theological thinking sought to bring the Church closer to the present, and so also registered the crisis of Western denominations and the growth of secularization in the most advanced societies. Thus, their entry point into the global discussion was precisely with the reconsideration of Orthodoxy as fundamentally different, and due to its archaic forms perhaps more resilient than Catholicism and Protestantism. Here the Orthodox crisis discourse was related to what was perceived as the "West" and, later, with the Bolshevik takeover in Russia and during the interwar period, it became universalized as an apocalyptic battle of religious tradition against the evils of secularization, rationalism, and communism.

The most important theoretician of crisis in the Russian religious context was doubtlessly Berdyaev.[103] While his earlier texts focused mainly on the crisis of Russian culture and society, after 1918 he reframed his position in terms of a more comprehensive spiritual crisis of Western civilization, searching for a way out precisely through Eastern Orthodox spirituality.[104] By the early 1930s, he saw crisis everywhere: "Everything in the contemporary world stands under the sign of crisis, not only in the social and economic sense, but in cultural as well as spiritual senses too."[105] He stressed that this crisis was not only that of secular or anti-Christian society but also of "historical Christianity." In fact, the central element of the unfolding crisis was precisely the decomposition of the secular belief in human progress that had replaced Christian belief in human salvation over the nineteenth century. Notably, he read Heidegger's *Sein und Zeit* as a symptomatic text indicating this metaphysical crisis.

Among the principal causes of crisis, Berdyaev singled out the inability of the European man to cope with the rise of mechanistic and technical civilization, irretrievably replacing the natural environment as the framework of human existence. This shift from "organism" to "organization" also led to a growing gap between the secular and religious spheres of life. This mechanization also manifested itself in social life, with the entrance of the masses into politics through the process of democratization. All this had resulted in the collapse of the higher ideals of life, which lingered in the form of crypto-religious movements such as communism. Totalitarian ideologies and movements were also crisis symptoms, manifesting the loss of faith in human liberty that characterized the post-Christian West. Totalitarianism can be understood not only as the culmination of the drive for rationalization and mechanization, but also as the revolt of the irrational core of human personality against them. Instead of these mass ideologies, Berdyaev advocated a "Christian personalist socialism," giving back the value of individual personality in one's relationship with God. The only way to resolve the contemporary crisis was to turn back to Christianity, but this about-face could not mean a return to a pre-existent spiritual and doctrinal arrangement. Berdyaev also pointed to a certain internal contradiction in historical Christianity—being unable to reveal the divine nature of the human being in its actual life. Thus, the central feature of the crisis Berdyaev detected was the threat of dehumanization, but crisis was also a chance for the revival of a richer spiritual existence for humankind in the form of "God-Manhood."

Crisis also became a key notion in the work of some Jewish authors reflecting on their faith and community. The second half of the nineteenth century saw a clash of modernist and traditionalist streams in this context as well, creating a strong liberal theological and social movement, aiming at the full emancipation and integration of the Jewish communities in their respective national contexts. However, these expectations and reforms suffered serious setbacks in the sense that anti-Semitism became a powerful political weapon at the turn of the century across Europe. In turn, there emerged Jewish critics of the liberal integration agenda, coining a national ideology that rejected assimilation and envisioned the creation of a Jewish nation-state or (mainly in the Russian imperial context) territorial autonomy. On theological grounds, then, a neo-traditionalist position sought to valorize Jewishness as a radical alternative to secular liberalism and socialism, while also rejecting the Zionist program. In the interwar years, with the further intensification of anti-Semitism in many contexts, and the gradual marginalization of liberalism, the cleavages among these positions became even deeper. Hence, both the critics of assimilation and the critics of Jewish spiritual traditions talked of the crisis of the Jewish collective self, albeit in very different terms.[106]

Romanian–Jewish journalist and political thinker Nicolae Steinhardt (1912–89), closely linked to the radical anti-modernist "generation of 1927" (comprising Mircea

66 Intellectuals and the Crisis of Politics

Eliade, Constantin Noica, Eugen Ionescu, and Emil Cioran, to mention those who subsequently became the most well-known from this *pléiade* of furious and exceptionally talented young Romanian intellectuals) developed his own crisis discourse related to Judaism. Steinhardt's *Essai sur une conception catholique du judaïsme* (1935), co-written with his brother-in-law Emanuel (Emanoil) Neuman (1911–95),[107] pointed to the crisis of the reformist and assimilationist strategies of the Jewish elites and came close to an anti-modernist vision (resonating with the French Catholic integralist discourse) arguing for the compatibility of Judaism and radical conservatism. However, in their subsequent *Illusions et réalités juives* (1937),[108] written in the context of the rise of the extreme right-wing and ferociously anti-Semitic Iron Guard, the authors moved toward a more open position toward liberal democracy, rejecting mysticism and depicting an either/or of liberalism or a "new Middle Ages." At the same time, they remained highly critical of what they considered to be the "abstract" universalist heritage of the Haskalah.

Going beyond the denominational discussion, the discourse of the crisis of religion was often framed in terms of a broader spiritual crisis. This could be constructed from a conservative perspective, deploring the rise of modernism as the cause of the loss of orientation and an overwhelming feeling of crisis. There were, however, alternative renderings that went against the logic of conservatism. As pacifist reform pedagogue Friedrich Wilhelm Foerster (1869–1966) argued in *Weltkrise und Seelenkrise*,[109] humankind faced a spiritual crisis that undermined the basic norms of human coexistence, as these norms had transcendental roots. In his understanding, there could be no human rights without divine right (*Gottesrecht*). The most disconcerting features of political modernity, such as nationalism, militarism, and the cult of the state were caused by the disorientation of religious sentiment, catalyzing an "apocalyptic struggle" between divine and "titanic" forces. The latter, for him, was exemplified by Bismarck, who created a unified (German) state by force. Here the conceptual sacralization clashed frontally with the logic of the nation-state.

In sum, if we consider the interwar period through the optics of the texts focusing on cultural and spiritual crisis analyzed here, we can find an interesting thread. Specifically, many of the analytical tools and categories appearing in post-Second World War scholarship on the idea and concept of crisis (among others, in the work of Reinhart Koselleck) pop up in these discussions, such as the coupling of critique and crisis, the idea of horizons of expectation, the question of the secularization of eschatological frameworks of historicity, the linking of the modern understanding of crisis to the transformative impact of the French Revolution, or the description of totalitarianism as a crisis symptom.

That said, a caveat is also due here. While these narratives had remarkable impact, as many of the authors mentioned in this chapter were among the most influential intellectual voices of the period, it would be misleading to limit the horizons of the discussion of the interwar crisis discourse to the cultural–philosophical register. The multiplicity of different spheres of knowledge production, and the myriad epistemic communities that converged in the discourse of crisis, entailed a variety of other approaches with divergent conceptual apparatuses and intellectual stakes. The following chapters look at different perspectives on the crisis of the economy, society, and the democratic political system, or of ideologies like liberalism and socialism, which unfolded in different (although not completely unrelated) segments of the public sphere. At the same time, their meta-historical frameworks were usually quite similar to the one described in this chapter, which was due exactly to the privileged position and powerful impact of the "grand narratives" developed by these cultural philosophers.

Notes

1. There are a number of important works on different aspects and contexts of interwar discourses of cultural crisis, see especially Vittorio Dini and Matthew D'Auria, eds., *The Space of Crisis: Images and Ideas of Europe in the Age of Crisis, 1914–1945* (Brussels: Lang, 2013); Moritz Föllmer and Rüdiger Graf, eds., *Die "Krise" der Weimarer Republik* (Frankfurt: Campus, 2005); Peter Fritzsche, "Landscape of Danger, Landscape of Design: Crisis and Modernism in Weimar Germany," in Thomas W. Kniesche and Stephen Brockmann, eds., *Dancing on the Volcano: Essays on the Culture of the Weimar Republic* (Columbia: Camden House, 1994), 29–46; Peter E. Gordon and John P. McCormick, eds., *Weimar Thought* (Princeton: Princeton University Press, 2013); Wolfgang Küttler, Jörn Rüsen, and Ernst Schulin, eds., *Geschichtsdiskurs*, vol. 4, *Krisenbewußtsein, Katastrophenerfahrungen und Innovationen 1880–1945* (Frankfurt a. M: Fischer, 1997); Miklós Lackó, *Válságok—választások* [Crises and Choices] (Budapest: Gondolat, 1975); Richard Overy, *The Morbid Age. Britain and the Crisis of Civilisation, 1919–1939* (London: Penguin, 2009); Hans Sluga, *Heidegger's Crisis. Philosophy and Politics in Nazi Germany* (Cambridge, MA: Harvard University Press, 1993).
2. This was pointed out by Jean-Louis Loubet del Bayle, "Une tentative de renouvellement de la pensée politique française," *MLN*, vol. 95, no. 4, French Issue (May, 1980): 807; see also his *Les non-conformistes des années 30. Une tentative de renouvellement de la pensée politique française* (Paris: Éditions du Seuil, 1969).
3. Edmund Husserl, *Die Krisis der europäischen Wissenschaften und die transzendentale Phänomenologie: Eine Einleitung in die phänomenologische Philosophie* (Belgrade: Ex officina Societatis "Philosophiae," 1936). Reprinted in 1954 as Edmund Husserl, *Husserliana*, vol. 6: *Die Krisis der europäischen Wissenschaften und die transzendentale Phänomenologie: Eine Einleitung in die phänomenologische Philosophie*, ed. Walter Biemel (Haag: Martinus Nijhoff, 1954).
4. Rudolf Pannwitz, *Die Krisis der europäischen Kultur* (Nuremberg: Hans Carl, 1917), written in 1915–16. On Pannwitz's book and its impact, see Jan Vermeiren, "Imperium Europaeum: Rudolf Pannwitz and the German Idea of Europe," in Mark Hewitson and Matthew D'Auria, eds., *Europe in Crisis: Intellectuals and the European Idea, 1917–1957* (New York: Berghahn Books, 2012), 135–54; as well as Paul Michael Lützeler, "Prophet der europäischen Krise," *Die Zeit*, no. 44, October 28, 1994, available online at https://www.zeit.de/1994/44/prophet-der-europaeischen-krise

68 Intellectuals and the Crisis of Politics

5. Ernst Troeltsch, "Die Krisis des Historismus," *Die neue Rundschau*, vol. 33, no. 1 (1922): 572–90; republished as Ernst Troeltsch, "Die Krisis des Historismus," in Friedemann Voigt, ed., *Lesebuch. Ausgewählte Texte* (Tübingen: Mohr Siebeck, 2003), 246–65.

6. For an introduction to the debate, see Guy Oakes, "Rickert and the Theory of Historical Knowledge," in *Weber and Rickert: Concept Formation in the Cultural Sciences* (Cambridge, MA: The MIT Press, 1990), 41–90; for a key primary source, see Heinrich Rickert, *The Limits of Concept Formation in Natural Science: A Logical Introduction to the Historical Sciences*, ed. and trans. Guy Oakes (Cambridge: Cambridge University Press, 1986).

7. Troeltsch, "Die Krisis des Historismus," in *Lesebuch*, 258.

8. Ibid., 260.

9. Ibid., 264.

10. Paul Valéry, "La crise de l'esprit" (1919), in *Variété I* (Paris: Gallimard, 1924), 11–31.

11. Othmar Spann, *Der wahre Staat. Vorlesungen über Abbruch und Neubau der Gesellschaft* (Jena: Gustav Fischer, 1938 [1921]).

12. Oswald Spengler, *Der Untergang des Abendlandes: Umrisse einer Morphologie der Weltgeschichte* (Munich: C.H. Beck, 1920).

13. Ibid., 65.

14. José Ortega y Gasset, *Esquema de las crisis* (Madrid: Revista de Occidente, 1942 [1933]).

15. Paul Hazard, *La crise de la conscience européenne, 1680–1715* (Paris: Boivin, 1935).

16. Pitirim Aleksandrovich Sorokin, *The Crisis of Our Age: The Social and Cultural Outlook* (New York: Dutton, 1941).

17. Wilhelm Röpke, *Die Gesellschaftskrisis der Gegenwart* (Erlenbach-Zürich: Eugen Rentsch Verlag, 1942); English translation: *The Social Crisis of Our Time* (Chicago: University of Chicago Press, 1950).

18. Hermann Keyserling, *Das Spektrum Europas* (Heidelberg: Kampmann, 1928).

19. Florian Znaniecki, *Upadek cywilizacji zachodniej* [The Fall of Western Civilization] (Warsaw: Wydawnictwo Uniwersytetu Warszawskiego, 2013).

20. Florian Znaniecki, *Ludzie teraźniejsi a cywilizacja przyszłości* [Present Humankind and the Civilization of the Future] (Lwów-Warsaw: Atlas, 1934).

21. Florian Znaniecki, "Polska w kryzysie światowym" [Poland in the World Crisis], in *Upadek*, 169–74. Originally published in *Dziennik Poznański*, no. 279 (December 3, 1933).

22. René Guénon, *The Crisis of the Modern World*, trans. Marco Pallis, Arthur Osborne, and Richard C. Nicholson (Hillsdale: Sophia Perennis, 2001). Original French edition: *La crise du monde moderne* (Paris: Bossard, 1927). On the intellectual roots and legacy of Guénon's "traditionalism," see Mark Sedgwick, *Against the Modern World: Traditionalism and the Secret Intellectual. History of the Twentieth Century* (Oxford: Oxford University Press, 2004).

23. Guénon, *The Crisis of the Modern World*, 1.

24. Ibid., 15.

25. Ibid., 22.

26. Ibid., 112–14.

27. Husserl, *Die Krisis der europäischen Wissenschaften*, 1–17.

28. José Ortega y Gasset, *The Revolt of the Masses* (London: Unwin, 1963 [1930]).

29. Ibid., 9.

30. Ibid., 10.

31. Ibid., 18.
32. Ibid., 138.
33. Ibid., 37.
34. Ibid., 58.
35. Ibid., 72.
36. Ibid., 114.
37. José Ortega y Gasset, *España invertebrada: Bosquejo de algunos pensamientos históricos* (Madrid: Revista de Occidente, 1971).
38. Ortega y Gasset, *The Revolt of the Masses*, 130.
39. Ibid., 137.
40. Ibid., 139.
41. Petre Andrei, "Criza culturii și rolul universității [The Crisis of Culture and the Role of the University] (1927)," in Iordan Chimet, ed., *Dreptul la memorie* [The Right to Memory], vol. 2, (Cluj-Napoca: Editura Dacia, 1992), 90–101.
42. Nicolae Bagdasar, "Criza culturii moderne [The Crisis of Modern Culture]," in *Din problemele culturii europene* [From the Problems of European Culture] (Bucharest: Societatea română de filosofie, 1931), 28–78.
43. On the critical reception of Spengler in Hungary and Romania, see Johannes Bent and Liisi Keedus, "Contesting German 'Crisis Literature': Oswald Spengler in Interwar Hungarian and Romanian Reviews," in Balázs Trencsényi, Lucija Balikić, Una Blagojević, and Isidora Grubački, eds., *East Central European Crisis Discourses in the Twentieth Century: A Never-Ending Story?* (New York: Routledge, 2025), 55–77.
44. Karl Jaspers, *Die geistige Situation der Zeit* (Berlin: de Gruyter, 1932).
45. Ibid., 68.
46. Oswald Spengler, *Jahre der Entscheidung* (Munich: C. H. Beck, 1933).
47. Ibid., 11.
48. Sluga, *Heidegger's Crisis*, 120.
49. Ibid., 179–205.
50. The history of the planned journal is carefully reconstructed by Erdmut Wizisla, *Walter Benjamin and Bertolt Brecht—The Story of a Friendship*, trans. Christine Shuttleworth (New Haven: Yale University Press, 2009), 66–97. Wizisla also documents that the journal project fit into a broader agenda (including attempts to form a Society of Materialist Friends of Hegelian Dialectics or a Marxist Club) of engaging with the burning social and philosophical issues of the day from a non-dogmatic Marxist perspective. See ibid., 41–43.
51. Benjamin's letter to Brecht, from 1931, quoted in ibid., 76.
52. Ibid., 74.
53. Ibid., 190.
54. Ibid., 92–3.
55. Ibid., 197.
56. Ibid., 88–9.
57. Georg Lukács, *Wie ist die faschistische Philosophie in Deutschland entstanden?* (Budapest: Akadémiai Kiadó, 1982). A later version was produced during the Second World War, in 1942, while Lukács was evacuated to Tashkent. Eventually, these manuscripts were used for the book Lukács published after the war, in a markedly different political and intellectual context shaped by the unfolding Cold War: *Die Zerstörung der Vernunft* (Berlin: Aufbau Verlag, 1954).

70 Intellectuals and the Crisis of Politics

58. Georg Lukacs, "Es geht um den Realismus," *Das Wort*, no. 6 (1938): 112–38. English translation in Ernst Bloch, Georg Lukacs, Bertolt Brecht, Walter Benjamin, and Theodor Adorno, *Aesthetics and Politics* (London: Verso, 1980), 32. Many thanks to Kateryna Lysenko for making me read this text.

59. Ibid., 37.

60. Karl Mannheim, *Ideology and Utopia: An Introduction to the Sociology of Knowledge* (London: Routledge & Kegan Paul, 1936). The first German edition was published in 1929. In his preface to the English translation, the American sociologist Louis Wirth explicitly contrasted Mannheim's "sober, critical, and scholarly analysis of the social currents and situations of our time" to the "extensive literature which speaks of the 'end', the 'decline', the 'crisis', the 'decay', or the 'death' of Western civilization." See ibid., xiii.

61. Ibid., 8.

62. Ibid., 36.

63. Ibid., 93.

64. Ibid., 42.

65. Ibid., 96.

66. Karl Mannheim, *Mensch und Gesellschaft im Zeitalter des Umbaus* (Leiden: A. W. Sijthoff's Uitgeversmaatschappij, 1935), 57–92. The revised English version came out in 1940.

67. Ibid., 2.

68. Johan Huizinga, *In the Shadow of To-morrow: A Diagnosis of the Spiritual Distempers of Our Time* (London: William Heinemann, Ltd., 1936). The Dutch original was published in 1935.

69. Ibid., 81.

70. Ibid., 64–5.

71. Béla Hamvas, "Krízis és katarzis" [Crisis and Catharsis] (1937), in *Krízis és katarzis* (Budapest: Medio, 2019), 25.

72. Ibid., 39.

73. Hamvas, "A jövő árnyéka" [The Shadow of the Future] (1936), in ibid., 41–56.

74. Hamvas, "Huizinga krízis-könyve" [Huizinga's Crisis Book] (1936), in ibid., 88.

75. Eric Voegelin, "Nietzsche, the Crisis and the War," *The Journal of Politics*, vol. 6, no. 2 (May 1944): 177–212.

76. Voegelin, "Nietzsche, the Crisis and the War," 178.

77. Marian Zdziechowski, *W obliczu końca* [On the brink] (Vilnius: Wydawnictwo Stanisława Turskiego, 1938).

78. See Teresa Wilkoń, *Katastrofizm w poezji polskiej w latach 1930–1939. Szkice literackie* [Catastrophism in Polish Poetry between 1930 and 1939. Literary Sketches] (Katowice: Wydawnictwo Uniwersytetu Śląskiego, 2016) as well as Urszula Osypiuk and Stefan Symotiuk, "The Decline of Poland as a 'Pre-Figure' of the Decline of Europe (On the Genesis of Witkacy's Catastrophism)," *Filosofija. Sociologija*, vol. 18, no. 1 (2007): 36–45.

79. Czesław Miłosz "A Song on the End of the World," trans. Anthony Milosz, available at https://www.poetryfoundation.org/poems/49451/a-song-on-the-end-of-the-world

80. Bogdan Radica, *Agonija Europe: Razgovori i susreti* [The Agony of Europe: Conversations and Encounters] (Zagreb: Disput, 2006). Originally published in 1940. On Radica's earlier writings, see Suzana Vuljević, "Order amid Chaos: The Crisis of Spirit and a Panoply of Pan-Balkan Solutions in Interwar Europe," in Trencsényi, Balikić, Blagojević and Grubački, eds., *East Central European Crisis Discourses*, 109–32.

Crisis of the Mind and Spirit **71**

81. Ibid., 26.
82. Bogdan Raditza, *Colloqui con Guglielmo Ferrero: Seguiti dalle Grandi Pagine* (Lugano: Nuove Edizioni Capolago, 1939).
83. Radica, *Agonija Europe*, 68.
84. Ibid., 158.
85. Ibid., 253.
86. Ibid., 180.
87. Ibid., 271.
88. On Tilgher's intellectual and political context see Alessandra Tarquini, *Il Gentile dei fascisti. Gentiliani e antigentiliani nel regime fascista* (Bologna: Il Mulino, 2009), 96–105. Tarquini points out that in the late 1920s Tilgher offered his services to the regime, but in the late 1930s he could be described as a "dissident" intellectual.
89. Ibid., 218.
90. Ibid., 225.
91. Ernest Renan, "La crise religieuse en Europe," *Revue des Deux Mondes*, vol. 1, no. 4 (1874): 752–79.
92. For contemporaneous interpretations of the phenomenon, see Gustav Krüger, "The 'Theology of Crisis': Remarks on a Recent Movement in German Theology," *Harvard Theological Review*, vol. 19, no. 3 (1926): 227–58; and Julius S. Bixler, "What, Then, is the Theology of Crisis?" *Christian Education*, vol. 14, no. 7 (1931): 735–40.
93. Karl Barth, *Der Römerbrief* (Bern: G. A. Bäschlin, 1919).
94. On the anti-historicist core of the theology of crisis, see Peter E. Gordon, "Weimar Theology: From Historicism to Crisis," in Gordon and McCormick, eds., *Weimar Thought*, 159.
95. Pope Pius X, "The Oath Against Modernism," available online at https://www.papalencyclicals.net/pius10/p10moath.htm
96. Emmanuel Mounier, *Manifeste au service du personnalisme* (Paris: Éditions Montaigne, 1936); English translation: *The Personalist Manifesto* (London: Longmans Green and Co., 1938).
97. Mounier, *The Personalist Manifesto*, 8.
98. Jacques Maritain, *Le crépuscule de la civilisation* (Paris: Editions les Nouvelles Lettres, 1939).
99. Ibid., 26.
100. See Vilius Kubekas, *The Quest for Unity in a Time of Crisis: Catholic Intellectuals and the Challenges of Political Modernity in Interwar Lithuania* (PhD Dissertation, Central European University, 2023), especially ch. 4.
101. Stasys Šalkauskis, "Ideologiniai dabarties krizių pagrindai ir katalikų pasaulėžiūra [The Ideological Foundations of Contemporary Crises and the Catholic Worldview]," in Juozas Eretas and Antanas Salys, eds., *Lietuvių katalikų mokslo akademijos suvažiavimo darbai 1936*, vol. 2 (Kaunas: Lietuvių katalikų mokslo akademija, 1937), 45–80.
102. See Maria Falina, *Religion and Politics in Interwar Yugoslavia. Serbian Nationalism and East Orthodox Christianity* (London: Bloomsbury, 2023).
103. Nikolay Berdyaev, *Духовный кризис интеллигенции* [Spiritual Crisis of the Intelligentsia] (St. Petersburg: Типография товарищества «Общественная польза», 1910).
104. For a transitional text, see Nikolay Berdyaev, *Кризисъ Искусства* [Crisis of Art] (Moscow: Изданіе Г. А. Лемана и С. И. Сахарова, 1918), which argues that the crisis symptoms in contemporary Western art were indicative of a broader cultural crisis.

72   Intellectuals and the Crisis of Politics

105. Nikolay Berdyaev, "Духовное состояние современного мира [The Spiritual State of the Modern World]," *Путь*, vol. 35 (1932): 56–68.

106. See Guy Miron, "A 'Usable Past' and the Crisis of the European Jews: Popular Jewish Historiography in Germany, France and Hungary in the 1930s," in Ezra Mendelssohn, Stefani Hoffman, and Richard I. Cohen, eds., *Against the Grain: Jewish Intellectuals in Hard Times* (New York: Berghahn, 2014), 213–39.

107. Nicolae Steinhardt and E. M. Neuman, *Essai sur une conception catholique du judaïsme* (Bucharest: Cultura Românescâ, 1935). Republished in a Romanian–French bilingual edition as Nicolae Steinhardt and Emanuel Neuman, *Eseu despre o concepție catolică asupra iudaismului. Iluzii și realități evreiești* (Iași: Polirom, 2011). The 2011 edition also includes their *Illusions et réalités juives* from 1937 (n. 108).

108. Nicolae Steinhardt and Emanuel Neuman, *Illusions et réalités juives. Considérations réalistes sur quelques problèmes juifs* (Paris: Lipschutz, 1937).

109. Friedrich Wilhelm Foerster, *Weltkrise und Seelenkrise* (Berlin: Zeitbücher-Verlag, 1932).

4
Crisis of Capitalism

An obvious context where the crisis discourse had a pivotal role in the interwar years was the debate on economy. Interestingly, from the perspective of the 1910s, this was less predictable than one might retrospectively think. In the second half of the nineteenth century, the idea that crises were constitutive elements of economic development had become prevalent, and different theories were put forward to offer a causal explanation for their recurrence. A famous example is the work of the English economist and logician William Stanley Jevons (1835–1882), linking economic crises to meteorological factors, such as the appearance of sunspots, which in turn affected agricultural production.[1]

However, with the development of quantitative methods, by the turn of the century the concept of crisis all but vanished from more professional works on economy, being taken over by the conceptual framework of cycles and conjunctures.[2] Thus, Albert Aftalion (1874–1956), the prominent French economist of Bulgarian Jewish roots, argued in his 1913 study that it was impossible to understand individual crises without inserting them into a more comprehensive framework of cycles (including periods of prosperity and depression) and advocated the use of "economic cycles" as a more scientific term.[3] In this sense, Joseph Schumpeter's (1883–1950) analysis of the "crisis of the tax state" (written during the final phase of the First World War) is more of an outlier. Schumpeter used the notion of "crisis" in terms of recurrent economic troubles but meant rather a meta-historical transformation of the overall economic system.[4] Sketching out a perspective of "fiscal sociology," Schumpeter stressed that it was not just the war that challenged the socioeconomic system:

> Even the simplest considerations show that, at most, the war could have brought to light a much more basic inadequacy of the particular society whose fiscal expression the tax state is; that, at most, it could have been the occasion which laid bare the structural weaknesses of our society and thus precipitated a collapse which was inevitable for deeper reasons.[5]

The modern "tax state" emerged from the crisis of the previous configuration, namely the feudal system, which by the sixteenth century proved completely unable to cover the growing costs of warfare. The formation of modern states was thus closely linked with financial needs, and the new political system—characterized by the clash of the king and the estates, usually resulting in the victory of the former in the form of absolute rule—evolved as a reaction to fiscal necessities. According to Schumpeter,

Intellectuals and the Crisis of Politics in the Interwar Period and Beyond. Balázs Trencsényi, Oxford University Press.
© Balázs Trencsényi (2025). DOI: 10.1093/9780198929512.003.0004

74   Intellectuals and the Crisis of Politics

this system underwent its most profound crisis in Austria before and during the war due to the exponential growth of state expenditures and the "uninhibited paper money economy." His proposal was to introduce a capital levy that would reduce inflated paper money and state bonds and would thus restore the parity between the amount of money and goods in the economy.

For Schumpeter, the relative success of the war economy was due to the contribution of the competitive sphere and not so much the intensification of state intervention. Consequently, he also expected entrepreneurial capitalism to play a key role in postwar recovery. The excessive bureaucratic control of the economy, which had only increased during the war, was not only dysfunctional but also retrograde from a socialist perspective: it prevented economic development that could eventually lead to socialism in the Marxian sense, namely the overcoming of the capitalist mode of production. Thus, the "crisis of the tax state" was an either/or of falling back to pre-capitalist bureaucratic control or opening the road toward a post-capitalist order:

> By and by, private enterprise will lose its social meaning through the development of the economy and the consequent expansion of the sphere of social sympathy. The signs of this are already with us and it was inherent in the tendencies of the second half of the nineteenth century, whose perhaps final aberration was all that which culminated in the World War. Society is growing beyond private enterprise and the tax state, not because but in spite of the war.[6]

Given the marginalization of the concept of crisis in the language of economists by the theory of economic cycles, it is not by chance that the only comprehensive study on the history of economic crises in the immediate aftermath of the First World War was written by a young Hungarian economist, Tivadar Surányi-Unger (1898–1973). Later, Surányi-Unger had a notable academic career in interwar Hungary, developing international connections in the United States and in the expert circles of Geneva, and—after his emigration in 1945—teaching in the United States and West Germany. But only 22 years old when writing his "Outline" of the history of economic crises, he was hardly a well-known scholar.[7]

Surányi-Unger sought to create a bridge between the methods of the German Historical School and the Austrian School, which became increasingly dominant after the First World War. In his sweeping historical reconstruction covering classical Antiquity, the Middle Ages, and the early modern and modern periods, Surányi-Unger stressed specific local factors such as the sudden overflow of bullion, speculative bubbles, and mistaken political decisions. He noted that from the nineteenth century onward, the growing interconnection of different national economies led to the rise of international crisis phenomena, resulting in the first "world economic crisis" in 1857.[8] While he did not develop any mathematical model of cyclical development, his interpretation was based on the observation of recurrent patterns of economic boom, the catalyzation of speculation, the growth of credit without adequate back-up, and eventually overproduction, resulting in sudden financial breakdowns and panic, depressed wages, and the growth of unemployment, all of which triggered political conflicts. Looking at the postwar situation, the Hungarian economist argued that socioeconomic hardship was not only due to four years of military conflict but had *sui generis* economic reasons too. Still, he stuck to the primacy of political motives, which became even more obvious in his short overview of the Hungarian situation where he derived the crisis mainly from territorial losses following the war and the conclusion of the peace treaties in Paris.

Perhaps the only theoretically solid text of the early and mid-1920s on economic crises was an extensive lexicon entry by German economist Arthur Spiethoff (1873–1957).[9] Spiethoff was a student of Gustav Schmoller and a representative of the German Historical School, but methodologically he was increasingly open to a dialogue with the Austrian School and he formed a good working relationship also with Schumpeter, while both of them were teaching in Bonn. His entry can also be considered part of this dialogue, keeping to the more "traditional" concept of crisis but in fact putting forward a theory of business cycles, building on the work of Ukrainian economist Mykhailo I. Tuhan-Baranovskyi (1865–1919). Spiethoff's analysis was based on the model of periods of economic boom catalyzing speculation and the abandonment of self-restraint, resulting in overproduction and the loss of balance between production and consumption. From this perspective, he defined crisis as the decisive stage of the transformation of an "ailing" economic situation, accompanied by sudden and violent symptoms (e.g., collapse of credits, bank runs).[10] The credit crisis also triggered other crisis phenomena, like speculation crisis or capital crisis. Along these lines, Spiethoff offered a combination of analytical and historical approaches to describe the unfolding of economic crises, using especially British, French, and German datasets (the changing price of individual products, production in different sectors of the economy, financial statistics, etc.). Rather than explaining everything mechanistically, he also paid attention to subjective factors, such as the loss of trust and overall anxiety concerning the economic system, which in turn impacts the overall economic dynamic as well (e.g., in the form of the escape of capital and precious metals from the given country). Nevertheless, the overall picture he painted was that of regularities, with the phases of stagnation, upswing, and crisis following each other in strict consistency and in some ways also reinforcing each other as stimuli to eventually impose more rational and efficient economic behavior.

In contrast to Surányi-Unger's and Spiethoff's focus on the concept of crisis and the historicity of crisis phenomena, the cutting-edge scholarly paradigm in the 1920s was the study of "economic conjunctures" (*Konjunkturforschung*) using a mathematical toolkit and an elaborate apparatus of data visualization.[11] There were comparable and simultaneous initiatives in the German, American, British, and Austrian contexts, also becoming increasingly aware of each other. Gradually, they turned into a transnational network of knowledge production and exchange of experience, assisted by the League of Nations and by the American Rockefeller and Carnegie foundations close to the League. While seemingly an inductive and descriptive approach, there were strong normative underpinnings behind this research branch rooted in the conviction that self-regulating price mechanisms constituted the underlying economic processes. From this perspective, the world economy was exposed to permanent fluctuations of conjuncture and disjuncture; moments of contraction also meant the restoration of equilibrium, from which point another cycle of growth could start. By contrast, the notion of crisis sounded overly emotional and pre-scientific. However, the Great Depression brought the concept of crisis back into public view as well as into scholarly discourse. The central question was whether the dramatic economic situation resulted from a normal cyclical downturn or a more general structural transformation, indicating the end of a hitherto known economic system and the beginning of something radically different.

The Great Depression and the Quest for "Irregular" Features

The dramatic events unfolding in the global economy after 1929 broke through the language of cycles and opened up the search for a new analytical framework that could grasp the difference between regular fluctuations and irregular processes, which could not be described in terms of disequilibrium.[12] An impressive international effort to mobilize expert knowledge for analyzing the key features of the economic depression was coordinated by the League of Nations in Geneva, resulting in a report by Swedish economist Bertil G. Ohlin (1899–1979).[13] The report employed the concept of crisis only sparingly, instead using "depression," a term that was considered more scientific. Ohlin relied on quantitative data gathered through members of the broad expert circle, many of whom were adepts of the new scientific paradigm of "conjuncture research," invited to assist the project. The Swedish economist, himself strongly committed to quantitative methods, was confident that his comparative analysis of business cycles provided a basis for understanding the nature of the economic downturn. He pointed to the devastating effects of the war, the ambiguous consequences of the economic upswing of the mid-twenties—rooted in rationalization and technological innovation—and the changing dynamic of capital exports in the late 1920s. He concluded that "the international financial position in the years before the depression was much less stable than before the war."[14] Nevertheless, Ohlin's report avoided a more comprehensive causal explanation beyond economic indicators. The general remarks at the end of the report were tentative and stressed that one of the main causes of the deepening of the depression was the expectation that commodity prices would further decline. The report exposed the need to counteract this (and pointed out some of the negative consequences of protectionist tariff regimes and the limitation of migration) but refrained from offering a more comprehensive picture and a direct criticism of state policies. The report only noted that there was "no doubt the extreme political instability and the general lack of confidence which has resulted therefrom have exercised a disturbing influence on international financial relations."[15]

The League of Nations report was intentionally restricted to the economic sphere, as engaging with the broader political context would have opened up a Pandora's

Box of competing national(ist) perspectives. By contrast, most individual observers who sought to explain to the international public the causes of the unexpectedly deep depression stressed the entanglement of economic and political causes. The concept of crisis reemerged at the very intersection of economic and political analyses. From 1930 onward, as the global dimensions of the depression became evident, there was a boom of studies and pamphlets trying to explain crisis to non-specialized audiences. As German economic expert Julius Hirsch (1882–1961) put it: "no one is guilty of the crisis . . . but no one will be spared its consequences."[16]

An influential overview along these lines, written in the midst of the Great Depression, is Paul Einzig's (1897–1973) *The World Economic Crisis*.[17] Of Transylvanian Jewish background, Einzig moved to England in 1919 and became a political and economic analyst with considerable resonance, gaining international visibility with his writings on economic policy in the early 1930s. Contrasting crisis and depression, he did not aim at providing an all-round explanation, but pointed to a number of dilemmas and puzzles related to the interpretation of crisis phenomena. Alluding to the failure of economists to predict the crisis and their inability to agree upon its main causes, he stressed the inadequacy of conventional interpretative frameworks of global economic processes. Einzig identified two major schools: one sought to insert the Great Depression into a recurrent cyclical movement of crisis and recovery, while the other argued that the actual phenomena were fundamentally different from "normal" cycles. This latter camp insisted that there were no intrinsic readjustments that could end the crisis. Reaching equilibrium at a lower level than the previous boom—but still at a higher level compared to previous stages of economic development—appeared inconceivable in the given circumstances.

Rather than opting for one of these models, Einzig sought to develop an interpretation that cut through their conflict. For him, the very question of the starting point of the crisis needed rethinking. One the one hand, the "seeming normality" of the mid-1920s was not necessarily in line with how periods of economic boom had been previously understood. On the other hand, most observers only realized that they were experiencing a crisis roughly a year after the appearance of phenomena usually identified as the unmistakable signs of a downward turn. What is more, many of the developments showed a wholly unpredictable dynamic: for example, the fall in interest rates did not lead to growth in commerce.

To understand the complexity of the situation, Einzig cataloged a huge variety of explanatory models. He identified a more traditional and mechanistic cyclical scheme; the idea that the depression was merely a return to more "natural" pre-war levels after the artificial growth of production and incomes due to "extra-economic" reasons (i.e., the Great War and its aftermath); theories of overproduction and underconsumption central to the German political–economic debate between socialists and conservatives; the idea of monetary causes; the focus on overcapitalization; the idea that it was mainly due to financial overspeculation; and the model stressing the unfortunate interference of independent factors catalyzing unprecedentedly virulent crisis symptoms.

In general, Einzig leaned toward the latter explanation of a "negative invisible hand," that is, the convergence of many factors reinforced by an endemic lack of cooperation among different actors and groups affected by the crisis. Rather than giving a final answer to the question of the ultimate cause, he was more interested in offering some hints at coping with the situation. His main suggestion was to encourage more cooperation and coordination on many levels—among producers, countries, employers, and employees. He stressed the importance of regulation by the authorities as well, to avoid overproduction, coordinate planning, and to alleviate some of the social effects of the depression. He was convinced that the era of *laissez-faire* had ended; instead, the new situation demanded a creative combination of cooperation and individual initiative. In this respect, he considered that the crisis had heightened the communist danger. By implementing state control without liberty, the communist offer was able to avoid the most visible effects of crisis (albeit with huge social costs), thus posing a powerful challenge to the capitalist world. Einzig warned that if there was no fundamental change in the way that political actors related to the economy and society in the West, the next crisis—with similar dimensions to that of 1929—might destroy the capitalist system.

Julius Hirsch, a German–Jewish left-liberal economic expert and professor at the Berlin commercial college (*Handelshochschule*), also sought to offer a "real-time" analysis of the unfolding crisis.[18] Being an insider in the German political system as a former State Secretary in the Ministry of Economy (*Reichswirtschaftsministerium*) in the early years of the Weimar Republic, he stressed the entanglement of political and economic factors and pointed to the irregularity of certain features of the economy already before the escalation of the Depression. As for the economic side, he emphasized the growing productivity and the disfunction of the price mechanism. While a normally functioning price mechanism would push down prices in cases of overproduction, after the Great War raw materials were not part of this price mechanism and thus could not adjust to the new situation.[19] Another factor where political and economic aspects were both present was the fall of foreign capital investment in Germany due to growing insecurity in the countries where these investments originated (mainly the United States and Great Britain). As a result, the proportional weight of reparations became much heavier. To these issues, Hirsch added the growth of antisystemic aggression, which in turn made any rational economic decision-making harder and engendered an overall crisis of social trust.[20] This last link in the chain triggered irrational behavior among consumers and producers alike.

As someone involved in practical politics, Hirsch also sought to offer remedies. While he shared the idea that crises were inherent in the long-term course of economic development—and thus it was impossible to eliminate them completely—he thought that conscious governmental intervention could influence their timing. He stressed that the general aim of policy making was to keep prices low and stable, and thus criticized cartelization as particularly dangerous for healthy economic life. He also argued that crisis management necessitated the modernization of the economy, meaning a move away from primary products, attracting new capital, and implementing certain social measures such as unemployment insurance.

Resonating with the culturalist crisis discourses, Hirsch held that the "normal" alternation of conjuncture and depression had turned into an unprecedented crisis also due to spiritual factors that went beyond mere economic causation. Finally, he noted the importance of engaging with crisis management on an international scale. After the catastrophic Depression, there was a need to regain domestic and international trust, which implied both economic cooperation and more exchange of information across the borders, for instance among bank presidents.

Emil Lederer (1882–1939) offered an analysis like Hirsch's, combining economic, political, and cultural causes, albeit with somewhat different accents. Lederer came from a Bohemian Jewish background, studied in Vienna, was influenced by Austro-Marxism, and made a spectacular academic career in Germany in the 1920s, succeeding Werner Sombart in his chair at the University of Berlin in 1931. After his emigration to the United States following the Nazi takeover, Lederer played a key role in setting up the University in Exile in New York, which then became part of the New School for Social Research. His influential *Ways Out of the Crisis* (*Wege aus der Krise*) was published in 1931.[21] A member of the Social Democratic Party (SPD), Lederer also subscribed to the image of economic crises having "normal" cyclical movements but contrasted this to the phenomenon of "universal crisis" triggered by the convergence of many—economic, political, and cultural—factors. Among these, he listed deflation, technological progress, the growth of agrarian productivity, the growth of population, and growth in the size of the working force, which had expanded due to the inclusion of women.

Lederer's analysis showed that growth in production without a related expansion of employment opportunities undermined the equilibrium which seemed to be restored after the Great War—though this was also due to the serious demographic losses caused by warfare. As a result, at the end of the conjuncture of the 1920s, there was no readjustment according to free market logic. Efforts were made to keep up the high prices of the previous phase, but the post-conjuncture fall in wages was not compensated by a fall in prices. Other factors Lederer considered as aggravating the situation, especially in the German case, were the growth of protectionism, the burden of war reparations, and the lack of internal political stability. His proposal for a way out of the crisis was a combination of liberal precepts with a certain dose of state intervention to let prices readjust to a new equilibrium while simultaneously triggering more consumption. He also agreed that the ongoing crisis offered an opportunity to separate competitive and less-competitive economic enterprises (functioning as a sort of selective struggle for survival, or commercial *Reinigungsprozess*). It also represented a turning point in the evolution from more competitive forms of capitalism to the firmer closure of national markets. Thus, overall, Lederer asserted that the crisis could be overcome if market laws were allowed to prevail, but at the same time he argued for the need to regulate "high capitalism" by a series of interventions that followed a coherent plan (e.g., linking wage cuts to price cuts). In many ways, this tension in Lederer's thinking was characteristic of the German social democrats, torn between their theoretical conviction of the necessary destructive features of the

80 Intellectuals and the Crisis of Politics

progress of capitalism that would eventually lead to socialism, and their commitment to ameliorate the plight of the working class hit by the Depression.

A particularly innovative argument which went against the social democratic orthodoxy was formulated by Russian-born Jewish economist Wladimir S. Woytinsky (Vladimir S. Voitinsky, 1885–1960). Woytinsky started out as a Bolshevik but moved closer to the Menshevik faction during the First World War and tried to resist with arms the October Revolution in 1917. For some time, he represented the Georgian social democratic government abroad. Settling in Germany, he became a prominent economic statistician (leading the statistic office of *Allgemeine Deutsche Gewerkschaftsbund*, the umbrella organization of socialist trade unions) in the 1920s. After the Great Depression hit Germany, he emerged as a protagonist in the public debate on crisis management. In his programmatic article from 1931 on the possible ways to cope with the crisis, he also started from the theory of business cycles (as most of his German colleagues), but categorically rejected the self-healing potential of the market, arguing that there was no automatic rebounding to an equilibrium situation. Instead, there was a need to intervene into the market mechanisms to limit the destructive potential of the crisis.[22] He argued in favor of a more systematic intervention by the state to manage the crisis. From a social democratic perspective, he rejected that the crisis of capitalism could immediately result in a socialist transformation. Instead, Woytinsky admitted that because of the growing unemployment that could be used as a "disciplining" instrument, crisis made the working class and the workers' movement more vulnerable.

Woytinsky also registered the demoralizing effects of crisis on the workers' movement; without a coherent economic action program, the social democrats could not be positioned as an active force in changing the dynamic.[23] He pointed to developments in economic analysis that led to better comprehension of the nature of short and long waves in the business cycle. At the same time, he believed that it was not necessary to develop a fully fledged crisis theory to work on the practical tasks of attenuating its effects. Along these lines, he distinguished between "meteorological" and "medical" intervention, arguing that while the first only seeks to describe and predict the phenomena, the second also tries to influence these processes. He argued that economic knowledge had reached a sufficient level to make such an engagement and considered the crisis phenomena unfolding as characteristic of a transitional period toward a new model of socioeconomic organization.

Woytinsky's analysis of the unfolding crisis focused on the subversion of the common liberal and conservative arguments for non-intervention. He rejected the idea of a "cleansing crisis" (*Reinigungskrise*, a concept popularized by Schumpeter) and the assumption that the fall in prices was an automatic catalyst of economic regeneration. In his understanding, a prolonged decrease of prices and incomes was rather a downward spiral, which could only be stopped by some sort of public intervention to stimulate private economic activity. If the causal connection between growing wholesale market prices and the revitalization of economic activity (and thus the fall of unemployment) held, then "medical" intervention implied a public investment (even based on a loan), which generated demand.[24] Deflation was thus always dangerous;

inflation, kept within reasonable limits, could also have positive effects. Importantly, Woytinsky also extended this interpretative framework to interstate relations. In his argument, even highly industrialized countries—seemingly affected less by the dramatic fall of agrarian prices—would have an interest in contributing to the revitalization of the economies of affected countries as well, thus opening or expanding markets for their own industrial products.

Woytinsky's theoretical work resulted in a comprehensive plan for a public work program, put forward together with Fritz Tarnow and Fritz Baade (hence the name "WTB plan") on behalf of the German trade union confederation. It was not taken up by the SPD as its official program, due especially to the resistance of the main economic theoreticians of the party, such as Rudolf Hilferding, who had a much more deterministic understanding of capitalist crises.[25] As a result, the WTB plan eventually failed, but its recommendations anticipated a variety of interventionist policies of crisis management, from the New Deal (Woytinsky actually emigrated to the United States after the Nazi takeover and worked for the Roosevelt administration) to the Nazi public work programs.

Arguably the most famous economist of the interwar years, John Maynard Keynes (1883–1946) also reacted to the unfolding crisis in "real time." However, as his biographer Robert Skidelsky points out, his response was less coherent and "Keynesian" (in the sense of supporting "deficit spending" to create jobs and thus reactivate the economic dynamic) than usually thought.[26] In his *Treatise on Money* (1930), as well as in his 1931 lectures delivered at the New School, he focused on high postwar interest rates (especially the move of the US Federal Reserve to raise interest rates in 1928 and 1929, cutting the economic boom of the 1920s) as a key catalyst of the economic downturn. As a result, he stood against the policy of cutting public budgets, and argued for monetary expansion, mainly by lowering interest rates. He distinguished the American and British situations, pointing out that there was no similar postwar boom in the United Kingdom. He argued in the Macmillan Committee on Finance and Industry and the Economic Advisory Council's Committee of Economists that this was due in part to the overvaluation of the pound following Britain's return to the gold standard in 1925.[27] Keynes also engaged in a debate in 1930 with liberal economists Lionel Robbins (a key figure in the development of neoliberal economic thought, 1898–1984) and Hubert D. Henderson (1890–1952). The contention centered on the question of whether wages were too high in the latter half of the 1920s because they had artificially outrun the level of productivity per worker, or whether this had resulted from a gap between the actual terms of British trade and its calculated equilibrium; Keynes argued for the latter.[28]

When the symptoms of the Depression became unmistakable, Keynes also addressed the specific socioeconomic problems it posed, describing it as "one of the greatest economic catastrophes of modern history."[29] At the same time, he was still convinced that depressions are sooner or later followed by recovery, comparing them to a "nightmare, which will pass away with the morning."[30] Keynes also shared the analytical position with regard to the exceptionality of the unfolding crisis, which pointed to the interference of a number of originally separate phenomena. This led

82 Intellectuals and the Crisis of Politics

to a situation where the traditional measures of crisis management proved ineffective because neither the restriction of output nor the reduction of wages could restore the equilibrium. In his opinion, the way out was the harmonization of the monetary sphere with the sphere of production:

> ... there cannot be a real recovery... until the ideas of lenders and the ideas of productive borrowers are brought together again; partly by lenders becoming ready to lend on easier terms and over a wider geographical field, partly by borrowers recovering their good spirits and so becoming readier to borrow.[31]

This required state intervention and international cooperation:

> ... the Central Banks of these three great creditor nations should join together in a bold scheme to restore confidence to the international long-term loan market; which would serve to revive enterprise and activity everywhere, and to restore prices and profits, so that in due course the wheels of the world's commerce would go round again.[32]

Key elements of this interpretative framework, combining liberal precepts with a call for selective and self-restraining state intervention—and stressing the interference of multiple causes in making the depression starting in 1929 truly exceptional—were also shared by some economists living in illiberal states, like fascist Italy. Pasquale Jannaccone (1872–1959) was professor of economics at Turin and member of the circle around the journal *La Riforma Sociale*. Jannaccone held important positions in the academic and expert field in the 1920s although he maintained a certain distance from fascism. In a text submitted as an expert opinion in a legal case, he accentuated the divergence of the meaning of crisis in different national contexts. For example, in the United States it entailed the collapse of financial markets, while in Italy it was related mainly to the (de)stabilization of the currency. Likewise, the timeline of economic crisis was also different, even if there were obvious interferences.[33] A key feature of the crisis in Jannaccone's understanding was the global fall of savings and lack of new investments in the postwar period. He derived this from the destruction caused by warfare and the tasks of nation-building, which undermined traditional economic centers and networks and led to a general condition of economic fragmentation. By contrast, the United States' economic rise led to exaggerated spending and consumption, which eventually also resulted in further imbalance. The implications of this analysis were that state intervention was needed to push economic actors into more rational behavior, but the over-étatization of the economy was equally dangerous, as it led exactly to the destruction of markets.

A key question among economic analysts was whether or not the actual crisis was part of a long-term cyclical movement. This was a central preoccupation of Ernst Wagemann (1884–1956), president of the Weimar-era Ministry of Economy's Statistical Office (*Statistisches Reichsamt*), director of the Institute for Conjuncture

Research (*Institut für Konjunkturforschung*), and author of a widely discussed crisis management plan from 1932. A main figure of the international research network on economic conjunctures, he also offered his analysis during the Great Depression.[34] In this work, he sought to bring together the idea of cyclicity with his conviction that there was no automatic recovery (rebounding). As he pointed out, short business cycles tended to be more intrinsic to the economic process, while longer cycles were more external to that process and were also linked to political and other circumstances, alien to the economic "automatism."[35] This also implied that certain measures of state intervention could alleviate the effects of the crisis. Going against Chancellor Heinrich Brüning's economic vision, in early 1932 Wagemann put forward a plan arguing for the partial suspension of the gold standard and the emission of small currencies used by internal transactions, thus stimulating both consumption and production. However, the government distanced itself from Wagemann's plan as it clashed with its deflationary policies and implied a devaluation of the currency, causing problems with the war reparations.

As Wagemann's 1935 book indicates, the discussion on the lessons of the Great Depression continued well into the mid-1930s. This was due partly to the rather protracted period of up- and downturns, which in different countries created a different temporality of the recovery from crisis, complicated also by the concomitant political events that often generated new socioeconomic crisis phenomena. In the French context, liberal economist Jacques Rueff (1896–1978) sought to draw the theoretical lessons of the crisis.[36] First, he stressed its unprecedented nature: "its breadth and length qualify it as a completely new phenomenon."[37] He contrasted this to the "quasi-equilibrium" before the First World War, characterized by a lack of permanent unemployment and the uninhibited regulative function of the price mechanism. Rueff blamed étatist meddling with prices during the war for upsetting the market mechanisms, pushing the economy toward the "slippery slope" of interventionism. Once the state broke with economic "realities", there was a need to implement more and more control, leading to a generalization of planning. The various projects mushrooming after 1929 regarding planned economy were thus symptomatic of a deeper disorientation and in turn contributed to the further deterioration of the situation. For Rueff, the collectivist political–economic configurations that had emerged as a response to the crisis were particularly dangerous. They fused "utopian idealism" (to eliminate all injustice on earth) with manipulative egoism (enforcing the interests of some groups who could "capture" the state with the pressure they could exert, e.g., cartels or trade unions), blocking the self-regulating functions of the market once for all and thus perpetuating the crisis.

Significantly, Rueff's position was far from uncontested even in his academic milieu. Charles Rist (1874–1955), another prominent economist of the period, criticized Rueff for idealizing the prewar conditions and pointed out that the economic system was far from being purely liberal. In contrast to the étatist measures undertaken during the war, he considered the postwar readjustment as the root of the crisis and stressed the conflict of economic and political liberalism, which Rueff has taken to overlap unproblematically. Likewise, legal scholar Henry Truchy

84   Intellectuals and the Crisis of Politics

(1864–1950) and economic expert Louis Marlio (1878–1952) also questioned the necessary link between interventionism and dictatorship. They challenged Rueff's monocausal explanation—which subordinated all other factors to the disruption of the price mechanism—and pointed to other important factors, such as economic nationalism resulting from the Wilsonian principle of nation-statism, as well as the growth of mass speculation as catalysts of the Great Depression.

The Terminal Crisis of Capitalism?

The similarities of the positions analyzed here indicate that even though economists placed their emphases in different areas when trying to grasp the roots of the crisis, the difference between liberal and social democratic experts was not so dramatic. Even if their country was more affected than most others by the economic depression, experts (like Lederer) close to German social democracy tended to believe in managing the crisis by surgical state interventions while allowing market mechanisms to do their destructive and constructive work. Lederer's position was thus very far from the radical Left, which stressed that the unfolding socioeconomic disaster was the indicator of a terminal crisis of capitalism. This position gained particular resonance because—rooted in the Marxian theories of cyclical development—communist crisis theory prefigured, and in some ways also predicted, the Great Depression.

Jenő (Eugen) Varga (1879–1964) was the most important communist theoretician of crisis. The Hungarian communist economist of Jewish background participated in international socialist discussions from the early 1910s onward, debating with the Austro-Marxists, particularly Otto Bauer. After his involvement in the 1919 Soviet Republic in Hungary, he was forced to emigrate, first to Vienna and then to Moscow, where he worked for the Comintern. Between 1922 and 1927, he was employed by the Department of Trade at the Soviet embassy in Berlin, experiencing first-hand the interaction between communist and capitalist economic regimes, thus having the opportunity to combine Marxist macro-theory and empirical observation.[38] Due to this duality of theory and practice, his writings often carried a tension between his political commitment to the Soviet project and his scholarly curiosity to understand economic dynamics with empirical tools.[39]

As his articles in *Kommunismus: Zeitschrift der Kommunistischen Internationale für die Länder Südosteuropas* (1920–21) witness, Varga was preoccupied with the problem of crisis already during his stay in Vienna.[40] In fact, other contributors to the journal, including a number of communist exiles from Hungary, Bulgaria, and Romania, also focused on the crisis symptoms of the postwar political and economic order. During his stay in Berlin after 1922, Varga observed the peak of German inflation, the process of economic consolidation, and the short economic boom of the mid-1920s. He interpreted these economic developments as the result of the clash of two antagonistic tendencies: the social democratic push for higher wages, and the "high capitalist" push for rationalization, aimed at the formation of monopolies, cutting costs, and fixing prices. In his opinion, eventually both tendencies were equally futile, as there was chronic disparity between production and consumption. Ongoing low levels of consumption did not allow production to rise to prewar levels. Even if the postwar German economy had reached its imperialist phase again, the absence of possibilities for colonial expansion would have made such a development particularly crisis ridden.[41] As a result, one could hardly speak of a full recovery.

For Varga, this period of late capitalism was marked by the continuation of the overall crisis with short-lived conjunctures and, consequently, rapid downturns. This framework allowed him to forecast the return of economic depression, the catastrophic dimension of which in turn seemed to validate his theory. Importantly, this model was also somewhat like Wolfgang von Kempelen's Mechanical Turk (evoked also by Walter Benjamin in his reflection on the Marxist theory of history): crisis always trumps all the other processes—at least until the socialist revolution, which would create a completely new and crisis-resistant historical situation.

Varga's early postwar analyses were written in the context of the first four World Congresses of the Comintern while Lenin was still alive and before the institution's Stalinization. Across this period, an extensive debate took place among communist theoreticians on whether the calamities after 1918 signaled just another cycle of crisis in an alternation of conjuncture and disjuncture, or whether capitalism had entered a different (and presumably terminal) period altogether.[42] Varga's 1921 *Crisis of the Capitalist World Economy*, written as part of his preparation for the Third Congress, focused on the question of the possibility of a new equilibrium in the context of the downturn of global revolutionary activism and the launching of the New Economic Policy in the Soviet Union, which introduced limited market mechanisms and to a certain extent relinked the Soviet economy with global commercial circulation.[43] Soon after, in his report delivered to the Fourth Congress, Varga linked political and economic factors to produce, drawing on the canonic socialist theoreticians—particularly Rosa Luxemburg—of the first decade of the century, his theory of "permanent crisis" in capitalist economies.[44]

Varga also paid special attention to the emerging paradigm of conjuncture research.[45] His chief theoretical ambition was to contrast the Marxist interpretation of crises with existent "bourgeois theories," showing the advantages of the Marxist framework, but also adopting certain insights and know-how from the more recent non-Marxist theoretical approaches. In this methodological dialogue and ideological competition, the concept of "crisis" was at the very center of his interpretation of capitalist economy. In a later article written already after the onset of the Great Depression, he argued that in contrast to the bourgeois theory of business cycles or conjunctures, in the Marxist framework, focusing on overproduction, every crisis brings the world economy closer to the final collapse of capitalism.[46] Citing the Rooseveltian economist Willard Thorp's (1899–1992) writings on economic conjuncture as his main reference, he blamed bourgeois theorists for not thinking systematically and rather focusing on disparate aspects, failing to see the global historical dynamism and thus even tending to erase the concept of "crisis" from their analysis, replacing it with "recession." This was also due to a difference in perspective rooted in class consciousness: for the workers, *any* economic depression triggering unemployment counts as a crisis, whereas for the capitalists it only sets in with bankruptcy.[47] Revisiting the theory of crisis developed by Karl Marx and Friedrich Engels, Varga argued that the novelty of their perspective was that they described crisis as the escalation of preexisting contradictions, bursting out in momentarily violent solutions. The main embedded contradiction was constant over-production by the capitalist-held means of production. This necessarily led to a disequilibrium, since markets are by default unable to absorb over-production given the ever-decreasing wages of the working class.

While Varga's general theoretical perspective was predicated upon the crisis-ridden nature of modern capitalism, his first reaction when the Great Depression set in was to follow the Hilferdingian paradigm, calculating that monopolies would put their weight on the workings of the crisis and there would be no credit collapse. Later, when banks started to fail, he had to readjust his position. He was also criticized for failing to predict a long depression, and as a result Varga performed a rather reluctant self-criticism in December 1931 and January 1932 for not being able to discern the depth of the crisis. Refining his theoretical approach, he developed an explanatory framework, often referred to as "Varga's law," asserting that it was technical innovation that generated unemployment and narrowed the markets. This position was in turn criticized by the mainstream of Stalinist economists as "Luxemburgism," which they contrasted to the orthodox Marxist theory of the cyclical reproduction of capital as the key cause of recurrent crises.

This debate had a special political importance as, after 1929, the Soviet leadership had to face the pressing question of how to relate to the dramatic global economic developments. Stalin's 1930 "The Growing Crisis of World Capitalism"[48] in a way reinforced Varga's original thesis that overproduction was the root cause of the economic crisis. Stalin combined this with the idea that, due to its non-capitalist mode of production, the Soviet Union was not affected by the crisis. The ongoing crisis was in many ways irregular, not the least because of the coincidence of the industrial and agrarian crises. This position was meant to give a boost to the self-confidence of the Soviet project (the catastrophic developments in Soviet agriculture following the kolkhozification campaign were conveniently glossed over). Thus, the Soviet Union was put forward as a viable economic alternative to the "decomposing" capitalist system. This also implied that the new cycle of crisis in capitalist countries could open the gates again for revolutionary agitation, which had otherwise been toned down after Lenin's death in 1924. This interpretation was echoed by Vyacheslav Molotov (1890–1986), the Chairman of the Council of People's Commissars and key figure of the Stalinist leadership. Molotov interpreted crisis as an international revolutionary factor, leaving only two possible directions for the capitalist world: communism or fascism.[49]

In the early 1930s, Varga was intimidated by a campaign orchestrated against him, although Stalin still held him in high esteem for his factual knowledge and analytical capacities. However, when, in 1934 Stalin asked him to express his opinion on global developments, Varga responded with an analysis that sought to harmonize his previous arguments with the Stalinist ideological agenda. He started from the cyclical model of crises of over-production, but rejected mechanistic repetition, stressing instead that every crisis had a specific historical place in the development of capitalism.[50] He thus tried to forge a crisis theory based on the theory of phases of capitalism, adding as new factors the agrarian crisis and global entanglements. Resonating with the conceptions of many "bourgeois" studies of crisis, his main point was that what had occurred since 1929 was not a "normal" crisis fitting into the usual cyclical pattern, but rather represented a qualitatively new phenomenon. He identified several specific factors: the interplay of industrial and agricultural crisis phenomena; currency devaluation; the credit and debt crunch; the stopping of capital transfers; crisis management measures on the part of the state; and monopoly capitalism. In contrast to previous periods, modern rationalization (symbolized above all by the Fordist conveyor belt) did not multiply production capacity but rather the intensity of work. As a result, the working class experienced growing unemployment, falling real wages, and declining social security. There were also specific factors that aggravated the crisis in particular contexts (e.g., the loss of colonies in the case of Germany), which made it impossible to put some of the economic burden on non-European populations as had previously been the case.

Overall, this configuration pointed toward an open and brutal class conflict, pushing the bourgeoisie to abandon the framework of liberal democracy and move toward open fascist dictatorship. As a result, Varga predicted a long depression rather than a swift recovery; the situation could well become a revolutionary crisis if domestic and international antagonisms reinforced each other. What he saw was a specific depression occurring on the basis of the general crisis of capitalism—and only a major historical reconfiguration, such as another world war, could break the cycle.[51] The Soviet "success story" was contrasted to this picture of economic and political destabilization: while between 1913 and 1932 capitalist production globally had fallen by 10%, the USSR could boast 200% growth over the same period. Although productive growth finally appeared in the West by 1933, according to Varga this was due mainly to military investment and inflation and not a real recovery. This interpretation evidently buttressed Stalin's vision, who turned it to his own political benefit in pursuing a precipitated state-managed industrialization program to prepare the Soviet state for the eventual showdown.

Varga's other key text from the period, *The Great Crisis and Its Political Consequences: Economics and Politics, 1928–34*,[52] was written in the context for the Seventh Congress of the Comintern in 1935, which opted for an anti-fascist cooperation with non-communist forces under the aegis of the Popular Front, reversing the previous policies of intransigent struggle against "social fascists" (i.e., social democrats) and bourgeois democrats. However, since the turn was rather abrupt, Varga's text showed a hesitation between a broader anti-fascist platform (which he seemed to support during the clashes within the Hungarian communist exile, as he gradually distanced himself from the more intransigent Béla Kun) and the idea of a looming proletarian revolution. Although the growth of production of machines for some time stimulated more employment, the technical advancement eventually led to the decrease of the need for working force, which triggered the growth of unemployment and the gradual fall of the capacity of consumption. This undermined the self-correcting capacity of contemporary capitalism but did not necessarily mean an imminent collapse.[53] While "healthy" capitalism was based on free trade and circulation of goods and capital, in the period of decadence, characterized by monopolist tendencies and state involvement, external commerce was falling, free trade was replaced by inter-state clearing agreements, and countries fell back on self-sufficiency, resulting in the collapse of world markets and the outburst of national conflicts. The more this form of monopoly capitalism prevailed, the less capacity for consumption the society could retain, thus getting closer and closer to its final crisis.

Turning to the agrarian question, Varga went so far as to correct Marx, arguing that the crisis of agrarian production was part of the general crisis of capitalism (although Varga later found a formula to claim that, from a higher perspective, he was right but Marx was also right, as agrarian crises could also be considered as crises of over-production).[54] He also argued that national economies could not be understood in a homogenized way, since different sectors had different dynamics. Thus, for instance, agrarian crises were not periodically recurrent in the same way as financial crises, but still, the general nature of capitalism affected all sectors, including the agrarian. To be sure, Engels's prediction about the universalism of agrarian crises eventually failed to materialize. Agrarian crises became endemic mostly in Europe and they could be attenuated with structural changes—shifting from wheat production to intensive farming and rationalization—although this only worked in ascending capitalism, when the consumption of agrarian products grew steadily.[55] But in a situation of labor market contraction, with an unprecedented fall in consumption power, the agrarian crisis of the late 1920s and 1930s could not be resolved within capitalist conditions. Social tensions necessitated growing repressive measures, and the crisis could only be managed by a state which controlled credit, labor, prices, and imports. There were two étatist models to this end: Soviet and fascist. The fascist model tried to save capitalism by suppressing democracy; the Soviet one broke with capitalism altogether and created a new form of democracy. Varga predicted that the coming historical period would be characterized by the clash of these two models.

Varga could already identify many signs of the approaching finale, asserting that the crisis management strategies of bourgeois states, which consisted of restricting the consumption power of the population, further aggravated the crisis. In this situation, the restoration of free trade only benefited the strongest states. Likewise, economic intervention by the capitalist state could not attenuate the deeper dynamic of disintegration. Varga pointed to the New Deal, arguing that it did not manage to create more growth than what was in line with the internal logic of capitalism, as counter-cyclical measures were eventually restricted by a higher economic logic.[56] Similarly, he criticized Keynes for believing that using state intervention to regulate currency and interest rates could resolve the crisis once for all.

Hence, Varga envisioned a struggle on two fronts for the communist movement— against both social and bourgeois democrats as well as fascists. In contrast, he suggested cooperating with colonial and agrarian movements against the representatives of the capitalist order. In the meantime, he was also tasked by the Comintern to open a front against socialist theoretician Henri de Man (1885–1953), whose "planism"—which sought to bring together some elements of capitalism and socialism—became extremely popular among leftist circles in Western Europe in the early 1930s. Varga dismissed de Man's ideas with the argument that planned economy was impossible within capitalist conditions. The only way toward real rationalization was through the elimination of profit altogether—that is, socialism.[57]

The ambiguities of Varga's argument about the predictability of a terminal crisis of capitalism and bourgeois democracy were due to the fact that although he always tried to develop a coherent interpretation, he often shifted his positions as he analyzed complex issues that defied the simplistic formulas preferred by the Stalinist political environment. The question of the predictability of the terminal crisis of capitalism continued to preoccupy him. After 1945, he returned to these questions, admitting that Western economies had proved more resilient than usually thought and thus the Soviet Union should prepare for a relatively long period of coexistence with global capitalism. This also implied a rather extensive transitional phase through people's democracy to socialism in the East Central European countries occupied by the Soviet Union. As had happened before, these ideas did not completely overlap with an increasingly intransigent party line and thus cost him his position. Forced into self-criticism, he was eventually spared of further consequences and managed to survive Stalin by more than a decade.

Among the radical leftist theoreticians, Varga had an ongoing controversy with Henryk Grossman (1881–1950). Grossman was of Galician Polish–Jewish provenance and studied in Kraków and Vienna. After the First World War, he taught in Poland, and in 1925 moved to Germany to become part of the Institute for Social Research in Frankfurt (the precursor of the Frankfurt School). Grossman's agenda was to revive the Marxian intellectual heritage in new postwar conditions, and along these lines he tried to reinterpret Marx's and Engels's work on crisis. He rejected the underconsumption theory popular among social democrats and stressed the dynamic of over-accumulation as an inherent contradiction that undermined capitalism. Responding to this, Varga criticized Grossman's model for being too mechanistic in stipulating that the collapse of capitalism could be exactly predictable.[58] Grossman's 1932 text offered a sophisticated rereading of the Marxian theory of value developed in the first two volumes of *Capital*, arguing that it was only a model, and could not be taken word by word to describe the high capitalist conditions, where one needed to pay special attention to production prices and profit rates as well.[59] From this perspective, Grossman argued that crises were due to the disproportionality of capital distribution, thus going against Bauer, Luxemburg, and Hilferding, who (in his understanding) all interpreted crisis exclusively from the perspective of value theory.[60] At the same time, he did not negate the relevance of value theory either, pointing out that it was completely neglected by bourgeois economists.

Varga and Grossman were highly influential, but surely not the only voices in the interwar Marxist debate on economic crisis. For instance, in her 1935 book, the Polish-Jewish economist living in Switzerland, Natalie Moszkowska (1886–1968) offered a broad panorama of competing theories of crisis within the ranks of the socialist intellectual and political camp.[61] She contrasted Marx's interpretation that the search for profit pushes down wages and saturates markets to the contemporary theories of crisis focusing on over-production and underconsumption. Carefully analyzing these theories and models, including Wagemann's conjuncture research—as well as a number of socialist authors ranging from Bauer and Lederer to Grossman—Moszkowska came to the conclusion that the main cause of the crisis was, in the final analysis, underconsumption: "In the capitalist system, crises and unemployment are the consequence of *profusion*, not any kind of shortage."[62] However, this could not be repaired with social protectionist measures. In the logic of late capitalism, the gap between production and consumption was prone to grow further until an escalation, which could on the one hand lead to a socialist transformation, and on the other hand to a fascist backlash.

It was not only the radical Left who sought to turn the image of the terminal crisis of capitalism against the bourgeois order. While most conservative revolutionary discourses were culturalist, and thus economic arguments were not at their core, we occasionally encounter representatives of this camp speculating on the catastrophic end of the capitalist era as the dawn of a new biologically rooted collectivism. A case in point is *End of Capitalism* by political journalist and member of the *Die Tat* circle, Ferdinand Fried (born Ferdinand Friedrich Zimmermann, 1898–1967).[63]

Fusing the more conventional spiritualist discourse of the radical conservative subculture he belonged to with an economic analysis, Fried embedded his argument into a cyclical metahistorical narrative. He thus compared the 1780s (the emergence of modern capitalism) to the early 1930s, describing the latter as a new turning point, but now away from capitalism. He listed a number of crisis symptoms that signaled this reconfiguration: the expansion of economic planning after 1918; the concomitant rise of state regulation and autarchic policies; monopolist tendencies undermining free trade; the collapse of negative correlation between prices and unemployment (due to the limitation of free market mechanisms by the cartels, the growth of prices could go together with the fall of employment); and the overall decline of technological innovation as talented youth gravitated toward the political sphere. According to Fried, the current elite was aged and spiritually barren, providing no basis for recovery and blocking the young generation from developing its creative energies.

Fried also came close to the communist understanding of the relationship between regular and irregular ("systemic") crises. He argued that while crises from 1815 onward were characterized by normal adjustment (*Anpassung*) processes and could be considered crises of growth (*Wachstumkrisen*), they also brought along a gradual concentration of capital and a contraction of the middle class. This development was also underpinned by a global transformation as the push toward industrialization in non-European countries began to undermine European economic hegemony.

Fried's proposed remedy was an odd combination of liberal and conservative precepts. He admitted that theoretically the optimal solution would be a return to "real capitalist principles" in the sense of "breaking up the cartels and the immediate and ruthless reduction of prices." However, there would be a very high social price to pay for this, in the sense of destroying too many companies. Restoring free market liberalism was thus politically impossible,[64] and the way out was to abandon the liberal economy altogether, which necessitated the obliteration of the global economic system supporting it. He argued that, due to global inequalities, many countries were interested in breaking these ties: reparations had forced Europe into a colonial dependence on the United States, the international debt crisis turned greater numbers of countries into the quasi-colonies of financial centers, and the agrarian population was hit heavily by further widening of the agricultural price gap ("price scissors"). The destruction of the global economy, with all its systemic inequalities, would also instantly liberate obligated countries as it was only the pressure to remain part of the global economy that made countries pay their debts.[65] Rather than global interdependence, this alternative path prioritized regional clearance agreements based on national interest, and Fried pointed to the projected (but eventually unrealized) Austrian–German customs union as a good start toward the creation of an autarchic *Mitteleuropa*.

Fried envisioned a global revolt against hegemonic liberal capitalism, subverting the international economic and power hierarchies along the lines of a vision not uncommon in conservative revolutionary circles, namely as some sort of geopolitical cooperation of Germany and Soviet Russia. Contrasting "the West" (*Abendland*) to the "Rest of the World," he associated the first with commercial advertisement; the gold standard; internationalization; global trade; the world stock exchange; and the pressure to export, coupled with huge debt and unemployment. The latter moved in the other direction: social compromise; liberation from debt; distrust of gold and of the concept of money; the assertion of the right to work; and the "right to life." It was an unintended irony of this vision—from the perspective of the geopolitical order emerging after 1945—that Fried described Germany as the very epicenter of the clash of these two models, arguing that the dividing line between the West and the "Rest" cut German territory to an Eastern and a Western zone, with Berlin as a Western enclave in the area marked by Eastern patterns!

Managing Economic Crisis in the Semi-periphery

As Fried's engagement with global inequalities also shows, interpretations of economic crisis were closely connected to the particular socioeconomic and geopolitical context where they were formulated. Therefore, we need to situate the texts coming from outside the centers of high capitalism in Western Europe with regard to the particular perspective they had on this "center–periphery" relationship. These discourses usually contrasted the highly industrialized Western core of capitalism to the dominantly agrarian and raw-material-producing ("underdeveloped") economies in the East and the South. They described the crisis in terms of further marginalization (due to widening agricultural price scissors), but in certain cases also as a possibility to reposition their societies by subverting the global hierarchy. This was coupled with a discussion on the need for universal or specific recipes of crisis management.

92 Intellectuals and the Crisis of Politics

Did the strategies proposed by theoreticians in London, Paris, or New York apply to Warsaw, Bucharest, or Lisbon as well? Or was there a need for specific local strategies?

Some of the authors from these "semi-peripheries" merely reproduced the intellectual frames and discourses of what they perceived as the "centers." Thus, under the title *World Crisis and Technocracy* (1933), Hungarian university professor of engineering and expert in railway design József Nemcsek (1893–1945) combined two seemingly incompatible threads: technocratic solutions and cultural criticism. He pointed to American models of rationalization as a way out from crisis, while relying on mainly the German conservative crisis discourse (especially Sombart and Spengler), contrasting culture and civilization, to describe the global situation.[66] What brought together these rather divergent references was his outspoken anti-liberalism and craving for a new social organization based on planning (his most radical claim was that instead of the gold standard, humankind should shift to "units of energy" as a universal monetary framework).

More interesting attempts to conceptualize crisis were made by experts involved in the actual economic and political decision-making of their countries. Prominent Czech economist and politician Karel Engliš (1880–1961) reflected on crisis management policies in Czechoslovakia (to a large extent implemented by himself, as he was Minister of Finance between 1925 and 1928, and again between 1929 and 1931), putting them into a comparative framework of Western and Eastern European experiences.[67] Analyzing the crisis unfolding after 1929, and discerning its multi-causal and multi-sectoral nature (e.g., monetary, agrarian, financial, employment, debt), Engliš tried to defend liberalism from the accusations that it was the very cause of the crisis: in reality it was exactly the exaggeration of regulation that caused the main disturbances.[68] Engliš also rejected the common claim that before the economic crisis extreme liberalism dominated Europe, pointing out that state involvement was strong everywhere after the Great War. It was also untenable that a regulated economy was completely crisis-proof, as certain factors, such as international conflicts or over-production, remained sources of insecurity.

At the same time, and like the interpretations of many liberal and most anti-liberal economic analysts studied here, Engliš admitted that the crisis erupting in 1929 was unusual, as there had been a great divergence between the dynamic of production and consumption. While it was aggravated by state intervention, a certain level of state interference was also needed to correct it. From this perspective, the Czech author tried to distinguish a fully-fledged regulated economy from corrective state intervention, arguing that while the first is to be rejected, in a crisis situation it is natural that a certain level of planning and state involvement is necessary in any economic system.[69]

Distinguishing between organized and regulated economy, Engliš argued that planning did not necessarily imply collectivism (as he put it with an inventive pun, *Wirtschaftsplan* was not equal to *Planwirtschaft*). The main theoretical task was exactly to demarcate the level of intervention and avoid such measures that in the long run would destroy the economic system. Along these lines, he was highly critical of socialism, citing the paradigmatic neoliberal argument about the price mechanism, and reviewing key authors linked to the socialist calculation debate, including Boris Brutskus, Friedrich von Hayek, Keynes, Fritz Machlup, Ludwig von Mises, Otto Neurath, and Václav Verunáč. He subscribed to the idea that it was impossible to relate prices and work directly to one another due to the incommensurability of different types of work. How can one hour of toiling at the assembly line be converted into accountancy or writing a novel? Intervention was needed not to bring the economy under state control, but rather to restore free competition and stimulate the revival of economy. Further, planning was needed not to limit the entrepreneurial spirit, but rather to coordinate different sectors and measures to avoid their potential clash. This could also lead to a new model that would synthesize liberal democracy and an emancipatory version of solidarism, making chances more equal via measures as a land reform, without however the collectivization of production or the state regulation of consumption. This would also entail the return to a more open economy as autarchic tendencies were, for Engliš, only prolonging the crisis.

Throughout the 1930s and early 1940s the problem of planning remained a central question for East Central European experts. One of the most interesting voices was Polish–Jewish sociologist Ferdynand Zweig (1896–1988). A member of the leading Polish economic "think tank" of the period, the Kraków Economic Society, Zweig published several studies in the early 1930s on the theoretical problems posed by the Great Depression. Escaping to England in 1939, he worked for the Polish government-in-exile and wrote a synthetic study, *Poland Between Two Wars*, which sought to assess the ways the Polish state and Polish society coped with the endemic political and economic crises of the interwar years.[70] In contrast to Engliš, Zweig argued that in the Polish case the 1929–33 economic crisis was managed on the basis of *laissez-faire* ideology, and planning became more prominent as a state policy only in the mid-1930s. He explained this resilience of the classical liberal doctrine with reference to Polish identity politics, which claimed to be the outpost of the Western world in Eastern Europe and thus stuck to Western economic orthodoxy, even if the economic situation was totally different.

Zweig derived the origins of Polish backwardness from the absence of a national state before 1918, which implied the lack of a mercantilist phase sheltering economic development from the competition of more advanced economies. After 1918, the re-emergence of Polish statehood created a high expectation of economic development but, overall, the society was unwilling to pay its price. In turn, the mid-1920s brought about a gradual professionalization of administration, the turn away from foreign models, and the adoption of indigenous solutions. At the same time, the new state continued to be ravaged by deep internal—territorial, generational, political, national, and social—cleavages. The decline of out-migration (due to the more restrictive immigration policies in the United States) and internal developments in Russia and Germany, which hindered Polish agrarian exports, created further social tensions.

Growing economic and social insecurity contributed to the delegitimization of parliamentarism and catalyzed the authoritarian turn that brought Józef Pilsudski, promising social and political stability, back to power. However, his regime was hit

94   Intellectuals and the Crisis of Politics

hard by the Great Depression, which had particularly destructive impact on the economies in Eastern Europe in general, and Poland in particular (resulting in a 50%—in real value 25%—decline in national income). Among the main factors of the depression in Poland, Zweig enumerated the opening of the agricultural price scissors, the outflux of capital, and the self-destructive impact of monetary orthodoxy sticking to overvalued national currency (*złoty*). He also registered a move toward state interventionism because of the depression (even though the crisis was not entirely overcome even after 1933), leading to étatization as entire strategic branches went bankrupt.

This étatist turn was most clearly manifested by Eugeniusz Kwiatkowski (1888–1974), who sought to industrialize central Poland. In Zweig's reading, this was akin to implementing a "New Deal" in an authoritarian context. The ambitious program changed the social structure of the country to a certain extent but could not eliminate the agrarian misery that remained endemic throughout the interwar years, due mainly to the structure of landownership, the fragmentation of the land, the loss of emigration opportunities, high taxation, disguised unemployment, and a general lack of capital and credit. Writing during the Second World War, Zweig, as did many other Polish intellectuals in exile and in the underground state at home, also sought to project an image of what postwar Poland could be. He envisioned a democratic and more integrated Polish state with access to the Baltic Sea, one which could develop a mutually profitable economic exchange with the Soviet Union, enter into a regional framework of integration with other East Central European nations, and profit from a more rational pooling of global resources.[71]

While the broader public discourse of the interwar years was saturated by the trope of economic crisis, we can see that the reconstruction focusing on the intellectual history of the period shows a somewhat different picture. In contrast to the general penchant of philosophers and cultural commentators for linking the different sectors of human existence into one comprehensive crisis discourse, economic experts (such as Hirsch, Lederer, or Engliš) were for a long time reluctant to describe the economic slump as a "crisis of capitalism." This was due both to the theoretical delegitimization of the concept of crisis before 1918 as against the theory of conjunctural cycles offering more quantitative exactitude, and the embeddedness of experts in economic decision-making bodies having a vested interest in calming down the public and pointing to a more technocratic solution. We can identify several such attempts combining conceptual de-contestation with emotional "de-dramatization." It is not by chance then that the crisis discourse would return to the center of political rhetoric of anti-systemic contenders.

One the one hand, communist theoreticians had both a political and intellectual fascination with the crisis of capitalism, combining the Marxian conception of the essentially crisis-ridden nature of capitalism with a vision of the transformation of capitalist economy from the late nineteenth century onward (characterized by monopolistic tendencies), which could be used as a legitimization of the Soviet project. On the other hand, there was also a niche for an extreme-right-wing economic analysis of crisis phenomena. Even though the professed anti-materialism of conservative revolutionary subcultures prevented the proliferation of an economic crisis discourse, economic aspects were integrated into a more comprehensive framework linking biological, spiritual, and social aspects.

In addition to the anti-liberals on the left and right, the crisis discourse also surfaced in the works of economic experts losing their grip on state institutions. These experts felt that the political establishment was fatally non-responsive to their clarion call for a fundamental change in economic policy. This was the case with some of the key figures of the emerging neoliberal project in the 1930s. However, quite predictably, they did not talk of the "crisis of capitalism" as such. Rather, some registered a transformation in the economy as a shift from the more competitive nineteenth-century forms of capitalist production to those of the twentieth century, marked by previously unheard-of levels of concentration. In general, however, they sought to address the problem of the crises of liberalism and democracy, subverting the usual subordination of economic aspects to political and spiritual causes by arguing that there was a mutual conditioning between the economy and political culture. Only by liberating the economy could there be potentially stable guarantees for political liberties. At the same time, from the perspective of observers from countries generally considered under-developed, the exclusivity of these neoliberal precepts could be relativized, and some elements of liberalism and planning seemed to be much more compatible ideologically as part and parcel of a strategy of crisis management.

Notes

1. William Stanley Jevons, "The Periodicity of Commercial Crises, and its Physical Explanation," *Journal of The Statistical and Social Inquiry Society of Ireland* 7, Part 54 (1878/1879): 334–42.
2. See Alexander Nützenadel, "Jenseits des Dualismus von Wandel und Persistenz? Krisenbegriffe der Sozial- und Kulturanthropologie," in Thomas Mergel, ed., *Krisen verstehen*, 59–78; György Kövér, *A növekedés terhe. Krízisek–csődök–ciklusok* [The Burden of Growth. Crises, Bankruptcies, Cycles] (Budapest: Osiris, 2018).
3. Albert Aftalion, *Les crises périodiques de surproduction* (Paris: M. Rivière, 1913).
4. Joseph Alois Schumpeter, *Die Krise des Steuerstaats* (Graz: Leuschner & Lubensky, 1918). In English: "The Crisis of the Tax State," in Alan T. Peacock et al., eds., *International Economic Papers*, vol. 4, trans. Wolfgang F. Stolper and Richard Abel Musgrave (London: Macmillan, 1954), 5–38.
5. Ibid., 6.
6. Ibid., 38.
7. Tivadar Surányi-Unger, *A gazdasági válságok történetének vázlata 1920-ig* [An Outline of the History of Economic Crises Until 1920] (Budapest: Szent István Társulat, 1921).
8. Ibid., 42.
9. Arthur Spiethoff, "Krisen," in *Handwörterbuch der Staatswissenschaften*, 4th edn., vol. 6 (Jena: Gustav Fischer, 1925), 8–91.
10. Ibid., 9.

96 Intellectuals and the Crisis of Politics

11. Analyzing the transnational entanglements of neoliberalism, Quinn Slobodian calls attention in a pioneering manner to the importance of data visualization in economic theory and policymaking. See Quinn Slobodian, *The Globalists: The End of Empire and the Birth of Neoliberalism* (Cambridge, MA: Harvard University Press, 2018).

12. To some extent, Schumpeter is an outlier also in the sense that his synthetic work on business cycles came out at the very end of the interwar period: Joseph A. Schumpeter, *Business Cycles. A Theoretical, Historical and Statistical Analysis of the Capitalist Process* (New York: McGraw-Hill Book Company, 1939). He used the word "crisis" in this book as well but noted that it was not a "technical term," and put forward instead "waves" and "cycles" as more adequate analytical categories.

13. Bertil G. Ohlin, *The Cause and Phases of the World Economic Depression. Report Presented to the Assembly of the League of Nations* (Geneva: Secretariat of the League of Nations, 1931). The expert network around the report included Friedrich von Hayek, German economist Ernst Wagemann, British liberal politician and economist Hubert D. Henderson, Polish socialist economist Edward Lipiński, Italian statistician close to the fascist regime, Corrado Gini, and Edgard Milhaud from the International Labour Organization, among others.

14. Ibid., 37.

15. Ibid., 313.

16. Julius Hirsch, *Die Wirtschaftskrise* (Berlin: Fischer, 1931), 9.

17. Paul Einzig, *The World Economic Crisis, 1929–1931* (London: Macmillan, 1931).

18. Hirsch, *Die Wirtschaftskrise*.

19. Ibid., 26–7.

20. Ibid., 41.

21. Emil Lederer, *Wege aus der Krise* (Tübingen: J. C. B. Mohr, 1931).

22. Wladimir Woytinsky, "Aktive Weltwirtschaftspolitik," *Die Arbeit*, 6 (June 1931): 413.

23. Ibid., 414.

24. Ibid., 422.

25. For an overview of Woytinsky's ideas and activities, see Sheri Berman, *The Primacy of Politics: Social Democracy and the Ideological Dynamics of the Twentieth Century* (Cambridge: Cambridge University Press, 2006), 111–15.

26. See the excellent analysis by Robert Skidelsky, "The Great Depression: Keynes's Perspective," in Harold James, ed., *The Interwar Depression in an International Context* (Munich: R. Oldenbourg, 2002), 99–112.

27. John M. Keynes, "The Macmillan Committee," in *The Collected Writings of John Maynard Keynes*, vol. 20: *Activities 1929–1931: Rethinking Employment and Unemployment Policies* (London: Royal Economic Society, 1978), 38–66, particularly 60, for his arguments at the Macmillan Committee; see Keynes, "The Committee of Economists," in ibid., 423–432, for his arguments at the Committee of Economists.

28. Keynes, "The Committee of Economists," 406–7.

29. John M. Keynes, "The Great Slump of 1930," in *The Collected Writings of John Maynard Keynes*, vol. 9: *Essays in Persuasion* (London: Royal Economic Society, 1978), 126–34.

30. Ibid., 126.

31. Ibid., 133.

32. Ibid. 134.

33. Pasquale Jannaccone, "Speculazione di Borsa" (1931), in *Prezzi e mercati* (Turin: Giulio Einaudi, 1951), 354–83.
34. Ernst Wagemann, *Zwischenbilanz der Krisenpolitik* (Berlin: Carl Heymanns, 1935).
35. Ibid., 10.
36. Jacques Rueff, *La Crise du Capitalisme* (Paris: Revue Bleue, 1935).
37. Ibid., 5.
38. For a collection of his writings on the Great Depression, see Jenő Varga, *A nagy válság* [The Great Crisis] (Budapest: Kossuth, 1978).
39. For a contextualization of Varga's early writings, see André Mommen, *Stalin's Economist: The Economic Contributions of Jenő Varga* (London: Routledge, 2011); for a selection of published primary sources translated into English, see Eugen Varga, *Selected Political and Economic Writings: From the Hungarian Revolution to Orthodox Economic Theory in the USSR*, ed. and trans. André Mommen (Leiden: Brill, 2020).
40. I thank Cody Inglis for calling my attention to the articles in *Kommunismus*, providing a context for Varga's early writings.
41. Varga, *A nagy válság*, 95.
42. These debates also filtered into the various theoretical journals of the Comintern; Varga, for example, published in *Kommunismus* (Vienna) between 1920–21 on the crisis-laden character of capitalist economies. For the published proceedings of the first four Congresses, see John Riddell, ed., *Founding the Communist International: Proceedings and Documents of the First Congress: March 1919* (New York: Pathfinder, 1987); idem., ed., *Workers of the World and Oppressed Peoples, Unite! Proceedings and Documents of the Second Congress, 1920*, 2 vols. (New York: Pathfinder, 1991); idem., ed., *To the Masses: Proceedings of the Third Congress of the Communist International, 1921* (Leiden: Brill, 2015); and idem., ed., *Toward the United Front: Proceedings of the Fourth Congress of the Communist International, 1922* (Leiden: Brill, 2012).
43. Eugen Varga, *Die Krise der kapitalistischen Weltwirtschaft* (Hamburg: Verlag der Kommunistischen Internationale, 1921). Republished as Varga, "The Crisis of the Capitalist World Economy," in *Selected Political and Economic Writings*, 343–92.
44. Eugen Varga, "The Process of Capitalist Decline (Report to the Fourth Congress of the Communist International)," in *Selected Political and Economic Writings*, 415ff, particularly 434–35.
45. Varga, "A konjunkturakutatás és a válságelmélet [Conjuncture Research and Crisis Theory] (1927)," in *A nagy válság*, 145–58.
46. Varga, "A gazdasági világválságok [The Economic World Crises] (1937)," in *A nagy válság*, 383–430.
47. Varga, "A konjunkturakutatás és a válságelmélet," 151.
48. J. V. Stalin, "The Growing Crisis of World Capitalism and the External Situation of the USSR," in *Works*, vol. 12, *April 1929–June 1930* (Moscow: Foreign Languages Publishing House, 1955), 242–69.
49. Vyacheslav Molotov, *The Developing Crisis of World Capitalism. The Revolutionary Crisis and the Tasks of the Comintern* (London: Modern Books, 1930).
50. Varga, "Új jelenségek a gazdasági válságban [New Phenomena in the Economic Crisis] (1934)," in *A nagy válság*, 195–276.
51. Ibid., 242.

52. Eugen Varga, *The Great Crisis and its Political Consequences: Economics and Politics 1928–34* (London: Modern Books, 1935). Republished in Varga, *Selected Political Writings*, 700–901.
53. Varga, *A nagy válság*, 282.
54. For an important study of the agrarian question in the Comintern context, see George D. Jackson, *Comintern and Peasant in East Europe, 1919–1930* (New York: Columbia University Press, 1966).
55. Varga, *A nagy válság*, 315.
56. Ibid., 325.
57. Eugen Varga, *Henri de Man et son plan* (Paris: Bureau d'éditions, 1934).
58. See André Mommen, "Eugen Varga: An Introduction to His Life and Works," in Varga, *Selected Political Writings*, 60–61.
59. Henryk Grossman, "Die Wert-Preis-Transformation bei Marx und das Krisenproblem," (1932) in *Aufsätze zur Krisentheorie*, Archiv sozialistischer Literatur, vol. 20 (Frankfurt a. M.: Verlag Neue Kritik, 1971), 43–75.
60. Ibid., 59.
61. Natalie Moszkowska, *Zur Kritik Moderner Krisentheorien* (Prague: Michael Kacha, 1935).
62. Ibid., 41.
63. Ferdinand Fried, *Das Ende des Kapitalismus* (Jena: Eugen Diederichs Verlag, 1931). On his ideas and background, see Joshua Derman, "Prophet of a Partitioned World: Ferdinand Fried, 'Great Spaces,' and the Dialectics of Deglobalization, 1929–1950," *Modern Intellectual History* 18, no. 3 (2021): 757–81.
64. Fried, *Das Ende des Kapitalismus*, 188–9.
65. Ibid., 247.
66. József Nemcsek, *Világválság és technokrácia* [World Crisis and Technocracy] (Budapest: Fővárosi Könyvkiadó Rt., 1933).
67. Karel Engliš, *Regulierte Wirtschaft* (Prague: Orbis, 1936). The Czech edition, *O řízeném hospodářství*, was published in 1935.
68. Engliš, *Regulierte Wirtschaft*, 78–85.
69. Ibid., 49.
70. Ferdynand Zweig, *Poland Between Two Wars: A Critical Study of Social and Economic Change* (London: Secker & Warburg, 1944). On Zweig's intellectual and institutional context in Kraków, see Marcin Chmielowski, "Economic Society in Kraków as Polish Prewar Pro Liberty Think Tank," in Federico N. Fernández, Barbara Kolm, Victoria Schmid, eds., *The Indispensability of Freedom. 8th International Conference—The Austrian School of Economics in the 21st Century* (Vienna: Friedrich A. von Hayek Institut, 2020), 103–13.
71. Zweig, *Poland Between Two Wars*, 158ff.

5
Crisis of Social Cohesion

While the economic depression was often studied on its own, diagnoses of societal crisis were typically associated with other faces of crisis. In his influential work *The Social Crisis of Our Time*, Wilhelm Röpke repeatedly argued that social, economic, and political symptoms were intertwined.[1] While the trope of the "crisis of society" was commonly linked to the analysis of economic developments, some observers argued that the process of social disintegration was perhaps the cause, and not the result, of the economic downturn. Within the social fabric, various loci (as well as social groups and patterns of behavior) were identified: the elites, the youth, the family (and gender roles), as well as social infrastructure (such as the "housing crisis").

Crisis also featured in some of the paradigmatic texts shaping the disciplines of sociology and anthropology at the turn of the century. Thus, Émile Durkheim (1858–1917) linked experiences of crisis to *anomie* and also analyzed the boom of anti-Semitism in France in the context of the sociopolitical crisis phenomena of the last decades of the nineteenth century.[2] Likewise, in his methodological manifesto ("The City: Suggestions for the Investigation of Human Behavior in the City Environment," 1915), American Robert E. Park (1864–1944), a student of Georg Simmel and founder of the "Chicago School" of urban sociology, employed crisis as a key interpretative term for understanding collective psychology: "What is the psychology of crisis? What is the cycle of events involved in the evolution of a crisis, political or economic. . . ."[3]

These theoretical discussions also resonated with *fin-de-siècle* visions of the decline and disintegration of the social fabric, necessitating urgent social reform. These critical discourses had both left-wing and right-wing modalities, but these could also overlap. For example, the eugenic discourse at the turn of the century was often used by social reformers on the left who linked their social hygienic programs to the idea of emancipation.[4] However, it became appropriated gradually by radical nationalists, especially after 1918. They contrasted the "racial decadence" of the present to their own visions of collective regeneration by violent means of purification.

There was also considerable change over time in the structure of this discourse. In the context of the relative stabilization of the 1920s, social crisis came to be framed more in terms of the collapse of predictability. In the conservative discourse this was linked to the disintegration of traditional social patterns and relationships, even deploring the growth of the living standard of the working class in comparison to its relative fall in the case of the middle class. By contrast, on the left, the social crisis

---

Intellectuals and the Crisis of Politics in the Interwar Period and Beyond. Balázs Trencsényi, Oxford University Press.
© Balázs Trencsényi (2025). DOI: 10.1093/9780198929512.003.0005

100 Intellectuals and the Crisis of Politics

was often explained by comparing promises and expectations of social progress and emancipation around 1918–19 with the ensuing social tensions. The postwar period also saw the radicalization of generational conflicts, which were prevalent already at the turn of the century, especially in the context of the different youth movements (*Jugendbewegungen*).

The Great Depression brought yet another transformation as the general collapse of the living standard, pauperization, proletarianization of the middle class and the intelligentsia, and the destabilization of the social position of traditional elites by new étatist leaderships made the feeling of crisis even more immediate across different social strata. However, in the context of political radicalization, endemic crisis could also be perceived as an exceptional opportunity for a fundamental social transformation. Here again, the radical left and right-wing agendas showed certain morphological similarities.

With the unfolding of different—democratic, autocratic, and totalitarian— strategies of crisis management, by the mid-1930s conceptualizations of social crisis again acquired somewhat different accents, as now it became both a framework of analyzing the persistent internal divisions within these societies as well as a counterconcept to new local and world orders in the making—seemingly emerging out of the crisis itself and thus supposedly capable of fencing it off in the future. In the following, this chapter analyzes a number of these societal crisis discourses both synchronically (in view of their different ideological and geographical localizations) and diachronically (considering the ever-changing sociopolitical context).

The Crisis of Elites and the Rise of Mass Society

One of the most common localizations concerned the crisis of elites, contrasted to the emergence of modern ("mass") societies. This theme was rooted in debates going back to the second half of the nineteenth century and focused on the decline of traditional ruling strata, especially the nobility, and (in some contexts) also the traditional urban patriciate. These debates were particularly sharp in East Central Europe (but not in the Balkans), where until that point the landed nobility had preserved its dominant position. Debates on social transformation thus focused on the failure of structural adaptation, contrasting Britain as the model with its capitalist gentry to the disintegration of the traditional elites and the rise of new (often ethnically "othered") contender groups. This situation also triggered yet another often discussed phenomenon—the move of these traditional elites into state administration, creating a rift between the old state-centered elites and the new economy-centered ones.

Obviously, this general dynamic of contestation between "old" and "new" elites had local peculiarities, depending on the way the state and society related to each other in different contexts (starting with the most obvious question of the relative position of the given elite group in its multiethnic imperial or homogenizing nation-state setting). It is enough to compare the Spanish, French, German, Polish, and Hungarian dynamic to see the convergences and divergences. For instance, the drive toward the legal profession and the army was quite common everywhere, but political parties had different functions. In France, after 1871, the bourgeois strata took over the political machine, while in the other countries traditional elites retained some of their power positions (related to the different electoral systems and levels of political participation). These discussions often occurred in terms of "questions," as analyzed by Holly Case, such as the "gentry question" prevalent in Polish and Hungarian debates, or in Italy the "Southern question," focusing on the de-modernization of the southern regions of united Italy, linked to the exploitation of state structures by the latifundia-owner class of the Italian south.[5]

The new social and political challenges in the interwar period twisted these discourses to a considerable extent. The socioeconomic decline of the middle classes following the Great War was coupled by what was described as the rise of "mass society," menacing the social and intellectual elites. In this context, there appears an overall morphological shift of the debate as the turn of the century "questions" were reframed in terms of crises,[6] for example, the debate on population. While the Malthusian frame of the "population question"—dominant at the turn of the century both among the Left and the Right—was abandoned, both overpopulation and depopulation could be described as crisis symptoms. Similarly, reframing the late nineteenth-century debates, the crisis of the middle class became central to the interwar social imaginary. While before the First World War the middle classes were on the rise (and were contrasted to traditional elites), the postwar socioeconomic context catalyzed a generalized narrative of their loss of prestige and overall material and spiritual decline.[7]

The discourse on the intelligentsia was yet another modality of the discussion on the transformation of elites, and it is remarkable that the rhetoric of crisis appeared almost simultaneously with that phenomenon toward the end of the nineteenth century. Assuming a transnational perspective that goes beyond the somewhat one-sided historiographical view locating the origins of intellectuals exclusively in the French context around the Dreyfus affair, one could even risk saying that the emergence of intellectuals as a normative group identity in Europe coincided deliberately with the emergence of the discourse of their crisis.

While the interwar period saw an unprecedented numerical expansion of the liberal professions all over Europe, this did not entail a growth of cultural and political prestige, let alone economic well-being. Rather, many voices (not only among the conservatives) became increasingly skeptical of public opinion. The irreversible expansion of mass society undermined the classical patterns of public discourse and circulation of information. The transformation of the public sphere was fundamental, often grasped in terms of Americanization. This perception of an expanding mass society was linked to—and absorbed by—narratives about the crisis of culture.

In contrast to discourses of the "crisis of the mind," which focused on the spiritual sphere in particular, the trope of the "crisis of society" pointed to the entanglement of the disfunctions of mass society, social transmission, values, and institutions. A case in point is Röpke's *Social Crisis of Our Time* from the end of our period (1942), written in neutral Switzerland and thus reflecting less on the devastating social impact

102 Intellectuals and the Crisis of Politics

of the Second World War, but looking instead back more to the interwar themes and debates.[8] Röpke used a medicalized language (*Krankheitszustand*) to describe the social malaise he sought to dissect and eventually to heal. However, while couching the problem in biological terms, Röpke argued for the primacy of the spiritual sphere, stressing that the crisis was rooted in the disorientation of values and emotions, moral–intellectual decadence, spiritual chaos, relativism, and agnosticism.

For Röpke, an important trigger was the collapse of the long period of peace, associated with liberal capitalism, as a result of the First World War. At the same time, he asserted that certain processes of disintegration had started well before the war, catalyzed by the democratization and massification of society in the late nineteenth century. Indeed, the key notions used by Röpke—*Vermassung, Massenmensch, Proletarisierung*—resonated with the conservative cultural criticism of modernity. However, Röpke did not argue for a return to any sort of patriarchal society, nor did he cultivate any illusions about the social conditions of the past. Rather, the question was how to create a new social framework capable of culturally and socioeconomically integrating the masses. Looking at the crisis-management policies of Europe in the mid-to-late 1930s, Röpke saw certain signs of recovery but also dangerous "pseudo-solutions," such as socialism, which in his opinion would only result in further proletarianization. He thus positioned himself as against both "extreme capitalism" and socialism, pointing out that irrespective of the differences in the proposed solutions, they had a common basis in subordinating all other spheres of life to that of economically driven materialism (*Ökonomismus*).

Crisis of Social Reproduction

Like the debate on the "crisis of the middle class," the interwar discussion on demography also had deep roots in the nineteenth century. Thematized as both a cause and an indicator of social transformation, demography was studied and debated both by professionals and the broader public, but the underlying theoretical framework was changing. It is indicative that in the early 1920s Italian leftist Adriano Tilgher conceived of the "demographic crisis" still in Malthusian terms, praising France for its decreasing birth rate and arguing that Germany would have won the war if it had a smaller population.[9] For him, the crisis of Europe was linked to overpopulation and suggested that the way out for Germans and Italians was to introduce measures to limit birth and thus reduce unemployment. A decade later, Swedish social democrat scholar Gunnar Myrdal (1898–1987) linked his sweeping proposal of social reform to a demographic crisis discourse from a pro-natalist perspective.[10] Starting in the early 1930s, and assisted by his wife Alva (1902–86), Myrdal published a number of texts culminating in the 1934 *Crisis in the Population Question* (though the title was actually provided by the editor).[11]

Shifting away from the neo-Malthusian argument, the Myrdals subscribed to an ideological construct of "the crisis of national health" that potentially included almost all political forces except for the extreme left. In many ways this overlapped with the reconfiguration of Swedish social democracy in the early 1930s under the leadership of Per Olov Hansson, whose *Folkshemmet* (people's home) ideology merged socialist and bourgeois components on a common reformist platform legitimized with biopolitical arguments. Thus, the Myrdals also argued that state intervention was necessary to defy the tendencies of depopulation and the concomitant growth of immigration, to achieve at least a demographic equilibrium. What distinguished their position from the traditional bourgeois nationalist discourse was that the Myrdals problematized the liberal capitalist framework as well, arguing that only a profound social transformation could restore the positive dynamics of social reproduction. "Crisis" here is conceptualized as an opportunity for such radical transformation, in a way mirroring (but also subverting) the right-wing nationalist discourses of crisis that had become increasingly dominant in continental Europe by the early 1930s.[12]

Continuing these arguments, Gunnar Myrdal's English-language *Population* argued that demography was a "life and death question of democracy."[13] He sought to challenge the Malthusian paradigm, which in his understanding was shared by conservatives, Manchester liberals, and "old-style" social democrats as well. The urgency posed by the decrease in population, especially visible in Western and Northern Europe, necessitated a new political approach. In contrast to the elitism of the conservative critics of modernity, Myrdal took mass society and representative democracy for granted, but considered it important to shape public opinion, since decisions needed to be based on objective knowledge. The way to achieve this was to make scientific knowledge available to the masses, and his framing of social problems in terms of crisis exemplified this approach. In contrast to the moral and/or metaphysical discourse of the conservatives and liberals, his understanding of crisis was more functionalist. When talking of the "crisis of opinion" unleashed by a decrease in population, Myrdal rather used "crisis" as a synonym for "conflict."[14] He pointed to the importance of studying crisis in a comparative setting, offering his case study on Sweden as a sort of "laboratory" for further research. He also analyzed retrospectively the debate of the early 1930s, referring to his own book as a spark. He argued that his call for action to revert negative demographic trends could be successful because it touched a sensitive nerve in Swedish public opinion, namely the "fear of the death of the nation," which in his interpretation was a "mild form" of nationalism—not an expansive drive, but rather an apprehension directed toward the possible loss of national homogeneity caused by immigration.

The Myrdals had remarkable success in attracting attention to their sociological theories clad in the discourse of societal crisis, linking the democratization of the public sphere to their suggested social reforms. They were proud of having forged a framework where conservatives and progressives could find common ground, even if they were attracted to different components. For conservatives, the aims were held in common, but the proposed remedies not; conversely, the progressives were uneasy about the demographic aims but supported the interventionist social policy suggested by the Myrdals. This was even more interesting regarding the envisioned common platform between feminists like Alva Myrdal and conservative advocates of

104 Intellectuals and the Crisis of Politics

traditional family values, who both agreed upon the need to protect women outside of the domestic environment.

This tactical convergence should not distract us from the Myrdals' sweeping horizons of expectation. They were convinced about the direction of historical development, stressing that there was no way back to patriarchy, and that the task was to link feminism to the widely shared sentiment of preserving the family and the nation. Maintaining this common ground required abandoning the dogmatic liberal positions that condemned state intervention. By using statistical data on the housing market, Gunnar Myrdal argued that the fall in the population led to less demand and less investment, eventually resulting in an economic slump. To achieve and sustain this new consensus, Myrdal considered it crucial to democratize the public sphere, but also to make it possible for expert opinions and rational scientific arguments to reach the masses.

A similar strategy was followed by feminist thinkers in East Central Europe as well, even if the political context was radically different (and their possible impact on the state much more limited).[15] In 1932, prominent Slovenian leftist activist and reform pedagogue Angela Vode (1892–1985) published a series of articles dedicated to the problem of the "crisis of family."[16] Vode rejected moralizing crisis discourses that pointed to the loss of Christian faith as a reason for the phenomena of social disintegration. Instead, she argued for the primacy of economic causes in triggering a fundamental social transformation. Vocally critical of the dominant conservative and nationalist discourses that blamed the emancipation of women for the demographic decline, she pointed instead to socioeconomic reasons stemming from the global depression and argued that reductions in social security had a direct impact on the willingness of families to have more children.

Crisis in this perspective was a highly ambiguous concept. Following the Marxist logic, Vode subscribed to the idea of irreversible long-term historical progress toward emancipation (understood both in economic and gender terms). At the same time, she was also conscious of the enormous suffering caused by the economic crisis for society in general, and for women and children in particular. In this context, she focused on the catastrophic social impact of the exponential growth of unemployment and argued that the social and economic emancipation of women was making the crisis more manageable: "[I]f both members of the family are economically independent, the conflict between them is usually less tragic."[17]

In the interwar period, the hottest debates on the crisis of social reproduction were linked to what was described as the clash of generations. Like the other themes analyzed in this chapter, generational conflict was also rooted in a pre-existing intellectual framework. Drawing also on romantic discursive traditions, *fin-de-siècle* youth movements pointed to the tension between antiquated and unnatural social conventions and the natural inclinations of the youth, envisioning a liberation of instincts and breaking off the fetters of tradition. They were aware of the tragic and self-destructive potentials of this clash, as exemplified by such paradigmatic literary works of the time as Frank Wedekind's 1891 *Spring Awakening* [Frühlings Erwachen]. The interwar period, with the war experience as a trigger, witnessed the further radicalization of this discourse, making the feeling of generational rupture even more fundamental, especially between those who had participated in the war, those who were too old to serve on the battlefields, and those who were too young to be drafted. The ensuing debate on generations cut across political camps and engendered heated discussions in many national contexts. Generational rhetoric could draw on a long history: a key topos of romantic nationalism was youth itself (Young Europe, etc.), and subsequent paradigm shifts in national liberalism were often framed in these terms (e.g., the Young Czechs as opposed to the Old Czechs). Finally, at the turn of the century, there was a proliferation of anti-political youth movements as well as radical nationalist groups both in Eastern and Western Europe, which all devised their mobilizing ideology in terms of the clash of old and young.[18]

This discord became even more influential as it was coupled with the experience of a global crisis of temporality: a fundamental rupture in time created by the Great War. Hence, in the early 1920s the ideologeme of generational conflict prevailed in most European contexts, even in those countries that did not participate in the war (e.g., Spain). It became a central discursive component of conservative revolutionaries, for example, when they proclaimed the need to break with the corrupted recent past to restore a deeper continuity with an earlier heroic one. This heroic past, in the terms of conservative revolutionaries, had been marked by high social coherence and cultural authenticity. But the radical left also rejected the recent past, which had been marked by the more moderate and evolutionary vision of the prewar social democratic leadership.

While it is possible to discern leftist and rightist tendencies, projecting a binary logic on these developments obliterates the considerable discursive similarity between statements stemming from diametrically opposed ideological camps. Note that in many cases this ideological polarization followed a relatively long period of co-existence when a common anti-political and anti-institutional rhetoric still provided cohesion for individuals who later chose radically divergent paths. This is most obvious in the late 1920s and early 1930s: 1927–28 roughly marked the point at which the first postwar cohort distinguished itself from the "war generation" that had been shaped by the *Fronterlebnis*. By contrast, members of the postwar generation had usually experienced the war only as children, developing an ambiguous relationship to it—remembering it but not being able to base their symbolic legitimacy on their participation. They came to maturity in the mid-1920s, in the context of a relative normalization compared to the previous decade, and usually turned toward culture instead of party politics and state-building. In the long run, however, this meta-political position was also prone to assume direct political connotations, often linked to political movements challenging institutionally established political forces.

A paradigmatic case where generational and crisis discourses intertwined was in Romania. There, the "Young Generation" or "Generation of 1927" brought together a plethora of highly original young intellectuals who later had a formative impact on their national culture.[19] The first programmatic articulation of this generation is

106 Intellectuals and the Crisis of Politics

usually linked to Mircea Eliade's (1907–86) *Spiritual Itinerary*, defining the search for spiritual experience as the agenda of the new post-war generation:

> One might say that a generation, as long as it exists, is a flowing continuum throbbing with life and, therefore, contradictions. It is, to say the least, unscientific to attempt to capture its contours, to isolate it, to render it in words. A generation's soul is hard to reconstruct, even with the help of time and history. Because a generation—and, of course, by this I understand the generation's elite—does not stand out unless it is marked by a catastrophic crisis. Such as, for instance, the war. Generations that are exposed to minor crises—a philosophy, a religion, a political doctrine, or an artistic experience—preserve their extreme mobility.[20]

Although there was a general anti-political thrust in most of these statements (e.g., rejection of party politics in the years following the war, blame laid on the old elite for "missing the chance" of radical political and spiritual transformation of the country), various political forces also tried step by step to use the generational discourse to their advantage. Eliade reflected on this ideological polarization in his 1935 "Crisis of Romanianism,"[21] where he defined Romanian national identification as natural and self-evident, and criticized both the "cosmopolitan" rejection of this identification (describing it as "spiritual death") and the compensatory overperforming of national belonging. Later, however, as Eliade himself became entangled with radical nationalism, he projected his vision of spiritual regeneration through ritualized violence on the Romanian ethnonational community.

The transformation of an individualist metaphysical revolt into a violent political program can be best observed in the writings of Emil Cioran (1911–95), who was at the periphery of the "young generation" at the time of its launch, being somewhat younger than its leaders. However, developing an idiosyncratic and radical style of thinking, he became one of the most characteristic figures of his cohort in the 1930s. In his essays written in the mid-1930s, and especially in his pamphlet on the "transfiguration of Romania," with its blending of existentialism and—both left and right-wing elements of—totalitarianism, we see him adapting a hypertrophic version of the generational discourse to an image of an all-encompassing crisis of national identity.[22] He extended the ideology of generational conflict to the entire nation-building project and launched the idea of "Romanian Adamism" involving the start of a real, "historical" existence initiated by the rejection of the "ahistoric-larval" way of life of the previous generations.

Crisis of the Peasantry

While in Scandinavia the debate about national reproduction increasingly focused on the urban population, in East Central Europe it was still the sizeable peasantry that was the center of attention, in view of both sociocultural and demographic processes. Representing a powerful political tradition all over the region, agrarian populism articulated itself through a crisis discourse contrasting East and West and subverting the traditional symbolic geographical hierarchy that envisioned the radiation of modernity from the European center. In contrast to the protagonists of the Conservative Revolution, however, the agrarian populists put more emphasis on socioeconomic relations, contrasting the industrialized Western European core to the rural peripheries. They argued that the crisis was largely due to the misunderstanding of this relationship on the part of local liberal elites (and their socialist opponents) who sought to catch up with the West by imposing industrialization and "pseudo-Western" urban modernity to the detriment of the rural classes who were kept in quasi-feudal dependence. Instead, they suggested focusing on the specific social interests and mentalities of the smallholder peasants who combined private property with a lack of capitalist exploitation (since they worked on their own land). This was reinforced by the argument that in contrast to industrial modernity, which was eminently crisis-ridden, the agrarian economy based on family farms was more resistant to crisis.[23]

A good example of this discourse is the work of the Romanian economic theoretician of the National Peasant Party, Virgil Madgearu (1887–1940), who went as far as to argue in favor of free trade against the sheltered industrialization project of the National Liberals.[24] As the Great Depression brought both an industrial and agrarian crisis, and the peasantry was hit particularly severely, Madgearu's position also changed. In the 1930s he pleaded for the realization of a "peasant state"—a social and political system that favored the peasantry as the most numerous and economically important stratum of society. The idea of a peasant state was ambiguous enough that it could be appropriated by different political projects. Thus, integral nationalist social philosopher Constantin Rădulescu-Motru (1868–1957) argued that, due to the specificity of development in Romania, the peasant state converged with the ideal of the "national state."[25] For him, peasantism, fascism, and Bolshevism formed part of a common anti-liberal and collectivist revolt that offered a way out of the crisis of political modernity.

However, agrarian populism should not be conflated with nationalism. Indeed, the agrarian populist agenda was prone to be put forward within a regionalist discursive framework, stressing the common needs of East Central European rural nations against the West. To make this even more complicated, many of the agrarian populists can still be considered selective Westernizers in the sense that they looked to the democratic Northern and Northwest European small states—characterized by highly productive traditions of farming agriculture and cooperativism (as in Denmark and the Netherlands)—for inspiration.

Most East Central European agrarians argued for a "Third Way," which cut across the alternative between liberal capitalism and communism. This often implied a geopolitical self-positioning between the advanced capitalist and overly individualistic West and the underdeveloped overly collectivistic East. Most often they also positioned themselves as highly critical of fascist and national socialist ideologies and movements, which suppressed democratic political frameworks supported by the agrarian populists—even if they were highly critical of actually existing party systems, which they considered to be non-representative of real social interests. Rather than subscribing to a passéist cult of premodern organic peasant society, these political activists and thinkers were also critical of the survival of feudal structures in their societies and sought to combine representative democracy with some cooperative structures of production and interest representation. Bulgarian writer and journalist Todor Vlaykov (1865–1943), who was shaped by the Russian *narodnik* ideas during his studies in Moscow, explained the postwar crisis in both political and social terms. He contrasted "alienated" and "organic" elites and envisaged a social transformation that would steer the country toward an organic development. However, parliamentarism was not "alien" in his view; rather, it was the natural means by which popular sovereignty was manifested, and thus he was critical of the left- and right-wing radicals whose attacks on the parliamentary system led to political autarchism. In this sense, he distanced himself from the agrarian radicalism of Aleksandar Stamboliyski and his followers, whose regime was increasingly critical of parliamentary democracy, the latter seen as formalist and unable to represent the interests of society.

Overall, however, the crisis of representative democracy was less central for the East Central European agrarians. It was always held by them to be problematic, even if some of the agrarian parties (in Romania, Poland, or Czechoslovakia) acted as defenders of the parliamentary regime against left- and right-wing autocratic movements. What was much more central was what Hungarian populist intellectual and politician Imre Kovács (1913–1980) described as the "collapse of the peasant form of life."[26] Kovács established this crisis diagnosis with the help of "sociographic" literature, which usually merged scientific (mainly sociological) analysis with some elements of literary reportage.[27] He compared the relevance of this method to that of dissection in nineteenth-century medical research—radically extending and deepening scientific knowledge. In this populist analysis, the central opposition was between the peasant masses and the inorganic/dysfunctional elites (including the middle class, which this perspective linked to the elite); Kovács's aim was thus to facilitate social and political mobility among the peasantry to create a more authentic new middle class. Crisis in this rendering denoted the growing gap between the rural and urban worlds, which seemed less and less bridgeable. Concomitantly, the further proletarianization of the peasantry seemed to undermine those normative features (the combination of individual responsibility toward one's own land and collective solidarity toward the community, dignity, honesty, health, fecundity, patriotism, etc.) that qualified the peasantry as the symbolic and biological reservoir of the nation. Thus, sociographical literature became "crisis literature," focusing on such symptoms as the growth of indebtedness, the fall of the fertility rate, self-destructive tendencies, and religious sectarianism.

This can be seen in the sociographic work of Croatian economist and peasantist politician Rudolf Bićanić (1905–68).[28] In assessing the devastating impact of the economic crisis on the peasantry, Bićanić pointed out the growing discrepancy between agrarian and industrial prices. He considered the expansion of financial capitalism particularly harmful to the peasants, making them dependent through indebtedness. In contrast to the liberal and Marxist visions (which both supported the further growth of capitalist production and eventually the proletarianization of the peasantry) Bićanić argued that the main aim of agrarian policy should have been precisely to prevent peasants' proletarianization, even at the expense of slowing down economic development. While the sociographic method he used was particularly suitable to document the material (and intellectual) "backwardness" of the countryside, Bićanić did not opt for passive resignation. Instead, he considered crisis as an opportunity to pressure people to cooperate. This implied both peasant self-organization and bringing Croatian urban elites closer to the rural population. There was also a national implication in this discourse: the Croatian peasantists considered the Serbian-dominated Yugoslav state bureaucracy as alien and parasitic. In this sense, facing the crisis also required the reinforcement of national solidarity, which fit the ideology of the Croatian Peasant Party, operating as a quasi-national party.

This case also shows that the contrast between "organic countryside" and "inorganic city" could be framed in ethnocultural terms, arguing either that the urban middle class and the elites were ethnically "alien" or that they became culturally or mentally "alienated." Especially in East Central Europe, where the pre-1918 imperial frames indeed set multicultural and multiethnic urban society against the rural *Hinterland*, this could be easily converted into a conflict about defining and representing the nation. It also carried the potential to turn the peasantist rhetoric into an exclusivist direction, targeting those groups who did not fit into the national frame (e.g., Jews) or remnants of the dominant pre-war elites (e.g., Germans or Hungarians).

A paradigmatic discussion on this issue took place among Hungarian agrarian populists in the late 1930s. For instance, writer and political activist Géza Féja (1900–1978) argued that, in the "feudal-capitalist" society of his country, Jews had necessarily become scapegoats of accumulated social aggression.[29] His proposed solution was to invite the Jews to switch sides and turn against the social and political elites of the authoritarian conservative administration of Miklós Horthy and take the side of the peasantry, "assimilating into the working people," as he put it. For others, however, on the right of the populist movement, the social interests of the peasantry were incompatible with those of the urban Jewry. In fact, even Féja's position oscillated between a more inclusive and a more exclusive stance during the Second World War.

While the social context and the national reference was different, and the numerical and symbolic dominance of the agrarian population was much less evident, agrarian populism also had a certain impact in Western Europe. Ernst Laur (1871–1964) was a key ideologist and social actor of Swiss peasantism with a strong resonance in the East and a crucial participant in the debates on economic crisis management in the early 1930s. Laur was also among the initiators of the *Kriseninitiative* of 1934–5, which proposed a number of interventionist social and economic measures to protect the social groups most affected by the Depression. His representative and comprehensive work on the Swiss peasant was prepared for the 1939 Zürich National Exhibition, organized in the shadow of the rapidly worsening international situation with the intention of boosting Swiss identity and pride in the socioeconomic resilience of the country.[30] Laur focused on the peculiarities of the Swiss peasantry as a key part of the nation, but did not claim that it was the only representative of authentic traditions, let alone the demographically dominant stratum. In fact, in contrast to his East Central European peers, Laur could not frame his homeland as a peasant country, as the agrarian sector produced only 13% of the national economy, and only 21% of Switzerland's population (including family members) could be counted as part of the peasantry. At the same time, however, he argued that Swiss political culture derived from the natural Alpine conditions that forced people to cooperate. This, however, did not imply a retrospective peasantist utopia. In fact, he subscribed to an evolutionary image of history, noting that it was only in 1848 that the last elements of feudalism were removed, and Swiss peasants became entrepreneurs by the late nineteenth century.

While Laur's description of the peasant economy also had strong technocratic components, there were also some features of his discourse that could be qualified as agrarian populist. Thus, he argued against "too much" federalism and the centralizing tendencies of the Swiss urban elites, contrasting the peasants' contact with nature, piety, patriotism, and democratic traditions with the alienation of the city. Along these lines, he also extolled the authentic peasant population, as a resource for national self-reproduction, as against the growing number of foreigners settling in Switzerland. (In the context of the late 1930s, when many political refugees from Germany tried to reach safety in Switzerland, this discourse also had sinister connotations.) Laur declared that peasants were the "source of vitality of the Swiss people,"[31] supplying healthy newcomers to the elites and boosting the falling natality rate of the urban population.

Furthermore, while Laur supported capitalism, he also promoted peasant cooperatives as an antidote to limitless competition and "extreme liberalism." He thus argued in favor of collective property but rejected socialism. Finally, he adhered to some populist cultural tropes, such as the defense of regional cultural differences against homogenized urban culture, and his eulogy for the "natural philosophers" among the common people, who possessed a more authentic knowledge about the world than many urbanites. At the same time, this agrarian populist cultural narrative did not go together with the idea of a radical political transformation comparable to the East Central European agrarian populists' vision of the "peasant state." Instead, his suggestions were pragmatic—such as setting up agricultural schools, credit institutions, and endorsing the state protection of agrarian production—but remained within the capitalist logic. In cultural terms, he set out to make peasant culture again independent from the city, though not in terms of full autarchy, but rather as creative adaptation, like the revival of some elements of Swiss folk dress as more functional alternatives to urban fashions. Eventually, the political direction of his populism was democratic and he argued that peasants were the defenders of Swiss democracy against an external totalitarian threat. In this sense, he "externalized" the crisis discourse, pointing to the explosive international situation that prompted Swiss society to reinforce its internal solidarity.

The other key figure mediating between Western and East Central European agrarian populism was Röpke, who settled in Switzerland after his emigration from Germany after the Nazi takeover and an interim stay in Turkey, and also drew on the Swiss experience in his political thinking. For him the agrarian issue was part of a broader picture, as he argued that the political and economic crises reinforced each other. The ensuing total crisis could result in totalitarianism, undermining all the civilizational achievements of human development. To fence off this crisis, Röpke argued for a "Third Way," which would transcend the alternatives of *laissez-faire* and collectivism. Like other neoliberals, Röpke considered the crisis of the Second World War as a possible new beginning for social regeneration along the lines of a reconfigured liberal agenda.[32]

Röpke stressed that his "Third Way" was not a neo-traditionalist project as he rejected medieval hierarchies and the corporatist visions that sought to restore a premodern order. Instead, he argued for the importance of the legacies of early modern movements that broke up the medieval (feudal) frameworks as well as the cultural impact of the Enlightenment. At the same time, he remained skeptical of "abstract rationalism" and—pointing to the Swiss, Scandinavian, and Anglo-Saxon models—he stressed that modern democracy emerged from the movements of peasants and burghers and not from the "speculations" of philosophers and lawyers. He also rejected secularization as the only way toward modern democracy and tried instead to draw a line of continuity between Christianity and the Enlightenment.

From this perspective, the French Revolution was also highly ambiguous—Röpke praised its break with feudalism but castigated revolutionary romanticism and Napoleon's expansionism as highly destructive. He was critical of the nineteenth century's *Megalolatrie* (cult of "bigness"), which was fascinated by the colossal in different political and cultural domains. To Röpke, this was clearly manifest in the doctrines of imperialism, socialism, monopoly capitalism, and étatism. Instead, adopting the cyclical logic of *Geistesgeschichte*, he argued for a return to the more human proportions of the eighteenth century, noting that the Classicism of the seventeenth century was closer to the bombastic aesthetics of the nineteenth. This periodization set Röpke apart from radical conservatives (e.g., Maurras in France) who contrasted Classicism favorably to Romanticism, playing down the eighteenth century and its Enlightenment heritage.

Coming closer to the present, Röpke contrasted neoliberalism—which more organically linked the past and the present—to classical liberalism, which he described as "dogmatic," absolutizing the market principle, and thus undermining its own dominance. Instead, he argued that a functioning market economy needed to be based on the moral integrity of citizens; a strong state able to protect itself from state capture by individuals or lobbies; a vigorous policing of the markets to hinder the formation of monopolies; and the protection of a legal order that makes it possible to prevent abuses of power by the economically strong. This was also linked to his vision of social mobility: while arguing for the importance of a "spiritual" hierarchy, he rejected the idea of the self-reproduction of privileged classes. At the same time, any intervention had to be "surgical" and could only be accepted if in

112 Intellectuals and the Crisis of Politics

the long run it contributed to the preservation of liberty. In this vein, Röpke pointed to the inherent tendency of the state to conquer all spheres: economic, social, and finally cultural. Hence, for Röpke, protecting economic liberty was a precondition of preserving political freedom.[33]

To sum up, this chapter shows that the criticism of (old and new) elites and the crisis discourses focusing on demography, generational transmission, and the peasantry were often closely interconnected. These tropes of the crisis of social coherence yielded themselves readily for populist discursive modalities because of the populist propensity to contrast the "organic community" with "inorganic," "artificial," or "alien" social actors, as well as the antipolitical overtones inherent to the biopolitical and generational discourses. This overview also indicates that it is futile to try to place these populist tropes on a one-dimensional left–right continuum. They could be used by very different projects and they often served precisely as mediators or even coagulants of new ideological combinations.[34] This also helps us to locate agrarian populism in the multidimensional spectrum of populist ideology, going beyond the binaries put forward by the classical works dealing with the topic, such as Margaret Canovan's contrast of political and agrarian populism,[35] or the counterposition of peasantism and agrarian populism in the influential edited volume by Ghiță Ionescu and Ernest Gellner.[36] Agrarian populism is thus one of the many varieties of populism, rather prominent in East Central Europe, and less so in Western Europe. Ethnopopulism (what could be described with the German term *Völkisch*) was equally present across the continent—usually not as an ideological *core* but more like a component of an ideological *mix*.

In some cases populism formed part of an anti-systemic ideology, but it could also become part of systemic right-wing authoritarian and even totalitarian projects (including fascism and national socialism), although in these cases it was usually subordinated to the palingenetic nationalist core. In turn, it could also be integrated into socialist political discourses. As discussed, it became part and parcel of the Swedish social democratic ideological framework in the early 1930s, making it eventually more resistant to the conservative counterattack, while in other countries it was the "Popular Front" ideology that catalyzed an interplay of socialist and populist elements.

Rather than just a critical position that set the people and the inorganic elites against each other, interwar populism merged several other motifs: the defense of private property; a support for democracy; a dislike of state bureaucracy and traditional party politics. Further, it addressed the idea that, even if the actual economic crisis hit the rural population more than the urban, this was unnatural, as the lifestyle of the self-employing peasantry was more resilient to crises than the employees of urban capitalist enterprises. From this perspective, agrarian populists attributed the horrible situation of the peasantry in the 1930s precisely to the egoism of the political and economic elites which had "captured" the state and imposed the whole burden of the crisis on them. Thus, the peasantry could not be held responsible for the crisis in any way. Likewise, the demographic crisis could be thematized by leftist critics of the political mainstream, combining radical reformism with a biopolitical discourse.

Members of the generational movements could also employ populist tropes, attacking the traditional elites for blocking social circulation and mobility. The core of their criticism of political and cultural institutions was that they were utterly hypocritical: neither participatory, nor representative. In this sense—and in most of the cases where it was evoked—the crisis of social cohesion pointed to another crisis, namely that of liberalism.

Notes

1. Wilhelm Röpke, *Die Gesellschaftskrisis der Gegenwart* (Zurich: Eugen Rentsch Verlag, 1942).
2. Chad Alan Goldberg and Emile Durkheim, "Introduction to Emile Durkheim's 'Anti-Semitism and Social Crisis,'" *Sociological Theory* 26, no. 4 (2008): 299–323.
3. Ken Gelder and Sarah Thornton, eds., *The Subcultures Reader* (London–New York: Routledge 1997), 22.
4. For the continuities and ruptures in the German context see Paul J. Weindling, *Health, Race and German Politics Between National Unification and Nazism, 1870–1945* (Cambridge: Cambridge University Press, 1989); in East Central Europe, see Marius Turda and Paul J. Weindling, eds., *Blood and Homeland: Eugenics and Racial Nationalism in Central and Southeast Europe, 1900–1940* (Budapest: CEU Press, 2006).
5. See Holly Case, *The Age of Questions* (Princeton: Princeton University Press, 2018).
6. Looking at the German and Swedish contexts, Nina Witoszek and Lars Trägårdh, eds., *Culture and Crisis: The Case of Germany and Sweden* (New York, Berghahn, 2002) pinpointed the shift from "question" to crisis in the late 1920s; see especially Yvonne Hirdman, "Crisis. The Road to Happiness?", 156.
7. Obviously, this does not necessarily mean that the middle classes lost ground economically after the First World War. See the classic study by Charles S. Maier, *Recasting Bourgeois Europe: Stabilization in France, Germany, and Italy in the Decade after World War I* (Princeton: Princeton University Press, 1975), as well as the recent work by Máté Rigó, *Capitalism in Chaos: How the Business Elites of Europe Prospered in the Era of the Great War* (Ithaca: Cornell University Press, 2022).
8. Röpke, *Gesellschaftskrisis*. On Röpke's oeuvre and intellectual contexts, see Patricia Commun and Stefan Kolev, eds., *Wilhelm Röpke (1899–1966): A Liberal Political Economist and Conservative Social Philosopher* (New York: Springer, 2018).
9. Adriano Tilgher, *La crisi mondiale* (Bologna: Zanichelli, 1921), 105ff.
10. On the way that the crisis discourse was used as a legitimization of étatist reforms in early 1930s Sweden and the crisis bill of 1930, see Hirdman, "Crisis," 156–7. On the intellectual origins of the pro-natalist project of the Myrdal family, see also Allan C. Carlson, *The Swedish Experiment in Family Politics: The Myrdals and the Interwar Population Crisis* (London: Routledge, 1990), which, however, needs to be used very critically.
11. Alva Myrdal and Gunnar Myrdal, *Kris i befolkningsfrågan* [Crisis in the Population Question] (Stockholm: Bonnier, 1934).
12. On the democratic revisionism of the Swedish Social Democrats in the interwar period, successfully integrating certain national references as well, see Sheri Berman, *The Primacy of Politics*, 152–76.

114 Intellectuals and the Crisis of Politics

13. Gunnar Myrdal, *Population: A Problem for Democracy* (Cambridge, MA: Harvard University Press, 1940). The Swedish edition is from 1938.

14. Myrdal, *Population*, 64ff.

15. For the Yugoslav context, see, e.g., Isidora Grubački, "Čija kriza? Feminizam i demokratija u Jugoslaviji 20-ih godina XX veka [Whose Crisis? Feminism and Democracy in 1920s Yugoslavia]," *Prispevki za novejšo zgodovino* 62, no. 2 (2022): 29–49.

16. Angela Vode, "Kriza družine [The Crisis of the Family]," *Jutro*, nos. 1–6 (January 18 and 25, and February 1, 8, 22, and 29, 1932). On Vode, see Karmen Klavžar, "Angela Vode," in Francisca de Haan, Krassimira Daskalova, and Anna Loutfi, eds., *A Biographical Dictionary of Women's Movements and Feminisms: Central, Eastern, and South Eastern Europe, 19th and 20th Centuries* (Budapest–New York: Central European University Press, 2006), 604–608.

17. Vode, "Kriza družine," (January 18, 1932), 6.

18. On the youth movements of the first half of the twentieth century in the German contexts, see Thomas Koebner and Rolf-Peter Janz, eds., *Mit uns zieht die neue Zeit: Der Mythos Jugend* (Frankfurt a. M.: Suhrkamp, 1985).

19. Matei Călinescu, "The 1927 Generation in Romania: Friendships and Ideological Choices (Mihail Sebastian, Mircea Eliade, Nae Ionescu, Eugène Ionesco, E. M. Cioran)," *East European Politics and Societies* 15, no. 3 (2001): 649–77.

20. Mircea Eliade, "Itinierariu spiritual [Spiritual Itinerary] (1927)," in *Profetism Românesc*, [Romanian Prophetism] vol. 1 (Bucharest: Editura Roza Vânturilor, 1990), 19; English excerpts in Diana Mishkova, Marius Turda, and Balázs Trencsényi, eds., *Discourses of Collective Identity in Central and Southeast Europe (1775–1945): Texts and Commentaries*, vol. 4, *Anti-Modernism. Radical Revisions of Collective Identity* (Budapest: CEU Press, 2014), 130.

21. Mircea Eliade, "Criza românismului?" [The Crisis of Romanianism?] in *Textele "legionare" și despre "românism"* [The "Legionary" Texts and about "Romanianism"] (Bucharest: Dacia, 2011), 117–19.

22. See Emil M. Cioran, *Singurătate și destin* [Loneliness and Destiny] (Bucharest: Humanitas, 1991); idem., *Schimbarea la față a României* [The Transfiguration of Romania] (Bucharest: Vremea, 1941). On Cioran's political writings, see Marta Petreu, *An Infamous Past: E. M. Cioran and the Rise of Fascism in Romania* (Chicago: Ivan R. Dee, 2005). Importantly, in his texts from the period Cioran did not use the concept of crisis, preferring other adjacent notions like agony, despair, passion, transfiguration, or revolution.

23. Overall, the agrarian populist political discourse was insensitive to intra-family inequalities regarding age and gender. At the same time, some representatives of the sociographic literature linked to the agrarian populist movement, such as the Romanian "Gusti school" or the Hungarian *népi írók* ("populist writers"), were more attentive to this problem. On various aspects and national contexts of Eastern European agrarian populism in the interwar years, and its interferences with other ideologies, see Georgi M. Dimitrov, "Agrarianism," in Feliks Gross, ed., *European Ideologies: A Survey of 20th Century Political Ideas* (New York: Philosophical Library, 1948), 396–450; Nissan Oren, *Revolution Administered: Agrarianism and Communism in Bulgaria* (Baltimore: Johns Hopkins University Press, 1973); Zigu Ornea, *Poporanismul* [Populism] (Bucharest: Minerva, 1973); Gyula Borbándi, *Der ungarische Populismus* (Mainz: Hase & Koehler, 1976); Augusta Dimou, *Entangled Paths Towards Modernity. Contextualizing Socialism and Nationalism in the Balkans* (Budapest: CEU Press, 2009).

24. See his collected studies: Virgil Madgearu, *Agrarianism, capitalism, imperialism. Contribuţii la studiul evoluţiei sociale româneşti* [Agrarianism, Capitalism, Imperialism: Contributions to the Study of Romanian Social Evolution] (Cluj: Dacia, 1999).

25. Constantin Rădulescu-Motru, *Românismul, catehismul unei noi spiritualităţi* [Romanism: Catechism of a New Spirituality] (Bucharest: Editura pentru Literatură şi Artă Regele Carol II, 1936).

26. Imre Kovács, *A parasztéletforma csődje* [The Collapse of the Peasant Form of Life] (Budapest: Bolyai Akadémia, 1940)

27. On the history of the sociographic method outside of the agrarian populist agenda, written by a contemporary, see Hans Zeisel, "Zur Geschichte der Soziographie," in Marie Jahoda, Paul F. Lazarsfeld, and Hans Zeisel, *Die Arbeitslosen von Marienthal. Ein soziographischer Versuch über die Wirkungen langandauernder Arbeitslosigkeit* (Frankfurt a. M.: Suhrkamp, 1980), 113–48. Originally published in 1933.

28. Rudolf Bićanić, *Kako živi narod. Život u pasivnim krajevima* [How the People Live. Life in the Passive Regions], vol. 1 (Zagreb: Tipografija, 1936).

29. Géza Féja, "A zsidók útja [The Way of the Jews]," *Magyarország* 45, no. 100 (May 5, 1938): 5.

30. Ernst Laur, *Le paysan suisse, sa patrie et son oeuvre: Conditions et évolution de l'agriculture suisse au vingtième siècle* (Brougg: L'union suisse des paysans, 1939).

31. Laur, *Le paysan suisse*, 701.

32. Röpke, *Gesellschaftskrisis*.

33. Eastern European agrarian populists were eager readers of Laur and Röpke. See, for instance, the overview of the Hungarian reception of Röpke in Péter Cserne, "Harmadik utak. Néhány szempont Röpke és Bibó összevetéséhez [Third Ways. Some Aspects of the Comparison of Röpke and Bibó]," *Magyar Tudomány* 6 (2003): 726–37. Simultaneously, Röpke was read as a protagonist of liberalism by the Polish political thinker Stefan Kisielewski after the Second World War. Laur's main practical work, *Landwirtschaftliche Betriebslehre für bäuerliche Verhältnisse* (1907), was translated into Polish (1928) and Czech (1937) as well.

34. The syncretic nature of populism was noted already by observers such as David Mitrany, who argued that it contained conservative, liberal, and socialist elements. See David Mitrany, *Marx Against the Peasant: A Study in Social Dogmatism* (Chapel Hill: University of North Carolina Press, 1951).

35. See Margaret Canovan, "Agrarian Populism in Perspective," in *Populism* (New York: Harcourt Brace Jovanovich, 1981), 98–135.

36. See Ghiţa Ionescu, "Eastern Europe," in Ghiţa Ionescu and Ernest Gellner, eds., *Populism: Its Meanings and National Characteristics* (Letchworth: The Garden City Press, 1969), 97–121.

6
Crisis of Liberalism

Closely linked to the discourses of spiritual, economic, and societal crisis, the debate on the decline of liberalism (both the ideology and its institutions) was among the most heated intellectual and political controversies of the interwar years. It was not the first time that liberalism seemed to be in crisis globally: already in the 1870s Ernest Renan remarked that "Pour le moment, le parti le plus vaincu en Europe, c'est le parti libéral."[1] From a different perspective, after the turn of the century, prominent British liberal political thinker J. A. Hobson (1858–1940) analyzed the "crisis of liberalism" in terms of the heightened conflict between the conservative Lords and the liberal-dominated Commons over the issue of the "People's Budget," which was meant to alleviate poverty by introducing new taxes on high income.[2] Crisis in Hobson's understanding was a future-oriented term, a dramatic transitional phase giving birth to a new ideological configuration, labeled by Hobson as "New Liberalism": "the substitution of an organic for an opportunist policy, the adoption of a vigorous, definite, positive policy of social reconstruction, involving important modifications in the legal and economic institutions of private property and private industry."[3] Hobson invited his readers to answer the question: "Will Liberalism, reformed and dedicated to this new, enlarged, and positive task of realising liberty, carry its adherents with unbroken ranks with persistent vigour along this march of social progress?"[4] His book was meant as a roadmap for this transformation, abandoning *laissez-faire* policies and reevaluating the role of the state in social policy.

The end of the First World War, with the United States having emerged as the new global power-center, seemed to open new opportunities for liberalism. But it also brought along new challenges, and the optimistic postwar mood was quickly replaced by a feeling of instability and disorientation. Since the normative framework of the new order emerging after the Great War was conceptualized as "liberal democracy," it is not easy to separate the diagnoses of the crisis of liberalism from those of the crisis of democracy. In fact, it is in the context of the postwar "Wilsonian moment" that the ideological combination of liberal democracy became prevalent and for some time also normative for the political elites that sought to fit into the new mainstream. At the same time, since liberals and democrats were not necessarily converging before the war, there were also different ideological streams of anti-liberalism and anti-democratism predating the interwar period, and they could also play the two ideologies against each other, for instance in the form of anti-democratic ("oligarchic") liberals or anti-liberal ("national") democrats. In the interwar years,

---

Intellectuals and the Crisis of Politics in the Interwar Period and Beyond. Balázs Trencsényi, Oxford University Press.
© Balázs Trencsényi (2025). DOI: 10.1093/9780198929512.003.0006

critics of the liberal democratic framework would also opt for setting democracy and liberalism directly against each other, advocating an illiberal democracy or an anti-democratic liberalism as a way out of the crisis of the political system.

The discourse of the crisis of liberalism that became prevalent after 1918 also entailed the disintegration of liberal nationalism, which, at the turn of the century, was still dominant in several political contexts. Some of its representatives became increasingly nationalistic and opted out of the liberal framework altogether, while others turned against what they perceived as an increasingly reactionary nationalism and came closer to a broadly conceived socialist position. In most contexts this amounted to the fragmentation of the liberal camp and the appearance of incompatible and often openly clashing liberal positions. This is memorably captured by Michael Freeden in view of the British context of the 1920s. Freeden wrote of "hairline cracks widened into rifts that would not heal" and the emergence of "liberalisms that could not be reduced to liberalism."[5] Going beyond the cleavage Freeden identified in the British case between the "progressive" (left and center) and "libertarian" streams, one could also point to a division between economic, cultural, and political liberalisms. It is then possible to denote positions which were, for instance, culturally liberal/progressive but economically anti-liberal, or economically liberal, but politically authoritarian and even ethno-nationalist.

Decline, Collapse, or Reconfiguration?

With the rise of mass politics and thus mass parties (social democrats, Christian socialists, and various sorts of nationalists) one could observe the weakening of liberal parties already before 1918 in many European contexts, from France to Sweden and Austria. There were cases, however, where the liberal political representation remained powerful, as in Britain, parts of Southeastern Europe (Romania and Greece), and to a certain extent Italy, where, during the First World War, the country's engagement on the side of the Entente was spearheaded by forces configured around the national liberal ideological pole. However, in these cases the liberal ideological component also gradually lost ground due to a growing polarization of the political sphere.

An important factor undermining the plausibility of liberalism was the breakdown of the evolutionary perception of history, which implied the abandonment of relative optimism about self-correcting mechanisms in society and culture.[6] If there was no guarantee for gradual progress, signs of disorder were not merely temporary setbacks but could be symptoms of an impending catastrophe and total disintegration, but also radical and unexpected leaps forward. This also triggered a competition of structurally often similar but politically incompatible futural projections, announcing a radical break with the recent past. Jörn Leonhard described this as *Utopienkonkurrenz* in the context of the final phase of the First World War.[7] In political terms, some of these projections, like Wilsonism, could remain within the liberal ideological framework, while others like Leninism and fascism were emphatically anti-liberal.

118   Intellectuals and the Crisis of Politics

In socioeconomic terms, this could be framed as the contrast of "regular" and "irregular" crises; while in sociocultural terms, as the breakthrough of an unprecedented social organization—mass society—which changed the rules of human existence and created a fundamentally new anthropological type ("mass man"). The Great Depression and its concomitant economic, social, and political phenomena of disintegration provided ample evidence for this vision of an "irregular" crisis, demonstrating that the conventional imagery of gradual human progress was inadequate.

The weakening of liberal political forces did not mean an immediate and total defeat. In fact, in the context of the economic and political stabilization around 1924 (most spectacularly in Germany, but there were several other stabilization programs implemented all over Europe) there was also a short period of liberal revival, although it is telling that the classical liberal formations were unable to regain their prewar position, not only in Germany but also in Great Britain. Gustav Stresemann's German People's Party and the left-liberal German Democratic Party, the two main pre-war liberal formations (in the 1912 Reichstag elections they received 25.4%), oscillated between 22.2% (1920) and 13.5% (1928), falling to 8.3% in 1930, and sinking to total insignificance by 1932. In the United Kingdom, votes for the Liberals rose from 13% in 1918 to 18.9% in 1922, but this was well below the landslide 48.9% of 1906. In 1923, they even reached 29.7%, but by 1924 they fell back to 17.8%, plummeting to 6.5% in 1931.[8]

During the late 1920s, precipitated by the devastating social consequences of the Great Depression but also due to the convergence of other, more local processes (e.g., the radicalization of national conflicts in Yugoslavia and Poland), liberal political forces and ideological positions were further weakened. It is telling that by 1934 almost the whole of East Central Europe was ruled by more or less autocratic governments (Hungary, Poland, the Baltic states, Yugoslavia, Bulgaria, Romania), as well as Italy, Austria, Portugal and arguably also Ireland (a "hybrid regime," mixing formal parliamentary democracy and Catholic authoritarianism). The only contrary example was the restoration of parliamentarism in Spain in 1931, which however did not result in a stable democratic system but catalyzed an ongoing internal strife eventually turning into a civil war.

In this context, the "crisis of liberalism" served as a key ideological trope for the intellectual supporters of the authoritarian and fascist takeovers. A case in point is the work by Eberhard Kautter (1890–after 1949?) on the "world crisis of liberalism," published in 1933 right after the Nazi capture of power.[9] A key figure of the *Bund Wiking*, a paramilitary organization led by Hermann Ehrhardt, who in turn competed with Hitler for the leadership of the German extreme right in the 1920s, Kautter refashioned himself just in time as an ideological supporter of the Nazis (demonstrating his allegiance by dedicating his book to Hitler). His offer was accepted, and, during the war, he was even tasked by Alfred Rosenberg to turn the International Institute of Social History into a Nazi think-tank in occupied Amsterdam.[10]

Unsurprisingly, for this seasoned extreme rightist, liberalism was the main culprit and the root cause of the *Totalkrise*, which affected religion, culture, politics, and economy alike. While he registered the economic and sociopolitical features of the unfolding crisis, his argument was that these were surface-level appearances, whereas the real causes were biological and cultural. He drew on Oswald Spengler to depict a cyclical image of history with recurrent transitional periods of disintegration caused by mismatches between the racial and spiritual basis of a given period. In the concrete German case, he argued that the crisis was ultimately due to the clash between the universalist precepts of Christianity and the inherent particularism of the *Volkstum* (ethnic character) which defined the social and political actions of a given community. In his rendering, the way out of this impasse was the regeneration of the national spirit, which implied the nationalizaton of religion. This had already started during the Reformation, which broke the link to Rome and laid the foundations of a "national Church." To Kautter, however, the import of liberalism in the early nineteenth century derailed this development toward spiritual autarchy and pushed back the German Soul toward a futile universalist aspiration, while also undermining the authority of the state. Further, modern liberalism catalyzed the rise of the "late capitalist" economy, based on international trade, cartelization, economic imperialism, forced industrialization, mechanization, and the destruction of indigenous agrarian production. All this made human work superfluous, triggering unemployment and the concomitant sharpening of internal social and external political conflicts.

Kautter thus announced a conclusive break with liberalism and the creation of an alternative socioeconomic order rooted in the spirituality of the *Volk*. He pointed to Italian fascist and some elements of Stalinist crisis management as examples to follow, although he categorically rejected the Soviet model as "state capitalist imperialism" and described both Italian fascism and Soviet communism as representing the terminal phase of liberal individualism rather than a way to overcome it.

For Germany, Kautter's "healing principle"[11] entailed the reintegration of racial and spiritual elements, together with new economic and social policies. As the bulk of his book was still written before 1933, the author was hardly able to fathom the immense possibilities of violent state intervention that the National Socialist regime would soon have at its disposal to transform society. Thus, his practical suggestions were still relatively timid, but the direction was obvious, following the logic of the Conservative Revolution: relying on the power of the modern state to restore organic social structures destroyed by political modernity. Rejecting the half-hearted protectionism practiced by the Weimar governments, which focused on certain sectors of the economy, Kautter advocated a selective support scheme for companies that fit his racial and spiritual criteria of eligibility. This could result in pushing down the price level; stabilizing the living standard of the population; resuscitating agriculture with the policy of new settlements; eliminating urban unemployment; and finally, reintegrating the rural and proletarian spheres by supporting workers to maintain an agricultural household.

The entanglement of the economic slump with political and institutional disturbances also prompted authors from East Central Europe to theorize on the crisis of liberalism. Mihail Manoilescu (1891–1950), the prominent economist and representative of the Romanian neoliberal stream of the early 1920s, sought to offer an alternative reading of the crisis from the perspective of the European periphery.[12]

While he started with the sobering statement that "concerning the world crisis, every-thing has already been said,"[13] he also sought to contribute his own ideas to the discussion, focusing on the difference of the crisis symptoms in industrial and agri-cultural countries. He stressed that the agrarian/industrial cleavage was still central to the European economy, as agrarian products provided a basis on which industrial countries were able to develop their trade and industry. At the same time, statis-tics indicated that industrial countries mostly traded with each other, and economic growth led to proportionally more export and import activities. Therefore, in the long run, it would have been the interest of the industrial countries not to hinder the indus-trialization of their agrarian peers, as the growth of productivity and income levels in these countries also created new markets for the industries of the most developed Western countries. In the short run, however, the loss of the industrial monopoly of the West could also lead to more competition due to the cheaper labor costs of the non-Western societies, and thus could result in the relative fall of the Western living standard.

Consequently, for Manoilescu, the growth of state interventionism and sheltered industrialization was a reaction to the growing imbalance between industrial and agrarian countries (which amounted to an "invisible exploitation").[14] In contrast to liberal critiques, for him, étatism was not the cause of the economic crisis but more of a reaction and a necessary instrument of crisis management. Manoilescu rejected the Smithian/Ricardian idea of comparative advantage and argued that if the productiv-ity of an industrial worker was ten or even twenty times higher than that of a peasant, by sticking to the idea of complementarity, agrarian countries would have been con-demned to keep reproducing their backwardness.[15] Along these lines, asserting that Western economic growth was rooted in the exploitation of non-industrial countries, he deemed it hypocritical to claim that differences in the global distribution of wealth were due to hard work and local innovation.

As economic growth required expansion to new markets, agrarian countries, who kept buying most of the industrial products from abroad without being able to pro-duce their own industrial goods, had increasingly unfavorable trade balances. Hence, they were pushed to control their external commerce to avoid the depreciation of their currency. As the agricultural price scissors were opening further with the con-tinuous fall of agrarian prices, the only way for these countries to survive was to cut imports and gradually create branches of local industry. In this situation pro-tectionism was fully reasonable even if on the surface it seemed counter-productive by comparing only the relatively higher local costs to the lower prices on the interna-tional markets. Manoilescu argued that even mining at relatively higher production costs was more profitable for the national economy than sending the miners back to the agrarian sector and buying coal from abroad.

From this perspective, Manoilescu criticized those liberal experts who saw the reopening of global free trade as the only viable solution to overcome the crisis; this was rather an exercise in defending the superordinate economic positions of their highly developed Western industrial societies. He could only accept the removal of tariffs if it went together with the closing of the agricultural scissors, which required a substantial drop in industrial prices. Rather than global free trade, he considered regional barter agreements that also extended to tariff rates as the only way forward.

In his passionate and subversive attack against Western economic dominance, Manoilescu went so far as to stress that, with the expansion of social legislation, the class inequalities detected by Marx could be gradually reduced, but the inequality between nations kept growing. It was the task of a new ideology of emancipation, a "socialism of nations," to achieve a global balance.[16] In the early 1930s, this program was still formulated more as a theoretical construct from the perspective of a scholar offering economic analysis and policy recommendations. But very soon Manoilescu turned in an openly political direction, entering the chaotic Romanian power struggle between King Carol II returning from exile, the traditional party structures, and the emerging radical right (exemplified by the Iron Guard). Along these lines, the "socialism of nations" could be reframed as "national socialism," and Manoilescu eventually became a key figure in Romanian politics in the early 1940s, tying his country's destiny to that of the Axis Powers.

While the political, cultural, and economic manifestations of liberalism in Germany, Italy, and most of East Central Europe became principal targets for autocratic regimes, on the European level both economic and cultural liberalism continued to have some influence and in the 1930s also showed a certain resilience in the face of the totalitarian threat. Reflecting on these new conditions, liberals formulated a sharp critique of planned economy, collectivism, and the total state, both on the left and on the right. Indeed, some of the genealogically non-liberal interwar political formations assumed more or less liberal agendas, such as the French Radicals, Czech Masarykians, some intellectuals around the British Labour Party, Central European social democrats, and even some Catholics inspired by Personalism.

However, this does not mean that those who opted for liberalism were uncritical. Importantly, the crisis of liberalism was diagnosed not only from anti-liberal perspectives but was reflected upon also within these liberal or crypto-liberal formations. Crisis could serve as a central notion of the liberals themselves, who relied on this trope to propose an upgraded version of their doctrine, seeking to heal the wounds caused by the étatist/collectivist/authoritarian "deviations" that were becoming especially prevalent from the late 1920s onward.[17] The different neoliberal projects of the early and mid-1930s centered on the concept of crisis and offered themselves as a remedy.[18] By contrast, political liberals who broke with the classical liberal economic doctrine and argued for planning also legitimized their position with the help of the crisis discourse.

The discussion on the crisis of liberalism was thus especially complex and was intertwined with crisis discourses formulated in the context of other cultural and political spheres, from philosophy to religion, national integration, and international cooperation. One might argue that the discourse of the crisis of liberalism functioned as an ideological glue weaving together the sectoral crisis discourses, and often culminating in a vision of "total crisis." Consequently, in this chapter, the discourse of the crisis of liberalism connects radical anti-liberal ideological positions with attempts to revive liberalism in the new and highly challenging conditions. Rather than being

122 Intellectuals and the Crisis of Politics

totally incompatible, this was often an osmotic relationship with many possible transitional positions between these two opposing poles. At the same time, the emerging discourse of "total crisis" was frontally opposed to liberal democracy, rejecting all components of political modernity as part and parcel of the same pathology, and this ultimately draws a line between the liberal and anti-liberal conceptions.

Anti-Liberal Entanglements: Fascist and Anti-Fascist Conceptualizations of Crisis

The radicalization of politics in the immediate postwar period saw the emergence of left- and right-wing streams of thought that had many common features, such as the contrast of "formal" and "real" democracy, and the claim that liberalism was the ideology of the nineteenth century and had nothing to offer for the new situation after the Great War. This in turn did not mean that certain elements of liberalism were not integrated into these new political-ideological streams, as for instance anti-democratic radical nationalism could also go together with economic liberalism.

The Italian context of the early 1920s is interesting in many ways, both in view of the similarities of the radical leftist and rightist discourses of the crisis of liberalism, but also because at the same time both directions could position themselves as the realization rather than the negation of some key liberal principles. For the radical left, Adriano Tilgher's *La crisi mondiale* from 1921 is one of the most paradigmatic texts focusing on the global crisis, describing it as the direct consequence of imperialism and the growth of social inequalities.[19] Tilgher came from an Italian–German mixed family background and was strongly critical of the pro-Entente involvement of his country during the war. His articles, written during the peace talks and in the context of postwar social and political storms, sought to challenge the prevalent nationalist interpretation of the situation and offer an alternative leftist internationalist reading, transforming the "great war of nations" into a class struggle of global dimensions.[20] With reference to George Bernard Shaw and Karl Kautsky, he rejected the common narrative of German aggression, describing it as a "myth" and offered an alternative rendering, focusing on the establishment of British hegemony over Europe, which sought to turn it into an "Anglo-Saxon colony." In an article from 1919, Tilgher went so far as to talk of "Finis Europae."[21] He added that the Wilsonian principles were ignored by the peacemakers, who relied on Machiavellianism instead, that is, a state-centered *Realpolitik* and the deification of the nation-state.

From this perspective (in line with the summary opinion of the Comintern at this point) the new polities created by the Versailles peace system (such as Yugoslavia) were "bourgeois and nationalist buffer states," while the Wilsonian program of protecting small nations became an instrument of the bourgeois great powers. The ensuing global dominance of the United States, Great Britain, and France was depicted by Tilgher in apocalyptic terms as the rise of the "New Leviathan." In contrast, he called for a "peace of the peoples" (*pace dei popoli*), overcoming the international "war of all against all." In the struggle to subvert the postwar order, Tilgher counted on a merger of the nationalism of the losers of the post-First World War peace system (especially the "proletarianized" nations: Germany, Russia, Japan, and Italy); the anti-colonial movements in India, China, and the Muslim world; and the proletarian internationalism of the socialists, pointing conspicuously to Spartacus as a common symbol of resistance. Tilgher advocated the idea of a "socialist Europe," which was meant to be a federal framework of socialist nations, resonating with the declared emancipatory line of Leninist nationality politics.

However, in Tilgher's understanding, the imminent conflict between revolutionary and reactionary forces was potentially destructive to the extreme. Any national clash in the era of total war could result in the breakthrough of barbarism. This merger of class war and civilizational conflict pushed Tilgher beyond the conventional narratives of socialist world revolution that promised the smooth victory of the proletariat. In his interpretation the global crisis was due to the human intellect's inability to control dark instincts and thus, rather than achieving universal harmony, humankind came close to destroying itself.[22] Nevertheless, as a socialist Tilgher still had a modicum of optimism, rooted not so much in the traditional vision of linear progress, but rather in a Marxist reinterpretation of the cyclical view of the history of civilizations, that is, hoping that the impending "second Middle Ages" would be followed by a "new Renaissance."

For Tilgher, the other side of the global crisis concerned the interplay of the moral and socioeconomic elements of the bourgeois civilization. While the Marxist theory of crisis focused on overproduction and impoverishment, in the postwar period it was the other way round: consumption capacity was growing, but production fell, which triggered inflation. The moral ideal of classical capitalism was work for work's sake, without a clear moment of satisfaction, but after the war work was subordinated to the search for fulfillment. These contradictions gradually undermined the existing order, resulting in a comprehensive crisis of values and institutions: "what is built for centuries now collapses like a building with its fundament being washed away."[23] It is symptomatic of the entanglement of leftist and rightist intellectual resources that Fichte, who also served a major point of orientation for the conservative revolutionaries seeking to destroy the "hypocritical" bourgeois system, was in this analysis a key reference.

Tilgher himself noted the similarities between leftist and rightist radicalism, arguing that the depth of the crisis in the Italian case was indicated by the very confusion of anti-systemic forces. But, for him, obviously, the resolution of the crisis was only possible by making a choice between *conservazione* and *rivoluzione*. Since liberalism was fundamentally rooted in capitalism, he saw no possible compromise with the liberal political forces. With reference to the Italian situation, he asserted that liberals were slipping toward imperialism, giving up their traditionally virulent anticlericalism and eventually becoming part and parcel of the "reactionary camp."

Tilgher linked this transformation to the formative experience of the petty bourgeoisie, losing most of its material and symbolic status during the World War. While not negating that the anti-systemic radicalism of this social stratum was still ideologically diffuse, with possible leftist and rightist directions, he asserted that the only consequently revolutionary class was the proletariat, characterized by an anti-historic, mythical, and apocalyptic mentality. However, the proletariat was also not immune to disorientation, as they lacked a clear picture of a new order to replace the bourgeois system, as if they were "walking in the Egyptian desert" without having any idea of their "Canaan." For some time, Tilgher toyed with the idea of an alliance of the proletariat with the radicalized petty bourgeoisie, bringing together the class struggle of the former with the organizational skills of the latter. However, by 1921, he became convinced that, with the rise of fascism it was precisely an alliance of high and petty bourgeoisie that was forming against the proletariat, even if their economic interests remained somewhat contradictory. Along these lines, he interpreted fascism as a merger of liberal, imperialist, and conservative elements.

The early fascist discourse of crisis displayed several similarities with this analysis even if the political conclusions drawn were diametrically opposed. The similarity was not merely structural but obviously also genealogical, given the ideological trajectory of Benito Mussolini and many of his early followers. It is thus less surprising than it first seems that Tilgher wrote his most influential study on Luigi Pirandello, who openly—though not unreservedly—supported Mussolini, while the younger brother of Antonio Gramsci, Mario, was a prominent fascist activist in Lombardy.

In the early postwar situation, Mussolini employed the concept of crisis to draw a symbolic dividing line between the traditional political elite and the "Italian people," stressing that the war was won by the people and not by the elites.[24] This anti-bourgeois sentiment remained part and parcel of the fascist ideological framework, even though various authors put their emphases differently. In these early texts, the discourse of crisis was used by Mussolini and his comrades to legitimize fascism as reaction to Italy's political and spiritual breakdown. Thus, in his diary entries from 1922, Italo Balbo (1896–1940)—who was close to the blackshirts and rejected parliamentary politics—pointed to the fascist takeover as the only way out of the political crisis.[25]

At the same time, some of these ideologists also talked of the "crisis of fascism" in the sense of reaching a turning point of its evolution, especially after the short-lived Pact of Pacification that Mussolini signed with the socialist leadership in August 1921. This duality is present in the work of essayist and sociologist Camillo Pellizzi (1896–1979), who argued that the "general crisis" helped the fascists to take power, while the Italian "internal crisis" was caused by the Pact of Pacification.[26] The Pact led to a clash between the rural *squadristi*, who considered the socialists as their main enemies, and Mussolini, who at that point still argued for a common anti-liberal front based on syndicalist principles.

Crisis thus became a central notion in the competing narratives of the essence of fascism. Dino Grandi (1895–1988), a representative of the radical stream in Mussolini's inner circle, sought to create a metahistorical narrative of the rise of the movement. He linked humanism, the *Risorgimento*, and fascism into a historical chain and pointed to the "spiritual crisis" before the Great War as the catalyst of the fascist idea, combining elements of modernism, syndicalism, and nationalism. By contrast, the main enemies of fascism in his reading were clericalism, liberalism, and socialism.

The idiosyncratic radical writer Curzio Malaparte (Kurt Erich Suckert, 1898–1957) created a wholly different genealogy.[27] For him, fascism was a revolt against the bourgeoisie, in terms of rejecting modernity, civility, and rhetoric. He turned to the Counter-Reformation as a model, comparing Mussolini to Ignatius Loyola, the founder of the Jesuits. Rather than the humanists or Giuseppe Mazzini (the Risorgimento activist), the Italian tradition Malaparte assumed (or tried to reinvent) linked classical antiquity, anti-liberalism, and anti-Europeanism. Along these lines, he drew a parallel between the Bolshevik and fascist anti-modern revolts, both of which were directed against a Europe dominated by the Nordic, Protestant, and Anglo-Saxon nations.

While the fascist crisis discourse, especially in the early years, tended to bring together some elements of the leftist and rightist ideological references on a common anti-liberal platform, there were also contrary interpretations, trying to steer fascism toward an alliance with the bourgeoisie. Journalist Massimo Rocca (1884–1973) was originally an anarchist who became a collaborator of Mussolini's during the Great War. In 1921, Rocca supported the Pact of Pacification and framed his position in terms of a crisis discourse, stressing that the internal debate between moderates and radicals on strategy was a "natural crisis of growth."[28] Rocca tried to harmonize liberalism and fascism and talked of fascism as a possible "Italian neoliberalism." Along these lines, he contrasted liberalism to democracy and argued that the former could be integrated into the new regime while the real enemies were the "collectivist" movements. This position clashed with the radicalism of the *squadristi* but was also an ambiguous defense of Mussolini's pact with the socialists. In Rocca's vision, fascism was a response to the postwar crisis of state and society, a continuation of national liberalism "by other means."

In this transitional moment, even Mussolini toyed with quasi-neoliberal ideas while he was moving away from his previous syndicalist position. Thus, in his 1922 Udine speech he castigated both socialist étatism and "liberal impotence," putting forward a program of a new state disentangled from various group interests (e.g., railway workers, postmen). Liberated from such particularisms, which also undermined its financial sustainability, this new state had to focus on its fundamental functions of policing, educating, and defending the nation.[29]

The discussion on crisis heated up again after Giacomo Matteotti was murdered on June 10, 1924. For many friends and foes alike, this was when the fascist regime seemed to have crossed a red line. The "revisionists" around the journal *Critica fascista*, like Rocca or Giuseppe Bottai, interpreted crisis as a moment of decision between further radicalization or consolidation. Predictably, Rocca argued for the second option: since the fascists had already claimed power, the task was now to organize the government competently and not to perpetuate revolutionary violence.[30] The shift from movement to regime, however, could not mean a return to liberal democracy of any sorts, as fascism was not a political faction but the politically active nation itself.[31]

After 1925, with the further reinforcement of the systemic features of fascism, the language of crisis gradually disappeared from fascist political discourse, or appeared there only in retrospect, explaining and legitimizing the rise of the movement, for example, Giovanni Gentile's (1875–1944) authoritative 1927 synthesis *Origini e dottrina del fascismo*. For the representative idealist philosopher of the regime, the Great War was not the cause, but more the culmination, of a profound spiritual crisis already mounting at the turn of the century. Gentile pointed to the *Risorgimento* as a model and Mazzini as the key figure who brought together thinking (*pensiero*) and action (*azione*), contrasted with subsequent generations of intellectuals (*literati*) who separated these spheres again.[32] Along the lines of the Hegelian tradition, describing the present in terms of a synthesis of contrary elements, Gentile also rejected the idea that fascism was merely anti-democratic and/or anti-liberal and argued instead for conceiving of it as the *Aufhebung* of bourgeois democracy and of liberalism, realizing substantial liberty in a more complete form than its liberal abstraction ever did.

The claim that Italian fascism emerged as a successful response to the political and spiritual crisis of the turn of the century thus made it hard to conceptualize crisis during the Great Depression. Writing in 1931, Delio Cantimori (1904–1966), the young fascist intellectual and future academic fellow traveler of the communists after 1945, talked of the "Italian crisis" in the past tense. He contrasted the period marked by the rise of fascism between 1919 and 1922 to the raging European crisis erupting in 1929.[33] This retrospective gaze did not imply that Cantimori proposed a conservative model; on the contrary, he tried to challenge the equation between reaction and fascism, negating that fascism was anti-modern (in the sense of passéism) or reactionary nationalism (in the style of the French royalists). Fascism was not a new type of restoration, but a new type of revolution and, in this sense, Cantimori found certain parallel traits with communism as both ideologies fought against the "old world." What made fascism distinctive was the corporatist solution that created a synthesis between collectivism and private property, thus offering a remedy to the all-European socioeconomic crisis.

A similar argument was put forward by Nello Quillici (1890–1940), a journalist and close collaborator of Balbo (who was on board when the fascist leader's plane was shot down). He argued that fascism itself was a response to the crisis of Italian history and consequently it offered an example of successful crisis management to the world with its programs of public work, organized industry, and state investment.[34] Tellingly, he felt the need to add that to a certain extent the Soviet Union could also boast of a similar resilience.

Indeed, as the Great Depression deepened globally, Italian fascist voices kept asserting that they lived under an ideal regime defying the crisis symptoms. Mussolini's own interpretation was that the loss of the dynamism of capitalism and the shift to monopolism culminated in the crisis of the liberal capitalist system worldwide. While this reading resonated with the contemporary Marxist (and Stalinist) conceptions of crisis, the remedies he proposed were naturally different: mixed economy, reinforced agriculture, and corporatism. Describing both capitalism and international socialism as equally crisis-ridden, Mussolini saw only one solution, creating a new synthesis between individualism and collectivism: fascism.[35]

Offering a more philosophical take in positioning fascism ideologically, Pellizzi—who lived in London during the 1920s and 1930s as a journalist and cultural representative of the regime, rubbing shoulders with like-minded British intellectuals such as Ezra Pound—talked of crisis not as a passing socioeconomic condition but as a "form of civilization."[36] He drew on the neo-Hegelian stream *à la* Gentile, depicting fascism as a synthesis of liberty and collectivism (contrasted to "one-sidedly collectivist" communism and "one-sidedly individualist" bourgeois liberalism). From this perspective, the erupting world crisis was a test of "our revolution" and an opportunity to universalize the Italian experience (convinced of the uniqueness of the "Italian synthesis," Pellizzi labeled Hitler a primitive "*squadrista*").

Crisis would resurface again as an element of the fascist discourse in the early 1940s toward the very end of the regime. Here it served as a platform for an intra-systemic critical position, drawing on the conceptual link between critique and crisis. Thus, looking back on his journal *Critica Fascista*, Giuseppe Bottai's essay on "twenty years of fascist criticism" described fascism as a sort of permanent revolution (with a penchant for destruction and reconstruction as well), set in motion by the original insurrection against bourgeois liberalism, but always facing new challenges that necessitated an avid "fascist criticism."[37] Bottai also argued that it was not fascism that was in crisis, but rather that fascism synthesized "the crisis of the whole Italian life." Crisis was thus not equal to decline, but instead was a ferment that created new and future-oriented historical forms.

While Bottai voted against Mussolini in 1943 and subsequently had to escape Italy (ending up in the ranks of the French Foreign Legion), supporters of the Italian Social Republic (who claimed to represent the true uncompromising spirit of fascism) also framed the split in the movement as a crisis, but with a different political agenda. Thus, in 1944, propagandist Bruno Stampanato wrote about the crisis of the fascist system in terms of the clash between "conformism" and activism and sought to reactivate the revolutionary potential of fascism against the ruling classes as a solution.[38] Likewise, corporatist theoretician and prominent politician of the Italian Social Republic Angelo Tarchi (1897–1974) stressed that it was a mistake to identify the fascist cause with that of the bourgeoisie, as the fascist revolution was essentially anti-bourgeois. Forming the policies of the reconstructed state based on this anti-bourgeois program could offer a solution to the internal cleavages ravaging the fascist movement: "The recognition of a past error could make a crisis . . . beneficial and productive."[39]

In many ways mirroring the fascist discourse, in the Italian liberal anti-fascist narrative crisis was also a keyword, but less loaded than in the radical leftist and rightist contexts. In his 1943 lectures on the history of the fascist movement, delivered in the United States, prominent Italian émigré Gaetano Salvemini (1873–1957) used "crisis" recurrently, but this was rooted precisely in the author's intention to delimit it conceptually.[40] In "The Crisis of the Postwar Period," his chapter on the rise of fascism, Salvemini argued that at the end of the war there was no fatal crisis, no

128 Intellectuals and the Crisis of Politics

real collapse of the economy, but rather a protracted and contradictory process of recovery. What he considered more fateful was the incomplete democratic transformation of Italy in the nineteenth century. Following Guglielmo Ferrero, Salvemini described the Italian pre-fascist system as a transitional form between absolutism and democracy that could well be characterized as an oligarchy. Coming from the radical left, Mussolini could rely on broader anti-systemic emotions, but successfully turned the language of class struggle into a national direction, pitting the Italian "proletarian nation" against the global hegemony of Western imperialist powers. Thus, from Salvemini's perspective, rather than being a response to the crisis, fascism was generating it, using existing tensions and disfunctions within the system to overhaul it completely.

Neoliberals Before Neoliberalism?

The crisis of liberalism was announced from various leftist and rightist political positions in the interwar years, but there were also remarkable intellectual efforts to turn this crisis into the starting point of a regeneration. Those who sought to reposition liberalism as a future-oriented doctrine often focused on the devastating effects of anti-liberal ideologies and regimes.[41] The logic of this argument was to admit that there was indeed a profound political and economic crisis; however, it was not caused by liberalism, but rather by the collectivist ideologies that claimed to offer a remedy to its actual or imagined deficiencies. Thus, instead of its total abandonment, it was the *renewal* of liberalism that could overcome the general crisis.

A foundational text to which many later authors reverted for arguments was Ludwig von Mises's (1881–1973) polemic book, *Socialism: An Economic and Sociological Analysis* (1922), written in the context of the postwar debates on protectionism and social rights in Austria. Its English translation, published in 1936, appeared in a very different context, namely at the peak of the confrontation of liberal and totalitarian visions of state and economy.[42] Mises argued that the purported socialist reorganization of society was unrealizable as it implied a return to self-sufficiency, while capitalism was rooted in the division of labor, which catalyzed socioeconomic progress. There was no way out of interdependence as more advanced social forms necessarily erased the more backward ones. For Mises, interdependence did not imply collectivism. Rather, the basis of every society was the individual and it was erroneous to talk of collective action in the terms that became fashionable both on the right (using the terminology of mass psychology) and on the left (relying on Marxist class theory). Further, the precondition of higher-level social and economic activity was the existence of private property. Hence, it was exactly ideologies that rejected private property that had triggered the crisis and undermined the whole edifice of human civilization.

Mises also suggested that the crisis of civilization occurred not so much because of socioeconomic processes per se, but because of the influence of ideas. Hence, he argued for the necessity of an ideological counterstrike to convince the population of the perniciousness of collectivist ideologies and their systems of social organization. Thus, in the conclusion of his book, he eloquently called all his readers to join the raging intellectual battles of their times and help regain the ideological hegemony of liberalism, which was the only guarantee of ever overcoming the crisis.

The agenda of renewing liberalism to respond to the challenges posed by the socioeconomic and political transformations brought about by the Great War and its aftermath was shared by political thinkers across the continent. One of the most interesting discussions took place in Romania, where one can also find the neologism of "neoliberal" well before it was launched as a self-descriptive notion at the 1938 Walter Lippmann Colloquium. Thus, remarkably, the conceptual link of neoliberalism and crisis preceded the outbreak of the Great Depression.

A protagonist of the Romanian discussion was the above-mentioned Mihail Manoilescu, who already called for an "ideological rebirth" of liberalism "after the crisis"—in 1922.[43] In order to face this challenge of adjustment to new conditions, it was necessary to define the "core of liberalism," which in Manoilescu's opinion was found in the principle that "every human being was an end in itself." From this perspective, the main aim of liberalism was not general happiness but general liberty, and Manoilescu also rejected the connection of liberalism to any normative vision of historical evolution comparable to the Marxist doctrine.

For Manoilescu, the central conflict of his time was the clash of liberty and equality, pitting liberalism and socialism against each other.[44] In this sense, his position was similar to that of the Austrian thinkers around Mises, even if he put more emphasis on economic interventionism already in his early post-1918 work. For him too, the crisis of liberalism consisted in the seemingly unstoppable growth of state influence. Referring to the German conservative liberal sociologist Leopold von Wiese, Manoilescu argued that the collapse of "old liberalism" was due to its inadequate answer to the problem of power. In his reading, it was the emergence of monopolies, limiting the free competition, that was chiefly responsible for the unfolding crisis. Along these lines, he contrasted "true democracy," where the preferences of the members of society prevail, to "deviant democracy," where the state is captured by some social groups (cartels on the side of employers, trade unions on the side of employees).

The way out of the crisis was to rethink the liberal doctrine from a neoliberal perspective, preserving what was essential and getting rid of what was accidental. Manoilescu even considered some elements of corporatism compatible with liberalism in the sense that it helped to avoid class struggle by mediating between different classes and preventing the expropriation of the state by a given class. At the same time, Manoilescu also criticized the hypocrisy of "old liberalism," which saw only individuals and rejected the realities of class. Along these lines, he asserted that the state needed to intervene beyond providing just the framework for market competition, first and foremost by balancing the unequal competition of strong and weak parties.

Neoliberalism in this sense entailed the harmonization of individual liberty and state intervention to make life supportable for as many individuals as possible. As a model, Manoilescu pointed to the British political scene with the convergence of Labour and the Liberals. He thus considered neoliberalism also compatible with some elements of socialism. However, it was not meant as a middle way between liberalism and socialism, but rather the program of achieving the original aims of liberalism "with other means." For instance, from his perspective, private property was a key expression of human liberty and a catalyst of development but was not untouchable. An "intelligent fiscal intervention" could correct the exaggerations of the free play of capitalism which would otherwise result in the extreme polarization of society. Seeking to create a more equitable and productive competitive environment, Manoilescu also favored measures like the introduction of progressive taxation.

There was yet another sphere where Manoilescu felt the need for state intervention, criticizing the alleged neutrality of "old liberalism" regarding the national question. Neoliberalism sought to realize the liberal agenda in a new context, where individual liberty had to be harmonized with national liberty. While in the early 1920s Manoilescu stressed the importance of integrating national minorities, there was also an obvious niche for a more nationalist rendering of neoliberalism. This can be seen in the writings of the other key ideologist of Romanian neoliberalism, Ştefan Zeletin (originally Motăş, 1882–1934).[45] In his 1927 book *Neoliberalism*, Zeletin tried to harmonize national integration and market liberalism, creating a historical argument asserting that in the nineteenth century liberalism was an ideology of "catching up" cultivated by the peripheral elites in Eastern and Southern Europe who sought to enter the global economic system. In the 1929 revised edition, Zeletin added further texts that focused on questions of centralization, interventionism, and developmental policies.

Referring explicitly to English "new liberals" like Hobson, Zeletin stressed that his conception of neoliberalism emerged out of the crisis of "old liberalism" and that its key feature was the support of certain types of intervention and a striving to harmonize the interests of different socioeconomic actors. This crisis had deeper roots than the individual mistakes and moral debasement of the political elite, which was often blamed for the inadequacy of the Romanian political system by leftist and rightist critics alike. Zeletin argued instead for a more encompassing framework of the evolution of capitalism, taken mainly from German economic sociologist Werner Sombart (1863–1941), who argued that capitalism always started from external human and capital resources, but gradually transitioned to the next phase characterized by the nationalization of the bourgeoisie and the indigenization of capital. Zeletin linked neoliberalism to this envisioned new developmental phase, which he also described as "financial imperialism." Remarkably, in his understanding this also entailed the realization of the socialist program in the sense of "taming" the social effects of capitalism.

In Zeletin's model, crisis was the transitional moment between two socioeconomic and ideological configurations, characterized by disorientation and contention but eventually resulting in the emergence of a new formation at a higher developmental level. Tellingly, in 1929, he still considered Great Britain more crisis-ridden than Germany and argued that it was precisely the resilience of the previous, but already superseded, model that made British society less adaptable to new challenges. In the

Romanian context, he described the 1923 Constitution as a neoliberal response to the postwar economic and political crisis, mediating between the principles of individual liberty and state intervention. But this was not merely a socioeconomic issue. For Zeletin, as well as for Manoilescu—steeped in the problems of the newly created Greater Romania, which included large territories of the defunct Romanov and Habsburg empires with their multiethnic populations—the main task of the postwar generation was to find a viable combination of liberalism and the imperative of nation-building.

Regarding the national ideology, Zeletin's "developmentalist" neoliberalism was clearly much more autarchic than the ideas put forward by his Austrian contemporaries, who—from the perspective of the former imperial center—pleaded for the reintegration of markets and castigated economic nationalism as a principal evil. At the same time, Zeletin also argued for opening up the economy, and thus rejected both protectionist tariffs and the global regulation of working hours and conditions, which in his opinion undermined the competitive advantage of Romania.[46] Regarding the internal Romanian political debate, his criticism commonly targeted, and also merged, the powerful conservative/organicist and leftist anti-liberal ideological traditions that had pervaded Romanian intellectual culture from the turn of the century (although national liberalism continued to dominate the Romanian party political scene well into the late 1920s).

Zeletin stressed the need to create a "national capitalism" alongside a more homogeneous middle class. From this perspective, he rejected the anti-bourgeois narodnik "deviation" in the agrarian populist stream, but at the same time, interestingly, opted for a populist party—the "People's Party" of General Alexandru Averescu—describing them as the closest to the spirit of neoliberalism, combining rural spirit and communitarian solidarity with liberal socioeconomic policies. Most of all, he praised the agrarian reforms implemented after the war by the Averescu government, which he saw as essentially neoliberal, that is, intervening into the economy with state power to create economic conditions conducive to more dynamic and competitive environment. However, he admitted that the new configuration was not resistant to crisis either, as it did not create a prosperous peasantry, and to pursue this aim he also allowed for further state intervention, for example, state guarantees on landed property.

In Zeletin's opinion, the economic crisis unfolding in the late 1920s was a transition not toward socialism or cooperativism—as in the socialist and agrarian populist perceptions—but rather toward a more advanced phase of capitalism. To manage this transition, it was necessary to rethink democratic praxis, too. Democracy, as it came to be practiced after the Great War, put too much pressure on governments to seek popularity with the masses, making them unable to implement long-term structural reforms. In Zeletin's vision, neoliberalism allowed state intervention into the democratic process, temporarily limiting popular sovereignty to achieve a modernizing leap forward. However, as with the economy, intervention was meant to be used surgically and, after a period of transition, state power was again to be restricted, like a "tutor who completed his mission."

132 Intellectuals and the Crisis of Politics

To be sure, the stakes of the Romanian discussion did not completely overlap with the considerations of Austrian, British, American, or French authors who, in the mid-1930s, put forward an internationally visible neoliberal agenda. Zeletin's and Manoilescu's stress on the agrarian question, the problem of the ethnic heterogeneity of the middle class in Romania, or the imperative of nation-state building was clearly rather divergent from the concerns of Mises, Lippmann, or Swiss academic and diplomat William Rappard. However, other elements were not alien to the "Western" discussion: the contrast between old and new liberalisms in view of different understandings of the role of the state in creating and preserving a framework where the creative forces of capitalism can freely unfold; the criticism of socialists as profoundly antidemocratic in the sense of subordinating the state to particular class interests; and the reproach to parliamentary democracy as inflexible and instrumentalized by particularisms could all fit the "Western" terms of the emerging neoliberal paradigm. The negotiation of neoliberalism and populism was much more explicit in the East Central European discussion than in Western contexts. On the one hand, Zeletin criticized the cooperativist agrarian populists for their anti-liberal propensities and, paradoxically, also for their advocacy of international free trade. This was specific to the Romanian discussion, where national liberals by contrast argued for protective tariffs to defend the budding local industry. On the other hand, he consciously integrated populist elements into his discourse, contrasting the interests of the "common people" to the particularism of the socialist and conservative elites and even focusing on the creation of a market-oriented and ethnically autochthonous upwardly mobile peasant stratum that could be the core of the newly unified modern nation-state.

The Neoliberal "Garden of Forking Paths"

The transnational discussion on the future of liberalism experienced a dramatic twist with the advent of the "Great Depression," which for many observers validated the claim of the bankruptcy of liberal principles. For others, however, it offered a pivotal position to critically reassess the economic and political dynamic of the entire postwar era and try to "update" liberalism to be able to face these challenges. Along these lines, the concern with rethinking liberalism became central for several prominent intellectuals and experts from Poland to Great Britain. A key development in this discussion was the redescription of the concepts of democracy and popular sovereignty along the lines of a market- and consumer-oriented model. In his 1931 lecture focusing on the causes of the economic crisis, Mises sought to forcefully rebut the accusation that the anarchic nature of capitalism was to blame for the catastrophic developments.[47] He argued rather that the market was the most reliable regulator, and capitalist market economy could be understood as a democratic mechanism, where every penny spent was a vote by the "sovereign consumer."

Von Mises conceptually transferred Renan's "daily plebiscite," constitutive of the nation, to the consumer, where it was constitutive of the market economy (remarkably, in the pages of his *Omnipotent Government* from 1944, Mises would eloquently praise Renan's interpretation of nationhood and nationalism as well). The result of this "daily plebiscite" was that those entrepreneurs whose pricing and quality satisfied the consumers would prevail over those who could not achieve this in the long run. This argument was embedded in a polemic with the leftist (social democratic and communist) and rightist (radical conservative) positions, which dominated the German public sphere by the early 1930s by way of reappropriating some of their key concepts and tropes. For instance, "democracy"—defined in terms of the sovereignty of a homogeneous community—had some resonance with the Schmittian conception. Mises went so far in employing this "illiberal democratic" conceptual framework that he identified the consumer as a member of the *Volk*, that is, a *Volksgenosse*, a concept with organicist overtones used both by the left and the radical right. He contrasted this to the "pseudo-democracy" of the trade unions, where the sovereign is the worker (i.e., a member of the minority) imposing his will on the consumers, who make up the whole population.[48]

Market mechanisms forced capitalists to satisfy the needs of consumers and thus by default serve the common good. When this mechanism was disturbed, crisis symptoms appeared. Regarding the economic depression starting in 1929, Mises pointed to the over-expansion of bank credit for political reasons, which artificially catalyzed production without demand. This resulted in a self-generating panic, followed by mass withdrawal of money from the banks and frantic hoarding. Thus, the quicker the credit expansion could be stopped, the smaller the crisis would become.

Going beyond the model of cyclical upturns and downturns, Mises subscribed to the idea—shared by many other analysts of the Great Depression—of the irregularity of the ongoing crisis. He stressed that, in contrast to cyclical recessions, it was not preceded by an economic boom. Furthermore, part of the intervention that aggravated it came not from the state but from the trade unions. Regarding the unions, he argued that in a market where the income level was "natural" there could be no real unemployment. The market's self-regulating mechanism would redistribute the employees to those branches where their work could be more profitable. However, the "artificial" growth of incomes imposed by the political power of the unions generated unemployment since, in having to pay higher wages, not every enterprise could offer its products at an acceptable price level and thus chose not to engage in production at all.[49] Importantly, Mises also admitted that such a mechanism only worked under the conditions of an internationally open market, as the imbalances in any given economy would be evened out by global migration. Consequently, he also blamed trade unions for sustaining the wage difference between the United States and Europe and thus eventually generating xenophobic reactions.

Apart from the trade unions, Mises also criticized the state for subsidizing unprofitable sectors and thus eventually harming consumers (i.e., the people) to satisfy particular segments of the society. In his view, the modern state took up "too many" responsibilities and thus created expectations that it could not fulfill.[50]

From this perspective, the ongoing economic crisis could also be interpreted as a "crisis of public finances."[51] Artificially generated growth, and the proliferation of unsecured credit—not tied to any collateral—only aggravated the crisis. Along these lines, Mises criticized "third way" discourses on the left and right, arguing that the market could not be regulated by political means. To the contrary: the only solution to the crisis was to allow the market's pricing mechanism to regulate production.

His long-term vision was the gradual elimination of global economic and structural differences, and, along these lines, he advocated the industrialization of countries that were still predominantly agrarian. In this sense, his horizons of expectation were not dissimilar from those of the Romanian neoliberals, who also argued for the industrialization of agrarian countries. However, Mises rejected protectionist measures while the Romanians considered them important in the "take-off" stage of indigenous industrialization.

The young Friedrich von Hayek's (1899–1992) analysis of crisis was similar but not identical. For him, the main cause of the post-1929 economic depression was overinvestment and the creation of an artificial boom in the 1920s.[52] He rejected the interventionist policies advocated by Keynes (e.g., the reduction of interest rates to stimulate more investment, and the creation of public works and public investment programs), arguing that the crisis was best overcome by self-recovery, restoring the equilibrium that was upset during the pre-crisis over-expansion period. In his interpretation, there was an inherent logic of "rebounding"—at a certain point of the crisis the scarcity of consumer goods would trigger the extension of production, which would lead to the hiring of new workers.

Inspired by the Austrian School's critical position toward state intervention (and having a key role in hiring Hayek at the London School of Economics), prominent young British economist Lionel Robbins also developed a complex crisis narrative.[53] Referring to the Depression as the "nineteenth year of world crisis," he compared it to earlier instances of economic slumps, which he considered much less destructive. Drawing on his primary expertise, he offered a dominantly economic interpretation of the main factors of the crisis, listing the disruption of world trade; the cartelization and rigidity of the job market; the social and economic effects of postwar inflation; the excessive interest rates in England which kept gold in the country; the prevention of capital export; the overheated US economy; the inflationary extension of credit; and the general problems of the gold standard.

Seeking to fit all these components into his model of the origins of the crisis, Robbins rejected monocausal explanations and argued instead that the Depression was caused by an uncommon convergence of many factors. Rejecting monocausality did not preclude the question of agency. Robbins started his political career on the left, but gradually moved to a more critical position not only toward socialism but also more moderate state intervention, eventually falling out with Keynes during their work as advisers to the Ramsay MacDonald government on managing the Depression. Therefore, by 1934, Robbins came to describe the state and the political elites ruling the state as the primary culprits of the crisis, who opted for protective tariffs and thus unleashed a chain reaction of mutual restrictions. Similarly, he saw the decision to keep wage rates up as particularly self-destructive; in his critical interpretation of the crisis-management measures of most governments, consumption was stimulated at the expense of capital investment, sustaining a wide range of "bad business positions" created during the boom.

Going beyond the enumeration of causal factors, the principal question Robbins sought to answer was why the Depression dragged on for so long. He identified several political aspects: internal and international instability; the framework of reparations; the improbable convergence of industrial depression and the fall of agricultural prices, all of which hindered what would have otherwise been a natural healing process. Importantly, while his political message was obviously different, Robbins's book shared an important feature with the radical leftist and rightist interpretations of the economic crisis—that it sought to offer a critical vantage point to fundamentally rethink the whole period preceding it and provide a comprehensive vision of regeneration based on this analysis. At the same time, for Robbins (as well as many of his liberal and conservative colleagues) the crisis was not a symptom of the failure of capitalism, but an opportunity for economic and social self-cleansing. Instead of allowing this process to unfold, politically motivated state intervention created a contrary dynamic: "We eschew the sharp purge," he argued, and rather prefer "the lingering disease."[54] Robbins thus rejected the trade unions' suggestions to reduce working hours and production. He was indebted especially to Mises, repeating almost word by word his argument linking unemployment to the "artificial" defense of high wages.[55] The conclusion of his book about the importance of ideological battles also resonated with that of Mises: the "masses think what they are taught to think by their thinkers," and while, in the short run, ideas might seem "unimportant and ineffective . . . in the long run they . . . can rule the world."[56]

Robbins also clearly followed the Austrian School when arguing that no state agency was able to determine prices better than the market. Perhaps the most important argument he shared with Mises (central to the Austrian economist's 1932 preface to the second German edition of his *Sozialismus*) was the idea of the consumers' ballot, drawing an analogy between democratic participation and consumers' participation in market mechanisms: "Every shilling spent is a vote for a particular commodity,"[57] evaluating the quality of the products and the profitability of the production process. Furthermore, Robbins drew explicitly on Hayek when criticizing the interventionist social housing policy of "Red Vienna," which he argued was a self-destructive strategy that amassed public debt and eventually triggered economic collapse.

Like the Austrians, Robbins criticized state intervention also on the level of meddling with international financial relations. Protectionist state actors continued to treat bad and good debts together and thus hindered the process of self-cleansing. While he praised Britain for resisting inflationary pressure, at the same time Robbins held that abandoning the gold standard undermined a key instrument of free trade and precipitated the global catastrophe, reinforcing the international disequilibrium.

136 Intellectuals and the Crisis of Politics

Likewise, he was bitterly critical of Roosevelt for overruling the World Economic Conference and pushing up US agrarian prices to gain the political support of the farmers at the cost of aggravating the crisis elsewhere.

Rather than protectionist state interference in the economy, which merely delayed the change and thus made the crisis more devastating, Robbins allowed for a "surgical" state intervention in restructuring the work force, setting the self-regenerating mechanisms of the market in motion. He was convinced that the market was a majoritarian instrument that mediated the general will through the aggregation of individual activities of buying and selling. He extended the argument that protectionism eventually hit all strata of consumers and that all citizens were first and foremost consumers, even if many of them also happened to be producers—all of which were forced to pay more for local products than would have been the case on global markets. Thus, Robbins made important steps toward identifying free markets with the *volonté générale*. Market mechanisms here merged with democratic mechanisms as a place of "continuous election with proportional representation."[58]

By identifying the interests of consumers with democracy, Robbins put forward arguments that resonated with the populist contrast of "inorganic minorities" seeking to impose their will on the majority versus the sovereign and undifferentiated "people"—the natural "organic" majority community. Further, he asserted that there was an unbridgeable cleavage between the perspectives of producers and consumers. Quoting Adam Smith, he argued that producers were prone to deceive (and eventually oppress) the public. He also used some anti-elitist tropes untypical in a liberal political language. For example, he contrasted the imperative of progress to the fantasies of "dilettante economists of wealthy universities" about social legislation, which benefited some individuals but eventually hindered development.[59] It was the interests of the common people that mattered over the interests of certain groups or the conceit of some theoreticians: "it is for the millions to whom a slice of bacon more or less, or a bus ride to the sea, still matter, to make the decision."[60] Nevertheless, what made this position different from conventional populist rhetoric is its inherent globalism—while the populist contrast of organic community and inorganic minority always referred to the condition of a "permanently divided mankind," Robbins and his circle raised this counter-position to global dimensions. Thus, national(ist) protectionism could also be redescribed as favoring the minority over the majority.

Rather than interventionism and protectionism, the task of the state was to constrain those political and economic actors who tried to impose their partial will. Along these lines, Robbins contrasted the situation of the unemployed to the minority of workers whose wages were protected by the state. Likewise, state interference to shield businessmen from failure placed their partial interests over the interest of the whole. For Robbins, an enterprise only deserved to survive if its activities eventually converged with public demand: "The property owner must learn that only by continually satisfying the demands of the consumer can he hope to maintain intact its value."[61]

Finally, Robbins also concurred with Mises and Hayek in depicting a "slippery slope" of interventionism and planned economy toward tyranny: "We may not all be socialists now, but we are certainly (nearly) all planners."[62] Planning, however, eventually amounted to socialism, even if most decision-makers did not understand this. His main theoretical argument against planning was clearly taken from the Austrian economists' position in the "calculation debate"—that the aggregation of information on the price preferences of individuals was impossible. Tastes and technologies changed all the time, so every attempt to plan always lagged behind real market processes, making it impossible to calculate what the adequate price for certain commodities could be. In contrast, relying on the market solved this problem: if costs are below the market price, this signals a demand, and eventually the market dynamics of costs and prices indicate what planners would like to calculate, and the "free market does the rest."[63]

Polemicizing with economists like Polish–Jewish émigré Oskar Lange (1904–65), who sought to bring socialism and market mechanisms together, Robbins argued that once the government starts to control some spheres, the drive toward socialism will unavoidably eliminate both the market and eventually also political liberties, as there was a basic incompatibility of planning and freedom. Thus, economic planning was directly responsible for the rise of socialist and national socialist economies and regimes. Therefore, a decision had to be made to stop intervention once for all to avoid the catastrophic political and social consequences of leftist and rightist collectivism. Rather than the beginning of the end of bourgeois liberalism, the unfolding crisis could serve as a "wake-up call" that presented societies with an either–or decision between freedom and tyranny.

Robbins was particularly concerned with the global dimensions of the crisis. The propensity toward planning had devastating consequences, catalyzing protectionist policies, dismantling global markets, and creating the "chaos of bilateralism," which went together with the rise of nationalism and civil strife. Following Mises, he was also convinced that it was futile to try to restore prosperity in one country alone, since an international equilibrium was needed. Furthermore, Robbins toyed with the idea of a unified international banking system to prevent naturally generated inflation; if this could not be implemented due to political fragmentation, what was needed (at the least) was the restoration of a common currency standard. He supported the gold standard as a potential solution, but his more basic concern was the restoration of a fixed currency exchange rate, even if it was tied to another natural resource.

Rejecting interventionism did not imply unconditional support for *laissez-faire*. Among others, Robbins allowed for limitations on private property and supported various forms of taxation. He argued that the aim of such measures was to make the state more efficient by limiting its activities and focusing instead on the tasks of governing. While he did not use the term "neoliberalism," Robbins anticipated most of the arguments that became central to this stream of thought in the second half of the 1930s. Importantly, however, his was not the only possible intellectual trajectory. German ordoliberalism, which developed its own interpretation of the crisis

138 Intellectuals and the Crisis of Politics

and a vision of economic and political regeneration simultaneously, also provided an alternative ideological path.

This tradition is usually linked to the work of economist Walter Eucken (1891–1950). He inherited the preoccupation with crisis from his father, philosopher and literature Nobel laureate Rudolf Eucken (1846–1926).[64] Walter also took from his father a holistic perspective, linking different spheres of life into one analytical framework. In his opinion, it was precisely the loss of the underlying unity of life that caused the spiritual and political crisis of the 1920s and 1930s.[65] Along these lines, he rejected a one-sided focus on any particular sphere of life, such as prioritizing the economy (*Ökonomismus*) or politics (*Politismus*). Instead, he linked the crisis of capitalist market economy, which had become visible already in the late nineteenth century, to the crisis of culture (*Kulturkrise*). As a response to this process of disintegration, the state came to replace religion (*Religionsersatz*), creating the preconditions of the total state, both in its fascist and communist manifestations.[66] Thus, in Walter Eucken's case, the criticism of the omnipotent and interventionist state was rooted in a metaphysical argument, going well beyond the question of economic expediency. Importantly, this holistic approach did not lead to a radically anti-liberal vision of *Totalkrise*, but to an attempt to identify a causal relationship between the different crisis phenomena and thus reconstruct a viable political and economic order, integrating the liberal elements into a new synthesis.

Walter Eucken was not the only critical voice in Germany regarding the idolatry of the state in the context of the economic and political instability of the early 1930s. Economic sociologist Alexander Rüstow (1885–1963) was another key figure of the debate on the rise of anti-liberalism and the chances for a liberal renewal. Rüstow started on the political left, but from the mid-1920s onward worked as an expert for the German Engineering Federation (VdMA) and fell under the intellectual influence of Carl Schmitt. In Rüstow's interpretation, published in the *Europäische Revue*, the economic crisis that erupted in late 1929 was not the beginning, but rather the culmination, of the demise of the German middle class following the Great War.[67] The ensuing socioeconomic misery catalyzed the rise of anti-capitalism, making planned economy attractive for intellectuals and masses alike, leading to political radicalization on the extreme left and right, and culminating in the rise of fascism, with its apocalyptic visions that attracted the politically disempowered strata.

Reflecting upon the economic causes of the Great Depression, Rüstow rejected most popular explanations. He was equally critical of interpretations pointing to some unforeseeable natural occurrence or to a cyclical pattern of economic development and stressed instead the importance of political agency. Rüstow also discarded the widely known explanation of Swedish economist Gustav Cassel, who linked deflation (and thus indirectly the global crisis) to the fall of the productivity of gold mining. Rüstow argued that there was enough gold reserve in the national banks to keep the global economy running. Furthermore, he rejected the claim of the German political right that postwar reparations were to blame for the crisis, but also the typical social democratic argument about underconsumption as the root cause.

Instead, Rüstow focused on the adverse effects of the postwar boom in productivity and technical innovation, leading to over-production, which in turn caused the fall of prices and the push for protectionist measures.

In line with the perspective of the VdMA, which was highly critical of state intervention (regulating prices and wages) in industry, Rüstow described the Great Depression as a crisis of "state socialism" and contrasted it to the "self-healing power" of the market. According to Rüstow, this was also true in the agricultural sphere, as the multitude of small-scale actors that relied on the free market were more resilient to crisis than a few large-scale economic conglomerates. This was due mainly to the fact that small-scale peasant properties engaged in intensive farming were much less exposed to market fluctuations than the extensive rye- and potato-producing latifundia in Eastern Prussia—whose representatives militated for protectionist measures.

The other central figure of the forming canon of *Ordoliberalismus* was Wilhelm Röpke. Like Eucken and Rüstow, Röpke linked social, economic, and cultural aspects in his analysis of crisis phenomena. As the Great Depression erupted and concomitant political and social problems sharpened, Röpke became even more engaged with the crisis discourse.[68] In his programmatic 1931 article, he pointed to the "growing cracks" in the building of the contemporary world, stressing unemployment as a key phenomenon.[69] At the same time, Röpke was wary of apocalyptic visions. Twisting the language of crisis, he used epidemiological metaphors to criticize these positions, referring to them as the "bacillus of fear of the future."[70] While he did not negate the severity of crisis, he was equally critical of the leftist (singling out the sociologist and cultural critic Siegfried Kracauer) and neo-conservative (referring to the *Tat* circle) versions of catastrophism.[71]

Turning to the economic causes of the crisis, Röpke subscribed to the idea of the exaggeration of investments as a key catalyst.[72] He suggested this wrought such havoc because more regular crisis phenomena had overlapped with irregular historical circumstances, which hit the agrarian, raw material-producing, and banking spheres simultaneously. He also pointed out that the conventional crisis-management policy of restricting both over-production and over-consumption to restore the markets' equilibria at lower levels in this case led to over-saving and deflation, triggering further contraction in a downward spiral. The unfolding chain reaction resulted in a circularity of indebtedness which eventually came to undermine the global economy. All of this, however, in Röpke's understanding, did not mean the end of capitalism—only a very serious challenge to it.

Röpke considered the economic crisis to be part and parcel of a more general civilizational disorientation.[73] Searching for possible remedies, he was critical of autarchic policies and argued instead for deeper international cooperation. His main concern was the rise of anti-democratic étatist ideologies that turned away from Western values of individualism and liberty. In contrast to the old-style adherents of *laissez-faire* and to the position of Mises, Röpke was more open toward state intervention to minimize the suffering of those who were most affected by the crisis. He stressed that the reluctance of governments to intervene, which resulted in deflation, was self-destructive and led not to purification but instead to ongoing illness, "contaminating" the healthy sectors of national economies as well. Instead, Röpke was open to the idea of counteracting deflation even by printing more money. Along these lines, he stressed that fears of inflation were exaggerated and lent his support to the 1932 "Papen Plan" for economic recovery, advocating the subsidization of public works to attenuate the devastating effects of the depression. It is important to mention that well into the early 1940s Röpke was appreciative of Keynes's ideas and only became more critical of him toward the end of the war, accusing him both of inspiring totalitarian economic policies and of representing a hyper-rationalist and quantitative bias in analyzing the economy.

Even from this short overview, it is possible to identify several common features shared by most of those who later were "canonized" as precursors of neoliberalism. However, there were also considerable divergences. Doubtlessly, they all agreed that liberal democracy had entered an unprecedentedly dangerous period of transition, which they framed as a crisis. Furthermore, they argued that the economic sphere needed to be understood in relationship to other spheres, such as politics, culture, and even religion. Along these lines, they became more skeptical of the statistical method dominant in the research of business cycles and economic conjunctures during the 1920s and developed "hybrid" approaches where economic analysis was linked to institutional, sociocultural, and even metaphysical considerations.

They also tended to draw a distinction between economic and political liberty, though not necessarily advocating the restriction of political liberty to preserve the economic one. Conversely, they could imagine both liberal and illiberal forms of democracy, considering the latter potentially (or actually) totalitarian. They also agreed that the main remedy proposed by political actors on the radical left and right—strengthening the state to intervene in all social and economic affairs of society—was damaging and potentially catastrophic, since, as they argued, it legitimized cynical power-maximizers who claimed to serve the common good but who aimed at tyrannical rule.

In contrast to planning, which—following Mises—they considered both theoretically and practically problematic, the fluctuation of market prices was held by them to be a much more reliable indicator of economic processes. They were also critical of "self-conceited intellectuals" who fell for various apocalyptic crisis scenarios or hoped to develop some comprehensive models of rational planning which could control all levels of the economy. Finally, even if some had an inclination toward political nationalism, they shared a criticism of isolationism and "economic nationalism." As Quinn Slobodian points out, they had a strong conviction that it was impossible to manage the crisis at the nation-state level, and the only long-term solution was to remove protectionist barriers from the global circulation of goods and capital.[74]

Where there was much less agreement was the evaluation of pre-existing liberal theory and practice. Here, Mises represented one extreme position, as he was quite close to nineteenth-century classical liberals in view of his repudiation of state intervention (earning himself the not-so-flattering label of "paleo-liberal" in the internal discussions of the forming neoliberal stream in the mid-1930s). Others were more open to involving the state as an important economic actor: Robbins assumed a characteristic in-between position and argued for the need to remove particularisms and hindrances to the smooth working of the market, for example, monopolies and cartels.

The German ordoliberals were even more forthcoming on some measures that were expected to attenuate the effects of the crisis in the spheres of monetary and social policies alike. In this context, Rüstow made an important distinction between those interventions that were and were not eventually compatible with the functioning of the market and its price mechanism. Ordoliberals also had a somewhat divergent understanding of society: while they were more interested in intermediary associations between the individual and the global level, Mises paid considerably less attention to them. Similarly, while these theorists were all critical of irrational tendencies in politics and advocated a rationalist approach, some of them, like Röpke, were also increasingly critical of "abstract" rationalism. Their historical meta-narratives were also divergent to some extent in identifying different moments as the roots of later calamities (thus, for instance, Röpke was especially critical of the French Revolution as a setback in the progress of civilization and the cause of liberty). Nevertheless, they tended to reject any retrospective utopia and set themselves the task of removing the obstacles from social and economic development. Furthermore, they were highly critical of emergent mass society and sought to preserve the value of individuality.

While the self-fashioning of postwar neoliberalism often constructed an image of a heroic uphill struggle against the domination of leftist and rightist adherents of planning and state intervention, the critiques of interventionism had strong intellectual and institutional positions even during the years of the Great Depression. For example, a seminar organized by the *Verein für Sozialpolitik* in 1932 was convened to assess the causes and main features of the economic crisis and brought together many leading figures of the German scene of social sciences, including Sombart, Eucken, Rüstow, and Röpke.[75]

The seminar's keynote speaker was Kyiv-born, Zürich-based economist Manuel Saitzew (1885–1951).[76] Drawing on Sombart's ideas, he linked industrialization and unemployment and argued that the process of mechanization replaced workers even if the machines were not profitable. All this was aggravated by interventionism, not only in the form of trade protectionism, but also regarding price policies and the politicization of wages. Resonating with Robbins and Rüstow, Saitzew also held that crisis symptoms such as unemployment were caused by politics and not economics. He criticized both leftist social politics and capitalist monopolies, holding up the self-regulation of the market as a fundamental value. At the same time, as did Robbins and Rüstow, he did not reject state intervention by default but pointed to the political actors' infatuation with it as particularly dangerous. Further, he inserted his criticism into a global context, stressing that the expansion of autarchism made German industry less exportable and thus aggravated the crisis. The "vicious circle of interventionism" led to a situation wherein everyone wanted to produce and to sell, but nobody wanted to buy.

142 Intellectuals and the Crisis of Politics

Saitzew's position was critically assessed by a well-known economist from Kiel, Gerhard Colm (1897–1968), who later emigrated to the United States and became a professor at the New School for Social Research. In contrast to his colleagues, who criticized intervention, Colm was convinced that the market could not overcome the crisis. In his interpretation, it was the progress of industrialization that made some sort of state intervention unavoidable. While small-scale industry could only create small-scale unemployment, the growing scope of industrial production necessitated state involvement in conjuncture policies to prevent the catastrophic social consequences of periodically occurring slumps.[77]

This exchange indicates that, beyond the thinkers who made it into the postwar neoliberal canon, there were many other authors who reflected on the possibilities of renewing liberalism in the mid-1930s as a response to the economic and political crisis. These debates also had repercussions in East Central Europe. For instance, Romanian Jewish lawyer and political thinker Emanuel Neuman linked the diagnosis of a "crisis of principles" of modern politics to the search for a renewal of liberalism in his 1937 doctoral dissertation on the limits of state power.[78] Neuman drew on the classical liberal tradition (above all Benjamin Constant) to argue for the need to limit popular sovereignty. At the same time, he came close to the neoliberal intellectual framework when alluding to the sovereignty of the consumer and pointing out—drawing on Ferrero—that the state had an important function in mediating between different social and economic actors. Contrary to the traditional liberal position, he stressed that it was exactly the weakness of the state that generated oppression through the privatization of state functions by various para-legal entities. While Neuman identified with the European liberal tradition, he was more ambiguous about such a basic democratic institution as universal suffrage. He argued that one could analytically separate political liberty and influence, and that liberty in some situations could be defended precisely by setting limitations on the omnipotence of the majority.

The Making of a Neoliberal "Synthesis"

Most of the key components of neoliberalism as a political doctrine were already present by the early 1930s, formulated as a response to the comprehensive social, economic, political, and cultural crises of the period. At the same time, in the early 1930s the different national contexts had their own dynamics and, even if neoliberal theoreticians had a strong penchant for thinking on a supra-national level, they did not completely break out of their local frameworks of reference and immediate political concerns. The situation changed after 1933, following the exile of several key figures from Germany upon the Nazi takeover, and the experience of a protracted crisis, triggering comparable étatist crisis-management policies that created a common framework of references and critical arguments across Europe. In this sense, the formative insight of neoliberalism (as it came to be known from the late 1930s) was precisely the structural similarity of crisis management in democratic countries and in autocratic and totalitarian regimes.

The sentiment of the omnipresence of étatist ideologies also radicalized the critics of these measures of crisis management and made more plausible the idea of convergence between different versions of étatism and interventionism. This also meant that the discussion on crisis, previously focusing mostly on the causes and consequences of the Great Depression, shifted toward the problem of totalitarianism even in societies that managed to preserve democratic institutions. The vision of an imminent breakthrough of collectivist tyranny was not necessarily connected to expectations of open political coups. Rather, it was linked to the irreversible transformation of the socioeconomic system and the mindset of the population—thus undermining the liberal democratic system from the inside.

A representative work along these lines was *Les mystiques politiques* by Louis Rougier (1889–1982), a French rationalist philosopher influenced by the ideas of the Viennese Circle.[79] This book was the central piece in a series of studies on the "mystique" of modernity (the other two volumes focused on democracy and the economy) and sought to deconstruct the illogical dogmatism underlying various ideological positions. Rougier started from the perspective that legitimacy was pursued by all regimes, even dictatorial ones, which often turned toward plebiscitary confirmation even if their underlying popular consent was "fabricated." According to Rougier, "political mystique" was precisely such a tool for legitimization—"a common irrational basis" of collective prejudices, passions, and mass sentiments.

Before 1918, monarchy and democracy were the two competing symbolic frameworks of legitimization. Referring to Marc Bloch (1886–1944) among others, Rougier developed a somewhat idiosyncratic historical interpretation, deriving both monarchic and democratic legitimacy from theological roots. He admitted that in the Old Testament theocracy was also present, but in his opinion it was more of a deviation. Later, this theocratic stream resurfaced in the caesaropapism of Eastern Christianity, whereas in the West the investiture struggle prevented its formation. Gradually, monarchic mystique withered away, and by the twentieth century nobody believed in royal *onction* any longer, not even the staunchest conservatives. Thus, after the Great War resulted in the demise of Eastern European monarchies, democracy became hegemonic in Europe and beyond. However, the triumph of the democratic principle was soon followed by the swift decline of democratic politics, which Rougier characterized as the first global crisis in the history of humankind.

Faced with this crisis, the younger generation became especially fascinated by millenarist and messianic political styles. Claiming to offer responses to the global crisis, the new ideological contenders (fascists and communists) of the postwar order had certain democratic features but rejected the liberal framework altogether. What they preached instead was nationalization, politicization, and the subordination of individual liberties to the collectivity. This resulted in a veritable backlash to the democratic wave that dominated Europe between 1808 and 1918, as the principle of popular sovereignty came to be challenged by the authoritarian *Führerprinzip*.

144 Intellectuals and the Crisis of Politics

Furthermore, while they seemed to be on the opposite ends of the ideological continuum, these ideologies had a complex entanglement, as fascism was often legitimized as a counter-reaction to the communist threat, thus aggravating the crisis even further. Importantly, both fascism and communism created an ideological universe that could be compared to religious faith (here Rougier also drew a parallel with Christianity), even though there were also certain differences, such as their foreign policies, as—lacking an adequate industrial basis—Stalinism was more prone to defensive warfare, while Hitler was more expansive: thus, the *"mystique naziste"* was more virulent and posed a perpetual danger for peace in Europe.

Rougier shared the idea often surfacing in the intellectual circles that came to be associated with neoliberalism that a central feature of the unfolding crisis was that the political elites trying to manage it operated only on a national level. However, it was only possible to overcome this crisis at the international level by restoring free trade and enhancing the collaboration of nations. Reflecting on the ideological disorientation of his contemporaries, Rougier admitted that there was a certain divergence between the principles of political, economic, and cultural liberalism, but he firmly asserted that economic liberalism was the precondition of the others. To illustrate this, he linked academic freedom to economic liberalism, arguing that dissent was possible when only some scholars were state employed, and a robust private sphere also had its share in supporting research and teaching.

Rougier also reiterated the argument about economy being a "daily plebiscite" by relying on the price mechanism, adding that in the long run planned economy was incompatible with civil liberties. In this context, he was highly critical of the Popular Front ideology, which sought to combine the defense of individual freedom with economic collectivism. While Rougier defended liberal democracy against its radical leftist and rightist contenders, he was skeptical of the actual state of parliamentarism, admitting that parties did not seem to be adequate representatives of different social groups. He also pointed to a certain self-destructive potential in the liberal democratic system, as the development of industry led to the creation of oligarchies (*feodalité financière*) and the formation of authoritarian regimes. Following their own particularistic interests, oligarchs sought protection from the state, promoting economic nationalism, generating inflation, and unleashing paramilitarism.

The totalitarian mystique and the rise of mass parties were responses to the insecurity felt by people in these precarious conditions.[80] Postwar societies lived in permanent anxiety, and their citizens demanded to be "liberated from the effort of thinking and self-directing."[81] The new type of police state emerging as a result of this craving for security destroyed the separation of powers and turned the mass party into a key actor of social organization, serving as police force, a praetorian guard, and a privileged class. Hence, the only way to avoid the totalitarian transformation of the whole of Europe was to return to liberalism in an institutionalist framework and open the world economy to undermine political projects based on autarchism. But the danger was imminent, wrote Rougier, doubtlessly under the shock of the violent clashes of the French left and right in the early 1930s that culminated in the half-hearted and eventually failed extreme right-wing coup in February 1934.[82] The deepening crisis exposed the imperative of urgent decision: "Time is pressing ... Gentlemen, you have to choose."[83]

The feeling that the crisis went even deeper than the cataclysm of the Great Depression and the concomitant disappointment with various recipes of crisis management, all promoting economic planning, brought together people from different subcultures to reflect on the future of liberalism. This collective thinking was enhanced by a series of initiatives to create a forum of transnational intellectual exchange and a platform to represent what, to its adherents, seemed to be a counter-hegemonic liberal alternative to étatist "orthodoxy." To this end, in 1936 the Rockefeller Foundation funded a conference on world economy, while in 1938 a colloquium on Walter Lippmann's *The Good Society* was organized in Paris. The latter came to be considered the birthplace of neoliberalism (although, as we could see, the notion existed well before).[84]

Doubtlessly, Lippmann's work had a powerful impact on this intellectual milieu. He was an integrative personality who brought together thinkers and intellectual positions not necessarily close to each other. It is telling that he thanked Hayek, Mises, and Keynes in the preface to his book. Coming from outside of Europe but having good local knowledge of the different academic cultures on the Old Continent, he was also able to mediate between the Austrian, German, British, and French networks and, as a former Wilsonian, he had a special link also to the intellectual milieu of the League of Nations in Geneva.

However, while he was critical toward étatist tendencies of different colors, Lippmann was open to certain forms of state intervention, and this attracted those who sought to defend liberalism but rejected *laissez-faire* economics. He was explicit about the obligation of powerholders to protect members of a society "from each other's injustice." It is not by chance that there was a considerable divergence of opinion among the colloquium organizers regarding whom exactly to invite to discuss the book and to assess its broader implications. This intellectual latitude, which could also be described as theoretical eclecticism, created the possibility for many different thinkers to identify with what they took to be the core of Lippmann's book.[85]

The American intellectual's rhetorical question about the roots of the decline of liberalism, and his answer stressing that the problem was not with the doctrine but with the actual performance—as "liberals failed to develop the promise of liberalism"—resonated with many thinkers and experts who still identified themselves with the liberal tradition in the context of surging anti-liberalism from left and right. Like Rougier, Lippmann also stressed the impact of economic and social instability: in such situations of distress, people who were asked to choose between security and liberty tended to opt for the former. Reflecting on the ideological disorientation of his time, Lippmann declared: "we belong to a generation that has lost its way."[86] While economic progress was previously linked to political emancipation, during the last decades political interference turned into a hindrance of progress. Eventually this became a vicious circle, with economic hardships triggering étatist policies and excessive state intervention triggering further economic hardships.

146 Intellectuals and the Crisis of Politics

"Crisis" came to be used as a conceptual legitimization of collectivist measures, which perpetuated the crisis and prompted more and more invasive actions. In this logic, as Lippmann put it, "the emergency never ends," even if some adherents of autocratic or totalitarian policies claimed to aim at restoring the previous constitutional regime. The politics of emergency also implied an obsession with unity, equating opposition with treachery. What is more, a totalitarian system was condemned to permanent mobilization: in the fascist socioeconomic framework, the living standard could only be maintained via expansion, keeping the "nation at arms," while in a Marxist dictatorship, class and regional differences persisted, thus generating newer and newer campaigns of violent homogenization.

It is in this context that Lippmann described the Soviet economy—drawing on Michael Polanyi's (1891–1976) analysis[87]—as monopolistic corporate capitalism, where class divisions were overtly reproduced by the cleavage between public officials deciding about the allocation of resources and the bulk of the population. The main difference between this system and "normal" capitalism was that in the latter, social advantages conferred political power, while in communism it was the other way round. Totalitarian states were eventually self-perpetuating war economies—in situations of scarcity it might have made sense to rely on planning for the allocation of resources, but it was impossible to plan abundance. Along these lines, while Lippmann allowed for some forms of state intervention, he categorically rejected planned society as a theoretical error that was incapable of being prosperous and peaceable. He identified the predilection for planning as a common denominator behind different anti-liberal movements—from communism to nationalism, progressivism, technocratism, fascism, and even some novel streams of liberalism. In his interpretation, their underlying vision of the "providential state" was built on the marriage of knowledge and force and went back to Plato for inspiration. It was re-actualized in the "neo-technical age" (per sociologist Lewis Mumford), resulting in étatism and enormous concentrations of power with the help of advanced technologies of control that premodern autocracies never imagined possible.

While their understanding of liberalism was rather divergent, Lippmann's arguments against planning were like those of Mises, pointing out the impossibility of collecting and aggregating adequate data and subordinating every process to centralized decision-making. Citing the example of his own "simple" breakfast, which brought together products from different continents and was the result of an intricate transnational entanglement of producers and merchants, he argued that this infinitely complex web could not be controlled from one privileged point as there were too many variables involved:

> It is not merely that we do not have to-day enough factual knowledge of the social order, enough statistics, censuses, reports. The difficulty is deeper than that. We do not possess the indispensable logical equipment—the knowledge of the grammar and the syntax of society as a whole—to understand the data available or to know what other data to look for.[88]

What made Lippmann's argument resonate with the circles that came to identify themselves with neoliberalism was not so much his broadly conceived antitotalitarian position, which was shared by various authors on the moderate left and the moderate right as well, but his criticism of what he labeled as "democratic collectivism" in terms of a "slippery slope" eventually resulting in political oppression. Far from being present only in countries with autocratic regimes, Lippmann pointed to Britain and the United States as contexts where this stance gained special currency. He argued that even if these policies were launched in the name of democracy, their reliance on planning overruled democratic deliberation and the introduction of protective tariffs also served particular interests that undermined democratic politics in the long run. Instead of creating more welfare, their outcome hindered progress and reproduced misery. The ensuing "social crisis" created by the growing gap between popular expectations and restricted productivity thus perpetuated backwardness and undermined democracy.[89]

This "politics of backwardness" became particularly virulent with the transformation of nationalism. Lippmann registered a shift in the status and morphology of nationalism: whereas, before 1870, political union preceded national unity, after 1870 nationalism became "centrifugal" (here Lippmann drew on the conceptual framework of Hungarian émigré political thinker Oszkár Jászi, 1875–1957, who analyzed the "centrifugal" features of nationalism in the process of the dissolution of the Habsburg Empire). This new nationalism was characterized by protectionism, collectivism, authoritarianism, and in certain situations—clashing with socialist variants of protectionism—it could evolve into fascism, seeking to divert class conflicts toward an external enemy and find new resources to exploit in the occupied territories.

All of this was aggravated by the rise of the ideology of total war, which replaced nineteenth-century liberal dominance mediated by the British imperial framework, the latter acting as some sort of global regulator. Lippmann concurred with Ferrero in describing the Napoleonic wars as precursors of the modern phenomenon of total war, and the Congress of Vienna as a return to a more humane global order. By contrast, the Versailles Treaty after the First World War generated a serious backlash, as it contained "terms appropriate to the conception of total war" and became an instrument in a struggle for supremacy rather than settling specific grievances.[90] For Lippmann, the main contradiction of the global order emerged in the early twentieth century between the actual interdependence of states, economies, and societies, and the tendencies of separation rooted in economic and political nationalism, isolationism, and aggressive expansionism. The solution to this global political and economic crisis was by restoring international circulation and allowing market mechanisms to shape the economic dynamic, facilitating progress and global interdependence.

From this perspective, the "cardinal fallacy" of nineteenth-century liberalism was that it did not defend the market as a "sovereign regulator" but rather sought to legitimize the miseries and injustices caused by capitalist economies. Lippmann was also highly critical of those "classical" liberals who delineated an imaginary social order and related to it as if it was real. The idea of *laissez-faire* was false, as the state was unavoidably involved in regulating certain social phenomena such as property rights—a key normative element in liberal economic thought. While liberals were generally correct, they were insensitive to the social misery, while collectivists were wrong in their theory, but had "a sympathy for the poor" and a "burning sense of the wrong."[91] However, economic recovery could only be rooted in the division of labor, and the division of labor was only productive if market forces were allowed to function. At the same time, Lippmann repudiated Mises's market fundamentalism and admitted that not every market was equally efficient, as the power difference of actors could grossly distort its output. The state was required to regulate the market precisely to avert these distortions, for example, by preventing the sale of harmful products. Pursuing this train of thought, Lippmann drew the general conclusion that the liberal state could not be neutral in the conflict between those who had too little bargaining power (typically employees) and those who had too much (typically employers) but had to guarantee justice in the very bargaining process.

The liberal state also needed to intervene in other spheres: preserving national heritage; building infrastructure; providing recreational facilities; raising the hygienic and educational level of society (Lippmann explicitly stated that schools should not be subordinated to market logic but to public authority); regulating inheritance or the means of capital-investment (thus, for instance, the state could sanction the retention of capital); and even control the business cycle to prevent too much deflation or inflation. He was also critical of the uprooting of the population in certain areas due to the decline of particular sectors of the economy and the attraction of richer countries or regions. While some level of migration was unavoidable, the movement of capital was to be preferred over the mass migration of people.

At the same time, he distanced himself from any sort of egalitarianism. Taxes were not to be spent on the poor but to make competition fair. Likewise, the aim was to reduce, but not eliminate, income differences, and to create a society where the majority belonged to the middle class. This was only possible if the international circulation of goods and capital was restored (forming an "interdependent Great Society") and economic nationalists were defeated. Describing this Great Society, Lippmann advanced several themes and key notions that were to have a remarkable influence on postwar American and European liberalism. He stressed the importance of education, as the Great Society was only viable if the nationalist mindset of the population could be changed. It was also extremely naïve to imagine a supranational planner who would be able to regulate the affairs of different states in an equitable manner. The realistic modality of transnational cooperation was the creation of a worldwide "civil society" that maintained the worldwide division of labor.

Regarding the form of government, Lippmann was critical of majoritarianism and argued for the importance of expert elites capable of steering the political system toward the best interests of society. Along these lines, he also rejected the "cynical plebiscites" practiced especially by fascists, with manufactured majority opinion being treated as the "will of the nation." "Pure" or majoritarian democracy tended to turn into authoritarianism, thus an intricate system of checks and balances was needed, however, this could not mean "obstructing" the popular will, but rather "refining it." A free society meant that the government did not unnecessarily intervene into the affairs of citizens but administered justice among them. The "rule of law" Lippmann advocated could be considered a "third way" between *laissez-faire* and collectivism. Rule of law, however, did not mean that laws were unchangeable, but rather that they were calculable and that powerholders were also under the law. Along these lines, he introduced the category of fairness as a regulatory idea. Liberalism should not be identified with a set of laws but more with an evolutionary process, and human rights were central to this evolution. Reaching back to the conflict between the English jurist Edward Coke and James I in the early seventeenth century, Lippmann contrasted common law to Roman/imperial law, arguing that the former was closer to the liberal ideal. He also linked common law to the intermediaries between the state and the individual (e.g., church, family, local communities).

Similar to other versions of the interwar crisis discourse, both liberal and conservative, Lippmann's analysis linked the socioeconomic disturbances of his time to a deeper, spiritual disorientation: "In the epochal crisis of our time the cause of civilization is being defended by men who possess a great tradition that has become softened by easy living, by men who have forgotten the necessities in which their principles were wrought."[92] He talked of the "collapse of certainties" and the "disruption of the natural order of things."[93] He contrasted periods of spiritual integrity, dominated by Buddhism and Christianity, to the "degradation of man" in the nineteenth century, characterized by rationalism, moral relativism, and the hesitation between the ideas of predestination and human providence (secular versions of which underlaid the agenda of planning). He derived the rise of totalitarian movements (fascism and communism) from this spiritual void, reducing humans to cogs or cells.

Written by a prominent American public figure with international prestige, Lippmann's book managed to synthesize many arguments circulating at the turn of the 1930s among various intellectual and expert groups into a sweeping political argument that could catch the attention of a broader audience beyond academic circles. This feature made it attractive for his European friends to organize a seminar around the book, bringing together the most prominent voices dealing with the problems Lippmann explored. While there was some hesitation regarding whom to invite (and even figures who were quite far from liberalism were considered), eventually the list of those invited was rather representative of the broader ideological orientation of "self-critical" liberals.

The colloquium took place in August 1938, when it was already a widely shared opinion that France's Popular Front government had failed both economically and politically. This provided an impetus to those liberals who felt uneasy with the either–or choice between a fascist and a leftist anti-fascist platform, as the latter was also dominated by supporters of planned economy and collectivism.[94] The seminar was introduced by Rougier, who reiterated the familiar argument that the crisis was not so much economic or social, but spiritual. Along these lines, he claimed that the contemporary political disorientation could be traced back to two false presuppositions: the mutually exclusive choice of socialism and fascism posited both by the

150 Intellectuals and the Crisis of Politics

adherents of the Popular Front and the radical right, and the identification of liberalism with the doctrine of *laissez-faire*. From Rougier's perspective, Lippmann's book challenged both presuppositions and thus helped to reposition liberalism on the ideological map. The third key argument Rougier took from Lippmann's book was that the liberal order was not the result of spontaneous development, but an intricate combination of the "plebiscite of prices" and the "concerted arbitrage of the state." Along these lines, Rougier stressed the importance of linking economic and political analyses, while at the same time, somewhat paradoxically, he argued against the politicization of culture.

In his response, Lippmann was also bitterly critical of nineteenth-century liberalism for failing to serve as a guide for the behavior of people. Consequently, he rejected any attempt to return to prewar liberalism and called instead for a fundamental revision. This was even more pressing as the collectivistic ideologies of communism, national socialism, and fascism posed a serious challenge, rejecting the limitation of power and moral universalism. Instead, they sought to subordinate all social institutions to the state—including religion, education, and science—and fundamentally break with the Western political tradition, which was built on the autonomy of these spheres.

In the different conversations following Lippmann's intervention, participants discussed various aspects of their intellectual agenda, including: the very name of the ideological stream they sought to launch; the question of monopolies; the limits of state intervention; economic nationalism; the question of war economy; the entanglement of economic and political freedom; the relationship of industrial and agrarian production; and the threat of totalitarianism. Indeed, there was significant divergence on most of these issues. One of the most heated debates was on the role of the state in regulating competition and the relationship of economic and extra-economic rationality. Rougier, Röpke, and Mises stressed that usually it was the state that distorted market mechanisms and created monopolies, while others (closer to Lippmann's argument) allowed for state regulation under certain conditions. Thus, for instance, Rüstow argued that a weak state was unable to police the market and guarantee the fairness of market competition. As a result, extra-market forces could be converted to economic advantages, distorting the market and eventually undermining the health of the economy.

From another perspective, French technocrat Auguste Detoeuf (1883–1947) considered state intervention indispensable for alleviating the misery of the population caused by *laissez-faire* policies. Similarly, economist Étienne Mantoux (1913–1945) argued that the state should assume part of the costs of the transition of the working force from one branch to another even if economic rationality dictated the immediate abandonment of certain industries. Here, Lippmann and Jacques Rueff entered a polemic, which in some ways anticipated the discussions of the late twentieth and early twenty-first centuries. Rueff stressed that the aim of an economic system is to give maximum benefits compatible with the state of production and any intervention to prevent certain branches from collapsing was counterproductive. From this perspective, he used the example of the Great Depression and argued that state intervention delayed its outbreak and thus in the long run aggravated it. Lippmann answered that the state can still diminish suffering, to which Rueff retorted that this was possible only within a balanced budget. That said, Rueff also admitted the theoretical necessity of intervention in certain situations.

Apart from the role of the state, there was also a discussion on trade unions and other organs that represented collective interests. Mises argued that unemployment, and thus the crisis, was caused by excessively high salaries. Hence, breaking the collective bargaining position of the trade unions would eventually lead to a better economic situation for the majority. From a different perspective, economic expert and industrialist Louis Marlio blamed syndicalism for blocking immigration to keep up high wages and thus disrupting the natural circulation of capital and the working force.

There were also several voices in favor of taking out certain branches from the market mechanism, for example, railways and other vital infrastructure. This discussion was also linked to the question of war economy, with Mantoux admitting that interdependence might be dangerous in some cases from the perspective of national defense. Austrian economic and military expert Stefan Possony (1913–1995)[95] argued that protectionism was counter-productive even in a situation of war preparation. Overall, for most participants at the colloquium, economic nationalism was a major trigger of the crisis, but there was less consensus on what caused it. For instance, Marlio pointed to the Versailles Treaty as its catalyst, while others linked it to *longue durée* processes, such as the transformation of national ideology in the nineteenth century.[96]

Reflecting on the relationship of the economic and non-economic spheres, there was also a certain tension between the liberal set of values and the subversive implications of the crisis discourse to which most participants of the colloquium subscribed. This tension created a critical distance for discussing liberalism not as the "only game in town," but as a highly contested doctrine in need of critical rethinking. Thus, while stressing the prevalence of economic rationality over extra-economical normative frameworks, many participants at the colloquium considered the crisis of the early 1930s not so much an economic depression, but (as Rüstow put it) "a vital crisis in general and a crisis of integration in particular."[97] Similarly, they identified unity and liberty as key values of liberalism, but their historical analysis pointed to the fact that, replacing the pre-modern hierarchies, the market destroyed pre-existing frameworks of solidarity, creating atomization, loss of security, and the rise of interest groups that disregarded the common good. Neglecting the irrational but vital needs of life, such as the craving for integration in a community, liberal modernity became particularly vulnerable to ideologies offering a "new totality." According to Michael Polanyi, while totalitarianism was clearly inferior to liberal democracy in economic terms, it had a remarkable spiritual advantage.[98]

Some elements of anti-modernist cultural criticism could also be found in the discussion on the peasantry. Röpke raised the question of agrarian production in relation to the problem of economic nationalism. He referred to the industrial/agrarian cleavage and argued for treating these spheres separately. Likewise, Rüstow made a distinction between workers and peasants and argued that in general the latter are more satisfied with the organic results of their work, adding that migration away from villages was due to the bizarre income differences between city and countryside and was not "natural."[99] In turn, Mises criticized Rüstow's "romantic idealization" of the peasantry while also answering to Polanyi, pointing out that the Soviet regime was not based on satisfying the spiritual or material needs of the population, and the identification of Soviet citizens with the regime was only due to propaganda and the isolation of the country, depriving its inhabitants of a comparative perspective.[100]

While these sharp exchanges made it evident that on certain issues the participants continued to hold divergent opinions, the experience of a rather broad common ideological platform was more fundamental and eventually came to exert a lasting impact on the evolution of this stream of thought and the network of intellectuals subscribing to it. They all agreed with Rougier's counter-position of liberal democracy, based on the sovereignty of the individual, and the Rousseauian model of anti-liberal democracy, based on mass sovereignty. They also tended to agree with Lippmann (although the details were debated and, finding himself in the minority, Mises expressed his wish to continue the debate after the colloquium) that the state had to create and sustain the legal framework regulating economic interaction and provide for national defense, social insurance, services, and education. They also rejected the idea of a perfect economic order, arguing instead (as Marlio put it) that one still had to choose between "better or worse" directions.

Finally, in line with the recommendations of Mises, Rougier, and Lippmann, the participants concurred on the need to wage an ideological struggle and (re)conquer the minds of the elites and the broader population, winning them over to their vision of a free economy and society. Along these lines, they launched a "Centre international d'études pour la Rénovation du Libéralisme," which did not have much direct impact in the shadow of the erupting Second World War, but structurally and ideologically it can be considered the precursor of the postwar Mont Pèlerin Society.

However, it would be incorrect to assess the influence of these discussions restrictively, focusing only on the canonic figures of the postwar neoliberal movement. For instance, Lippmann's work, and the debates around it, resonate in the writings of political thinker and journalist Imre Csécsy (1893–1961). A friend of Jászi, Csécsy and his "civic radical" intellectual group sought to rethink liberalism in the Hungarian political context, which was becoming increasingly anti-liberal and authoritarian. In his studies from the mid-1930s—especially in the 1935 essay provocatively titled "Has Democracy Failed?"—Csécsy argued for a synthesis of liberalism and democracy, stressing the difference between the "old" doctrine of democracy (i.e., majoritarianism) and the modern one incorporating the protection of minorities.[101] An emphatic liberal component appeared in his argument in favor of competition both in the economic and political spheres. In his understanding, the two spheres were closely linked, and thus the suppression of economic liberty in the form of monopoly capitalism necessarily resulted in étatism. However, competition was not an aim for Csécsy but was linked to the ideal of "economic democracy." These ideas were directly linked to the discussions around Lippmann's book, since Jászi drew Csécsy's attention to *The Good Society* already in 1937, while in 1938 Csécsy published Jászi's review article of the book in his journal *Századunk*, and for some time they even entertained the idea of preparing a Hungarian translation.[102]

Furthermore, like Röpke and Rüstow, Csécsy also tried to link liberal values and the agrarian sphere, arguing for land reform—distributing the latifundia and creating family farms—that would also make the peasantry economically more competitive. This was particularly important in the Hungarian context of the 1930s, where the left liberal "urbanite" stream (*urbánusok*) clashed with the agrarian populist movement (*népi mozgalom*) exactly on the question of the peasantry.[103] Csécsy's attempt to harmonize liberalism with the demand of an agrarian reform was thus an offer to find common ground in a moment marred by irritation between the two groups, not least because of the anti-Semitic overtones from key interlocutors of the populist discourse. It is also in this context that Csécsy stressed the entanglement of national independence and the cause of liberty, thus providing a broader anti-fascist platform that could accommodate liberals, social democrats, agrarian populists, and even moderate conservatives.[104]

New Challenges and Opportunities during the Second World War

The discussion obviously did not stop with the closing of the Walter Lippmann Colloquium and the creation of a tentative transnational institutional and ideological platform to renew liberal thinking. Different participants continued to pursue their own intellectual and academic careers while their existential situation and political choices turned out to be highly divergent, especially during the probing years of the Second World War. This was especially dramatic in the case of the French protagonists of the network, many of whom made a somewhat surprising (although not completely illogical) U-turn to support the "national revolution" of Philippe Pétain, while projecting some of the neoliberal ideological matrix on the neo-conservative reformism of the Vichy regime.[105] Others opted for various streams of the *Résistance*, adopting their political discourse to that of their allies (and generally accepting the importance of a more emphatic state involvement in economic and social processes). This flexibility was due primarily to the (ideological and often also generational) entanglement of various "neo-" doctrines, from neoliberalism to neo-socialism and neo-conservatism.

The interplay of neoliberalism with other new ideological streams on the eve of the Second World War is apparent in the work of economist and political adviser Gaëtan Pirou (1886–1946).[106] Pirou originally came from a corporatist milieu, subsequently becoming part of the neoliberal intellectual network (acting as a co-editor of the *Revue d'économie politique* with Charles Rist). He contrasted neoliberalism to corporatism and socialism, but also to "classical liberalism," which he characterized

154 Intellectuals and the Crisis of Politics

by the principles of price mechanism, market equilibrium, and the idea of progress. For Pirou, a principal problem with classical liberalism was that market competition was often eliminated by the producers themselves and thus a *laissez-faire* logic could eventually lead to the collapse of free markets. This became even more threatening as the twentieth century saw the rise of a new type of capitalism characterized by overproduction, the concentration of capital, the bureaucratization of big enterprises, and monopolistic tendencies. The crisis starting in 1929 amply showed that the inherent logic of modern capitalism contradicted the principle of the common good: it tended to privatize benefits (accumulating personal wealth) while collectivizing losses (asking society and the state to alleviate the social costs of economic growth and to support those who were affected by the economic crises).

What was new in the neoliberal vision according to Pirou was the conviction that in the case of crisis the state could not remain neutral. Instead, it had to prevent social catastrophe and salvage economic competition itself. Referring to the Lippmann Colloquium, Pirou stressed that neoliberalism allowed the state to initiate and implement structural reforms and to regulate the uneven relationship of economic actors with legal means. As peasants and workers did not have the same power as capitalists in their "exchange" of labor for monetary compensation, there was a need to protect them, for example, by creating cooperatives. Pirou also stressed that Lippmann allowed for progressive taxation, provided that the tax revenue was used to create more activity and not just boost consumption.

Remarkably, Pirou registered the rise of interest in liberalism after the Colloquium and the growing disillusionment with directed economy.[107] For him, the main "selling point" was that the French public remained open to cultural and political liberalism even if it was highly critical of classical liberalism of the *laissez-faire* type. Neoliberalism seemed to be a possible synthesis of these branches, reestablishing economic liberalism by adapting it to the conditions of contemporary capitalism, defending the market also from the hegemonistic tendencies of the monopolists. At the same time, he also allowed for the theoretical possibility that not all monopolies were necessarily harmful for the society.

While competing with neoliberalism, neo-corporatism, according to Pirou, also emerged as a reaction to the economic crisis. Its main aspiration was to establish professional corporations that could mediate between the state and the individual. Overall, Pirou admitted that the logic of corporatism led toward some sort of planned economy. There was, however, a divergence between the different versions of the corporatist doctrine, according to whether these corporations were meant to be only economic or also political, and which boiled down to the clash between the supporters of autonomous and subordinated corporations, the latter being prevalent in fascist regimes. He also identified corporatist elements in non-corporatist regimes, where the drive toward homogenization and discipline created similar arrangements, such as the collective bargaining agreements in France, which were becoming increasingly more binding. Also, with time, some of the economic branches—such as sugar production or fishing—became virtually closed, and thus showed corporatist features even if the broader economic environment was still based on non-corporatist principles.

Finally, Pirou also registered neo-socialism as a product of crisis—both of the traditional Marxist doctrine, based on historical materialism and price–value theory (undermined by marginalism), and of the entire socioeconomic framework in the early 1930s.[108] As Marxism was challenged by a variety of revisionist and revolutionist schools as well as syndicalism, and a number of new theoretical and political positions emerged, one of the most coherent alternatives was neo-socialism. Pirou pointed to Henri de Man, Werner Sombart, and G. D. H. Cole as its main sources and referred to the debate between those theoreticians (such as Mises and Albert Aftalion) who rejected social and economic planning by arguing that it was impossible to calculate its effects adequately, and those who tried to harmonize the market and socialist planning. Aside from Oskar Lange, Pirou mentioned French economist Robert Mossé (1906–73), who based his counterargument on the fact that even in the Soviet Union, money and the market continued to exist.

Describing neo-socialism as an attempt to create a new synthesis, Pirou pointed to radical MP Gaston Bergery (1892–1974) and his program as paradigmatic in trying to delimit the public, controlled, and free economic spheres. He also referred to the 1935 General Confederation of Labour (CGT) plan, promoting socialism without nationalization, as well as to the cooperativist stream around economist Bernard Lavergne (1884–1975) as inspirations for neo-socialism. In political terms, Pirou described neo-socialism as a response to the success of the fascist regimes, drawing on the insight that the intensification of the class struggle between the proletariat and the other strata did not give birth to socialism. To the contrary: alienating the middle classes opened the way to fascist backlash. Thus, to outcompete fascism ideologically and reconquer the middle classes, neo-socialism also opted for a nationalist rhetoric.[109]

The most interesting aspect of Pirou's analysis was his remark on the convergence between the three "neo" movements: while neoliberalism was moving toward some form of interventionism, neocorporatism formulated the idea of self-limitation of the state, and neo-socialism was trying to salvage and even stimulate private initiative.[110] While he did not negate their philosophical and political differences, Pirou thought that, in the atmosphere of national mobilization for an imminent global conflict, all societies gravitated toward a more nationalist and corporatist direction and the expansion of state control was unavoidable even in democracies. In this sense, as a response to the general political and economic crisis, the future synthesis of these ideologies was not at all inconceivable.

While the war years were hardly propitious for liberalism, the discussions on the renewal of liberalism, which started a decade earlier, continued both in the context of the debate on the desirable postwar order (especially among the experts and intellectuals advising or seeking to advise the decision-makers of the Allies), as well as on the relationship of (neo)liberalism and authoritarianism. Indeed, during the Vichy regime, references to neoliberalism survived in the academic subculture while

156 Intellectuals and the Crisis of Politics

some of its key representatives chose to collaborate with the regime. These discussions are reflected by the dissertation defended by the Romanian Mihai Mărculescu (Michel Marculesco) in occupied Paris in 1943, having one of the protagonists of the Lippmann Colloquium, the economist Louis Baudin, on his defense committee.[111] Notably, Mărculescu was the nephew of former prime minister of Romania Gheorghe Tătărescu (1886–1957), who himself was the leader of the faction of "young liberals" in the National Liberal Party, which combined support for free trade with authoritarian politics.[112]

Mărculescu started his thesis with a picture of declining liberalism: as the *laissez-faire* doctrine of the nineteenth century lost its revolutionary potential, it became retrograde. In this context, the author saw the contribution of neoliberalism in realizing that market competition did not necessarily take place among equals, and thus the state needed to intervene to make these conditions more equitable. He also pointed out that, even in the heyday of capitalism, during the nineteenth century the concentration of capital was not the outcome of free competition but the result of pre-existing imbalances of forces among economic actors. This was even more so in the twentieth century. With the decline of individualism, the masses became central to economic processes, for instance, in speculation or hoarding products. Mărculescu quoted Lippmann and argued that instead of competition and natural selection, modern capitalist economy was about concentration and over-production. Further, in many novel economic formations, such as the big holdings, the price mechanism simply did not function at all.

In this crisis of ideas and practices, neoliberals tried to save what they considered to be liberalism's core. Neoliberalism in this context became "*libéralisme dirigé*," not eliminating the possibility of crises, but making them "inoffensive" by finding a middle road between individualism, corporatism, and socialism. This interpretation implied a skeptical stance toward neoliberalism as a unique path toward universal regeneration: Mărculescu did not hide the "weak points," for example, the rise of joint stock companies and cartels as part and parcel of the modern economy which restricted free competition. In his response to the dissertation, Louis Baudin argued even more openly that certain monopolies could be beneficial.

While the discussion registered by Mărculescu did not indicate a fundamental break with the paradigms established in the second half of the 1930s, the personal and political choices of many protagonists showed a considerable shift., For example, Baudin himself, already in the mid-1930s expressed his sympathy for António de Oliveira Salazar's (1889–1970) Portuguese corporatist regime as a way out of the endemic economic and social crises on the mainland Europe. It was along these lines that Baudin chose to collaborate with the Vichy regime, and in 1941 published a work on the corporatist model as the solution to all the problems created by uncontrolled liberalism.[113]

Another key figure already mentioned, Louis Rougier, travelled to London in 1940 with the nebulous agenda of negotiating an agreement between Pétain and the British government. When this mission failed, he moved to the United States and assumed a vocally anti-Gaullist position. After the war, he persisted in legitimizing his own wartime position and accusing Charles de Gaulle of dividing the nation, subordinating its interests to the Anglo-Saxons, and even preparing the ground for the communists. Eventually, he became an important intellectual mentor of the emerging *Nouvelle Droite* in the 1960s, providing a framework for a European pan-nationalism against the Soviets, the Americans, and the non-white postcolonial population, and rejecting the postwar consensus politics engineered by the center right and the center left.

Due to the ideological disorientation and institutional disintegration of the French pole of the neoliberal network, and the emigration of many European scholars to Great Britain and the United States, the epicenter of the discussion moved to these two countries during the war. Hayek was a key figure who relocated from Austria to the LSE upon the invitation of Lionel Robbins already in the early 1930s. He was also on the faculty of the Geneva Graduate Institute where he rubbed shoulders with many other key figures of the transnational liberal network, such as Mises, Mantoux, Rappard, and Ferrero.

Hayek also took part in the Lippmann Colloquium, but since he did not speak French, his contributions were not reproduced in the edited version of the discussion. Continuing the conversation, a year later he coordinated and co-authored a collective volume on planned economy and collectivism, published by Librairie de Médicis, the same publisher as that of the Colloquium (and founded by Rougier and Baudin to popularize the neoliberal cause).[114] In his introduction, Hayek stated that the debate on socialism was dominated by ethical and psychological considerations, and he sought to bring in the economic perspective. Reflecting on the state of economic science, he argued that in the mid-nineteenth century common economic knowledge was on a higher level than after the First World War, but the collapse of classical theory and the rise of the Historical School erased theoretical reflection and prepared the ground for the dominance of "pseudo-scientific theories" on the left and the right. Along these lines, he linked Marx also to the Historical School (which resonated with Mises's earlier claim that Marx was a relativist, rejecting the universal validity of logic).

In this text and his further work, synthesized in *The Road to Serfdom* (written between 1940 and 1943), Hayek reformulated the previous arguments against planned economy and turned them into the very core of his polemic, targeting socialism as the main enemy and stressing that even a minor and seemingly innocent step toward central planning eventually led to fully fledged totalitarian control.[115] At the same time, he asserted that he was not necessarily for *laissez-faire* as the legal framework of market economy needed to be guaranteed by the state power. Rejecting Lange's trial-and-error method of market socialism, Hayek contended that the transition to socialism could not start with prices formed by capitalism. He also stressed the difference between the economic behavior of individual entrepreneurs and central planners and argued that in a centrally planned economy, risk-taking would be minimized, which would also limit the developmental potential. Furthermore, he also reiterated the idea of the sovereignty of the consumer.

158 Intellectuals and the Crisis of Politics

Hayek's argument in *The Road to Serfdom* took from the crisis discourse of the mid-1930s the key idea that opting for planning or economic freedom was an either–or decision where there was no middle way or compromise. The urgency of this decision was linked to the global situation, with the advancing of various collectivist regimes that threatened the "free world" with subjection. From this perspective, the Nazi and Soviet policies could seem similar, being rooted in the same aspiration for planning and total state control over the economy. Appealing to the sentiment of national specificity among his British target audience and shaped by the liberal anti-totalitarian discourse on national character promoted by public figures like Ernest Barker during the interwar period,[116] Hayek also referred to the idea of planning as a "foreign import." Instrumentalizing the isolationist reflexes of his audience, this Central European émigré intellectual thus warned of the political and intellectual danger of dragging Britain into the "European crisis" allegedly imported by fellow Central European émigré intellectuals like Karl Polanyi (1886–1964) and Karl Mannheim.

In contrast to Hayek's position, which contrasted planning to political freedom, yet another wartime Central European liberal refugee in England, Ferdynand Zweig, used the crisis discourse to synthesize arguments in favor of the compatibility of these two principles from a developmentalist perspective.[117] Zweig considered rational planning as a principal lesson the world had to draw from the interwar economic and political crises and declared that "planning is the child of crisis."[118] It was also a rational response to global inequalities and backwardness.[119] While highly industrialized rich countries were able to turn free trade to their advantage, countries trying to launch a program of modernization or seeking to defend themselves in an insecure international situation simply could not avoid some level of planning. If there were no external resources available for industrialization, rational planning was the only way to allocate resources to the sectors that needed them most. This did not mean that Zweig was an uncritical adherent of planning. He was very much aware of the counterarguments coming from the neoliberal camp (he referred mostly to Hayek) about planning as a "slippery slope" toward authoritarianism. Therefore, in his understanding, the task was to harmonize freedom, democracy, and the application of rationalistic principles in designing economic policies. In his opinion, this did not necessarily entail autocratic power concentration. Since it was technically impossible to centralize all decision making anyhow, planning provided more a direction of development than total control: "Planning imposes on a country a certain order, which emanates from a particular leading idea."[120]

Admitting that planning was hardly apolitical, Zweig distinguished between different—socialist, nationalist, and technocratic—ideological frameworks of planned economy. At the same time, he also pointed to certain common traits, and these were like those identified by the neoliberal critics, albeit from a different normative position. Zweig admitted that planning could tend toward detaching the national economy from its transnational interrelationships, uniformization, and the limitation of the entrepreneurial spirit. However, he considered this to be part of a global dynamic of economic history, with the stages of economic development passing through mercantilism, liberalism, and eventually neo-mercantilism. Planned economy was entangled with the transition away from free market economy, being both the cause and the result of autarchic tendencies. In this sense, his position was similar to the Romanian neoliberals, even if he did not draw comparably nationalist conclusions. At the same time, rather than just focusing on the intrinsic development of the economic doctrines, Zweig paid more attention to the collective experiences that made economic planning more plausible than before, linked to the "Great Emergency" of the First World War and the ensuing crisis-ridden period, which called for decisions under extreme time pressure.

Zweig was convinced that, even after the end of the Second World War, this feeling of emergency would remain. Drawing on Mannheim's ideas, he reiterated that even free societies needed planning to manage an increasingly complex economy with growing public debt and direct taxation while facing the danger of galloping inflation. However, he considered planning a useful tool but not a panacea. It could help reduce social differences, but it could only work if there was a high level of social consensus. No ideal society could be created by rational planning only—life was an endless struggle full of unpredictable turns. Citing a variety of theoretical references from Lange and Henry Dickinson (1899–1968) to Soviet and even Nazi experts, Zweig argued that the process of planning was also based on a method of trial and error (for example, in establishing the right relation of different types of labor). While in the world of machines it was possible to fully control the processes, this was much harder where there was a more significant human factor involved. The best way was to avoid direct pressure and coercion and achieve the desired aims by education, responsible leadership, and good information provided to the population. In this respect, Zweig had no illusions about the efficiency of the Stalinist project of forced industrialization, coupled with accelerated Five-Year Plans: he stressed that irrespective of the propaganda statements about the USSR being immune to the crisis, and thus being on the way to overtake Western European economies, the Soviet economy only reached the pre-war Russian level of growth in 1935–6.

Trying to harmonize planning and political freedom, Zweig rejected the inference that planning necessarily resulted in the nationalization of property, arguing that one could imagine an unplanned socialist economy (like the New Economic Policy in the Soviet Union) and a planned capitalist economy based entirely on private property. What is more, certain forms of private property, such as public utility companies and cooperatives, were eminently compatible with planned economy. At the same time, it was impossible to imagine a society completely excluding market mechanisms. Planning should not be identified with concentrated ownership; to the contrary, regional planning might involve decentralization. Planning was also not uniform, as different economies required very different types of planning: in general, national economies of a larger size tended to be more in need of it. During the socialist calculation debate, Hayek and Mises stood against planning on the argument that planners are unable to aggregate information about individual transactions and thus artificially distort the price mechanism. Zweig responded by arguing that there was space for price control, combining market and public preferences, even from a marginalist perspective. He

160 Intellectuals and the Crisis of Politics

also responded to Hayek's criticism of the idea of planning *ex nihilo*, arguing (like Lange) that there was always a historically given starting point and a certain price level of a certain product which could then be related to other products. Finally, he also considered planning compatible with transnational cooperation, envisioning an international clearing currency that would take over the role of the gold standard, capable of integrating national economies on a higher level.

To sum up, while a central theme of the interwar crisis debate, the crisis of liberalism was rarely analyzed in separation from other "faces of crisis." What made the feeling so prevalent that liberalism was in crisis was the widely shared conviction (also among liberals themselves) that it was impossible to continue what many observers described as "nineteenth-century" liberalism. This conviction catalyzed a common framework of references for positions which were otherwise, in political terms, hardly compatible, and offered a possibility to shift from liberal to anti-liberal perspectives—and back again. Looking at the broader intellectual landscape also puts neoliberalism into a different perspective. Rather than a linear process of emergence or crystallization, what we see is a multiplicity of alternative positions seeking to renew liberalism from within. Further, the presence of competing liberalisms (for example, economic, political, social, cultural, national, "neo-") came to be perceived by many observers as a crisis phenomenon that became increasingly central to the discussion on the viability of liberal democracy.

However, these liberalisms were not completely isolated, and there were many entanglements and overlaps. In this sense, neoliberalism and social liberalism were far from being incompatible antagonists, rather partially overlapping and partially competing configurations. Importantly, the same argument could have very different acoustics in different contexts, depending on the place of the given community in the symbolic and economic hierarchies within Europe. Thus, planning and economic nationalism could be radical "others," but also possible complementary components of interwar liberal projects that sought to respond to what they perceived as an unprecedented crisis of economy, politics, and culture. This insight also offers a possibility to dissolve the unitary image of neoliberalism cherished both by its adherents and foes in the twenty-first century. Rather than a doctrine of autonomous free markets from the beginning, it could be described more as an attempt to find a way out from the crisis of liberalism by redefining the role of the state as an important partner in forming policies and sustaining a legal and institutional framework for the socially and economically most productive unfolding of individual freedom.[121]

Notes

1. Ernest Renan, "La crise religieuse en Europe," *Revue des Deux Mondes (1829–1971), troisième période* 1, no. 4 (1874), 752–79, 775.
2. John Atkinson Hobson, *The Crisis of Liberalism: New Issues of Democracy* (London: P. S. King & Son, 1909), vii.
3. Ibid., xi.

Crisis of Liberalism   161

4. Ibid., xiv.
5. Michael Freeden, *Liberalism Divided: A Study in British Political Thought 1914–1939* (Oxford: Clarendon, 1986), 1.
6. On the link of the collapse of the evolutionary vision and the crisis of liberalism see also Anselm Doering-Manteuffel and Jörn Leonhard, "Liberalismus im 20. Jahrhundert—Aufriss einer historischen Phänomenologie," in Anselm Doering-Manteuffel and Jörn Leonhard, eds., *Liberalismus im 20. Jahrhundert* (Stuttgart: Franz Steiner Verlag, 2015), 23.
7. Jörn Leonhard, "Der Liberalismus 1914–1918 im internationalen Vergleich," in ibid., 72.
8. It is much harder to quantify this in the French context as there was no nominally liberal political force in the interwar period and the division between Left and Right actually cut across the liberal ideological camp, with some of the Radicals opting for cooperation with the Left while the republican Right gradually moving closer to the anti-systemic authoritarian conservatives. See Klaus-Peter Sick, "Vom *Opportunisme* zum *Libéralisme autoritaire*. Die Krise des französischen Liberalismus im demokratisierten Parlamentarismus 1885–1940," *Geschichte und Gesellschaft* 29, no. 1 (2003): 66–104.
9. Eberhard Kautter, *Deutschland in der Weltkrise des Liberalismus* (Stuttgart: Kohlhammer, 1933).
10. Karl Heinz Roth, "The International Institute of Social History as a Pawn of Nazi Social Research," *International Review of Social History* 34, suppl 1 (1989): 1–24.
11. Kautter, *Deutschland in der Weltkrise*, 231.
12. Mihaïl Manoïlesco, *L'Impératif de la crise* (Bucharest: Chambre de commerce internationale, Comité national roumain, 1933).
13. Ibid., 3.
14. Mihaïl Manoïlesco, *L'Équilibre économique Européen* (Bucharest: Imprimeria naţională, 1931).
15. Mihaïl Manoïlesco, *Une nouvelle conception du protectionnisme industriel* (Bucharest: Imprimeria naţională,1931).
16. Manoïlesco, *L'Équilibre économique*, 13.
17. H. G. Wells, *After Democracy: Addresses and Papers on the Present World Situation* (London: Watts and Co., 1932); William E. Rappard, *The Crisis of Democracy* (Chicago: University of Chicago Press, 1938).
18. Ludwig von Mises, *Socialism: An Economic and Sociological Analysis* (London: Jonathan Cape, 1936 [1922]); Louis Rougier, *Les Mystiques politiques contemporaines et leur incidences internationales* (Paris: Sirey, 1935); Alexander Rüstow, "Der Weg durch Weltkrise und deutsche Krise," *Europäische Revue* 6, no. 12 (1930): 873–84; see also Serge Audier, ed., *Le Colloque Lippmann. Aux Origines du néo-libéralisme* (Lormont: Le Bord de l'eau, 2008).
19. Adriano Tilgher, *La crisi mondiale e saggi critici di marxismo e socialismo* (Imola: Nicola Zanichelli, 1921).
20. Ibid., 43.
21. Tilgher, "Finis Europae (May 29, 1919)," in ibid., 35.
22. Ibid., 43.
23. Ibid., 56.
24. Benito Mussolini, "Discorso per la fondazione dei Fasci di Combattimento" (March 23, 1919), in Renzo De Felice, ed., *Autobiografia del fascismo. Antologia di testi fascisti 1919–1945* (Torino: Einaudi, 2004), 15.

162 Intellectuals and the Crisis of Politics

25. Italo Balbo, "Diario 1922" in ibid., 109. Later, Balbo emerged as an internal alternative to Mussolini within the fascist leadership, assuming the governorship of Libya in 1934, and eventually dying in somewhat unclear circumstances, as his airplane was shot down by "friendly fire" from the Italian artillery.
26. Camillo Pellizzi, "Problemi e realtà del fascismo" in De Felice, *Autobiografia*, 132.
27. Curzio Suckert (Malaparte), "Ragguaglio sullo stato degli intellettuali rispetto al Fascismo," in De Felice, *Autobiografia*, 151–4.
28. Massimo Rocca, "Un neo-liberalismo?" in De Felice, *Autobiografia*, 86.
29. Benito Mussolini, "Discorso pronunciato a Udine il 20 settembre 1922," in De Felice, *Autobiografia*, 124.
30. Giuseppe Bottai, "Dichiarazioni sul revisionismo," in De Felice, *Autobiografia*, 191.
31. Maurizio Maraviglia, "Discorso al V. Congresso del PNF," in De Felice, *Autobiografia*, 211.
32. Giovanni Gentile, "Origini e dottrina del fascismo," in De Felice, *Autobiografia*, 262.
33. Daelio Cantimori, "Fascismo, nazionalismi e reazioni," in De Felice, *Autobiografia*, 297.
34. Nello Quillici, "Crisi o rivoluzione?" in De Felice, *Autobiografia*, 313.
35. Benito Mussolini, "Discorso pronunciato al Consiglio Nazionale delle Corporazioni il 14 novembre 1933," in De Felice, *Autobiografia*, 333.
36. Camillo Pellizzi, "Tre lettere e una postilla," in De Felice, *Autobiografia*, 323.
37. Giuseppe Bottai, "Vent'anni di Critica Fascista," in De Felice, *Autobiografia*, 434–45.
38. Bruno Stampanato, "Considerazioni sui fatti d'Italia," in De Felice, *Autobiografia*, 488–9.
39. Angelo Tarchi, "La nostra rivoluzione," in De Felice, *Autobiografia*, 514.
40. Gaetano Salvemini, *Le origini del fascismo in Italia* (Milano: Feltrinelli, 1975).
41. The last two decades saw a veritable and to some extent also predictable boom of works on the history of neoliberalism. My work was inspired mainly by the authors who looked at intellectual networks and dialogues rather than starting from a normative definition or reading these texts as merely the legitimization of class domination. Among the most innovative works along these lines are Philip Mirowski and Dieter Plehwe, eds., *The Road from Mont Pèlerin. The Making of the Neoliberal Thought Collective* (Harvard: Harvard University Press, 2009); Angus Burgin, *The Great Persuasion: Reinventing Free Markets Since the Depression* (Cambridge, MA: Harvard University Press, 2012); Quinn Slobodian, *Globalists: The End of Empire and the Birth of Neoliberalism* (Cambridge, MA: Harvard University Press, 2018); and Niklas Olsen, *The Sovereign Consumer: A New Intellectual History of Neoliberalism* (London: Palgrave Macmillan, 2019).
42. Ludwig von Mises, *Socialism: An Economic and Sociological Analysis*, trans. J. Kahane (Indianapolis: Liberty Classics, 1981 [1936]). The original German version was published as *Die Gemeinwirtschaft: Untersuchungen uber den Sozialismus* (Jena: Gustav Fischer, 1922).
43. Mihail Manoilescu, "Neoliberalismul (1922)," in *Dreptul la memorie*, vol. 2, 180–227.
44. Ibid., 186.
45. Ştefan Zeletin, *Neoliberalismul* (Bucharest: Pagini Agrare şi sociale, 1927); modern ed. *Burghezia română. Neoliberalismul* (Bucharest: Nemira, 1997), 279–489.
46. Ibid., 417.
47. Ludwig von Mises, *Die Ursachen der Wirtschaftskrise: ein Vortrag* (Tübingen: Mohr, 1931).
48. Ibid., 8–10.
49. Ibid., 31.
50. Ibid., 27.

51. Ibid.
52. See Antonio Magliulo, "Hayek and the Great Depression of 1929: Did He Really Change His Mind?" *The European Journal of the History of Economic Thought* 23, no. 1 (2016): 31–58.
53. Lionel Robbins, *The Great Depression* (London: Macmillan, 1934). Robbins was the head of LSE's Department of Economics from 1929 to 1940, then following the Second World War from 1945 to 1961.
54. Ibid., 73.
55. Ibid., 82.
56. Ibid., 199–200.
57. Ibid., 149.
58. Ibid.
59. Ibid., 141.
60. Ibid., 143.
61. Ibid., 190.
62. Ibid., 145.
63. Ibid., 152.
64. Michael Schäfer, "Kapitalismus und Kulturkrise. Walter Eucken und die Philosophie Rudolf Euckens," in Swen Steinberg and Winfried Müller, eds., *Wirtschaft und Gemeinschaft. Konfessionelle und neureligiöse Gemeinsinnsmodelle im 19. und 20. Jahrhundert* (Bielefeld: Transcript, 2014), 303–18.
65. Walter Eucken, "Staatliche Strukturwandlungen und die Krisis des Kapitalismus," *Weltwirtschaftliches Archiv* 36 (1932): 297–321.
66. Ibid., 309.
67. Alexander Rüstow, "Der Weg durch Weltkrise und Deutsche Krise," *Europäische Revue* 6, no. 12 (1930): 873–83. The *Europäische Revue* was the intellectual project of the idiosyncratic conservative pan-Europeanist aristocrat Karl Anton Rohan. On the *Revue*, see Guido Müller, "Von Hugo von Hoffmannsthals 'Traum des Reiches' zum Europa unter nationalsozialistischer Herrschaft—Die 'Europäische Revue' 1925–1936/44," in Hans-Christof Kraus, ed., *Konservative Zeitschriften zwischen Kaiserreich und Diktatur. Fünf Fallstudien* (Berlin: Duncker & Humblot, 2003), 155–86.
68. For a selection of Röpke's political texts, see Wilhelm Röpke, *Marktwirtschaft ist nicht genug. Gesammelte Aufsätze*, ed. Hans Jörg Hennecke (Waltrop: Manuscriptum, 2009). On Röpke's economic ideas, see Samuel Gregg, *Wilhelm Röpke's Political Economy* (Cheltenham: Edward Elgar, 2010).
69. Röpke, "Der Weg des Unheils" (1931), in *Marktwirtschaft ist nicht genug*, 39–44.
70. Ibid., 41.
71. Röpke, "Die Katastrophensüchtigen" (1931), in ibid., 45–46.
72. Röpke, "Der derzeitige Geld- und Finanzkrisis" (1932), in ibid., 47–66.
73. Röpke even used the concepts of *Totalkrise* and *Gesamtkrise*, pointing to the civilizational underpinnings of the economic, social, and political crisis symptoms, but kept stressing that the different manifestations of crisis can and should be analytically separated and it is possible to establish causal relationships between them. See his lecture from 1938, where he also links Lippmann to the German "ordoliberals": Wilhelm Röpke, "Die entscheidenden Probleme des weltwirtschaftlichen Verfalls," *Zeitschrift für schweizerische Statistik und Volkswirtschaft* 74 (1938): 493–506.
74. Slobodian, *Globalists*, 91–120, 263–88.

164 Intellectuals and the Crisis of Politics

75. Franz Boese, ed., *Deutschland und die Weltkrise* (Munich and Leipzig: Duncker und Humblot, 1932).

76. Manuel Saitzew, "Deutschland und die Weltkrise. Industrialisierung und Arbeitslosigkeit," in ibid., 15–35.

77. Gerhard Colm, "Deutschland und die Weltkrise. Die Industrialisierung als Ursache von Gleichgewichtsstörungen," in Boese, *Deutschland und die Weltkrise*, 36–41.

78. Emanuel Neuman, *Limitele puterii statului* [The Limits of State Power] (Bucharest: Universitatea din Bucureşti, 1937).

79. Louis Rougier, *Les mystiques politiques contemporaines et leurs incidences internationales* (Paris: Librairie du Recueil Sirey, 1935). On Rougier's complex intellectual trajectory see Angus Burgin, *The Great Persuasion*, 67–79.

80. Rougier, *Les mystiques politiques*, 79.

81. Ibid., 80.

82. On the collapse of the French political consensus in the early 1930s and the radical polarization resulting in the violent clashes of 1934, see Michel Winock, *La fièvre hexagonale. Les grandes crises politiques de 1871 à 1968* (Paris: Calmann-Lévy, 1986).

83. Rougier, *Les mystiques politiques*, 121.

84. Walter Lippmann, *The Good Society* (Boston: Little, Brown and Company, 1937). The presentations at the colloquium were republished in Serge Audier, ed., *Le colloque Lippmann*.

85. József Takáts shows the complexity of the discussion around Lippmann's book that goes well beyond the actual participants of the Colloque. He documented the exchange between Oszkár Jászi, the Hungarian civic radical émigré teaching at Oberlin College, and Lippmann himself. Jászi had read Lippmann's work as an attempt to find a "third way" between Marxist socialism and classical liberalism and so to create a non-dogmatic socialism that could accommodate the principles of private property and market competition. He also connected his younger friend Michael (Mihály) Polanyi (a natural scientist who was inspired by Keynes and was searching for a way out of the deadlock of liberal orthodoxy in the 1930s) with Lippman. Polanyi eventually participated in the Paris meeting; Jászi, whose main concern was the liberalization of socialism, did not. József Takáts, "Jászi és a jó társadalom. A Lippmann-felfedezés és -csalódás története [Jászi and the Good Society. The History of His Discovery of and Disappointment with Lippmann]," *BUKSZ—Budapesti Könyvszemle* [BUKSZ—The Budapest Review of Books] 24, no. 3–4 (2012): 220–9.

86. Lippmann, *The Good Society*, 21.

87. In contrast to his brother Karl (Charles, Károly) Polanyi, Michael became increasingly critical of the Western left for its penchant for collectivism, which in his understanding had potential totalitarian consequences. While he started as a natural scientist, he became interested in the way the Soviet system had limited academic freedom in favor of its ideological and pragmatic aims and published several polemic studies on the topic. In 1935, he also published a pioneering analysis of the Soviet economic system. See Michael Polanyi, "U.S.S.R. Economics: Fundamental Data, System, and Spirit," *The Manchester School of Economic and Social Studies* 6 (November 1935): 67–89. For a good overview of the intellectual history of interwar Hungarian emigration, see Lee Congdon, *Seeing Red: Hungarian Intellectuals in Exile and the Challenge of Communism* (DeKalb: Northern Illinois University Press, 2001).

88. Lippmann, *The Good Society*, 31.

89. Ibid., 131.
90. Ibid., 154.
91. Ibid., 204.
92. Ibid., 371.
93. Ibid., 370.
94. On the importance of the timing, see François Denord, "French Neoliberalism and Its Divisions: From the Colloque Walter Lippmann to the Fifth Republic," in Mirowski and Plehwe, *The Road from Mont Pèlerin*, 45–67.
95. After the *Anschluss*, Possony first moved to France and eventually to the United States, where he became a well-known foreign policy and national security expert. He lived long enough to be a key figure in preparing Ronald Reagan's "Star Wars" program.
96. Audier, *Le colloque Lippmann*, 305–6.
97. Ibid., 324.
98. Ibid., 328.
99. Ibid., 318–19, 332.
100. Ibid., 331.
101. Imre Csécsy, "Megbukott-e a demokrácia [Has Democracy Failed]?" in Tibor Valuch, ed., *Radikalizmus és demokrácia. Csécsy Imre válogatott írásai* [Radicalism and Democracy. The Collected Writings of Imre Csécsy], ed. (Szeged: Aetas, 1998), 111–34.
102. Oszkár Jászi, "A jó társadalom [The Good Society]," *Századunk* 13, no. 4–5 (1938): 122–32. See Takáts, "Jászi és a jó társadalom," 227. *Századunk* was the intellectual successor to *Huszadik Század* [Twentieth Century], the main outlet of the *fin-de-siècle* progressive intelligentsia in Hungary which Jászi had edited until it ceased publication in late summer 1919.
103. On the urbanite-populist conflict, see Gyula Borbándi, "Entstehung des Populismus," in *Der ungarische Populismus* (Mainz: Hase & Koehler, 1976), 88–104.
104. See especially his "A *magyar Gironde* vagy jótanács a jobboldalnak [The Hungarian Girondins: Or, Some Advice to the Right]," in Valuch, *Radikalizmus és demokrácia*, 163–72. Originally published under the same title in *Századunk* 14, no. 1 (1939): 1–11.
105. Olivier Dard, "Louis Rougier: Itinéraire intellectuel et politique, des années vingt à Nouvelle École," *Philosophia Scientiæ* 7 (2007): 50–64.
106. Gaëtan Pirou, *Néo-libéralisme, néo-corporatisme, néo-socialisme* (Paris: Gallimard, 1939).
107. Ibid., 48.
108. On the debates around the idea of neo-socialism, see "The Identity Crisis of Social Democracy" in Chapter 8.
109. Pirou, *Néo-libéralisme*, 165.
110. Ibid., 175ff.
111. Michel Marculesco, *La critique du libéralisme d'après les auteurs néo-libéraux* (Paris: Faculté de Droit, 1943).
112. Tătărescu was reputedly flexible ideologically: he worked with King Carol II to establish the royal dictatorship in 1938, while after 1945 he was an important fellow-traveler of the communists.
113. Louis Baudin, *Le Corporatisme. Italie, Portugal, Allemagne, Espagne, France* (Paris: Librairie générale de droit et de jurisprudence, 1941).

114. N. G. Pierson, Ludwig von Mises, Georg Halm, and Enrico Barone, and Friedrich A. von Hayek, *L'Économie dirigée en régime collectiviste: études critiques sur les possibilités du socialisme* (Paris: Librairie de Médicis, 1939).
115. Friedrich A. von Hayek, *The Road to Serfdom* (London: Routledge, 1944).
116. See Julia Stapleton, *Englishness and the Study of Politics: The Social and Political Thought of Ernest Barker* (Cambridge: Cambridge University Press, 1994).
117. Ferdynand Zweig, *The Planning of Free Societies* (London: Secker & Warburg, 1942), 9.
118. Ibid., 9.
119. Ibid., 70.
120. Ibid., 19.
121. See also Serge Audier's introductory notes to *Le colloque Lippmann*, where he points out that, up to the 1950s, self-regulating markets were not the core of neoliberalism.

7
Crisis of Democracy

The turn of the twentieth century brought about several highly conflictual situations in European parliamentary political systems from Italy to Austria–Hungary to England, all of which were framed as "political crises" by contemporaries. These were usually rooted in the clash of various loci of power (the parliament, the government, and the monarch) and often led to the strengthening of the executive branch, although they did not result in a fully-fledged authoritarian turn.[1]

In turn, the end of the First World War was often perceived as the triumphant moment of the principle of democratic self-determination, with historian James Bryce (1838–1922) counting in 1921 more than 100 representative assemblies in the world.[2] However, already in the early 1920s, representative democracy was often bitterly criticized for failing to provide an adequate manifestation of the common good and becoming instead the instrument of the uncontrollable and irrational masses. This criticism was not unprecedented, as it was rooted in the negative evaluations of mass democracy already prevalent at the turn of the century, formulated by such luminaries of social thought as Georges Sorel, Vilfredo Pareto, Gustave Le Bon, and Robert Michels, among others.[3] Their ideas gained further resonance in the early 1920s, when the proliferation of parliamentary regimes went together with the experience of permanent infighting and chronic instability, soon to be challenged by authoritarian projects.[4]

Indeed, Carl Schmitt's (1888–1985) sweeping criticism of parliamentary democracy—arguably the most complex interwar theoretical assault on liberal democracy and by implication on the whole political framework of the Weimar Republic—was not the product of the "Great Depression," but had been formulated in the early and mid-1920s.[5] Interestingly, in the preface to the first edition of his 1923 study on parliamentary democracy, crisis was not yet a keyword. Schmitt focused instead on parliamentarism's "loss of moral and intellectual foundations."[6] In the preface to the 1926 edition, however, crisis came to play a much more prominent role, as he asserted that the crisis of the parliamentary system sprang from the circumstances of modern mass democracy. While Schmitt made an analytical distinction between the crisis of parliamentarism, the crisis of the modern state, and the crisis of democracy, he also remarked that they reinforced each other.

Schmitt defined democracy not in terms of its "political content" but as an organizational form, as a "machinery" based on the majoritarian principle, aiming at "validating the general will." In his opinion, this implied that a functioning democracy required a substantial homogeneity of society (the identity of the governed and

---

Intellectuals and the Crisis of Politics in the Interwar Period and Beyond. Balázs Trencsényi, Oxford University Press.
© Balázs Trencsényi (2025). DOI: 10.1093/9780198929512.003.0007

168 Intellectuals and the Crisis of Politics

governing) as the outvoted also had to identify with it, otherwise the majoritarian decisions would sooner or later completely disintegrate the political community.

Democracy for Schmitt was not to be equated with parliamentarism or liberalism. Liberalism and democracy only seemed to be identical during their common struggle against royal absolutism, but with the emergence of modern democratic institutions this convergence was naturally undermined as there was an "inescapable contradiction of liberal individualism and democratic homogeneity."[7] Democracy did not necessarily overlap with parliamentarism either, and the will of the people was not necessarily best expressed by aggregating opinions, as a system based on acclamation or some other form of direct democracy could well be more powerful than that mediated by parliaments. Thus, democratic components could be linked to different ideological positions, from socialism to conservatism. Along these lines he added that, although Bolshevism and fascism were evidently anti-liberal, they were not necessarily anti-democratic, which also implied the possibility of democratic dictatorships, as "Caesaristic methods" could be the "direct expression of democratic substance and power." For Schmitt, while Bolshevik practices contradicted the democratic principle, Bolshevism as an ideology was compatible with it. Conversely, Italian fascism challenged democracy in ideological terms, but its concept of legitimacy remained democratic.

Arguing that the degradation of parliamentarism predated the rise of fascism and Bolshevism, Schmitt also inferred that these ideologies emerged as possible solutions to the crisis of liberal democracy.[8] Furthermore, autocratic tendencies were not something unprecedented in democracy, as historical precursors of modern democracy (e.g., English Levellers) also had such features. According to Schmitt, nor were supporters of the Weimar Republic exempt from this, as they condoned certain autocratic measures to defend the democratic political framework. Schmitt could thus envisage both a dictatorial democracy and a democratic dictatorship, legitimizing the sovereign by democratic acclamation or educating the people to democracy by undemocratic means. From this perspective, in his interpretation, crisis was a breaking point that laid bare the artificiality of the liberal democratic political order, imposed by the creators of the Weimar Republic in their striving to comply with the ideological expectations of the victors of the Great War.

The Institutional Crisis of Parliamentary Democracy and its Remedies

That said, until the mid-1920s, the "crisis of democracy" was still considered to be specific for certain national contexts. Even critiques of specific systems rarely referenced a systemic crisis of democracy as such. Instead, they discussed dysfunctions to be remedied and excesses to be trimmed based on thorough institutional analyses. Another target of criticism was the moral level of political elites and societies, allegedly not yet mature enough to respect the democratic rules of the game. Thus, in 1925, French jurist and political writer Émile Giraud (1894–1965) reflected upon the seemingly paradoxical situation that the geographical and quantitative expansion of the democratic form of government coincided with the loss of self-confidence of democratic regimes. Giraud had a broadly transnational perspective as he worked for the League of Nations (and, after the Second World War, he contributed to the drafting of the Universal Declaration of Human Rights). Hence, he could start his book with a sweeping comparative analysis, pointing out that the weakening of democratic convictions was detectable even in countries that had a rather long democratic history behind them.[9] Giraud also pointed to the rise of a new type of anti-democratic doctrine combining nationalism and elitism, exemplified by the Action Française, and stressed the common features between the extreme right (fascist) and left (Bolshevik) critiques of democracy.

Along these lines, the French author rebutted some of the accusations against the democratic system, such as anarchy and the volatility of political preferences, accentuating instead several other problems, such as legislative impotence and temporizing, which in his understanding were responsible for the loss of faith in democratic institutions. Overall, in his opinion, the root of the unfolding crisis was in the inefficiency of parliamentary legislation and the fragmentation caused by individual and partisan interests. He called for a reform of the structure of parliament, moving toward more proportional representation and a restricted number of inclusive parties or party blocs that could stabilize the political system. In addition, he argued for the creation of a representative organ (of a quasi-corporatist type) based on the professional principle, which could focus its legislative efforts on the economy.

Another expert of parliamentary politics, internationally well-known German–Jewish liberal economist and political writer Moritz Julius Bonn (1873–1965) sought to reach beyond the German context and give a comprehensive interpretation in his 1925 *Crisis of European Democracy* published in the United States. He was among the first to describe the rise of a monstrous "New Leviathan," a new type of autocracy that posed an existential threat to liberal democracy.[10] Bonn acknowledged the disappointment with liberal democratic rule all over Europe and the appearance of new threats after 1918. He was particularly worried that, with the First World War, the Age of Reason had ended and the cult of violence became part and parcel of politics, both domestically and in the colonies.

Overall, in Bonn's rendering, democracy was relatively new and had limited experience in coping with crisis. The series of collective disappointments following the Great War, including the catastrophic consequences of the defeat of the Central Powers, socioeconomic hardships that hit winners and losers alike, and, in general, the eternal postponement of the promised "social millennium" to eliminate exploitation made people increasingly impatient with democratic institutions. As a result, they started to look for "shortcuts"—a dictator who could, with an act of will, simultaneously transform society and politics. Bonn linked this to the rise of a new type of political ideology, based on voluntarism, shared by such otherwise politically conflicting ideologists as Lenin and Mussolini—both of whom were inspired by the Sorelian critique of Marxist evolutionism. A novelty of these ideologies and emerging regimes was that they brought together democracy and oppression: while previous tyrannies were based on the domination of a minority, here the majority acted as the oppressor and the minorities were the principal targets. Bonn also stressed the entanglement between fascism and Bolshevism: they acted as a mutual trigger, pointing to the other as an existential threat to the community that could only be countered by total mobilization and the ruthless use of political violence. Their intertwining and similarities notwithstanding, Bonn admitted that these two ideologies were far from being identical. For example, Mussolini had no vision of an ideal social order, whereas Lenin and his followers had a well-defined final aim they strove to achieve: communism.

When, four years later, the Sudeten German member of the Czechoslovak Senate (for the Christian-Social People's Party, a conservative formation, which accepted the political framework of the Czechoslovak Republic and actively participated in its political life), Wilhelm Medinger (1878–1934) reviewed the discussions at the Inter-Parliamentary Union on the crisis of parliamentary democracy, the landscape was even more sobering as, in the meantime, many postwar democratic governments were replaced by autocratic regimes (Italy in 1922; Spain in 1923; Greece in 1925–6, Poland, Lithuania, and Portugal in 1926; and Yugoslavia in 1929).[11] Having multiple political socializations and loyalties, Medinger was sensitive to the contested nature of the concept of crisis. While in the German political discourse it became a central notion, Czech political actors tended to play it down, asserting with president Tomáš G, Masaryk (1850–1937) that crisis symptoms were only "child illnesses" (*Kinderkrankheiten*) that would be overcome as time passed and the organism grew.

To be sure, Medinger was more pessimistic, reminding his audience that before the *Marcia su Roma* no one could imagine the terminal crisis of Italian democracy. Going beyond analyzing the democratic ups and downs of individual national contexts, he also stressed that the problems he saw had universal relevance. Like Bonn, he contrasted the high expectations connected to the expansion of parliamentarism in the early 1920s and the subsequent disenchantment, pointing out that the only exceptions where the prestige of parliamentary democracy grew were in Sweden and Switzerland.

According to Medinger, a key feature of the loss of public trust was the bureaucratization of parliamentary factions that had lost touch with socioeconomic realities. Contrary to Giraud, who stressed the need to strengthen the executive, Medinger argued that it was the loss of the controlling function of parliament and its subordination to the executive that had fatally undermined the former's authority. The disenchantment with parliamentarism was thus essential to a broader process of the delegitimization of state structures. In contrast to the private sector, state institutions took no responsibility and could not be held accountable for spending public money and amassing public debt. The remedy Medinger suggested was *grosso modo* liberal, without insisting on the label: the privatization of certain sectors of the economy as well as regionalization/decentralization (notably, the latter point was in line with his political function of being a parliamentary representative for the German national minority in Czechoslovakia). He also favored the clear separation of political and technocratic functions in administration.

According to Medinger, another factor contributing to the delegitimization of parliamentary democracy was that, in the democratic political logic, short-term interests tended to dominate over long-term issues. At the same time, the survival of the political system required more lasting policies and commitments. In his opinion, this could only be achieved by creating durable structures, such as longer-term nominations for office, the immunity of members of parliament, or setting up a professional second chamber. Furthermore, drawing on his experience as a Sudeten German representative, he also argued for more inclusive politics, co-opting minorities into the government to avoid the creation of "permanent minorities" who would lose their motivation to participate in the political system. Finally, while accepting that modern democracy was built on universal suffrage, he argued against a totally proportional system, which he believed led to fragmentation, and suggested instead the personalization of political orientations, creating a system of "*Spitzenkandidaten*" with whom voters could identify more than with the impersonal party machines.

Giraud, Bonn, and Medinger can all be considered "internal" critics of liberal democracy who sought to revitalize it in a new context. They stressed that the crisis of parliamentarism was only part of a broader postwar crisis complex, and therefore unrepairable via merely technical changes. It required a more comprehensive response. At the same time, these thinkers rejected the idea of a "total crisis" and tried to demarcate institutional questions from more general cultural criticism. Their strategy was to create a more self-reflective democratic position and correct the exaggerated expectations of the early 1920s to prevent a growth in frustration with those who thought that democracy would immediately bring along an ideal socioeconomic and cultural order. However, toward the late 1920s, in the context of the rise of powerful anti-systemic forces (not only in Germany but also in many other national contexts), this strategy seemed less and less plausible. The generalization of the crisis discourse observed in the Weimar context still did not mean that the collapse of democracy would become a dominant scenario all over Europe. Nevertheless, the destabilization of Germany became a powerful argument for those who depicted the situation in terms of an existential crisis of democracy and of political modernity as such.[12]

Back in the mid-1920s, however, Germany was not the central point of reference for discussions on alternatives to liberal democracy. Parliamentary democracy crumbled earlier in Poland, where the May 1926 coup of Marshal Józef Piłsudski dismissed the president and the prime minister, affecting mainly the right-wing ethnonationalist National Democrats, who had formed the majority in the *Sejm*. Historian and syndicalist politician Kazimierz Zakrzewski (1900–41), who supported Piłsudski's coup, reflected on the rise of authoritarianism all over Europe in his book on the "crisis of democracy," coming up with a conceptualization of "anti-liberal democracy."[13] He pointed to the Italian fascist notion of "demoliberalism," which lumped liberalism and democracy together into a common enemy image, and argued that in reality these two ideological traditions were far from overlapping. To support his argument, he evoked Rousseau and the French revolutionary radicals who created an anti-liberal system of "democratic tyranny." In turn, he added, liberalism (which he linked to capitalism) could also be anti-democratic. He delineated these traditions historically as competing rather than converging: liberalism was the ideology of the oligarchy, challenged by populist democratic movements. Regarding the present, he described Bolshevism and fascism as anti-liberal but still essentially democratic doctrines. In general, anti-liberal democracy for Zakrzewski presupposed a direct link of people and government, excluding institutional mediation. Its main features were plebiscitary legitimization of power, personalized decision making, and the integration of organic social formations.[14] As a leftist supporter of Piłsudski's *Sanacja* regime, Zakrzewski's position was highly ambiguous: he rejected liberal democracy and was highly critical of parliamentarism—but not from a right-wing authoritarian and nationalist perspective. Rather, he was trying to save a secular and relatively tolerant political framework by restricting a pluralism dominated by Polish nationalists. This dilemma of limiting actual democracy to save its essence would be posed even more dramatically in the early 1930s in the German context when the Weimar Republic was challenged by anti-systemic forces on the radical right and radical left.

Facing the "New Leviathan": Intellectual Crisis Managers of Liberal Democracy

Lawyer and political thinker Hermann Heller (1891–1933) was a leading defender of parliamentary democracy in the last years of the Weimar Republic. He was close to the social democrats, even if his opinions were not always completely overlapping with those of the party leadership. He linked the idea of the existential crisis of democracy to the rise of fascism already in the second half of the 1920s, that is, before Nazism became a dominant force in German politics.[15] Converging with the earlier analyses of the loss of trust in democratic institutions, and entering into a complex critical dialogue with Schmitt's anti-democratic arguments, Heller also noticed that Bolshevism and fascism became especially attractive for those whose belief in the possibility of parliamentary democracy was shaken.[16]

Heller defined politics as the organization of contrary wills on a common basis. Hence, democratic politics was predicated upon the consensus of the population, that is, citizens agreeing to be ruled by a majority decision even if they did not concur with a particular policy in question. However, such a consensus was not that easy to create and maintain, as there were few features that connected all members of a modern society. Premodern religious unity was clearly lost, and was replaced by cultural community, which in turn was challenged by class differences. Likewise, the legal system needed to be based on some values that transcended it, as it was impossible to derive norms just from the legal system itself. Here Heller clashed head-on with legal positivism and especially with Austrian jurist Hans Kelsen (1881–1973), its main proponent and theoretician in the interwar period.

In contrast to Kelsen and coming close to Schmitt's position, Heller argued that only rules motivated by normative content could possess authority. The ongoing crisis of European politics in this understanding was precisely due to the dissolution of these underlying normative frameworks. He considered Pareto a paradigmatic thinker, who articulated the lack of normative bases of politics and described ideologies as the self-deceit of different parties who were contending for power. From this perspective, society was indeed a *bellum omnium contra omnes*, with competing elites seeking to control politics and manipulate the masses. Heller held that it was this non-normative vision (which in Pareto's case could be described as neo-Machiavellian, stating that the act always preceded the norm) that served as the principal inspiration for Mussolini and meant the most serious challenge to democratic politics.

Heller also identified other challenges that undermined the hitherto existing value system, such as the rise of new (post-positivist) scientific paradigms which challenged the rationalist worldview, rooted in natural law and Newtonian physics. In this dynamic moment of transformation, conservatism could not aim at preserving the social and cultural values of the recent past but had to turn more "revolutionary" and impose its irrationalist organicism and corporatist vision on society by force. Key intellectual representatives of this "counter-revolutionary revolution" were Schmitt, the Stefan George circle, Oswald Spengler, and the Conservative Revolutionaries, labeled by Heller as "epigons of Nietzsche."

At the same time, the left also moved toward irrational philosophy, as the widespread cult of Sorel indicates. Heller pointed out the structural similarity between leftist and rightist radicalism, referring to similarities in the ideas of Sorel and Action Française: irrationalism, anti-parliamentarism, anti-pacifism, and the rejection of bourgeois optimism. For Heller, both the right-wing and left-wing irrationalists suffered from the same normlessness. Their claim of universal regeneration was flawed, promising a sort of "pseudo-Renaissance," since they did not believe in the transcendence of the classical values they claimed to cultivate, as the case of Action Française showed. The political Catholicism of Maurras and his followers was based not on belief in God but on the craving for a hierarchical Church.

Overall, Heller considered these ideologies as imitative and incoherent; drawn from different second-hand sources; mixing mechanistic thinking and irrationalism; cultivating an "oppositional resentment" against the system and craving for a stable system at the same time (thus oscillating between incompatible positions and making voluntaristic shifts—"like a chameleon changes its colors") when political expediency demanded it. This argument was remarkable also because Heller sought to turn Schmitt's accusations against liberal democracy—as being devoid of a core and thus engaging in an endless alternation of contradictory positions—upside down.

For Heller, the attraction of fascism was in its rejection of "nomocratic thinking." Depending on the situation it could imply the rejection or deification of the state, support of socialism or capitalism, syndicalism or centralism, Catholicism or paganism.[17] Seeking to contextualize it in relation to Italy, he pointed to Italy's lack of internal integration during the nineteenth century, meaning the absence of common values and the especially divisive nature of class conflicts. This was aggravated by the failure of the constitutional state (the *Rechtsstaat* in Heller's terms) to

174 Intellectuals and the Crisis of Politics

enforce its norms, thus providing the opportunity for Mussolini and his followers to grab power. In Heller's understanding the image of a "heroic struggle" against the bourgeois system, perpetuated by fascist propaganda, was a myth.

Having no ideological core, Heller characterized fascism as having an "internal void."[18] Rather than the unfolding of a political ideology, its history could thus be equated with the "biography of Mussolini." Along these lines, Heller contrasted the 1919 fascist program to fascist ideological statements of the early 1920s, pointing out the shift from a leftist to an integral nationalist key. In his opinion, organicist ideas were only a veneer, whereas in reality Mussolini remained a subversive individualist-syndicalist, albeit turning away from popular sovereignty toward the idea that the only sovereign was the dictator himself.

Being based on the "normless will" (*normlose Willen*) that replaced the positivist "will-less norm" (*willenlose Norm*), fascism only pretended to rule by laws. This is where Heller engaged in battle with Kelsen and argued that while on the surface a fascist regime might well look like a constitutional state (*Rechtsstaat*), it was not (only a "formal nomocracy"). To support his case, Heller quoted Mussolini's 1929 speech in which he described his regime as "disciplined democracy," keeping the democratic surface, but rejecting its core idea of rule through the freely given consent of the citizens. Along these lines, Heller put Schmitt's concept of "plebiscitary democracy" into the same category as well. The fascist regime effectively constrained the democratic choice of citizens by exerting a monopoly over the press and directing the press with oral commands, limiting freedom of opinion and setting up special courts to prosecute critics of the government. Irrespective of the formal similarities, the dictatorial party was not rooted in real social functions but rather served as a *pars pro toto* of the regime and eventually a conduit for the personal will of the dictator. To Heller, this was completely different from the function of democratic parties, which aimed at organizing a plurality of wills into a common framework. In a dictatorial regime, on the other hand, state corruption becomes systemic and centralized, in contrast to the more accidental nature of corruption in a democratic system, where the public sphere still exerts a certain level of control.

Regarding fascist economic policies, Heller stressed the centrality of the corporatist idea, which was meant to overwrite class conflict, depoliticize society, and preserve capitalism but suppress socioeconomic or political self-management. In exchange, it created an "absolutist" welfare state that offered certain provisions, for example, some social protection and access to consumer goods, leisure activities, and the development of infrastructure. While Heller did not assert the complete convergence of fascism and Bolshevism, he still found comparable tendencies in the Soviet Union, which he characterized not so much as a socialist regime, but as the universalization of state capitalism, relying on "Manchesterian" forms of exploitation.

How was it possible to survive the crisis of democracy without falling into the trap of false solutions offered by these dictatorial regimes? Heller was committed to the defense of parliamentary democracy, using all possible means and perhaps also suspending some of the political rights of the outright enemies of the democratic order. To this end, he spelled out an early version of the idea of "militant democracy," the name of which was coined by German émigré Karl Loewenstein after the Nazi takeover.[19] Heller also hoped to create a rather broad social platform against the fascists, involving also the Church, which would have a vital interest in fighting the fascist normlessness and its cult of violence. In ideological terms, he hoped to find a common denominator among liberalism (rejecting the "Manchesterian" vision but supporting the liberalism of "basic rights"), social democracy, and national belonging (stressing the need for a certain homogeneity of wills while rejecting ethnic nationalism).

Heller eventually had an opportunity to try some of his ideas in practice, while seeking to defend the Weimar constitutional order against the Nazi takeover. He represented the Prussian social democratic government against the German state in the famous 1932 court case *Preußen contra Reich*, where Schmitt, his main political and intellectual adversary, advised the central government. Here, the crisis discourse was converted into the language of the state of exception, as both sides argued in need of exceptional measures to defend the constitutional order, albeit with contrary political implications. The Prussian social democrats sought to legitimize the continuation of their state-level government even if they lost their parliamentary majority, whereas the supporters of the central authorities and *Reichspräsident* von Hindenburg stressed the need for exceptional measures to prevent what they considered an unconstitutional move by the Prussian state government, invoking the famous Article 48 of the Weimar Constitution providing special powers to the president to defend the legal order and the unity of the state. While Article 48 was used in the early 1920s by social democrat Friedrich Ebert to fence off the extreme leftist and rightist attempts to undermine the Republic, it now became an instrument in the hands of those who would demolish the last institutionally powerful bastion of resistance against the Nazi takeover. The Constitutional Court ruled in favor of the central government and thus the last episode of the Weimar constitutional debate ended with the victory of Schmitt and the emigration (and subsequent premature death) of Heller.

Gerhard Leibholz (1901–1982) was another key defender of the democratic constitutional framework in the terminal period of the Weimar Republic. He was a student of prominent liberal professor of law Richard Thoma (1874–1957) and like Heller or Bonn, Leibholz also came from a highly integrated German–Jewish family. In his 1933 book, Leibholz sought to provide a theoretical framework for understanding the German developments that led to the demise of the liberal democratic order.[20] Leibholz started from the perspective that every state form had a metaphysical basis, resonating with the ideas of Max Weber (theorizing on the religious roots of modernity) and Louis Rougier (writing on "political mystique"), and to some extent also with Heller's argument about the normative basis of the legal-political system. In addition, Leibholz also referred to Thoma and Masaryk as important theoretical sources of his analysis.

From this perspective, it was the belief in freedom and equality that formed the metaphysical basis of democracy. Linking individualism and collectivism, democracy also combined the idea of popular sovereignty with the need for the state to

176 Intellectuals and the Crisis of Politics

guarantee individual freedoms. There existed, however, different types of democracy: their variation depended on the many divergent understandings of equality. The dominant form of modern democracy was the "mass-democratic party-state" (*massendemokratische Parteienstaat*). This variant was based on the majoritarian principle, being somewhat softened by the rotation of offices—making the inevitable clash of majority and minority more oblique. Leibholz stressed that if this mediation failed, the relationship of the majority and the minority could escalate into violent conflict.

Like Carl Schmitt, Leibholz admitted that the link between democracy and liberalism was not self-evident: they could converge, but also turn against each other.[21] One could imagine many divergent forms of democracy as a result: some of them compatible with liberalism and the defense of minorities, while others markedly anti-liberal. If unrestrained majoritarian rule and the Rousseauian *volonté générale* became core elements, the ensuing variant became an absolutist democracy, assuming such forms as Bonapartism, dictatorship, the rejection of the constitutional state (*Rechtsstaat*), and even outright tyranny. At the same time, like Heller, Leibholz also noted that the meaning of liberalism changed over time; thus, the relationship of liberalism and democracy needed to be conceived dynamically: elements that seemed compatible in the nineteenth century might well have become incompatible in the twentieth.

Written with the experience of the collapse of the Weimar system in mind, Leibholz's argument also concurred with Heller's on another point: a substantialist interpretation of the *Rechtsstaat*. It was not enough to base the *Rechtsstaat* on the unbreakability of laws, as "law" (*Gesetz*) and "right" (*Recht*) did not necessarily overlap. Leibholz framed this opposition as the conflict of legality and legitimacy, with reference to Schmitt. He also followed Schmitt when arguing that liberalism was based on value-relativism and was only possible in social systems that had an underlying layer of absolute values.[22]

Regarding Germany's crisis of parliamentary democracy, Leibholz pointed out that it could be related to the gradual relativization and eventual dissolution of the value system that had emerged originally from the religious sphere to be carried over into a secular system of normativity. He cited Kelsen, criticized both by Schmitt and Heller, as an example of this relativization. Leibholz also linked this relativization to a social transformation marked by the emergence of "bourgeois society" characterized by depersonalization and the separation of the spheres of production and producers (here referring to Marx). The result was that the *citoyen* was "lost" and only the "bourgeois remained." This transformation had an impact on the political and ideological coherence of society. While in 1918 there was still a level of consensus rooted in relative social and political homogeneity (here Leibholz drew on Heller's analysis), by the early 1930s hope had diminished that the fundamental conflicts of society could be resolved by means of parliamentary democracy (i.e., through discussion mediated by institutions).[23] As the crisis unfolded, a dialectical movement emerged between economic individualization and the growth of popular pressure to limit individuality by a repressive state.

Thus, in a way, mass democracy was undermined by those social groups who had previously been emancipated by liberalism. The emerging crisis-ridden form of government rejected institutional mediation and created a plebiscitary democracy where party movements dominated, and the parliament was turned into a mere "plebiscitary auxiliary body" (*plebiszitarer Hilfsorgan*). Following the loss of the transcendental basis of life, people started to search for faith in politics, sacralizing their political leaders (in a footnote, Leibholz referred to the cult of the "new man" in "Hitlerism"). With politics becoming a new religion of sorts, it became impossible to forge any compromise or make any lasting coalition—since every coalition was necessarily based on compromise, which in turn undermined the absolute nature of any participating political force.

The emerging "post-individual" state had different variants. In the case of authoritarianism, some elements of democracy could go together with a new understanding of the state and the will of the majority remained central to the legitimization of the regime, even if the institution of democratic elections was abandoned. In contrast, the totalitarian state invaded all spheres of life and aimed at the physical destruction of its enemies. For Leibholz, the question was whether the new regime installed in 1933 would opt for an authoritarian or totalitarian direction. He had mixed feelings. On the one hand, he registered the tendency of National Socialists to create a one-party state, eliminating all residual liberal and democratic elements. On the other hand, pointing to the German cultural and political tradition (going back to ancient and medieval "Germanic freedom"), he was ultimately skeptical of the possibility of completely collectivizing the individual and massifying the spirit.

By the early 1930s, the exponential growth of anti-democratic sentiments in Germany attracted vivid interest among external observers as well. Importantly, most of these authors analyzed this growth in terms of a "*Sonderweg*." For example, in his book on the "German crisis" French philosopher and Sorbonne professor Albert Rivaud (1876–1955), who—in contrast to Leibholz's anti-authoritarian reading—derived the failure of modern democratic institutions from the German historical tradition. He pointed to the more superficial Christianization of Germanic tribes in comparison to the Latins as well as the powerful collectivistic ideological traditions that subordinated individuality to the community, present in the thought of Kant, Hegel, and "political and social romanticism."[24]

Taking such a *longue durée* perspective, Rivaud argued that the economic hardships escalating at the turn of the decade were far from being the root cause of the decomposition of the Weimar Republic. There were underlying "moral and mental crises" that extended back into the pre-1914 period and that had triggered these postwar developments.[25] Thus, from the late nineteenth century onward, German society lost its sense of proportion and set out on a course of unlimited expansion, in both a political and economic sense, which could only lead to a catastrophic ending. This argument also implied that it was not the postwar political dynamic, let alone the Versailles Treaty, that was responsible for the fragility of German democracy. Rather, Rivaud claimed that European peace depended on defending the Versailles settlement. Along these lines, he questioned the overall commitment of German society to these democratic values and pointed to the authoritarian mentality of the German bureaucracy as well as the expansionism of industry as key factors of instability. He also considered the economic consolidation after 1924 as deceptive, creating an expectation of limitless growth that was financed mainly by state credits without real economic backing. He described this "artificial growth" as yet another manifestation of the overall loss of moderation, which thus prepared the ground for even more distorted reactions, "disregarding the facts, the lessons of experience and abandoning themselves to the obscure forces of life" when this economic growth stalled in the late 1920s.[26] The outcome was the collapse of the more moderate parties and the rise of the extreme right, which threatened the entire Western hemisphere.

Seeing little (if any) difference between the German establishment and the Nazi contenders, Rivaud stood for keeping to the restrictive policies of military and monetary control pursued by postwar French governments, and by implication he resented the British and American voices, which called for a more lenient treatment of Germany, given its economic and political hardships. This position *grosso modo* corresponded to the mainstream French conservative public opinion of the period. The ambiguities of this stance become more obvious when, by 1940, like some of these conservatives, Rivaud abandoned his liberal democratic position and opted to support Pétain's efforts of national regeneration in an—uneasy—alliance with Hitler's Germany.

Even if in other Western European contexts the danger of the collapse of democracy seemed less imminent, the feeling of urgency, related to the shaking of the democratic consensus, still existed and the discussions centered on the necessary social and ideological measures to defend this consensus. Having broad transnational horizons, British writer and social reformer H. G. Wells (1866–1946) was one of the prophets of such democratic self-defense worldwide. In his 1931 highly emotional talk "Our World in Fifty Years' Time", he declared that "[i]nstead of progress there is crisis everywhere."[27] Already in the 1920s, Wells repeatedly pointed to the inherent tensions of the modern democratic system. To fight back, he stressed the necessity of "clarifying the ideas" and forming an idealistic elite group (described as the "competent receiver") that would stimulate the transformation. Wells did not hide his admiration of totalitarian techniques and the existential commitment shown by members of such movements. Consequently, he called for a similarly total identification with the liberal democratic cause. Pointing to the communists and the Nazis as models to emulate, Wells called for militant activism to defend scientific, social, and political liberalism. By contrast, he was scornful of the Labour Party for having "empty minds and principles" and being unable to offer a compelling vision of the future.

Wells argued that the crisis of liberal democracy could only be overcome by creating a "world state" that could unify the creative energies of different nations and eliminate ethnic conflicts. This world state should also guarantee free speech as a basic precondition of progress. The main problem of anti-liberal doctrines and movements was that they suppressed the plurality of opinions and fomented national hatred, thus hindering evolution toward a truly human commonweal. Wells stressed that liberalism should not be understood as the ideology of the rich: traditionally it was the "friend of the debtor, the downtrodden, the masses."[28] It used to have a universalist aspiration, and it could thus be described as the "mental quality of all intelligent men in the world," whereas its main competitor—conservatism—was local and parochial.[29]

In Wells's interpretation, the main reason for the marginalization of liberalism by the early twentieth century was nationalist particularism. Consequently, he sought to challenge nationalism, pointing out that—contrary to the conservative organicist argument—it was a recent and artificial phenomenon. Along these lines, he was also critical of Woodrow Wilson for placing the principle of national sovereignty into the center of political legitimization and castigated the Versailles peace system for furthering, rather than preventing, national fragmentation.[30] The liberal militants ("liberal fascists, enlightened Nazis") he imagined were supposed to fight against national limits, creating a "common vision of the world" and a "common conception of history and morals."[31] As key features of the "good society," they should fight for a mixture of classical liberal values with those that could be considered socialistic: the defense of free speech, honest government, suppressing private weapons, and the progressive socialization of the collective economic affairs of mankind.

Key components of this move toward a universal government were setting up a world bank and creating a world currency. But it was not enough to change the economic preconditions: it also needed to focus on the cultural and spiritual transformation of mankind. In his 1929 address to the *Reichstag*, Wells used the concept of *Kulturkampf* in an abstract sense of "culture war" (i.e., not linked to the original meaning, which referred to the fight between the German *Reich* and the Catholic Church in the second half of the nineteenth century), defining it as a struggle "to control the education of the ordinary people."[32] Along these lines, he argued for the need to develop a new history, focusing not on nations but on mankind, and the writing of new school textbooks to raise new generations in this spirit.

As the global economic and political crisis seemed to be deeper than ever, Wells felt increasingly justified in his call for radical transformation. At the same time, there was still a gap between his mobilizing rhetoric and the course he expected world history to take. In his ominously titled "Crystal Gazing" from October 1932, he expressed his hope that, if the world got through the crisis without a major cataclysm until January 1, 1933, then "we shall have got through the worst."[33] Needless to say, the irony of history did not spare Wells. Less than a month after his prospective deadline, Adolf Hitler was appointed German Chancellor.

To be sure, the rise of Hitler to power was watched closely by political writers and was understood as a fundamental turn by many external observers, including French journalist Pierre Musat (?–1958). In his 1933 book *From Marx to Hitler*, Musat's main question was why it was Germany that experienced the most acute political crisis and consequently produced the most virulent political formation.[34] Seeking an answer, he inserted the Depression and the rise of Hitler within a broader framework of political and economic crisis, paying special attention to the post-First World War strategies of Germany, including the state's attempts to cut reparations, finance

180   Intellectuals and the Crisis of Politics

its economic reconstruction from external credits, and boost its domestic volume of economic production by adopting Taylorist methods. All of this resulted in global overproduction and consequently the growth of unemployment. This went together with the growing crisis of the middle class, torn between a more self-conscious stratum of unionized workers and their capitalist employers. As the groups in between (e.g., small property-holders and functionaries who, taken together, made up one-sixth of the productive population) lost their security, they gradually abandoned their traditional liberal creed. Their ranks were further bolstered by a growing number of unemployed university graduates. In this context, Musat pointed to the apparent paradox wherein the more particular social groups became proletarianized, the more they wanted to distance themselves from the proletariat. This frustration was reinforced among various strata of the population by widespread nostalgia for the lost empire. These factors came together in a profound multi-layered crisis, which was skillfully exploited by Hitler and his movement. Musat laconically declared: "The crisis is called Hitler".[35]

Another early reflection on the Nazi takeover came from Russian-born Pavlovian psychologist living in France, Wladimir Drabovitch (1885–1943).[36] He stressed the total character of modern dictatorships and linked the crisis of democracy to an overall "crisis of the spirit" (drawing also on the works of Guglielmo Ferrero, Karl Jaspers, and Paul Valéry). What he added to these analyses was a stress on individual and collective psychology and an emphatic comparative dimension. Referring to Italian anti-fascist Francesco Nitti (who claimed that "all tyrannies are the same system"), Drabovitch also drew a comparison between Lenin and Mussolini as examples of manipulative leaders who instilled fanaticism in their followers. This mobilization was based on a homogeneous enemy image and created a political system that went well beyond the power concentration of autocracies from the times of the *ancien régime*.

For Drabovitch, liberal democracy was undermined by the mental and moral deterioration of the society, which had lost its capacity to defend itself against tyrannical aspirations on the left and on the right. Pacifism (including conscientious objection), the doctrine of non-resistance, and the "enthusiasm for servitude" (a notion taken from French philosopher and historian Élie Halévy) were symptoms of its deterioration. Instead, Drabovitch advocated for the creation of an "authoritarian democracy" that could overcome the actual crisis. He argued that his model would preserve basic values—liberty of thought, conscience, and scientific research—but restrict certain rights that could be exploited by the enemies of democracy. He also called for the exclusion of left- and right-wing anti-liberal forces from the political framework as part of the legitimate self-defense of democracy and called for the creation of a unified "Bloc de liberté militante." This was an alternative to the "*front commun*" of socialists and communists on an anti-fascist basis, since he considered the communists as one of the extremist forces who sought to undermine liberal democracy. In turn, he also attacked those French intellectuals who argued for an empathetic stance toward what the pacifist philosopher Alain (Émile-August Chartier, 1868–1951) had called the "German spiritual revolution."

The delegitimization of democracy, its relationship to liberalism, and the rise of totalitarianism became central topics of the 1934 Prague World Philosophical Congress.[37] The illustrious list of participants of the plenary session on the "crisis of democracy" included Czech intellectuals and active political figures like Emanuel Rádl (1873–1942) and Edvard Beneš (1884–1948), prominent French thinkers such as Rougier, the liberal political thinker and professor of Germanistics of Hungarian-Jewish background, Victor Basch (1863–1944), cooperativist Bernard Lavergne, and legal philosopher (and future collaborationist) Joseph Barthélemy (1874–1945), with a colorful variety of national delegates ranging from Italian fascist Emilio Bodrero (1874–1949) to German liberal Paul Feldkeller (1889–1972).

The range of attendees and their opinions created a palpable tension between the actual divergence of political positions and the universalist conception of philosophical debate subscribed by many (but not all) of the participants. It was most eloquently expressed by Czech writer and public intellectual Karel Čapek (1890–1938), who called upon those present to preserve the freedom of mind, universalism, and a shared humanity as a common intellectual and moral framework. It was quite clear that from this perspective the outcome of the clash of democratic and anti-democratic tendencies was not at all indifferent, as the universalistic commitments clearly implied a democratic orientation. It however remained a question, what exactly democracy meant for the participants. Indeed, most of the texts engaging with the crisis of democracy began with an attempt to define democracy and clarify its relationship to other ideological streams or political systems (e.g., liberalism or parliamentarism). While for many participants liberalism essentially overlapped with democracy, others considered them very different.

However, irrespective of the actual political position of the contributors, there was a broad consensus that after the Great War democracy had been a dominant if not hegemonic ideological framework. Further, the feeling was that by the early 1930s, with the rise of powerful ideological alternatives—especially fascism and communism—this dominance was gone. Most of the participants (especially the Czechoslovak and French delegates) still argued in favor of democracy, but also agreed that there was a gap between the democratic principle as such and the functioning of "really existing" democratic regimes. In this respect, the identification of democracy with parliamentarism was repeatedly challenged, and several participants sought to offer an alternative to the "partocratic" parliamentary systems, suggesting alternative models. For example, Lavergne proposed dual representation of the citizens as producers and consumers, while American William P. Montague argued for the strengthening of the executive branch toward a democratically controlled temporary dictatorship (modeled on Roosevelt's arrogation of extraordinary powers to impose the New Deal). Most of these contributions addressed the crisis of democracy in terms of the clash of liberal democracy and its totalitarian contenders and stated the need for a more systematic engagement with the similarities and differences between democratic political cultures and autocratic contenders. However, the philosophical discourse itself tended to remain on an abstract level.

182 Intellectuals and the Crisis of Politics

Returning to these questions two years later, a member of the organizing committee of the World Congress, Zionist political thinker from Prague Felix Weltsch (1884–1964)—a friend of Max Brod and Franz Kafka—sought to offer a more systematic defense of liberal democracy against both the leftist and rightist radical doctrines, which he considered to be convergent on many levels.[38] Weltsch's liberalism was based on a belief in the compatibility of individual freedom and common good. He contrasted this to the anti-liberal doctrine (which he modeled on Schmitt's Hobbesian position) rooted in the principle of the permanent struggle of all against all, *homo homini lupus*, to be held in check by a monopoly of violence exercised by an autocratic leader.

Rejecting the Schmittian counter-position of liberalism and democracy, Weltsch argued that the two were intimately linked, as democracy followed from the liberal principle.[39] Along these lines, he called for an active defense of democracy in the context of the ravaging crisis. At the same time, he was explicit about the weak points of democracy that were targeted by right- and left-wing radicals: the protracted nature of decision making; the unwillingness to sacrifice; "partocracy"; the problem of selection; and the incapacity of self-defense. In his opinion, most of the resentment against the workings of democratic politics was due to the conflation of democracy with the majoritarian principle. By contrast, he argued that democracy's central aspiration was linked to distributive justice; majoritarianism was only an instrument of decision making, not its normative core. From this perspective, Weltsch argued that in case of an existential threat to liberal democracy, it was possible to suspend democratic procedures to defend the liberal democratic essence.[40] This position had many elements in common with the German émigré authors, particularly Loewenstein, who tackled the question of democratic self-defense in terms of "militant democracy."[41]

Explaining his central metaphor of "the middle," Weltsch sought to assume a position between individualism and collectivism. However, he stressed that this could not be an arithmetic middle between extreme left and extreme right, but rather a systemic alternative to the cult of struggle and violence that characterized both branches of radicalism. He pointed to the Masarykian doctrine of realism as an example to follow and employed the concept of humanity (another key notion of Masaryk as well as his other intellectual source, Henri Bergson) as a mediator between individualism and collectivism. In political terms, this implied a middle road between liberalism and socialism, while seeking to preserve the core values (*Wertkerne*) of both. Conscious of the fact that not every middle position was equally capable of mediating, Weltsch stressed that he did not envision a "compromise" but more a creative synthesis: "the middle is not a property but a task."[42]

By the mid-1930s, there was enough empirical research conducted that it became possible to devise a more comprehensive transnational comparative framework for interpreting the contemporary challenges to democracy. The 1936 overview prepared at the *Centre de documentation sociale* of the *École normale supérieure*, with the participation of Élie Halévy and Raymond Aron (1905–83), among others, sought to use the methodology of "inductive sociology" to analyze the different national contexts and dynamics, focusing especially on the entanglement of societal crisis and national ideologies.[43]

Looking at England as the paradigmatic liberal political culture, Halévy registered the divergence between political and economic liberalism. He also stressed the shift in public mood toward protectionist policies and the rise of collectivist tendencies in the religious sphere. He inserted this into a broader historical framework, linking the rise of anti-liberalism to the ascendance of Louis-Napoléon Bonaparte to power. Halévy described the French politician as the precursor of fascism, even if in the later years of his rule he turned toward an Anglo-Saxon liberal direction. At the same time, the 1870s witnessed the end of British liberal ideological hegemony, indicated by the successes of Bismarckian politics and the popularity of Benjamin Disraeli's social conservatism in the British political community itself. With the transformation of capitalism, the state became a central economic actor, managing both export and import policies. For Halévy this development was not a decline but a necessary change as he thought that it was possible to harmonize political liberalism and economic socialism. From this perspective, the program and policies of the Labour Party could be read as a rational compromise between these two ideologies and could also serve as an example for other European polities.

Considered a leading French expert in German political thought, young Raymond Aron contributed to the volume with an analysis on the "ideology and reality of national socialism," interpreted in terms of an "anti-proletarian revolution" resonating with Musat's analysis.[44] While he pointed to the longer prehistory of anti-democratic and anti-occidental thinking, he focused mainly on the immediate context of the rise of Nazism and argued that crisis "made people accessible to the Hitlerist propaganda."[45] Aron stressed that in order to understand its emergence, a class-based analysis did not seem adequate, as the common element of the groups that were most receptive to Nazism—the youth, white collar workers, intellectual proletariat, small shopkeepers, peasantry—was their fear of proletarianization and hatred of liberal capitalism. The Nazis offered a way out of this trap without subverting the total societal fabric, while the communist program of revolution alienated many people who also contested the existing order but were afraid of revolutionary chaos.

Aron was highly critical of the left for its Marxist belief in class-based politics and that historical dynamics would automatically lead to socialism. Rather than class-consciousness, it was resentment, common hope, and a shared ideological outlook that worked as chief group-creating factors. Nazism was able to promise something to every disaffected social subgroup: employment to the youth; moral dignity to the victims of capitalism; protection to the artisans, etc. Its ideology was based on rejecting equality, choice, rationalism, liberalism, parliamentarism, internationalism, and offering instead an "authoritarian and plebiscitary democracy."

Aron stressed that Hitler did not take power by force but became a chancellor after a compromise with the capitalist elite. The Nazis' anti-crisis economic measures were

184 Intellectuals and the Crisis of Politics

not unique and had parallels not only in fascist Italy but also in Roosevelt's New Deal. However, what was less typical was the virulence of hatred against the external world as such, which went together with the preparation of society for an impending open conflict.

Regarding the New Deal as a possible model of crisis management, economist and future architect of the European Economic Community Robert Marjolin (1911–86) argued that the crisis that began in 1929 undermined the American myth of exceptionalism, turning the United States in a similar direction as other countries: "the mirage disappeared."[46] Roosevelt's strategy was marked by the duality of individualist ideology, deeply rooted in the American tradition and the realities of mechanized work, which became more and more widespread in the industrial sector, hardly corresponding to the classical American self-image of Jeffersonian yeomanry. What is more, Roosevelt also had to find a balance between economic freedom and state intervention, especially since he was trying to get votes from both Southern rural areas as well as Midwestern farmers. From this perspective, Marjolin linked the New Deal to previous instances of popular mobilization critical of uncurbed capitalism, including late nineteenth-century rural (populist) movements.

The discussion also went beyond "Western" horizons. Evincing the divergence of interpretative angles and political positions in the volume and in the French academic community in general, sociologist Georges Friedmann's (1902–77) analysis of the Soviet Union was an apologetic piece, presenting it almost as an "affirmative action empire" and focusing on the emancipatory policies directed toward the nationalities previously suppressed under Tsarism.[47] What is more, Friedmann depicted the Stalinist policies in terms of normalization, going against the forced egalitarianism of the immediate post-revolutionary period. In this view, even Stakhanovism was praised as part of a broader policy of involving the workers in innovation. In a sense, Friedmann confirmed the Stalinist narrative that the Soviet Union was able to avert the crisis that hit Western capitalist societies with full force.

Étienne Dennery's (1903–79) analysis of Japanese fascism focused on the socioeconomic and mental preconditions of national radicalization. A key aspect of his analysis was the stress on the fundamental ambiguity of the Japanese stance toward the West, combining idolization and resentment. While not completely overlapping with Aron's analysis of German national socialism, there were interesting parallels. Dennery pointed to the collapse of rural patriarchy and the unevenness of industrialization, which led to the growth of social differences and the over-production of young intelligentsia without secure positions. While the system was also contested by the radical left, communist ideology was effectively trumped by popular nationalism. Japanese fascism built on this popular nationalism but, in contrast to Europe, its main carrier was not a mass party but secret societies seeking to subvert parliamentarism, relying on the army and the peasantry as their social basis.

Finally, philosopher and Durkheimian sociologist Célestin Bouglé (1870–1940), director of ENS at the time, contributed a piece on France.[48] He was markedly optimistic in view of the revival of liberalism. While he registered the anti-liberal turn of the French left in economic terms, he stressed that regarding social, political, and intellectual questions the liberal consensus still held. He questioned how it was possible to turn the anti-fascist popular mobilization (*rassemblements populaires*) into a more coherent political force that would contribute to the stabilization of liberal democracy in a moment when there were powerful external totalitarian pressures.

Apart from France, Czechoslovakia was the other European country that followed the German developments and the rise of totalitarianism with particular concern. Given the strong democratic agenda of the Masarykian state-building project, but also the sizable German minority—which after 1933 became increasingly dominated (both financially, organizationally, and ideologically) by the Nazis via Konrad Henlein's (1898–1945) *Sudetendeutsche Partei*—,the Czechoslovak intellectual discussion on the features of German National Socialism was very complex and multi-dimensional. A key theoretician of democracy and nationalism and a prominent natural scientist, Emanuel Rádl looked at the rise of Nazism from the perspective of the crisis of democracy.[49] Rádl distinguished between three conceptions of democracy—organic, majoritarian, and liberal—and pointed to the significant contextual differences between various national cases. While the Anglo-Saxon model of liberal democracy emerged from structures of privilege-based self-government, turning civic associations into the basis of democratic life and the limitation of the state as its main agenda, in France the very same privileges turned into noble self-defense and thus eventually democracy emerged as an étatist project that overruled social divisions. Rádl was even more critical of the German context, where he detected a strong anti-liberal and anti-universalist tradition both on the left and the right that subordinated the individual to the collective, thus contributing to the rise of totalitarian movements.

Rádl's anti-totalitarianism did not mean an uncritical stance toward classical liberalism. He was particularly critical of the econocentrism of liberals and, as a specialist on the nationality question, made powerful arguments against the individualist understanding of minority rights typical for the liberal script, embodied in the existent legislation on minorities, rather arguing for a need to think of them in terms of collectivities and confer collective rights upon them.

In Rádl's understanding the solution to the crisis of democracy was linked to rethinking the relationship between majority and minority, as well as the relationship between morality and legal formalism. Rádl argued that modern liberalism allowed for a break from formal law in the name of a higher moral standard and the defense of truth against the majoritarian principle. Following José Ortega y Gasset, Rádl also criticized mass rule as a pathway to tyranny and stressed the importance of "creative minorities" as catalysts of human progress. Eventually, his argument was that the tyranny of the majority should not be conflated with democracy: even if it appealed to a mass base, Nazism had nothing to do with democracy since democracy could not be conceived as the negation of individual liberty.

"End of the Postwar Period": Premonitions of Catastrophe and Glimpses of a New Order

As with the other sectoral discourses of crisis, the debate on democracy also received a new impetus toward the end of the 1930s. As it became more and more obvious that the postwar international framework was prone to collapse, the world seemed to have entered a highly explosive period, and a new set of political principles was needed to construct a fundamentally new order.

This was expressed by French political essayist Robert Aron (1898–1975, older brother of Raymond) whose book title announced "the end of the postwar period" in 1938.[50] Tellingly, at this point, the Great Depression ceased to be in the focus of the crisis discourse. For Robert Aron, a new historical period began with the Munich Agreement, which destroyed the system of alliances France had been carefully weaving together after the end of the First World War. A violent critic of the French political mainstream in the early 1930s, emerging from the ranks of the radical movement of "nonconformists," Robert Aron considered the interwar system inherently faulty and thus did not regret its collapse. However, he admitted that its demise created a new and dangerous situation in need of careful analysis. In his opinion, the postwar order was based on the idea of national self-determination that emerged in the second half of the nineteenth century. However, the principle of self-determination was used in a highly restrictive way, being identified with the rights of majorities and thus leading to a homogeneous understanding of nation-states. This, in his opinion, prepared the ideological ground for totalitarianism, also based on the rejection of the rights of minorities.

Robert Aron was bitterly critical of Czechoslovak President Beneš and his French supporters for leaving it to Hitler to deconstruct this "false state." Obviously, Aron's passion was not matched by his "local knowledge" (or perhaps his local knowledge was as one-sided as that of most French political writers who fervently supported Czechoslovakia in the 1920s as a beacon of Western civilization in the East). He thus summarily labeled Milan Hodža Beneš's "agent," even if the Slovak agrarian politician was perhaps the president's most important critic and competitor, who developed a federalist vision that stood in stark contrast to the centralism of the Czechoslovak political mainstream.

Describing Hitler as a "man of the nineteenth century," Robert Aron evidently did not sympathize with the German dictator even though the "third way" intellectual milieu he belonged to in the early 1930s had a highly ambiguous stance toward Hitlerism.[51] This was especially true in the first period after the *Machtergreifung*, as evinced by the infamous "Letter to Hitler," most probably written by Aron's friend Alexandre Marc, but expressing the position of the broader subculture, which included also Aron and Denis de Rougemont.[52] At the same time, while stressing that one needed to "understand Hitler, not to follow him," Aron considered the destruction of the postwar order fully justified. An ardent supporter of federalism, Aron also gave credit to Hitler's 1937 proposal to federalize Czechoslovakia. As a point of fact, the only possible solution for the "disorder" Robert Aron perceived in Central and Eastern European was a federal Danubian Union.

The either–or of the interwar crisis, as formulated by Robert Aron, thus cut across the right–left and fascist–anti-fascist alternatives that seemed to be omnipresent in interwar French politics. For him, the real cleavage was rather between centralist and federalist visions of politics. Overall, he considered the postwar period a failure precisely because of its inclination toward political and economic centralization. Aron held that centralist democracy (even if nominally liberal) was much closer to the totalitarian model than its adherents were ready to admit. The interwar crisis thus posed a choice between totalitarian all-inclusion (which had different—capitalist, imperialist, Stalinist, fascist, and planist—versions) and the "community of spirit," that is, a democracy built on a federal basis.[53] Along these lines, scrutinizing the future of French democracy, Robert Aron rejected power concentration both on the state and private levels, criticizing oligarchies, stock-holding companies, and the "state capitalism" advocated by socialists. Instead, he argued for free and coordinated cooperation of limited and autonomous enterprises.[54] He praised the Czech Baťa company as a model for the future, to be extended to financial and administrative self-government.

Finally, in view of the future of Europe, Robert Aron also saw a fateful either–or situation: if power concentration and the nineteenth-century logic of politics prevailed, a new conflagration was unavoidable: he quite conspicuously used the term "interwar" a year before the Second World War started.[55] The only way out of this self-destructive course was integration into a new federal Europe. As it happened, Robert Aron's intuition was correct regarding the plausibility of both scenarios, except that they proved not to be bound in a mutually exclusive either–or dichotomy but rather became sequential events in twentieth-century European history.

The crisis of the interwar democratic order was also central motif in William Rappard's (1883–1958) work. The Swiss economic expert and co-founder of the Graduate Institute of International Studies in Geneva argued that it was a basic mistake to take the hegemony of democracy for granted after the Great War: "the triumph of democracy seemed as easy to explain as impossible to avoid."[56] While in the early 1920s popular power was universally "welcomed, extolled, and worshipped," afterward a dramatic anti-democratic reaction set in. Considering all this, Rappard called for a profound reassessment of the idea of democracy, which was not to be confused with the rule of the people or of the majority. Rather, it referred to governance in accordance with the will of the people and with the individual rights of each citizen being respected.

Rappard also suggested that historical processes of democratization mattered immensely as anti-democratic tendencies were evidently stronger in countries that had no pre-existing democratic traditions before the World War. At the same time, he warned of equating modern dictatorships with prewar autocratic regimes. These dictatorships were popular in origin, (ab)using the contradictions of modern democracy between the principles of liberty, equality, and efficiency. While, after 1917, the establishment of democracy in Europe was considered to be a principal war aim of the Entente—and the war did end with the seeming triumph of democracy—Rappard considered the package much more contradictory. The total war of 1914–18 also brought about the fall of individualism, the growth of power-concentration, the

188 Intellectuals and the Crisis of Politics

expansion of censorship, and the rise of state-managed economies. From this perspective, both Bolshevism and fascism were outcomes of the social dislocation and demoralization caused by the World War. The peace treaties were also important factors in this analysis, leaving many national movements deeply frustrated and turning them against the postwar order. Thus, the transformation which started with the World War meant a double bind between democratization and the totalitarian anti-democratic backlash. Had it not been a democratic drive first, monarchies and multinational empires would have still existed—but no totalitarianism.

Highly critical of collectivistic tendencies, Rappard argued that the problem was not about democratic principles as such, but rather about the functioning of institutions, such as the party system in the case of France. Referring to Lippmann, Rappard stressed that political and economic liberty were necessarily interlinked. Consequently, he castigated France's Popular Front government for conceding to revolutionary trade unionism. That said, he was optimistic about the survival chances of democracy in countries where it had long-term historical roots. He pointed out that it was mainly the unconsolidated democracies that turned anti-democratic after a short postwar democratic intermezzo.[57] Fascism was particularly attractive in countries that were heavily in debt and ravaged by unemployment. It promised a way out of the socioeconomic crisis at the price of the militarization of society. Converging with Raymond Aron's analysis, in Rappard's opinion, this drive toward militarization was likely to result in a new war. Rappard was also convinced that this new war would be won by the democracies, but he was worried about the nationalist tendencies catalyzed by global militarization. Further, preparing for the war was by default destructive of the democratic system: "democracy is a child of peace and cannot live apart from its mother."[58]

Rappard's defense of democracy did not mean that he did not see any need for readjustment. The main task was to find a compromise between efficiency and responsiveness to the will of the people while not endangering individual liberty.[59] In any case, freedom of the opposition and the absolute independence of the judiciary was to be protected against any incursion. But he stressed that the most important precondition of a functioning democracy was not so much constitutional organization but the character, temper, and education of the people.

In the very same year, Paul Mantoux (1877–1956), Rappard's Geneva colleague and co-founder of the Graduate Institute, edited a volume on the world crisis, based on a colloquium funded by the Rockefeller Foundation.[60] One of the contributors, Belgian legal scholar Maurice Bourquin (1884–1961) wrote a piece on the "crisis of democracy" seeking to offer a liberal democratic redefinition. He rejected the idea of *volonté générale*, and argued that it was not enough to base democracy on public opinion either, for even authoritarian regimes had some sort of public opinion. He emphasized that this opinion needed to be the fruit of individual liberty, and likewise, liberalism necessarily formed part of the democratic framework. The key feature of liberal democracy, in contrast to various autocratic projects, is that it was not afraid of opposition, and even solicited it. In fact, the key figures of human progress, such as Socrates, the early Christians, Galileo, or Pasteur were all "in opposition." By contrast, in a dictatorship, public opinion is crystallized around a hegemonic doctrine, while opposition is considered a state crime.

Like his liberal colleagues, Bourquin also pointed to the failure of the postwar wave of democratization, which he linked to inflated expectations and the mistaken idea of "democracy export," arguing that, in contrast to the expectations of the peacemakers in 1919–20, a war was not a propitious occasion for democratic transformation. Like Rappard, he also stressed that there was no robust tradition of democracy in countries where dictatorships emerged in the twenties and early thirties, whereas in the countries which had been democratic before 1914, democratic government remained intact. This did not mean that there were no disfunctions in this latter group of countries, as certain crisis symptoms were present even before 1914, especially regarding those political parties which failed to fulfill their original function to aggregate divergent interests.

The prevalent sentiment and occasional explicit discourse of the "end of the inter-war period" can be read as a gesture of self-historicization, used mostly by liberal critics of the post-World War order. While the postwar reorganization of the world was held to follow a liberal democratic script, these authors, in responding to the perceived crisis in the 1930s, tried to salvage liberal democracy as an ideal but also distance themselves from what they saw as a failed project. On the one hand, they stressed that some of the roots of the actual crisis predated 1914, such as the dynamic of centralization and autarchic nationalist aspirations. On the other hand, for most of these authors, rather than an episode in the story of universal democratization as the Wilsonians would have it, the First World War triggered illiberalism and anti-liberalism, thus brutalizing social relationships, dismantling frameworks of civility, and reinforcing étatist tendencies in politics as well as in the economy. They were also highly critical of the postwar international framework, which created expectations that were impossible to meet. Consequently, they derived the rise of totalitarian challenges both on the left and on the right from this experience of violence and frustration, pointing to the complex entanglement between the two extremes.

At the same time, it is not true that these interwar defenders of liberal democracy completely identified communism and fascism. In the 1920s, fascist Italy was generally considered to be marginal to European developments while communism seemed a fundamental negation of liberalism, but by the mid-1930s fascism and especially National Socialism turned out to be formidable systemic competitors to liberal democracy. In this context, many observers considered the fascist regimes more stable and crisis-resistant than the Soviet model, and they also expected the next worldwide conflict to unfold between liberal democracies and fascist powers (while having rather limited insight about the geopolitical orientation of the Soviet Union).

Most importantly, many analysts who sought to defend liberal democracy tended to distinguish between the final goals of fascism and communism. In general, they stressed that fascism had no vision of the "end of history" while the communist vision was rather clear. The historical goal of communism was not inherently incompatible with Western civilization, but the proposed way to achieve this was self-destructive

190 Intellectuals and the Crisis of Politics

from the perspective of these (self-critical) interwar European liberal democrats. This was, to a certain extent, a difference between them and those economic liberals (most famously Mises) who, in the 1920s, considered fascism a violent but perhaps necessary way to crush the enemies of capitalism in countries characterized by a high level of contention between the working class and the bourgeoisie. For them, communism was a negation of Western development and a road toward civilizational collapse. Merging these positions, neoliberals from the mid-1930s stressed the slippery slope of any concession to collectivism, eventually leading to analogous patterns of dictatorship, but this conception became widely recognized and even popular only with Hayek's *The Road to Serfdom*, written during the Second World War. Thus, this position had less impact on European interwar crisis debates, and rather became a central narrative of the Western European and North American Cold War-era liberal political imaginary.

In fact, the late interwar discussions about the crisis of democracy also continued into the years of the Second World War. For many committed democrats, the global conflagration that pitted fascist and anti-fascist camps against each other meant a horrible ordeal but also seemed to offer a chance for the revitalization of the democratic idea. Serbian literary critic and liberal intellectual Milan Grol (1876–1952) used the crisis discourse to link two phenomena: the "Yugoslav crisis" (i.e., the collapse of the unitary state due to the centrifugal dynamic of its components) and the "crisis of democracy."[61] Drawing on French neo-Thomist philosopher Yves Simon and Catholic writer Charles Péguy, both of whom aimed at a synthesis of modern democracy and Christian tradition, Grol was far from being uncritical of the functioning of modern democratic institutions but assumed a vocal anti-totalitarian position. He pointed out that fascism attacked democracy at its "weakest point," that is, parliamentarism, which indeed was dysfunctional, clearly demonstrated by the Yugoslav interwar experience before the 1929 royal dictatorship. At the same time, the state's authoritarian bureaucracy was even more corrupted and oppressive.

Regarding the future of liberalism, even those authors who tried to save it as a relevant ideological tradition became skeptical of the possibility of "exporting" liberal democracy to societies that had limited or no historical preconditions for it. What is more, even in societies where liberal democracy was relatively resilient, they stressed that, rather than the constitutional form, what mattered more was the spirit of government. In this sense, the previously strong theoretical link between liberalism and institutionalism was (to a certain extent) severed.

Revisiting these discussions makes it clear that many key elements of later discussions, which resurfaced after 1989, were already solidly part of the interwar reflections on the crisis of liberal democracy. The experience of the opening rift between liberalism and democracy (and the phantom of "illiberal democracy"), the stress on the need for underlying absolute values to sustain a liberal system with epistemic pluralism and limited moral relativism, the dilemma of formal versus substantial democracy, or the contrast of authoritarianism and totalitarianism are excellent examples of ideas that would have a remarkable career at the end of the twentieth century. What is key in understanding these reflections is the feeling that the convergence of liberalism and democracy was challenged from various directions. In this respect a central point was the critique of majoritarianism and plebiscitary forms of democracy, pointing out that such a reduction of the democratic principle to the act of legitimizing political rule opened the gates to tyranny. This was often framed in terms of a broader cultural/philosophical discourse of crisis caused by the dominance of mass society. A key trigger of this in the eyes of these defenders of liberal democracy was doubtlessly the First World War, which undermined the civilizational standards of the West based on the creative energies of the individual, and turned Europe toward cultural, political, and economic collectivism.

Notes

1. For a case study on Italy and Great Britain, see Giulia Guazzaloca, "Due sistemi al vaglio di una crisi: La crisi di fine secolo nella rappresentazione di alcune riviste italiane ed inglesi (1899–1911)," in Paolo Pombeni, ed., *Crisi, legittimazione, consenso* (Bologna: Il Mulino, 2003), 15–80.
2. James Bryce, *Modern Democracies*, vol. 1 (New York: The Macmillan Company, 1921), 4.
3. For instance, as Jens Hacke points out, Michels mentions the "crisis of democracy" already in 1911 in his *Soziologie der Parteiwesens*. Jens Hacke, *Existenzkrise der Demokratie* (Berlin: Suhrkamp Verlag, 2018), 205.
4. Renzo de Felice, *Autobiografia del fascismo* (Turin: Einaudi, 2004), 34.
5. Carl Schmitt, *The Crisis of Parliamentary Democracy*, trans. Ellen Kennedy (Cambridge, MA: MIT Press, 1988). The English title is somewhat misleading as the book was originally published as *Die geistesgeschichtliche Lage des heutigen Parlamentarismus* (Leipzig: Duncker & Humblot, 1923), perhaps more directly translated as *The Intellectual-Historical Situation of Contemporary Parliamentarism*.
6. Ibid., 21.
7. Ibid., 17.
8. Ibid.
9. Émile Giraud, *Crise de la démocratie et les réformes nécessaires du pouvoir législatif* (Paris: M. Giard, 1925).
10. Moritz J. Bonn, *The Crisis of European Democracy* (New Haven, CT: Yale University Press, 1925).
11. Wilhelm Medinger, *Die internationale Diskussion über die Krise des Parlamentarismus* (Vienna: W. Braumüller, 1929).
12. Jens Hacke, in his *Existenzkrise der Demokratie*, gives an intriguing analysis of the liberal camp of the Weimar Republic from this perspective.
13. Kazimierz Zakrzewski, *Kryzys demokracji* (Warsaw: G. Kryzel, 1930).
14. Ibid., 33.
15. Hermann Heller, *Europa und der Fascismus* (Berlin: De Gruyter, 1929).
16. On the context and the arguments of this debate, see David Dyzenhaus, *Legality and Legitimacy: Carl Schmitt, Hans Kelsen and Hermann Heller in Weimar* (Oxford: Clarendon, 1997).
17. Heller, *Europa und der Fascismus*, 64.
18. Ibid., 59.

19. Karl Loewenstein, "Militant Democracy and Fundamental Rights," *The American Political Science Review* 31, no. 3 (1937): 417–32.

20. Gerhard Leibholz, *Die Auflösung der liberalen Demokratie in Deutschland und das autoritäre Staatsbild* (Munich: Duncker & Humblot, 1933).

21. Ibid., 21.

22. Ibid., 36. This argument was developed further after the Second World War in the discussions on the underlying values of the liberal democratic order, most famously in the work of Ernst-Wolfgang Böckenförde, strongly influenced by Carl Schmitt.

23. Ibid., 49–50.

24. Albert Rivaud, *Les Crises allemandes* (Paris: A. Colin, 1932), 197.

25. Ibid., 14.

26. Ibid., 196.

27. H. G. Wells, *After Democracy: Addresses and Papers on the Present World Situation* (London: C. A. Watts & Co., 1932), 215.

28. Wells, "Liberalism and the Revolutionary Spirit," in ibid., 21.

29. Ibid.

30. Wells, "Money and Mankind," in ibid., 93.

31. Wells, "A Liberal World Organization," in ibid., 31.

32. Wells, "The Common-Sense of World Peace," in ibid., 63.

33. Wells, "Crystal Gazing," in ibid., 226.

34. Pierre Musat, *De Marx à Hitler* (Paris: Felix Alcan, 1933).

35. Ibid., 128.

36. Wladimir Drabovitch, *Fragilité de la liberté et séduction des dictatures* (Paris: Mercure de France, 1934). On the author, see Annick Ohayon, "Between Pavlov, Freud, and Janet: The Itinerary of a Russian Gentleman who Emigrated to France: Wladimir Drabovitch (1885–1943)," *Bulletin de psychologie* 521, no. 5 (2012): 479–85.

37. Marián Sekerák, "Czechoslovak Intellectual Debate on the Crisis of Democracy in the 1930s," *Studies in East European Thought* 75 (2023): 33–51, see especially 40–42. For an impressionistic contemporary overview by the future star of logical positivism, see Ernest Nagel, "The Eighth International Congress of Philosophy," *The Journal of Philosophy* 31, no. 22 (1934): 589–601. The contributions were published in *Actes du Huitième Congrès International de Philosophie à Prague, 2–7 septembre 1934* (Prague: Orbis, 1936), available at https://www.pdcnet.org/wcp8

38. Felix Weltsch, *Das Wagnis der Mitte* (Ostrava: Kittl, 1936).

39. Ibid., 82.

40. Ibid., 87.

41. In the second part of his article, Loewenstein offers a series of cases studies for the self-defense of democratic regimes and anti-fascist legislation with a special focus on Czechoslovakia. See Karl Loewenstein, "Militant Democracy and Fundamental Rights, II," *The American Political Science Review*, 31, no. 4 (1937): 638-658.

42. Weltsch, *Das Wagnis*, 171.

43. Élie Halévy, Raymond Aron, A. Bernard, Georges Friedmann, Robert Marjolin, and Étienne Dennery, *Inventaires: La crise sociale et les idéologies nationales* (Paris: Alcan, 1936). The Centre was funded by the French–Jewish philanthropist Albert Kahn, known for initiating "The Archives of the Planet."

44. Raymond Aron, "Une *révolution antiprolétarienne*. Idéologie et réalité du national-socialisme," in ibid., 25.

45. Aron, "Une *révolution antiprolétarienne*," 36.
46. Robert Marjolin, "Les expériences Roosevelt et la Philosophie sociale américaine," in ibid., 135.
47. Georges Friedmann, "Quelques traits de l'esprit nouveau en URSS," in ibid., 82–126.
48. Célestin Bouglé, "Destinées de l'individualisme en France," in ibid., 164–93.
49. Emanuel Rádl, *O německé revoluci; K politické ideologii sudetských Němců* [On the German Revolution: On the Political Ideology of the Sudeten Germans] (Prague: Masarykův ústav AV ČR, 2004). The text is originally from 1933, while the modern edition also contains another text from 1935, entitled *Zur politischen Ideologie der Sudetendeutschen.*
50. Robert Aron, *La fin de l'après-guerre* (Paris: Gallimard, 1938).
51. On this milieu see the classic study by Jean-Louis Loubet del Bayle, *Les non-conformistes des années 30: Une tentative de renouvellement de la pensée politique française* (Paris: Editions du Seuil, 1969). See also Gilbert Merlio, ed., *Ni gauche ni droite: Chassés-crises idéologiques des intellectuels allemands et français dans l'entre-deux guerres* (Bordeaux: Presses de la Maison de Sciences de l'Homme, 1995).
52. Robert Aron et al., "Lettre à Hitler," *L'Ordre nouveau* 1, no. 5 (1933): 3–32.
53. Aron, *La fin de l'après-guerre*, 165.
54. Ibid., 110.
55. Ibid., 169.
56. William Rappard, *The Crisis of Democracy* (Chicago: University of Chicago Press, 1938).
57. Ibid., 244–5.
58. Ibid., 265.
59. Ibid., 266–7.
60. Paul Mantoux, William E. Rappard, Maurice Bourquin, Guglielmo Ferrero, Georges Kaeckenbeeck, Hans Kelsen, Ludwig von Mises, Pitman B. Potter, Wilhelm Röpke, Hans Wehberg, John B. Whitton, Paul Guggenheim, and Michael A. Heilperin, *The World Crisis* (London: Longmans Green, 1938).
61. Milan Grol, *Iskušenja demokratije* [The Temptations of Democracy] (Belgrade: Naučna knjiga, 1991). Grol's text was only published posthumously, part of the revival of the interwar Serbian democratic publishing series *Biblioteka Politika i društvo* (Politics and Society Library).

8
Crisis of Socialism

Liberalism was far from being the only ideological stream described as eminently crisis-ridden in the interwar years. There was also an extensive discussion on the crisis of socialism, ravaged by its division between revisionist, syndicalist, and communist orientations from the late 1910s onward. Socialism was also challenged by the rise of fascism and National Socialism, which meant an existential threat not only in terms of the violent repression of socialist movements wherever the political context allowed for reliance on extra-legal means, but also the enticement of a significant part of its social base.

From Revolutionary Crisis to the Crisis of the Revolution

The idea of crisis within the socialist movement did not emerge as a reaction to the 1917 Bolshevik Revolution. Rather, it had already appeared in the title of Lenin's emotional polemic with the Menshevik Yuri Larin in the context of the debate on the shipwrecked 1905 Revolution within the Russian socialist movement.[1] Lenin contrasted here the "crisis of Menshevism" caused by "bourgeois opportunism" with the immunity to crisis that characterized the Bolsheviks in his opinion. In turn, in his political articles from 1908–9, Lenin argued against the revisionist thesis according to which the advancement of capitalism and the expanding workers' movement made economy and society increasingly crisis-resistant.

During the First World War, Rosa Luxemburg's (1871–1919) powerful polemic *Krise der Sozialdemokratie* (written in 1915, published in early 1916 under the pseudonym Junius) focused on the existential decision the socialist movement had to make in view of the revolutionary situation which had opened up due to the international wartime crisis.[2] In Luxemburg's rendering, the rise of imperialism and the unprecedented brutality of the war posed an either–or question for humankind: the victory of socialism or "regression into barbarism" (a notion she took from Friedrich Engels) and the annihilation of civilization.[3] Along these lines, Luxemburg criticized the "passive fatalism" of the social democratic leadership, putting its trust merely into the impersonal forces of historical development, and called instead for an "active class politics" capable of driving the crisis "far beyond its original extent."[4] At the same time, as her later analyses of the Russian October Revolution show, Luxemburg remained ambiguous about the Leninist solution to the crisis. She deplored the voluntarism of the Bolshevik leaders, who attempted the forceful

---

Intellectuals and the Crisis of Politics in the Interwar Period and Beyond. Balázs Trencsényi, Oxford University Press.
© Balázs Trencsényi (2025). DOI: 10.1093/9780198929512.003.0008

socialist transformation of a society that had barely embarked on a high capitalist phase and criticized the anti-democratic traits of the Bolshevik understanding of proletarian dictatorship.[5]

Lenin also employed the concept of crisis strategically in the ideological buildup to the Bolshevik Revolution. His 1917 "Lessons of the Crisis," written in the spring after his return from Switzerland to Russia in a sealed train, started with the dramatic sentence: "Petrograd and the whole of Russia have passed through a serious political crisis, the first political crisis since the revolution."[6] The crisis was caused by the clash of the Provisional Government, representing the "capitalists" seeking to pursue Russia's military engagement on the side of the Entente, and the proletariat, refusing further involvement in the "predatory war." Thus, for Lenin, the true meaning of crisis was that it brought the class antagonism underlying political differences to surface in its naked reality. While he was far from calling for an immediate revolutionary transformation at this point, Lenin saw the possibility of radicalization. However, in his understanding, the transformation was supposed to unfold in a global framework: "The world situation is growing more and more involved. *The only way out is a world workers' revolution, a revolution which is now more advanced in Russia than in any other country*, but which is clearly mounting (strikes, fraternization) in Germany too."[7]

As "dual power" became increasingly contested in Russia and the socialist movements across Europe radicalized, Lenin wrote another text on the terminal crisis of the capitalist order, describing Russia as the *avant-garde* of the global revolutionary movement.[8] He argued that the peasant revolt, as well as the soldiers' refusal to continue the war, were clear symptoms of a revolutionary situation and he criticized those Bolshevik leaders who advocated a more careful position. Failing to act quickly in such a crisis situation would mean renouncing the revolution and betraying the Russian and international proletariat.

In turn, from a social democratic perspective, it was the Bolshevik revolution and the general political radicalization in Europe that could be perceived as a crisis threatening the survival of the socialist movement. For instance, Hungarian economic sociologist Pál (Paul) Szende (1879–1934), rooted in the Austro-Marxist tradition and having experienced the failure of the 1918 Hungarian democratic revolution and the ensuing waves of the White Terror and the Red Terror, analyzed the Central European situation in terms of an endemic "crisis of revolution."[9] Szende focused on the militarization and brutalization of societies because of the First World War and the ensuing torrents of revolutions and counter-revolutions. The outcome was the departure of a significant part of socialist political forces from the original agenda of eliminating oppression (which Szende identified with the core of the Marxian program) and the rise of voluntarist revolutionary movements, which neglected the socioeconomic preconditions in their respective countries and relied on pure coercion to enforce their envisaged socialist transformations. In this sense, Szende came close to the idea of the convergence and mutual reinforcement of radical left- and right-wing forces, thus anticipating the anti-totalitarian critique that became an ideological weapon of the social democrats from the mid-1920s.

196 Intellectuals and the Crisis of Politics

Overall, the three main issues debated in the context of the crisis of socialism in the early 1920s were the division of the workers' movement, the ideological conflicts between different interpretations of the Marxian heritage, and the divergence of strategic insights regarding revolutionary action. It was from this perspective that leading Austro-Marxist politician and ideologist Max Adler (1879–1934) linked the critique of Bolshevism with general frustration toward the collapse of the unity of the workers' movement.[10] For Adler, the "crisis of socialism" became manifest with the disintegration of the (Second) International at the outbreak of the First World War, but, in a sense, it was also the outcome of an already-existing crisis of the socialist doctrine that had been long simmering under the surface: "The crisis is essentially a crisis of proletarian intellectual life itself, and is therefore inadequately expressed by the popular opposition of 'reformism' and 'revolution.'"[11]

For Italian socialist leader Pietro Nenni (1891–1980), reflecting on the rise of fascism and the collapse of the Italian left in his Paris exile, the "socialist crisis" was the result of the paralysis of the movement following the Russian Revolution and the end of the First World War. In this dramatic period, the different socialist factions—with incompatible programs and divergent assessments of the situation—turned against each other, eventually destroying the unity of the socialist movement and undermining its political power.[12] For Nenni, the creation of a separate communist party was " . . . a disaster. From that moment on any common action became impossible for the proletariat."[13] He continued: "From January 1921, the socialist party passed from one crisis to another; however, the new communist party, which had a sectarian character, was unable to profit from its internal decomposition."[14] Eventually, this division of forces and the divergence of strategies left the proletariat defenseless in the face of the repressive actions of the fascists, openly or tacitly supported by various political forces of the bourgeoisie.

In contrast, while describing the internal friction within the European socialist movement after the end of the Great War as the central feature of the "crisis of world socialism,"[15] French radical socialist political journalist Paul Louis (original surname: Lévy, 1872–1955) blamed mainly the social democratic side for it. The first sentence of his book declares that "world socialism is undergoing a new crisis, and a deeper one than most of the other ones that preceded it."[16] Louis went on to specify that crisis in his reading was not a synonym for civilizational decline, but a period of fundamental transformation and a catalyst of progress, "a manifestation of force, a phase of growth, and the expulsion of the harmful principles which normally attack the entire organism."[17]

Louis analyzed the political history of the socialist movement from the late nineteenth century onward and pointed toward the social and political downturn after 1914, which made reformism increasingly untenable, even if during the war they seemed to achieve strong positions due to their cooperation with the bourgeois parties. The crisis became manifest in the spectacular failure of these parties to prevent the outbreak of the war. In turn, the "revolutionary crisis" unfolding after 1917 meant the return of the socialist movement to its true origins and "fundamental maxims,"[18] as a "socialism of doctrine and of action,"[19] which was obfuscated by the Second

International. In contrast, the emerging Third International was legitimized by the correct prediction of the crisis: "The essential concept of the communist International was that the revolutionary crisis had arrived, for the entire world, the way as it was prophesied by the 1848 Manifesto."[20] On the whole, Louis sought to prove that the Soviet leaders were faithfully following the Marxian line, including the role of the revolutionary elites and the break with parliamentary democracy.

However, the collapse of the revolutionary wave outside of Russia (Bavaria, Austria, Hungary) implied that this crisis was not just a short transitional phase toward global socialism. What was needed was concerted action by the socialist movement, breaking with the ideological deviations and mistaken practices of the Second International and returning to the uncorrupted principles of the First. The only representative of Marxist orthodoxy in this context was Moscow: "One cannot claim to be a Marxist without adhering to the theses of Moscow, and, conversely, one cannot adhere to the theses of Moscow without relying on Marxism and without acknowledging the absolute identity of these theses with the immortal manifesto of 1847."[21] Although Louis predictably emerged as an early adherent of the communist party in France, he soon became a target of criticism for remaining a "bourgeois journalist" by the radical left wing of the party, and eventually departed from the movement, forming his own minor party between the communists and the socialists.

While Louis wavered between the agenda of a global revolutionary transformation and the reality of the construction of socialism in one state, in the early 1920s the European radical left linked the crisis of the socialist movement mainly to a loss of faith in the imminent world revolution.[22] Italian socialist Adriano Tilgher's crisis discourse contained a self-critical thread that asserted that the postwar period was also a crisis of the global socialist movement.[23] For him, the lack of solidarity among European socialist parties toward the German and Hungarian "proletariat" (in the given context this denoted the German and Hungarian communists), seeking to induce revolution in their countries following the Russian example, indicated the moral collapse of international socialism after the war.

Thus, in Tilgher's rendering, the crisis of socialism equaled the decline of revolutionary dynamism in the Western hemisphere. The Italian case exemplified this crisis in a paradigmatic way. The proletariat was not immune to the petty bourgeois value system: Italy was a small country, bourgeois at heart, so many proletarians also craved to become bourgeois. The crisis of Italian postwar politics was due exactly to this in-betweenness: the socialists broke with the liberals, but being incapable of implementing socialism, they were left in limbo. A reviewer in the socialist journal *Avanti!*— journalist and politician Alessandro Schiavi (1872–1965)—interpreted Tilgher's book as profoundly ambiguous, itself signaling a crisis: calling for a break with the bourgeois parties but also fearing that capitalism did not reach its limits, and the socialist idea did not penetrate the proletariat deeply enough, preventing a successful revolutionary transformation.[24]

This trope could also be instrumentalized to delegitimize the Socialist Party as such by former socialists who changed gears during the war and opted for fascism. A case in point is Maria Rygier (1885–1953), a Polish-born Italian political writer and activist, who had a particularly colorful biography, oscillating ideologically between feminism, syndicalism, anarchism, anti-militarism, interventionism, fascism, and anti-fascism, and finishing her life as a monarchist. Inspired by Sorelian ideas, Rygier became a close collaborator of Mussolini during the war and used her remarkable prestige as a former political prisoner and charismatic agitator to legitimize the fascist project as a synthesis of socialist and individualist drives. In her 1920 article on the "crisis of socialism," Rygier announced that the "official socialist party without doubt goes through a profound and decisive crisis."[25] Here the concept of crisis implied not so much a transition from one stage to another, but an either–or of transformation (and alignment with nationalist aims) or dissolution because of the pro-communist takeover of the party leadership. Reflecting on the ambiguities of communist internationalism, and evidently drawing on her Polish sensibilities, Rygier also pointed out that the Soviets were hardly anti-nationalists, but rather followed Russian geopolitical interests and thus the internationalism of their Italian comrades was a self-deception.

Crisis famously featured as a key concept in Antonio Gramsci's (1891–1937) writings as well. An important early conceptualization is his article on the "Italian crisis" from 1924.[26] The young Gramsci described fascism as a product of the crisis of capitalism, offering a seeming solution for the petty bourgeoisie threatened by the economic depression and the virulence of the workers' movement. However, fascism could not overcome the crisis of capitalism, as it only offered a more straightforward use of violence to suppress the protests about the falling living standard. In fact, in the volatile period after the June 1924 murder of Giacomo Matteotti, the fascist leadership seemed to have lost its unity and self-confidence, which opened a possible window of opportunity for the anti-fascist opposition to challenge Mussolini's rule. In his work from this period, Gramsci argued that the regime was much less stable than it seemed. Thus, the general Italian crisis was also manifested by the "crisis of fascism." Given this crisis-ridden nature of the regime, Gramsci anticipated a prolonged power fight between the fascists and the bourgeois anti-fascist coalition. He considered the communist movement still unprepared to enter this struggle with a chance of prevailing over the whole bourgeois camp and advocated a cautious strategy of gathering strength until it could command most of the proletariat, sidelining the reformist socialists. In turn, the Italian communist theoretician also argued in favor of a struggle against the radical leftists who sought to provoke a premature confrontation. From Gramsci's point of view, the only viable strategy was to meticulously penetrate the working class, from the factories to the villages, with intensive political education, under the leadership of qualified communist organizers, and to use the trade unions as seeds for future revolutionary power structures. Only such a mass movement could aspire to successfully resolve the crisis in a revolutionary way. Importantly, this future revolution could not be an isolated event, but only part and parcel of a European and even global socialist transformation. When and how this would eventually unfold remained unclear in the text.

Rather than this earlier and more straightforward article, interpretations of Gramsci's concept of crisis usually point to his *Prison Notebooks* as the key source. Given the peculiar circumstances of the birth of these texts,[27] Gramsci used a coded language, which has made it notoriously hard to agree upon an unequivocal interpretation of his argument and has provoked discussions ever since the first edition in 1948. Hence, his oft-quoted sentence about crisis—"the old is dying and the new cannot be born; in this interregnum a great variety of morbid symptoms appear"—has generated many different readings.[28]

It is important to bear in mind that the *Notebooks* were written in 1929–35, when crisis indeed became a central theme of political discourse all over Europe. The fascist regime, like Stalin's Soviet Union, declared itself immune to crisis, but it could not completely negate the signs of economic depression, culminating in robust state intervention in the early 1930s. In the context of growing socioeconomic and political tensions, the Comintern also shifted gears, and from 1928 onward it broke with the "united front" tactics and started to frontally attack social democrats (labeled "social fascists") as but another face of bourgeois reaction, essentially converging with fascism. This resulted in an internal cleavage in the communist camp as well, with Gramsci taking a more moderate position compared to the leadership of the Italian Communist Party around Palmiro Togliatti (1893–1964), who implemented a Stalinist ideological transformation within the party.

Developing a veritable meta-theory of crisis, Gramsci himself used the concept in different contexts, from the socioeconomic sphere (e.g., "commercial crisis") to education and "traditional culture."[29] However, he reiterated that these phenomena were ramifications of a more comprehensive "organic crisis."[30] Along these lines, he distinguished between "organic" and "conjunctural" causal relationships shaping historical reality, pointing out that they were often conflated by previous analysts who either sought to explain away deeper transformations by pointing to individual political agency, or had overstressed mechanistic/deterministic explanatory schemes. The analysis of crisis situations is therefore central to the work of the socialist theoretician and has a direct link to political action, as its main task is the consolidation of forces (making them "ever more homogeneous, compact and self-aware")[31] that can achieve political change.

Such crises of authority or hegemony for Gramsci are rooted in the opening of the gap between the representatives and the represented, undermining the legitimacy of the political system. The ruling classes try to reinforce their rule by unifying hitherto competing political forces on their side into a unitary party. If this fails, then the rise of a charismatic individual leader might create a new but often fragile equilibrium between conservative and progressive social forces (as in the case of Louis Bonaparte, analyzed by Marx).[32] Thus, in Gramsci's *Prison Notebooks*, crises were not static moments but rather intertwining processes that characterized an "interregnum" that would eventually converge into a comprehensive transformation. From this perspective, his condensed entry on the "'Wave of Materialism' and the 'Crisis of Authority'" reflects his belief in a window of opportunity for communists to create a new culture while the previously dominant culture is disintegrating. In this sense, although the conceptualization became more sophisticated, Gramsci's overall political diagnosis in the *Prison Notebooks* remained quite similar to his early text in the sense that the socialist transformation, and thus the resolution to the crisis, was only possible if communists could achieve a cultural and political hegemony among the working class, and that this could not be accomplished overnight, but only with systematic and sustained effort.

Gramsci's position was comparable to some of the heterodox communist thinkers of the 1920s, such as Karl Korsch (1886–1961). Coming from a German reformist leftist intellectual milieu, Korsch's views radicalized in the context of the First World War. After 1920, he became a prominent communist leader in Thuringia, also acting as a minister of justice in the short-lived social-democratic/communist coalition government. His key theoretical work from the early 1920s was *Marxismus und Philosophie*, an ingenuous attempt to use the Marxist historical method for interpreting the development of Marxism.[33] Importantly, trying to grasp the historical process in its entirety, Korsch rejected the perception that philosophy and ideas in general were merely epiphenomena of a socioeconomic basis, arguing instead to consider them genuine "expressions of reality" that needed to be carefully analyzed in order to understand history in its totality. Although not a central notion in the book, Korsch repeatedly mentioned the "crisis of Marxism," referring mainly to the fatal division of the workers' movement after 1917. Interpreting this crisis with the Marxist tools of historical analysis, Korsch described the Second International as a manifestation of the counter-revolutionary developmental phase of the workers' movement and conceived of the period starting with the Great War as a general crisis that could eventually lead to the consummation of philosophical thought by turning it into revolutionary praxis.

By the early 1930s, the situation changed radically. Korsch was expulsed from the Stalinized Communist Party of Germany (KPD) and became one of the leading leftist dissidents. His 1931 study "Theses for the Debate on the 'Crisis of Marxism'" was an attempt to clarify his own intellectual position. However, due to the sensitive nature of the problem he raised, touching the very legitimacy of the Marxian heritage, it was not published during his lifetime.[34] The text opened with the dramatic sentences: "Marxism today is in the midst of an historical and theoretical crisis. It is not simply a crisis within the Marxist movement, but a crisis of Marxism itself."[35] The aim here was thus not to restore the authentic meaning of Marxism, but to historicize the Marxist doctrine as such and pose the question whether the failures of the movement might have signaled the shortcomings of the theory. This gripping question could point to the intellectual responsibility of the "founding fathers" for the deviations of the socialist movement, and the possibility of a new revolutionary phase eventually "going beyond" Marxian philosophical insights. The use of Marxist interpretative tools could thus potentially undermine the validity of Marxism as such, even if the text finished with the seemingly reassuring statement that "in a more fundamental historical sense, the theory of proletarian revolution, which will develop anew in the next period of history, will be an historical continuation of Marxism."[36]

Korsch could not resolve these painful dilemmas, but raising these very questions meant a radical departure from the Marxist orthodoxy, both in its Kautskyan social democratic exegetic form and its Leninist (and Stalinist) rendering. While the impact of his ideas in the context of the collapse of the Weimar Republic and the failure of the Stalinized communist parties in Europe to stave off the fascist wave was limited, Korsch's historicization of Marxism, criticism of ossified dogmatism, and emphasis on revolutionary praxis bring him close to the post-Second World War streams of "Marxist humanism," which—not so accidentally—also turned to the concept of the "crisis of socialism" to articulate their critical positions.[37]

The Identity Crisis of Social Democracy

The Great Depression and the political–institutional convulsions from 1929 put the entire postwar order into question, and this meant a particular challenge to the German social democrats who arguably identified themselves most completely with the Weimar Republic. In his analysis of the "current political crisis" jurist and diplomat Otto Landsberg (1869–1957) fought a characteristic two-front battle.[38] A former member of the revolutionary Council of the People's Deputies in 1918–19 and close collaborator of Friedrich Ebert, Landsberg rebutted the "*Dolchstoss* legend" of the radical right as well as the accusations of the radical left, who claimed that the republicans followed their narrow bourgeois class interests against the proletarian masses. Thus, Landsberg interpreted the 1918 revolution as a reaction to—rather than the cause of—the collapse of the Bismarckian empire, which in his understanding was less stable than it seemed, being torn by several internal structural contradictions. At the same time, responding to the criticism of the radical left, he also tried to defend social democrats against the accusation that they did not exploit the revolutionary situation to create a fundamentally new socioeconomic framework.

Citing the United States, Great Britain, and France as examples, Landsberg remained convinced that parliamentarism was globally the most successful model of government and inserted the Weimar Republic into this framework. He was ready to admit that the criticism of the intellectual level of debates in the *Reichstag* was justified, but also pointed out that the aim of parliament was to represent social forces and not to gather the most intelligent people. His relative optimism was also exemplified by the fact that, when he published his book in 1931, he did not consider the Nazi challenge to the Republic as an imminent danger. In line with his efforts to de-dramatize and contain the crisis, he argued for separation of the political and economic spheres, as the economic and political crises had different roots. In his reading, the political crisis was due to the dysfunctions of the party system, characterized by the lack of a clear majority and the unnatural proliferation of parties, most of them not being rooted in real social processes and needs. But he also noted the widespread discontent with parliamentarism that emerged from the popular antipathy toward capitalism. Hence, the final aim of social democrats should be to transcend capitalism and create socialism, but this could only be a gradual process and should be achieved democratically. Along these lines, he contrasted the "*Realpolitik*" of his camp with the revolutionary "*Romantik*" of the enemies of democracy both on the right and on the left.

202 Intellectuals and the Crisis of Politics

While Landsberg still preserved a feeling of "business as usual" with regard to advancing the socialist agenda, as time passed there were increasing numbers of voices who questioned the very core of socialist party politics as it had operated on the basis of Marxist ideas roughly since the 1890s. A key voice in the debate was Belgian theoretician Henri de Man. Deeply rooted both in the German and French intellectual milieux, he formulated an alternative to what he perceived as the "orthodox Marxism" that had shaped the politics of the socialist parties of Western Europe.[39] He argued that the Marxist reading of history was too mechanistic, believing in the automatic victory of socialism, downplaying human agency and psychological factors. Along these lines, he diagnosed the socialist movement as undergoing a "crisis of conscience" that resulted in the emergence of two radical wings: the left, who put their faith uncritically into Marxist dogmas (that is, upholding the doctrine but neglecting the practice) and the right (committed to a practice without doctrine), whose rejection of Marxism led them toward an uncritical cooperation with bourgeois parties.[40]

The way out of this impasse was a "spiritual revival"—a "moral revolt" against the bourgeois order rallying different social groups around the socialist cause. Trying to define the content of this spirituality, de Man described the socialist movement as the true successor of the Christian ideals corrupted by the Catholic Church and the successor of democratic ideals corrupted by the bourgeoisie. His support for democratic institutions as a key component of the socialist struggle—as against the radical left, which rejected these institutions as mere instruments of bourgeois class power—was combined with certain features of elitism. Most importantly, he stressed the importance of intellectuals, and of elites in general, capable of articulating these ideas of renewal, since the masses were unable to formulate a vision of socialist transformation for themselves because they also were bound to their consumption needs. Finally, de Man also tried to find a "third way" between nationalism and cosmopolitanism, stressing the importance of national consciousness as a constitutive element of social solidarity but rejecting the absolutization of the nation. While these ideological characteristics did not predetermine his wartime trajectory toward collaboration with the German occupiers, they nevertheless underwrote his rejection of the traditional division of the political left and right, which could open the possibility of making unconventional (and in his case eventually self-destructive) alliances.

In the 1930s, de Man had a truly transnational resonance way beyond his native Belgium.[41] His criticism converged largely with that of other political thinkers and activists across Europe who also sought to put forward an alternative agenda to the mainstream leftist and rightist positions. This can be seen in the writings of the Italian anti-fascist émigré political thinker Carlo Rosselli (1899–1937).[42] Rosselli had been preoccupied with the "intellectual crisis" of the socialist movement since the early 1920s, as attested by his article from 1923, where he stressed the necessity of open debate within the party to regain the political initiative.[43]

Witnessing the comprehensive defeat of the anti-fascist camp in Italy and forced to emigrate, Rosselli turned to the task of the intellectual renewal of the left, developing a vision of liberal socialism.[44] He drew on de Man's criticism of the deterministic worldview of mainstream socialist political elites and rejected the reduction of the socialist doctrine to the idea of class struggle. In his opinion, socialism was not equal to the socialization of the means of production, nor to the rise of the proletariat to domination, and not even material equality, but rather to the "progressive realization of the idea of liberty and justice among humans."[45] This implied the compatibility of liberal and socialist ideas, which in turn required a break with antiquated conceptions inherent to both ideologies. Thus, Rosselli criticized both "bourgeois liberalism" and the dogmatic Marxist framework of analyzing politics and society as anachronistic and "frozen in time," namely, in the nineteenth century. In his opinion, the Marxist theory of the "immanent crisis" of capitalism proved to be mistaken (a "false realism"[46]); further, the actual moments of crisis did not lead to a revolutionary transformation but, to the contrary, they reinforced the unity of the bourgeoisie and thus triggered the emergence of fascist backlash.

Perhaps the most resounding intellectual and political challenge to the socialist mainstream came from France, which was unsurprising, as the consolidation of a Marxist mass party was relatively late and never complete there. As a result, alternative ideological references—such as anarcho-syndicalism—continued to have considerable impact throughout the period in question. This debate also unfolded in close connection to the experience and discourse of crisis in the early 1930s, after the effects of the Great Depression also reached France. Leading socialist politician Léon Blum (1872–1950) developed his vision of the tasks of socialism in facing the economic and political crisis in a lecture from 1932.[47] Blum subscribed to the idea of a universal crisis rooted in the transformation of the nature of capitalist society.[48] He argued (quite accurately) that the French should not count on escaping the crisis just because effects of the Depression on Germany and the United States had not yet appeared in France. Interpreting the crisis phenomena in the framework of an overall reconfiguration of capitalism and the entrance into an era of rationalization, Blum was convinced that no country could escape the consequences of the crisis due to its common roots.

Rejecting the "theory of over-production" advanced by most bourgeois analysts, Blum argued that the crisis was linked instead to the "fundamental, essential and irreconcilable contradictions of the capitalist propriety regime."[49] The central contradiction in his understanding was between the acceleration of technological progress and the need for a smaller workforce, generating ever more unemployment. From this perspective, Blum also rejected several competing theories of crisis and their concomitant models of crisis management. The classical liberal understanding stipulated that, in certain moments of disequilibrium, crisis was a necessary purging process that erased unsustainable economic and social forms and reinforced those that were profitable, thus following the Darwinian logic of the survival of the fittest. For Blum, this position was inhumane and had already been superseded by the evolution of the modern state, which was far from the nineteenth-century ideal of *laissez-faire*. He also criticized those technocratic liberals (exemplified by American President Herbert Hoover) who themselves abandoned the non-interventionist position but considered that the main task of the state in times of crisis was to preserve the private ownership of the means of production and thus lay the groundwork for the next economic upswing. Finally, he also deplored the solution, subscribed to by some conservatives, that entailed the reduction of production, describing it as anti-modern and going against the direction of progress.

He was convinced that these theories of "the physicians of capitalism" were unable to offer a "cure" for the contradictions created by capitalism,[50] but even socialists could not offer a complete treatment for an incurable illness. Rather, these contradictions could only be overcome in the transition to socialism, where the contradiction of consumption and production would disappear, and crisis would become inconceivable. At the same time, in contrast to the communist interpretation (which put the emphasis on growing polarization and antagonism that could only be resolved through revolution), Blum argued that the workers' movement achieved some social and legal positions that made it more resilient and not merely left to the mercy of property owners. The socialist solution was thus to augment the buying power of the population through loans, public works, and international cooperation and not to escalate an armed conflict between the bourgeoisie and the proletariat.

Blum's analysis was carefully balanced, and his arguments against the recipes of liberal crisis management were pertinent. However, his vision of the solution was rather sketchy and did not seem particularly compelling. His most emotional lines were connected to the missed possibility of a much better global position for the socialist movement, had the Bolsheviks not opted for dividing the international workers' movement into competing socialist and communist camps.[51] This uchronic perspective in some ways foreshadowed Blum's Popular Front agenda from 1935, but also showed the serious limitations of the socialist imaginary in capturing the fantasy of those groups who assumed a more radical stance toward the actually existing socioeconomic and political order.

The ensuing congress of the French socialist party in July 1933 revealed a particularly sharp internal cleavage articulated by the protagonists as the crisis of the socialist movement. Several important politicians of the younger generation openly clashed with the leadership around Blum.[52] The most well-known among them was Marcel Déat (1894–1955), an influential radical intellectual with philosophical and sociological training. Their starting position was in a way a non-conventional revisionist criticism of the party line: they argued for cooperation with the progressive part of the bourgeoisie (in party political terms this meant mainly the bourgeois democratic Radical Party) to have a real say on the social and political conditions of the country. But this went together with a penchant for an anti-systemic radicalism resonating with the generational ideologies of the time, present on both the left and the right. This was all combined with a strong étatism (again with rightist and leftist parallels in fascism and Stalinism) asserting that real change could only be achieved through controlling state institutions and their resources.

The differences of opinion erupted in the debate on the budget vote in parliament when a minority of the socialist party around Déat voted with the Radicals and defied the party orthodoxy which rejected a close cooperation with the bourgeois left even if the growing polarization of political life seemed to dictate such a collaboration to prevent right-wing forces from coming to power.[53] Defending their dissident position, Déat and his colleagues also turned to the concept of crisis, which necessitated a break with conventional political wisdom and the search for new alliances and political strategies.

Déat's close collaborator, the deputy Barthélemy Montagnon (1889–1969) described the crisis of the socialist movement (*la crise socialiste*) as being entangled with a "general crisis" that subsumed global political life in both moral and material senses. What is more, this overlapped with a "doctrinal crisis" caused by the open-ended nature of the crisis of capitalism unfolding after 1929, which posed the question whether the working class was ready to take over the government and the means of production. Montagnon's speech was saturated by the concept of crisis: he talked of the "crisis of old forms," the "crisis of ideas," and the "crisis of transition"[54]—but, interestingly, he did not tie it conceptually to the Great Depression.

In this vision of "total crisis," the main task of socialist politicians was to study those contemporary political projects that sought to overcome it (e.g., Bolshevism, fascism, "Hitlerism," and the New Deal). Montagnon found a common denominator among these streams in their effort to strengthen the state, in contrast to bourgeois democracy and parliamentarism, which he characterized as doctrines preferring a "weak state." He also found a common ground between his own vision of socialism and fascism in syndicalism, which he considered a genuine socialist doctrine hijacked by the extreme right. While his imagery of the devastating effects of crisis was very dramatic, the proposals for a way out were far less clear. Merging Sorelian influences with de Man's "planism" Montagnon suggested reshaping parliamentarism, strengthening the state, and mobilizing people for a total transformation in the syndicalist manner with the "mystique of a plan."

His colleague Adrien Marquet (1884–1955), the popular mayor of Bordeaux, also focused on the crisis of the socialist movement, which in his opinion had reached an impasse since the First World War. This was proven by a decades-long stagnation in numbers: in 1914 it had 104 MPs and 100,000 activists; in 1932, merely 130 MPs and 120,000 activists. For Marquet, this meant that the strategy of the orthodox Marxist party leadership—committed to the idea of gradual but steady growth toward the final takeover of power—was becoming increasingly counter-productive. Rather than an unstoppable evolution toward socialism, modern Western societies experienced "a raging crisis all over the place."[55] This crisis did not catalyze a socialist revolution, but "worked for the reaction." Marquet pointed to the German example to support his argument that the unemployed were not potential revolutionaries, but more the auxiliary troops of reaction, many of them turning to support Hitler. The solution to the crisis was cooperation with the progressive bourgeois side to stabilize the economy, prevent currency devaluation (which had undermined the left-wing government in 1926), introduce protective tariffs, and reorganize the economy in a "national framework" (*cadre national*), eventually creating a "new order" (*ordre nouveau*). These key notions also indicated that the protagonists of French *néo-socialiste* criticism integrated many elements of the radical anti-establishment "third way" discourse of the "young generation" emerging in the context of the Great Depression, while at the same time envisaging a move toward the political center. This combination seemed highly dubious for the party leadership: Blum summarily labeled Marquet's position as "almost fascist."

In the raging theoretical and political debate, Déat—the most important intellectual of the neo-socialists—put forward a quasi "revisionist Marxist" formula, arguing that Marxism was a method and not a dogma. He proposed using the Marxist framework to interpret fascism, conceding that the main reason for fascist ascendance was the economic crisis, leading to the proletarianization of the middle classes.[56] This went together with the paralysis of the state, undermining the prestige of parliamentarism. Along these lines, however, he turned against the radical leftist understanding (most memorably formulated by Bulgarian communist politician Georgi Dimitrov, 1882–1949) that fascism was the conspiracy of the most reactionary elements of the high bourgeoisie and pointed instead to a "chain reaction," with the crisis of international capitalism catalyzing the crisis of international socialism, creating space for a new contender. To contain the fascists, Déat suggested rejecting the idea of a unified proletarian front with the communists and cooperating with the middle classes instead. This, however, did not imply a liberal common ground. To the contrary: Déat opted for a radically anti-liberal voluntarist rhetoric. Responding to Blum, he stressed that it was possible to combine the program of reform and revolution in a new way, but instead of the passivity of orthodox Marxists, fixated on the Hegelian dialectics of history eventually resulting in a synthesis, he pleaded for active engagement, mobilizing disaffected social groups and the young generation against the system: "we want to act, we want to transform the world in which we are."[57]

Déat and his comrades sought to take over the Socialist Party, but their position (i.e., insisting on cooperation with the Radicals) remained in the minority at the party congress and their group eventually seceded. While they fervently contested Blum's accusation of fascist sympathies, their political trajectory indeed led them toward the radical right (and eventually to collaboration with the Nazi occupiers during the Vichy regime), thus retrospectively validating the accusation of the socialist leader— or perhaps also turning it into a self-fulfilling prophecy. Importantly, and for some time, Rosselli also sympathized with the French *néo-socialistes* and even praised Déat for his daring criticism of the socialist mainstream. But the Italian anti-fascist network eventually accepted Blum's position, considering the neo-socialist current dangerously close to fascism.

The debate on the orientation of the French party also had broader international repercussions in the context of the general shock caused by the Nazi *Machtergreifung* in January 1933 and the subsequent decomposition of the socialist organizational structures in Germany. The main report at the conference of the Socialist International, seeking to give guidance in this dramatic moment, was prepared by Otto Bauer (1881–1938), who focused on Germany but also had in mind the dire situation of the social democrats in his native Austria.[58] The concept of crisis played an important role in Bauer's analysis as well. He thus referred to the "economic crisis in Germany" as a key factor in the rise of Nazism.[59] He connected this to other crisis phenomena, namely the wider "crisis of capitalism," the "crisis of parliamentarism," and the "crisis of democracy,"[60] pointing to the emergence of a new type of capitalism which was interlinked with anti-democratic politics.

Bauer's report defended democracy as a key value but rejected its formalist understanding and argued that it could only be maintained as a "revolutionary force," and not as a tool of conserving existing power and economic relations. The report also commended Blum's policy of the "unification of the proletariat" (preparing the Popular Front ideology that came to determine French socialist politics in the mid-1930s) as an adequate response to the advance of the extreme right. The crisis of democracy was thus not merely a moment of danger but could lend a new dynamic to the socialist movement. However, as socialist party leaderships tried to react to the new challenges, their self-criticism and proposed remedies were often found to be "too little too late" by their radical leftist critics.

Considering the rapid deterioration of the position of the Austrian social democrats in the early 1930s, Bauer's position was far from being uncontested. In fact, the criticism of the socialist mainstream for its too mechanistic image of history and too proceduralist understanding of democracy did not necessarily imply a turn toward a "neither right nor left" stance but could feed into a position which still tried to stay within the social democratic tradition, albeit with a very different political agenda. The most resounding criticism of the Austro-Marxist mainstream came from the journalist and writer Ernst Fischer (1899–1972), who emerged into the position of the leader of the internal opposition within the Social Democratic Workers' Party of Austria (*Sozialdemokratische Arbeiterpartei*, SDAP). His intellectual-political manifesto, entitled "The Crisis of the Youth," merged an emotional criticism of the social democratic mainstream with a generational crisis discourse, pointing to an unbridgeable rift between the young and the old.[61] As befitting a radical socialist, however, he did not anchor the generational crisis merely in spiritual or biological differences, but also pointed to the crisis of capitalism as an underlying substructure. In Fischer's understanding, capitalism as a system failed to fulfill its promise to provide enough goods for consumption, and thus generated widespread disaffection. But he went beyond the conventional schemes of economic determinism when he pointed out that he did not talk merely about the crisis of capitalist economy but rather the "chronical crisis of the capitalist world," manifested in combined economic, sexual, and ideological disorientation.[62] It destroyed the old civilizations, but did not create a universal culture and, instead, made the world more variegated and at the same time more monotonous, turning it richer and poorer at the same time, with every success linked to a new catastrophe...[63]

Fischer sought to overcome this crisis with a radical existential revolt against the moribund social and mental structures which continued to dominate the world even if they became evidently dysfunctional. However, crisis itself had a paralyzing effect on society—dire necessity made people less capable of articulating their interests, and the growth of unemployment undermined the social-political achievements of the working class as it made them much more dependent on power, while atomization made it impossible to resist repression.

208 Intellectuals and the Crisis of Politics

Apart from the generational discourse which was used by the radical left (and the radical right as well) at the turn of the 1930s, another point where Fischer diverged fundamentally from the typical social democratic political vision was his praise for the Soviet Union as the only country spared from the world economic crisis.[64] Yet, he was also far from communist rhetoric which tended to describe the communist state in utopian terms: he stressed instead that the birth conditions of the Soviet Union were highly disadvantageous and thus were conducive to many different crises, but the hope in a better future overwrote the actual misery. Overall, the belief in a future social transformation was central for Fischer as it gave sense to political action: "the crisis of capitalism is meaningless if it is not conducive to its death."[65]

As for the other components of the crisis, Fischer also put forward rather atypical ideas from the perspective of the social democratic party elite. He deemed the crisis of sexuality a key manifestation of the cultural and social crisis, pointing to the tension between the social realities of bourgeois family life, based on hierarchy and exploitation, and the idealized and spiritualized cult of "pure love." He linked the emancipation of women to the crisis of the war and argued in favor of the liberation of women from the domination of "masculine society."[66] At the same time, he rejected radical ideas of sexual liberation which threatened the institution of monogamous family life with dissolution. Once again, he pointed to the Soviet experience (especially in its early Stalinist phase) as paradigmatic, combining legal emancipation with respect for the family as the central unit of social responsibility.

What was perhaps the most heretical idea for a socialist was Fischer's argument that all the crisis phenomena formed part of a fundamental crisis of worldview (*Weltanschauung*) ravaging Western societies. He linked this to the collapse of the idea of progress after the First World War, which undermined those political and civilizational visions which believed in gradual but irreversible improvement. This also meant the delegitimization of rationalism and the decay of social trust, making democracy philosophically and culturally implausible as well. Democracy promised more than it could deliver, and its necessary orientation toward compromise resulted in a feeling that all social and political actors considered their interests only partially represented. In this situation, the young generation of proletarians felt naturally excluded from the democratic process and became increasingly prone to seek the transformation of the system by turning to violent means.

Generational revolt was thus legitimate, both against the system in general, and within the socialist movement, against a fossilized party apparatus preaching moderation. If there was no irreversible progress toward socialism, then the self-limiting institutionalist strategy of the Austrian social democratic leadership around Bauer was not only mistaken but straightforwardly self-destructive. Lacking revolutionary pathos and mobilizing drive, the social democrats lost the radicalized youth precisely to their most lethal enemies, the extreme right. Fascist parties had no coherent program, for they were torn by the contradiction between their anti-capitalistic rhetoric and close links to high capitalist circles who used them to get rid of the socialist "menace." For Fischer, then, the only way to defeat the pseudo-revolutionary mobilization on the right, which appealed to national solidarity against ethnic others—especially the Jews—was to release the revolutionary energies of the socialist side as well: "The only answer is the Deed (*Tat*)!"[67]

The Breakthrough of Totalitarianism and the Revival of Democratic Socialism

As the conflict between left and right sharpened, the debate in the Austrian socialist movement became increasingly heated. Bauer still sought to remain within the Austrian republican constitutional framework, waging an increasingly desperate struggle to prevent open conflict, while the party opposition advocated a strategy of radical contestation and preparation for illegal action. Hitler's rise to power in Germany and the shift toward authoritarianism in Austria was interpreted by the opposition as the writing on the wall, legitimizing their contestation of the middle-of-the-road leadership. A dramatic text by the Austrian leftist social democratic theoretician and feminist activist Käthe Leichter (1895–1942) from 1933 offered a comprehensive criticism of the socialist movement as being incapable of finding a way out of the impasse.[68] Similar to the French neo-socialists, Leichter also drew on de Man to castigate the determinism of socialist doctrine, which relegated struggle to an inherent historical dynamism: "we were mesmerized by the determining processes and lost our faith in the creative power of the workers' movement itself, our confidence in their own ability to organize and act."[69] Speaking on behalf of the disaffected activist youth wing of the SDAP (grouped around Ernst Fischer), Leichter pointed to the world economic crisis as precisely an opportunity for action which was missed by the social democratic leadership around Bauer, too much steeped in theoretical debate:

> And isn't it characteristic that the time of this first great shock of the world economic crisis, the time to unleash anti-capitalist enthusiasm, has been chiefly spent discussing whether this is only one crisis of capitalism or the last one, without finding the courage to tell the masses that we, the Socialists, are going to make it the last by releasing all the enthusiasm of anti-capitalism and reshaping it as enthusiasm for Socialism?[70]

Not mobilizing the masses was not only a missed opportunity, but also a tragic error in the sense that the same anti-systemic energies came to be channeled by the extreme right:

> To the masses shaken by the first shock of the crisis we have offered academic explanations, so that they slipped into resignation, the more so as they'd been hurled out of the productive sector and into the anti-capitalist demagoguery of the Nazis, either directly or after persistent periods of unemployment, without a socialist perspective.[71]

210   Intellectuals and the Crisis of Politics

Leichter rejected the legalist position of the party leadership, who insisted on forming a coalition government with bourgeois parties, limiting the revolutionary energies of the working class and the party activists: "But isn't precisely that the fundamental mistake, that we never thought of the power we were to exercise as socialist power, but from the outset only as that of a coalition government within the framework of the capitalist order?"[72] Leichter thus called for a mobilization of revolutionary energies as the only way out: "Less faith in the automatic nature of capitalism and the inevitability of its cycles from crisis to recovery; more boldness to stress our uncompromising will to exploit the crisis for the collapse of capitalism..."[73]

Postwar capitalist "rationalization" (another key analytical category in de Man's work) led to the proletarianization of large masses, but, in contrast to the orthodox Marxist expectation, this proletarianization did not boost the ranks of the socialist movement; to the contrary, the most marginalized groups opted for fascism, promising them a more immediate and radical action. The task of socialists was to prepare for confrontation both with the capitalist order and the government, captured by right-wing authoritarian groups. But transitioning from the democratic parliamentary routine to such a confrontative political style was extremely hard. Be that as it may, in contrast to the right-wing of the party which still hoped to achieve some sort of compromise with Dollfuß, Leichter advocated preparing for illegality, anticipating that the Austrofascist leadership would soon ban the activities of democratic parties.[74]

The events of 1933 in Germany and 1934 in Austria came as an intellectual shock and triggered a spatial reconfiguration of the discussion on the rise of fascism, creating new diaspora hubs of Central European leftist intellectuals. In 1934, Bauer moved to Brno/Brünn in Czechoslovakia and tried to rethink the postwar story of the Austrian socialist movement from the vantage point of the intertwined economic, political, and social crises that had derailed the development toward democratic socialism.[75] In terms of his analytical framework, he drew on his previous work from 1931 on socialism and capitalism after the war.[76] In the meantime, the political situation changed radically and his position also became more radical, approaching that of his former leftist internal critics. An evident sign of this intended reconciliation was his book's dedication to the "revolutionary socialists."

Bauer looked to the early 1920s for an explanation of the emerging crisis. The short postwar conjuncture was overcome by growing instability, making the masses susceptible to radical right-wing mobilization. The depression starting in 1929 went well beyond the usual dynamic of previous, nineteenth-century economic crises and now catalyzed heated social conflicts never before seen. This was caused not least by the overlap of industrial and agrarian crises, making it impossible for the countryside to absorb urban workers. What is more, in this entangled crisis situation, industrial and agrarian countries all opted for policies that were meant to reduce their interdependence. Agrarian countries opted for protectionist measures to develop an industrial sector, while industrial countries were fascinated with the idea of agricultural self-sufficiency. The capitalist recipe for crisis management was a push for deflationary policy. However, in this protracted crisis situation, leading to impoverishment, it was only possible to implement this policy fully with the help of open violence, paralyzing the resistance of workers. Thus, the crisis became a catalyst for the convergence of capitalism and fascism.[77] Fascism eventually also meant étatist control over the economy, first regulating foreign trade and gradually also interfering with the internal market. The authoritarian state achieved a certain level of stability with a set of welfare measures, which however only served the interests of power holders and were implemented with the help of a veritable militarization of the productive classes. "Crisis" thus provided the state with the opportunity to subjugate both the working class and capital.

This argument implied that Bauer went beyond the usual Marxist understanding of fascism as an instrument of the capitalists and developed a more complex model where political and economic dynamics reinforced each other. What is more, in some ways, his description of the "slippery slope" toward autarchic policies resonated with the emerging neoliberal criticism of state intervention. At the same time, obviously, he did not negate the linkage between capitalism and fascism, only pointing out that there was a gap between the anti-capitalist rhetoric of fascists and their actual policies, which only abandoned the liberal form of capitalism.[78] The new political order could be described as "neomercantilism," in a way returning to the pre-liberal absolutist logic.

Bauer was convinced that the crisis could be overcome. He evoked Marx's phrase from the *Theories of Surplus Value* that "there are no permanent crises (*Permanente Krisen gibt es nicht*)." For him, the socialist transformation would put an end to cyclical crises. In contrast to the growing convergence of capitalist crisis management and fascist mobilization, in Bauer's understanding the Soviet Union was spared from the crisis and could thus serve as a model for socialists all over the world, irrespective of the doctrinal differences of social democrats and communists. In this sense, the exiled Austro-Marxist theoretician moved quite close to the communist position, considering the Soviet model and the Soviet geopolitical presence as the only potent counterweight to the rise of fascism and National Socialism.

Departing for London from Vienna after the Nazi takeover, Karl Polanyi (1886–1964) also engaged with the problem of the crisis of the socialist movement and the rise and morphology of fascism.[79] Searching for a synthesis of socialism and Christianity in his new British intellectual milieu and captivated by the idea of "guild socialism," he linked the downfall of the European socialist movement to the end of Christianity (subverting the usual accusation that socialism was actually responsible for the decline of religiosity).[80] At the same time, he accepted the characterization of Austrian Catholic radical conservative sociologist Othmar Spann, who described socialism as a form of individualism, as opposed to the anti-individualism of the fascists. In Polanyi's opinion, fascism was rooted in those philosophical doctrines (from Hegel to Nietzsche) that erased the dividing line of state and society. While not negating that Marxism also aimed at a reintegration of the individual and the community, Polanyi reverted to Luxemburg's contrast of progress versus regression and argued

212 Intellectuals and the Crisis of Politics

that socialists envisioned a future reintegration, whereas fascism was regressive, seeking to insert the achievements of modernity into an "vitalist" vision of past social harmony.

For Polanyi, the fundamental root of the "social crisis of our time" was the "mutual incompatibility" of democracy and capitalism, which resulted in an alternative of socialism and fascism.[81] This incompatibility also set liberalism and democracy against each other, the first leading to fascism while the second to socialism. Arguing that fascism was the logical continuation of liberalism, Polanyi linked Mussolini, Hitler, and Mises as defenders of the capitalist order: "Fascism is condoned as the safeguard of liberal economics."[82] The solution to the crisis was the extension of democracy to economics and the elimination of an autonomous economic sphere (in *The Great Transformation*, his subsequent masterpiece, this became conceptualized as "re-embedding").

However, Polanyi's anti-liberal turn was far from being the only possible ideological option on the left for rethinking the relationship of democracy and liberalism. In fact, the mid-1930s saw several intellectual projects that sought to create a synthesis of liberalism and socialism as an antidote to the totalitarian menace. In some ways similar to the leftist opposition to the Austrian social democratic mainstream, Hungarian–Jewish social democratic journalist Ferenc Fejtő (1909–2008; after the Second World War, in French exile, and under the name François Fejtő, he became a leading expert of communism in Eastern Europe and an influential public intellectual) criticized the inertia of the socialist movement in the 1930s, which in the Hungarian case was also aggravated by the repercussions of the failed 1919 Soviet Republic and the ensuing radical right-wing backlash.[83] Reflecting on the rise of the totalitarian menace as a crisis of the socialist movement, in the mid-1930s Fejtő became increasingly convinced that democratic values could not be subordinated to any abstract socialist objective and pointed out that ideologically Lenin was closer to Sorel than to Marx (which also implied that Lenin was arguably closer to Mussolini than to the socialist classics). Fejtő thus reverted to the Marxian vision in his polemic against the Stalinists, stressing that socialism's precondition was embourgeoisement, so the revolutionary mobilization of masses with overwhelmingly rural backgrounds against the underdeveloped capitalist economy in Eastern Europe could hardly result in a socialist triumph: rather the contrary. Along these lines, he also pointed out the similarities between socialist and fascist anti-bourgeois discourses and stressed instead the need of a more inclusive "popular front" ideology, including liberals, social democrats, and radical leftists, if they accepted a common platform of democratic values and practices.

Finally, the radical leftist critique of Stalinism could also employ the discourse of crisis, for example, in Lev Trotsky's (1879–1940) "Transitional Program" from 1938, developed in dialogue with the American Socialist Workers Party and published as discussion material for the founding congress of the Fourth International.[84] Trotsky's assessment of the situation evoked Lenin's 1917 writings and stressed the maturing of the crisis on a global level and an imminent socialist revolution, while he rejected the political and economic experiments that tried to "manage" the crisis with state intervention and a combination of socialist and capitalist measures: "The present crisis, far from having run its full course, has already succeeded in showing that 'New Deal' politics, like Popular Front politics in France, opens no new exit from the economic blind alley."[85] As Lenin lumped together the Social-Revolutionaries and Mensheviks with those Bolshevik leaders who sought to reach a temporary compromise with the Provisional Government, Trotsky also coined the umbrella term "crisis of leadership," which referred to the "centrist," "reformist," and Stalinist political positions alike and pointed to the principal impediment to the successful socialist revolution: "The historical crisis of mankind is reduced to the crisis of the revolutionary leadership."[86] However, this crisis was to be resolved by the "objective laws" of development:

> ... the laws of history are stronger than the bureaucratic apparatus. No matter how the methods of the social betrayers differ—from the "social" legislation of Blum to the judicial frame-ups of Stalin—they will never succeed in breaking the revolutionary will of the proletariat. As time goes on, their desperate efforts to hold back the wheel of history will demonstrate more clearly to the masses that the crisis of the proletarian leadership, having become the crisis in mankind's culture, can be resolved only by the Fourth International.[87]

Bringing together social democrats, communists, fascists, Trotskyists, and many other ideological subcultures, the debate on the crisis of socialism was particularly interesting due to the intellectual resonance between politically incompatible positions. A case in point is the criticism of the bureaucratization and mechanization of the socialist movement (often drawn from the writings of de Man), which could be formulated from revisionist social-democratic, radical socialist, communist, "neo-socialist," and fascist direction as well. Because of these similarities, it is important to go beyond the convenient binaries (left vs. right, progressive vs. conservative, moderate vs. radical) traditionally used for describing the ideological dynamic of the interwar years and reflect on the entanglements between seemingly incompatible ideological settings. Rather than just a matter of morphological similarity between politically opposed ideological positions, the discourse of crisis can thus be understood also as a bridge across which affinities and even new alliances could be created. Eventually this could lead to dismantling the democratic political system (shown by the convergence of the neo-socialists with the radical right during the Vichy regime) but could also buttress the critical rethinking of positions that prepared the ground for a more inclusive socialist political platform (in the anti-fascist resistance during the war as well as in the post-war context). Sharing the criticism of the traditional social democratic model of gradual and irreversible progress toward socialism with the radical left and the radical right, and stressing the importance of will and agency, representatives of this position opted for creating some sort of synthesis between socialism and liberalism. They entered a dialogue with some of the liberals who came to reject the nineteenth-century *laissez-faire* doctrine and searched for a

214 Intellectuals and the Crisis of Politics

more socially inclusive rendering of their ideology, developing models of democratic socialism that came to have repercussions across Western, Southern, Northern, and East Central Europe as well.

Notes

1. Vladimir Lenin, "Кризис Меньшевизма [The Crisis of Menshevism]," (1906). Republished in English as V. I. Lenin, *Collected Works*, vol. 11, *June 1906–January 1907* (Moscow: Progress Publishers, 1972), 341–64, available at https://www.marxists.org/archive/lenin/works/1906/crimensh/index.htm
2. Rosa Luxemburg [Junius], *Die Krise der Sozialdemokratie* (Munich: Futurus, 1916).
3. Ibid., chap. 7. In English: https://www.marxists.org/archive/luxemburg/1915/junius/ch07.htm
4. Ibid.
5. Rosa Luxemburg, *Die Russische Revolution* (Berlin: Gesellschaft und Erziehung, 1922). Published in English as *The Russian Revolution* (New York: Workers Age Publishers, 1940).
6. Vladimir I. Lenin, "Lessons of the Crisis," *Collected Works*, vol. 24 (Moscow: Progress Publishers, 1964), 213–16; Written on April 22 (May 5), 1917, published on April 23 (May 6), 1917, in *Pravda*, no. 38; available at https://www.marxists.org/archive/lenin/works/1917/apr/22b.htm
7. Ibid.
8. Vladimir I. Lenin, "The Crisis Has Matured," *Collected Works*, vol. 26 (Moscow, Progress Publishers, 1972), 74–85. Written in early October 1917, available at https://www.marxists.org/archive/lenin/works/1917/oct/20.htm
9. Paul Szende, *Die Krise der mitteleuropäischen Revolution: Ein massenpsychologischer Versuch* (Tübingen: Mohr, 1921).
10. Max Adler, "Vladimir Iljitsch Lenin," *Der Kampf* 17, no. 3 (1924): 81–89. I am grateful to Cody Inglis for identifying this text and pointing out its relevance.
11. Ibid., 82.
12. Pietro Nenni, *Sei anni di guerra civile in Italia. Un libro bruciato dai nazisti* (Rome: Arcadia Edizioni, 2023); original edition: *Six ans de guerre civile en Italie* (Paris: Valois, 1930). Part IV of the book is entitled "La crisi socialista." Already present in the socialist political discourse in 1914–15 in the context of the debate on interventionism, the "crisi socialista" trope was used copiously in the early 1920s as well. See, for example, Alberto Malatesta, *La crisi socialista* (Milano: Sonzogno, 1923).
13. Ibid., 58.
14. Ibid.
15. Paul Louis, *La crise du socialisme mondial de la IIe à la IIIe Internationale* (Paris: Librairie Félix Alcan, 1921).
16. Ibid., 1.
17. Ibid.
18. Ibid., 35.
19. Ibid., 4.
20. Ibid., 127.
21. Ibid., 192.

Crisis of Socialism 215

22. Rüdiger Graf, "*Optimismus* und Pessimismus in der Krise—der politisch-kulturelle Diskurs in der Weimarer Republik," in Wolfgang Hardtwig, ed., *Ordnungen in der Krise: Zur Politischen Kulturgeschichte Deutschlands 1900–1933* (Berlin: De Gruyter, 2007), 115–40.

23. Adriano Tilgher, *La crisi mondiale e saggi critici di marxismo e socialismo* (Bologna: N. Zanichelli, 1921). On Tilgher's intellectual position see also "Anti-Liberal Entanglements: Fascist and Anti-Fascist Conceptualizations of Crisis," in chapter 7.

24. Alessandro Schiavi, "Crisi mondiale," *Avanti!* 25, no. 225 (September 22, 1921): 1. In the late 1920s, Schiavi became a promoter of de Man's critical ideas about the need to renew the socialist movement, while after the Second World War he became a prominent supporter of the European federalist project.

25. Maria Rygier, "La crisi socialista," *Tirrenio* (October 17, 1920), available at https://collections.library.yale.edu/catalog/10651772

26. Antonio Gramsci, "La crisi italiana," in Renzo Pecchioli, ed., *Da Gramsci a Berlinguer, La via italiana al socialismo attraverso i congressi del Partito comunista italiano*, vol. 1, *1921–1943* (Venice: Edizioni del Calendario, Marsilio Editori, 1985), 238–46. The text was originally written as a report for the Central Committee of the Communist Party in 1924, first published in *L'Ordine Nuovo.*

27. See Quintin Hoare and Geoffrey Nowell Smith, "Introduction," in Quintin Hoare and Geoffrey Nowell Smith, eds., *Antonio Gramsci: Selections from the Prison Notebooks* (New York: International Publishers, 1971), lxxxvii–xcvi.

28. Antonio Gramsci, "'Wave of Materialism' and 'Crisis of Authority,'" in *Selections*, 276. There is a recent upsurge in the academic discussion on the concept of crisis in Gramsci. See Milan Babic, "Let's Talk about the Interregnum: Gramsci and the Crisis of the Liberal World Order," *International Affairs* 96, no. 3 (2020): 767–86; Aaron Bernstein, "The State, Crisis, and Working-Class Strategy in Antonio Gramsci's Prison Notebooks," *Notebooks: The Journal for Studies on Power* 1, no. 1 (2021): 19–43; Gilbert Achcar, "Morbid Symptoms: What Did Gramsci Really Mean?" *Notebooks: The Journal for Studies on Power* 1, no. 2 (2022): 379–87.

29. See, e.g., Gramsci, *Selections*, 40, 67.

30. Ibid., 210–18.

31. Ibid., 185.

32. Karl Marx, "Der achtzehnte Brumaire des Louis Bonaparte," in Karl Marx and Friedrich Engels, *Werke*, vol. 8, (Berlin: Dietz Verlag, 1960), 111–207. First published in *Die Revolution*, no. 1 (1852).

33. Karl Korsch, *Marxismus und Philosophie* (Leipzig: C. L. Hirschfeld, 1923). Modern edition by Erich Gerlach (Frankfurt a. M.: Europäische Verlagsanstalt, 1966). For a recent interpretation of the text, see Nicholas Devlin, "Karl Korsch and Marxism's Interwar Moment, 1917–1933," *History of European Ideas* 48, no. 5 (2022): 574–93.

34. Karl Korsch, "Thesen zur Diskussion über 'Krise des Marxismus,'" in Michael Buckmiller, ed., *Gesamtausgabe*, vol. 5, *Krise des Marxismus: Schriften 1928–1935* (Amsterdam: IISG, 1996), 141–7. In English: "The Crisis of Marxism," trans. Otto Koester, *New German Critique* 3 (1974): 7–11.

35. Ibid., 7.

36. Ibid., 11.

37. See Una Blagojević, "The Cunning of Crisis and the Yugoslav Marxist Revisionists," in Balázs Trencsényi, Lucija Balikić, Una Blagojević and Isidora Grubački, eds., *East Central European Crisis Discourses in the Twentieth Century. A Never-Ending Story?* (London: Routledge: 2024), 245.

216 Intellectuals and the Crisis of Politics

38. Otto Landsberg, *Die politische Krise der Gegenwart* (Berlin: Dietz, 1931).
39. Henri de Man, *Au-delà du marxisme* (Bruxelles: L'Églantine, 1927). For a contemporaneous overview of de Man's ideas on the crisis of the socialist movement and ideology, see André Philip, *Henri de Man et la crise doctrinale du socialisme* (Paris: J. Gamber, 1928).
40. Philip, *Henri de Man*, 20.
41. Erik Hansen, "Depression Decade Crisis: Social Democracy and Planisme in Belgium and the Netherlands, 1929–1939," *Journal of Contemporary History* 16, no. 2 (1981): 293–322; and most recently Tommaso Milani, *Hendrik de Man and Social Democracy: The Idea of Planning in Western Europe, 1914–1940* (New York: Palgrave Macmillan, 2020).
42. On Rosselli, see Carmelo Calabrò, *Liberalismo, democrazia, socialismo: L'itinerario di Carlo Rosselli* (Florence: Firenze University Press, 2009).
43. Carlo Rosselli, "La crisi intellettuale del partito socialista," in J. Rosselli, ed., *Socialismo liberale* (Turin: Einaudi, 1973), 91.
44. Carlo Rosselli, *Socialisme libéral*, trans. and ed. Serge Audier (Lormont: Le Bord de l'Eau, 2008); originally published as Carlo Rosselli, *Socialisme libéral*, trans. Stefan Priacel (Paris: Librairie Valois, 1930). In English, Carlo Rosselli, *Liberal Socialism*, ed. Nadia Urbinati, trans. William McCuaig (Princeton: Princeton University Press, 1994). On the intellectual history of Rosselli's anti-fascist resistance group *Giustizia e Libertà* [Justice and Liberty], see Marco Bresciani, *Quale antifascismo? Storia di "Giustizia e Libertà"* (Rome: Carocci, 2017).
45. Rosselli, "La crisi intellettuale," 94.
46. Ibid., 144.
47. Léon Blum, *Le socialisme devant la crise* (Paris: Librairie Populaire du Parti Socialiste, 1933).
48. Ibid., 7.
49. Ibid., 15.
50. Ibid., 29.
51. Ibid., 38–9.
52. For the key discourses of this internal revolt, see Barthélemy Montagnon, Adrien Marquet, and Marcel Déat, *Néo-socialisme?: Ordre, autorité, nation*, with preface and commentaries by Max Bonnafous (Paris: B. Grasset, 1933).
53. On the broader intellectual context of Déat and his links to de Man, see Richard Griffiths, "Fascism and the Planned Economy: 'Neo-Socialism' and 'Planisme' in France and Belgium in the 1930s," *Science & Society* 69, no. 4 (2005): 580–93.
54. Montagnon et al., *Néo-socialisme*, 20, 27.
55. Ibid., 44.
56. Ibid., 74.
57. Ibid., 98.
58. *Après la catastrophe allemande: les résolutions de la Conférence Internationale de l'I.O.S., à Paris août 1933* (Paris: Éditions de l'Internationale Ouvrière Socialiste, 1933).
59. Ibid., 4.
60. Ibid., 8–12.
61. Ernst Fischer, *Krise der Jugend* (Vienna–Leipzig: Hess & Co, 1931).
62. Ibid., 9–10.
63. Ibid., 14.
64. Ibid., 31.

65. Ibid., 32.

66. Ibid., 53.

67. Ibid., 104.

68. On the political context, see Anson Rabinbach, *The Crisis of Austrian Socialism: From Red Vienna to Civil War, 1927–1934* (Chicago: University of Chicago Press, 1983), 151–4.

69. Käthe Leichter, "Die beste Abwehr [The Best Defense] (1933)," in *The Red Vienna Reader*, trans. Paul Werner, 3. Available at http://theorangepress.com/redviennareader/leichter/Leichter%20The%20Best%20Defense.pdf

70. Ibid.

71. Ibid.

72. Ibid., 4.

73. Ibid.

74. Leichter remained committed to her analysis. After the civil war of 1934, she left the country for Switzerland, subsequently returning to Austria to work in the illegal socialist press. After the *Anschluss*, she was arrested by the Gestapo and was eventually murdered in 1942.

75. Otto Bauer, *Ausgewählte Schriften*, vol. 2, *Zwischen zwei Weltkriegen? Die Krise der Weltwirtschaft, der Demokratie und des Sozialismus* (n.p.: Thomas Gimesi, 2017). The original was published in Bratislava by Prager-Verlag in 1936.

76. Otto Bauer, *Kapitalismus und Sozialismus nach dem Weltkrieg*, vol. 1, *Rationalisierung—Fehlrationalisierung* (Vienna: Wiener Volksbuchhandlung, 1931).

77. Bauer, *Zwischen zwei Weltkriegen*, 20–21.

78. Ibid., 65.

79. Karl Polanyi, "The Essence of Fascism," in Karl Polanyi, John Lewis, and Donald K. Kitchin, eds., *Christianity and the Social Revolution* (London: V. Gollancz, 1935), 359–94. On Polanyi's interpretation of crisis and democracy see Gábor Scheiring, "Sustaining Democracy in the Era of Dependent Financialization: Karl Polanyi's Perspectives on the Politics of Finance," *Intersections. East European Journal of Society and Politics* 2, no. 2 (2016): 84–103.

80. Ibid., 359.

81. Ibid., 391.

82. Ibid., 392.

83. Ferenc Fejtő, *Szép szóval* [With Beautiful Words], ed. Ágnes Széchenyi (Budapest: Századvég Kiadó, 1992).

84. Leon Trotsky, "Агония капитализма и задачи Четвертого Интернационала [The Agony of Capitalism and the Tasks of the Fourth International]," *Бюллетень Оппозиции (Большевиков-Ленинцев)* [Bulletin of the Opposition (Bolsheviks-Leninists)] 66/67 (May–June 1938): 1–18. English trans., *The Death Agony of Capitalism and the Tasks of the Fourth International: The Mobilization of the Masses around Transitional Demands to Prepare the Conquest of Power. "The Transitional Program"* (1938), ed. Dimitri Verstraeten (Leon Trotsky Internet Archive, 2002), available at https://www.marxists.org/archive/trotsky/1938/tp/transprogram.pdf

85. Ibid., 1.

86. Ibid., 2.

87. Ibid., 4.

9
Crisis of the Nation-State and the International System

The end of the First World War and the ensuing framework of peace treaties was hailed as the triumph of the principle of national self-determination and thus the universalization of the model of nation-statehood. However, the postwar polities proved to be increasingly conflict-ridden and the nation—and especially the nation-state—came to be affected by a deepening crisis of legitimacy. A common criticism concerned national fragmentation and particularism, which could be formulated from various perspectives. Remarkably, such critical voices appeared in liberal globalist, leftist universalist, anti-modernist (or conservative) anti-totalitarian, as well as totalitarian imperialist discursive settings.

On another level, the crisis of the nation-state was often described in terms of the rift between institutions (and elites) and the people (*Volk* in the rightist version; "working class" on the left), projecting a way toward regeneration in terms of a possible social overhaul or reintegration. All this could be encapsulated into an even broader framework of the crisis of the international system (here the paralysis of the League of Nations, increasingly unable to mediate and overrule national conflicts, provided ample food for thought). With the rise of authoritarian regimes that openly rejected the postwar order, the crisis of the international community came to be linked with the collapse of the postwar framework of liberal democracies created by the cooperation of the United States, Great Britain, and France. Along these lines, the dysfunctions of the international order could also be explained with the philosophical analysis of the crisis of values, converging in visions of the "crisis of the European idea."

The Ambiguities of Nation-Statehood

After 1918, the nation-state seemed to be the preferred model, but it is important to note that most of the East Central European states which (re)emerged after the Great War did not operate as nation-states but as sorts of mini empires.[1] They had sizeable minorities and experienced deep internal tensions between their centers and peripheries.

Intellectuals and the Crisis of Politics in the Interwar Period and Beyond. Balázs Trencsényi, Oxford University Press.
© Balázs Trencsényi (2025). DOI: 10.1093/9780198929512.003.0009

Crisis of the Nation-State and the International System 219

Predictably, the trope of the crisis of the nation-state framework, pointing to the contradiction of the principles of nationhood and statehood, was especially prevalent in the discourse of the losers of the postwar geopolitical order. German neo-conservative Max Hildebert Boehm (1891–1968) wrote about a "crisis of statehood" in terms of the contrast between the national homogenization drive of successful states and the existence of sizable minorities in many countries.[2] Here the crisis of statehood could be resolved by turning to the principle of the *Volk* as a more organic type of community, abandoning the liberal understanding of statehood and nationhood and reintegrating the German ethnic community in one political framework. In the German radical conservative discourse of the early 1930s, crisis became conceptually linked to the agonizing expectation of a revolutionary breakthrough by the *Volksgemeinschaft* (the ethnocultural community). In his influential article from 1932, Hans Zehrer (1899–1966)—the editor of the neo-conservative flagship journal *Die Tat*—talked about a "creeping crisis"—a protracted transitional phase characterized by ideological confusion and the emptying out of the traditional political center.[3] Zehrer contrasted the moribund political and state structure of the Weimar Republic to an envisioned new ethnocultural community, and described two anti-systemic forces on the extreme right (*Sturmabteilung*, SA) and extreme left (*Roter Frontkämpferbund* or *Rotfront*, RFB) as the carriers of this revolutionary transformation: "both army columns are but the wings of a great united movement."[4] While on the surface these two forces were antagonistic, their violent clashes signaled the radical transformative will each of their adherents shared and opened the way to a new ideological synthesis of "German socialism," which could also have global repercussions.[5] Such an envisioned transformation meant not only a political "changing of the guards" but the complete overhaul of the very framework of politics, eliminating the "intermediate" organizations that had divided society and replacing the liberal principle of nation-statehood with the organic *Volksgemeinschaft*.

Similarly, the rising Italian radical right was highly critical of what they perceived to be an anachronistic liberal model of nation-statehood. Piero Marsich (1891–1928), an Italian journalist and leader of the Venetian fascists—linked to D'Annunzio and the activist branch of the movement, who eventually broke with Mussolini and accused him of abandoning the revolutionary core of fascism—spoke of the "crisis of the nation-state," which in his opinion was not only institutional but spiritual.[6] Torn by mutually reinforcing tendencies of bureaucracy and anarchy, the state underwent an existential crisis, which was only possible to overcome by stepping outside of the confines of the law. In another article, like Zehrer, Marsich talked of the inevitable conflict of the "vital" nation and the "languid" state, contrasting activist radicals (including the anti-fascist *arditi di popolo*) as representatives of the former with the high bourgeoisie and the bureaucratic leadership of the Italian Socialist Party as the representatives of the establishment.[7]

The anti-liberal discourse of the crisis of the nation-state also had strong repercussions in Eastern Europe, but the actual use of it depended also on the agenda of the given national movement. The post-First World War writings of the Ukrainian émigré ideologist Dmytro Dontsov (1883–1973)—who started as a Marxist but

220 Intellectuals and the Crisis of Politics

already in the early 1910s shifted toward a more nationalistic stance—exemplifies the case of those national movements that did not have a nation-state framework to which they could appeal. Here, the crisis of nation-statehood was not meant to be resolved by the reinforcement of the organic element of the *Volk*, but the other way round: only a truly national state could overcome the decline of the national body. Assuming various positions during the short-lived independent Ukrainian state at the end of the Great War, Dontsov emigrated and became extremely critical of the left-wing populist ideological framework that dominated the Ukrainian public sphere in the war's tumultuous aftermath. He described this period as a crisis of national ideology and stressed the need to find a new ideal to replace the democratic Pan-Slavism that animated the Ukrainian political and cultural elites in 1918–20. This implied firstly the assertion of the antagonism between Russian and Ukrainian national aspirations and the program of "active nationalism" overwriting individual and class interests and capable of challenging the status quo that prevented the formation of a Ukrainian nation-state.[8] Rather than socialism or liberal democracy, the only solution for the Ukrainians was by adopting the principles of integral nationalism, where the ethnocultural and political understanding of nationhood could finally converge. However, this was only possible if the actual state-system of Eastern Europe could be radically subverted.

The crisis of the nation-state model was also formulated by liberals who increasingly felt that the high hopes of the postwar liberal democratic ascendance were fading. The conservative liberal Alfred Weber (1868–1958, Max Weber's younger brother) offered a complex and multi-faceted picture in his 1925 book *The Crisis of the Modern State Idea in Europe*.[9] Weber linked the emergence of modern statehood to the rise of capitalism and described it as the product of the disintegration of the medieval *oikumene*. He considered the modern state and its contentious relationship with society a *sui generis* Western configuration, contrasted to the "oriental fusion" of these two spheres.

For Weber, the modern state idea (*Staatsgedanke*)—characterized by the norms of human rights, the majoritarian principle, and the idea of nationality—evolved gradually. In the first phase (linked to the Enlightenment, and most paradigmatically present in the works of Jean-Jacques Rousseau) the concepts of "people" and "state" merged in the idea of popular sovereignty. The second phase, starting with the 1870s, was marked by the emergence of separate state and economic spheres and the assumption of a more violent role by the state in military expansion. This was accompanied by an ideological transformation, with cultural nationalization, the fashion of Nietzscheanism, and the cult of active power. This transformation of the national idea entailed a split from the sphere of the Spirit, with its sentiment of humanity (*Humanitätsgefühl*) and consciousness of culture (*Kulturbewusstsein*), and a move toward biologization. Weber considered the post-First World War period as the culmination of these tendencies, resulting in a crisis of statehood and of the European tradition, catalyzed by the entangled processes of economization (*Ökonomisierung*), mechanization, and militarization. In contrast to mercantilism, in this case it is the economy that regulates the state. Reaching the end of the expansive phase of capitalism triggered a push for the redistribution of markets and the concomitant militarization of Europe. The growing tensions also catalyzed a new type of politics, importing the American organization of party machinery and focusing on the personality of the party leader (*Führer*).[10]

Thus, for Weber, the European and the German crises of statehood were closely interrelated: "the European state crisis is our crisis, an existential crisis for us Germans."[11] He argued that the reconstruction of Germany was only possible in a broader framework—that of the recovery of the spiritual Europe (*geistige Europa*). While this argument overlapped with the neo-conservative criticism, in some key points Weber also diverged from their perspective. Most importantly, he defended democracy and rejected the accusation that the triumph of democracy after 1918 was but a cover of imperialist state interests seeking to weaken Germany. Democracy was the only modern framework of legitimation imaginable—the doctrine of legitimism organizing the medieval and early modern state system (and surviving in the imperial systems of the Habsburg, Hohenzollern, and Romanov empires until the end of the First World War) was effectively dead.

Weber also reflected on the threat posed by Bolshevism and fascism, which in his opinion had many common traits, both being essentially forms of rule by minority with a quasi-religious cult of the leader and the sacral exclusion of "heretics of doctrine." While they were rooted in specific political contexts, they also resonated in other societies that experienced a crisis. Weber registered the contradictory dynamic of the expansion of democratic principles: while outside of Europe there was an upsurge in democratization, in most of Central and Eastern Europe, democracy lost its support.[12] He linked this delegitimization to the disappointment with the postwar regimes, caused by the weakness of the state, and its capture by strong economic and political interest groups. The rise of autocratic government was thus rooted in a misguided popular craving for a more efficient state. Along these lines, the remedy Weber proposed was to reinvigorate the state, but not by returning to premodern patterns of authority; rather, he suggested combining parliamentarism and some elements of corporatism. All this also had a transnational dimension in the sense that he was critical of the proliferation of small nation-states in Central Europe and advocated instead some sort of regional integration where the most developed and powerful nation, namely Germans, were supposed to play a leading role.

The crisis of the nation-state was also central to the 1920s writings of Italian liberal dissident Guglielmo Ferrero. His 1924 political essay "Discourse to the Deaf" was full of metaphors like "crisis," "universal chaos," or "aesthetic and political anarchy."[13] In his reading, the crisis of the European state system had its roots in the nineteenth century, closely linked to the rise of "quantitative civilization" and the breakthrough of democratic forms of government in the mid-nineteenth century. All this meant an unprecedented power concentration, incomparable to the premodern absolutist or despotic states (be it ancient Babylon or the monarchy of the Sun King). These states claimed to have control over their subjects, but could hardly impose their will on them due to a lack of adequate resources and infrastructure.[14]

222 Intellectuals and the Crisis of Politics

However, the growth of the power of the modern state did not go together with the growth of its authority. This became obvious after 1918, when the formation of democratic governments did not result in political and economic stability. Like Alfred Weber, Ferrero characterized the overall situation of the postwar period as transitional: the monarchic principle lost its legitimacy, but the democratic one was unable to consolidate new regimes. Ferrero described this liminality in terms of a crisis, and the main symptoms of this crisis were the transitional forms mixing monarchic and democratic elements, giving birth to dictatorships that claimed to represent the popular will, but eventually subdued it.

The rise of dictatorships was replicated by the structural transformation of the economic sphere: the "tyranny of iron giants" (i.e., modern industrial organization) was forcing everyone to work and consume ceaselessly. In this general political and economic disorder, it was this highly mechanized industrial complex that kept the system running, but it was an illusion to believe that this would last forever. A sign of the impending radical transformation was the global revolt against European domination, which (in Ferrero's opinion) could not be repressed, but only tamed. Eventually, the endemic fear different social and ethnic groups had of each other could only be overcome by moving toward the planetary unity of mankind.[15]

Crisis of European Supremacy

Most authors analyzed in the previous section argued that the crisis of individual states was closely linked to the crisis of the European state framework. While the crisis of Europe was of course often raised in a culturalist key, several works went beyond providing autopsies of European civilization and focused instead on the causes of the loss of European economic and political dominance, suggesting a framework of (re)integration as a remedy. This debate had repercussions especially in France, which had the strongest public interest in cementing a European security framework to prevent the repetition of the catastrophic dynamic of the First World War by generating various projects of European cooperation.

In his 1920 book, Sorbonne professor of social geography Albert Demangeon (1872–1940), who was heavily involved in the preparation of the postwar peace settlement, took up a soberingly critical perspective.[16] Depicting the Europeanization of the world and its ambiguities, he cited Paul Valéry's famous essay on the "crisis of the spirit" to support his argument that the general crisis of Europe was rooted in a crisis of the global entanglements of Europe. In Demangeon's understanding, the loss of European hegemony became manifest right after the end of the Great War. He described this transformation with the help of generational metaphors, contrasting the "aging" and "decadent" European nations to the non-European "young peoples," such as the United States and Japan, both motivated by an ideology of "chosen nation."

The decline of the European empires and the rise of anti-colonial movements all over the world meant that the problem of nations came to be overwritten by the problem of races. This could have been a naïve imperialist argument stressing the need for reinforcing the racial hierarchies, but in Demangeon's text it had a strong component of self-criticism; he also admitted that colonial rule was economically exploitative and did not aim at civilizational progress. He stressed that the monoculturalism pursued by the imperial distribution of labor contributed to the destruction of local economies. As a result, the oppressed groups and nations were trying to turn the Western ideas of rights and liberty against the West. In this context, Demangeon pointed to the Afro-Americans, Egyptians, and Indians as the most successful instances of anti-Western mobilization. In addition to Western ideology (such as the ideas of Cavour, Mazzini, Kossuth, and Parnell—all used by Indian nationalists), Western technology was also assimilated by non-Western cultures and gradually made them capable of posing a challenge to global hierarchies. For example, it was the British-built railway systems in India that made mass Hindu pilgrimages possible. From this perspective, Demangeon's main question was whether the ensuing crisis of Europe was a crisis of hegemony or a crisis of existence. Remarkably, he was not against the loss of European primacy in principle, if it did not also imply a loss of "European vitality." In this respect, he was particularly worried by demographic decline in his native France, which undermined the possibility of national self-reproduction.

Crisis was thus equated with a global transformation of economic and political connections and, among its key symptoms, Demangeon listed the "crisis of production" and "debt crisis" as key indicators. Coping with this crisis required new socioeconomic policies from European nations: revitalizing agriculture and returning to the sea. But the main task was to reshape colonial empires taking into account the transformation described earlier, allowing for gradual economic and judicial emancipation. In his vision, rather than exploited subjects, the colonies could provide producers and consumers for their European centers and thus create a mutually profitable new relationship.

A decade later, François Delaisi (1873–1947) continued this line of thought in the context of a new crisis looming at the horizons: the Great Depression.[17] A prominent pacifist, economic expert with a syndicalist orientation, and secretary of the French section of the Pan-European Union, Delaisi was a vocal critic of financial capitalism. He was originally aligned with the political left but, as many of the syndicalists, after 1941 he collaborated with the Vichy regime, turning his anti-capitalism into an anti-Semitic direction. To fathom the multiplicity of possible trajectories, it is enough to mention that the preface to his 1929 book was by Dannie Heineman (1872–1962), a Belgian industrialist and natural scientist with a strong humanitarian inclination, who—in contrast to Delaisi—took part in saving Jews during the Second World War. In Heineman's interpretation, the destructive force of the erupting European crisis was due to the merger of industrial and agrarian components. He linked this to the transformation of the energy regime with the shift from carbon to electricity, undermining the previous frameworks of production.[18]

In contrast to Heineman's holistic take, Delaisi focused on the contextualization of the economic crisis in view of the cleavage between what he labeled as

"Europe A" and "Europe B," divided by the "Stockholm, Danzig, Budapest, Florence, Barcelona line."[19] Within the two zones, he noticed similarities that transcended national frontiers, such as common mentality and even clothing. The main factors of difference were energy resources, capitalization, and know-how. Delaisi's Europe A was the zone of industrial development, while Europe B was marked by the continuous presence of self-sufficient peasants. These economic and structural differences had consequences in many spheres of life, such as scholarship and education (Delaisi noted that in the humanities the difference was less tangible), as well as the political system (e.g., the way elections were organized, where Europe B was characterized by the capture of parties by local oligarchies).[20]

By the twentieth century, this division largely became globalized due to the emigration wave at the turn of the century and the concomitant transfer of capital from Europe especially to the United States and Latin America. This led to the formation of a sort of "Europe C" overseas, and the gradual disappearance of the dividing lines between the continents. Merging the traditional socialist analysis of over-production and the emerging neoliberal focus on the centrality of the consumer, Delaisi argued that the solution to the crisis was the expansion of Europe A into Europe B, which would stimulate the growth of production and consumption. Following this train of thought in the early 1930s, he proposed a European public works scheme that focused on transportation infrastructure to make the markets more accessible for the agrarian products of Europe B and thus to generate economic growth and eventually convergence.[21]

While the discourse of the "crisis of Europe" was often linked to a pacifist–leftist pan-European agenda, there were also alternative projects of "Europeanization" from the right (and even from the extreme right). In 1932, the Italian Academy convened a conference on the current crisis and future direction of European cooperation. The proceedings were supported by the Alessandro Volta Foundation, which sponsored the representative international cultural events of the fascist regime.[22] The program called attention to the "enormous historical crisis" of the continent, "not only in political and economic life, but also in its value and global prestige."[23] Typical for the conservative crisis discourses, the conveners of this conference argued that the causes of the crisis were not material and economic but rather cultural and spiritual. At the same time, in line with the general patterns of the fascist discourse of crisis, they suggested that under Mussolini's charismatic leadership, Italy had successfully overcome crisis back in the early 1920s. To that end, the Italian organizers set the stage for the discussion by asserting that crisis was either in the past or "elsewhere," and thus, "European chaos" could be conveniently contrasted with "Italian stability." Indeed, the invitees were mostly from intellectual circles who were sympathetic to the Italian fascist regime, but some openly anti-totalitarian thinkers were also invited, whose anxious voices about the future of Europe were particularly resounding, such as Alfred Weber, Stefan Zweig, John M. Keynes, Friedrich Meinecke, Virgil Madgearu, and Salvador de Madariaga. However, only Weber traveled to Rome from this group; many of them excused themselves in writing. For his part, Zweig sent a powerful message, evidently intended to challenge the radical conservative ideological hegemony of the conference organizers.

The participants were invited to respond to a set of questions framed by the organizers regarding the geopolitical and historical dividing lines of Europe. Renowned geographer, explorer, and faithful adherent of Mussolini, Giotto Dainelli (1878–1968) identified three geopolitical zones (West, East, and an intermediary central one) but also suggested that there was only one (Western) civilization and eventually all nations converged toward it.[24] British conservative historian (with Jacobite leanings) Sir Charles Petrie (1895–1977)—who was openly supportive of Mussolini and published a biography of the dictator in 1931—also addressed the question of European unity. He linked it to the common heritage of Roman civilization and Christianity which had been destroyed by the French Revolution. He described the fascist project as a restoration of the classical values of religion, discipline, and family, and accepted the curbing of parliamentarism and individual rights and the introduction of corporatism as the adequate means to achieve this renewal.[25]

Other voices also assumed an essentialist understanding of Europe. For instance, Romanian philomath historian and nationalist politician Nicolae Iorga (1871–1940), famous for his research on the Ottoman Empire and Southeastern Europe, contrasted European activity with Asian passivity.[26] Some speakers, such as English Catholic historian Christopher Dawson (1889–1970), warned against racializing this contrast. Others, such as Gerard Wallop, Viscount Lymington (1898–1984), a promoter of organic farming close to the British Fascists, subscribed to a framework of racial hierarchy and exclusion. The conference also featured Alfred Rosenberg (1893–1946), the key racial ideologist of the rising Nazi movement, who had recently published his synthesis *The Myth of the Twentieth Century*. Rosenberg talked about "incompatible" races and described the rejection of the non-assimilable biological enemy as a basic law of existence (*Lebensgesetz*). Predictably, he identified Bolshevism as the ideological cover of this biological enemy.

Most of the participants, however, kept to a discourse of spiritual rather than biological crisis. Representing a more pluralist position, famous Italian orientalist Giuseppe Tucci (1894–1984) analyzed the oriental counter-reaction to Occidentalization, expanding on the topos that rising non-European social and national movements only took Western technology without its spirit and used it to reinforce their local cultures. As a cultural relativist, Tucci rejected the possibility of real interaction between autarchic cultural systems and argued instead for mutual empathy. This also implied the impossibility of resolving the Western crisis from the outside: the solution was through a comprehensive spiritual revival, returning to the metaphysical roots of European culture.

Swiss conservative Gonzague de Reynold also depicted the convergence of economic, spiritual, and political problems in an unprecedented and comprehensive crisis hitting Europe. He envisioned the reorganization (although hardly a supranational unification) of Europe, based on the cooperation of elites, as a solution to the problem. He stressed the responsibility of intellectuals to create the ideological preconditions of this cooperation, contrasting the destructive "conspiracy of philosophers" (which started with idealism, but resulted in materialism) with the constructive work needed to create the new European order (*nouvel ordre européen*).[27] This new order was supposed to be a synthesis of tradition and modernity, transcending bourgeois civilization.

Most participants of the conference subscribed to some version of radical anti-liberalism. For instance, leading Italian fascist journalist Francesco Coppola (1878–1957) focused on the contrast between the European core—created by Roman civilization and characterized by hierarchy and order—and the various "anti-Europes" (Bolshevism, Islam, the United States), challenging this.[28] In his understanding, the principal danger was the disintegration from inside caused by the "vermin" of democracy and free thinking (becoming manifest in the Reformation and triggering the French Revolution) undermining authority. This narrative indicated an ideological fusion of Italian fascist discourse with the neoclassicist (and anti-Protestant) anti-individualism of the Action Française, which provided the most accessible radical conservative intellectual platform for various rightist subcultures in Europe. Likewise, German economist Erwin von Beckerath (1889–1964), leader of the German–Italian cultural institute (the *Petrarca-Haus*) and one of the future protagonists of *Ordoliberalismus*, labeled liberalism and socialism as straightforwardly "un-European."[29]

In turn, French rightist historian and journalist Pierre Gaxotte (1895–1982), who was close to the Action Française and famous for his criticism of the French Revolution, pointed to the rise of mass democracy as the root of the European crisis. He argued that democracy catalyzed national separatism, economic impoverishment, and the rise of anti-colonial movements; thus, abandoning democracy completely was the only solution to the global crisis.[30]

Among the few participants who did not reject liberalism, the most resounding contribution was from Austrian writer Stefan Zweig (1881–1942), who did not participate in person (although, two years later, he would travel to Rome to the Fourth Volta Congress on Theater, organized by the prominent modernist writer and fascist fellow-traveler, Luigi Pirandello), but sent his lecture. Zweig offered a crisis narrative diametrically opposed to the vision of the majority of participants, referring to the medical connotations of the concept of crisis and employing a metaphoric language to describe nationalist hatred as an "illness" similar to dependence on narcotics.[31] In Zweig's rendering, it was Rosenberg's (and his ideological cronies') antagonistic perspective of one group perceiving the other as an irreconcilable enemy that could be described as pathological. The task Zweig set for humankind was "moral detoxification," but there was no chance for immediate recovery—a "*magna therapia sterilisans*"—only gradual healing promised by the rise of a new generation. Focusing on this new generation, Zweig's main preoccupation was with a new type of historical education, shifting the emphasis from the divisive political pasts to the common cultural heritage. Along these lines, he talked of a "common European fatherland" (*Heimat Europa*) with symbolic heroes like Albert Einstein. Zweig's most interesting

Crisis of the Nation-State and the International System **227**

practical recommendation was the promotion of student exchange even in secondary schools, as well as setting up a European University and a European Academy. To change the public spirit, he also proposed a common European journal and even a supranational legal instance to prevent the circulation of "fake news" from breeding violence.

Swiss liberal journalist and historian William Martin (1888–1934) also argued for the political unification of Europe as a way out of the crisis. Using Delaisi's metaphor of Europe A and B, he suggested that, with the removal of protectionist barriers, there could be a mutually beneficial cooperation that could obliterate national tensions. Interestingly, for a functionary of the League of Nations, Martin unfavorably contrasted the global interconnectedness of European states (resulting in bilateral preferential treatments) with an envisioned pan-European economic integration.

Alfred Weber, a more reserved defender of liberal principles, chose to maintain a theoretical stance. He offered a broad historical overview of the constitutive elements of European culture and focused on the tension of the chivalric (conquest) and the Christian (resignation) principles.[32] He considered it the task of the European elites to preserve a certain kind of balance between these two elements, which in the modern ideological sphere entailed the synthesis of collectivism and personalism.

Even if their political assessment differed, most participants of the Volta conference—from the conservative liberal Weber to the Catholic conservative de Reynold, from the Austrian aristocratic pro-European publicist and Nazi fellow-traveler Karl Anton Rohan (1898–1975) to the pro-fascist Gaxotte and Coppola—argued that the cultural–political crisis preceded the economic disaster and that the European crisis had global entanglements. They also concurred with the idea that the current crisis would catalyze a radical transformation of Europe and eventually of the whole world. In this context, conservative Catalonian regionalist Joan Estelrich (1896–1958) made an interesting conceptual distinction between decadence and crisis, stressing that the latter is more open-ended.

Social scientists participating at the conference also emphasized the interplay of different crisis phenomena in different spheres, without necessarily prioritizing the spiritual aspect. Moderate conservative, Czech legal scholar, and statistician František Weyr (1879–1951) pointed to the entanglement of political and economic factors, while Werner Sombart focused on the European crisis "from an economic perspective" pointing to precedents in late Antiquity and the early modern period. For Sombart, crisis was a sign of transition toward a new form of economic organization, and he argued that the way out of the current crisis was the planned economy.[33] While the era of liberalism was marked by the domination of economics over politics, politics should now retrieve its primacy over economic "super-capitalism."

Paolo Orano (1875–1945) was an Italian political scientist who moved from the radical socialist camp to fascism and became a key proponent of anti-Semitism in the late 1930s. Orano reiterated the typical 1930s fascist discourse of crisis, stressing that, in Italy, the crisis was already overcome in the 1920s and thus the global depression did not really affect Italian society. He recommended the Italian étatist

228 Intellectuals and the Crisis of Politics

model of crisis management for other nations as well, envisioning a future Europe based on the peaceful coexistence of totalitarian countries.

Most non-Italian economic experts present struggled to find some sort of balance between the rejection of free trade and the critique of autarchy, which was likely to catalyze further crises in the future. Thus, economic analyst and journalist Paul Einzig castigated Great Britain for moving away from Europe and for the revival of preferential treatment for the members of the Commonwealth. Rather than suggesting the restoration of the free market economy, Hungarian–Jewish economic expert Elemér Hantos (1880–1942), who worked for Austrian and German business circles and was close to Richard Coudenhove-Kalergi's (1894–1972) Pan-European movement, argued for the revival of European economic cooperation based on a "French–German entente" as its core.

For those few experts present from East Central Europe, this dilemma was particularly pressing: they considered the era of liberal ideological dominance as finished, but also saw that the fragmentation of the world economy had devastating consequences for their countries. Bilateralism could also be dangerous because the negotiating position of small, semi-peripheral countries—producing mainly raw materials and agricultural goods—was weak. Thus, Croatian economist Ivan Frangeš (1899–1972) argued for more intensive economic interaction between Eastern and Western Europe, while at the same time moving away from free trade and toward a system of complementarity. Without this type of arrangement, there was the danger of the dominance of autarchic tendencies—which had caused the economic crisis—and/or a geopolitical turn toward the East (implying the Soviet Union).

Mihail Manoilescu, a Romanian corporatist theoretician with a growing international reputation, who gravitated toward the extreme right in the early 1930s, offered a more historically informed interpretation. He pointed to the devastating consequences of nineteenth-century economic development in Eastern Europe, which had proceeded under the aegis of Westernization. Pursuing the agenda of integration into the world economy, the intellectual and political elites of these countries exposed their countrymen to Western economic exploitation. Manoilescu linked this to the "hypocrisy" of liberal democracy: free competition was the ideology of the strong, used to make the weak even weaker.[34] The social impact of capitalism was very different in the West (where it was already functioning) than in the East (where it was only imported). Thus, rather than bringing welfare to all, capitalism became an instrument to reinforce on a global scale the division between exploiters and exploited. In Manoilescu's reading, both fascism and Bolshevism emerged as responses to this global inequality and the permanent crisis it generated.

Manoilescu returned to the Congress and his rendering of the discussions in a review article published in the French political journal *L'année politique*.[35] Going beyond an overview of the conference, Manoilescu tried to use this platform to recapitulate his own suggestions for overcoming the European crisis. He also took up Delaisi's idea of "two Europes" and argued that the crisis of Europe could only be solved if the interests of Europe B, characterized by adaptation and assimilation of the Western models, were taken seriously. But, in contrast with Delaisi, he rejected the idea that Europe A could eventually expand to include Europe B.

Manoilescu declared that the nineteenth-century European synthesis of individualism, liberalism, and capitalism had lost its rationale: individualism was only the side product of economic prosperity, but the radical transformation of economic conditions now necessitated a more collectivistic social order. In this sense, even if he argued for the importance of economic factors, he stressed the primacy of spiritual factors. His vision of recovery looked to the importance of Christianity as the basis of the restored European order and projected a fusion of Christian corporatism and fascism as the new synthesis. He also registered the ambiguity of Russia in relation to the European tradition: if individualism was Europe's foundation, then Russia was incompatible with it. But if a new collectivism emerged in Europe, then Russia could be considered an "*avant-Europe*" (not in its Bolshevik outfit, but rather in view of the collectivist Orthodox spiritual tradition, which resonated with the neo-Orthodoxism of the emerging Romanian extreme-right).

The crisis of the European state system continued to preoccupy intellectuals throughout the 1930s. Reflecting on the rise of totalitarianism as a response to the economic and political chaos, French political scientist and geographer André Siegfried offered a comprehensive interpretation of the European crisis by addressing the topics raised by Demangeon, Delaisi, and Manoilescu of the loss of global dominance and the internal divides within Europe.[36] Siegfried's main argument was that the hegemony of Northern and Western Europe, prompted by the industrial revolution, was affected by different, partly overlapping, crises: the First World War, the postwar transformation, and the Great Depression. The postwar economic boom created exaggerated expectations and promoted democratization without inculcating the feeling of responsibility. Siegfried also subscribed to the argument about the non-cyclical features of the Great Depression. The ongoing global reconfiguration of production was not part of the usual cyclical development of the economy, and rather signaled a shift away from the economic framework of free trade, marked by the uneven relationship between countries producing raw materials and those producing industrial goods. In this sense, the global economy—dominated by European economic and technical culture and facilitated by British imperial infrastructure—was much more fragile than it seemed. These tensions became visible with the "double crisis" of European leadership (Siegfried referred to the liberal Valéry and the integral nationalist Maurice Barrès as his inspiration) caused by non-Europeans' challenges to the embedded racial hierarchy with the white race on the top, and the rise of the United States as a new global economic center of gravity.

Importantly, from this perspective, the Great War was far from being the main trigger of the crisis: English hegemony was already weakening in the 1880s and by the turn of the century economic nationalism was on the rise. However, the war amplified some of these processes, causing a boom in imports and a fall in exports within the war-waging countries. Furthermore, the disintegration of the global economic framework led to the emergence of competing spheres of influence. In contrast to most conservative authors who saw the relationship of the West to the rest of the

230 Intellectuals and the Crisis of Politics

world in terms of a clear hierarchy, Siegfried was more cautious and rejected the idea of Western spiritual primacy and argued that the East also had its own respectable traditions. This also implied that the crisis of the West was not necessarily a global crisis: from a non-Western perspective, it could even be perceived as a chance for emancipation. At the same time, he also rejected the idea that the expansion of non-Western economies and societies by default implied a zero-sum game. The rise of local industry in non-Western countries was based on Western investment and necessitated European machines and know-how. Directing the global flow of capital investment, London could preserve its position as the financial capital of the world. Meanwhile, the fall of Western exports posed serious social challenges like unemployment. On the whole, the acceleration of globalization triggered the crisis of European societies, finding themselves at a crossroads between two possible paths: toward further expansion, where both the Western and the non-Western parts could profit from growing demand, or toward contraction, due to competition from countries with lower wages, higher levels of exploitation, and a lack of social protection.

In this context, Siegfried called on European elites to rethink their relationship to the world. The ongoing crisis was an invitation to take stock of available resources and reflect on future development. While the expansion of industrialization outside of the Old Continent was seemingly unstoppable, and there was an obvious tendency toward the leveling of living standards (implying a fall in Europe and growth elsewhere), European creative energy and culture remained an important asset and thus the picture was not completely bleak. But this potential could only be realized if European cooperation developed further, and these countries stopped undermining each other's positions globally. Writing in 1935 (after the Nazi takeover but before Hitler could start realizing his vision of territorial expansion) Siegfried did not yet feel the stirrings of another global conflagration, and hoped that common interests would prevail even among ideologically antagonistic European partners. However, there was a tangible anxiety about the future of Old Continent in his text.

Managing the Crisis of International Relations

By the 1930s, the entanglement of the European crisis with global processes became a widely shared assumption. Some of the authors discussed here contrasted the European interests to those of the non-Europeans (in the case of the incipient movements of decolonization or the cross-continental preferential trade agreements, undermining the intra-European economic cooperation), while others became convinced that the European crisis could only be understood and eventually overcome via a global framework. Many of the latter were linked, in one way or another, to the intellectual milieu of the League of Nations and the Geneva Graduate Institute, which emerged as a focal point of strategic thinking. Associated with it were experts of international economic and political relations like Maurice Bourquin, Carl Burkhardt, Guglielmo Ferrero, Paul Guggenheim, Michel A. Heilperin, Hans Kelsen, Paul Mantoux, Ludwig von Mises, Pitman Potter, William Rappard, and Hans Wehberg.

William Rappard was a central figure of the circle of intellectuals and experts linked to these institutions and repeatedly returned to the question of the tasks of the League in facing the "world crisis." In a paper read before the Geneva Graduate Institute in 1932, he argued that the unfolding world crisis defied the usual ways of crisis management.[37] Similar to the (neo)liberal critics of autarchic economic tendencies, Rappard castigated the national selfishness of the member states, enforcing policies at the expense of their neighbors, which led to the destabilization of the League. He also registered the clash between the League of Nations's bureaucracy and national politicians, who pushed responsibility for the paralysis of international relations onto each other. He argued that a higher level of integration, moving toward a single European market, would make it easier to fend off the crisis. He also praised initiatives that set forth a blueprint for integration, for example, Nobel Peace Prize winner and French Foreign Minister Aristide Briand's (1862–1932) proposal for European unification from 1929. It was clear from Rappard's analysis that, although he also considered economic nationalism as the primary culprit, he sought to go beyond purely economic instruments of crisis management. He remarked that the analysis of the crisis commissioned by the League and prepared by Swedish economist Bertil G. Ohlin (1899–1979) only addressed economic processes and that there was a need to extend the scope to political and institutional aspects as well. This implied that even the economic crisis could not be contained by merely economic means.

The Geneva Graduate Institute continued to serve as a primary hub for reflection on the international crisis and its remedies. In the volume on "world crisis" edited by Paul Mantoux (1877–1956), the Institute's co-founder, Mantoux's own contribution offered a retrospective analysis of the failure of the League to settle international conflicts.[38] He looked back to the case of Vilnius, contested by Poland and Lithuania in the early 1920s, and showed that both neighbors and the international observers were unable to settle on a consensual framework of mediation and eventually this failure undermined their trust in supranational institutions. This analysis was given a historical dimension but also a moderate anti-modernist twist by Ferrero's contribution to the volume.[39] The Italian thinker returned to his earlier analysis of "*anarchie internationale*" linked to the modern doctrine of total war, starting with Napoleon as contrasted to the more humane eighteenth-century understanding. Previously, war aims and sacrifices were proportional, and peace was concluded when the costs of going beyond the *status quo* had become disproportionate compared to possible gains. But in the Napoleonic logic, the sacrifices came to legitimize the aims, and thus warfare became potentially interminable.

Looking at various interpretations of international crisis, it becomes clear that most authors pleaded for supranational integration, but there was no consensus as to the depth and breadth of it. Somewhat surprisingly, many conservative and even extreme right-wing authors went beyond the nation-state framework in search of a remedy to the crisis. At the same time, in contrast to the liberal and socialist visions of gradual political unification, their main quest was for a common spiritual principle that could restore Europe to its past glory. In contrast to the right-wing radicals, whose combination of ethno-nationalism and supranationalism often culminated in some sort of hierarchic and expansive *Lebensraum*-based integration, moderate conservatives (in a way sticking to the conservative paradigm from before the turn of the century) pleaded for a transnational—and often pre-national—organizing principle. They criticized national self-centeredness but rejected a united Europe without regional divergences, let alone a global convergence, and sought to find some sort of common ground between the sub-national, national, and supranational layers. Furthermore, their supranationalism was not future-oriented, but rather based on the idea that the nationalist confrontation experienced during and after the First World War was a pathological deviation from a more harmonious European framework of coexistence. In contrast, some of the liberals opted for a European federalism, envisaging both an economic and a political integration and the creation of a European "supranation." They were also more future oriented and hardly could find a model of coexistence in the *ancien régime*. In contrast to the Eurocentrism of the conservatives, there were also more globalist tendencies in the liberal camp, both based on a vision of economic interdependence and on the expectation of a reform of international institutions, in turn rendering them capable of mediation among individual nations from different continents.[40]

There exist also interesting outliers who do not fit into this model, coming especially from the left. As the post-1918 international system proved increasingly fragile, the theoretical principles underlying the League of Nations were challenged in terms of a permanent crisis of international relations not only from the authoritarian right. Arguably the most sweeping criticism from the winning side of the Great War was put forward by English diplomat, historian, and political commentator Edward Hallett Carr (1892–1982). His *The Twenty Years Crisis, 1919–1939* came at the very end of the interwar period and represented a radical break with the mainstream liberal internationalism that was shaping the American, British, and French public spheres.[41]

Carr's book, which has been credited as a foundational text of the realist approach in the theory of international relations, was built on the contrast of rationalist "utopianism" (characterizing the liberal internationalist vision) and "realism" (focusing on power relationships). Searching for a way out of what he diagnosed as a profound intellectual and political crisis, Carr focused his energies on challenging the liberal position, describing it not only as hypocritical (in terms of covering actual power imbalances) but also self-destructive. A good indicator of this for him was the fall of democratic governments established after the First World War:

When the theories of liberal democracy were transplanted, by a purely intellectual process, to a period and to countries whose stage of development and whose practical needs were utterly different from those of Western Europe in the nineteenth century, sterility and disillusionment were the inevitable sequel. Rationalism can create a utopia but cannot make it real. The liberal democracies scattered throughout the world by the peace settlement of 1919 were the product of abstract theory, stuck no roots in the soil, and quickly shriveled away.[42]

The outcome of this loss of touch with reality was a deep structural crisis: "The breakdown of the nineteen-thirties was too overwhelming to be explained merely in terms of individual action or inaction. Its downfall involved the bankruptcy of the postulates on which it was based."[43] Following liberal moral imperatives did not result in universal harmony, but, on the contrary, opened up an abyss under the entire global political system: "The inner meaning of the modern international crisis is the collapse of the whole structure of utopianism based on the concept of the harmony of interests."[44] Eventually, for Carr, totalitarianism was a crisis symptom, rather than its catalyst, laying bare the unfounded normativity of the liberal political doctrines.

Although his text came to be cherished by those who tried to create a genealogy of realism in international relations, Carr was far from being uncritical of the "other side." He admitted that "realism, though logically overwhelming, does not provide us with the springs of action which are necessary even to the pursuit of thought."[45] Eventually, an extreme realist position would only legitimize existing power relations and arrest any further progress. Hence, he was far from being an adept of pure power politics and instead argued for rethinking the relationship of normative and analytical aspects as a basis for political action:

> Periods of crisis have been common in history. The characteristic feature of the present crisis, seen in the light of the twenty years between 1919 and 1939, has been the abrupt descent from the visionary hopes of the first post-War decade to the grim despair of the second, from a utopia which took little account of reality to a reality from which every element of utopia seems rigorously excluded.[46]

It was the new synthesis of these two competing doctrines that could lead to an *Aufhebung* of the crisis as "any sound political thought must be based on elements of both utopia and reality."[47] In practical terms, the political order Carr advocated was reverting to a federalist arrangement, replacing the ill-fated Wilsonian principles of self-determination, which (in his opinion) created permanent instability. Carr maliciously described this as the victory of Friedrich Naumann (the author of the wartime German geopolitical vision of *Mitteleuropa*) over Woodrow Wilson. As formal sovereignty had lost its value, there was a need to build the international order "on a unit of power sufficiently coherent and sufficiently strong to maintain its ascendancy without being itself compelled to take sides in the rivalries of lesser units."[48]

Since he did not see the possibility of one such all-encompassing unit of power, the logic of this argument led him toward accepting power blocs and spheres of influence as a key structuring agent. Due to his passionate fury against the post-First World War international order, this could turn him into an advocate of appeasement in 1938, condoning Hitler's subversion of the East Central European states. However, his real model was increasingly the Soviet Union, both as a pole of geopolitical integration and as a socioeconomic model of crisis management. Thus, while starting out as a liberal, Carr gradually became a staunch supporter of the Soviet

234 Intellectuals and the Crisis of Politics

geopolitical position and a committed leftist, inspired by Marx and the Russian revolutionary Mikhail Bakunin (1814–76). Overall, for Carr the Stalinist model came to represent a successful synthesis of utopia and realism, and a potential post-liberal model that transcended the ideological dividing lines and focused on social stability as against the liberal imperative of seeking economic profit. It is rather logical that, during the Second World War, with his series of articles published in *The Times*, Carr emerged as one of the most influential spokesmen of a postwar division of Europe, subordinating the East Central European zone to the Soviet power center.

Importantly, the main theoretical response to Carr's provocative work, coming from the naturalized British historian and political analyst of Jewish-Romanian background, David Mitrany (1888–1975), who became famous for devising a functionalist theory of international institutional cooperation, was also linked to the crisis discourse. Writing in 1943, Mitrany agreed that the interwar collapse of liberal internationalism showed that the normative supranationalism promoted by the League of Nations was highly problematic. Even though—in contrast to Carr—he shared the League's underlying value-system, Mitrany also considered the federalist solutions self-defeating.[49] He believed instead that a working peace system depended on the creation of a global web of international institutions that linked the different states together:

> Promissory covenants and charters may remain a headstone to unfulfilled good intentions, but the functional way is action itself and therefore an inescapable test of where we stand and how far we are willing to go in building up a new international society. It is not a promise to act in a crisis, but itself the action that will avoid the crisis.[50]

The feeling of crisis of the European state system triggered by the unprecedented brutality of the Second World War became a starting point for various projects searching for an alternative principle of international coexistence to that of nation-statehood. A foundational text in this regard is "The Ventotene Manifesto" by two Italian antifascists, Altiero Spinelli (1907–1986) and Ernesto Rossi (1897–1967) on the crisis of European civilization and the state system.[51]

Confined to internal exile to the island of Ventotene in the Tyrrhenian Sea, the two authors put forward a daring vision of a federal Europe coupled with a profound social transformation. Spinelli and Rossi came from different ideological traditions, Spinelli starting out as a communist but breaking with the party during the Stalinist show trials, while Rossi, a nationalist, moved toward social liberalism. To create a broad common platform, the duo refrained from going into details about the future sociopolitical organization of the country. They started instead from the supranational perspective, diagnosing the crisis of European civilization and sought to offer a remedy to it, transcending the national specificities. They believed the main cause of crisis was the ambiguity of national self-determination. While rooted in the fundamental principle of liberty, nation-statehood could also deteriorate into the legitimization of ethnic hatred and imperialistic pretensions and reaching its pinnacle in the totalitarian merger of national homogenization and state repression.

The authors' federalism was far from the "liberal utopianism" characterizing the immediate post-World War years, exemplified in the activities of the League of Nations and castigated by Carr and other critics of the postwar arrangement. Nor was it rooted merely in an idealist vision of supranational unification characteristic of the pan-European movement—more in a fear of the reemergence of antidemocratic nationalism after the war if nation-statehood were to remain the main principle of collective political existence. Furthermore, rather than a hierarchical vision of "civilized" Europe and "uncivilized" others, for the authors such a democratic European supranational polity also seemed to offer guarantees for peaceful cooperation and eventually also a promise of a global federation in the "distant future."

They also sought to learn from the mistakes of the post-First World War radical left, which pushed for a dictatorship of the proletariat and triggered a devastating backlash preparing the ground for the fascist takeover. While the authors sought to refrain themselves from making too many concrete political suggestions to preserve the unity of the anti-fascist coalition of forces, their program for the federalization of Europe was also linked to a vision of socioeconomic democratization. This included the limitation of capitalist market mechanisms in certain basic sectors of the economy, the guarantee of social rights, and state intervention to prevent the formation of monopolies of economic or political power (including the dominance of the Catholic Church). To implement this, the authors did not shy away from adopting radical methods in the projected postwar "revolutionary crisis" to break through the confines of "formal democracy" allegedly triggering endless discussion and thus quickly consuming the popular legitimacy of the new regime. At the same time, they warned of the communist instrumentalization of the class struggle of the proletariat, which would result in the self-destructive polarization of the political system, as in the early 1920s. Their proposed solution to the interwar crisis was thus a comprehensive rethinking of the principles of national and international politics triggering the interwar European "civil war" and breaking with the logic of mutually exclusive positions to create a more inclusive social and political framework based on an anti-totalitarian consensus:

> The moment has arrived to know how to discard old onerous burdens, how to be ready for the new *changements* that are coming and that will be so different from what we expected; to put aside the inept among the old, and create new energies among the young. Today those who have perceived the reasons for the present crisis in European civilization are seeking each other, and are trying to plan [the] future. In fact they are gathering the inheritance left by all those movements which worked to raise and enlighten humanity, and which failed because of their incapability to understand the purpose to be achieved or the ways how to achieve it.[52]

236 Intellectuals and the Crisis of Politics

East Central European political thinkers also suggested ideas of supranational reorganization as a solution to the economic and political crisis that hit their region particularly hard in the interwar years. In the early 1930s, a number of experts, such as the above-mentioned Elemér Hantos, argued in favor of an economic reintegration of the region as an antidote to the economic and political crisis triggered by fragmentation (he used the notion *Balkanisierung*) and protectionism after the collapse of the Habsburg Empire.[53] However, these projects usually remained limited to the economic sphere, and did not entail an agenda of political unification, which would have been unacceptable for most stakeholders. What was more typical was meso-regional visions of integration, especially pan-Balkanism,[54] in its leftist, liberal, and even conservative authoritarian iterations, and to a certain extent also a similar pan-Baltic orientation in the first half of the 1930s.

The war years brought a new wave of federalist thinking. A paradigmatic example, in some ways also comparable to the "Ventotene Manifesto," was *Federation in Central Europe*, written by Slovak émigré politician and former Czechoslovak prime minister Milan Hodža (1878–1944).[55] The book can also be read as a political testament, where Hodža recapitulated his own struggles from the turn of the century as he sought to achieve national rights for the Slovaks in a broader framework of transforming the Habsburg Empire into a federation and then, in the interwar period, arguing for the decentralization of the newly formed Czechoslovak state.[56] Carefully analyzing the series of economic and political crises hitting East Central Europe in general, and Czechoslovakia in particular, he considered the ongoing Second World War the occasion of an either–or decision: it could entail a fundamental reconfiguration of the region into a federal state (following the American and Swiss models), which would in turn fill in the geopolitical vacuum between Germany and Soviet Russia, or fall back into the international anarchy and toxic nationalist agitation that had undermined the European order in the 1930s.

Like the Italian anti-fascists, Hodža also linked this transformative vision to a comprehensive social reform agenda, but the content of this agenda was obviously different, being rooted in the regional sociopolitical context upon which he reflected. Thus, his main concern was the future of the prevalently agrarian societies characterizing the region (he also referred to Delaisi's idea of "two Europes" in this context).[57] Drawing on his analysis of the economic crisis of the early 1930s, he argued that the export-oriented heavy industry in the Czech lands was hit exceptionally hard due to the fragmentation of its markets and high protective tariffs (and thus contributed also to the radicalization of the Germany minority, which made up a significant part of the industrial proletariat in Czechoslovakia). While he argued that the agrarian sector was quicker to recover by comparison, the recovery was still protracted due to the lack of a common regional trade framework. A federal solution would have solved many of these problems, both creating a more integrated common market for the intra-regional circulation of agricultural and industrial products and making the negotiating position of the region much better in relation to Western Europe by replacing individual competition among national economies with a regional bilateralism. Finally, Hodža considered that a federal solution could also prevent the return of the crisis of democracy, which had characterized the region in the 1930s. As a result of this projected transformation, the agrarian middle class—which was a natural ally of any moderate politics against the leftist and rightist authoritarianisms and was inimical to radical nationalism—would be strengthened in the whole region. He argued that this agrarian project was the Central European counterpart to the liberal democratic (or liberal socialist) synthesis put forward by Western progressive thinkers during the war, rejecting *laissez-faire* economic frameworks but preserving the liberal values of individual dignity and economic initiative within a cooperative framework.

To sum up, the problematization of the nation-state as the principal unit of political community became a recurrent theme of interwar crisis discourses. Like the debates on liberalism or democracy, the seeming hegemony of this model in the early 1920s was also challenged by various contenders on the left and on the right. This provided a possibility of linking different levels of the discussion, most obviously in the context of the crisis of liberalism, which also undermined the liberal nationalist ideological framework underlying the post-1918 reorganization of East Central Europe. The experience of the Great Depression exposed the problem of economic nationalism and protectionism, while the geopolitical reconfiguration of the 1930s made the discourse of national self-determination increasingly problematic, if not completely illusory. Likewise, the debate on the crisis of socialism made the pre-1918 socialist federalist projects obsolete and exposed the need for new models. The extensive discussion on the crisis of European civilization, especially regarding the specific European combination of the principle of nation-statehood and transcontinental imperialism/colonialism, put all of this into an even more encompassing perspective. Importantly, except for the fascist rendering, the perceived entanglement of all these levels and spheres rarely produced a vision of total crisis and offered instead a vantage point to reflect on the interplay of the internal (societal) and supranational problems of integration.

The entanglement of the federalist projects described here with the analysis of the socioeconomic and political crisis phenomena also indicates that it would be misleading to read the interwar crisis discourses as doomsday scenarios or merely rhetorical exercises. Especially during the Second World War, the concept of crisis provided a "space of experience" regarding the devastating consequences of the economic depression, resulting in the delegitimization of democracy. Further, it opened a "horizon of expectation" in the sense of posing an either–or situation where the right choice might open a fundamentally new trajectory of development that went beyond the endemic national conflicts. Making a wrong choice would proliferate these conflicts further, until the next, even more encompassing crisis.

Notes

1. See also Peter Judson's analysis in *The Habsburg Empire: A New History* (Cambridge, MA: The Belknap Press, 2016), 388. He uses the concept of "little empires."

2. Max Hildebert Boehm, "Staat und Minderheit" *Europäische Revue* 6 (1930): 724–34.

3. Hans Zehrer, "Der Sinn der Krise," *Die Tat* 23, no. 12 (1932): 937–57. On the broader context, see the classic work by Kurt Sontheimer, *Antidemokratisches Denken in der Weimarer Republik. Die politischen Ideen des deutschen Nationalismus zwischen 1918 und 1933.* (Munich: Deutscher Taschenbuch-Verlag, 1994 [1962]).

4. Zehrer, "Der Sinn der Krise," 939.

5. Ibid., 941.

6. Piero Marsich, "La posizione teorica e pratica del Fascismo di fronte allo Stato" (1921), in Renzo de Felice, ed., *L'autobiografia del fascismo: Antologia di testi fascisti (1919-1945)* (Turin: Einaudi, 2004), 39.

7. Marsich, "Fra le due morse," in ibid., 76.

8. Dmytro Dontsov, *Підстави нашої політики* [The Foundations of Our Politics] (Vienna: Видавництво Донцових, 1921). On Dontsov's ideological shift, see Trevor Erlacher, "The Birth of Ukrainian 'Active Nationalism': Dmytro Dontsov and Heterodox Marxism before World War I, 1883-1914," *Modern Intellectual History* 11, no. 3 (2014): 519–48. On Dontsov's political ideas in the interwar years, see Oleksander Zaitsev, *Націоналіст у добі фашизму: Львівський період Дмитра Донцова, 1922-1939. Начерк інтелектуальної біографії* [Nationalist in the Time of Fascism. The Lviv Period of Dmytro Dontsov, 1922-39. Towards an Intellectual Biography] (Kyiv: Критика, 2019).

9. Alfred Weber, *Die Krise des modernen Staatsgedankens in Europa* (Stuttgart: Deutsche Verlags-Anstalt, 1925).

10. On the entanglements between the conceptions of *Führerdemokratie* by the two Weber brothers, see Eberhard Demm, "Max and Alfred Weber II: From *Führerdemokratie* to *Führernation*. A Comparative Synthesis of Their Political Sociology," *Max Weber Studies* 22, no. 1 (January 2022): 13–54.

11. Weber, *Die Krise*, 113.

12. Ibid., 122.

13. Guglielmo Ferrero, *Discours aux sourds* (Paris: Sagittaire, 1924).

14. Ibid., 82.

15. Ibid., 162.

16. Albert Demangeon, *Le déclin de l'Europe* (Paris: Payot, 1920).

17. François Delaisi, *Les deux Europes* (Paris: Payot, 1929).

18. Ibid., 9.

19. Ibid., 21.

20. Interestingly, Delaisi used "*caciques*," a metaphor taken from Spanish political terminology (originally denoting Latin American indigenous elites) to denote the local party elites who controlled the political machinery, which became a terminus technicus in comparative political science in the 1960s and 1970s.

21. See Frank Schipper, *Driving Europe: Building Europe on Roads in the Twentieth Century* (PhD dissertation, Technische Universiteit Eindhoven, 2008), 85–100, 117–18.

22. *Convegno di scienze morali e storiche: 14-20 novembre 1932-XI, tema: l'Europa*, vol. 1, *Atti preliminari, processi verbali* (Roma: Reale Accademia d'Italia, 1933). On the intellectual and political context of the *Convegno*, especially from the perspective of the entanglements of the Italian fascist regime and the Nazis, see Monica Fioravanzo, *L'Europa fascista: Dal "primato" italiano all'asservimento al Reich (1932-1943)* (Milano: FrancoAngeli, 2022), 43–55.

23. Convegno, 14.
24. Ibid., 83.
25. Ibid., 97.
26. Ibid., 107.
27. Ibid., 113.
28. Ibid., 254–7.
29. Ibid., 633. In 1936, Beckerath edited Mussolini's theoretical writings on economy in German. During the war, however, he became increasingly critical of National Socialist official policies, and he kept contact with dissident circles. After the war, he was among the key experts of economic policymaking in the Federal Republic.
30. Ibid., 398.
31. Ibid., 399–400.
32. Ibid., 114.
33. Ibid., 421.
34. Ibid., 209.
35. Mihaïl Manoïlesco, "L'inquiétude européenne et le Congrès de Rome," *L'année politique* 8, no. 2 (June 1933): 197–211. The cooperativist Bernard Lavergne, who was the editor of the journal, distanced himself from Manoilescu's interpretation and political agenda in an editorial note.
36. André Siegfried, *Die Krise Europas*, trans. Willi Reich (Zürich–Leipzig: Rascher, 1935).
37. William Rappard, "The League in Relation to the World Crisis," *Political Science Quarterly* 47, no. 4 (1932): 481–514.
38. Paul Mantoux, "A Contribution to the History of the Lost Opportunities of the League of Nations," in Paul Mantoux, William E. Rappard, Maurice Bourquin, Guglielmo Ferrero, and Pitman B. Potter, eds., *The World Crisis* (London: Longmans, Green, 1938), 3–35.
39. Guglielmo Ferrero, "Forms of War and International Anarchy," in ibid., 85–97.
40. For an overview of the interwar and early postwar conceptualizations of European unity and their underlying temporal modalities, see Mark Hewitson and Matthew D'Auria, eds., *Europe in Crisis: Intellectuals and the European Idea, 1917–1957* (New York: Berghahn, 2012).
41. Edward H. Carr, *The Twenty Years Crisis, 1919–1939: An Introduction to the Study of International Relations* (London: Macmillan, 1939).
42. Ibid., 25.
43. Ibid., 38–9.
44. Ibid., 61.
45. Ibid., 114.
46. Ibid., 283.
47. Ibid., 117.
48. Ibid., 100.
49. David Mitrany, *A Working Peace System. An Argument for the Functional Development of International Organization* (London: Royal Institute of International Affairs, 1943).
50. Ibid., 55.
51. The text was written in 1941, various versions of it were published in 1943 and 1944. Available at http://www.altierospinelli.org/manifesto/manifesto_en.html
52. Ibid. This English translation of the Ventotene Manifesto was prepared by Emma Urgesi for CIFE Italia.

240　Intellectuals and the Crisis of Politics

53. Elemér Hantos, *Denkschrift über die Wirtschaftskrise in den Donaustaaten* (Vienna: St. Norbertus, 1933), and *Der Weg zum neuen Mitteleuropa* (Berlin: Mitteleuropa-Verlag, 1933). See also Nils Müller, "Die Wirtschaft als 'Brücke der Politik': Elemér Hantos' wirtschaftspolitisches Programm in den 1920er und 1930er Jahren," in Carola Sachse, ed., *"Mitteleuropa" und "Südosteuropa" als Planungsraum: Wirtschafts- und kulturpolitische Expertisen im Zeitalter der Weltkriege* (Göttingen: Wallstein Verlag, 2010), 87–114.

54. Pavlos Hatzopoulos, *The Balkans Beyond Nationalism and Identity. International Relations and Ideology* (London: I. B. Tauris, 2008), 69–152.

55. Milan Hodža, *Federation in Central Europe: Reflections and Reminiscences* (London: Jarrolds, 1942).

56. The book also reflected Hodža's ongoing polemic with Edvard Beneš, the exiled president of the country, whose position on the Czechoslovak political system was centralistic and who opted for a closer cooperation, both strategically and ideologically, with the Soviets during the war.

57. Hodža, *Federation*, 167.

10
Long Shadows of the Interwar Crises

In the mainstream European historiographic narratives of the twentieth century, 1945 has been usually perceived as a fundamental turning point that obliterated most of the interwar political and ideological structures. Arguably, the concept of crisis also became much less central to political discourse than in the interwar years.[1] Albeit with different normative connotations, the experience of this rupture was indeed constitutive for the self-images of postwar Western European and North American liberal democratic consensus politics and Eastern European state socialism alike.[2] In the last decades, however, historiography became more sensitive to the continuities that linked the pre- and post-Second World War periods both structurally and ideologically. Studies started to bridge seemingly incompatible configurations, for example, interwar right-wing national authoritarianism and state socialism, or the Nazi-dominated supranational integration of war economies and the economic federalism of the emerging European Community.

This chapter does not intend to reconstruct the complex and multilinear story of the concept and discourse of crisis from 1945 up to the early twenty-first century in its entirety. Rather, it seeks to identify some of the turning points and paradigmatic discursive patterns and pays special attention to their entanglement with the pre-1945 discourses analyzed in previous chapters. Apart from helping to trace the roots of some elements of the present political imaginary, on a meta-level such a perspective can also offer clues regarding the relevance of historical knowledge in facing contemporary challenges to democracy—a question heavily debated in connection with the analogies between past and present anti-liberal contenders. For instance, is the populism that we have come to know since the 1990s in any way related to the populisms of the late nineteenth century or the interwar years? Or is it merely an accidental identity of labels? And in a broader sense: what do the structural analogies and genealogical links to the interwar collapse of liberal democracies tell us about our current predicament?

As references to populism and neoliberalism were becoming ubiquitous in the public sphere after 2008, many observers referred to them as something fundamentally new. At the same time, several excellent historical studies have been published which sought to trace these ideological traditions back in time. Still, there was often a sizable gap between historical reconstruction and the analysis of contemporary configurations, which pertained more to the domain of political science. Likewise, historical production on interwar crisis phenomena and the contemporary debate on

---

Intellectuals and the Crisis of Politics in the Interwar Period and Beyond. Balázs Trencsényi, Oxford University Press.
© Balázs Trencsényi (2025). DOI: 10.1093/9780198929512.003.0010

"permacrisis" intersect mainly in the sphere of journalistic commentaries that point to—often alarming—analogies, but rarely develop into a more meticulous analysis.

To get a more nuanced picture, we need to combine a diachronic perspective on the transformation and recontextualization of certain ideological elements (such as the contrast of the common people and the "alienated elites") and a structural analysis of the similarities between genealogically unrelated past and present arguments and discourses. Thus, my aim is not to prove that we live in a "new interwar period" or that manifestations and conceptualizations of neoliberalism or populism at different historical points of time are identical. Instead, I argue that these ideological streams, even if in many ways anti- or ahistorical in their own self-perception, still have their own accumulated historicity. The formative experiences shaping them at a given moment might have rather long-term repercussions, even if the socioeconomic conditions that once gave birth to them, and the discursive frameworks through which they were articulated, changed radically in the meantime. In my view, both neoliberalism and populism carry the experience of the interwar crises with them, and, in turn, their self-legitimization is also deeply entangled with the discourse of crisis. Consequently, analyzing them in view of this context makes it possible to discern continuities and ruptures in their historical trajectory as well as to reflect on the entanglements of these two seemingly antagonistic ideological streams.

After the Anno Zero: *New Beginning or Endemic Crisis?*

Preparing for the expected defeat of the Axis powers during the Second World War, policymakers and advisors of the Allies began to discuss the desired postwar global order. In doing so, they sought to consider the lessons learnt from the mistakes of the peacemakers after the First World War. However, the postwar situation turned out to be dramatically different from these projections. With the advancement of the Red Army way beyond any previous confines of the Russian imperial sphere of interest in the final phase of the war, the political field began to separate into pro-communist and anti-communist camps all over the continent. These developments were perceived by many observers as an acute political crisis right after the end of open warfare. This was not only the case in Soviet-occupied East Central Europe, but also in Western and Southern European countries with strong left-leaning anti-fascist movements, like France, Italy, and especially Greece, the latter of which plunged into a civil war immediately after the end of the Second World War.[3]

Thus, although there were high hopes among various political groups, from socialists to moderate conservatives, that the victory over fascism would create the possibility to establish ideologically and socially inclusive democratic regimes all over Europe, divergent understandings of democracy and the ensuing—often violent—postwar conflicts created a new setting for the crisis discourse. This situation prompted some of the key figures of the interwar political debates to reformulate or retune their previous analyses, often in a completely new political and cultural setting.

Wilhelm Röpke reflected on the "international crisis" in his article from 1945, trying to discern the lessons learned from the two World Wars.[4] He saw the rise of collectivism as a key feature of modern political and cultural trends, becoming especially palpable after the decline of classical liberalism from the mid-nineteenth century onward. From this perspective, Röpke's central question was whether it was possible to recreate a common ideological ground—accommodating liberals, moderate conservatives, and even moderate socialists—to find a way out of the impasse of two incompatible orientations: one considering state intervention and centralization as the only remedy to all socioeconomic and political problems, the other rejecting any involvement of the state whatsoever, abandoning society to the free play of economic forces. Crisis was here reformulated not as a choice between two options, but precisely as the "unnatural" pressure to choose. Resolving the crisis necessitated the rejection of this "false alternative."

Trying to steer toward such a "third way," Röpke had a considerable impact on East Central European political thinkers who rejected the alternative of Soviet-type communism and "*laissez-faire* capitalism." Many of them were themselves adherents of some form of a third-way ideology already in the interwar years. From a very different geopolitical vantage point than Röpke's—but in many ways resonating with (and influenced by) the German scholar's analysis—left-leaning Hungarian agrarian populist political thinker István Bibó (1911–79) published an essay on the crisis of Hungarian democracy in October 1945, barely half a year after the end of the war on Hungarian territory.[5] The essay was a powerful analysis of the fragility of the postwar democratic order in the East Central European countries "liberated" by the Red Army. It relied on Bibó's sweeping interpretation, developed during the war years, of the collapse of democratic politics and the breakthrough of extremist nationalism all over Europe. Key concepts in Bibó's work linked to crisis were "hysteria" (resonating with Röpke's contrast of *Vernunft* and *Hysterie*) denoting the loss of the sense of reality and proportions, then triggering an escalation of social and political aggression, as well as "fear," taken from Guglielmo Ferrero, whose classes he attended in 1935 at the Graduate Institute in Geneva.

While registering the profound ambiguities of Hungary's "liberation" by Stalin's Red Army from the German occupation—and its zealous Hungarian collaborators—Bibó hoped that the end of the war would offer a chance to break the vicious circle of violence and restore a pluralistic political system with its corresponding democratic ethos. However, he was increasingly worried that the tensions between political forces could undermine the consolidation of democratic politics:

> Under constant fear, Hungarian democracy has come to a crisis. Two kinds of fear gnaw at it: the fear of the dictatorship of the proletariat and the fear of reaction. Neither fear has objective grounds: it is an insignificant minority of Hungarians who want the dictatorship of the proletariat or the return of reaction, and no external

244 Intellectuals and the Crisis of Politics

forces would be pleased by such a turn. It is, however, in the nature of political fear that, even in the lack of objective conditions, through its sheer sway, it is capable of conjuring up the dreaded danger.[6]

Bibó used the concept of crisis strategically to alarm his audience. Since multi-party democracy had only been restored recently (after the long-lasting autocratic Horthy regime and the short-lived rule of the fascist Arrow Cross Party), invoking a crisis implied that the renewal of democracy—a program to which all legal political forces nominally subscribed—was in danger.[7] While on paper the immediate postwar coalition government seemed to be a rather stable and representative arrangement, the internal tensions (i.e., between communists and anti-communists; between those who understood democracy as a representative system based on the division of branches of power and those who defined it as the direct rule of the "people"; between parties focusing on the urban versus the rural electorates; between those who categorically rejected nationalism and those who tried to instrumentalize it) were visible from the very beginning.

Bibó argued that the endemic fear of all political actors prevented them from turning the 1945 regime change into a true experience of liberation. As the communists were aware of their limited social support, they were afraid of being ejected from the government by the other political forces. Thus, they had to rely on the occupying Soviet troops to manipulate the political system. A mere two years later, the elections would be infamously rigged, tilting the power balance toward the extreme left. On the other hand, the non-communist forces, and especially the Smallholders (who, in 1945, received 57% of the vote and named the first president and prime minister) were dazed by the danger of a communist takeover and thus integrated those who were inimical to the communists into their ranks, including the sizable base of the interwar authoritarian regime. To make this even more complicated, some of the former fascists were recruited by the communists, who appealed to their anti-bourgeois radicalism and promised them indemnity in exchange for their political U-turn. Thus, instead of working out a democratic consensus, the political system fell hostage to the polarizing drive of the two main forces, both fearing the other's dominance, which would fatally undermine the precarious balance.

Bibó's suggestion for escaping the crisis was the consolidation of the political center of the coalition, made up of two other parties: the social democrats and the agrarian populists. Both had certain connections to the left and the right, as well as an ideological commitment to self-government in contrast to the centralism of the communists and the interwar authoritarian right. Overcoming the crisis was thus conditional on setting the democratic process in motion, where both citizens and political parties could experience the accountability of powerholders.

Bibó's essay had powerful repercussions, including a critical rejoinder by György Lukács, who defended a binary opposition of "progressive" and "reactionary" forces—even though he did not argue for an immediate communist takeover, as he rather envisaged a prolonged transition period toward socialism.[8] What made

Bibó's position illusory in the end was the shift in communist tactics. The communist leadership's increasing obsession with total power in the context of the unfolding Cold War, and the marginalization not only of other political forces but even those figures in their own ranks who supported a more pluralist version of "popular democracy," erased any possibility of democratic consensus politics. In the international communist movement, this was prefigured by the showdown with Eugen Varga in the Soviet Union, who, in his 1946 book *The Economic Transformation of Capitalism at the End of the Second World War*,[9] still argued for a prolonged transition to socialism and long-term coexistence with the capitalist world.

Bibó's hopes for cooperation between the social democrats and the agrarian populists also proved unrealistic. These two parties were set apart by a powerful cultural divide, with most key figures of the agrarian populist movement resonating with some ethno-nationalist tropes—describing the "ethnically pure" peasantry as the main source of national regeneration, contrasted to the "ethnically mixed" urban population—whereas the social democrats focused on the working class and part of the intelligentsia, in turn irritated by the "folkish" political language of the former. This ideological divergence ironically prompted both parties to cooperate more with the communists than with each other. The peasantists found them congenial, as they also employed an anti-elitist and anti-bourgeois rhetoric to mobilize the most disaffected layers of the society, while many social democrats still viewed them as a working class "brother party," committed to industrialization and the overall modernization of society as against the "village romanticism" of the National Peasant Party.

Writing at roughly the same time in Great Britain, Michael Polanyi also described the political and intellectual situation of his adopted *patria* as dangerously crisis-ridden due to the growth of polarization:

> The situation is dangerous; not because freedom is infringed by direction of labour and the like, but because freedom depends on the agreed coherence of society. A society which is split into irreconcilable camps can be maintained only by violence [...] The fight for freedom must aim at the unending task of those who value liberty. For life in society can never cease to produce new dissensions and the citizens of a free society can never pause in their search after new harmonious solutions to ever recurring conflicts.[10]

For Polanyi, as for Bibó, the solution to the endemic crisis was some sort of "third way" that combined socialism and capitalism.[11] This also required the repositioning of the bourgeoisie from a privileged ruling class to an elite that organized society through its moral engagement and technological knowhow:

> More humane, more tolerant and more firmly principled than today, it must go out to overcome the spirit of class war and restore the fundamental agreement on which society is based. At home, at the office, in business, in politics, everywhere the bourgeoisie should surrender its unpaired privileges, reconcile disaffected followers and reassert its leadership.[12]

246 Intellectuals and the Crisis of Politics

On two sides of the descending Iron Curtain, Bibó and Polanyi both employed the concept of crisis to warn their readers of the dynamic of civil war, becoming increasingly threatening with the eruption of the Cold War. This global polarization prevailed within a relative geopolitical equilibrium, created at the heavy price of direct repression of non-communist political forces in the Eastern part of the continent and the less bloody—barring the Greek Civil War, where the Western Allies supported the royalist camp, which had integrated former pro-Axis collaborators—but still rather brutal marginalization of the radical left in Western Europe.

In this context, crisis could reemerge as a notion denoting the challenges to Cold War geopolitics. Perhaps the most well-known cases are the three conflicts unfolding almost simultaneously and having multiple entanglements in autumn 1956: the "Polish Crisis," the "Hungarian Crisis," and the "Suez Crisis." While international political observers used the notion of crisis copiously regarding these events, it was surprisingly much less common in the public discourse "on the ground" in Poland or Hungary. As tensions built up in summer 1956, local actors close to the regime employed the notion only sparingly, mostly in the negative, stressing that there was actually "no crisis" and that it was only the "concoction" of bourgeois ideologists.[13] In turn, reformers focused much more on the notion of critique, but shied away from pairing it conceptually with crisis, as the main stake of the public debate at that point was precisely to draw the line between "legitimate" and "anti-Party" criticism.

As the conflict of reformers and "Party conservatives" became more and more open, the notion of crisis also turned out to be more prevalent in public discourse. This can be seen in the resolution of the communist Union of Polish Youth (*Związek Młodzieży Polskiej*, ZMP), which referred to a "serious ideological and moral crisis" in a "large part of the younger generation."[14] However, it was still mainly external observers and political actors who employed this terminology. Tellingly, the October 23, 1956 editorial of the Yugoslav party journal *Borba* spoke of a "difficult crisis, one which this great European country [i.e., Poland] has experienced for a number of years," praising the new reform communist leadership for having successfully overcome it.[15] By contrast, actors on the ground still preferred other terms. Symptomatically, in his radio address to the Hungarian people, revolutionary prime minister Imre Nagy (1896–1958) used the concept only in reference to the "housing crisis."[16] Instead, the prevalent terms used by the Hungarian revolutionaries to describe the situation ranged from "popular uprising" to "revolution," while the pro-Soviet side (which gained the upper hand with the invasion of the Red Army) often resorted to the seemingly neutral term of "events," gradually adopting the explicitly condemnatory label of "counter-revolution."[17]

In Western Europe, with gradual political stabilization and economic growth in the 1950s, the concept of crisis seemed to have lost its previous preeminence in internal political debates. "Normal" politics was increasingly about avoiding domestic crises; crisis thus became a notion reserved for the international arena. It denoted the local manifestations of the global political division (as was the case with the 1954–8 Taiwan, 1958–61 Berlin, and 1962 Cuban Missile crises) and the process of decolonization (the 1954 "Algerian Crisis," 1960–5 "Congo Crisis," 1967–70 "Biafran Crisis," etc.). Even Hollywood reflected on this, as can be seen from the 1950 film by Richard Brooks (1912–1992), *Crisis*, co-written by Hungarian-Jewish émigré George Tabori (1914–2007), who had his share of crisis experience while living in Germany and working with Bertolt Brecht during the crumbling of the Weimar Republic. Tellingly, the film merged the medical and political connotations of crisis, culminating in a surgical and moral "either/or": the main hero, an American brain surgeon on an exotic vacation played by Cary Grant, is forced to operate on a fatally ill Latin American dictator while his wife is kidnapped by the resistance movement to pressure the doctor to commit a "mistake" and thus kill the tyrant. No matter how pressing for the individuals caught up in this quagmire, crisis in this film as well as in public discourse, was projected outside of the "West" to the fuzzy peripheries. The ironic final image of the trailer, a hand-written note stating that "We are all enthusiastic about *Crisis*" (referring both to the title of the film but also the concept itself) could only work for those viewers who no longer felt its imminence in their own life.

While the immediate domestic political implications were increasingly played down, crisis became a central concept in historical analyses of different periods and configurations. Already in 1949, the French medievalist and former resistance fighter Edouard Perroy (1901–74) published an article seeking to synthesize the different features of financial and monetary crisis in the fourteenth century.[18] In turn, in his *Crisis of the Early Italian Renaissance* (1955), German–Jewish-born American historian Hans Baron (1900–88) depicted the transformation of Florentine political thought at the turn of the fifteenth century as a response to the threat of the emergence of autocratic territorial states, leading to the creation of a new "civic humanist" discourse that offered a new participatory understanding of politics.[19] While this argument could have been read as purely historical, it is important to bear in mind that, as a young intellectual and a student of Ernst Troeltsch in the 1920s, Baron himself took part in the debate on the crisis of the Weimar Republic. Thus, his search for a successful republican reframing of the political community in times of crisis had obvious implications for the discussion on the resilience of democratic regimes both in the interwar and the Cold War contexts.

Crisis became a useful analytical term in view of later historical periods as well. Yet another prominent historian of German–Jewish cultural background, Eric Hobsbawm (1917–2012), launched a long-lasting debate in 1954 with "The General Crisis of the European Economy in the 17th Century".[20] Working within the Marxist paradigm, Hobsbawm focused on the economic substructure of the crisis. His interpretation was extended but also challenged by Hugh Trevor-Roper (1914–2003) in "The General Crisis of the 17th Century," published five years later.[21] Trevor-Roper pointed to a combination of economic, political, and institutional aspects to argue for an even more comprehensive crisis in the mid-seventeenth century, going well beyond the economic sphere, thus also problematizing the Marxist interpretative framework.[22]

While the historical dynamic in early modern England and France was markedly different from that of Eastern Europe, the crisis paradigm shaping the work of Hobsbawm also found prominent adherents in Marxist historiography on the other

248   Intellectuals and the Crisis of Politics

side of the Iron Curtain. From the perspective of these authors, the main question was precisely the divergence of Western and Eastern paths of development in the early modern period. While the West was transformed by bourgeois and industrial revolutions, the Eastern part of the continent experienced an economic and political stagnation that resulted in the reinforcement of feudal ties to the detriment of urbanization and social mobility. The interpretative model emerging to explain this divergence focused on the concept of "second serfdom" present already in the works of Marx and Engels, but significantly extended and reworked by Polish Marxist economic historians Witold Kula (1916–88) and Marian Małowist (1909–88), as well as Hungarian Zsigmond Pál Pach (1919–2001) from the mid-1950s onward.[23]

In their interpretation, the sixteenth and seventeenth centuries witnessed an overall "crisis of feudalism" in Europe, to which Western European countries responded by creating a global economic circulation through colonization that facilitated their successful leap forward toward embourgeoisement and the dissolution of feudal ties. The modern (absolutist) state was thus rooted in the alliance of the king and upwardly mobile strata of society (basically the bourgeoisie) and opened the way toward extra-European expansion. The Eastern part of the continent saw a contrary dynamic. Finding markets for its agricultural products in the West, the nobility reinforced its control over the peasantry and, for some time, also gained the upper hand over the king (most obviously in the Polish case), preventing the formation of efficient state structures. The "either–or" inherent in the concept of crisis was thus translated by these historians into two possible trajectories of European economic and political development (in a way returning to the interwar categorization of Europes "A" and "B"). The political implication was that only the revolutionary socialist transformation could propel the East back into the main line of European development and resolve the historical crisis, at least retrospectively.

While emerging from a totally different intellectual subculture, Reinhart Koselleck's *Kritik und Krise* also falls into the historiographical context of the 1950s, marked by the growing interest in the concept of crisis as an analytical tool, rather than an openly political instrument.[24] Working on his dissertation project in the early 1950s, Koselleck was part of a conservative intellectual milieu preoccupied with the historical morphology and explanatory value of crisis.[25] This is evidenced by the work of Koselleck's friends and fellow-members of the circle around Carl Schmitt: Nicolaus Sombart (1923–2008) and Hanno Kesting (1925–75). For them, crisis was both an analytical concept to understand past historical configurations as well as a permanent feature of political modernity.[26] Conceptualizing crisis thus also meant perpetuating it, even though this argument was not taken to its logical endpoint in reflecting on the crisis discourse of interwar conservative revolutionaries (and Schmitt in particular) as an instrument to transcend political modernity.

What was common in these liberal, Marxist, and conservative historicizations was the understanding of crisis as a powerful historical catalyst of change. In many interpretations this was coupled with a "grand narrative" of historical development, even if there could be deviations from the norm, as the various *Sonderweg* conceptions prevalent in the postwar period indicated. But these exceptions only reinforced the normativity of the "proper" path of development. Importantly, as the cases of Koselleck or Baron indicate, most of the intellectuals who sought to employ "crisis" as an analytical term were deeply steeped in the interwar discussion and often had personal exposure to key authors of the crisis debates of the 1920s and 1930s. Their turn toward this notion was not accidental and had important political implications, too. Regarding Eastern European Marxist historians, this implied the legitimization of the socialist transformation as a way out of the crisis-ridden historical *Sonderweg* of their societies. For them, the path of crisis culminated in the interwar and/or wartime authoritarian/fascist regimes (although, in the case of Kula for example, this did not mean an uncritical stance toward "really existing" socialism). In the West, it implied a debate on the entanglement of the emergence of bourgeois modernity with social, political, and cultural conflicts and especially the question of the roots of the German National Socialist *Götterdämmerung*.

Crises of "Really Existing" Socialism and Capitalism

As we could see, the post-Second World War interpretative frames of crisis were not devoid of meta-political subtexts. However, the overall tendency toward the historicization of the concept could be interpreted as a sign of its gradual depoliticization. The early and mid-1960s seemed to be a period of relative stability (even though the Cuban Missile Crisis in October 1962 raised the specter of a global conflagration). The period was marked by the expansion of the welfare state both in Western and Eastern Europe, creating the sentiment of a systemic convergence of socialism and capitalism. In Western economic theory, the fine-tuning of monetary policy based on "vulgar Keynesianism" (i.e., pumping money into the economy and lowering interest rates when a counter-cyclical economic downturn materialized) led to a belief that it was possible to avoid economic crises altogether. Of course, the economic policies which emerged in the context of the "economic miracles" of the 1950s, implemented by the dominant center-right and center-left political elites of the time, were not purely Keynesian by any means. Instead, they were a strange mixture of Keynesian and neoliberal/*Ordoliberal* precepts—even if the chief ideologists of neoliberalism considered themselves to be utterly marginalized from economic policymaking.

Crisis nevertheless appeared in the political language of the time, although less centrally than before. In this sense, Hannah Arendt's (1906–1975) essays from the 1950s and 1960s (starting with "The Crisis in Education" from 1954,[27] followed by "The Crisis in Culture" from 1960,[28] and four other pieces, eventually published together in 1972 as *Crises of the Republic*[29]) stand out. "The Crisis in Education" starts with a dramatic image of an all-pervasive crisis: "The general crisis that has overtaken the modern world everywhere and in almost every sphere of life manifests itself differently in each country, involving different areas and taking on different forms."[30] Arendt's radical use of the concept with a trans-sectoral reference to a "general" crisis resonated with the interwar philosophical ideas of Karl Jaspers and Martin

Heidegger, both of whom had an enormous impact on her intellectual development, albeit in different ways, while it was much less typical for American intellectual milieux. The power of her argument was augmented by using the concept of crisis in the American context dominated by a broad consensus about the direction of the political and socioeconomic evolution of the West, contrasted to the repressive methods and economic scarcity of the Soviet-ruled countries (a counter-position also fed by Arendt's own conceptualization of totalitarianism). Rather than an indicator of irreversible civilizational decline, for Arendt, crisis was first and foremost a window of opportunity, "which tears away facades and obliterates prejudices,"[31] thus making it possible to confront the "essence of the matter" and exercise the human capacity of judgment: "A crisis forces us back to the questions themselves and requires from us either new or old answers, but in any case direct judgments. A crisis becomes a disaster only when we respond to it with preformed judgments, that is, with prejudices."[32]

The 1960s and 1970s, however, brought both the oil crisis and the previously unimaginable phenomenon of "stagflation," that is, the convergence of two phenomena which, according to the Keynesian understanding, should not have come together. It roughly coincided with the radicalization of the generational conflict, culminating in the student movements in 1968, with somewhat divergent ideologies and stakes in the Eastern and Western parts of the continent. All of this undermined the general confidence in the postwar welfare state's immunity from crisis. Different societies managed this differently and employed divergent conceptual frameworks to describe these developments. But overall, the discourse of crisis became much more prevalent by the early 1970s, especially in the context of the erupting "energy crisis" and the concomitant "ecological crisis." In this context, the crisis discourse of the Club of Rome, founded in 1968, which sought to integrate different crisis phenomena (environment, health, economy, criminality) into one model with the help of systems theory and quantitative methods, had considerable impact, way beyond the expert community.[33] The main message of the Club of Rome's fundamental text, *The Limits to Growth*, was that disparate crisis symptoms might be visible but are only recognized as such (becoming a "crisis point") when they actually become irreversible: "Symptoms of the crisis will begin to appear long before the crisis point is reached" and "the human race may have very little time to react to a crisis resulting from exponential growth in a finite space."[34] The discursive proliferation of crisis in the early 1970s was also reflected upon by contemporary observers, such as Edgar Morin, who started to talk about the "inflation" or even the "crisis" of the very notion.[35]

The shaking of the consensus around unlimited progress in the 1970s also reshaped economic thought, amplifying the voice of neoliberals who had been critical of the interventionist policies which characterized the postwar projects of welfare state-building since the 1940s. This also rekindled the discussion on the history of the Great Depression and the lessons to be drawn from it. Friedrich von Hayek and Milton Friedman were both at the forefront of these discussions that focused on inflation and challenging the Keynesian argument that economic crises were necessarily tied to deflation.[36] At the same time, Hayek revisited his own earlier positions, and became more critical of deflationary measures, castigating monetary authorities for aggravating the crisis. Antonio Magliulo argued that, while Hayek did not change his overall position about finding the roots of the Great Depression in protectionist measures which distorted the market, he admitted that misplaced deflationary politics indeed made the situation worse in the second phase of the crisis, contributing to the shrinking of "aggregate demand."[37]

In the German academic context of the early 1970s, too, crisis became a key analytical notion, especially in the work of Jürgen Habermas and Claus Offe. Drawing on systems theory, these authors stressed the importance of political institutions in crisis management, thus going beyond the Marxist economic determinism still powerfully present in the German leftist intellectual milieu. Habermas stressed that the "application of the Marxian theory of crisis to the altered reality of 'advanced capitalism' leads to difficulties."[38] While their positions did not completely overlap, the two scholars agreed that the state had the capacity to develop efficient policies to attenuate the consequences of crisis. Still, they pointed to the paradoxical situation that exactly this type of efficient crisis-management would raise ever-growing expectations on the part of the population, ones which the state could not fulfill and thus would become inescapably affected by a general "legitimation crisis."[39]

Written from a markedly different political perspective, the report of the French sociologist of organizations Michel Crozier (1922–2013), American political scientist Samuel P. Huntington (1927–2008), and Japanese political sociologist Joji Watanuki (1931–2015), also focused on the legitimacy crisis of democratic institutions, registering the growing gap between expectations and realities. The authors defended the democratic system from the communist criticism; at the same time, they formulated serious reservations with respect to the increase of political participation.[40] Dramatizing the intellectual and political stakes of the venture, Zbigniew Brzezinski (1928–2017), the director of the Trilateral Commission and close friend of Huntington, went so far as to evoke Spengler's *Decline of the West* when comparing the crisis-ridden mood of the 1970s to that of the early 1920s in his introduction.

As the three authors of the report argued, the "problems of inflation, commodity shortages, international monetary stability, the management of economic interdependence, and collective military security"[41] had combined with the development of an "adversary culture" of intellectuals and a fundamental shift in the value-orientation of the population away from "materialistic work-oriented, public-spirited values." This contributed to the pervasive loss of trust in—and the consequent destabilization of—political institutions even in the most developed countries, such as the United Kingdom, Japan, or the United States. The authors went even further in expressing their irritation with "value-oriented intellectuals" taking no responsibility for public affairs but formulating moral criticism, considering the danger that they posed potentially comparable to the fascist movements and communist parties in the past. The main problem they detected, however, was that democracy was

252 Intellectuals and the Crisis of Politics

not a self-regulating system and it had an intrinsic tendency toward self-destruction, resulting in the "breakdown of traditional means of social control, a delegitimation of political and other forms of authority, and an overload of demands on government."[42]

There were substantial differences between the three authors (with Crozier being more critical of the structural inequalities in society than his colleagues and putting more emphasis on the cultural features of crisis) and the three contexts analyzed (Japan experienced a period of economic boom and the rule of the Liberal Democratic Party seemed unchallenged). Eventually, however, the report boiled down to a diagnosis that these societies were becoming "ungovernable." Available resources were insufficient to satisfy growing societal demands, which resulted in the loss of the common aims—the agenda of economic reconstruction and the Cold War security threat—that kept society together in the quarter century after the end of the Second World War.

Roughly in the same period, state socialist countries also experienced a series of systemic challenges resulting in sharpening conflicts between reformist and conservative forces within the party and society. These conflicts reached their peak in the stormy year of 1968 in political terms, but also continued to have repercussions well into the 1970s, as the global economic downturn was felt on the other side of the Iron Curtain as well. Here again, the concept of crisis became central to many interventions, and overall, one can identify a shift from the elaboration on the Marxist theory of crisis to the idea of the "crisis of Marxism."

Perhaps the most complex polemic argument along these lines was put forward by Czech philosopher Karel Kosík (1926–2003). His "Our Current Crisis" is a veritable treasure trove of the revisionist Marxist "crisis discourse" with manifest links to previous conceptualizations of crisis in Czech and European intellectual culture.[43] In Kosík's understanding, what happened in 1968 was "not merely a political crisis," but "simultaneously a crisis of politics" that questioned "not just a certain political system, but, at the same time and above all . . . the sense of politics."[44] Most importantly, Kosík problematized the mismatch between the democratic aspirations of society and the lifeless dogmatism of the Communist Party of Czechoslovakia. Consciously alluding to Masaryk's use of the concept of crisis, Kosík argued that it was not only a crisis of different social groups, but more importantly of social and cultural coherence in general: "Our current crisis is one of all sectors and classes of society, while, at the same time, it is a crisis of their mutual interaction. The words reiterated a thousand times over regarding the unity and alliance of the workers, peasants, and intelligentsia have become an empty affirmation."[45]

The original Masarykian idea of "our current crisis" was linked to the "Czech Question" in terms of the search for meaning of the existence of small nations in general and the Czech nation in particular. Along these lines, Kosík also linked the "current crisis" to national existence, projecting a possible loss of the national self under the homogenizing communist rule:

In the current crisis the nation is exposed to a three-way danger. It can lose its force for change as an historical subject and become an historical object molded by others. It can disappear as a political nation that renews and affirms itself by thinking through its own platform and by public debate about the meaning of its own existence, and slip into being a populace that speaks Czech and produces steel and wheat. Finally, it can trade the three-dimensional quality of its historical existence for a unidimensional one of merely vegetating and, thereby, forfeit its memory and perspective.[46]

Like Masaryk, Kosík described the national crisis as having universal implications: "the national crisis in Czechoslovakia is the crux of the crisis in Europe, and ... within the Czech crisis the European crisis emerges."[47]

Crisis meant here a dramatic turning point: "The radical resolution of this crisis is possible only if the system of a police-bureaucratic or a bureaucratic dictatorship is replaced by a system of socialist democracy."[48] Facing this crisis, Czechoslovak society could regain its agency and possibly even open the road to universal regeneration with its model of "socialism with a human face," or else it would fall back into the line of Sovietized societies and perpetuate the inertia characteristic of post-Stalinism. Kosík also described the crisis situation as a platform for the "philosopher politician" as against the "political pragmatist," focusing on "apparatus" and "transmission" (the allusions to the Jaspersian analysis, written almost four decades before, are unmistakable here):

> The political pragmatist can resolve only some social problems and only certain kinds of crises, but he is powerless in relation to the reality that exceeds his horizon and possibilities: he can attempt the resolution of an economic and civic-legal crisis, but he remains impotent when faced with a moral crisis.[49]

Significantly, crisis is directly linked by Kosík to critique: "Critical opinion does not seek to replace inefficient phrases with more updated ones nor to focus its attention on the result. Its goal is to get to the heart of the issue and to reveal the basis from which our behavior and thinking are derived."[50]

Constructing the model of the "philosopher politician" capable of this systemic critique, Kosík linked key political thinkers of the communist tradition (Luxemburg, Lenin, and Gramsci) to Masaryk, indicating a conscious effort to valorize the local "progressive" (not only Marxist, but also "bourgeois democratic") traditions, inserted into a broader historical contrast of democratic but unevenly modernized Central Europe versus autocratic and underdeveloped Russia. This framing opened the path toward the re-evaluation of the Central European cultural and political heritage after the crushing of the Prague Spring. However, in contrast to the implications of Kundera's later metaphor of a Europe *kidnappée*, Kosík did not affirm the superiority of an ideal Western civilization. Remaining a reform communist, Kosík argued that the Czechoslovak crisis was part and parcel of a deeper disorientation of humankind, a general crisis of modernity, as it were. "The modern age is an age of crisis because its foundations are in crisis."[51] As a result, humankind is torn between two ideological positions which were in many ways equally distorted: "Reality itself is cut in two by this crisis, because neither of these two systems provides a true alternative to the roots of modern subjectivism-nihilism."[52]

That "crisis" became a veritable *Kampfbegriff* in this period is also visible from the emotional rejoinder of Czech Marxist humanist philosopher Ivan Sviták (1925–94), who criticized the reform communist mainstream for seeking to preserve the monopoly of power while allowing for a broader social exchange of ideas and yielding to pressure from outside of the party. With his exclamation that it was not society that was in crisis but the "comrades," Sviták sought to turn the concept of crisis against the reform communist elites, drawing a symbolic line between the party and society and arguing instead for more complete democratization, including institutional plurality, as a way out of the impasse.[53]

Crisis also became a strategic concept for the dissident movements of the 1970s all over East Central Europe. They pointed to the systemic dysfunctions of "really existing" socialism, which could not be corrected by the reforms and adjustments usually put forward by the pragmatic/technocratic wings of the party elites but required much deeper structural transformation (even though many dissidents continued to make a distinction between socialist "ideals" and "practice"). Overall, most East Central European critics increasingly focused on the dysfunctionality of the socialist political and economic system and the inadequacy of the Marxist interpretative framework to analyze the situation and offer ways out of the impasse. In his analysis of the Polish intellectual scene, Raymond Taras described this as a gradual transition from the diagnosis of the "crisis of ideology" formulated by revisionist Marxist thinkers to a proliferation of "ideologies of crisis," which transcended the revisionist paradigm.[54] Thus, in the mid-1960s Polish context, Jacek Kuroń (1934–2004) and Karol Modzelewski (1937–2019) still linked the crisis of the socialist regime to an expectation of proletarian revolution—one that would sweep away the bureaucratic superstructure and create a more authentic socialist system. By contrast, two decades later, dissident political sociologist Jadwiga Staniszkis (1942–2024) described the systemic crisis as a root cause of the emergence of the Solidarity movement. While the latter challenged the socialist ideological hegemony, communist technocrats argued that the catastrophic socioeconomic situation necessitated depoliticized crisis management. Crisis was no longer conceptualized as a possible turning point toward the creation of a more authentic socialism, but rather as a trigger to (openly or tacitly) break with socialist principles.

This change was underpinned by the philosophical writings of dissidents turning to phenomenology and existentialism as an alternative referential framework to Marxism, transcending the socialist framework with their crisis discourse. Like Kosík, they often emphasized the presence of a more comprehensive crisis of modern man, of which the crisis of state socialism was only one aspect. Václav Havel's (1936–2011) work from the mid-1970s was inspired by Jan Patočka (1907–1977), the key philosopher of Czechoslovak dissent and Husserl's student. Havel relied on Patočka's critical perspective (with its roots in the late 1930s) on the mechanization and dehumanization of modern culture and society and described state socialism as a particularly repressive version of political modernity. In his speech (delivered by Tom Stoppard, as Havel was not allowed to leave Czechoslovakia) written in 1984 on receiving an honorary doctorate in Toulouse, Havel declared that:

> ... totalitarian systems warn of something far more serious than Western rationalism is willing to admit. They are, most of all, a convex mirror of the inevitable consequences of rationalism, a grotesquely magnified image of its own deep tendencies, an extreme offshoot of its own development and an ominous product of its own expansion. They are a deeply informative reflection of its own crisis. Totalitarian regimes are not merely dangerous neighbors and even less some kind of an avant-garde of world progress. Alas, just the opposite: they are the avant-garde of a global crisis of this civilization, first European, then Euro-American, and ultimately global.[55]

These modalities of the philosophical crisis discourse used by dissidents were rooted in the interwar criticism of instrumentalized rationalism. They were targeting not only Marxist ideological dogmatism but also the bureaucratism underpinning the regimes of "normalization" installed after the suppression of the movements toward democratization in the late 1960s. Nor did the consumerism of the Western welfare state escape this criticism.

By contrast, when reform-oriented technocrats turned to the concept of crisis, they looked to the West for a model to follow. They usually argued for the need to overhaul comprehensively the state's economic framework during the growing credit crunch of the late 1970s. This was felt strongly in many socialist countries, which had used the cheap money circulating globally after the oil price boom to finance their increasingly unprofitable economy. These resources were used to subsidize the production of industrial goods that could not be sold on the global market for hard currency, as well as to purchase Western consumer goods to sustain the feeling of a growing living standard and thus to secure political stability, since these regimes increasingly felt the loss of their legitimacy. It was in this context that some neoliberal ideas came to be adopted in the milieu of economic experts, especially around the financial apparatus and various planning institutes that orbited around the party leadership.[56]

In the 1980s, the perception of crisis became endemic in East Central Europe. It was used to denote both the systemic deterioration of the socioeconomic framework, and (like the situation of 1956 and 1968) the erupting political conflicts which challenged the Cold War *status quo*. Both meanings of crisis were simultaneously present in the Polish context. The latter was employed by the dissidents adhering to the Solidarity movement, emphasizing the moral and political disorientation of the country, while the former was used mainly by reformist experts who pushed for the depoliticization of the economy and pragmatic measures of crisis management. At the same time, those who defended the increasingly indefensible *status quo* sought to push the notion out of the public sphere. It is not accidental that the leading Polish punk band of the time chose the name *Brygada Kryzys* (Crisis Brigade), releasing

256   Intellectuals and the Crisis of Politics

their first, self-titled album in 1982, one year after the introduction of martial law. The authorities subsequently insisted they change their name, and as a result, they appeared for some time as *Brygada K.*

There were, however, more sophisticated apologists of the socialist regime who tried to subvert the anti-systemic connotations of crisis. In the context of the martial law, Aleksander Bocheński (1904–2001), a prominent intellectual fellow-traveler of the Polish communist regime who was socialized in the interwar conservative revolutionary milieu, published a volume ominously entitled *The Polish Crisis and the Crisis of Humanity.*[57] He did not deny that the country had undergone a serious political and economic crisis, but sought to put responsibility on the external and internal enemies of the regime: the Reagan administration and Solidarity. He drew on interwar nationalist tropes and intellectual references, including key ethno-nationalist ideologue Roman Dmowski (1864–1939), to castigate Polish society and especially the trade unions and the intelligentsia (i.e., the two main bases of the opposition) for undermining social discipline and thus exposing the Polish nation-state to an existential threat (Bocheński pointed to "German revanchism" as a source of danger). The period of martial law introduced by General Wojciech Jaruzelski (1923–2014) was thus a necessary measure of crisis management in Bocheński's view, and its Western critics, who appealed to human rights, dealt in double standards since they were much less eager to condemn the state of emergency introduced by the British government in Northern Ireland. The way out of the crisis, according to Bocheński, required the creation of a common platform between members of the Polish United Workers' Party and the broader non-communist masses and intelligentsia on a common national(ist) basis. The goal, then, would be to implement necessary economic reforms and create a synthesis of democracy and strong leadership, overcoming the traditional Polish propensity to anarchy.

The author did not stop at the borders of Poland and extended his interpretation toward recognizing a general crisis of humankind, manifested by the growing gap between rich and poor countries. Economic and scientific progress only served the interests of the select few, while others remained bound to the satisfaction of basic, biologically conditioned needs. In this way, a Catholic anti-modernist discourse could be conveniently merged with communist anticolonial rhetoric, morphing into some sort of anti-Western geopolitics and creating an ideological bridge between the interwar period and late socialist ethno-nationalism, both full of *ressentiment* against the "hypocritical West." Actually, the merger of these elements came to shape the "new right" in East Central Europe after the fall of the communist regime with lasting political consequences (and Bocheński himself lived long enough to have some personal impact on the re-emerging Polish radical right after 1989).

Apart from Poland, another pivotal context where crisis became a self-descriptive term (and, arguably, a self-fulfilling prophecy) of both the dissident and technocratic groups in the last decade of state socialism was Yugoslavia. Here, the national, economic, and institutional layers were intertwined in a particular way, making it possible to perform a mental shift from the analysis of a particular social, cultural, or economic sphere to an apocalyptic vision of the dissolution of the state.

Such visions appeared with greater frequency on the horizons of expectation of both the elites and the broader population, especially after the death of Tito in 1980.

By the mid-1980s, crisis indeed became a central notion of the Yugoslav political debate, reflecting both national and socioeconomic tensions.[58] One of the most resounding interventions linking these spheres was the book *System and Crisis*, written by Zagreb-based Serbian political scientist Jovan Mirić (1934–2015).[59] Mirić skillfully wove socioeconomic and institutional analyses together, frontally challenging the "inert" political system created by the 1974 Constitution that had introduced decentralization without democratization. He argued from a Yugoslavist position, which envisioned the gradual convergence of the constitutive units of the federal state into a common political and cultural entity. He contrasted the dynamic of European unification unfolding from the 1950s onward to the political and economic atomization of his own country: "While in the world today we bear witness to the integration of former enemies, we demonstrate 'Balkanization'—primitivism and disintegration."[60] In his understanding, the unfolding political, national, cultural, and economic crisis implied an "either–or" of thoroughgoing structural reforms versus the eruption of national divisions and eventually the collapse of the state.

With hindsight, this analysis was remarkably perceptive. Mirić identified the most powerful centrifugal forces that eventually played a role in the collapse of the state: the autarchic economic policies of the republics; paralysis in the decision-making system due to the veto power of each entity; the shrinking of the common public sphere; and the essentially non-democratic selection procedure of deputies in the federal parliament. However, his suggested remedies were problematic, overrating spontaneous processes of national homogenization (pointing to the growing number of citizens defining themselves as Yugoslavs, living especially in the big cities), and underrating popular commitment to the symbols and institutions of national self-government, describing them merely as instruments of the "natiocratic" elites who were empowered by the new constitution but were detached from the "real needs" of society. As such, Mirić's work exemplified a key feature of the crisis discourse of the late socialist intellectual elites, who could identify most of the key factors of the decomposition and delegitimization of the system but were torn between seeking to preserve whatever was worth preserving and suggesting a radically new alternative. As a result, their sophisticated conjectures were eventually overtaken and swiftly relegated to the past by the acceleration of historical time bringing along the cataclysmic changes of 1989–90.

History is Dead—Long Live Crisis?

The end of the Cold War and of the division of Europe in 1989 was rarely conceptualized in terms of crisis. The conceptual cluster of "revolution"—for example, "Self-Limiting Revolution," "Velvet Revolution," "Televised Revolution," "Negotiated Revolution," as well as the more skeptical *Nachholende Revolution*, that is,

258   Intellectuals and the Crisis of Politics

"Rectifying" or "'Catching-up' Revolution"—seemed to be more in line with the transformative intentions of key actors, who rather opted for the classical nineteenth-century imagery of removing an anachronistic political construction to open up an unlimited future (which in this case was meant to converge with that of "the West").

In the general euphoria over the rather unexpected fall of the Iron Curtain, various partisans of liberal democracy put forward their vision of a world that was supposed to overcome, once for all, systemic crises in the absence of any viable ideological alternative and in the context of the seemingly unstoppable expansion of globalization. At the same time, considering the growing awareness of the limitedness of resources, the future-oriented developmental vision proved increasingly untenable. Therefore, the triumphant global capitalist world order seemed to be suspended in the eternal present rather than striving for a final aim of history. In any case, for a short moment, the return of crisis on a global scale seemed to be unimaginable. At the same time, at the local level, it could be seen everywhere, not only in the post-communist East, which underwent a complex (and never-ending) process of readjustment to market economy (and in some cases also violent state disintegration), but also in some of the less predictable contexts. For example, Finland suddenly lost its profitable mediating position between the two camps from before 1989 and came to face an unexpectedly deep economic slump marked by the collapse of several banks and the palpable growth of social inequalities.[61]

While many of the local crises erupting in the late 1980s were eventually declared to have been overcome—or at least contained—those caused by the disintegration of Yugoslavia and the Soviet Union were left simmering, to be rekindled periodically. Further, the 1990s and 2000s saw the proliferation of crisis discourses in many different contexts, starting with the 1990–91 "Gulf Crisis." With its acute experience of the entanglement of external (geopolitical) and internal (political and socioeconomic) instability, Russian public discourse in the 1990s was particularly saturated by the tropes of crisis, chaos, and catastrophe.[62] Hitting the country in a moment of seeming stabilization, the 1998 financial crisis had particularly strong repercussions. A literary reflection of this is the self-styled poetic "rock opera" *Awful Crisis Super Star* by Andrey Voznesenskiy (1933–2010), the leading Russian poet of the late socialist and early post-transition period.[63] Ironically playing with the pop-cultural commodification of Jesus, Voznesenskiy painted a tableau of the omnipresence of crisis in Russian society, penetrating all spheres of life: "New melody, like a spiral, coils in the boulevard./We all are rock opera characters: Awful Crisis Super Star."[64]

But these discourses were not limited to the (semi-)peripheries of the new world order. Remarkably, Jan Marco Sawilla counted almost 3,000 publications appearing between 1990–2011 having crisis in the title.[65] At the same time, there was also an important shift: while most of the crises were geographically localized in the 1990s (even if they had transnational repercussions), after the turn of the millennium, the Great Recession of 2008 and the Covid-19 pandemic contributed to the globalization and synchronization of the crisis discourse, transcending national and disciplinary boundaries alike.

The expansion and "routinization" of the crisis discourse is also visible from the way it gradually became part of the language of policymaking. Thus, for instance, in 2021 the European Union's External Action Service issued the white paper "Cultural Heritage in Conflicts and Crises,"[66] while the New European Bauhaus project launched by the European Commission to tackle the challenges of climate change has been constantly framed in terms of the imagery of crisis. In one of her short introductory speeches on the project, Ursula von der Leyen recycled an apocryphal sentence by Einstein that went viral in the 2010s: "This pandemic changes the way we live and work. It changes our perspective on many things. But in every crisis also lies an opportunity."[67] Along these lines, crisis increasingly became a preferred buzzword of academic funding on the European level. For example, the Collaboration of Humanities and Social Sciences in Europe (CHANSE) and the Humanities in the European Research Area (HERA) issued a new call in 2023 entitled "Crisis—Perspectives from the Humanities" in order to "understand" crisis, problematize the concept, shape resilience in the face of crises, and assess the role of humanities in escalating and de-escalating them.[68]

The veritable flood of such texts and utterances in the last two decades should not be taken automatically as an indicator of a general crisis as such, rather the diffusion of the notion across the most variegated spheres, including economy, politics, sociology, social anthropology, psychology, and the environmental sciences. Arguably, this was also caused by transformation of the underlying temporal vision of contemporary social and political thinking, that is, a shift in the emphasis from the trope of progress/evolution to that of stagnation/suspension.[69]

In this context, different authors, representing highly divergent political positions, have come up with a variety of interpretations of the crisis of the liberal democratic world order that not long ago still seemed to be hegemonic, having emerged triumphantly from the Cold War. In fact, some of these voices derived crisis precisely from this seeming hegemony. A case in point is David Runciman's argument about the potentially self-defeating internal contradictions of the global ascendance of liberal democracy. In his reading, the current crisis "was born out of the success of democracy, not out of some ongoing external threat to it. In the first decade of the twenty-first century democracy confronted no serious ideological rivals."[70] According to Runciman, the cause of this crisis was thus inherent to the way democratic political cultures handle challenges:

> The period from 1989 to 2008 was marked by continuity and rupture. The continuity was in economic affairs. The rupture was in international affairs. Continuity is bad for democracies because it produces complacency and drift. Rupture is bad for democracies because it produces impulsiveness and aggression. The combination proved toxic.[71]

At the same time, Runciman did not intend to create an image of general doom: he admitted that the impact of crisis "was neither consistent nor uniform: some democracies fared much better than others."[72]

By contrast, writing in the immediate aftermath of the 2008 Financial Crisis, David Harvey drew on Marxist theoretical precepts to describe crisis as a transformative moment in socioeconomic development: "Financial crises serve to rationalise the irrationalities of capitalism. They typically lead to reconfigurations, new models of development, new spheres of investment and new forms of class power."[73] Along these lines, for Harvey, the principal question was whether it was possible to turn this global crisis into a starting point of a structural change to overcome capitalism: "Whether we can get out of this crisis in a different way depends very much upon the balance of class forces. It depends upon the degree to which the mass of the population rises up and says, 'Enough is enough, let's change this system."[74]

Operating with yet another historical and theoretical model, Elemér Hankiss (1928–2015), a Hungarian cultural sociologist and prominent political analyst of the transition period, also turned to crisis as a key interpretative framework of European civilization. In some ways, he extended his pre-1989 crisis discourse focusing on "really existing socialism" to more global dimensions, developing an holistic philosophical anthropology and linking the interwar references, such as Jaspers or Ortega y Gasset, to the critical social theories of the 1980s and 1990s.[75] Along these lines, Hankiss emphasized the need to add a historical dimension to the analysis of the economic, social, and cultural features of crisis, thus inserting them into a more comprehensive landscape of civilizational transformation and putting forward the idea of a "new axial age." Tellingly, for the Hungarian author the transitions of 1989–90 still signaled the moment of the triumph of modernism (characterized by a feeling of a stable "world order," "Pax Americana," "global peace," the possibility of "unlimited progress," etc.), which he contrasted to global "chaos," the loss of Western dominance, "unsustainable development," and the rise of new nationalisms and fundamentalisms.

The omnipresence of the crisis discourse, especially after 2008, thus raised the question of the relevance of historical references, especially regarding the interwar discussions, for understanding contemporary developments. The parallels drawn between the interwar economic crisis and the developments of the early twenty-first century were perceived as increasingly plausible. For example, in the updated version of his 1999 *The Return of Depression Economics* (which originally focused on the Asian financial crisis), Paul Krugman accentuated the many parallels between the interwar and the post-2008 situation, describing "depression economics" in terms of dealing with the "failures on the demand side of the economy."[76] Krugman's straightforward practical recommendations to attenuate the crisis ("get credit flowing again and prop up spending")[77] also resonated with at least one possible reading of the lessons of the Great Depression.

Back in the 1990s, such historical parallels between interwar and post-1989 phenomena were pointed out much less frequently. An early occurrence was Rogers Brubaker's heuristic metaphor of "Weimar Russia"[78] which turned out to be highly relevant well after the academic discussion around it had ended in the late 1990s. When the analogies with interwar phenomena became more prevalent in the early 2000s in other contexts too, several common traits were identified (e.g., political polarization, radical nationalism, ideological disorientation, international instability and fragmentation, economic protectionism, and the decline of liberalism). Underlying it all was the conceptual proliferation of the notion of crisis in all possible spheres of life. Thus, one can find not only analyses of political, ecological, or economic crises, but also references to the crisis of all imaginable and unimaginable human activities and commodities, from the "crisis of care"[79] to the "cost of living crisis"[80] and down to the "crisis of French foie gras."[81] Second, as in the interwar period, the idea that different sectoral crises are converging, and thus mutually catalyzing each other, has become increasingly dominant.[82] Third, there is an increasing theoretical effort on the meta-level focusing on the art of crisis-management as a central political competence.[83]

Tellingly, already back in 2004, BBC Two aired a "role-playing interactive drama documentary" with the title *Crisis Command*, where the players had to assume the role of "ministers" tasked with responding to various imaginary crisis situations (a terrorist attack, a natural disaster, an epidemic) in consultation with (real) military and communication experts.[84] At the same time, with all of this anticipation of crisis in political thought and in popular culture, there seems to be no comprehensive theory of crisis available—also because it is increasingly hard to say what would be a "non-crisis."[85] Thus, on the whole, crisis has turned into an underlying condition and permanent reference point for most spheres of life without, however, too much intellectual engagement with its actual meaning. In fact, even the inference from the Koselleckian interpretation that the proliferation of notions of crisis might well indicate (or even constitute) the crisis (of political modernity) seems to be rather infrequently made.

Continuities, Ruptures, and Entanglements from an "Enlarged" European Perspective

Arguably, one of the main reasons for this seemingly contradictory situation—the omnipresence of the crisis discourse and the relatively limited theoretical engagement and conceptual rigor—is the powerful presence of two ideological streams: neoliberalism and populism. These streams focus on, and in some ways are genealogically linked to, the concept of crisis. Precisely because the concept of crisis is so constitutive for their self-legitimization and self-perpetuation, it is also a blind spot that cannot be critically examined from within these ideological contexts. Further, it is precisely through this discursive framework of crisis that these ideological streams, usually considered to be diametrically opposed, are entangled.

In fact, after 2000, it has been repeatedly pointed out by observers representing different disciplinary and ideological traditions that the discourse of crisis provided a conceptual framework for ideological streams that seemed to be mutually incompatible at first sight. Moreover, their adherents often perceived each other as the main cause of the crisis. This was not unrelated to the fact that, as mentioned in previous chapters, these two ideological streams exerting a major impact on the post-1989 world had a special relationship with the interwar crisis discourse. They were rooted in a historical moment considered particularly crisis-ridden, and their adherents tended to frame them as the only possible solution to this crisis.

Thus, the question of the actual continuities with the interwar forms of these ideological streams and movements is a particularly hard nut to crack. To be sure, recent secondary literature, especially in the domain of political science, often describes both as radically new. If we take populism, there has been a widely shared assumption that, to understand the politics of Pim Fortuyn, Silvio Berlusconi, Christoph Blocher, Viktor Orbán, Jörg Haider, or Jean-Marie and Marine Le Pen, it is more or less irrelevant to look at previous political movements or actors who called themselves populist (*völkisch, narodnik, népi*, etc.). This argument is often predicated upon the understanding that populism is a question of attitude—a specific political style that can parasitize any content precisely because it contains no ideological core whatsoever.

More interestingly, scholars with a keen historical sense, who considered populism to possess a certain ideological profile and historicity also questioned the relevance of the longer-term ideological traditions shaping these notions. Devising a morphology based on a normative definition of populism, Jan-Werner Müller made a strong case for excluding the two late nineteenth-century movements (the American Populists and the Russian *narodniki*) from his analysis, both of which arguably lent their names to this contemporary ideological stream.[86] Likewise, while seeking to reconstruct the French conceptual threads, Pierre Rosanvallon had a hard time establishing a link between modern populism and the concept of *populiste* in the French interwar context, as the notion appeared mainly in the literary milieu (here, Rosanvallon pointed to the 1929 *Manifeste du roman populiste* of Léon Lemonnier, 1890–1953). The *Prix Eugene Dabit*, established in 1931 to reward "populist writers," could hardly serve as a reliable ideological compass either, since it was subsequently given to writers like Jean-Paul Sartre.[87]

On the other hand, a hyper-historicizing tendency that locates populism in all possible modern and pre-modern contexts is visible, drawing a line from "*populariter agere*" in ancient Roman urban politics through Machiavelli and Savonarola all the way to National Socialism as parts of a *longue durée* populist tradition.[88] Such an effort at historicization might eventually become ahistorical, as it makes it very hard to take any context into account and thus the referentiality to the very notion of the people as the common thread becomes rather thin. (What connects the ancient Roman *populus*, the French revolutionary *peuple*, and the racial understanding of the German *Volk*?)

Beyond the question of historical roots and continuities, any interpretation of populist discourse is further complicated by significant regional divergences. In Western and Northern Europe, populist components were identified across various competing interwar ideological camps, from social democracy to conservatism and fascism. In East Central Europe, however, populism emerged, mainly within the framework of agrarian populism, as a separate ideological stream. Consequently, East Central European scholars tended to be more keen on establishing the continuities of these ideological threads, since the discursive tropes that constituted the turn-of-century and interwar agrarian and ethnopopulist traditions could be easily recognized in the political discourse of the anti-systemic contenders of the 1990s.[89] For a Hungarian observer, the resonance of the discourse of the post-transition radical right with interwar populist (*népi*) ideology did not require much elucidation, since the actors themselves often framed their discourse in terms of such a continuity. Likewise, for a Serbian historian, both the systemic and the anti-systemic versions of the ethno-populist ideology of the 1990s showed affinities with the populist tradition of the late nineteenth century and with the People's Radical Party (*Narodna radikalna stranka*) in particular.[90] However, these resonances were less obvious for scholars beyond the East Central European historiographical orbit due to the persistent dividing lines of competence that survived well after the fall of the Iron Curtain. It is symptomatic that, while Ernest Gellner and Ghiţă Ionescu's 1969 edited work on populism remained a staple reference for most scholars dealing with the phenomenon, the substantial part of the book dealing with Russia and Eastern Europe was usually neglected in deference to a more general interpretations of populism—even though the editors themselves both had East Central European roots.[91]

What further complicated the question of continuities, even in the East Central European context, is the ambiguous relationship between agrarian and ethnic populism: in the interwar context, agrarian populists could be highly critical of nationalism. This ambiguity contributed to the academic debate launched by Gellner and Ionescu on the question whether agrarianism (alternatively termed "peasantism") could be equated with populism at all. Further, the resonance of interwar populist ideologies and movements was predicated upon the existence of dominantly agrarian societies, that were substantially transformed and partly eliminated after 1945. After 1989, then, populists rarely focused on the peasantry alone, even if some of them still led nominally "agrarian" parties (as was the case with Hungarian József Torgyán and his Independent Smallholders' Party in the 1990s). Overall, due to programs of forced industrialization and urbanization, in these countries the agrarian majority gradually evaporated. While in the interwar period 75% of Poland's population could be qualified as rural, in the 1960s it was around half; in 2010 it was just below 40%, which was still the highest in the European Union. All of this made it increasingly problematic to sustain a political discourse that identified the peasantry with the people as the holder of national (or even state) sovereignty.

Beyond East Central Europe, the agrarian connections of modern populism were less obvious, although not completely missing. For instance, the Swiss People's Party (*Schweizerische Volkspartei*, SVP)—one of the paradigmatic populist parties in Europe after 1990—adopted peasantist elements from its institutional predecessor, the *Bauern-, Gewerbe- und Bürgerpartei*, founded in 1936 on the basis of various cantonal peasant parties. While the genealogical lineage is more complicated, the Freedom Party of Austria (*Freiheitliche Partei Österreichs*, FPÖ) can also be linked to the interwar agrarian populist *Landbund* through the former's post-Second World War offshoot, the *Verband der Unabhängigen*.

This mismatch of historical points of reference was also caused by further divergences in the ideological alliances of modern populists in different national contexts. While the left-wing links and components of populism were more obvious for scholars in and of Eastern Europe or Latin America (and to some extent also of Southern Europe), in the Western European cases the most studied entanglement of populism has been with far-right agendas. Attempts to extend this to other ideological types, for example, framing it as part of a family of "beyond left and right" discourses, has been less common, although not entirely missing. For instance, German political scientist and historian Karin Priester (1941–2020) described populism as a "third way" ideology, which in her understanding meant a curious mixture of political anarchism and a conservative way of thinking (*Denkstil*).[92] However, left-wing associations remained less plausible for most scholars focusing on Western Europe, and only with the rise of movements like the Greek Syriza and the Spanish Podemos was the discussion extended to investigate the link between populism and leftist ideological streams.[93]

In contrast to populism (on the surface at least), the historical trajectory of neoliberalism bridging the interwar and postwar periods was less controversial. This is mainly because its key interwar representatives, both in the Anglo-American and the German political and intellectual contexts, also played an important role in the debate about the desirable limits of state intervention in the 1950s and 1960s. In scholarly literature, after Michel Foucault's pioneering investigations, a series of authors contributed to tracing the continuities and networks of neoliberalism, moving well beyond one-sided condemnatory or hagiographic approaches.[94]

These divergences in historicization and localization made it rather complicated for scholars to devise a common framework of interpretation for populism and neoliberalism. At the same time, from the 2000s onward, there was an increasing sentiment of such an entanglement in the political life of various countries. A recurrent interpretative strategy seeking to identify possible causal links between populism and neoliberalism is based on the assumption that the triumph of neoliberal politics in the 1980s was the trigger for the emergence of populism.[95] In the East Central European context, this was articulated in a compelling way by Ivan Krastev and Stephen Holmes, who derived the rise of populism and the disintegration of the liberal consensus from a "deep-seated disgust at a perceived post-1989 imitation imperative."[96]

However, many observers pointed to the mutual interdependence of these two streams, notwithstanding the seeming causal relationship of neoliberalism being the catalyst of the populist backlash. According to Michael A. Wilkinson, "Authoritarian liberalism is now fomenting the politics of an authoritarian populism that it was meant to prevent, but with which it appears to be mutually dependent."[97] A more radical argument along these lines is that populism and neoliberalism are the two sides of the same coin of (post-)modern politics. An influential intervention along these lines, linking them to the crisis *problématique*, is Zygmunt Bauman's (1925–2017) and Carlo Bordoni's dialogical book *State of Crisis*,[98] in which the authors point to the fall of Keynesianism as the context in which a new crisis-ridden politics emerged, with citizens losing their agency and turning to pseudo-solutions providing an "illusion of participation." Neoliberalism contributed to this by delegating most responsibilities of the welfare state to the private sector. For Bordoni, this indicates a crisis of modernity, marked by the withdrawal of its promises of security, control over nature, and vision of a welfare state. For Bauman, it is rather the illusions of modernity that are abandoned. The authors added to this the crisis of the nation-state (for Bordoni, the "post-Westphalian state model"), that is, an endemic conflict between the national electorate and global politics. According to the authors, the rise of global threats, without an adequate institutional and mental framework to respond on a global level, generated a retreat to national solutions which in turn aggravated the crisis.

Central to Bauman and Bordoni's argument is that in the postmodern condition crisis is not a transitional phenomenon, but rather something that is permanent and prone to catalyze recurrent waves of anti-systemic populism. However, due to its focus on postmodern politics, Bauman and Bordoni's analysis of the interplay of populism and neoliberalism lacked a more longitudinal historical perspective going beyond the last few decades, and the authors did not engage with the longer-term entanglements of these two streams.

The intimate link of these ideologies to crisis discourses was noticed by other scholars as well. Priester called populism the "child of crisis," resulting from broken communication channels between elites and the people.[99] Rather than describing populism as a mere counter-reaction to neoliberalism, Priester also observed that there were deeper similarities, most importantly the affinity with the neoliberal push for deregulation and the rejection of the Keynesian ("social democratic") state. She also pointed to several populist sub-streams and politicians whose anti-étatist drives resonated with neoliberalism, especially Berlusconi and France's Bernard Tapié, whom she described as "anarcho-capitalists." In turn, Rosanvallon distinguished quasi-leftist and quasi-neoliberal variants of populism, which he believed had many conceptual convergences even though their stance to immigration remained a dividing line between them.[100] From his perspective, Jean-Marie Le Pen's critique of "too much state" is indicative of right-wing populism's possible (neo)liberal direction, while Marine Le Pen's emphasis on protectionism points the other—étatist—way.

Informed by the experience of Trumpism, Adam Przeworski reframed the causal model and derived the "crisis of democracy" precisely from the entanglement of neoliberalism and populism[101] while asserting that "populism is an ideological twin of neo-liberalism."[102] However, in contrast to Bauman and Bordoni, for Przeworski (who pointed to Gramsci's *Prison Notebooks* for an analogous understanding) crisis is more of a "state of suspension" between old and new forms with an open-ended outcome—an ominous period marked by the possibility, although not necessarily the actuality, of radical transformation.[103] In this sense, he did not associate the crisis of democracy with an imminent collapse, but more with a slow erosion due to creeping illiberal tendencies. While he also stressed the importance of inserting different crisis phenomena into a historical framework, in Przeworski's interpretation historical reconstruction served more as a basis for a diachronic comparison with previous instances of destabilization rather than the analysis of continuities and ruptures.[104] Tellingly, the key factors of crisis he identified were structural, for example, the collapse of the traditional party system, the rise of xenophobia, and the decline of popular support for democratic politics.

Moving beyond the commonly scrutinized contexts of the Western hemisphere gives an even more complex picture. While the intimate relationship of populism

266 Intellectuals and the Crisis of Politics

and neoliberalism was noticed relatively recently by scholarship dealing with Western Europe and the United States, it was much more central in literature dealing with Latin America or Eastern Europe. Among the experts on Latin America, this "intimate relationship" was already part of scholarly discussion in the 1990s, with the rise of populist politicians like Peru's Alberto Fujimori (in office 1990–2000) or Argentina's Carlos Menem (in office 1989–99), who both combined a commitment to free-market ideology (in reality peppered with crony capitalism); a focus on the "common people" counterposed to the traditional elites; a propensity for personalized and mediatized politics; and often a strong cultural and political narrative that hammered against local leftist traditions, labeling them all summarily as "communist."[105]

In East Central Europe, the 1990s were dominated by a liberal consensus that was institutionalist and anti-populist. These positions were determined by a fear of the possible demagogical instrumentalization of the economic hardships of the transition by former communists and the "old–new" nationalists. In turn, the most emblematic autocratic populists of the period (e.g., Slovakia's Vladimír Mečiar or Serbia's Slobodan Milošević) were markedly anti-liberal in cultural, political, and economical terms. As a result, the discussion on the intertwining of populism and neoliberalism only became more vivid after 2000.[106] On the one hand, some critics of the transition from the left (both locally and in international academic milieux) argued that the emerging populist backlash was due to the liberal transition elites' insensitivity (or "betrayal") of the social issue and their focus mainly on political and human rights while neglecting the plight of the working class, hit by rapid de-industrialization after 1989. On the other hand, the region experienced a significant rise in populist authoritarianism after the turn of the millennium, going together with several specific institutional practices (e.g., workfare, the crushing of free education, and selective austerity measures used as a weapon against the adversaries of these regimes), which catalyzed a growing literature on the concealed or overt neoliberal features of these regimes. In this context, Hungary and Poland were the most unexpected (and therefore most discussed) cases in terms of an autocratic backlash, sometimes together with Serbia,[107] and several other—arguably less coherent and less successful—authoritarian regime-building attempts in Slovenia, North Macedonia, Bulgaria, and Slovakia.

All this became increasingly palpable in Western Europe as well. In fact, from this transnational perspective, phenomena like the intertwining of the far-right Alternative for Germany (AfD) with the Ordoliberal tradition—through Bayreuth professor of economics Peter Oberender (1941–2015), co-editor of the journal *Ordo*, critique of the Euro, and supporter of the liberalization of organ trade—becomes less surprising. Importantly, the 2005 "Hamburg Appeal" initiated by future AfD founder Bernd Lucke and signed by 243 economists, among them Oberender, started with the image of a "deep structural crisis" in Germany, demanding "drastic and painful reforms."[108] The text was full of neoliberal ideological references, such as the support for globalization, critique of high wages, and arguments for cutting taxes to make the society more competitive. Furthermore, Oberender was *Doktorvater* to

Long Shadows of the Interwar Crises   **267**

Alice Weidel, a key politician of the extreme-right wing German party. In her parliamentary interventions, Weidel also keeps referring to crisis and more dramatically to "long-lasting crisis" (*Dauerkrise*), which could only be overcome by "returning to reason": stopping mass immigration, social subsidies, state funding for climate projects, and international development help.[109]

In all these cases, the concept of crisis plays an important role both in the legitimization of these authoritarian projects and the interpretative literature on them. As a rule, the political positions of apologists for these autocratic regimes and ideological streams were diametrically opposed to those of academic analysts. But they did concur when it came to the idea that these anti-liberal endeavors signaled the crisis of the transplantation of liberal democratic institutions and ideologies from "the West" to contexts with markedly different political traditions and economic preconditions. Further, they also tended to agree that the apparent failure of this process was part and parcel of the global crisis of the liberal democratic model of government.

This interplay of perceived local and global crisis phenomena both in the ideological and analytical literature exposes the need to consider the multiplicity of perspectives and regional dynamics when trying to assess the complex entanglement of populism and neoliberalism with each other and with the discourse of crisis. If one seeks to devise a truly European story, one should not extrapolate from a single case but try to compare various trajectories and remain open to surprises coming from unexpected geographical or intellectual directions. Such a perspective also has moral and political implications in the sense that it makes it less convincing to pathologize certain contexts from the comfortable position of assumed "normality." Contexts beyond Western Europe can thus serve not as "peripheries" of the mainstream paradigms, but laboratories of ideas and practices (both liberal and illiberal) that might have global repercussions. There is no "safe space" in this respect. The entanglements of populism and neoliberalism with crisis discourses, analyzed in this book, are present as actualities or potentialities everywhere in Europe, and engaging with them critically remains imperative for political thought and action in the North, South, West, and East of the continent alike.

Notes

1. In his "Die Krise als epochenmachende Begriff," for instance, Rüdiger Graf talks about the "decline" of this discourse after 1945.
2. On the postwar political and intellectual reconfiguration of Europe, Tony Judt's *Postwar: A History of Europe Since 1945* (New York: Penguin Press, 2005) remains a compelling master-narrative.
3. President Harry Truman's 1947 speech asking Congress for military and economic assistance for Greece and Turkey, which is considered to be the articulation of what came to be known as "Truman Doctrine," also used the notion of crisis to underpin the urgency of American engagement. See https://www.archives.gov/milestone-documents/truman-doctrine (accessed on April 30, 2023).

268 Intellectuals and the Crisis of Politics

4. Wilhelm Röpke, "Die Natur der Internationalen Krisis" (1945), in *Marktwirtschaft ist nicht genug: Gesammelte Aufsätze* (Lüdinghausen: Manuscriptum, 2009), 29–38.

5. István Bibó, "A magyar demokrácia válsága [The Crisis of Hungarian Democracy]," *Valóság* 1, no. 2–4 (1945): 5–43.

6. Ibid., 5. An unpublished English translation, used here, was prepared by Péter Pásztor. The more literal translation of the first sentence would be: "Living in fear, Hungarian democracy is in crisis."

7. In 1945, Hungary had a postwar coalition government which included all major parties: the communists, social democrats, agrarian populists, and the centrist "Smallholders." Traditional right-wing parties were not allowed to contest the elections. On the political context, see Peter Kenez, *Hungary from the Nazis to the Soviets: The Establishment of the Communist Regime in Hungary, 1944–1948* (Cambridge: Cambridge University Press, 2006).

8. For the debate on Bibó's article, see György Lukács et al., "Vita demokráciánk válságáról [Debate on the Crisis of Our Democracy]," *Valóság* 2, no. 1–2 (1946): 86–103.

9. See E. Varga, Изменения в экономике капитализма в итоге второй мировой войны [Changes in the Capitalist Economy as a Result of the Second World War] (Moscow: Госполитиздат, 1946).

10. Michael Polanyi, "British Crisis (1947?)," *Polanyiana* 23, no. 1–2 (2014): 64.

11. See Michael Polanyi, "Social Capitalism," *Time and Tide* 13 (April 13, 1946): 341–2.

12. Polanyi, "British Crisis," 64.

13. Paul E. Zinner, ed., *National Communism and Popular Revolt in Eastern Europe: A Selection of Documents on Events in Poland and Hungary, February–November 1956* (New York: Columbia University Press, 1956), 30.

14. Ibid., 189.

15. Ibid., 263.

16. Ibid., 430.

17. See *Ellenforradalmi erők a magyar októberi eseményekben* [Counter-Revolutionary Forces in the Hungarian October Events], vols. 1–4 (Budapest: Magyar Népköztársaság Minisztertanácsa Tájékoztatási Hivatala, 1957).

18. Edouard Perroy, "À l'origine d'une économie contractée: les crises du XIVe siècle," *Annales E.S.C.* 4 (1949): 167–82.

19. Hans Baron, *The Crisis of the Early Italian Renaissance: Civic Humanism and Republican Liberty in an Age of Classicism and Tyranny* (Princeton: Princeton University Press, 1955).

20. Eric J. Hobsbawm, "The General Crisis of the European Economy in the 17th Century," *Past & Present* 5 (1954): 33–53.

21. Hugh R. Trevor-Roper, "The General Crisis of the 17th Century," *Past & Present* 16 (1959): 31–64. See also the discussion on the text, with a rejoinder from Hobsbawm, in "Discussion of H. R. Trevor-Roper: 'The General Crisis of the Seventeenth Century,'" *Past & Present* 18 (1960): 8–42.

22. On the historiographical use of the concept of crisis in the 1950s, see Cesare Cuttica, László Konlter, and Clara Maier, "Introduction," in Cesare Cuttica and László Kontler, with Clara Maier, eds., *Crisis and Renewal in the History of European Political Thought* (Leiden: Brill, 2012), 1–22.

23. For a good overview of the Polish debate, see Anna Sosnowska, *Explaining Economic Backwardness. Post-1945 Polish Historians on Eastern Europe* (Budapest: CEU Press,

2019). In the 1950s, these economic historians also took part in the debate on the agrarian crisis of the fourteenth century, arguing that the crisis in the Western part of the continent was more dramatic. See, e.g., Marian Małowist, "Zagadnienie kryzysu feudalizmu w XIV i XV w. w świetle najnowszych badań," [The Problem of the Crisis of Feudalism in the 14th and 15th Centuries in the Light of Recent Studies] *Kwartalnik Historyczny* 60, no.1 (1953): 86–106.

24. Reinhart Koselleck, *Kritik und Krise: Ein Beitrag zur Pathogenese der Bürgerlichen Welt* (Freiburg–Munich: Alber, 1959). Koselleck submitted his dissertation to the University of Heidelberg in 1954.

25. On the intellectual context of Koselleck's early work, see Sebastian Huhnholz, *Von Carl Schmitt zu Hannah Arendt? Heidelberger Entstehungsspuren und bundesrepublikanische Liberalisierungsschichten von Reinhart Kosellecks* Kritik und Krise (Berlin: Duncker & Humblot, 2019).

26. See, e.g., Nicolaus Sombart, *Krise und Planung: Studien zur Entwicklungsgeschichte des menschlichen Selbstverständnisses in der globalen Ära* (Frankfurt: Europa Verlag, 1965).

27. Hannah Arendt, "The Crisis in Education," in *Between Past and Future: Six Exercises in Political Thought* (New York: The Viking Press, 1961), 173–96.

28. Hannah Arendt, "The Crisis of Culture: Its Social and Its Political Significance," in ibid., 197–226. Parts were originally published as "Society and Culture," *Daedalus* 89, no. 2 (1960): 278–87.

29. Hannah Arendt, *Crises of the Republic* (New York: Harcourt Brace & Company, 1972).

30. Arendt, "The Crisis in Education," 173.

31. Ibid., 174.

32. Ibid.

33. See Philippe Braillard, "New Political Values for a World in Crisis: The Approach of the Club of Rome," *International Political Science Review* 3, no. 2 (1982): 238–45.

34. Donella H. Meadows, Dennis L. Meadows, Jørgen Randers, and William W. Behrens III, *The Limits to Growth: A Report for the Club of Rome's Project on the Predicament of Mankind* (New York: Universe Books, 1972), 52, 51.

35. Edgar Morin, "Pour une crisologie," *Communications* 25 (1976): 149–63. This issue was dedicated to "La notion de crise."

36. See Angus Burgin, *The Great Persuasion: Reinventing Free Markets Since the Depression* (Cambridge, MA: Harvard University Press, 2012), 152–85. It is indicative of the shift of intellectual trends in the 1970s that Hayek received the Nobel Prize in 1974 (shared with the social democratic Gunnar Myrdal), while Friedman received it in 1976.

37. On Hayek's changing intellectual position, see Antonio Magliulo, "Hayek and the Great Depression of 1929: Did He Really Change His Mind?" *The European Journal of the History of Economic Thought* 23, no. 1 (2016): 31–58, here 52ff.

38. Jürgen Habermas, *Legitimation Crisis* (Cambridge: Polity Press, 1988 [1973]), 1.

39. Tanja Klenk and Frank Nullmeier, "Politische Krisentheorien und die Renaissance von Konjunkturprogrammen," *dms—der moderne staat—Zeitschrift für Public Policy, Recht und Management* 2 (2010): 275–6.

40. Michel Crozier, Samuel P. Huntington, and Joji Watanuki, *The Crisis of Democracy: Report on the Governability of Democracies to the Trilateral Commission* (New York: New York University Press, 1975).

41. Ibid., 4.

42. Ibid., 8.

270 Intellectuals and the Crisis of Politics

43. Karel Kosík's "Naše nynejší krize" was published as a series in *Literární listy* in 1968, republished in English translation as Karel Kosík, "Our Current Crisis," in James H. Satterwhite, ed., *The Crisis of Modernity: Essays and Observations from the 1968 Era* (Lanham: Rowman & Littlefield Publishers, 1995), 17–51.

44. Kosík, "Our Current Crisis," 17.

45. Ibid., 25.

46. Ibid., 30.

47. Kosík, "Socialism and the Crisis of Modern Man," in ibid., 53.

48. Ibid., 18.

49. Ibid., 24.

50. Ibid., 32.

51. Ibid., 50.

52. Ibid., 44.

53. Ivan Sviták, "Vaše nynější krize [Your Current Crisis]," in *Kulatý čtverec: Dialektika demokratizace 1968–1969* [The Round Square: Dialectics of Democratization, 1968–69] (Prague: Naše vojsko, 1990), 53. It was delivered as a speech on April 18, 1968. Note the play on Kosík's (and Masaryk's) original title.

54. Raymond Taras, "The Crisis of Ideology and the Ideology of Crisis: Marxist Critiques of the Polish Socialist System 1956–90," in Michael E. Urban, ed., *Ideology and System Change in the USSR and East Europe: selected papers from the Fourth World Congress for Soviet and East European Studies* (New York: St. Martin's Press, 1992), 162.

55. The essay first appeared in Czech in 1984. Erazim Kohák and Roger Scruton translated it into English for the *Salisbury Review* 2 (January 1985).

56. Joanna Bockmann, *Markets in the Name of Socialism: The Left-Wing Origins of Neoliberalism* (Stanford: Stanford University Press, 2011); Attila Antal, *Chicago a Dimitrov téren: Neoliberalizmus és a Kádár-rendszer* [Chicago at Dimitrov Square: Neoliberalism and the Kádár Regime] (Budapest: Napvilág Kiadó, 2021).

57. Aleksander Bocheński, *Kryzys Polski i kryzys ludzkości* [The Polish Crisis and the Crisis of Humanity] (Warsaw: Państwowy Instytut Wydawniczy, 1982).

58. An excellent overview of the changing horizons of expectation in the Serbian context is Jasna Dragovic-Soso, *Saviours of the Nation: Serbia's Intellectual Opposition and the Revival of Nationalism* (Montreal: McGill-Queen's University Press, 2002).

59. Jovan Mirić, *Sistem i kriza: Prilog kritičkoj analizi ustavnog i političkog sistema Jugoslavije* [System and Crisis. A Contribution to the Critical Analysis of the Constitutional and Political System of Yugoslavia] (Zagreb: Cekade, 1984).

60. Ibid., 87.

61. For an overview of the "Finnish crisis" in a Nordic comparative context, see Seppo Honkapohja, "The 1990's Financial Crises in Nordic Countries," *Bank of Finland Research Discussion Papers* 5 (Helsinki: Bank of Finland, 2009). For the somewhat comparable Swedish context, leading to the crumbling of the social democratic welfare-state, see Jane Jenson and Rianne Mahon, "Representing Solidarity: Class, Gender and the Crisis in Social-Democratic Sweden," *New Left Review* 201 (1993): 76–100.

62. For an analysis of the ways crisis was framed and managed in the post-transition Russian context, see Olga Shevchenko, *Crisis and the Everyday in Postsocialist Moscow* (Bloomington: Indiana University Press, 2009).

63. Andrey Voznesenskiy, *Жуткий Crisis Супер стар: Новые стихи и поэмы, 1998—1999* [Awful Crisis Super Star: New Poetry and Poems] (Moscow: Teppa, 1999).

64. Translation and contextualization by Olga Shevchenko in her "Awful Crisis Superstar: Disasters and Routinization," *Etnografia e Ricerca Qualitativa* 2 (2015): 301.

65. Jan Marco Sawilla, "Zwischen Normabweichung und Revolution—'Krise' in der Geschichtswissenschaft," in Carla Meyer, Katja Patzel-Mattern, and Gerrit Casper Schenk, eds., *Krisengeschichte(n). 'Krise' als Leitbegriff und Erzählmuster in kulturwissenschaftlicher Perspektive* (Stuttgart: Franz Steiner Verlag, 2013), 145–72.

66. European External Action Service, "Cultural Heritage in Conflicts and Crises: A Component for Peace and Security in European Union's External Action," April 19, 2021, available at https://data.consilium.europa.eu/doc/document/ST-9962-2021-INIT/en/pdf

67. Ursula von der Leyen, "Speech by President von der Leyen to the Global Forum of Local Governments on the New European Bauhaus," Brussels, December 3, 2020, available at https://ec.europa.eu/commission/presscorner/detail/en/SPEECH_20_2298

68. Humanities in the European Research Area (HERA), "Crisis: Perspectives from the Humanities," Proposal Announcement, January 16, 2024, available at https://heranet.info/funding/current-funding-opportunities/crisis-perspectives-from-the-humanities/

69. Helge Jordheim and Einar Wigen, "Conceptual Synchronisation: from Progress to Crisis," *Millennium: Journal of International Studies* 46, no. 3 (2018): 421–39.

70. David Runciman, *The Confidence Trap: A History of Democracy in Crisis from World War I to the Present* (Princeton: Princeton University Press, 2015), 266.

71. Ibid., 268.

72. Ibid., 27.

73. David Harvey, *The Enigma of Capital and the Crises of Capitalism* (New York: Oxford University Press, 2010), 11.

74. Ibid., 12.

75. Elemér Hankiss, "Európa, két világ közt [Europe, Between Two Worlds]," *Magyar Tudomány* 174, no. 11 (2013): 1386–95.

76. Paul Krugman, *The Return of Depression Economics and the Crisis of 2008* (New York: Norton, 2009), 182.

77. Ibid., 184.

78. Rogers Brubaker, *Nationalism Reframed: Nationhood and the National Question in the New Europe* (Cambridge: Cambridge University Press, 1996), 107–47.

79. Emma Dowling, *The Care Crisis. What Caused It and How Can We End It?* (London: Verso, 2022).

80. In 2022 alone, see, e.g., Kat Watson et al., "Cost of Living Crisis: Relying on Food Handouts and Moving Country," *BBC News*, May 30, 2022, available at https://www.bbc.com/news/world-61584608; John Harris, "The Decade That Broke Britain: The Disastrous Decisions That Left Millions in a Cost of Living Crisis," *The Guardian*, June 1, 2022, available at https://www.theguardian.com/politics/2022/jun/01/the-decade-that-broke-britain-the-disastrous-decisions-that-left-millions-in-a-cost-of-living-crisis; and Laura Howard, "Cost of Living Crisis: Second Cost of Living Payment Rolls Out to Low Income Households," *Forbes Advisor*, article updated November 8, 2022, available at https://www.forbes.com/uk/advisor/energy/cost-of-living-crisis. In addition, the *Financial Times* maintains a sub-categorization of its articles entitled "Cost of Living Crisis," available at https://www.ft.com/cost-of-living-crisis

81. Xu Xiaofei, "Michelin Menus in Turmoil as France Faces Foie Gras Crisis," *CNN Travel*, May 7, 2022, available at https://edition.cnn.com/travel/article/france-foie-gras-crisis/index.html

82. For a concise argument along these lines, see Jeremy Adelman and Anne-Laure Delatte, "The Crisis of Our Crises," *Project Syndicate*, September 7, 2015, available at https://www.project-syndicate.org/commentary/global-crises-international-integration-by-jeremy-adelman-and-anne-laure-delatte-2015-09

83. One can even purchase crisis management software for one's company at https://murphysolution.com/

84. See "Crisis Command," BBC, TV Series, 2004, available at https://www.imdb.com/title/tt0426344/

85. See Michael Freeden, "Crisis? How Is That a Crisis!?" *Contributions to the History of Concepts* 12, no. 2 (2017): 15.

86. See Jan-Werner Müller, *What is Populism?* (Philadelphia: University of Pennsylvania Press, 2016).

87. Pierre Rosanvallon, *Le siècle du populisme: histoire, théorie, critique* (Paris: Seuil, 2020).

88. Thorsten Beigel and Georg Eckert, eds., *Populismus. Varianten von Volksherrschaft in Geschichte und Gegenwart* (Münster: De Gruyter, 2017).

89. On East Central European populist ideological traditions, see Joseph Held, ed., *Populism in Eastern Europe: Racism, Nationalism and Society* (Boulder, CO: East European Monographs, 1996); Latinka Perović, *Srpsko-ruske revolucionarne veze: Prilozi za istoriju narodnjaštva u Srbiji* [Serbo-Russian Revolutionary Connections: Contributions to the History of *Narodnik* Ideas in Serbia] (Belgrade: Službeni list, 1994); Miklós Lackó, *Sziget és külvilág* [Island and Outer World] (Budapest: MTA Történettudományi Intézet, 1996). For a comparative overview of the Northern and Southeastern European dynamics, see Diana Mishkova, Balázs Trencsényi, and Marja Jalava, eds., *"Regimes of Historicity" in Southeastern and Northern Europe, 1890–1945: Discourses of Identity and Temporality* (Basingstoke: Palgrave Macmillan, 2014).

90. Dubravka Stojanović, *Populism: The Serbian Way* (Belgrade: Peščanik, 2017).

91. Ernest Gellner and Ghiţa Ionescu, eds., *Populism: Its Meanings and National Characteristics* (London: Weidenfeld & Nicolson, 1969).

92. Karin Priester, *Populismus: Historische und aktuelle Erscheinungsformen* (Frankfurt a. M.: Campus Verlag, 2007).

93. One of the pioneering contributions, looking both to the left and the right of the political spectrum, is by Cas Mudde, "The Populist *Zeitgeist*," *Government and Opposition* 39, no. 4 (2004): 541–63.

94. Michel Foucault, *The Birth of Biopolitics: Lectures at the Collège de France, 1978–1979*, ed. Michel Senellart, trans. Graham Burchell (New York: Palgrave Macmillan, 2008). On Foucault's interpretation of neoliberalism, see Serge Audier and Michael C. Behrent, "On Neoliberalism Through Foucault's Eyes," *History and Theory* 54, no. 3 (2015): 404–18. For an intellectual history of neoliberalism and its links to Foucault's thought see Daniel Rodgers, *Age of Fracture* (Cambridge, MA: Harvard University Press, 2011).

95. This is the overall picture emerging from the volume by Gregor Fitzi, Juergen Mackert, Bryan Turner, eds., *Populism and the Crisis of Democracy*, vol. 1, *Concepts and Theory* (Milton Park: Routledge, 2019).

96. Ivan Krastev and Stephen Holmes, *The Light that Failed: A Reckoning* (London: Allen Lane, 2019), 74.

97. Michael A. Wilkinson, *Authoritarian Liberalism and the Transformation of Modern Europe* (Oxford: Oxford University Press, 2021).

98. Zygmunt Bauman and Carlo Bordoni, *State of Crisis* (Cambridge, MA: Polity Press, 2014).

99. Priester, *Populismus*, 28.

100. Rosanvallon, *Le siècle du populisme*, 81ff.

101. Adam Przeworski, *Crises of Democracy* (Cambridge: Cambridge University Press, 2019).

102. Ibid., 87.

103. Ibid., 10.

104. Ibid.

105. See Kenneth M. Roberts, "Neoliberalism and the Transformation of Populism in Latin America: The Peruvian Case," *World Politics* 48, no. 1 (1995): 82–116. For an early attempt to compare the Latin American and Eastern European contexts from this perspective, see Kurt Weyland, "Neoliberal Populism in Latin America and Eastern Europe," *Comparative Politics* 31, no. 4 (July 1999): 379–401.

106. See, e.g., David Ost, *The Defeat of Solidarity: Anger and Politics in Postcommunist Europe* (Ithaca: Cornell University Press, 2006); Attila Antal, *The Rise of Hungarian Populism: State Autocracy and the Orbán Regime* (Bingley: Emerald Group, 2019); and Gábor Scheiring, *The Retreat of Liberal Democracy: Authoritarian Capitalism and the Accumulative State in Hungary* (Cham: Palgrave, 2020).

107. See Mitchell A. Orenstein and Bojan Bugarič, "Work, Family, Fatherland: The Political Economy of Populism in Central and Eastern Europe," *Journal of European Public Policy* 29, no. 2 (2020): 176–95. Note that such a triangular comparison would have been inconceivable in the 1990s, when Poland and Hungary were the exemplary liberal transition countries, while Serbia was perceived as a paragon of ethnonationalism. After the 2023 Polish elections, the comparison obviously lost most of its cogency.

108. Available at https://web.archive.org/web/20130226021243/http://www.wiso.uni-hamburg.de/fileadmin/wiso_vwl_iwk/paper/appell.pdf

109. Speech on November 28, 2023, available at https://dserver.bundestag.de/btp/20/20139.pdf

11
Conclusion

The Politics of Crisis

Reading the interwar discourses on crisis and the post-2000 uses of the concept synoptically seems particularly instructive, as it can shed light on the underlying "regimes of historicity" that shape political ideologies and systems. The argument is often that the current predicament of crisis—catalyzing "illiberal" ideologies—is rooted in the collapse of the modernist imaginary and of evolutionary models of development.[1] Symptoms of disorientation have also been frequently linked to the "postmodern condition," which came to be philosophically and aesthetically articulated from the late 1970s onward (as against the modernist/developmentalist visions that dominated the 1950s and 1960s).[2] However, in the history of political thought this transformation is somewhat more complicated and multi-layered. We cannot identify a single moment when the modernist framework of representation was replaced by something radically different. The trajectory was more ambiguous and not so one-directional: the modernist understanding of time and historicity itself has internal contradictions between projections of continuity and experiences of rupture.

The Underlying Temporalities of the Contemporary Crisis Discourse

The interwar years witnessed the shaking of the modernist futural vision and the rise of alternative—anti-modernist—modalities, rejecting historical progress as constitutive of social and political values.[3] Significantly, while they did not completely overlap, there was substantial resonance between the anti-modernist and postmodernist political and aesthetic sensitivities, for example, in the work of key authors who bridged the two paradigms (e.g., T. S. Eliot, Mircea Eliade, Louis-Ferdinand Céline, Paul de Man, or Jorge Luis Borges) even if the political subtexts and implications of their works were fairly divergent.[4] At the same time, the 1950s and 1960s saw a revival of modernist sensitivities both in the socioeconomic and the artistic spheres. Furthermore, while the 1980s and 1990s were the heyday of philosophical and aesthetic postmodernism, the collapse of the Cold War division of the world, and the proliferation of liberal democratic "transition scripts," brought a more linear modernist imaginary back to the fore, even if only some were enchanted by the neo-Hegelian construction of Francis Fukuyama and his less-original epigons.

Intellectuals and the Crisis of Politics in the Interwar Period and Beyond. Balázs Trencsényi, Oxford University Press.
© Balázs Trencsényi (2025). DOI: 10.1093/9780198929512.003.0011

Conclusion: The Politics of Crisis   **275**

The entanglement between anti-modernism and postmodernism might well yet provide another reason why some of the interwar ideological modalities started to attract special attention in the last decades. Importantly, the ascendance of populism and neoliberalism was also intertwined with the shaking of the linear modernist vision. In some ways these ideological streams are rooted in "*Sonderweg*" discourses or visions of "alternative modernities." Thus, both populists and neoliberals reject the image of an inherent and irreversible historical evolution toward greater liberty and consider the actual tendencies (toward centralization and étatism) extremely dangerous; they assert the need to return to an abandoned path of organic development (even though they understand organicity very differently). This search for an alternative modernity was already present in the discourse of nineteenth-century populists (such as the narodniks of the Russian Empire), who questioned both the liberal belief in the historical convergence of economic and existential liberty and the Marxist vision of development toward communism through the unfolding of capitalism. Likewise, interwar neoliberals were critical of the "mechanistic" vision of historicity that, in their understanding, characterized classical liberals and Marxists alike. In contrast, both populists and neoliberals stressed the centrality of a quasi-transcendent meaning-constitutive and self-regulating principle: populism's "will of the people" and neoliberalism's "market mechanism" and "spontaneous order." Such a principle creates its own historicity characterized by an alternation between periods of purity or unrestricted realization versus times of ideological and social contamination (by "alien elites" or planners).

Resonance or even genealogical links of course do not imply full convergence. The changing meanings and discursive functions of the very notion of crisis over the last hundred years is a case in point. Rather than indicating a decision of life and death, or pointing to a dramatic transformative process, in the last decades crisis has come close to a shorthand for identifying a problem area with no solution in sight. In Myriam Revault d'Allonnes's words: "there is nothing to settle, nothing to decide, as the crisis became permanent."[5] This transformation of the understanding of crisis is also reflected in the attempt to give "crisis scholarship" a separate academic identity, with a focus on "creeping crises" that have no clear beginning or ending and that are defined against the conventional definition of crises as dynamically unfolding and having well-defined beginnings and ends.[6]

This all fits into a broader transformation of the underlying temporalities of political discourse characterizing the decades around the turn of the millennium. One might even describe it as yet another *Sattelzeit*, in some ways returning to the interwar dynamic of atemporalization, serialization, hierarchization, biologization, and sacralization. To be sure, these terms imply different things now than they did a century ago. It is not so much the past (although parahistorical narratives made considerable advances over professional historical knowledge production) and the future (notwithstanding the proliferation of catastrophic scenarios of extinction) that is in the center of attention, but the present. In this sense, atemporalization means that the present does not function as an interface of the past and the future (or a "gap" from where it is possible to reflect on them, as Hannah Arendt would have it), but is projected on both: hence, we can imagine less and less our past and future as being different from our present. Serialization also turns into a feeling of eternal repetition: "we have seen this before." This does not mean, however, that this time we will handle this challenge better, as our experience is not cumulative. Hierarchization is also becoming presentist: domination is not legitimized by narratives about the past or by collective futural projections. In its stead, it is based on "ruling the moment," a phrase used by a propagandist of Viktor Orbán to formulate the essence of the governmentality of his boss. Biologization refers here to preservation rather than proliferation, and the increasingly omnipresent organic metaphor is extinction, which needs to be avoided. Youth is not perceived as a phase in human life which can be a basis of radical subversion of the political order, but something to be perpetuated as "eternal youth." It thus becomes a conservative drive to fence off change, as change can only be for the worse. Likewise, sacralization is decoupled from the linearity of salvation stories and is separated from the prospect of death and resurrection, becoming instead the sacralization of the self. In politics, this amounts to the mediatization of individual and collective narcissism, where the leader figure and the followers mutually confirm each other's self-images of "greatness." While this could imply a time horizon that projects a glorious past onto the future (making something "great again"), both the past and the future in this construction are ahistorical. What matters is rather the mechanistically reproduced charisma of the leader as a *pars pro toto* of his supporters in the present. Along these lines, crisis is not a phase of development, nor is it possible to overcome eventually with a right decision. It is something to be perpetuated as an amalgamating agent of this conjunction.

The disappearance of the temporal limits of crisis as a liminal process, with a discernible beginning and end, is similar and interrelated with the resemanticization of the concept of "transition." In the political science literature of the 1980s and 1990s, transition denoted a dynamic process where a given society or sector shifts from one more or less fixed framework to another (e.g., authoritarian to democratic). More recently, however, it came to signify a permanent condition. Tellingly, the European Union now annually issues its *Transitions Performance Index*, which measures all countries in the world along four axes of transition: economic, social, environmental, and governance.[7] The index is meant to determine the relative position of EU member states in a global context, but without positing firm points of departure or arrival in the process of transition—neither locally nor globally.

"Ruling the Moment": The Confluence of Populist and Neoliberal Crisis Discourses

The omnipresence of the concepts of crisis or transition in public and expert discourses should not be taken to indicate that the world is in permanent crisis or in transition. Likewise, the proliferation of the concept of "philosophy" (with everyone, from a marketing agency to a football manager, claiming to "have a philosophy") has

Conclusion: The Politics of Crisis **277**

evidently not made the world more philosophical.[8] Simultaneously, our reflective and unreflective uses and abuses of these terms still signal a transformation of sensitivities and mentalities, which indeed impacts our political and social practices. By describing a situation as a crisis, these terms define the spaces and limits of individual and collective action. In their analysis of African "subjectivities of crisis," Achille Mbembe and Janet Roitman also point to the entanglement between enunciation and action:

> . . . by relegating the crisis to the realm of the inexplicable, people likewise simultaneously circumscribe a field of both constraints and possible, reasonable and legitimate action. Through acting on the basis of these rationalities, in the midst of these entangled fields of action, they themselves end up participating in the very process of the production of the crisis: a self-referring chain.[9]

In this rendering, speaking *about* the crisis is indeed *part of* the crisis, but this does not imply that just using the concept could create a crisis *ex nihilo*. Rather, this self-referentiality can become a loop, resulting in the perpetuation of crisis. The classical understanding of crisis perceived it as transformative and transitional, thus asserting that crisis referred to the end of a certain configuration and the beginning of something new. However, with the destabilization of the sequence of past–present–future, crisis lost its temporal limits and became circular (or even atemporal). In an interview from 2013 expanding on Koselleckian motifs, Giorgo Agamben declared: "Today, however, judgement is divorced from the idea of resolution and repeatedly postponed. So, the prospect of a decision is ever less, and an endless process of decision never concludes."[10] It is precisely in this perpetuated present that crisis turns from a transitional phase of destabilization of order into "an instrument of rule" that serves "to legitimize political and economic decisions that in fact dispossess citizens and deprive them of any possibility of decision."[11]

If we perceive our society and all its subsystems to be in permanent crisis or constant transition, it becomes increasingly hard to envision a consensual framework regarding certain common aims, for which different social and political actors—professing different values and seeking different group interests—might strive. Agreement on such aims can only be the result of a lasting dialogue following certain procedural rules that regulate such a negotiation. But in the temporal framework of permanent crisis, it is hard to imagine any space and time for such a deliberative process. Instead, we are left with short-term tactical alliances and strategies of muddling through under the leadership of technocratic "crisis managers" who rise with the promise of removing the burden of decision from the shoulders of the community. Eventually, however, these "managers" fall when they are physically and morally consumed by recurrent (and apparently insurmountable) crisis phenomena. Their professed *raison d'être* is usually an aspiration to prevent something worse from happening: the total breakdown of the political system. Therefore, they do not seek to "resolve" the crisis once for all, or "complete" the transition, but only to avoid an impending catastrophe.

278 Intellectuals and the Crisis of Politics

As a number of observers, such as Paul Taggart, have pointed out, such a self-limitation of political deliberation ("unpolitics") might catalyze an anti-systemic (or "revolutionary") anti-politics that rejects institutional procedures altogether.[12] The challengers of the system can capitalize on social fatigue with measures of permanent crisis management, pointing to the fundamental "distortion" of the political, social, and cultural order and promising its radical overhaul—"draining the swamp" as it were. In their anti-systemic crusade, at least rhetorically, they often revert to (and sometimes—consciously or unconsciously—also draw on) the interwar understanding of crisis as an either–or situation, stipulating an "existential decision" that will irrevocably change the political system.

However, when these anti-systemic contenders become increasingly systemic (as with some of the virulent autocratic projects from the Philippines, Serbia, and Hungary), they predictably never reach the envisaged point of consolidation and instead opt for the "routinization of crisis." Rather than declaring that, by their coming to power, the crisis was finally resolved, they tend to amplify the crisis discourse. For them, sovereignty is not so much the legal power to introduce a fully-fledged state of exception and suspend the constitution as such (which might push them out of the international frameworks upon which they still depend), but a tool to "slow cook" democracy by institutionalizing the emergency policies deriving from the crisis while applying the label of "enemy" to those who are critical of these measures. They can thus limit political competition without completely abandoning democratic forms.

All of this means a reorganization of the political field according to a binary model, making it impossible to take up indeterminate positions. Moreover, these formerly anti-systemic contenders can hardly describe credibly their defeated (and constantly disparaged) competitors as the very source of this fundamental existential threat to the community. They create instead an apocalyptic enemy image, where local opponents are only proxies of a much more extensive and sinister camp—a global "shadow power" of unfathomable proportions. They can thus continue to capitalize on the energies and symbolic resources of anti-systemic mobilization, even if they are the uncontestable power holders. Tellingly, with reference to the Hungarian political tradition, Viktor Orbán calls this a "freedom struggle" while Recep Tayyip Erdoğan and Vladimir Putin, both with powerful post-imperial resentment, employ anti-colonial rhetoric against the West. Pointing to this looming threat—be it the influx of non-white refugees as part of the plan of "great replacement," the alleged "conspiracy" of civil activists dubbed as "Soros agents" or their association of demographic decline with the expansion of LGBTQ+ rights, etc.—contemporary authoritarians turn internal political competitors into "foreign agents," first symbolically, and eventually legislatively too.

On this basis they might introduce a rhetorical (or, by "hacking" the legal system, sometimes real) state of exception, suspending the regular temporality of the political system and restricting the agency of political actors unconnected to those who hold power. In a way, they redistribute the time pressure of crisis among members of the society: they alleviate democratic pressure on themselves (by limiting checks and balances with reference to the emergency), but at the same time use the full weight of the majoritarian principle to demotivate, demobilize, and eventually pulverize the opposition. This is an advanced and generalized version of the policies of selective austerity noticed by Kim Lane Scheppele when analyzing Orbán's "crisis management" after he came to power in 2010, which resulted in an economic and legal reconfiguration that has turned Hungary into the first autocracy in the European Union.[13]

In this context, there is a tendency to use the crisis discourse internationally to legitimize measures normally held to be incompatible with the common European value system. Orbán has been ready to use this copiously at any opportune moment. In his letter to Ursula von der Leyen, he wrote:

> In light of the urgent and severe crisis, I ask the Commission to propose adapting the legal framework to the new realities and most urgently discontinue enforcing the obsolete and obstructive regulations in place and suspend all infringement procedures that undermine Member States' actions.[14]

Orbán sought here to instrumentalize the tension created by Alexander Lukashenko (with whom he otherwise cultivates a cordial relationship), who transported Syrian refugees to the Polish border as a retaliation for the EU's—otherwise rather inefficient—support for the 2021 Belarusian opposition movement.

The proliferation of the crisis discourse is thus intertwined with the changing temporality of politics, both in the sense that references to crisis create an atmosphere of urgency, as well as that the very feeling of acceleration of political developments itself is often interpreted as the core of the crisis. Thus, we can also detect important similarities as well as differences between the present and the interwar period. While extreme time pressure is obviously not new and has characterized tense political situations in the past as well, the contemporary technological apparatus, which makes it possible to synchronize events happening in faraway locations, creates a completely different logic of political action and its underlying models of causality.

The first half of the twentieth century already experienced features of this synchronization, for example, the global snowball impact of the 1929 Wall Street crash. Eight decades later, this became intensified further by the unprecedented virtualization and deterritorialization of economic processes. In the spring of 2022, seconds after the freshly reelected Orbán mentioned in parliament his government's intended interventionist economic policies, the Hungarian forint drastically fell in value due to the anxious reaction of investors tens of thousands of kilometers away.

An even more dramatic case of the compression of temporal horizons is inherent to the very nature of nuclear deterrence. In case of a false alarm, the survival of humankind depends on the speed by which the American and Russian militaries can clarify the situation by a hotline before both sides unleash a preventive nuclear strike. This became more aggravated in the context of the full-scale Russian invasion of Ukraine, which exposed the possibility of escalation due to an—intended or unintended—Russian missile attack on a NATO member state.

This increase in temporal compression affects our models of causation, as the conventional linear temporal and spatial coordinates of political action are dissolved due to the global entanglement of synchronically occurring factors. For instance, the internal economic and political calamity in Sri Lanka in summer 2022 was aggravated by the disruption of global networks of food supply and the collapse of tourism because of the Russian invasion of Ukraine. But due to the multiplicity of factors and transmitters, it became difficult to assess the actual line of causes and effects here. In some ways this might recall Walter Lippmann's breakfast in *The Good Society*, used as an illustration of the infinitely complex interconnectedness of innumerable threads of production and transportation activities. Temporal and spatial compression brings along an extremely mediated relationship of cause and effect. While things that normally follow each other synchronize, people who share the same political space, but exist in parallel informational and discursive bubbles, desynchronize, making it increasingly hard to describe societal processes in any comprehensive way.

Accordingly, several interpreters of the crisis discourse pointed to the growing rift between causes and consequences in the representation of events.[15] In the loop of crisis, the same phenomenon can be both a catalyst and a result at the same time. The destabilization of frameworks of explanation is thus one of the key collective experiences that signal a general cognitive disorientation. Such a disorientation is both a cause and a consequence of the proliferation of crisis as a conceptual framework for describing reality and acting upon it. Furthermore, due to their interconnectedness, any local crisis can turn into a global predicament and any remote crisis can have immediate local repercussions. In this situation, it also becomes increasingly hard to employ basic concepts of political ethics, such as "agency" and "responsibility."

In the interwar period, thinkers of such different political positions as José Ortega y Gasset and Carl Schmitt, and in the postwar era the young Koselleck too, derived the turn of crisis into a "permanent condition" of modernity from the loss of the "capacity of decision." Indeed, Nadia Urbinati points out that, from a decisionist perspective, dissent among citizens is also perceived as a symptom of crisis.[16] Challengers to the status quo thus often claim to represent the "silent majority" and seek to enforce a decision that would finally change the political system. In the political discourse of the post-2000s, this is legitimized with reference to crisis as an existential threat (migration, demographic decline, climate change, global epidemic, etc.) to the community, necessitating immediate reaction. In this context, the urgent decisions made by those in power under the agenda of "saving the community" also shape the lives of those who do not share the same vision of crisis and do not want to be "saved." As a result, practically every election could be framed as a fatal "either–or": a potential point of no return regarding mutually exclusive scenarios of crisis, reshaping not only the near future of the political system, but its deep structures as well. The routinization of these either–or questions is channeled into zero-sum games where there are only potential losers and winners and no space for compromise or proposing a "third way."

In some cases, actual political developments indeed validated this perspective, for example, Brexit, which eventually forced even its staunch opponents to envision the future of their country outside of the European Union. In other cases, especially with the victory of political forces that belonged to the traditional political elite, even if they also frame their position in terms of crisis management (as it happened at the last two French presidential elections in 2017 and 2022) it just seemingly adjourns the conflict to the next round of confrontations. In this sense, the discourse of crisis becomes an engine of political polarization that gradually erodes the various explicit or tacit divisions rooted in the pillarization processes that had consolidated multi-party democracy in the 1950s and 1960s in Western Europe, and—much less so—in post-1989 East Central Europe.

The most destructive blend is the combination of a feeling of permanent crisis rooted in the fading away of the future as a possible horizon of resolving it mingled with a compulsive urge to make radical decisions, constantly reshaping the whole community. The crisis loop here is based on the suffocating experience of the eternal present, where decisions do not open new trajectories; it rather catalyzes a counter-reaction in the form of seemingly returning to the underlying temporality of the interwar years, where the concept of crisis was linked to a radical choice between mutually exclusive ideological options. However, in the current regime of historicity, with an evanescent sense of the future, every decision that seems to resolve a crisis just perpetuates it, deepening and multiplying the social and political ruptures. This is very visible in the current populist political discourse and practice, which operates with a restorative modality (recovering something lost—homogeneity, sovereignty, security, stability, greatness, etc.) and depicts the future mainly as a source of threat. It is also increasingly present in the neoliberal ideological framework that was historically more future-oriented (as it is the case with the evolutionism underlying Hayek's idea of spontaneous order). However, contemporary neoliberals are also less future-oriented, not the least because they lost the universalizing drive of their interwar predecessors and seem to have opted for the idea of "neoliberalism in one country," that is, some sort of economic nationalism (this dynamic could be observed, for example, in the post-transition mutation of neoliberalism in East Central Europe, such as former Czech president Václav Klaus, as well as in the buildup of the pro-Brexit campaign that mixed neoliberal and restorative/isolationist arguments).

In this situation, crisis indeed seems to be everywhere and nowhere at the same time. Anyone and anything can be found to be crisis-ridden and anyone or anything can be identified as a cause of crisis. It becomes omnipresent rhetorically, both as a legitimizing instrument of systemic and anti-systemic ideological positions and in the self-narration of decision makers and citizens. Everyone is permanently exposed to any crisis wherever it might originate, due to global political, economic, or even demographic connectivities. To stay with Lippmann's breakfast metaphor, the expansion of global economic and political connections has resulted in a complexity that not only precludes rational planning but also brings the repercussions of innumerable local crises among faraway populations to the kitchen table (as well as to the wallet and even the mind). Thus, it is increasingly problematic to frame the further advance of globalization as a possible resolution of these crises. At the same time, attempts to disconnect from these transnational and global frameworks also can be seen as catalysts of different types of crisis phenomena.

282 Intellectuals and the Crisis of Politics

These two possible options of crisis management—expanding and disconnecting—can be linked to the neoliberal and populist ideological positions, with the former advocating globalization and the latter spearheading deglobalization. Their enemy images are often reciprocal, as adherents of these positions tend to point precisely to the perseverance of the other pole as the main culprit for the ongoing crisis. However, this does not exclude a confluence of the two positions. Remarkably, we can find various hybrids, such as "neoliberal populists" and "populist neoliberals." The former advocate for a political system based on an organic community; consequently, they reject the negotiation of competing moral, economic, and social visions typical of a pluralistic liberal democratic system while at the same time employing neoliberal economic and social engineering strategies that limit or even eliminate the collective bargaining power of employees or distributing welfare provisions as "workfare." By contrast, the latter—the "populist neoliberals"—claim to stand for liberal capitalism but define the political community in an exclusivist way. They appeal to the popular spirit when legitimizing a market-based socioeconomic framework characterized by a relative homogeneity of insiders who compete for comparative advantages but start from a similar position both economically and socioculturally. The homogeneous in-group of "sovereign consumers" is contrasted to the heterogeneous outsiders, the subaltern and/or intruding "others" who, in this rendering, aim at the irretrievable transformation (or straightaway "replacement") of the community. It is in this context that Walter Ötsch and Stephan Pühringer talk of a dual concept of a "divided world" as a common ground linking "right-wing populism" and "market fundamentalism."[17]

Indeed, after 2008, with the generalization of the discourse of crisis and the expansion of "unorthodox" measures to contain the economic depression, it became less and less possible and meaningful to discern those who moved toward neoliberalism from populism, and vice versa. This made some observers opt for the other extreme and argue for the intrinsic identity of populism and neoliberalism, pointing to their shared antipathy toward redistributive welfare policies, resonance with racial arguments, propensity for decentralization, or the complicity between populism and "big business."

The result (so far) of this co-evolution has not necessarily been the formation of a binary "either liberal democracy or autocracy" situation in all polities. But in those cases where it did occur—often at the expense of the center-right political position or by its coopting of the radical right (characterizing some East Central European countries that have transitioned toward competitive autocracy, but to some extent also the United States, Italy, and Israel)—crisis has become routinized as a framework of mobilization and a self-fulfilling prophecy. This dynamic of polarization within a framework of perceived existential crisis of the community also explains how both ideological streams, which were traditionally rather skeptical of charismatic individual leadership, opted for leader figures that personalized the collective that craved efficient "crisis management."[18]

Conclusion: The Politics of Crisis **283**

This confluence has traceable historical roots. Thomas Frank named it "market populism" back in 2000,[19] and more recently, Niklas Olsen reconstructed the discourse of the "sovereign consumer" based on the argument that since every citizen is by necessity a consumer, allowing market forces to prevail was more democratic than any kind of interventionism that appealed to the "common good."[20] As previous chapters show, while the neoliberal ideological mainstream was critical of "economic nationalism," certain neoliberal streams were ready to accept fascist violence to remove impediments from the beneficial unfolding of market forces, others were open to ethno-populism or even racism, and some substreams of the interwar radical right toyed with the idea of using political violence to create a "true capitalism," which could also go together with the removal—or extermination—of some of the actual capitalists. Therefore, from a historical perspective, the increasing convergence between these streams in the last three decades seems unsurprising.

Recovering the Concept of Crisis

Having revisited the problem of analogies and genealogies with regard to the ideological streams of populism and neoliberalism, it is time to return to the book's initial question: is it possible to learn something more from the historical reconstruction of debates on crisis than merely registering the variegated uses of this concept by different political actors? Conversely, having confronted the mind-boggling plurality of the uses of the term, can we rely on "crisis" as an analytical tool at all? If so, can we apply it to the current political situation in any productive way? Is liberal democracy in crisis, or more in crisis than it ever was?

This book, which focuses mostly on the interwar period, points to the recurrence of this notion in various contexts: from abstract philosophical analyses to the most concrete and empirical discussions about institutions or sociocultural and demographic processes. The term crisis has been used strategically by many actors to position themselves within ongoing debates and to underline the urgency and importance of the issues they addressed. In this sense, the sheer frequency and intensity of the use of the concept does not mean that there is necessarily a crisis of any magnitude "out there." However, if we take the authors studied in this book seriously, and follow them in their analyses of the crisis of the political sphere, we can identify a certain pattern of decomposition of the democratic political order from the early 1920s to the late 1930s—a period that is highly relevant also for an observer in the 2020s.

While it is misleading to draw a fully-fledged parallel between the interwar years and the period after 1989—as the end of the First World War was surely a very different historical moment than the end of the Cold War—it is still remarkable that in both periods populism and neoliberalism became important contenders after a seemingly irreversible liberal democratic transformation and a subsequent autocratic backlash.[21] Further, the destabilization of the liberal democratic framework

284 Intellectuals and the Crisis of Politics

happened in both periods in a concatenation of events and processes, which came to be described by those who experienced them as economic, social, political, and cultural crises, converging into a "general crisis."

The political and philosophical perspectives of the authors employing the crisis discourse were extremely divergent, but in their own ways they all registered the intensification of the tension between the principles of liberalism and democracy. The historical memory of the separate existence and often antagonistic relationship between the liberal and democratic ideological traditions was obviously much more vivid in the 1920s and 1930s, when liberal democracy was perceived as a novel doctrine and political framework, and it has coagulated only relatively recently. By contrast, liberal democracy in the early 2000s seemed to be a historically deeply rooted institutional framework of politics—at least in the "Global North"—even if ideologically there were always contenders on the radical left and radical right. As argued by many observers who asserted the stability of the post-Second World War Western liberal democratic framework, in practical terms—cynically or sincerely—most contenders also relied on the political freedoms guaranteed by liberal democracy when propagating their creed. In this sense, the post-First World War brutalization and paramilitarization of politics, with many groups rejecting the democratic framework much more consciously and demonstratively, is hard to compare with what we witnessed in the last two decades (although the post-Yugoslav societies had comparable experiences of paramilitarization in the 1990s, and sinking into its imperial war of aggression, Putinist Russia is becoming increasingly comparable with the interwar authoritarian/fascist regimes). Similarly, a fundamental difference between the interwar years and the decades after 1989 is that the socialist/communist challenge that structured the political field after the Bolshevik Revolution and thus also shaped the populist and neoliberal discourses (both rejecting the socialist regime of property and historicity) has all but disappeared.

Nevertheless, even in the period following the First World War the political mainstream of most European countries perceived the interrelation of liberalism and democracy for some time as the universal norm, or at least a consensual "best practice." Although in most countries liberals lost their importance at the very center of the party system (between the socialist left and the conservative nationalist right), liberal principles seemed to have permeated the political framework, often confirmed by new constitutional documents, and to some extent also subscribed to by the erstwhile ideological enemies (conservatives, agrarian populists, or socialists) of liberalism. Likewise, it became almost impossible to argue against the democratic principle as constitutive of the political system, even if the modalities of representation and the very contours of the demos (defined ethnically or politically) remained heavily contested.

However, with the growing internal and international anxiety in the 1920s, there were ever more critics of the liberal democratic model who considered these two ideologies incompatible. On the one hand, radical left- and right-wing voices contrasted democracy (understood in terms of a majoritarian or metaphysical, i.e., representing the "true spirit" of the people, manifestation of popular sovereignty) with liberalism (understood as a doctrine focusing on individual competitiveness and consequently lacking any solidarity toward the losers of this competition and the sociopolitical community as such). On the other hand, proponents of economic competition felt increasingly constrained by what they considered to be extra-economic incursions by the political and social spheres and especially by the representatives of labor who imposed their will with reference to democratic principles and thus distorted the "natural" market relations.

From both directions, liberal democracy looked increasingly hypocritical, concealing the underlying fundamental conflicts (and thus the very nature of politics) and unable to mediate the vital forces (the "spirit of the people" or the "self-regulating market") that animated political, social, and economic life. However, the competition of these positions was not even: the dominance of collectivist (populist, fascist, and communist) ideas in the 1930s almost completely overshadowed the neoliberal project, which only became more visible retrospectively with the revival of its criticism of state intervention in the 1970s. Note also that not all branches of neoliberalism were equally critical of liberal democracy in principle, although they were usually very disaffected by the actual workings of the leading Western democracies.

Previous chapters showed how this disaffection with liberal democracy, expressed through the discourse of crisis, often grew into veritable abhorrence, so much so that in some configurations the detractors of "really existing" democracies were ready to forge new alliances, even if their criticism was expressed from a diametrically opposite position. Examples include the mixture of *völkisch* and ordoliberal ideas in Germany during the early 1930s, the free market liberalism of the ethnonationalist Polish National Democrats, or the rallying of French neoliberals to the Vichy regime. This convergence was one of the triggers (but also the result) of the proliferation of crisis discourses. While the policy recommendations of the representatives of these streams were usually divergent, their assessment of the situation was often strikingly similar. They agreed about the urgency of action, pointing to the socioeconomic and moral disintegration of the late 1920s, and the inadequacy of the institutional system, especially parliamentarism. They also agreed that the renewal of the political and economic order could entail the limitation of political rights among the population—rights that seemed to have been consensual in the first wave of democratic enthusiasm after 1918.

Eventually, these insights might help us recover the political meaning of the concept of crisis beyond identifying it as a recurrent *Kampfbegriff*. While it would have made little sense to look for a "Platonic idea" of crisis behind the innumerable articulations and seeming manifestations, we can still identify certain common traits between the political contestations of the interwar and post-1989 periods, which help us draw some preliminary conclusions about the political usability of this concept. One important inference is that the liberal democratic framework is more fragile both institutionally and ideologically than many of its adherents are prone to concede. The liberal and democratic ideologies as they historically emerged do have many common traits and co-evolved since the late nineteenth century, but to some extent they have different core values and can also be played out against each other. In this sense

286 Intellectuals and the Crisis of Politics

the concept "illiberal democracy" has a certain analytical value in the sense that it is possible to imagine a democratic doctrine that rejects liberalism. Historically, we can find many instances of this, particularly before 1945.

What the modern partisans of this position (e.g., Orbán) as well as the critics who use the term (from Fareed Zakaria to Jacques Rupnik) tend to overlook is the negotiation and merger of liberalism and democracy after 1945, which reshaped both ideological streams. Liberalism and democracy changed considerably because of the traumatic experiences in the 1930s and 1940s. This means that positing illiberal democracy as an ideological option means not only putting two different and theoretically equally plausible types of democracy alongside each other, but also contrasting two temporalities by negating the evolution of European politics after the Second World War that sought to overcome the civil wars and authoritarian legacies of the interwar years. While this evolution only took place in postwar Western Europe, there was an awareness of it in the thinking of reformers and dissidents beyond the Iron Curtain, and the "liberal democratic consensus" of the 1989 regime changes can be considered its localization.

If we were to accept this evolution as constitutive of postwar European political culture, it is impossible to envision a democracy that is not liberal in the modern understanding of providing for the autonomy of the individual as well as protecting the personal and political liberties of citizens. In contrast to a pure majoritarian understanding of democracy, minorities who cannot enforce their will through the regular democratic process are also to be protected. Furthermore, there are provisions to make sure that democratic participation not only takes place through voting in elections, but also through various other modalities that make it possible for the citizens to consult with and control those in power, as well as receive adequate information about political and social processes.

However, if we bracket off the Western European political development after 1945, it is possible to imagine a democracy that does not share the liberal value system in the broader sense described here, and also to imagine a liberal project that rejects democratic norms. It is particularly easy to do so in political cultures without a lasting liberal democratic consensus, saturated instead by "illiberal" variants of democracy. Such variants ranged from the post-Second World War idea of "popular democracy," considered as a transitory phase to socialism (while excluding liberal, Christian Democratic, and conservative forces from the political process) to the idea of "democratic centralism" (which in practice meant the power concentration of the party bureaucracy under state socialism). But the cracks in the liberal democratic framework also became apparent outside of the former socialist countries, especially in cases (e.g., Italy) where this consensus was always half-hearted, and the political system was maintained by the fear of a radical leftist contender.

Therefore, those who talk about "illiberal" democracy do not simply "innocently" assert the theoretical possibility of yet another sub-type of democracy. Seeking to (re)create it, they negate the postwar European evolution and opt for a possible but unrealized ("uchronic") trajectory, that is, the continuation of the interwar polarization without heeding the lessons of the Second World War and its aftermath.

The recurrence of the concept of crisis in public discourse thus indicates that the disintegration of the liberal democratic synthesis becomes increasingly imaginable. Conversely, the discourse of crisis serves as a key instrument for adherents of populism and neoliberalism and promotes their ideological position as a solution to the political impasse. While their practical recommendations are opposed, they employ the crisis discourse similarly to challenge the principle of liberal democracy as a unitary framework and thus to legitimize their assault. Consequently, their envisioned future largely coincides with the pre-Second World War past of European politics.

This "dialectic" relationship also means that crisis is neither merely the cause nor the consequence of populism or neoliberalism, but rather their self-perpetuating and self-legitimizing symbolic framework. In this sense, the frequent appearance of the discourse of crisis transcends the world of representations and becomes indicative of a real emergency—that of the growing rift between liberal and democratic principles. The consequences of this rift can be very tangible and painful in our everyday experience of the workings of political institutions. Populists and neoliberals both reflect this split in their ideology and seek to widen it even further by offering their understanding of democracy and liberalism, respectively, as a way out of the crisis. But, as I argue, they are part of the problem and not the solution. In some ways, this dynamic of self-perpetuating deterioration can be compared to the pattern that early modern political thinkers established when using the concept of "corruption." While the factors considered by these early modern authors were obviously different, their warnings about the mutual conditioning of the concentration of power in the executive branch and the loss of civic virtue remains relevant. As J. G. A. Pocock recapitulated this argument: "if ever Parliament or those who elect them—for corruption may occur at this point too—should be wholly corrupt, then there will be an end of independence and liberty."[22]

Nevertheless, the fixation on crisis by those who seek to undermine liberal democracy should not mean that we must abandon the concept as wholly "contaminated." Drawing on the historical parallels analyzed in this book, we can also make some inferences regarding the possible use of the rhetoric of crisis for defending liberal democracy. Historically, as we could see in the chapters on the interwar years, it is not true that every single author who turned to the concept of crisis sought to undermine liberal democracy: many registered signs of disorientation and conflict, but thought that their critical position might contribute to the regeneration of the liberal democratic political system in their country (or even globally). In this sense, crisis can also become a strategically used mobilizatory concept that alerts the political community to the growing tension between liberal and democratic principles and urges action. The intention of the speaker who employs the crisis discourse thus can be the very opposite of those who support authoritarian projects. An important marker distinguishing the liberal democratic crisis discourse from the illiberal and antidemocratic ones lies in the causal scheme employed: most of the interwar authoritarian crisis discourses combined the image of a general crisis with an explanatory model pointing to one single root cause, be it spiritual or material. In their vision, crisis is literally omnipresent and threatens the community with dissolution, but it is possible to overcome it finally by engaging with it at one fundamental sphere of life—cauterizing the severed neck of the Hydra, as it were. In contrast, liberal democratic crisis discourses are much more sensitive to the differences between individual spheres of life, remain much more skeptical of the possibility of immediate recovery, and use the concept of crisis diagnostically to localize the dysfunctions of culture and society. When these authors talk about multi-sectorial crisis, they do not presume that, via one master stroke, all can be overcome; rather, they seek to disentangle the connections and interferences between these crisis phenomena.

However, for the retrospective gaze it is challenging to discern the differences between the two (liberal democratic and authoritarian) discourses of crisis because certain ideological subcultures (or even individual authors) oscillated between them. Adherents of conservative traditionalism, radical socialism, agrarian populism, and even liberalism could change positions regarding the liberal democratic framework—first by attacking it in the name of a metaphysical truth, class struggle, organic community, or the self-regulating market, but then, in the face of the totalitarian threat, reverting to a more inclusive position. Conversely, they could start with a critical but still integrative position but then, in the storm of the radical ideologies around them, assume a stance that rejected the compatibility of liberal and democratic elements altogether. This perspective allows us to make a more nuanced judgment of individual oeuvres and ideas, avoiding those all too simplistic labels (left vs. right, progressive vs. reactionary) that are often put on certain authors or subcultures. Many of these authors changed their opinion over time, assuming positions that were more compatible with a liberal democratic orientation, while others challenged it. Similarly, many of those who eventually opted for a neoliberal or populist position after 1989 began with a more empathetic criticism of the existing political system and only gradually assumed an intransigent stance. Further, I tried to show how these traditions themselves are multi-layered and change over time and space: some neoliberals were more (or less) democratic, and some populists were more (or less) liberal than others. Thus, a historically embedded reconstruction might also offer a possibility for populists and neoliberals to reflect on their own positionality and reframe their criticism of the existing political, cultural, and economic practices in a way that remains compatible with a liberal democratic framework where these criticisms can be articulated and negotiated. There exist several instances of populist projects compatible with liberal democracy, from the bulk of the Italian Cinque Stelle to Volodymyr Zelenskyy. Conversely, as Poland or Slovakia show, certain neoliberals can be important allies against authoritarian ethno-protectionism.

This also means that, rather than repudiating neoliberals or populists by default as responsible for the decomposition of liberal democracy, it is better to engage them in a debate and try to convince them that their justifiable disappointment with certain features of the political system can be channeled into political action within the liberal democratic framework (which would actually reinforce the political structure rather than undermine it). This imperative of dialogue has been increasingly neglected by the mainstream adherents of populism or neoliberalism who have become critical not only of the political elites and the "class" of intellectuals whom they accuse of being detached from reality, but also of the very fabric of the political system seeking to mediate between different positions. But there is also a deficit of dialogue on the part of those elites and intellectuals subscribing to the liberal democratic "playbook" who consider that rationality is by default on their side and any critical voice coming from outside eventually threatens the legitimate political and cultural order where they feel reasonably comfortable. Securitization in the name of an emergency, precluding any meaningful discussion, and seeming depoliticization, appealing to the lack of legitimate alternatives, have become all too convenient tools also for the defenders of liberal democratic values.

The imperative of dialogue should not be confused with merely adopting populist positions to revitalize the democratic political system, advocated by some of the left-wing anti-liberals following in the footsteps of Ernesto Laclau (1935–2014).[23] Taking populist or neoliberal criticism seriously does not mean assimilating their perspective. Further, the viability of this dialogue also defines the limits of democratic tolerance for those who challenge the liberal democratic framework. The idea of "militant democracy,"[24] which has gained new relevance in the context of the authoritarian upsurge in the 2010s, implies a commitment to protecting the democratic order from those who cynically try to instrumentalize liberal democratic principles (freedoms of speech, gathering, press, etc.) to destroy it. But it can only use force when it has already tried all other means to keep its adversaries within the framework of liberal democracy. First, it is an obligation to engage in a debate with the aim of restoring trust in the liberal democratic framework as a common space where it is possible to argue while accepting the possibility of disagreement. Democracy cannot survive without democrats, and the socialization of democrats requires agonistic situations. They can only learn to agree if they also learn to disagree. In turn, if militant democrats decide to opt for violence in order to suppress their adversaries without having exhausted all other means, then they too become a threat to liberal democracy by escalating violence and opening the possibility for an endless cycle of coups and counter-coups. At that point, they become part and parcel of the crisis they tried to overcome.[25] Thus, militant democracy by default needs to be self-limiting.

Along these lines, a democratic politics of crisis too can only be self-limiting both conceptually and in terms of its actions. The concept of crisis as a mobilizing term can be used when one considers that the very values and institutions of liberal democracy are in danger. In fact, failing to mobilize in these situations, watching idly the subversion of these values and institutions, contributes to the delegitimization (and eventual collapse) of liberal democracy. It sends the message that its challengers, who declare the rottenness and impotence of the system, are in fact right. At the same time, if every political contestation is framed as crisis by the defenders of liberal democracy and every radical contender is considered by default anti-systemic, the notion loses its meaning and the "immune system" of the political community loses its resilience; it is unable to tell false alarm from real.

The liberal democratic discourse of crisis is thus necessarily self-reflective. It scrutinizes the dysfunctions of the system and identifies the challengers. Following the imperative of debate, its adherents need to listen carefully to criticism irrespective of its political background. Problems need to be localized to avoid the generalizations of the discourse of "general crisis," which tends to be the underlying argument of those who seek to destroy the liberal democratic framework altogether. They must seek the integration of criticism without necessarily assimilating it, while remaining open to engage with components of the radical challenges to the liberal democratic framework without accepting their underlying narrative of "total crisis," irretrievable decline, or impending civilizational collapse.

At the same time, it is not sufficient for liberal democratic politics to be merely reactive. One of the most self-defeating features of interwar liberals as well as their post-1989 East Central European peers was that they allowed authoritarian challengers to take up the initiative and appropriate the space for criticism of the political system. This was allowed to proceed to the extent that these liberals became indistinguishable from the system itself (even if the system in its actual working was far from being liberal). By consequence, the system's destabilization necessarily undermined their own positions as well, and vice versa, the demise of the liberal elites also meant the end of the liberal democratic institutions.

The reactive nature of liberal democratic politics is even more self-destructive in the context of hybrid authoritarian regimes, which launch newer and newer waves of attacks on the remnants of liberal democratic institutions and milieux. The autocrats' strategy to legitimize these attacks is precisely to point to the general crisis that necessitates unconventional measures. To respond to this merely by negating the crisis and sticking conventionally to the "status quo" is self-defeating. In situations where a large part of society shares feelings of disorientation, any project that seeks to reinforce or restore democracy requires "unconventional" steps to reshuffle the cognitive frames of political thinking and action. Hence, surprise, humor, and unpredictability are the strongest strategic weapons of those who face seemingly all-powerful autocrats. Acting in a crisis mode in this sense means stepping outside of the established "division of labor" of the political system, which leaves an ever shrinking sphere of freedom for the critics of the regime. In a world that is increasingly abandoning the idea of progress as the principal futural modality, crisis as a speech act might reopen the future by shattering the deep frozen time of autocrats.

Unconventional, however, does not mean unprecedented. In fact, the playbooks of would-be autocrats and democrats are not unlimited. Seeking to defend or revive democracy thus also entails a synchronic and diachronic engagement with other instances of similar contestation, sometimes quite distant in time and/or space. In fact, reflecting on these cases (and thus opening the compressed horizons of temporality and spatiality entailed by the crisis discourse) might well be one of the most efficient antidotes to claims about the general and unprecedented nature of the crisis, which is a recurrent trope used by the challengers of liberal democracy everywhere. The applicability of the discourse of crisis for defending these values depends on being conscious of its limitations and relationality. Not every crisis discourse responds to the same threats and catalyzes the same actions. Thus, we can learn from others' conceptualizations and reactions (both successful and unsuccessful), but we also need to reflect on what makes our current predicament different from other contexts.

A comparative and transnational historical gaze, making us assess the plurality of crises across contexts as well as their common threads, creates both empathy and distance, inviting us to recognize ourselves in others and reflect their predicament in us. This book is meant as a modest contribution to this never-ending process.

Notes

1. See, e.g., Timothy Snyder's contrast of "politics of inevitability" and "politics of eternity" in his *The Road to Unfreedom: Russia, Europe, America* (New York: Tim Duggan Books, 2018).
2. Jean-François Lyotard, *La condition postmoderne: Rapport sur le savoir* (Paris: Minuit, 1979). Lyotard speaks of the "crisis of narratives" while defining postmodernity as an "incredulity towards metanarratives," linking it also to the "crisis of scientific knowledge."
3. On anti-modernism as an analytical category in the history of political thought, see Antoine Compagnon, *Les Antimodernes: De Joseph de Maistre à Roland Barthes* (Paris: Gallimard, 2005), as well as Sorin Antohi and Balázs Trencsényi, "Introduction: Approaching Anti-Modernism," in Diana Mishkova, Marius Turda, and Balázs Trencsényi, eds., *Discourses of Collective Identity in Central and Southeast Europe (1770–1945)*, vol. 4, *Anti-Modernism: Radical Revisions of Collective Identity* (Budapest: CEU Press, 2014), 1–43.
4. While all of them expressed sympathies toward radical right-wing regimes or movements, their level of engagement was rather divergent. Céline, de Man, and Eliade qualified as openly pro-totalitarian during the Second World War; T. S. Eliot was lured by the political aesthetics of Italian fascism during its ascendance; Borges openly distanced himself from Nazism in the 1940s but later in his life made some positive gestures toward the Argentinian military junta, while despising the populism of the Peronists.
5. Myriam Revault d'Allonnes, *La crise sans fin: Essai sur l'expérience moderne du temps* (Paris: Seuil, 2012), 10.
6. See Arjen Boin, Magnus Ekengren, and Mark Rhinard, eds., *Understanding the Creeping Crisis* (London: Palgrave Macmillan, 2021).
7. Most recently, see European Commission (EC), "Transitions Performance Index 2021: Towards fair and prosperous sustainability," 2022, available at https://ec.europa.eu/assets/rtd/tpi/2021/index.html
8. Indicatively, www.philosophy.com is a cosmetic company.
9. Achille Mbembe and Janet Roitman, "Figures of the Subject in Times of Crisis," *Public Culture* 7 (1995): 323–52. I am grateful to Olga Shevchenko for calling my attention to this article.
10. Giorgio Agamben, "The Endless Crisis as Instrument of Power: In Conversation with Giorgio Agamben," *Verso Books Blog*, June 4, 2013, available at http://www.versobooks. com/blogs/1318-the-endless-crisis-as-an-instrument-of-power-in-conversation-with-giorgio-agamben (originally published in German: *Frankfurter Allgemeine Zeitung*, May 24, 2013). I am grateful to the anonymous reviewer of Oxford University Press for this reference.

11. Ibid.
12. Paul Taggart, "Populism and 'Unpolitics,'" in Gregor Fitzi, Jürgen Mackert, and Bryan Turner, eds., *Populism and the Crisis of Democracy*, vol. 1: *Concepts and Theory* (Abingdon: Routledge, 2019), 79–87.
13. Kim Lane Scheppele, "Hungary and the End of Politics," *The Nation*, May 6, 2014, https://www.thenation.com/article/archive/hungary-and-end-politics/
14. Marton Kasnyik, "Hungary's Orban Asks EU to End Lawsuits, Citing Border Crisis," *Bloomberg*, November 22, 2021, available at https://www.bloomberg.com/news/articles/2021-11-22/hungary-s-orban-asks-eu-to-end-lawsuits-citing-border-crisis, accessed June 1, 2022.
15. See, for example, Jan Marco Sawilla's point about the tension between causes and effects (*Trennung zwischen Ursachen und Wirkungen*) in Jan Marco Sawilla, "Zwischen Normabweichung und Revolution: 'Krise' in der Geschichtswissenschaft," in Carla Meyer, Katja Patzel-Mattern, and Gerrit Jasper Schenk, eds., *Krisengeschichte(n): "Krise" als Leitbegriff und Erzählmuster in kulturwissenschaftlicher Perspektive* (Stuttgart: Steiner, 2013), 145–72, 148.
16. Nadia Urbinati, *Me the People: How Populism Transforms Democracy* (Cambridge, MA: Harvard University Press, 2019), 11.
17. Walter Ötsch and Stephan Pühringer, "The Anti-Democratic Logic of Right-Wing Populism and Neoliberal Market-Fundamentalism," *Working Paper Series Ök-48* (Cusanus Hochschule für Gesellschaftsgestaltung, Institut für Ökonomie, 2019).
18. Nadia Urbinati argues that while older research on populism, such as Margaret Canovan's influential book, characterized populism in modern societies as a movement without a leader, there were many versions of populism that also entailed a leadership cult, starting with Italian fascism. See Urbinati, *Me the People*, 5.
19. Thomas Frank, *One Market under God: Extreme Capitalism, Market Populism, and the End of Economic Democracy* (New York: Doubleday, 2000).
20. Niklas Olsen, *The Sovereign Consumer: A New Intellectual History of Neoliberalism* (Cham: Palgrave Macmillan, 2019).
21. In the last couple of years, there has been an extensive discussion on the parallels between the interwar era and the post-1989 period, especially in view of the rise of populism. See, e.g., Sheri Berman, "Populism Is Not Fascism: But It Could Be a Harbinger," *Foreign Affairs* 95, no. 6 (2016): 39–44; Jeffry Frieden, "International Cooperation in the Age of Populism," in Luis Brites Pereira, Maria Eugénia Mata, and Miguel Rocha de Sousa, eds., *Economic Globalization and Governance: Essays in Honor of Jorge Braga de Macedo* (Cham: Springer, 2021), 303–14; and Martyn Hammersley, "Karl Mannheim on Fascism: Sociological Lessons About Populism and Democracy Today?" *Sociological Research Online*, October 28, 2021, available at https://doi.org/10.1177/13607804211042032. The "new interwar period" is an important metaphor also in Bruno Latour and Nikolaj Schultz, *On the Emergence of an Ecological Class: A Memo* (Cambridge: Polity, 2022), 92.
22. J. G. A. Pocock, *Politics, Language, and Time: Essays on Political Thought and History* (Chicago: University of Chicago Press, 1989), 125.
23. Ernesto Laclau, *On Populist Reason* (London: Verso, 2005).
24. Originating with Karl Loewenstein's "Militant Democracy and Fundamental Rights," part 1 in *The American Political Science Review* 31, no. 3 (1937): 417–32, and part 2 in *The American Political Science Review* 31, no. 4 (1937): 638–58.

25. Violence, even in defense of liberal democracy against its authoritarian challengers, is always a second-best solution. As István Bibó argued in his tape-recorded "political testament," entitled "The Meaning of European Social Development" (from 1971–2): "there is a disarming gesture for every aggression, and this is what we ought to seek. If we cannot find it, all we can do is protect those entrusted to us with all our might and, as a worse option, with violence, but force is always the worse option." Hence, gestures of political violence "are never final and necessary; though helpful or useful, they are far from the best possible actions in a given situation." István Bibó, *The Art of Peacemaking. Political Essays by István Bibó*, ed. Iván Zoltán Dénes, trans. Péter Pásztor (New Haven: Yale University Press, 2015), 395–6. See also Aurelian Craiutu, *Faces of Moderation: The Art of Balance in an Age of Extremes* (Philadelphia: University of Pennsylvania Press, 2017).

Select Bibliography

Achcar, Gilbert, "Morbid Symptoms: What Did Gramsci Really Mean?" *Notebooks: The Journal for Studies on Power* 1, no. 2 (2022): 379–87.

Actes du Huitième Congrès International de Philosophie à Prague, 2–7 septembre 1934 (Prague: Orbis, 1936).

Adelman, Jeremy and Anne-Laure Delatte, "The Crisis of Our Crises," Project Syndicate (September 7, 2015), available at https://www.project-syndicate.org/commentary/global-crises-international-integration-by-jeremy-adelman-and-anne-laure-delatte-2015-09

Adler, Max, "Vladimir Iljitsch Lenin," *Der Kampf* 17, no. 3 (1924): 81–89.

Aftalion, Albert, *Les crises périodiques de surproduction* (Paris: M. Rivière, 1913).

Agamben, Giorgio, "The Endless Crisis as Instrument of Power: In conversation with Giorgio Agamben," versobooks.com, available at http://www.versobooks.com/blogs/1318-the-endless-crisis-as-an-instrument-of-power-in-conversation-with-giorgio-agamben

Année académique... Institut universitaire de hautes études internationales (Geneva: Graduate Institute of International Studies, 1932–39).

Antal, Attila, *The Rise of Hungarian Populism: State Autocracy and the Orbán Regime* (Bingley: Emerald Group, 2019).

Antal, Attila, *Chicago a Dimitrov téren: Neoliberalizmus és a Kádár-rendszer [Chicago at Dimitrov Square: Neoliberalism and the Kádár Regime]* (Budapest: Napvilág Kiadó, 2021).

Arendt, Hannah, *Between Past and Future: Six Exercises in Political Thought* (New York: The Viking Press, 1961).

Arendt, Hannah, *Crises of the Republic* (New York: Harcourt Brace & Company, 1972).

Aron, Robert et al., "Lettre à Hitler," *L'Ordre nouveau* 1, no. 5 (1933): 3–32.

Aron, Robert, *La fin de l'après-guerre* (Paris: Gallimard, 1938).

Audier, Serge, *Le colloque Lippmann: aux origines du néolibéralisme* (Paris: Le Bord de l'Eau, 2008).

Audier, Serge, and Michael C. Behrent, "On Neoliberalism Through Foucault's Eyes," *History and Theory* 54, no. 3 (2015): 404–18.

Babic, Milan, "Let's Talk About The Interregnum: Gramsci and the Crisis of the Liberal World Order," *International Affairs* 96, no. 3 (May 2020): 767–86.

Bagdasar, Nicolae, *Din problemele culturii europene* (Bucharest: Societatea română de filosofie, 1931).

Bambach, Charles, *Heidegger, Dilthey, and the Crisis of Historicism* (New York: Cornell University Press, 1995).

Baron, Hans, *The Crisis of the Early Italian Renaissance: Civic Humanism and Republican Liberty in an Age of Classicism and Tyranny* (Princeton: Princeton UP, 1955).

Barth, Karl, *Der Römerbrief* (Bern: G. A. Bäschlin, 1919).

Baudin, Louis, *Le Corporatisme. Italie, Portugal, Allemagne, Espagne, France* (Paris: Librairie générale de droit et de jurisprudence, 1941).

Bauer, Otto, *Kapitalismus und Sozialismus nach dem Weltkrieg, vol. 1, Rationalisierung—Fehlrationalisierung* (Vienna: Wiener Volksbuchhandlung, 1931).

Bauer, Otto, *Après la catastrophe allemande: les résolutions de la Conférence Internationale de l'I.O.S., à Paris août 1933* (Paris: Éditions de l'Internationale Ouvrière Socialiste, 1933).

Bauer, Otto, *Zwischen zwei Weltkriegen? Die Krise der Weltwirtschaft, der Demokratie und des Sozialismus, Ausgewählte Schriften, Band 2*, ed. Thomas Gimesi (Vienna: Thomas Gimesi, 2017).

Bauman, Zygmunt, and Carlo Bordoni, *State of Crisis* (Cambridge, MA: Polity Press, 2014).

Bebermayer, Renate, "'Krise'-Komposita—verbale Leitfossilien unserer Tage," in *Muttersprache* 90 (1980): 189–210.

Beigel, Thorsten and Georg Eckert, eds., *Populismus. Varianten von Volksherrschaft in Geschichte und Gegenwart* (Münster: De Gruyter, 2017).

Bell, John D., *Peasants in Power: Alexander Stamboliski and the Bulgarian Agrarian National Union, 1899–1923* (Princeton, NJ: Princeton University Press, 1977).

Benjamin, Walter, *Illuminations: Essays and Reflections*, ed. and trans. Harry Zohn, with an introduction by Hannah Arendt (New York: Schocken Books, 1999).

Berdiaev, Nikolai, Sergei Bulgakov, Mikhail Gershenzon, Bogdan Kistiakovskii, Petr Struve, Semen Frank, and Aleksandr Izgoev, *Vekhi (Landmarks)*, eds. and trans. Marshall S. Shatz and Judith E. Zimmermann (London: M. E. Sharpe, 1994).

Berdyaev, Nikolay, *Духовный кризис интеллигенции [Spiritual Crisis of the Intelligentsia]* (St. Petersburg: Типография товарищества «Общественная польза», 1910).

Berdyaev, Nikolay, *Кризисъ Искусства [Crisis of Art]* (Moscow: Издание Г. А. Лемана И С. И. Сахарова, 1918).

Berdyaev, Nikolay, "Духовное состояние современного мира [The Spiritual State of the Modern World]," *Путь*, 35 (1932): 56–68.

Berend, Iván T., *Válságos évtizedek: Közép- és Kelet-Európa a két világháború között [Decades of Crisis: Central and Eastern Europe between the Two World Wars]* (Budapest: Gondolat, 1982).

Berman, Sheri, *The Primacy of Politics: Social Democracy and the Ideological Dynamics of the Twentieth Century* (Cambridge: Cambridge University Press, 2006).

Berman, Sheri, "Populism Is Not Fascism: But it Could Be a Harbinger," *Foreign Affairs* 95, no. 6 (2016): 39–44.

Bernstein, Aaron, "The State, Crisis, and Working-Class Strategy in Antonio Gramsci's Prison Notebooks," *Notebooks: The Journal for Studies on Power* 1, no. 1 (2021): 19–43.

Besomi, Daniele, "Clément Juglar and his Contemporaries on the Causes of Commercial Crises," *Revue européenne des sciences sociales*, XLVII, no. 143 (2009): 17–47.

Bibó, István, "A magyar demokrácia válsága [The Crisis of Hungarian Democracy]," *Valóság* 1, no. 2–4 (1945): 5–43.

Bibó, István. *The Art of Peacemaking. Political Essays by István Bibó*, trans. Péter Pásztor, ed. Iván Zoltán Dénes (New Haven: Yale University Press, 2015).

Bićanić, Rudolf, *Kako živi narod. Život u pasivnim krajevima [How the People Live. Life in the Passive Regions]*, vol. I., (Zagreb: Tipografija, 1936).

Bideleux, Robert, "The Peasantries and Peasant Parties of Interwar East Central Europe," in Sabrina P. Ramet, ed., *Interwar East Central Europe, 1918–1941* (Abingdon: Routledge, 2020), 281–331.

Biondich, Mark, *Stjepan Radić, the Croat Peasant Party, and the Politics of Mass Mobilization, 1904-1928* (Toronto: University of Toronto Press, 2000).

Bixler, Julius S., "What, Then, is the Theology of Crisis?" *Christian Education* 14, no. 7 (1931): 735–40.

Bloch, Ernst, Georg Lukacs, Bertolt Brecht, Walter Benjamin, and Theodor Adorno, *Aesthetics and Politics* (London: Verso, 1980).

Blum, Léon, *Le socialisme devant la crise* (Paris: Librairie populaire du Parti socialiste, 1933).

Blyth, Mark, *Great Transformations: Economic Ideas and Institutional Change in the Twentieth Century* (Cambridge: Cambridge University Press, 2002).

Bocheński, Aleksander, *Kryzys Polski i kryzys ludzkości [The Polish Crisis and the Crisis of Humanity]* (Warsaw: Państwowy Instytut Wydawniczy, 1982).

Bockmann, Joanna, *Markets in the Name of Socialism: The Left-Wing Origins of Neoliberalism* (Stanford: Stanford University Press, 2011).

296   Select Bibliography

Boehm, Max Hildebert, "Staat und Minderheit," in *Europäische Revue* 6 (1930): 724–34.

Boese, Franz, *Deutschland und die Weltkrise. Verhandlungen des Vereins für Sozialpolitik* (Munich: Duncker & Humblot, 1932).

Boin, Arjen, Magnus Ekengren, and Mark Rhinard, eds., *Understanding the Creeping Crisis* (Cham: Palgrave Macmillan, 2021).

Bonn, Moritz J., *The Crisis of European Democracy* (New Haven: Yale University Press, 1925).

Borbándi, Gyula, *Der ungarische Populismus* (Mainz: Hase & Koehler, 1976).

Boyce, Robert, *The Great Interwar Crisis and the Collapse of Globalization* (Basingstoke: Palgrave Macmillan, 2009).

Braibant, Marcel, *D'abord la terre! Le salut par les paysans* (Paris: Denoël et Steele, 1935).

Braillard, Philippe, "New Political Values for a World in Crisis: The Approach of the Club of Rome," *International Political Science Review* 3, no. 2, (1982): 238–45.

Bresciani, Marco, *Quale antifascismo? Storia di "Giustizia e Libertà"* (Rome: Carocci, 2017).

Breuer, Stefan, *Die Völkischen in Deutschland. Kaiserreich und Weimarer Republik* (Darmstadt: Wissenschaftliche Buchgesellschaft, 2008).

Brubaker, Rogers, *Nationalism Reframed. Nationhood and the National Question in the New Europe* (Cambridge: Cambridge University Press, 1996).

Brubaker, Rogers, "Why Populism?" *Theory and Society* 46, no. 5 (2017): 357–85.

Bryce, James, *Modern Democracies*, vol. 1 (New York: The Macmillan Company, 1921).

Burckhardt, Jacob, *Weltgeschichtliche Betrachtungen*, ed. Jakob Oeri (Pfullingen: Neske, 1949).

Burgin, Angus, *The Great Persuasion: Reinventing Free Markets Since the Depression* (Cambridge: Harvard University Press, 2012).

Burrow, John W., *The Crisis of Reason: European Thought, 1848–1914* (New Haven: Yale University Press, 2000).

Calabrò, Carmelo, *Liberalismo, democrazia, socialismo: l'itinerario di Carlo Rosselli* (Florence: Firenze University Press, 2009).

Călinescu, Matei, "The 1927 Generation in Romania: Friendships and Ideological Choices (Mihail Sebastian, Mircea Eliade, Nae Ionescu, Eugène Ionesco, E. M. Cioran)," *East European Politics and Societies* 15, no. 3 (2001): 649–77.

Canovan, Margaret, *Populism* (New York: Harcourt Brace Jovanovich, 1981).

Cappoccia, Giovanni, *Defending Democracy: Reactions to Extremism in Interwar Europe* (Baltimore: Johns Hopkins University Press, 2005).

Carey, John, *The Intellectuals and the Masses: Pride and Prejudice Among the Literary Intelligentsia, 1880–1939* (London, Boston: Faber and Faber, 1992).

Carlson, Allan C., *The Swedish Experiment in Family Politics: The Myrdals and the Interwar Population Crisis* (London: Routledge, 1990).

Carr, Edward H., *The Twenty Years Crisis, 1919–1939: An Introduction to the Study of International Relations* (London: Macmillan, 1939).

Case, Holly, *The Age of Questions: or, a first attempt at an aggregate history of the Eastern, social, woman, American, Jewish, Polish, bullion, tuberculosis, and many other questions over the nineteenth century, and beyond* (Princeton: Princeton University Press, 2018).

Charle, Christophe, *Naissance des "intellectuels", 1880–1900* (Paris: Minuit, 1990).

Chimet, Iordan, ed., *Dreptul la memorie*, vols. I–IV. *[The Right to Memory]* (Cluj: Dacia, 1993).

Chirot, Dan, "Neoliberal and Social-Democratic Theories of Development: The Zeletin–Voinea Debate Concerning Romania's Prospects in the 1920s and Its Contemporary Importance," in Kenneth Jowitt, ed., *Social Change in Romania 1860–1940: A Debate on Development in a European Nation* (Berkeley: Institute of International Studies, 1978), 31–52.

Churchill, Winston, *The World Crisis*, vols. 1–5 (London: Thornton Butterworth and Charles Scribner's Sons, 1923–31).

Cioran, Emil M., *Schimbarea la față a României [The Transfiguration of Romania]* (Bucharest: Vremea, 1941).

Cioran, Emil M., *Singurătate și destin [Loneliness and Destiny]* (Bucharest: Humanitas, 1991).

Commun, Patricia and Stefan Kolev, eds., *Wilhelm Röpke (1899-1966): A Liberal Political Economist and Conservative Social Philosopher* (New York: Springer, 2018).

Compagnon, Antoine, *Les Antimodernes: de Joseph de Maistre à Roland Barthes* (Paris: Gallimard, 2005).

Congdon, Lee, *Seeing Red: Hungarian Intellectuals in Exile and the Challenge of Communism* (DeKalb: Northern Illinois University Press, 2001).

Convegno di scienze morali e storiche: 14–20 novembre 1932—XI, tema: l'Europa. Vol. 1. Atti preliminari, processi verbali (Roma: Reale Accademia d'Italia, 1933).

Craiutu, Aurelian, *Faces of Moderation: The Art of Balance in an Age of Extremes* (Philadelphia: University of Pennsylvania Press, 2017).

Crozier, Michel, Samuel P. Huntington, and Joji Watanuki, *The Crisis of Democracy. Report on the Governability of Democracies to the Trilateral Commission* (New York: New York University Press, 1975).

Csécsy, Imre, *Radikalizmus és demokrácia. Csécsy Imre válogatott írásai [Radicalism and Democracy. Selected Writings of Imre Csécsy]*, ed. Tibor Valuch (Szeged: Aetas, 1998).

Cserne, Péter, "Harmadik utak. Néhány szempont Röpke és Bibó összevetéséhez [Third Ways. Some Aspects for Comparing Röpke and Bibó]," *Magyar Tudomány* 6 (2003): 726–37.

Cuttica, Cesare and László Kontler, with Clara Maier, eds., *Crisis and Renewal in the History of European Political Thought* (Leiden: Brill, 2021).

Dard, Olivier, "Louis Rougier: Itinéraire intellectuel et politique, des années vingt à Nouvelle École," *Philosophia Scientiae* 7 (2007): 50–64.

Daskalov, Roumen and Diana Mishkova, eds., *Entangled Histories of the Balkans, vol. 2: Transfers of Political Ideologies and Institutions* (Leiden: Brill, 2013).

Deczki, Sarolta, *Meredek sziklagerincen: Husserl és a válság problémája [On a Steep Cliff Edge: Husserl and the Problem of Crisis]* (Budapest: L'Harmattan, 2014).

de Felice, Renzo, *L'autobiografia del Fascismo* (Torino: Einaudi, 2004).

de Haan, Ido, "Third Ways Out of the Crisis of Liberalism: Moderation and Radicalism in Germany, 1880–1950," in Ido de Haan and Matthijs Lok, eds., *The Politics of Moderation in Modern European History* (London: Palgrave Macmillan, 2019), 131–50.

Delaisi, François, *Les deux Europes* (Paris: Payot, 1929).

de Man, Henri, *Au-delà du marxisme* (Bruxelles: L'Églantine, 1927).

Demangeon, Albert, *Le déclin de l'Europe* (Paris: Payot, 1920).

Demm, Eberhard, "Max and Alfred Weber II: From *Führerdemokratie* to *Führernation*. A Comparative Synthesis of Their Political Sociology," *Max Weber Studies* 22, no. 1 (January 2022): 13–54.

Derman, Joshua, "Prophet of a Partitioned World: Ferdinand Fried, 'Great Spaces', and the Dialectics of Deglobalization, 1929–1950." *Modern Intellectual History* 18, no. 3 (2020): 1–25.

Devéze, Marius, *La Crise du Parlementarisme* (Paris: Ficker, 1932).

Devlin, Nicholas, "Karl Korsch and Marxism's Interwar Moment, 1917–1933," *History of European Ideas* 48, no. 5 (2022): 574–93.

Diamond, Jared, *Upheaval: How Nations Cope with Crises (or Don't)* (London: Allen Lane, 2019).

Dimitrov, Georgi M., "Agrarianism," in Feliks Gross, ed, *European Ideologies: A Survey of 20th Century Political Ideas* (New York: Philosophical Library, 1948), 396–450.

Dimou, Augusta, *Entangled Paths Towards Modernity. Contextualizing Socialism and Nationalism in the Balkans* (Budapest: CEU Press, 2009).

298   Select Bibliography

Dini, Vittorio, and D'Auria, Matthew, eds., *The Space of Crisis: Images and Ideas of Europe in the Age of Crisis, 1914–1945* (Bruxelles: Lang, 2013).

Doering-Manteuffel, Anselm and Jörn Leonhard, *Liberalismus im 20. Jahrhundert* (Stuttgart: Franz Steiner Verlag, 2015).

Doliesen, Gerhard, *Die polnische Bauernpartei "Wyzwolenie" in den Jahren 1918–1926.* (Marburg: Herder-Institut, 1995).

Dontsov, Dmytro, *Підстави нашої політики [The Fundaments of Our Politics]* (Vienna: Видавництво Донцових, 1921).

Dostál, Vladimír, *Agrární strana. Její rozmach a zánik [The Rise and Fall of the Agrarian Party]* (Brno: Atlantis, 1998).

Dowling, Emma, *The Care Crisis. What Caused It and How Can We End It?* (London: Verso, 2022).

Drabovitch, Wladimir, *Fragilité de la liberté et séduction des dictatures* (Paris: Mercure de France, 1934).

Dragovic-Soso, Jasna, *Saviours of the Nation: Serbia's Intellectual Opposition and the Revival of Nationalism* (Montreal: McGill-Queen's University Press, 2002).

Dyzenhaus, David, *Legality and Legitimacy: Carl Schmitt, Hans Kelsen and Hermann Heller in Weimar* (Oxford: Clarendon, 1997).

Edelstein, Dan, Stefanos Geroulanos, and Natasha Wheatley, eds., *Power and Time: Temporalities in Conflict and the Making of History* (Chicago: University of Chicago Press, 2020).

Eellend, Johan, "Agrarianism and Modernization in Inter-War Eastern Europe," in Piotr Wawrzeniuk, ed., *Societal Change and Ideological Formation Among the Rural Population of the Baltic Area 1880–1939* (Huddinge: Södertörn University Press, 2008), 35–56.

Einzig, Paul, *The World Economic Crisis, 1929–1931* (London: Macmillan, 1931).

Eliade, Mircea, *Profetism Românesc [Romanian Prophetism]*, vol. 1 (Bucharest: Roza Vânturilor, 1990).

Eliade, Mircea, *Textele "legionare" și despre "românism" [Legionary Texts and Texts on "Romanism"]* (Bucharest: Dacia, 2011).

Ellenforradalmi erők a magyar októberi eseményekben [Counter-Revolutionary Forces in the Hungarian October Events], vols. 1–4 (Budapest: [Information Office of the Council of Ministers of the Hungarian People's Republic] Magyar Népköztársaság Minisztertanácsa Tájékoztatási Hivatala, 1957).

Ene, Ernest, *Spre statul țărănesc [Towards the Peasant State]* (Bucharest: Eminescu, 1932).

Engliš, Karel, *Regulierte Wirtschaft* (Prague: Orbis, 1936).

Erdei, Ferenc, *Magyar város [The Hungarian City]* (Budapest: Athenaeum, 1939).

Erdei, Ferenc, *Magyar falu [The Hungarian Village]* (Budapest: Athenaeum, 1940).

Erlacher, Trevor, "The Birth of Ukrainian 'Active Nationalism': Dmytro Dontsov and Heterodox Marxism before World War I, 1883–1914," *Modern Intellectual History* 11, no. 3 (2014): 519–48.

Eucken, Walter, "Staatliche Strukturwandlungen und die Krisis des Kapitalismus," *Weltwirtschaftliches Archiv*, vol. 36, (1932): 297–321.

Falina, Maria, *Religion and Politics in Interwar Yugoslavia. Serbian Nationalism and East Orthodox Christianity* (London: Bloomsbury, 2023).

Féja, Géza, "A zsidók útja [The Way of the Jews]," *Magyarország* 45, no. 100 (1938): 5.

Féja, Géza, *Márciusi front [The March Front]* (Budapest: Mundus, 2002).

Fejtő, Ferenc, *Szép szóval [With Beautiful Words]*, ed. Ágnes Széchenyi (Budapest: Századvég Kiadó, 1992).

Fernández, Federico N., Barbara Kolm, and Victoria Schmid, eds., *The Indispensability of Freedom. 8th International Conference – The Austrian School of Economics in the 21st Century* (Vienna: Friedrich A. von Hayek Institut, 2020).

Ferrero, Guglielmo, *Discours aux sourds* (Paris: Sagittaire, 1924).

Fillafer, Franz Leander, "The Enlightenment on Trial: Reinhart Koselleck's Interpretation of *Aufklärung*," in Q. Edward Wang and Franz Leander Fillafer, eds., *The Many Faces of Clio: Cross-Cultural Approaches to Historiography: Essays in Honor of Georg G. Iggers* (Oxford: Berghahn Books, 2007), 322–45.

Fioravanzo, Monica, *L'Europa fascista. Dal "primato" italiano all'asservimento al Reich (1932–1943)* (Milano: FrancoAngeli, 2022).

Fischer, Ernst, *Krise der Jugend* (Vienna: Hess & Co, 1931).

Fitzi, Gregor, Juergen Mackert, and Bryan Turner, eds., *Populism and the Crisis of Democracy: Concepts and Theory: Volume 1: Concepts and Theory* (Abingdon: Routledge: 2019).

Foerster, Friedrich Wilhelm, *Weltkrise und Seelenkrise* (Berlin: Zeitbücher-Verlag, 1932).

Föllmer, Moritz and Rüdiger Graf, *Die "Krise" der Weimarer Republik. Zur Kritik eines Deutungsmusters* (Frankfurt am Main: Campus, 2005).

Foucault, Michel, *The Birth of Biopolitics: Lectures at the Collège de France, 1978–1979*, ed. Michel Senellart, trans. Graham Burchell (New York: Palgrave MacMillan, 2008).

Frank, Thomas, *One Market Under God: Extreme Capitalism, Market Populism, and the End of Economic Democracy* (New York: Doubleday, 2000).

Freeden, Michael, "Crisis? How Is That a Crisis!? Reflections on an Overburdened Word," *Contributions to the History of Concepts* 12, no. 2 (2017): 12–28.

Freeden, Michael, *Liberalism Divided: A Study in British Political Thought, 1914–1939* (Oxford University Press, 1986).

Freeden, Michael, *Ideologies and Political Theory: A Conceptual Approach* (Oxford: Clarendon Press, 1996).

Fried, Ferdinand, *Das Ende des Kapitalismus* (Jena: Eugen Diederichs Verlag, 1931).

Frieden, Jeffry, "International Cooperation in the Age of Populism," in L. Brites Pereira, Maria Eugénia Mata, and Miguel Rocha de Sousa, eds., *Economic Globalization and Governance: Essays in Honor of Jorge Braga de Macedo* (Cham: Springer, 2021), 303–14.

Friedewald, Boris, *Die Engel von Paul Klee* (Cologne: DuMont, 2011).

Fritzsche, Peter, "Historical Time and Future Experience in Postwar Germany," *Ordnungen in der Krise: zur politischen Kulturgeschichte Deutschlands 1900–1933*, ed. Wolfgang Hardtwig (Munich: Oldenbourg, 2007), 141–64.

Fritzsche, Peter, "Landscape of Danger, Landscape of Design: Crisis and Modernism in Weimar Germany," in Thomas W. Kniesche and Stephen Brockmann, eds., *Dancing on the Volcano: Essays on the Culture of the Weimar Republic* (Columbia: Camden House, 1994), 29–46.

Gellner, Ernest and Ghiţa Ionescu, eds., *Populism. Its Meanings and National Characteristics*, (London: Weidenfeld & Nicolson, 1969).

Gelder, Ken and Sarah Thornton, eds., *The Subcultures Reader* (London: Routledge, 1997).

Ghervas, Stella, *Conquering Peace: From the Enlightenment to the European Union* (Cambridge, MA: Harvard University Press, 2021).

Gijsenbergh, Joris, Saskia Hollander, Tim Houwen and Wim de Jong, eds., *Creative Crises of Democracy* (Bruxelles, New York: Peter Lang, 2011).

Gilbert, Andrew S., "Conceptual Histories and Critical Theories," *Thesis Eleven: Critical Theory and Historical Sociology* 132, no. 1 (2016): 87–101.

Gilbert, Andrew S., *The Crisis Paradigm: Description and Prescription in Social and Political Theory* (Cham: Palgrave Macmillan, 2019).

Giraud, Émile, *Crise de la démocratie et les réformes nécessaires du pouvoir législatif* (Paris: M. Giard, 1925).

Goldberg, Chad Alan and Emile Durkheim, "Introduction to Emile Durkheim's 'Anti-Semitism and Social Crisis'," *Sociological Theory* 26, no. 4 (2008): 299–323.

300 Select Bibliography

Gollwitzer, Heinz, ed., *Europäische Bauernparteien im 20. Jahrhundert* (Stuttgart: Gustav Fischer Verlag, 1977).

Gordon, Peter E., and John McCormick, eds., *Weimar Thought: A Contested Legacy* (Princeton: Princeton University Press, 2013).

Graf, Rüdiger, and Konrad H. Jarausch, "'Crisis' in Contemporary History and Historiography," Docupedia-Zeitgeschichte, available at http://docupedia.de/zg/graf_jarausch_crisis_v1_en_2017

Graf, Rüdiger, *Die Zukunft der Weimarer Republik. Krisen und Zukunftsaneignungen in Deutschland 1918–1933* (Munich: Oldenbourg, 2008).

Graf, Rüdiger. "Die Krise als epochemachender Begriff im 20. Jahrhundert," in Frank Bösch, and Martin Sabrow, eds., *ZeitRäume. Potsdamer Almanach des Zentrums für Zeithistorische Forschung* (Göttingen: Wallstein Verlag, 2016): 20–37.

Graf, Rüdiger, "Either-Or. The Narrative of 'Crisis' in Weimar Germany and in Historiography," *Central European History* 43, no. 4 (2010): 592–615.

Graf, Rüdiger, "Optimismus und Pessimismus in der Krise—der politisch-kulturelle Diskurs in der Weimarer Republik," in Wolfgang Hardtwig, ed., *Ordnungen in der Krise: zur politischen Kulturgeschichte Deutschlands 1900–1933* (Munich: Oldenbourg, 2007), 115–40.

Gramsci, Antonio, *Selections from the Prison Notebooks*, eds. Quintin Hoare and Geoffrey Nowell Smith (New York: International Publishers, 1971).

Gramsci, Antonio, "La crisi italiana", in Renzo Pecchioli, ed., *Da Gramsci a Berlinguer, La via italiana al socialismo attraverso i congressi del Partito comunista italiano, vol. I, 1921–1943* (Venezia: Edizioni del Calendario, Marsilio Editori, 1985), 238–46.

Gregg, Samuel, *Wilhelm Röpke's Political Economy* (Cheltenham: Edward Elgar, 2010).

Griffiths, Richard, "Fascism and the Planned Economy: 'Neo-Socialism' and the 'Planisme' in France and Belgium in the 1930s," *Science & Society* 69, no. 4 (2005): 580–93.

Grol, Milan, *Iskušenja demokratije [Temptations of Democracy]* (Belgrade: Naučna knjiga, 1991).

Grossman, Henryk, *Aufsätze zur Krisentheorie* (Volume 20 of Archiv sozialistischer Literatur). (Frankfurt a. M: Verlag Neue Kritik, 1971).

Grubački, Isidora, "Čija kriza? Feminizam i demokratija u Jugoslaviji 20-ih godina XX veka [Whose crisis? Feminism and Democracy in Yugoslavia in the 1920s]," *Prispevki za novejšo zgodovino* 62, no. 2 (2022): 29–49.

Grunwald, Henning, and Manfred Pfister, eds, *Krisis! Krisenszenarien, Diagnosen und Diskursstrategien* (Munich: Fink, 2007).

Guénon, René, *The Crisis of the Modern World*, trans. Marco Pallis, Arthur Osborne, and Richard C. Nicholson (Hillsdale: Sophia Perennis, 2001).

Gusy, Christoph, ed., *Demokratie in der Krise: Europa in der Zwischenkriegszeit* (Baden-Baden: Nomos, 2008).

Habermas, Jürgen, *Legitimation Crisis* (Cambridge: Polity Press, 1988).

Hacke, Jens, *Existenzkrise der Demokratie. Zur politischen Theorie des Liberalismus in der Zwischenkriegszeit* (Berlin: Suhrkamp, 2018).

Hadzhiyski, Ivan, *Оптимистична теория за нашия народ. Избрани съчинения в три тома [An Optimistic Theory for Our People. Selected Works in Three Volumes]* (Sofia: Лик, 2002).

Halévy, Élie, Raymond Aron, A. Bernard, Georges Friedmann, Robert Marjolin, and Étienne Dennery, *Inventaires: la crise sociale et les idéologies nationales* (Paris: Alcan, 1936).

Hammersley, Martyn, "Karl Mannheim on Fascism: Sociological Lessons About Populism and Democracy Today?" *Sociological Research Online*, 28, no. 2. (2021): 320–35.

Hamvas, Béla, ed., *A világválság — Die Weltkrise [Aktuális kérdések irodalma a Fővárosi Könyvtárban. Literatur von Zeitfragen in der Stadtbibliothek Budapest]*, 53. (Budapest: Budapest Székesfőváros Házinyomdája, 1938).

Hamvas, Béla, *Krízis és katarzis—Esszék, tanulmányok, előadások, hozzászólások II (1936–1939)* [*Crisis and Catharsis—Essays, Studies, Lectures, Contributions II (1936–1939)*] (Budapest: Medio, 2019).

Hankiss, Elemér, "Európa, két világ közt [Europe between Two Worlds]," *Magyar Tudomány* 174, no. 11 (2013): 1386–95.

Hansen, Erik, "Depression Decade Crisis: Social Democracy and Planisme in Belgium and the Netherlands, 1929–1939," *Journal of Contemporary History* 16, no. 2 (1981): 293–322

Hantos, Elemér, *Denkschrift über die Wirtschaftskrise in den Donaustaaten* (Vienna: St. Norbertus, 1933).

Hantos, Elemér, *Der Weg zum neuen Mitteleuropa* (Berlin: Mitteleuropa-Verlag, 1933).

Hardtwig, Wolfgang, "Die Krise des Geschichtsbewusstseins in Kaiserreich und Weimaerer Republik und der Aufstieg des Nationalsozialismus," in Wolfgang Hardtwig, ed., *Hochkultur des bürgerlichen Zeitalters* (Göttingen: Vandenhoeck & Ruprecht, 2005), 77–102.

Harre, Angela, *Wege in die Moderne. Entwicklungsstrategien rumänischer Ökonomen im 19. und 20. Jahrhundert* (Wiesbaden: Harrassowitz Verlag, 2009).

Harvey, David, *The Enigma of Capital and the Crises of Capitalism* (New York: Oxford University Press, 2010).

Hatzopoulos, Pavlos, *The Balkans Beyond Nationalism and Identity. International Relations and Ideology* (London: Tauris, 2008).

von Hayek, Friedrich A., N. G. Pierson, Ludwig von Mises, Georg Halm, and Enrico Barone, *L'Économie dirigée en régime collectiviste: études critiques sur les possibilités du socialisme* (Paris: Librairie de Médicis, 1939).

von Hayek, Friedrich A., *The Road to Serfdom* (London: Routledge, 1944).

Hazard, Paul, *La Crise de la conscience européenne, 1680–1715* (Paris: Boivin, 1935).

Heinrich, Walter, *Grundlagen einer universalistischen Krisenlehre* (Jena: G. Fischer, 1928).

Held, Joseph, ed., *Populism in Eastern Europe: Racism, Nationalism and Society* (Boulder, CO: East European Monographs, 1996).

Heller, Hermann, *Europa und der Fascismus* (Berlin: De Gruyter, 1929).

Herceg, Rudolf, *Seljački pokret u Hrvatskoj [The Peasant Movement in Croatia]* (Zagreb: Herceg, 1923).

Herf, Jeffrey, *Reactionary Modernism: Technology, Culture, and Politics in Weimar and the Third Reich* (Cambridge: Cambridge University Press, 1984).

Heurtaux, Jérôme, Rachel Renault, and Federico Tarragoni, eds., "États de crise," *Tracés: États de crise* 44 (2023), 9–27.

Hewitson, Mark and Matthew D'Auria, eds., *Europe in Crisis: Intellectuals and the European Idea, 1917–1957* (New York: Berghahn, 2012).

Hinde, John R., *Jacob Burckhardt and the Crisis of Modernity* (Montreal: McGill–Queen's University Press, 2000).

Hirsch, Julius, *Die Wirtschaftskrise* (Berlin: Fischer, 1931).

Hitchins, Keith, "A Rural Utopia: Virgil Madgearu and Peasantism," in *The Identity of Romania* (Bucharest: Encyclopaedic Publishers, 2009), 119–45.

Hobsbawm, Eric J., "The General Crisis of the European Economy in the 17th Century," *Past & Present* 5 (May 1954): 33–53.

Hobsbawm, Eric, "C (for Crisis)," *London Review of Books* 31, no. 15 (2009), 12–3.

Hobson, John Atkinson, *The Crisis of Liberalism: New Issues of Democracy* (London: P. S. King & Son, 1909).

Hodža, Milan, *Federation in Central Europe* (London: Jarrolds, 1942).

Hoffmann, Stefan-Ludwig, *"Der Riss in der Zeit". Kosellecks ungeschriebene Historik* (Berlin: Suhrkamp, 2023).

Hölscher, Lucian, *Die Entdeckung der Zukunft* (Frankfurt am Main: Fischer, 1999).

302 Select Bibliography

Honkapohja, Seppo, *The 1990's Financial Crises in Nordic Countries. Bank of Finland Research Discussion Papers 5* (Helsinki: Bank of Finland, 2009).

Howard, Laura, "Cost of Living Crisis: Second Cost of Living Payment Rolls Out to Low Income Households," Forbes Advisor, updated November 8, 2022, available at https://www.forbes.com/uk/advisor/energy/cost-of-living-crisis.

Huhnholz, Sebastian, *Von Carl Schmitt zu Hannah Arendt?: Heidelberger Entstehungsspuren und bundesrepublikanische Liberalisierungsschichten von Reinhart Kosellecks Kritik und Krise* (Berlin: Duncker & Humblot, 2019).

Huizinga, Johan, *In the Shadow of To-morrow: A Diagnosis of the Spiritual Distempers of Our Time*, trans. J. H. Huizinga (London: William Heinemann, 1936).

Husserl, Edmund, *Die Krisis der europäischen Wissenschaften und die transzendentale Phänomenologie: Eine Einleitung in die phänomenologische Philosophie* (Belgrade: Ex officina Societatis "Philosophiae", 1936).

Imbriano, Gennaro, *Der Begriff der Politik. Die Moderne als Krisenzeit im Werk von Reinhart Koselleck* (Frankfurt am Main: Campus, 2018).

Jachymek, Jan and Waldemar Paruch, eds., *Więcej niż Niepodległość. Polska myśl polityczna 1918–1939 [More than Independence. Polish Political Thought, 1918–1939]* (Lublin: UMCS, 2001).

Jackson, George D., Jr. *Comintern and Peasant in East Europe, 1919–1930* (New York: Columbia University Press, 1966).

Jacobson, Arthur J. and Bernhard Schlink, eds., *Weimar: A Jurisprudence of Crisis* (Berkeley: University of California Press, 2000).

Jahoda, Marie, Paul F. Lazarsfeld, and Hans Zeisel, *Die Arbeitslosen von Marienthal. Ein soziographischer Versuch über die Wirkungen langandauernder Arbeitslosigkeit* (Frankfurt am Main: Suhrkamp, 1980).

James, Harold, *The German Slump: Politics and Economics, 1924–1936* (Oxford: Clarendon Press, 1986).

Jannaccone, Pasquale, *Prezzi e mercati* (Torino: Giulio Einaudi, 1951).

Jaspers, Karl, *Die geistige situation der Zeit* (Berlin: de Gruyter, 1932).

Jászi, Oszkár, "A jó társadalom *[The Good Society]*," *Századunk* 13, no. 4–5 (1938): 122–32.

Jedlicki, Jerzy, "Trzy wieki desperacji. Rodowód idei kryzysu cywilizacji Europejskiej [Three Centuries of Desperation: The Origin of the Idea of the Crisis of European Civilization]," *Znak*, 48, nr. 1 (1996): 4–25.

Jenson, Jane and Rianne Mahon, "Representing Solidarity: Class, Gender and the Crisis in Social-Democratic Sweden," *New Left Review* 201 (1993): 76–100.

Jevons, William Stanley, "The Periodicity of Commercial Crises, and its Physical Explanation," *Journal of The Statistical and Social Inquiry Society of Ireland*, Vol. VII, Part 54 (1878/1879), 334–42.

Jordheim, Helge and Einar Wigen, "Conceptual Synchronisation: From *Progress* to *Crisis*," *Millennium—Journal of International Studies* 46, no. 3 (2018): 421–39.

Jovanović, Dragoljub, *Seljak - svoj čovek [The Peasant is His Own Man]* (Belgrade: Institut za noviju istoriju Srbije, 1997).

Judson, Peter, *The Habsburg Empire: A New History* (Cambridge, MA: Belknap Press, 2016).

Judt, Tony, *Postwar: A History of Europe Since 1945* (New York: Penguin Press, 2005).

Juhász, Gyula, *Uralkodó eszmék Magyarországon, 1939–1944 [Ruling Ideas in Hungary, 1939–1944]* (Budapest: Kossuth, 1983).

Karaömerlioğlu, Asım, "Agrarian Populism as an Ideological Discourse of Interwar Europe," *New Perspectives on Turkey* 26 (2002): 59–93.

Kasnyik, Marton, "Hungary's Orban Asks EU to End Lawsuits, Citing Border Crisis," Bloomberg, November 22, 2021, available at https://www.bloomberg.com/news/articles/2021-11-22/hungary-s-orban-asks-eu-to-end-lawsuits-citing-border-crisis

Select Bibliography 303

Kautter, Eberhard, *Deutschland in der Weltkrise des Liberalismus* (Stuttgart: Kohlhammer, 1933).

Kenez, Peter, *Hungary from the Nazis to the Soviets: The Establishment of the Communist Regime in Hungary, 1944–1948* (Cambridge: Cambridge University Press, 2006).

Keynes, John M., *The Collected Writings of John Maynard Keynes, Vol. 9: Essays in Persuasion* (London: Macmillan, 1972).

Keynes, John M., *The Collected Writings of John Maynard Keynes*, vol. 20: *Activities 1929–1931: Rethinking Employment and Unemployment Policies* (London: Royal Economic Society, 1978).

Keyserling, Hermann, *Das Spektrum Europas* (Heidelberg: Kampmann, 1928).

Kjaer, Poul F. and Niklas Olsen, *Critical Theories of Crisis in Europe: From Weimar to the Euro* (Lanham: Rowman & Littlefield, 2016).

Kjellén, Rudolf, *Studien zur Weltkrise* (Munich: Bruckmann, 1917).

Klavžar, Karmen, "Angela Vode," in Francisca de Haan, Krassimira Daskalova, and Anna Loutfi, eds., *A Biographical Dictionary of Women's Movements and Feminisms: Central, Eastern, and South Eastern Europe, 19th and 20th Centuries* (Budapest–New York: Central European University Press, 2006), 604–8.

Klenk, Tanja and Frank Nullmeier, "Politische Krisentheorien und die Renaissance von Konjunkturprogrammen," *dms—der moderne staat—Zeitschrift für Public Policy, Recht und Management* 2 (2010): 273–94.

Koebner, Thomas and Rolf-Peter Janz, eds., *Mit uns zieht die neue Zeit: der Mythos Jugend* (Frankfurt am Main: Suhrkamp, 1985).

Korsch, Karl, *Marxismus und Philosophie* (Leipzig: C. L. Hirschfeld, 1923).

Korsch, Karl, "Thesen zur Diskussion über 'Krise des Marxismus'," in Michael Buckmiller, ed., *Gesamtausgabe*, vol. 5, *Krise des Marxismus: Schriften 1928–1935* (Amsterdam: IISG, 1996), 141–7.

Koselleck, Reinhart, *Kritik und Krise: Ein Beitrag zur Pathogenese der Bürgerlichen Welt* (Freiburg and Munich: Alber, 1959).

Koselleck, Reinhart, "Krise," in Otto Brunner, Werner Conze, and Reinhart Koselleck, eds., *Geschichtliche Grundbegriffe: Historisches Lexicon zur politisch-sozialen Sprache in Deutschland, vol. 3: H–Me* (Stuttgart: Klett-Cotta, 1982), 617–50.

Koselleck, Reinhart, *Futures Past: On the Semantics of Historical Time* (Cambridge, MA: MIT Press, 1985).

Koselleck, Reinhart, *Critique and Crisis: Enlightenment and the Pathogenesis of Modern Society* (Cambridge, MA: MIT Press, 1988).

Koselleck, Reinhart, *Zeitschichten: Studien zur Historik* (Frankfurt am Main: Suhrkamp, 2000).

Koselleck, Reinhart and Michaela W. Richter, "Crisis," *Journal of the History of Ideas* 67, no. 2 (2006): 357–400.

Kosík, Karel, *The Crisis of Modernity: Karel Kosík's Essays and Observations from the 1968 Era* (Lanham, MD: Rowman & Littlefield, 1994).

Kovács, Imre, *Néma forradalom [The Silent Revolution]* (Budapest: Cserépfalvi, 1937).

Kovács, Imre, *A parasztéletforma csődje [The Collapse of the Peasant Form of Life]* (Budapest: Bolyai Academy, 1940).

Kovács, Imre, *Népiség, radikalizmus, demokrácia [Populism, Radicalism, Democracy]* (Budapest: Gondolat/Nyilvánosság Klub/Századvég, 1992).

Keller, Márkus, György Kövér, and Csaba Sasfi, eds., *Krisen/Geschichten im mitteleuropäischem Kontext: sozial- und wirtschaftsgeschichtliche Studien zum 19./20. Jahrhundert/Válság/történetek közép-európai összefüggésben: társadalom- és gazdaságtörténeti tanulmányok a 19-20. századról* (Vienna: Institut für Ungarische Geschichtsforschung in Wien/Balassi Institut, Collegium Hungaricum Wien, 2015).

304 Select Bibliography

Kövér, György, *A növekedés terhe [The Burden of Growth]* (Budapest: Osiris, 2018).

Krastev, Ivan and Stephen Holmes, *The Light that Failed: A Reckoning* (London: Allen Lane, 2019).

Krüger, Gustav, "The 'Theology of Crisis': Remarks on a Recent Movement in German Theology," *Harvard Theological Review* 19, no. 3 (1926): 227–58.

Krugman, Paul, *The Return of Depression Economics and the Crisis of 2008* (New York: W.W. Norton & Company, 2009).

Kubekas, Vilius, *The Quest for Unity in a Time of Crisis: Catholic Intellectuals and the Challenges of Political Modernity in Interwar Lithuania* (PhD Dissertation, Central European University, 2023).

Kutnar, František, *Generace Brázdy [The Brázda Generation]* (Prague: Historický Klub, 1992).

Küttler, Wolfgang, Jörn Rüsen, and Ernst Schulin, eds., *Geschichtsdiskurs, vol. 4.: Krisenbewußtsein, Katastrophenerfahrungen und Innovationen 1880–1945* (Frankfurt a. M: Fischer, 1997).

Lackó, Miklós, *Válságok—választások [Crises and Choices]* (Budapest, Gondolat, 1975).

Lackó, Miklós, *Sziget és külvilág [Island and Outside World]* (Budapest: Akadémiai, 1996).

Laclau, Ernesto, *On Populist Reason* (London: Verso, 2005).

Landsberg, Otto, *Die politische Krise der Gegenwart* (Berlin: Dietz Nachf, 1931).

Laqueur, Walter, *Weimar: A Cultural History, 1918–1933* (New York: Capricorn Books, 1976).

Latour, Bruno and Nikolaj Schultz, *On the Emergence of an Ecological Class: A Memo* (Cambridge: Polity, 2022).

Laur, Ernst, *Le paysan suisse, sa patrie et son oeuvre: conditions et évolution de l'agriculture suisse au vingtième siècle* (Brougg: L'Union Suisse des Paysans, 1939).

Lederer, Emil, *Wege aus der Krise* (Tübingen: J. C. B. Mohr, 1931).

Lehmann, Hartmut and James Van Horn Melton, eds., *Paths of Continuity: Central European Historiography from the 1930s to the 1950s* (Washington, DC: German Historical Institute, 1994).

Leibholz, Gerhard, *Die Auflösung der liberalen Demokratie in Deutschland und das autoritäre Staatsbild* (Munich: Duncker & Humblot, 1933).

Leichter, Käthe, "Die beste Abwehr [The Best Defense] (1933)," in *The Red Vienna Reader*, trans. Paul Werner. Available at http://theorangepress.com/redviennareader/leichter/Leichter%20The%20Best%20Defense.pdf

Lenin, Vladimir I., "The Crisis of Menshevism," *Collected Works*, vol. 11, ed. Clemens Dutt (Moscow: Progress Publishers, 1972), 341–64.

Lenin, Vladimir I., "Lessons of the Crisis," *Collected Works*, vol. 24, ed. Bernard Isaacs (Moscow: Progress Publishers, 1964), 213–16.

Lenin, Vladimir I., "The Crisis Has Matured," *Collected Works*, vol. 26, ed. George Hanna, trans. Yuri Sdobnikov and George Hanna (Moscow, Progress Publishers, 1972), 74–85.

Lippmann, Walter, *The Good Society* (Boston: Little, Brown and Company, 1937).

Loewenstein, Karl, "Militant Democracy and Fundamental Rights," *The American Political Science Review* 31, no. 3 (1937), 417–32.

Loewenstein, Karl, "Militant Democracy and Fundamental Rights, II," *The American Political Science Review*, 31, no. 4 (1937): 638–58.

Lorenz, Thorsten, ed., *Cooperatives in Ethnic Conflicts: Eastern Europe in the 19th and Early 20th Century* (Berlin: Berliner Wissenschafts-Verlag, 2006).

Loubet del Bayle, Jean-Louis, *Les Non-conformistes des années 30: une tentative de renouvellement de la pensée politique française* (Paris: Seuil, 1969).

Loubet del Bayle, Jean-Louis, "Une tentative de renouvellement de la pensée politique française," *Modern Language Notes* 95, no. 4, French Issue (1980): 789–807.

Louis, Paul, *La crise du socialisme mondial de la IIe à la IIIe Internationale* (Paris: Librairie Félix Alcan, 1921).

Lüdders, Marc, *Die Suche nach einem dritten Weg: Beiträge der deutschen Nationalökonomie in der Zeit der Weimarer Republik* (Wien: Peter Lang, 2004).

Lützeler, Paul Michael, "Prophet der europäischen Krise," *Die Zeit* 44 (October 28, 1994), available at https://www.zeit.de/1994/44/prophet-der-europaeischen-krise

Lukács, György et al., "Vita demokráciánk válságáról [Debate on the Crisis of our Democracy]," *Valóság* 2, no. 1–2 (1946): 86–103.

Lukács, Georg, *Die Zerstörung der Vernunft* (Berlin: Aufbau Verlag, 1954).

Lukács, Georg, *Wie ist die faschistische Philosophie in Deutschland entstanden?* (Budapest: Akadémiai Kiadó, 1982).

Luxemburg, Rosa [Junius], *Die Krise der Sozialdemokratie* (Munich: Futurus, 1916).

Luxemburg, Rosa, *Die Russische Revolution* (Berlin: Gesellschaft und Erziehung, 1922).

Lyotard, Jean-François, *La condition postmoderne: rapport sur le savoir* (Paris: Minuit, 1979).

Madgearu, Virgil, *Agrarianism, capitalism, imperialism. Contribuţii la studiul evoluţiei sociale româneşti [Agrarianism, Capitalism, Imperialism. Contributions to the Study of Romanian Social Evolution]* (Cluj: Dacia, 1999).

Maeztu, Ramiro de, *Authority, Liberty and Function in the Light of the War. A Critique of Authority and Liberty as the Foundations of the Modern State and an Attempt to Base Societies on the Principle of Function* (London: G. Allen & Unwin, 1916).

Magliulo, Antonio, "Hayek and the Great Depression of 1929: Did He Really Change His Mind?," *The European Journal of the History of Economic Thought* 23, no. 1 (2016): 31–58.

Maier, Charles S., *Recasting Bourgeois Europe: Stabilization in France, Germany, and Italy in the Decade after World War I* (Princeton: Princeton University Press, 1975).

Malatesta, Alberto, *La crisi socialista* (Milano: Sonzogno, 1923).

Małowist, Marian, "Zagadnienie kryzysu feudalizmu w XIV i XV w. w świetle najnowszych badań [The Issue of the Crisis of Feudalism in the 14th and 15th Centuries in the Light of the Latest Research]," *Kwartalnik Historyczny* 60, no.1 (1953): 86–106.

Mannheim, Károly, *Lélek és kultúra [Soul and Culture]* (Budapest: Benkő, 1918).

Mannheim, Karl, *Mensch und Gesellschaft im Zeitalter des Umbaus* (Leiden: A. W. Sijthoff's Uitgeversmaatschappij, 1935).

Mannheim, Karl, *Ideology and Utopia: An Introduction to the Sociology of Knowledge* (London: Routledge & Kegan Paul, 1936).

Manoïlesco, Mihaïl, *L'Équilibre économique Européen* (Bucharest: Imprimeria naţională, 1931).

Manoïlesco, Mihaïl, *Une nouvelle conception du protectionnisme industriel* (Bucharest: Imprimeria naţională, 1931).

Manoïlesco, Mihaïl, *L'Impératif de la crise* (Bucharest: Chambre de commerce internationale, Comité national roumain, 1933).

Manoïlesco, Mihaïl, "L'inquiétude européenne et le Congrès de Rome," *L'année politique* June (1933), 197–211.

Manoilescu, Mihail, *Die einzige Partei als politische Institution der neuen Regime* (Berlin: Stollberg, 1941).

Mantoux, Paul, William E. Rappard, Maurice Bourquin, Guglielmo Ferrero, and Pitman B. Potter, eds., *The World Crisis* (London: Longmans, Green, 1938).

Marculesco, Michel, *La critique du libéralisme d'après les auteurs néo-libéraux* (Paris: Faculté de Droit, 1943).

Maritain, Jacques, *Le crépuscule de la civilisation* (Paris: Editions les Nouvelles Lettres, 1939).

Marlio, Louis, *Dictature ou liberté* (Paris: Flammarion, 1940).

Marx, Karl, "Lohnarbeit und Kapital," in Karl Marx and Friedrich Engels, *Werke*, Vol. 6, (Berlin: Dietz Verlag, 1959), 397–423.

306 Select Bibliography

Marx, Karl, "Der achtzehnte Brumaire des Louis Bonaparte," in Karl Marx and Friedrich Engels, *Werke*, vol. 8 (Berlin: Dietz Verlag, 1960), 111–207.

Marx, Karl, "Theorien über den Mehrwert," in Karl Marx and Friedrich Engels, *Werke*, vol. 26, no. 2 (Berlin: Dietz Verlag, Berlin, 1967).

Masaryk, Tomáš G., *Naše nynější krize. Pád strany staročeské a počátkové směrů nových [Our Current Crisis. The Fall of the Old Czech Party and the Beginnings of New Directions]* (Prague: Čas, 1895).

Masaryk, Tomáš G., *The Problem of Small Nations in the European Crisis: Inaugural Lecture at the University of London, King's College* (London: The Council for the Study of International Relations, 1916).

Mbembe, Achille and Janet Roitman, "Figures of the Subject in Times of Crisis," *Public Culture* 7 (1995): 323–52.

McMahon, Darrin M. and Samuel Moyn, eds. *Rethinking Modern European Intellectual History* (Oxford: Oxford University Press, 2014).

Meadows, Donella H., Dennis L. Meadows, Jørgen Randers, and William W. Behrens III, *The Limits to Growth. A Report for the Club of Rome's Project on the Predicament of Mankind* (New York: Universe Books, 1972).

Medinger, Wilhelm, *Die internationale Diskussion über die Krise des Parlamentarismus* (Wien: W. Braumüller, 1929).

Mergel, Thomas, ed., *Krisen verstehen. Historische und kulturwissenschaftliche Annäherungen* (Frankfurt: Campus, 2012).

Merlio, Gilbert, ed., *Ni gauche ni droite. Chassés-crises idéologiques des intellectuels allemands et français dans l'entre-deux guerres* (Bordeaux: Presses de la Maison de Sciences de l'Homme, 1995).

Meyer, Carla, Katja Patzel-Mattern, and Gerrit Jasper Schenk, eds, *Krisengeschichte(n). "Krise" als Leitbegriff und Erzählmuster in kulturwissenschaftlicher Perspektive* (Stuttgart: Franz Steiner Verlag, 2013).

Michalski, Krzysztof, ed., *Über die Krise (IWM Castelgandolfo-Gespräche II, 1985)* (Stuttgart: Klett-Cotta, 1986).

Milani, Tommaso, *Hendrik de Man and Social Democracy: The Idea of Planning in Western Europe, 1914–1940* (New York and Basingstoke: Palgrave Macmillan, 2020).

Miller, Daniel E., *Forging Political Compromise. Antonín Švehla and the Czechoslovak Republican Party, 1918–1933* (Pittsburgh: University of Pittsburgh Press, 1999).

Miłosz, Czesław, "*A Song on the End of the World*," trans. Anthony Milosz, available at https://www.poetryfoundation.org/poems/49451/a-song-on-the-end-of-the-world

Mirić, Jovan, *Sistem i kriza. Prilog kritičkoj analizi ustavnog i političkog sistema Jugoslavije [System and Crisis. A Contribution to the Critical Analysis of the Constitutional and Political System of Yugoslavia]* (Zagreb: Cekade, 1984).

Miron, Guy, "A 'Usable Past' and the Crisis of the European Jews: Popular Jewish Historiography in Germany, France and Hungary in the 1930s," in Ezra Mendelssohn, Stefani Hoffman, and Richard I. Cohen, eds., *Against the Grain, Jewish Intellectuals in Hard Times* (New York: Berghahn, 2014), 213–39.

Mirowski, Philip and Dieter Plehwe, eds., *The Road from Mont Pèlerin. The Making of the Neoliberal Thought Collective* (Harvard: Harvard University Press, 2009).

von Mises, Ludwig, *Socialism: An Economic and Sociological Analysis*, trans. J. Kahane (Indianapolis: Liberty Classics, 1981).

von Mises, Ludwig, *Die Ursachen der Wirtschaftskrise: ein Vortrag* (Tübingen: Mohr, 1931).

Mishkova, Diana, and Balázs Trencsényi, "Conceptualizing Spaces within Europe. The Case of Meso-Regions," in Willibald Steinmetz, Michael Freeden, and Javier Fernández Sebastián, eds., *Conceptual History in the European Space*, (New York: Berghahn, 2017), 212–35.

Select Bibliography **307**

Mishkova, Diana, Marius Turda, and Balázs Trencsényi, eds., *Discourses of Collective Identity in Central and Southeast Europe (1775–1945): Texts and Commentaries, Volume IV: Anti-Modernism. Radical Revisions of Collective Identity* (Budapest: CEU Press, 2014).

Mishkova, Diana, Balázs Trencsényi, and Marja Jalava, eds., *Regimes of Historicity in Southeastern and Northern Europe: Discourses of Identity and Temporality, 1890–1945* (Palgrave Macmillan, 2014).

Mitrany, David, *A Working Peace System: An Argument for the Functional Development of International Organization* (London: Royal Institute of International Affairs, 1943).

Mitrany, David, *Marx against the Peasant: A Study in Social Dogmatism* (Chapel Hill: University of North Carolina Press, 1951).

Mladenatz, Gromoslav, *Histoire des doctrines coopératives* (Paris: Presses universitaires de France, 1933).

Molotov, Vyacheslav, *The Developing Crisis of World Capitalism. The Revolutionary Crisis and the Tasks of the Comintern* (London: Modern Books, 1930).

Mommen, André, *Stalin's Economist: The Economic Contributions of Jenő Varga* (London: Routledge, 2011).

Montagnon, Barthélemy, Adrien Marquet, and Marcel Déat, *Néo-socialisme?: ordre, autorité, nation,* preface and commentaries by Max Bonnafous (Paris: B. Grasset, 1933).

Morin, Edgar, "Pour une crisologie," *Communications* 25 (1976): 149–63.

Moser, Charles A., *Dimitrov of Bulgaria: A Political Biography of Dr. Georgi M. Dimitrov* (Ottawa: Caroline House, 1979).

Moszkowska, Natalie, *Zur Kritik Moderner Krisentheorien* (Prag: Michael Kacha, 1935).

Mounier, Emmanuel, *Le Manifeste au service du personnalisme* (Paris: Éditions Montaigne, 1936).

Moyn, Samuel, and Andrew Sartori, eds., *Global Intellectual History* (New York: Columbia University Press, 2013).

Mudde, Cas, "The Populist *Zeitgeist,*" *Government and Opposition* 39, no. 4 (2004): 541–63.

Mudde, Cas and Cristóbal Rovira Kaltwasser, *Populism: A Very Short Introduction* (Oxford: Oxford University Press, 2017).

Müller, Dietmar, *Agrarpopulismus in Rumänien. Programmatik und Regierungspraxis der Bauernpartei und der Nationalbäuerlichen Partei Rumäniens in der Zwischenkriegszeit* (Sankt Augustin: Gardez!-Verlag, 2001).

Müller, Guido, "Von Hugo von Hoffmannsthals 'Traum des Reiches' zum Europa unter nationalsozialistischer Herrschaft – Die 'Europäische Revue' 1925–1936/44," in Hans-Christof Kraus, ed., *Konservative Zeitschriften zwischen Kaiserreich und Diktatur. Fünf Fallstudien* (Berlin: Duncker & Humblot, 2003), 155–186.

Müller, Jan-Werner, *Contesting Democracy: Political Ideas in Twentieth Century Europe* (New Haven: Yale University Press, 2011).

Müller, Jan-Werner, *What is Populism?* (Philadelphia: University of Pennsylvania Press, 2016).

Müller, Nils, "Die Wirtschaft als 'Brücke der Politik': Elemér Hantos' wirtschaftspolitisches Programm in den 1920er und 1930er Jahren," in Carola Sachse, ed., *"Mitteleuropa" und "Südosteuropa" als Planungsraum: Wirtschafts- und kulturpolitische Expertisen im Zeitalter der Weltkriege* (Göttingen: Wallstein Verlag, 2010), 87–114.

Müller, Tim B. and Adam Tooze, eds., *Normalität und Fragilität. Demokratie nach dem Ersten Weltkrieg* (Hamburg: Hamburger Edition HIS, 2015).

Murgescu, Bogdan, *Romania and Europe: Modernization as Temptation, Modernization as Threat* (Bucharest: Allfa Körber-Stiftung, 1998).

Musat, Pierre, *De Marx à Hitler* (Paris: Felix Alcan, 1933).

Myrdal, Alva, and Gunnar Myrdal, *Kris i befolkningsfrågan [Crisis in the Population Question]* (Stockholm: Bonnier, 1934).

308 Select Bibliography

Myrdal, Gunnar, *Population: A Problem for Democracy* (Cambridge, MA: Harvard University Press, 1940).

Nagel, Ernest, "The Eighth International Congress of Philosophy," *The Journal of Philosophy* 31, no. 22 (1934): 589–601.

Narkiewicz, Olga A., *The Green Flag: Polish Populist Politics, 1867–1970* (London: Croom Helm, 1976).

Nemcsek, József, *Világválság és technokrácia [World Crisis and Technocracy]* (Budapest: Fővárosi Könyvkiadó Rt., 1933).

Nenni, Pietro, *Sei anni di guerra civile in Italia. Un libro bruciato dai nazisti* (Rome: Arcadia Edizioni, 2023).

Neuman, Emanuel, *Limitele puterii statului [The Limits of State Power]* (Bucharest: Universitatea din Bucureşti, 1937).

Niculae, Vasile, Ion Ilincioiu, and Stelian Neagoe, eds., *Doctrina ţărănistă în România [Peasantist Doctrine in Romania]* (Bucharest: Editura Noua Alternativă, 1994).

Nye, Robert A., "Degeneration and the Medical Model of Cultural Crisis in the French Belle Époque," in Seymour Drescher, David Sabean, and Allan Sharlin, eds., *Political Symbolism in Modern Europe: Essays in Honor of George L. Mosse* (Somerset: Taylor & Francis Group, 1982), 19–43.

Oakes, Guy, *Weber and Rickert: Concept Formation in the Cultural Sciences* (Cambridge, MA: The MIT Press, 1990).

O'Donnell, Guillermo A., "The Perpetual Crises of Democracy," *Journal of Democracy* 18, no. 1 (2007): 5–11.

Ohayon, Annick, "Between Pavlov, Freud, and Janet. The Itinerary of a Russian Gentleman who Emigrated to France: Wladimir Drabovitch (1885–1943)," *Bulletin de psychologie* 521, no. 5 (2012): 479–85.

Ohlin, Bertil G., *The Cause and Phases of the World Economic Depression. Report Presented to the Assembly of the League of Nations* (Geneva: Secretariat of the League of Nations, 1931).

Olsen, Niklas, *History in the Plural: An Introduction to the Work of Reinhart Koselleck* (New York: Berghahn Books, 2012).

Olsen, Niklas, *The Sovereign Consumer: A New Intellectual History of Neoliberalism* (Cham: Palgrave Macmillan, 2019).

Olsen, Niklas, "Spatial Aspects in the Work of Reinhart Koselleck," *History of European Ideas* 49, no. 1 (2023): 136–51.

Oren, Nissan, *Revolution Administered: Agrarianism and Communism in Bulgaria* (Baltimore: Johns Hopkins University Press, 1973).

Orenstein, Mitchell A., and Bojan Bugarič, "Work, Family, Fatherland: The Political Economy of Populism in Central and Eastern Europe." *Journal of European Public Policy* 27, no. 3 (2020): 1–20.

Ormos, Mária, *A gazdasági világválság magyar visszhangja 1929–1936 [The Hungarian Echo of the World Economic Crisis 1929–1936]* (Budapest: Eötvös Kiadó – PolgART Könyvkiadó, 2004).

Ornea, Zigu, *Poporanismul [Populism]* (Bucharest: Minerva, 1972).

Ortega y Gasset, José, *Esquema de las crisis* (Madrid: Revista de Occidente, 1942).

Ortega y Gasset, José, *Man and Crisis*, trans. Mildred Adams (New York: Norton & Company, 1958).

Ortega y Gasset, José, *The Revolt of the Masses* (London: Unwin, 1963).

Ortega y Gasset, José, *España invertebrada: bosquejo de algunos pensamientos históricos* (Madrid: Revista de Occidente, 1971).

Orth, Ernst Wolfgang, "Krise", in Christian Bermes und Ulrich Dierse, eds., *Schlüsselbegriffe der Philosophie des 20. Jahrhunderts* (Hamburg: Meiner, 2010), 149–73.

Osborne, Peter, *The Politics of Time: Modernity and Avant-Garde*, (London: Verso, 1995).

Select Bibliography **309**

Ost, David, *The Defeat of Solidarity: Anger and Politics in Postcommunist Europe* (Ithaca: Cornell University Press, 2006).

Osypiuk, Urszula and Stefan Symotiuk, "The Decline of Poland as a 'Pre-Figure' of the Decline of Europe (On the Genesis of Witkacy's Catastrophism)," *Filosofija. Sociologija*, 18, no. 1 (2007): 36–45.

Ötsch, Walter and Stephan Pühringer, *The Anti-Democratic Logic of Right-Wing Populism and Neoliberal Market-Fundamentalism*. Working Paper Series Ök-48 (Koblenz: Cusanus Hochschule für Gesellschaftsgestaltung, Institut für Ökonomie, 2019).

Overy, Richard, *The Morbid Age: Britain and the Crisis of Civilisation, 1919–1939* (London: Penguin, 2009).

Paine, Thomas, "The American Crisis," December 23, 1776, available online at https://www.ushistory.org/Paine/crisis/c-01.htm

Pannwitz, Rudolf, *Die Krisis der Europaischen Kultur* (Nuremberg: Hans Carl, 1917).

Perović, Latinka, *Srpsko-ruske revolucionarne veze. Prilozi za istoriju narodnjaštva u Srbiji [Serbian–Russian Revolutionary Ties: Contributions to the History of Narodnik Ideas in Serbia]* (Belgrade: Službeni list, 1994).

Perroy, Edouard, "À l'origine d'une économie contractée: les crises du XIVe siècle," *Annales E.S.C.* 4 (1949): 167–82.

Pešelj, Branko M., "Peasantism. Its Ideology and Achievements," in C. Black, (ed.) *Challenge in Eastern Europe* (New Brunswick: Rutgers University Press, 1954), 109–31.

Pessoa, Fernando, *Páginas de pensamento político*, Vol. 2, *1925–1935*. ed. António Quadros (Lisbon: Europa-América, 1986).

Petreu, Marta, *An Infamous Past: E. M. Cioran and the Rise of Fascism in Romania* (Chicago: Ivan R. Dee, 2005).

Peukert, Detlev J. K., *The Weimar Republic: The Crisis of Classical Modernity* (New York: Hill & Wang, 1992).

Philip, André, *Henri de Man et la crise doctrinale du socialisme* (Paris: J. Gamber, 1928).

Pietrini, Daniela and Kathrin Wenz, eds., *Dire la crise: mots, textes, discours/Dire la crisi: parole, testi, discorsi/Decir la crisis: palabras, textos, discursos: Approches* (Peter Lang, 2016).

Pirou, Gaétan, *Néo-libéralisme, néo-corporatisme, néo-socialisme* (Paris: Gallimard, 1939).

Pocock, John G. A., *Politics, Language, and Time: Essays on Political Thought and History* (Chicago: University of Chicago Press, 1989).

Polanyi, Karl, "The Essence of Fascism," in Karl Polanyi, John Lewis, and Donald K. Kitchin, eds., *Christianity and the Social Revolution* (London: V. Gollancz, 1935), 359–94.

Polanyi, Michael, "U.S.S.R. Economics: Fundamental Data, System, and Spirit," *The Manchester School of Economic and Social Studies* 6 (1935): 67–89.

Polanyi, Michael, "British Crisis (1947?)," *Polanyiana* 23, no. 1–2 (2014): 59–64.

Polanyi, Michael, "Social Capitalism," *Time and Tide* 13 (April 13, 1946): 341–2.

Pombeni, Paolo, ed., *Crisi, legittimazione, consenso* (Bologna: Il Mulino, 2003).

Priester, Karin, *Populismus: historische und aktuelle Erscheinungsformen* (Frankfurt a. M.: Campus Verlag, 2007).

Przeworski, Adam, *Crises of Democracy* (Cambridge: Cambridge University Press, 2019).

Rabinbach, Anson, *The Crisis of Austrian Socialism: From Red Vienna to Civil War, 1927–1934* (Chicago: University of Chicago Press, 1983).

Radić, Stjepan, *Politički spisi, govori i dokumenti [Political Writings, Speeches and Documents]* (Zagreb: Dom i svijet, 1994).

Radica, Bogdan, *Agonija Europe: razgovori i susreti [The Agony of Europe: Conversations and Encounters]* (Zagreb: Disput, 2006).

Raditza, Bogdan, *Colloqui con Guglielmo Ferrero: seguiti dalle Grandi Pagine* (Lugano: Nuove Edizioni Capolago, 1939).

310 Select Bibliography

Rádl, Emanuel, *O německé revoluci; K politické ideologii sudetských Němců [On the German Revolution; On the Political Ideology of the Sudeten Germans]* (Prague: Masarykův ústav AV ČR, 2004).

Rădulescu-Motru, Constantin, *Românismul, catehismul unei noi spiritualități [Romanism: The Catechism of a New Spirituality]* (Bucharest: Editura pentru Literatură şi Artă Regele Carol II, 1936).

Rădulescu-Motru, Constantin, *Scrieri politice [Political Writings]* (Bucharest: Nemira, 1998).

Rákosník, Jakub, Matěj Spurný, and Jiří Štaif, *Milníky moderních českých dějin: krize konsenzu a legitimity v letech 1848–1989 [Milestones of Modern Czech history: The Crisis of Consensus and Legitimacy in the Years 1848–1989]* (Praha: Argo, 2018).

Ralea, Mihai, *Fenomenul românesc [The Romanian Phenomenon]* (Bucharest: Albatros, 1997).

Raphael, Lutz, "'Gescheiterte Krisen': Geschichtswissenschaftliche Krisensemantiken in Zeiten postmoderner Risikoerwartung und Fortschrittskepsis," in Friedrich Wilhelm Graf, Edith Hanke, and Barbara Pich, eds., *Geschichte intellektuell. Theoretische Perspektiven*, eds. (Tübingen: Mohr Siebeck GmbH & Co., 2015), 78–92.

Rappard, William, "Democracy vs. Demagogy: I." *Political Science Quarterly* 38, no. 2 (1923): 290–306.

Rappard, William, "The League in Relation to the World Crisis," *Political Science Quarterly* 47, no. 4 (1932): 481–514.

Rappard, William, *The Crisis of Democracy* (Chicago: University of Chicago Press, 1938).

Reckwitz, Andreas, and Hartmut Rosa, *Spätmoderne in der Krise. Was leistet die Gesellschaftstheorie?* (Berlin: Suhrkamp, 2021).

Reinhoudt, Jurgen and Audier, Serge, eds., *The Walter Lippmann Colloquium. The Birth of Neo-Liberalism* (Cham: Palgrave Macmillan, 2018).

Renan, Ernest, "La crise religieuse en Europe," *Revue des Deux Mondes, Troisième Période* 1, no. 4 (1874): 752–79.

Revault d'Allonnes, Myriam, *La crise sans fin. Essai sur l'expérience moderne du temps* (Paris, Seuil, 2012).

Rickert, Heinrich, *The Limits of Concept Formation in Natural Science: A Logical Introduction to the Historical Sciences*, ed. and trans. Guy Oakes (Cambridge: Cambridge University Press, 1986).

Riddell, John, ed., *Founding the Communist International: Proceedings and Documents of the First Congress: March 1919* (New York: Pathfinder, 1987).

Riddell, John, ed., *Workers of the World and Oppressed Peoples, Unite! Proceedings and Documents of the Second Congress, 1920, 2 vols.* (New York: Pathfinder, 1991).

Riddell, John, ed., *To the Masses: Proceedings of the Third Congress of the Communist International, 1921* (Leiden: Brill, 2015).

Riddell, John, ed., *Toward the United Front: Proceedings of the Fourth Congress of the Communist International, 1922* (Leiden: Brill, 2012).

Rigó, Máté, *Capitalism in Chaos: How the Business Elites of Europe Prospered in the Era of the Great War* (Ithaca: Cornell University Press, 2022).

Ringmar, Erik, "The Institutionalization of Modernity: Shocks and Crises in Germany and Sweden," in Nina Witoszek and LarsTrägårdh, eds., *Culture and Crisis: The Case of Germany and Sweden* (New York: Berghahn, 2002), 24–47.

Rivaud, Albert, *Les Crises allemandes* (Paris: A. Colin, 1932).

Robbins, Lionel, *The Great Depression* (London: Macmillan, 1934).

Roberts, Henry L., *Rumania. Political Problems of an Agrarian State* (Hamden: Archon Books, 1969).

Roberts, Kenneth M., "Neoliberalism and the Transformation of Populism in Latin America: The Peruvian Case," *World Politics* 48, no. 1 (1995): 82–116.

Rodgers, Daniel, *Age of Fracture* (Cambridge, MA: Harvard University Press, 2011).

Roitman, Janet, *Anti-Crisis* (Duke University Press, 2013).

Röpke, Wilhelm, "Die entscheidenden Probleme des weltwirtschaftlichen Verfalls," *Zeitschrift für schweizerische Statistik und Volkswirtschaft* 74 (1938): 493–506.

Röpke, Wilhelm, *Die Gesellschaftskrisis der Gegenwart* (Erlenbach-Zürich: Eugen Rentsch Verlag, 1942).

Röpke, Wilhelm, *Marktwirtschaft ist nicht genug: Gesammelte Aufsätze*, ed. Hans Jörg Hennecke (Waltrop: Manuscriptum, 2009).

Rosanvallon, Pierre, *Le siècle du populisme: histoire, théorie, critique* (Paris: Seuil, 2020).

Rosselli, Carlo, *Socialismo liberale*, ed. J. Rosselli (Turin: Einaudi, 1973).

Rosselli, Carlo, *Socialisme libéral*, ed. and trans. Serge Audier (Lormont: Le Bord de l'Eau, 2008).

Rössler, Reto, "'Krise' und 'Kap': Figurationen Europas in/als Literatur- und Kulturtheorie (Husserl/Derrida)," in Wolfgang Johann, Iulia-Karin Patrut, and Reto Rössler, eds., *Transformationen Europas im 20. und 21. Jahrhundert* (Bielefeld: transcript Verlag, 2019), 69–92.

Roth, Karl Heinz, "The International Institute of Social History as a Pawn of Nazi Social Research," *International Review of Social History* 34, suppl 1 (1989): 1–24.

Rougier, Louis, *Les mystiques politiques contemporaines et leurs incidences internationales* (Paris: Librairie du Recueil Sirey, 1935).

Rousseau, Jean-Jacques, "Considérations sur le Gouvernement de Pologne, et sur sa réformation projetée," in *Collection complète des oeuvres* (Geneva, 1782), vol. 1, 415–540.

Rousseau, Jean-Jacques, *Emile, or Education*, trans. Barbara Foxley (London: J.M. Dent and Sons, 1921).

Rueff, Jacques, *La Crise du Capitalisme* (Paris: Revue Bleue, 1935).

Runciman, David, *The Confidence Trap: A History of Democracy in Crisis from World War I to the Present* (Princeton: Princeton University Press, 2015).

Rüstow, Alexander, "Der Weg durch Weltkrise und Deutsche Krise," *Europäische Revue* 6, no. 12 (1930): 873–83.

Rygier, Maria, "La crisi socialista," *Tirrenio* (October 17, 1920), available online at https://collections.library.yale.edu/catalog/10651772

de Saint-Simon, Claude-Henri, *The Political Thought of Saint-Simon*, ed. Ghita Ionescu (Oxford: Oxford University Press, 1976).

Šalkauskis, Stasys, "Ideologiniai dabarties krizių pagrindai ir katalikų pasaulėžiūra [Ideological Foundations of Current Crises and the Catholic Worldview]", in Juozas Eretas and Antanas Salys, eds., *Lietuvių katalikų mokslo akademijos suvažiavimo darbai* [Proceedings of the Congress of the Lithuanian Catholic *Academy of Sciences*], vol. 2, 1936 (Kaunas: Lietuvių katalikų mokslo akademija, 1937), 45–80.

Salvemini, Gaetano, *Le origini del fascismo in Italia* (Milano: Feltrinelli, 1975).

Sawilla, Jan Marco, "Zwischen Normabweichung und Revolution—'Krise' in der Geschichtswissenschaft," in Carla Meyer, Katja Patzel-Mattern and Gerrit Casper Schenk, eds., *Krisengeschichte(n). "Krise" als Leitbegriff und Erzählmuster in kulturwissenschaftlicher Perspektive* (Stuttgart, 2013), 145–72.

Schäfer, Michael, "Kapitalismus und Kulturkrise. Walter Eucken und die Philosophie Rudolf Euckens," in Swen Steinberg, and Winfried Müller, eds., *Wirtschaft und Gemeinschaft. Konfessionelle und neureligiöse Gemeinsinnsmodelle im 19. und 20. Jahrhundert* (Bielefeld: transcript, 2014), 303–18.

Scheiring, Gábor, "Sustaining Democracy in the Era of Dependent Financialization: Karl Polanyi's Perspectives on the Politics of Finance," *Intersections. East European Journal of Society and Politics* 2, no. 2 (2016): 84–103.

Scheiring, Gábor, *The Retreat of Liberal Democracy: Authoritarian Capitalism and the Accumulative State in Hungary* (Cham: Palgrave, 2020).

312 Select Bibliography

Scheppele, Kim Lane, "Hungary and the End of Politics." *The Nation* (May 2014), available at https://www.thenation.com/article/hungary-and-end-politics/

Schiavi, Alessandro, "Crisi mondiale," *Avanti!* 25, no. 225 (1921): 1.

Schipper, Frank, *Driving Europe: Building Europe on Roads in the Twentieth Century* (PhD dissertation, Technische Universiteit Eindhoven, 2008).

Schleifer, Ronald, *Modernism and Time: The Logic of Abundance in Literature, Science, and Culture, 1880–1930* (Cambridge: Cambridge University Press, 2000).

Schmidt, Jochen, *Populismus oder Marxismus. Zur Ideengeschichte der radikalen Intelligenz Rumäniens 1875–1915* (Tübingen: Verlag der Tübinger Gesellschaft, 1992).

Schmitt, Carl, *The Crisis of Parliamentary Democracy*, trans. Ellen Kennedy (Cambridge, MA: MIT Press, 1988).

Scholem, Gerschom, *On Jews and Judaism in Crisis: Selected Essays* (New York: Schocken Books, 1976).

Schorske, Carl, "Politics in a New Key: An Austrian Trio," in *Fin-de-Siecle Vienna: Politics and Culture* (New York: Vintage Books, 1981), 116–80.

Schultz, Helga and Eduard Kubů, eds., *History and Culture of Economic Nationalism in East Central Europe* (Berlin: Berliner Wissenschaftsverlag, 2006).

Schulz-Forberg, Hagen, ed., *Zero Hours: Conceptual Insecurities and New Beginnings in the Interwar Period* (Brussels: Peter Lang, 2013).

Schumpeter, Joseph Alois, *Die Krise des Steuerstaats* (Graz: Leuschner & Lubensky, 1918).

Schumpeter, Joseph Alois, *Business Cycles. A Theoretical, Historical and Statistical Analysis of the Capitalist Process* (New York: McGraw-Hill Book Company, 1939).

Sedgwick, Mark, *Against the Modern World: Traditionalism and the Secret Intellectual History of the Twentieth Century* (Oxford: Oxford University Press, 2004).

Sekerák, Marián, "Czechoslovak Intellectual Debate on the Crisis of Democracy in the 1930s," *Studies in East European Thought* 75 (2023): 33–51.

Shariatmadari, David, "A Year of 'Permacrisis'", Collins Language Lovers Blog, November 1, 2022, available at https://blog.collinsdictionary.com/language-lovers/a-year-of-permacrisis/

Shelton, Anita K., *The Democratic Idea in Polish History and Historiography: Franciszek Bujak, 1875–1953* (Boulder, CO: East European Monographs, 1989).

Shevchenko, Olga, *Crisis and the Everyday in Postsocialist Moscow* (Bloomington: Indiana University Press, 2009).

Shevchenko, Olga, "Awful Crisis Superstar: Disasters and Routinization", in *Etnografia e Ricerca Qualitativa* 2 (2015): 301–20.

Sick, Klaus-Peter, "Vom *Opportunisme* zum *Libéralisme autoritaire*. Die Krise des französischen Liberalismus im demokratisierten Parlamentarismus 1885–1940," *Geschichte und Gesellschaft* 29, no. 1 (2003): 66–104.

Siegfried, André, *Die Krise Europas*, trans. Willi Reich (Zürich: Rascher, 1935).

Skidelsky, Robert, "The Great Depression: Keynes's Perspective," in Harold James, ed., *The Interwar Depression in an International Context* (Munich: Oldenbourg, 2002), 99–112.

Slobodian, Quinn, *Globalists: The End of Empire and the Birth of Neoliberalism* (Cambridge, MA: Harvard University Press, 2018).

Sluga, Hans, *Heidegger's Crisis: Philosophy and Politics in Nazi Germany* (Boston: Harvard University Press, 1993).

Snyder, Timothy, *The Road to Unfreedom: Russia, Europe, America* (New York: Tim Duggan Books, 2018).

Sombart, Nicolaus, *Krise und Planung: Studien zur Entwicklungsgeschichte des menschlichen Selbstverständnisses in der globalen Ära* (Vienna: Europa Verlag, 1965).

Sontheimer, Kurt, *Antidemokratisches Denken in der Weimarer Republik: Die politischen Ideen des deutschen Nationalismus zwischen 1918 und 1933* (Munich: Deutscher Taschenbuch-Verlag, 1994).

Sorokin, Pitirim Aleksandrovich, *The Crisis of Our Age: The Social and Cultural Outlook* (New York: Dutton, 1941).

Sosnowska, Anna, *Explaining Economic Backwardness: Post-1945 Polish Historians on Eastern Europe* (Budapest: CEU Press, 2019).

Spann, Othmar, *Der wahre Staat: Vorlesungen über Abbruch und Neubau der Gesellschaft* (Jena: Gustav Fischer, 1938).

Spengler, Oswald, *Der Untergang des Abendlandes: Umrisse einer Morphologie der Weltgeschichte* (Munich: C. H. Beck, 1920).

Spengler, Oswald, *Jahre der Entscheidung* (Munich: C. H. Beck, 1933).

Spiethoff, Arthur, "Krisen," in *Handwörterbuch der Staatswissenschaften*, 4th edn., Vol. 6, (Jena: Gustav Fischer, 1925), 8–91.

Spinelli, Altiero and Ernesto Rossi "The Ventotene Manifesto," available at http://www.altierospinelli.org/manifesto/manifesto_en.html

Stahl, Henri H., *Gânditori şi curente de istorie socială românească [Thinkers and Currents of Romanian Social History]* (Bucharest: Universităţii, 2001).

Stalin, J. V., "The Growing Crisis of World Capitalism and the External Situation of the USSR," in *Works*, vol. 12, *April 1929–June 1930* (Moscow: Foreign Languages Publishing House, 1955), 242–69.

Stapleton, Julia, *Englishness and the Study of Politics: The Social and Political Thought of Ernest Barker* (Cambridge: Cambridge University Press, 1994).

Stedman-Jones, Daniel, *Masters of the Universe: Hayek, Friedman, and the Birth of Neoliberal Politics* (Princeton: Princeton University Press, 2012).

Steinberg, Swen, and Winfried Müller, eds., *Wirtschaft und Gemeinschaft. Konfessionelle und neureligiöse Gemeinsinnsmodelle im 19. und 20. Jahrhundert* (Bielefeld: transcript, 2014).

Steinhardt, Nicolae and Emanuel Neuman, *Eseu despre o concepţie catolică asupra iudaismului. Iluzii şi realităţi evreieşti [Essay on a Catholic Conception of Judaism. Jewish Illusions and Realities]* (Iaşi: Polirom, 2011).

Stern, Fritz, *The Politics of Cultural Despair: A Study in the Rise of the Germanic Ideology* (Berkeley: University of California Press, 1974).

Sternhell, Zeev, *Neither Right nor Left* (Princeton: Princeton University Press, 1996).

Stojanović, Dubravka, *Populism: The Serbian Way* (Belgrade: Peščanik, 2017).

Surányi-Unger, Tivadar, *A gazdasági válságok történetének vázlata 1920-ig [Outline of the History of Economic Crises up to 1920]* (Budapest: Szent István Társulat, 1921).

Sviták, Ivan, *Kulatý čtverec. Dialektika demokratizace 1968–1969 [Round Square. The Dialectic of Democratization 1968–1969]* (Prague: Naše vojsko, 1990).

Szabó, Dezső, *Az egész látóhatár [The Entire Horizon]* (Budapest: Magyar élet, 1939).

Szabó, Miklós, *Az újkonzervativizmus és a jobboldali radikalizmus története, 1867–1918 [A History of Neoconservatism and Right-Wing Radicalism, 1867–1918]* (Budapest: Új Mandátum, 2003).

Széchenyi, Ágnes, ed., *Válasz, 1934–1938 [Answer: 1934–1938]* (Budapest: Magvető, 1986).

Szende, Paul, *Die Krise der mitteleuropäischen Revolution: Ein massenpsychologischer Versuch* (Tübingen: Mohr, 1921).

Takáts, József, "Jászi és a jó társadalom. A Lippmann-felfedezés és -csalódás története [Jászi and the Good Society: The History of His Discovery of and Disappointment with Lippmann]," *BUKSZ: Budapesti Könyvszemle* 24, no. 3–4 (2012): 220–29.

Taras, Raymond, "The Crisis of Ideology and the Ideology of Crisis: Marxist Critiques of the Polish Socialist System 1956–90," in Michael E. Urban, ed., *Ideology and System Change in the USSR and East Europe: Selected Papers from the Fourth World Congress for*

314 **Select Bibliography**

Soviet and East European Studies, Harrogate, 1990 (New York: St. Martin's Press, 1992), 162–82.

Tarquini, Alessandra, *Il Gentile dei fascisti: Gentiliani e antigentiliani nel regime fascista* (Bologna: Il Mulino, 2009).

Tikos, Laszlo M., "Waiting for the World Revolution: Soviet Reactions to the Great Depression," *Journal of Contemporary History* 4, no. 4 (1969): 87–99.

Tilgher, Adriano, *La crisi mondiale e saggi critici di marxismo e socialismo* (Imola: Nicola Zanichelli, 1921).

Tomašić, Dinko, *Društveni razvitak Hrvata: rasprave i eseji [Social Development of Croats: Discussions and Essays]* (Zagreb: Hrvatska naklada, 1937).

Tooze, Adam, *The Deluge: The Great War and the Remaking of Global Order, 1916–1931* (London: Penguin Books, 2015).

Tooze, Adam, "Welcome to the World of the Polycrisis" *Financial Times* (October 28, 2022).

Trencsényi, Balázs, "The Faces of Crisis: Rethinking a Key Concept in View of the Transnational Intellectual History of Europe," in Marjet Brolsma, Alex Drace-Francis, Krisztina Lajosi, Enno Maessen, Marleen Rensen, Jan Rock, Yolanda Rodríguez Pérez, and Guido Snel, eds., *Networks, Narratives and Nations: Transnational Approaches to Cultural Nationalism in Modern Europe and Beyond* (Amsterdam: Amsterdam University Press, 2022), 211–22.

Trencsényi, Balázs, Maciej Janowski, Mónika Baár, Maria Falina, Luka Lisjak-Gabrijelčič, and Michal Kopeček, *A History of Modern Political Thought in East Central Europe*, vols. I–II (Oxford: Oxford University Press, 2016–18).

Trencsényi, Balázs, Lucija Balikić, Una Blagojević and Isidora Grubački, eds., *East Central European Crisis Discourses in the Twentieth Century. A Never-Ending Story?* (London: Routledge, 2024).

Trevor-Roper, Hugh R., "The General Crisis of the 17th Century," *Past & Present* 16 (1959): 31–64.

Troeltsch, Ernst, "Die Krisis des Historismus," *Die neue Rundschau* 33, no. 1 (1922): 572–90.

Troeltsch, Ernst, *Lesebuch. Ausgewählte Texte*, ed. Friedemann Voigt (Tübingen: Mohr Siebeck, 2003).

Trotsky, Lev, "Агония капитализма и задачи Четвертого Интернационала [The Agony of Capitalism and the Tasks of the Fourth International]," *Бюллетень Оппозиции (Большевиков-Ленинцев)* 66/67, May–June (1938): 1–18.

Turda, Marius, *Modernism and Eugenics* (London: Palgrave Macmillan, 2010).

Turda, Marius and Paul J. Weindling, eds., *Blood and Homeland: Eugenics and Racial Nationalism in Central and Southeast Europe, 1900–1940* (Budapest: CEU Press, 2006).

Urbinati, Nadia, *Me the People: How Populism Transforms Democracy* (Cambridge, MA: Harvard University Press, 2019).

Valéry, Paul, "La Crise de l'esprit" (1919), in *Variété I* (Paris: Gallimard, 1924), 11–31.

Varga, Eugen, *Die Krise der kapitalistischen Weltwirtschaft* (Hamburg: Verlag der Kommunistischen Internationale, 1921).

Varga, Eugen, *Henri de Man et son plan* (Paris: Bureau d'éditions, 1934).

Varga, Eugen, *Selected Political and Economic Writings: From the Hungarian Revolution to Orthodox Economic Theory in the USSR*, ed. and trans. André Mommen (Leiden: Brill, 2020).

Varga, Jenő, *A nagy válság [The Great Crisis]* (Budapest: Kossuth, 1978).

Varga, Evgeniy, *Изменения в экономике капитализма в итоге второй мировой войны [Changes in the Capitalist Economy as a Result of the Second World War]* (Moscow: Госполитиздат, 1946).

Veber, France, *Idejni temelji slovanskega agrarizma [Ideological Foundations of Slavic Agrarianism]* (Ljubljana: Kmetijska tiskovna zadruga, 1927).

Veres, Péter, *Szocializmus, nacionalizmus [Socialism, Nationalism]* (Budapest: Mefhosz, 1939).

Vode, Angela, "Kriza družine [Crisis of the Family]," *Jutro* I–VI (18, 25 January; 29 February 1932).

Voznesenskiy, Andrey, *Жуткий Crisis Супер стар. Новые стихи и поэмы, 1998–1999 [Awful Crisis Super Star: New Poems and Verses, 1998–1999]* (Moscow: Teppa, 1999).

Wagemann, Ernst, *Zwischenbilanz der Krisenpolitik* (Berlin: Carl Heymanns, 1935).

Warriner, Doreen, "Urban Thinkers and Peasant Politics in Yugoslavia 1918–1959," *The Slavonic and East European Review* 38 (1959): 59–81.

Weber, Alfred, *Die Krise des modernen Staatsgedankens in Europa* (Stuttgart: Deutsche Verlags-Anstalt, 1925).

Weindling, Paul, *Health, Race and German Politics Between National Unification and Nazism, 1870–1945* (Cambridge: Cambridge University Press, 1989).

Wells, H. G., *After Democracy: Addresses and Papers on the Present World Situation* (London: Watts & Co., 1932).

Weltsch, Felix, *Das Wagnis der Mitte* (Ostrava: Kittl, 1936).

Werner, Michael and Bénédicte Zimmermann, "Beyond Comparison: Histoire Croisée and the Challenge of Reflexivity," *History and Theory* 45, no. 1 (2006): 30–50.

West, Alick, *Crisis and Criticism* (London: Lawrence and Wishart, 1937).

Weyland, Kurt, "Neoliberal Populism in Latin America and Eastern Europe," *Comparative Politics* 31, no. 4 (1999): 379–401.

Wilkinson, Michael A., *Authoritarian Liberalism and the Transformation of Modern Europe* (Oxford: Oxford University Press, 2021).

Wilkoń, Teresa, *Katastrofizm w poezji polskiej w latach 1930–1939. Szkice literackie [Catastrophism in Polish Poetry in the Years 1930–1939: Literary Sketches]* (Katowice: Wydawnictwo Uniwersytetu Śląskiego, 2016).

Winock, Michel, *Le siècle des intellectuels* (Paris: Seuil, 1997).

Winock, Michel, *La fièvre hexagonale. Les grandes crises politiques de 1871 à 1968,* (Paris: Calmann-Lévy, 1986).

Witoszek, Nina and Lars Trägårdh, eds., *Culture and Crisis: The Case of Germany and Sweden* (New York: Berghahn Books, 2002).

Wizisla, Erdmut, *Walter Benjamin and Bertolt Brecht: The Story of a Friendship*, trans. Christine Shuttleworth (New Haven, CT: Yale University Press, 2009).

Woytinsky, Wladimir, "Aktive Weltwirtschaftspolitik," *Die Arbeit* 6 (1931): 413–40.

X-Crise, *Centre polytechnicien d'études économiques, De la récurrence des crises économiques: son cinquantenaire 1931–1981* (Paris: Economica, 1982).

Xiaofei, Xu, "Michelin Menus in Turmoil as France Faces Foie Gras Crisis," *CNN Travel* (May 7, 2022), May 7 https://edition.cnn.com/travel/article/france-foie-gras-crisis/index.html

Zaitsev, Oleksander, *Націоналіст у добі фашизму: Львівський період Дмитра Донцова, 1922–1939. Начерк інтелектуальної біографії [Nationalist in the Time of Fascism. The Lviv Period of Dmytro Dontsov, 1922–39. Towards an Intellectual Biography]* (Kyiv: Критика, 2019).

Zakrzewski, Kazimierz, *Kryzys demokracji [Crisis of Democracy]* (Warsaw: G. Kryzel, 1930).

Zdziechowski, Marian, *W obliczu końca [On the Brink]* (Vilnius: Wydawnictwo Stanisława Turskiego, 1938).

Zehrer, Hans, "Der Sinn der Krise," *Die Tat* 23, no. 12 (1932): 937–57.

Zeletin, Ştefan, *Burghezia română. Neoliberalismul [Romanian Bourgeoisie. Neoliberalism]* (Bucharest: Nemira, 1997).

Zinner, Paul E., ed., *National Communism and Popular Revolt in Eastern Europe: A Selection of Documents on Events in Poland and Hungary, February–November 1956* (New York: Columbia University Press, 1956).

316 Select Bibliography

Znaniecki, Florian, *Ludzie teraźniejsi a cywilizacja przyszłości [People of Today and the Civilization of the Future]* (Warsaw: Atlas, 1934).

Znaniecki, Florian, *Upadek cywilizacji zachodniej [The Fall of Western Civilization]* (Warsaw: Wydawnictwo Uniwersytetu Warszawskiego, 2013).

Zweig, Ferdynand, *The Planning of Free Societies* (London: Secker & Warburg, 1942).

Zweig, Ferdynand, *Poland Between Two Wars. A Critical Study of Social and Economic Change* (London: Secker & Warburg, 1944).

Index

Action Française, 58, 169, 173, 226
Adler, Max, 196
Aftalion, Albert, 73, 155
Agamben, Giorgio, 277
Agrarianism, 114n, 263 (see also agrarian populism)
angels, 1
anti-Semitism, 65–6, 99, 153, 223, 227
apparatus, 46, 208, 213, 253, 255, 279
Arendt, Hannah, 249–50, 275
Argentina, 266
aristocracy. *See* nobility
Aron, Raymond, 6, 182–3
Aron, Robert, 186–7
assimilation, 65–6
Austria, Austrians, 35, 74, 128–9, 206, 210–2, 228, 263
Austrian School (in Economics), 74, 75, 134, 135
Austro-Marxism, 79, 84, 195–6, 207, 211
authoritarianism, 23, 49, 56, 118, 147, 148, 155, 158, 171, 177, 190, 209, 237, 241, 266
Averescu, Alexandru, 131

backward, backwardness, 42, 93, 109, 120, 128, 147, 158
Baeumler, Alfred, 47, 52
Bagdasar, Nicolae, 43
Balbo, Italo, 124, 126
Balkans. *See* Southeastern Europe
Barker, Ernest, 158
Baron, Hans, 247, 249
Barrès, Maurice, 229
Barth, Karl, 62
Baudin, Louis, 156, 157
Bauer, Otto, 6, 84, 89, 206–11
Bauman, Zygmunt, 264–5
Beckerath, Erwin von, 226, 239n
Benda, Julien, 58
Beneš, Edvard, 181, 186, 240n
Benjamin, Walter, 6, 13n, 47–8, 85
Berdyaev, Nikolay, 6, 52, 54, 56–7, 60, 64–5
Bergery, Gaston, 155
Bergson, Henri, 56, 182
Berlin, 47, 48, 57, 78, 84, 91, 246
Berlusconi, Silvio, 262, 265
Bibó, István, 6, 243–5, 246, 293n
Bićanić, Rudolf, 108–9
Bismarck, Otto von, 56, 61, 66, 183, 201
Bloch, Ernst, 10, 47

Bloch, Marc, 143
Blum, Léon, 203–7, 213
Bocheński, Aleksander, 256
Boehm, Max Hildebert, 219
Bolshevism, 41, 42, 54, 57, 59, 60, 63, 64, 107, 168, 172, 174, 188, 196, 221, 225, 228
Bonaparte, Louis-Napoléon (Napoleon III), 55, 183
Bonaparte, Napoleon 35, 55, 111, 147, 231
Bonn, Moritz J., 169–70, 171
Bordoni, Carlo, 264–5
Borges, Jorge Luis, 274, 291n
Bottai, Giuseppe, 125, 127
Bouglé, Célestin, 184
bourgeoisie, 49, 59, 87, 123–5, 127, 130, 190, 196, 198, 202, 203, 204, 206, 219, 245, 248
Bourquin, Maurice, 188–9
Boyce, Robert, 4
Brecht, Bertolt, 47–8, 247
Brubaker, Rogers, 260
Brunner, Otto, 10
Bryce, James, 167
Bulgaria, Bulgarians, 84, 108, 118, 206, 266
Burckhardt, Jacob, 21, 35, 44, 52
bureaucracy, 45, 74, 109, 112, 154, 170, 178, 190, 213, 219, 253, 254, 255, 286

Caesar, Iulius, Caesarism, 42, 54–5, 60, 168
Canovan, Margaret, 112, 292n
Cantimori, Delio, 126
Čapek, Karel, 181
capitalism, 20, 48–9, 56, 73–95, 102, 107, 109, 110, 111, 123, 126, 128, 130–2, 135, 138, 139, 146, 152, 154, 156, 157, 172, 174, 183, 184, 187, 190, 194, 197, 198, 201, 203–12, 220, 221, 223, 227–9, 243, 245, 249, 251, 260, 266, 275, 282–3
Carr, Edward H., 232–4
Case, Holly, 14n, 101
Cassel, Gustav, 138
Catastrophism, 49, 54, 139
Catholicism, 39, 54, 58–64, 66, 118, 121, 173, 202, 235, 256
Céline, Louis-Ferdinand, 274, 291
character (national), 158
China, Chinese, 123
Christianity, 33, 35, 54, 56, 57, 58, 64–5, 111, 119, 144, 149, 211, 225, 229
Church, 57, 61–4, 119, 149, 173, 175

318 Index

Churchill, Winston, 23
Cioran, Emil M., 66, 106, 114n
citizens, 111, 136, 144, 149, 152, 172, 174, 181, 187, 244, 245, 257, 264, 277, 280, 281, 283, 286
city, 42, 99, 109, 110, 152
city-state, 42, 55
civic, civility, 125, 185, 189, 253, 287
civilization, 3, 32, 36–43, 45, 46, 51, 55, 63, 65, 92, 111, 123, 127, 141, 149, 191, 208, 221, 223, 225, 226, 260
   crisis/decline of civilization 22, 37, 38, 44, 52, 54, 58, 59, 70, 128, 139, 190, 194, 196, 207, 250, 255, 290
   European civilization, 23, 36, 44, 55, 56, 222, 234, 235, 237, 260
   Western civilization, 32, 36–9, 42, 58, 64, 186, 189, 253
Club of Rome, 250
Cold War, 27, 190, 245–7, 252, 255, 257, 259, 274, 283
Colm, Gerhard, 142
common law, 149
communism, 49, 56, 62, 64, 65, 86, 107, 119, 126, 127, 144, 146, 149, 150, 170, 181, 189, 190, 212, 243, 275
communists, 126, 143, 157, 178, 180, 197, 199–200, 206, 211, 213, 244, 245, 266
conceptual history (*Begriffsgeschichte*), 7, 11, 15n, 18, 28n
Congress of Vienna, 55, 147
conjunctures (economic), 73–6, 79, 82–3, 85, 90, 94, 140, 142, 210
conservatism, conservatives, 5, 9, 16n, 21, 25, 27, 32, 33, 35, 37, 38, 40, 43, 45–6, 48, 51, 52, 53–4, 57, 58, 59, 60, 62, 66, 77, 80, 90, 91, 92, 99, 101–4, 105, 109, 111, 112, 116, 124, 126, 129, 131, 132, 133, 135, 139, 143, 149, 153, 168, 170, 173, 179, 179, 183, 199, 204, 211, 213, 218, 219, 220, 221, 224–7, 229, 231–2, 236, 242, 243, 246, 248, 252, 256, 262, 264, 276, 284, 286, 288
constitution, 19, 131, 149, 174–6, 188, 190, 209, 257, 278, 284
consumption, 20, 85, 88–92, 93, 123, 202, 204, 207, 224
continuity, 9, 24–5, 27, 44, 46, 51, 55, 105, 111, 241, 242, 259, 261–5, 274
Conze, Werner, 104
Coppola, Francesco, 226, 227
corporatism, 23, 64, 111, 126–7, 129, 153–6, 159, 173, 174, 221, 225, 228–9
corruption, 60, 174, 190, 287
Coudenhove-Kalergi, Richard, 228
Croatia, Croatians, 54, 108–9
Croce, Benedetto, 56
Crozier, Michel, 251–2

Csécsy, Imre, 152–3
currency, 82–3, 87, 88, 94, 120, 137, 147, 160, 179, 205, 255
cycles, 9, 19, 36, 73–6, 77, 79, 99, 111, 119, 123, 289
   civilizational cycles, 36, 43, 46, 52
   economic cycles, 20, 73–7, 80, 82–8, 94, 96n, 133, 138, 140, 148, 210–1, 229
Czechs, 23, 105, 121, 170, 181, 187, 236, 252–4
   Czechoslovakia 92, 108, 170, 181, 185–6, 210, 236, 252–5

Dainelli, Giotto, 225
Dawson, Christopher, 225
Déat, Marcel, 204–6
decadence, 36, 38, 40, 41, 88, 99, 102, 227
de Gaulle, Charles, 156
de Man, Henri, 89, 155, 202, 205, 209, 210
de Man, Paul, 274, 291n
Delaisi, François, 223–4, 227, 228, 229, 236
Demangeon, Albert, 222–3, 229
democracy, 88, 95, 103, 110, 111, 112, 118, 122, 125, 126, 128, 129, 131, 132, 133, 136, 143, 147, 148, 152, 158, 167–91, 197, 201, 205, 207, 208, 212, 221, 226, 235, 237, 241, 242, 243, 244, 251, 256, 259, 278, 281–90
   liberal democracy, 66, 87, 93, 116, 122, 125, 140, 144, 151, 152, 160, 169, 171, 172, 173, 178–82, 185, 188–91, 220, 228, 232, 258, 265, 282–90
   "militant democracy," 175, 182, 289
   illiberal democracy, 11, 117, 133, 171, 172, 190, 286
   people's democracy, 89, 245
demography, 3, 7, 22, 79, 102–4, 106, 110, 112, 223, 278, 280, 281, 283
depression, 73, 76–88, 94, 99, 104, 151, 198–9, 237, 260, 282
   Great Depression, 40, 48, 76–88, 93, 94, 96n, 107, 118, 126, 129, 132–3, 138–41, 143, 145, 150, 167, 186, 201, 203, 205, 206, 223, 229, 237, 250–1, 260
Detoeuf, Auguste, 150
Dickinson, Henry, 159
Die Tat, 90, 219
Dmowski, Roman, 256
Dontsov, Dmytro, 219–20
Drabovitch, Wladimir, 180
Duhamel, Georges, 57
Durkheim, Émile, 99, 184

East Central Europe, 28, 42, 63, 89, 93, 94, 100, 104, 106–9, 111, 112, 118, 119, 121, 132, 142, 214, 218, 228, 233, 234, 236, 237, 242, 243, 254, 255, 256, 262–3, 264, 266, 281, 282, 290

Index 319

education, 18, 41, 42, 47, 148, 150, 152, 159, 179, 188, 198, 199, 224, 226, 249, 266
Einstein, Albert, 226, 259
Einzig, Paul, 77–8, 228
Eliade, Mircea, 66, 106, 274, 291n
Eliot, Thomas S., 274, 291n
elites, 9, 10, 21, 34, 39–40, 43, 56, 58, 62, 66, 90, 99, 100–13, 116, 124, 130, 132, 135, 144, 148, 152, 168, 178, 183, 197, 202, 203, 208, 218, 220, 225, 227, 228, 230, 238n, 242, 245, 249, 254, 257, 265, 266, 275, 280, 288, 289, 290
Engels, Friedrich, 86, 88, 89, 194, 248
England, English, Great Britain, 19, 23, 34, 37, 49, 57, 75, 78, 81, 100, 117, 118, 121, 122, 129, 130, 132, 134, 135, 145, 147, 157–8, 167, 183, 201, 211, 223, 225, 228, 229, 245, 247, 256
Engliš, Karel, 92
Enlightenment, 2, 8–9, 18–9, 36, 39, 43, 44, 46, 55, 60, 111, 220
Entente, 23, 117, 122, 187, 195
equilibrium, 37, 60, 76, 77, 79–86, 103, 134, 137, 139, 153, 203, 246
esotericism, 39
Estelrich, Joan, 227
étatism, 83, 88, 94, 100, 111, 120, 121, 125, 139, 142–6, 152, 185, 189, 204, 211, 227, 265, 275
Eucken, Rudolf, 138
Eucken, Walter, 138–9, 141
Eugenics, 9, 22, 99

family, 52, 99, 104, 107, 110, 114, 149, 153, 208, 225
fascism, fascists, 5, 22, 25, 41, 48, 49, 55–60, 62, 63, 82, 86, 87, 88, 90, 107, 112, 117, 118, 119, 122–8, 138, 143, 144, 146, 147, 148, 149, 150, 154, 155, 161n, 168, 170, 172, 173–5, 181, 183, 184, 187–90, 194, 196–201, 203, 204–6, 208, 210–3, 219, 221, 224–8, 229, 235, 237, 242, 244, 249, 251, 262, 283, 284, 285
    anti-fascism, 55, 56, 58, 87, 127, 149, 153, 180, 185, 187, 190, 198, 213, 219, 235, 242
    Austrofascism, 210
fear, 1, 103, 139, 140, 183, 222, 235, 243–4, 266, 286
Federalism, 57–9, 110, 186–7, 232–7, 241
Féja, Géza, 109
feminism, 104, 198, 209
Ferrero, Guglielmo, 35, 54–6, 128, 142, 147, 157, 180, 221–2, 230, 231, 243
feudalism, 110, 111, 248
Fichte, Johann Gottlieb, 44, 46–7, 58, 123
Finland, 258
Fischer, Ernst, 207–8, 209
Foerster, Friedrich Wilhelm, 66
Folkshemmet, 103
Foucault, Michel, 264, 272n

France, French, 9, 19, 21, 22, 33, 37, 38, 43, 49, 57, 58–9, 61, 63, 83, 99, 101, 102, 111, 117, 121, 122, 126, 144, 145, 149, 153–4, 157, 161n, 164n, 178, 180–5, 186–8, 197, 201, 202–5, 206, 213, 218, 222, 223, 228, 232, 242, 247, 262, 265, 281, 285
Frangeš, Ivan, 228
Frank, Thomas, 283
Freeden, Michael, 24, 30n, 31n, 117
Fried, Ferdinand, 90–1
Friedmann, Georges, 184
Fujimori, Alberto, 266
future, 18, 37, 38, 40, 41, 42, 45, 50, 53, 55, 59, 116, 117, 127, 128, 139, 178, 187, 208, 224, 228, 230, 232, 235, 236, 258, 274–6, 277, 280, 281, 287, 290

Gaxotte, Pierre, 226, 227
Gellner, Ernest, 115, 263
General Confederation of Labour (CGT), 155
generations, generational conflict, 9, 22, 55, 65, 90, 93, 100, 104–6, 112–3, 131, 143, 145, 153, 179, 204, 206–8, 222, 226, 246, 250
Geneva Graduate Institute 157, 187, 188, 230–1, 243
Gentile, Giovanni, 126
George, Stefan, 32, 173
Germany, Germans: 3, 16n, 19, 23, 33, 34, 37, 43, 45–9, 53, 56, 61, 62, 63, 64, 66, 77, 78, 79, 80, 81, 85, 87, 91, 92, 93, 102, 113n, 118–9, 122, 130, 133, 138, 141, 142, 172, 175–80, 184–6, 195, 197, 200, 201, 203, 205, 206, 210, 221, 226, 228, 233, 236, 249, 251, 256, 266, 285
    Sudeten Germans 170–1, 185
Giraud, Émile, 168–9, 170, 171
Gogarten, Friedrich, 62
gold standard, 81, 83, 91, 92, 134, 135, 137, 160
Graf, Rüdiger, 24
Gramsci, Antonio, 124, 198–200, 215n, 253, 265
Grandi, Dino, 124
Greece, Greeks, Hellenes, 9, 34, 43, 246, 264
Grol, Milan, 190
Grossman, Henryk, 89
Guénon, René, 38–9, 52
Gu Hongming, 32

Habermas, Jürgen, 251
Habsburg Empire 131, 147, 236
Halévy, Élie, 180, 182–3
Hamvas, Béla, 7, 52–3
Hankiss, Elemér, 260
Hansson, Per Olov, 103
Hantos, Elemér, 228, 236
Harvey, David, 59–60
von Hayek, Friedrich, 134, 135, 137, 157–8, 159, 190, 250–1, 269n, 281

320 Index

Hazard, Paul, 36
Hegel, Georg Wilhelm Friedrich, 37, 49, 126, 127, 177, 206, 211, 274
Heidegger, Martin, 32, 35, 46–7, 65, 250
Heineman, Daniel, 223
Heinlein, Konrad, 185
Heller, Hermann, 172–6
Hilferding, Rudolf, 81, 86, 89
Hinduism, 38
Hirsch, Julius, 77, 78–9, 94
historicity, 12, 26, 66, 75, 242, 262, 274–5, 281, 284
Historicism, 9, 16n, 33, 56
Hitler, Adolf, 58, 118, 127, 144, 177, 179–80, 183, 186, 205, 209, 212, 233
Hobsbawm, Eric, 15n, 247
Hobson, John Atkinson, 116, 130
Hodža, Milan, 186, 236–7
Hollywood, 247
Huizinga, Johan, 51–3
Humanism, 35, 38, 44, 56, 58, 63, 124, 125, 247
Hungary, Hungarians, Magyars 7, 69n, 74–5, 84, 87, 101, 108–9, 114n, 152–3, 195, 197, 212, 243–4, 246, 262, 266, 278–9
Huntington, Samuel P., 251
Husserl, Edmund, 32, 39, 43, 45, 51, 254
hybrid regimes, 11, 118, 282, 290

India, 32, 123, 223
individualism, 32, 35, 62, 119, 127, 139, 156, 168, 175, 182, 187, 211, 226, 229
inflation, 81, 84, 87, 123, 134, 135, 137, 140, 144, 148, 159, 250, 251
intellectuals, intelligentsia, 6, 7, 10, 21, 22, 33, 34, 37, 47–9, 63, 66, 94, 100, 101, 106, 126, 138, 140, 155, 184, 202, 210, 226, 245, 249, 251, 252, 256, 288, 289
International, First, 197
    Second, 196–7, 200
    Third (Comintern), 48, 84, 85, 87, 89, 122, 199
    Fourth, 212–3
interventionism, 81, 83–4, 94, 103, 109, 120, 129–30, 134–8, 141, 143, 155, 198, 203, 214n, 250, 279, 283
Ionescu, Ghiţă, 112, 263
Iorga, Nicolae, 225
Iron Guard, 66, 121
Islam, Muslims, 38, 39, 123, 226
Italy, Italians, 22, 37, 59, 82, 101, 102, 117, 118, 119, 121, 122–8, 167, 168, 170, 171, 173, 180, 184, 189, 191n, 196–9, 202, 206, 219, 221, 224–8, 234, 282, 286, 288, 291n, 292n

Jannaccone, Pasquale, 82
Japan, 46, 123, 184, 222, 251, 252
Jaspers, Karl, 44–5, 180, 249, 253, 260
Jászi, Oszkár, 147, 152–3, 164n

Jevons, William Stanley, 73
Jews, Judaism, 65–6, 109, 209, 223
Juglar, Clément, 19–20
Junimism, 22

Kautter, Eberhard, 118–9
Kelsen, Hans, 172, 174, 176
Kesting, Hanno, 248
Keynes, John M., 81, 88, 93, 134, 140, 145, 224, 249, 250, 264, 265
Keyserling, Hermann, 37
Kjellén, Rudolf, 22–3
Klee, Paul, 1
Korsch, Karl, 200–1
Koselleck, Reinhart, 2–4, 8, 10–11, 16n, 18, 26, 66, 248, 249, 261, 277, 280
Kosík, Karel, 252–4
Kovács, Imre, 108
Kracauer, Siegfried, 47, 139
Krastev, Ivan, 264
Krise und Kritik, 47–8
Kriseninitiative, 109
Krugman, Paul, 260
Kwiatkowski, Eugeniusz, 94

Laclau, Ernesto, 289
laissez-faire, 50, 78, 93, 111, 116, 137, 139, 145–50, 154, 156, 157, 203, 213, 237, 243
Landsberg, Otto, 201–2
Lange, Oskar, 137, 155, 157, 159
Larin, Yuri, 194
Laur, Ernst, 109–10
Lavergne, Bernard, 155, 181, 239n
League of Nations, 75, 76, 145, 169, 218, 227, 230–2, 234, 235
Lederer, Emil, 79, 84, 90, 94
legitimacy, legitimation, 43, 105, 143, 168, 176, 199, 200, 218, 221–2, 235, 251, 255
Leibholz, Gerhard, 175–7
Leichter, Käthe, 209–10
Lenin, Vladimir I., 85, 86, 169, 170, 180, 194–5, 212–3
von der Leyen, Ursula, 259, 279
liberalism, 11, 12, 23, 25, 27, 40, 41, 43, 45, 56, 57, 58, 63, 65–6, 67, 83, 91, 92, 95, 105, 110, 111, 113, 116–60, 168, 171, 172, 175–91, 203, 212, 213, 226, 227, 229, 234, 237, 243, 260, 264, 284–2
    conservative liberalism, 53, 220, 227
    illiberalism, 189
    liberal nationalism, 16n, 23, 64, 117, 237
Lippmann, Walter, 63, 132, 145–53, 154, 156, 157, 163n, 164n, 188, 280, 281
Lippmann Colloquium, 129, 145, 149–52, 154, 156, 157
Lithuania, Lithuanians, 63, 170, 231

Loewenstein, Karl, 175, 182, 192n
London, 127, 156, 211, 230
London School of Economics, 134
Louis, Paul, 196–7
Lukács, Georg (György), 48–9, 69n, 244
Luxemburg, Rosa, 85, 89, 194–5, 253
Lyotard, Jean-François, 291n

Maceina, Antanas, 64
Madariaga, Salvador de, 57, 224
Madgearu, Virgil, 107, 224
Maeztu, Ramiro de, 23
majoritarianism, 11, 136, 148, 152, 167–8, 176,
    182, 185, 191, 220, 284, 286
Malaparte, Curzio (Kurt Erich Suckert), 125
Małowist, Marian, 269
Malthusianism, 101, 102, 103
Mann, Thomas, 48, 56
Mannheim, Karl (Károly), 23–4, 49–50, 158, 159
Manoilescu, Mihail, 119–21, 129–30, 131, 228–9
Mantoux, Étienne, 150
Mantoux, Paul, 188
Marc, Alexandre, 186
Marculesco, Michel, 155–6
Maritain, Jacques, 52, 58, 60, 63
Marjolin, Robert, 184
markets, 120, 129, 130, 131, 132–42, 147–160,
    164n, 211, 221, 224, 228, 231, 235, 236, 248,
    251, 255, 258, 266, 275, 282–3, 285, 288
Marlio, Louis, 84, 151, 152
Marquet, Adrien, 205–6
Marsich, Pietro, 219
Martin, William, 227
Marx, Karl, Marxism, 3, 20, 42, 48, 59, 74, 79,
    84–90, 94, 104, 109, 121, 123, 126, 128, 129,
    146, 155, 157, 169, 176, 183, 195–7, 199,
    200–3, 205–6, 210, 211, 213, 234, 247–9, 251,
    252–5, 259, 275
Masaryk, Tomáš G., 23, 25, 121, 170, 175, 182,
    185, 252, 253
mass society, 21, 22, 24, 41, 43, 46, 56, 100–3, 118,
    141, 191
Matteotti, Giacomo, 125, 198
Mauriac, François, 58
Mazzini, Giuseppe, 58, 125, 126, 223
Mbembe, Achille, 277
Medinger, Wilhelm, 170–1
Menem, Carlos, 266
Mensheviks, Menshevism, 80, 194, 213
Merezhkovskiy, Dmitriy, 60
Middle Ages, 18, 34, 35, 43, 51, 63, 64, 66, 74, 111,
    123, 177, 220, 221, 247
middle class, 90, 99–101, 108, 109, 113n, 131, 132,
    138, 148, 155, 180, 206, 237
Miłosz, Czesław, 54

minority (national, ethnic, political), 9, 40, 43,
    130, 133, 152, 170–1, 176, 185–6, 204, 218–9,
    221, 236, 243, 286
Mirić, Jovan, 257
Mises, Ludwig von, 93, 128–9, 132–5, 137, 139,
    140, 141, 145, 146, 148, 150–2, 155, 157, 159,
    190, 212, 230
Mitrany, David, 234
Mitteleuropa, 23, 91, 233
modernism, 124, 260
    anti-modernism 9, 10, 26, 27, 35, 38, 43, 49, 52,
        53, 61–4, 65, 66, 125–6, 151, 204, 218, 231,
        256, 274, 275, 291n
    theological modernism 54, 61–4, 66
modernity, 2, 6, 9, 10, 11, 18, 21, 22, 26, 27, 33,
    34–9, 43, 50, 52, 53–4, 60, 61, 64, 66, 102, 103,
    107, 119, 122, 125, 143, 151, 171, 175, 212,
    226, 248, 249, 253, 255, 261, 264, 275, 280
Molotov, Vyacheslav, 86
monarchy, 55, 59, 143, 188, 221–2
monopolies, 49, 84, 86–8, 90, 94, 111, 120, 126,
    129, 141, 146, 150, 152, 154, 156, 174, 182,
    235, 254
Montagnon, Barthélemy, 205
Morin, Edgar, 14n, 250
Mont Pèlerin Society, 152
Moscow, 48, 57, 63, 84, 108, 197
Moszkowska, Natalie, 89–90
Mounier, Emmanuel, 62
Müller, Jan-Werner, 262
Musat, Pierre, 179–80, 183
Mussolini, Benito, 55, 124–8, 169, 170, 173–4,
    180, 198, 212, 219, 224, 225
Myrdal, Alva, 102–4
Myrdal, Gunnar, 102–4
mystique, 143–4, 175, 205

natality, 110
nationalism, 22, 33, 37, 39, 42, 53, 54, 58, 60, 61,
    66, 103, 107, 123, 125, 133, 137, 146, 147,
    157, 169, 175, 179, 184, 185, 202, 220, 235,
    244, 256, 260, 263
    economic nationalism, 84, 131, 140, 144, 150,
        151, 160, 229, 231, 281, 283
    liberal nationalism, 64, 117
    radical nationalism, 56, 59, 106, 122, 237, 243,
        260
    romantic nationalism, 105
national socialism, Nazism, 16, 45–8, 53, 58, 62,
    63, 64, 79, 81, 111, 118, 142–4, 158–9, 172,
    175, 178–85, 201, 206, 209, 211, 225, 227,
    230, 241, 291n
Naumann, Friedrich, 23, 233
Nemcsek, József, 92
Nenni, Pietro, 196

322 Index

neoliberalism, neoliberals, 11, 12, 25, 26, 27, 28, 63, 81, 92, 95, 96n, 111, 119, 121, 125, 128–160, 162n, 190, 211, 224, 241, 242, 249, 250, 255, 261, 264–7, 275, 276, 281–9
Netherlands, Dutch, 61, 107
Neuman, Emanuel, 66, 142
New Deal, 81, 88, 94, 181, 184, 205, 213
Nietzsche, Friedrich, 32, 44, 47, 49, 52, 53, 56, 173, 211, 220
nobility, 40, 100–1, 227, 248

Oberender, Peter, 266
Offe, Claus, 251
Ohlin, Bertil G., 76
Olsen, Niklas, 283
Orano, Paolo, 227
Ordoliberalism, 137, 139, 141, 226, 249, 266, 285
Ortega y Gasset, José, 36, 40–2, 43, 44, 51, 52, 55, 57, 185, 260, 280
Orthodoxy, Eastern Christianity, 52, 60, 64, 143, 229

Paine, Thomas, 19
pan-Europeanism, 32, 223, 224, 227, 228, 235
Pannwitz, Rudolf, 32–3
Papini, Giovanni, 59–60
Paris, 56, 145, 156, 196
parliaments, parliamentarism, 43, 46, 54, 93, 108, 118, 144, 167–8, 170–3, 181, 183, 184, 190, 201, 205–7, 221, 225, 285
peasant, peasantry, 37, 43, 106–13, 120, 131, 132, 139, 151–3, 154, 183, 184, 194, 224, 245, 248, 252, 263
Pellizzi, Camillo, 124, 127
permacrisis, 11
Personalism, 57, 61–3, 64, 121, 227
Peru, 266
Petrie, Charles, 225
Phenomenology, 32, 45, 254
Pirandello, Luigi, 124, 226
Pirou, Gaétan, 153–5
Pius IX, Pope, 61
Pius X, Pope, 62
planning, 50, 78, 83, 90, 92–3, 95, 121, 137, 140–1, 145–7, 149, 155–60, 255, 281
   planned economy, 83, 121, 137–8, 144, 149, 154–9, 227
Pocock, John G. A., 287
Poland, Polish, 9, 19, 37–8, 54, 89, 93–4, 100–1, 108, 118, 170, 171, 172, 197–8, 231, 246, 248, 254–6, 263, 266, 279, 285, 288
Polanyi, Karl (Károly), 158, 211–2
Polanyi, Michael (Mihály), 146, 151–2, 164n, 245–6
Popular Front, 87, 112, 144, 149, 188, 204, 207, 212, 213

populism, 11, 22, 25–8, 110, 112, 132, 241, 242, 261–7, 275, 282–3, 287, 288
   agrarian populism, 42, 107–112, 114n, 131, 132, 153, 243–5, 262, 263, 284, 288
   ethnopopulism 112, 262–3
Portugal, Portuguese, 118, 170
positivism, 9, 26, 30n, 61, 173–4
   legal positivism, 172
Possony, Stefan, 151, 165n
postmodernism, 265, 274–5
Prague, 181–2, 253
prices, 75–6, 78–84, 88, 89, 90–4, 108, 119–21, 133, 135–41, 144, 150, 153, 155–7, 159, 188, 255
Priester, Karin, 264–5
progress, 10, 19–21, 22, 34, 40–1, 44, 50–1, 55, 64, 79, 100, 104, 116, 117, 118, 123, 128, 136, 141, 145, 147, 153, 178, 185, 188, 196, 203–4, 208, 211, 213, 223, 233, 250–60, 274, 290
protectionism, 57, 59, 76, 79, 90, 119–20, 128, 131, 134–7, 139, 140, 141, 147, 151, 183, 210, 227, 236–7, 251, 260, 265
   ethno-protectionism, 288
Protestantism, Reformation, Calvinism, 33, 34, 38, 58, 61–2, 119, 226
   Counter-Reformation, 125
Prussia, 9, 139, 175
Przeworski, Adam, 265

Quillici, Nello, 126

race, 42, 46, 47
   racism, 46, 52, 59, 283
Radica, Bogdan, 54–60
Rádl, Emanuel, 181, 185
Rădulescu-Motru, Constantin, 107
Rappard, William, 131–2, 157, 187–8
rationalism, 33, 36, 43, 49, 52, 61, 62, 64, 111, 140, 141, 143, 149, 158, 173, 183, 208, 232, 255
   irrationalism, 49, 58, 173
realism, 182, 203, 232–4
regeneration, 19, 24, 39, 47, 52, 53–64, 80, 99, 106, 111, 119, 128, 135, 138, 218, 287
   national regeneration, 178, 245
   universal regeneration, 1, 56–7, 60, 156, 173, 253
Reichstag, 118, 179, 201
religion, 37, 51, 61, 62, 66, 106, 118, 119, 121, 138, 140, 150, 177, 225
Renaissance, 9, 32, 34, 35, 38, 39, 43, 44, 58, 60, 63, 64, 123, 247
Renan, Ernest, 42, 61, 116, 133
Revault d'Allonnes, Myriam, 275

revolution, 18, 20, 37, 48, 49, 51, 57, 59, 85–7, 111, 123–7, 156, 173, 183, 184, 188, 194–209, 210, 212, 213, 219, 235, 246, 248, 254, 257–8, 262, 278
    conservative revolution, 27, 33, 45, 48, 60, 90–1, 95, 105, 107, 119, 123, 173, 248, 256
    French Revolution 8, 44, 54, 66, 111, 141, 171, 225, 226
    Russian Revolution (1905), 21–2
    Russian Revolution (1917), 60, 80, 196
Reynold, Gonzague de, 54, 59, 225
Risorgimento, 124, 125, 126
Rist, Charles, 83, 153
Rivaud, Albert, 177–8
Robbins, Lionel, 81, 134–7, 141
Rocca, Massimo, 125
Rohan, Karl Anton, 163n, 227
Roitman, Janet, 277
Romania, Romanians, 22, 65–6, 105–6, 107–8, 117, 118, 119–21, 129–32, 134, 156, 229
Romanticism, 9, 46, 55, 111, 177
    Political Romanticism, 10
    "village romanticism," 245
Rome, 57, 224, 226
Roman civilization, Roman Empire, Romans, 34, 37, 42, 43, 46, 54, 55, 149, 225, 226, 262
Roosevelt, Franklin D., 81, 136, 184
Röpke, Wilhelm, 28, 36, 99, 101–2, 111–2, 139–41, 150, 151, 153, 163n, 243
Rosanvallon, Pierre, 26, 262, 265
Rosenberg, Alfred, 49, 118, 225–6
Rosselli, Carlo, 202–3, 206
Rossi, Ernesto, 234
Rougemont, Denis de, 186
Rougier, Louis, 143–5, 149–50, 152, 156, 157, 175, 181
Rousseau, Jean-Jacques, 18–9, 44, 46, 58, 152, 171, 176, 220
Rueff, Jacques, 83–4, 150–1
Runciman, David, 259
Russia, Russians, 12, 21–2, 31, 36, 37, 54, 57, 60, 64, 93, 108, 123, 194–5, 197, 198, 220, 229, 242, 253, 258, 260, 262, 263, 275, 279, 280, 284
Rüstow, Alexander, 138–9, 141, 150, 151, 152, 153
Rygier, Maria, 197–8

Saint-Simon, Claude-Henri de, 19
Saitzew, Manuel, 141
Šalkauskis, Stasys, 63–4
Salvemini, Gaetano, 127–8
Sanacja, 172
Sattelzeit, 9, 16n, 18, 26, 275
Sawilla, Jan Marco, 258
Scandinavia, 106, 111
Scheppele, Kim Lane, 279

Schiavi, Alessandro, 197
Schmitt, Carl, 10, 17n, 46, 52, 63, 133, 138, 167–18, 172–6, 182, 248, 280
Schumpeter, Joseph, 73–4, 75, 80, 96n
Serbia, Serbians, 22, 109, 190, 257, 263, 266, 273n, 278
Sforza, Carlo, 58
Siegfried, André, 57, 229–30
Skidelsky, Robert, 81
Skvireckas, Juozapas, 63
"slippery slope," 61, 83, 137, 147, 158, 190, 211
Slobodian, Quinn, 96n, 140
Slovakia, Slovaks, 236
Sluga, Hans, 46–7
social democracy, 48, 49, 79–80, 84, 89, 102–5, 112, 113n, 117, 121, 133, 138, 153, 175, 194–6, 199, 200, 201–9, 211, 212, 213, 244–5, 262, 270
socialism, 11, 25, 45, 57, 65, 67, 74, 80, 89, 92, 102, 110, 111, 121, 125, 127, 128, 129, 130, 131, 134, 137, 139, 149, 153, 155, 157, 157, 164n, 168, 173, 182, 183, 194–214, 220, 226, 237, 241, 244, 245, 249–57, 286, 288
    neo-socialism, 153–5, 205–6, 209, 213
sociography, 108–9, 114n, 115n
Sombart, Nicolaus, 248
Sombart, Werner, 79, 92, 130, 141, 155, 227
Sonderweg, 27, 35, 177, 248, 249, 275
Sorel, Georges, 167, 169, 173, 198, 205, 212
Sorokin, Pitirim Aleksandrovich, 36
soul, spirit (national), spirituality, 19, 21, 22, 23, 24, 25, 32–67, 79, 90, 95, 101, 102, 106, 111, 116, 119, 124, 126, 127, 131, 138, 149, 151, 177, 179, 180, 187, 190, 202, 207, 219, 220, 221, 222, 224, 225, 227, 229–30, 231, 282, 284, 285, 287
Southeastern Europe, 2, 64, 100, 117, 225
Soviet Union, 64, 85–6, 89, 94, 126, 155, 159, 174, 184, 189, 199, 208, 211, 228, 233, 245, 258
Spain, Spanish, 23, 36, 41, 55, 57, 58, 100, 105, 118, 170, 264
    Spanish Civil War, 58
Spann, Othmar, 35, 211
Spengler, Oswald, 25, 35–6, 40, 42–3, 45–6, 49, 51, 54, 69n, 92, 119, 173, 251
Spiethoff, Arthur, 75
Spinelli, Altiero, 234
squadristi, squadrismo, 124, 125, 127
Stalin, Iosif V., 85–7, 213, 243
Stalinism, 48, 49, 85–6, 89, 119, 126, 144, 159, 184, 187, 199, 200–1, 208, 212, 213, 234, 253
Steinhardt, Nicolae, 65–6
Sternhell, Zeev, 22
Stoppard, Tom, 255
Struve, Piotr, 21
Surányi-Unger, Tivadar, 74

324 Index

Sviták, Ivan, 254
Sweden, Swedes, 102–4, 113n, 117, 170
Switzerland, Swiss, 101, 109–11, 170, 236, 263
Syriza, 264
Szende, Paul, 195

Tabori, George, 247
Tarchi, Angelo, 127
Tătărescu, Gheorghe, 156
technocracy, technocrats, 92, 94, 110, 146, 150, 158, 170, 203, 254
theology of crisis, 62, 71n
"third way," 23, 62, 107, 111, 134, 149, 164n, 186, 202, 206, 243, 245, 264, 280
Tilgher, Adriano, 59, 102, 122–4, 197
Tolstoy, Leo, 33
Tooze, Adam, 4–5, 11
totalitarianism, 8, 43, 51, 53, 55–58, 62, 63, 65, 66, 100, 106, 110, 111, 112, 121, 128, 140, 143–51, 157, 158, 164n, 177, 178, 181, 185–90, 195, 209–12, 218, 224, 228, 229, 233, 235, 250, 255, 288, 291n
transition, 25, 26, 36, 55, 80, 89, 116, 119, 122, 125, 128, 130, 131, 140, 150, 157, 158, 197, 198, 204, 205, 210, 212, 219, 222, 227, 244–5, 254, 258, 260, 262, 265–6, 274, 276–7, 281
Trevor-Roper, Hugh R., 247
Troeltsch, Ernst, 33–4, 247
Trotsky, Lev, 212–3
Tucci, Giuseppe, 225
Tuhan-Baranovskyi, Mykhailo, 75

Ukraine, Ukrainians, 12, 75, 219–20, 279, 280
Unamuno, Miguel de, 58
United States of America, 6, 34, 36, 37, 53, 74, 78, 82, 91, 93, 116, 122, 133, 147, 157, 184, 201, 203, 218, 222, 224, 226, 229, 251, 266, 282
urban, urbanity 21, 43, 99, 106–10, 112, 119, 153, 210, 244, 245, 248, 263
Urbinati, Nadia, 280, 292n
utopia, 40, 50, 53, 83, 110, 141, 208, 232–4, 235

Valéry, Paul, 34, 40, 42, 43, 180, 222, 229
Varga, Jenő (Eugen), 84–9, 97n, 245
Ventotene Manifesto, 234–5, 236
Verein für Sozialpolitik, 141
Versailles Treaty, 122, 147, 151, 177, 179
Vichy regime, 153–6, 206, 213, 223, 285
Vienna, 53, 79, 84, 89, 135, 147, 211
village, 152, 198, 245
Vilnius, 231
Vlaykov, Todor, 108
Vode, Angela, 104
Voegelin, Eric, 53

Volta Conference, 224–230
Voznesenskiy, Andrey, 258

Wagemann, Ernst, 82–3, 90
Wallop, Gerard (Viscount Lymington), 225
Watanuki, Joji, 251–2
Weber, Alfred, 220–1, 224, 227
Weber, Max, 175, 220
Weidel, Alice, 267
Weimar Republic, 3, 25, 45, 46, 49, 78, 119, 167, 168, 171, 172, 175, 176, 177, 201, 219, 247
Wells, H.G., 178–9
Weltsch, Felix, 182
Werner, Michael, 7
Western Europe, 2, 6, 21, 57, 58, 60, 89, 91, 105, 107, 109, 112, 159, 178, 190, 202, 228, 229, 232, 236, 241, 246, 248, 263, 264, 266, 267, 281, 286
Weyr, František, 227
Wilson, Woodrow, 84, 116, 117, 122, 145, 179, 189, 233
Witkacy (Stanisław Ignacy Witkiewicz), 54
women, 79, 104, 208
workers, working class, proletariat, 20, 59, 80, 85–7, 99, 100, 102, 119, 123, 124, 134, 136, 141, 148, 151, 154, 155, 180, 183, 184, 190, 194–8, 200–8, 210, 211, 213, 218, 235, 236, 243–5, 252, 254, 266
proletarianization, 20, 100, 102, 108–9, 123, 180, 183, 206, 210
World War I, 5, 10, 22, 23, 32, 34, 37, 38, 40, 46, 54, 55, 58, 60, 73, 74, 80, 83, 89, 101, 102, 116, 117, 123, 147, 157, 159, 167, 169, 179, 186, 189, 191, 194, 195, 196, 200, 205, 208, 218, 219, 220, 221, 222, 229, 232, 233, 235, 242, 283, 284
World War II, 27, 53, 54, 66, 94, 102, 109, 111, 152–60, 169, 187, 190, 201, 212, 223, 234, 236, 237, 241, 242, 286
Woytinsky, Wladimir, 80–1

youth, 44, 99, 100, 104, 105, 183, 207–9, 246, 276
Yugoslavs, Yugoslavia, 22, 109, 118, 122, 170, 190, 246, 256–7, 258, 284

Zakrzewski, Kazimierz, 171–2
Zdziechowski, Marian, 54
Zehrer, Hans, 219
Zeletin, Ştefan, 130–2
Zimmermann, Bénédicte, 7
Zionism, 65, 182
Znaniecki, Florian, 37–8, 39
Zweig, Ferdynand, 93–4, 158
Zweig, Stefan, 226